EASTERN BROOK TROUT: *Salvelinus fontinalis* (Mitchill).

Painting from life of a female fish 16¾ inches long, taken in Rangeley Stream, Oquossoc, Maine.

AMERICAN FOOD AND GAME FISHES. A POPULAR ACCOUNT OF ALL THE SPECIES FOUND IN AMERICA NORTH OF THE EQUATOR, WITH KEYS FOR READY IDENTIFICATION, LIFE HISTORIES AND METHODS OF CAPTURE

BY

DAVID STARR JORDAN, PH. D.

AND

BARTON WARREN EVERMANN, PH.D.

DOVER PUBLICATIONS, INC., NEW YORK

Published in Canada by General Publishing Company, Ltd., 30 Lesmill Road, Don Mills, Toronto, Ontario.

Published in the United Kingdom by Constable and Company, Ltd., 10 Orange Street, London WC 2.

This Dover edition, first published in 1969, is an unabridged republication of the last revised edition, as published by Doubleday, Page and Company in 1923. The first ten illustrations listed on page xiii were reproduced in color in the previous edition.

Standard Book Number: 486-22196-2
Library of Congress Catalog Card Number: 71-84702

Manufactured in the United States of America
Dover Publications, Inc.
180 Varick Street
New York, N.Y. 10014

PREFACE

THIS volume upon American Food and Game Fishes is one of a series of books treating of the natural history of North America in its varied and more popular aspects. Its scope includes all the species of fishes north of Panama which are used by man as food or which are sought by anglers for the sport which their capture affords.

In its preparation the authors have made free use of their various published writings upon fishes, especially their "Fishes of North and Middle America." They have also made equally free use of the vast store of valuable information contained in the numerous Reports and Bulletins of the United States Fish Commission, and the "Fisheries and Fishery Industries of the United States" by the late Dr. George Brown Goode and associates. The reports of the Fish Commissions of the different States and Canada, as well as the files of the many valuable outing magazines have been consulted.

To the many individuals who have assisted us in one way or another we wish to express our thanks and appreciation. First of all we are indebted to the Hon. Geo. M. Bowers, U. S. Commissioner of Fish and Fisheries, and to Dr. H. M. Smith, Mr. W. de C. Ravenel, Dr. W. C. Kendall, Mr. E. L. Goldsborough, and Mr. C. H. Townsend, of the Fish Commission, for many courtesies extended and assistance given. The excellent coloured plates in this volume are from the splendid paintings by C. B. Hudson and A. H. Baldwin, and we are able to use them through the kind permission of Mr. Bowers.

To Dr. Richard Rathbun, Assistant Secretary of the Smithsonian Institution, we are indebted for the privilege of using as text figures many of the illustrations from Bulletin 47, U. S. National Museum.

The numerous excellent and artistically beautiful photographs of live fishes were all taken by Mr. A. Radclyffe Dugmore, who has, with infinite patience and skill, achieved such marvellous results in photographing wild animals. These photographs were taken by Mr. Dugmore expressly for this work at Key West, Lake Maxinkuckee, and at the Pan-American Exposition; and it is doubted if such excellence had ever before been attained in this line of live animal photography.

To numerous angling and sportsmen friends who have aided us with kindly advice and counsel we are duly grateful.

In conclusion we may say that our aim has been to make a book which will prove useful and entertaining to anglers; to commercial fishermen and dealers in fish and fishery products; to teachers and others who wish to inform themselves regarding our vast array of food and game fishes; and to the multitude of intelligent men and women who have an interest in Nature and Nature Study.

David Starr Jordan
Barton Warren Evermann

April the tenth
Nineteen hundred and two

TABLE OF CONTENTS

Table of Contents

LIST OF ILLUSTRATIONS

PLATES

HALFTONES

xiii

xiv

xv

LIST OF TEXT ILLUSTRATIONS

xix

INTRODUCTION

"Of Recreation there is none
So free as Fishing is alone;
All other Pastimes do no less
Than Mind and Body both possess;
    My Hand alone my Work can do,
So I can fish and study too."

A

THE aim of this book is to furnish that which well-informed men and women, and those who desire to become well informed, might wish to know of the food and game fishes which inhabit American waters. Though primarily a popular treatise, its method is in part technical, for the characters we call "technical" are the ones we can trust in distinguishing one fish or group of fishes from another. These distinctions are the ones established by Nature herself, and the study of natural objects is useful to us in the degree that we are willing to overlook artificial or temporary characters in our search for real ones. Thus to know that a salmon has red flesh and a pike white flesh is to know nothing about either salmon or pike. The real differences appear on comparison of the fins, the teeth, the skeleton, and the facts we have gained as to the origin of the different forms. The use of technical terms therefore finds its justification in that the facts they set forth would be unintelligible without them. But the technical terms used in describing a fish are no more difficult to understand than those used in describing anything else.

Head, snout, maxillary, jaw, fins, and the like are quite as simple as head, nose, arm and foot used in naming the parts of our own body; or petal, stamen, stem, leaf and pistil in describing a flower. To understand or to be able to study any subject one must necessarily know something of the language of that subject. A book which does not take for granted a certain amount of intelligence on the part of the reader has no excuse for being. This book presupposes on the part of the reader a knowledge of ordinary English, as used by Americans of fairly good education, and a willingness to make an honest effort to find out more about the food and game fishes of our country.

The aim has been to make a book by the aid of which any one of average intelligence may easily and readily identify any American fish that is used as food or game, and the book is technical only to that extent. For those who do not care for these facts the part of the text which refers to them has been printed in smaller type. The small type is therefore for those who would study fishes with specimens in hand; the large type for those who would read about fishes, whether the fishes themselves are present or not.

The second purpose of the book is to give individuality to the different kinds of fishes treated, by some account of their geographic distribution, habits, life histories, commercial and food value, and interest to the angler.

These facts and discussions are, indeed, those which are given greatest prominence in the book.

About 12,000 different species of fishes are now known, besides a vast and varied assemblage of forms now extinct. These 12,000 species are arranged in about 200 groups called families. The families are of very unequal size, some containing hundreds of species, others but few or even only one. In some cases the group is now at its height, more forms existing than ever before. In other cases one poor little species may be the sole survivor of a once mighty race.

Of the species of fishes which are known about one-fourth (3,300) are found in the waters of North America, that is north of the Isthmus of Panama. All of these the present writers have described in detail in a book of four volumes and 3,313 pages, called "The Fishes of North and Middle America," to which those who wish to study our fishes more seriously are referred. The present volume covers the same geographic area, but its treatment is limited to those families containing fishes useful as food or interesting to the angler from their display of those qualities we call "game." Not all the species of any family are of equal value as food or game; indeed, many families, containing most excellent food and game species, contain others of no value whatever for either of those purposes. Then again, some species, as the tarpon, possess game qualities in a high degree, but are not valued as food. We have, however, usually included mention at least of all the species of those families any of whose members are game or food for man; and, it is believed, that any one who really cares to do so, can, with this book, accurately identify any specimen he may obtain, if it belongs to a family containing any American food or game-fish.

We have left out the vast array of little fishes, too small to be worth eating—except to bigger fish. These swarm in all waters— minnows and darters in the brooks, silversides and killifishes in the estuaries, anchovies in the surf, and many even in the open sea, the prey of the mackerel, the bluefish, and other pelagic pre- daceous species. We have left out or briefly mentioned rare fishes, those which occasionally appear on our coasts. We have not con- sidered the many strange fishes of the depths, soft-bodied, black in colour, and often provided with luminous spots which serve as lan- terns in the watery darkness. These would be food-fishes if we could get at them, and game-fishes likewise, for they will take the hook at the depth of half a mile, with ferocity and persistence. But the reader of this book will seldom angle for them, and, if he does, he will know how to look elsewhere for their descriptions.

Then, too, we omit the groups which lie below the true fishes—the lampreys without limbs or jaws, which are not true fishes themselves, but merely fish-like animals that live by sucking the blood of real fishes; the sharks and rays or skates, with large fins and often with large teeth, and a skeleton of cartilage. It is true that lampreys are much eaten in Europe and sometimes in America, for we ourselves have eaten canned lamprey on the Col- umbia River and found it excellent; that from the fin-rays of certain sharks the Chinaman prepares a delicious soup; and that the skate with brown butter, *raie au beurre noir*, is a delicacy of the French chef. But in the United States none of these is a food-fish. Our people are too well fed to care for the coarse rank flesh of sharks, however much its flavour may be disguised by the ingenious cook. Other coarse-grained fishes, such as the sea catfish, we have omitted or noticed only in passing.

There are certain fishes whose flesh contains poisonous alka- loids which, in the tropics, become greatly developed, and, when eaten, producing the dangerous disease called "Ciguatera." These are the file-fishes, trigger-fishes, globe-fishes, porcupine-fishes and puffers. In Hawaii one of these species, *Tetraodon gibbosus*, is known as *Muki Muki*, or Deadly Death, its flesh being poisonous in the highest degree. In general, however, these fishes cease to

xxv

be venomous in the colder waters of our northern coasts. They are by no means food-fishes, and are mentioned here only that they may be avoided.

Setting aside, then, all these, the small, the lean, the coarse, the poisonous, the rank, the rare, and the inhabitants of the oceanic abysses, we still have left a royal assemblage of food and game-fishes, and all these are treated in the present volume. Of these, the total number of species is about one thousand, fully one-third of all the food and game-fishes of the world, or nearly one-third of all the fishes of whatever kind known from American waters. A few which may be called unimportant are important to some-body and are therefore included, even though scarcely mentioned in any other work. Thus the great catfish of the Rio de las Balsas in Mexico (*Istlarius balsanus*) is important to the natives of Morelos, though unknown to every one else. On the other hand, we may have omitted species important to somebody because they do not concern the reader and have never interested us. The line between those we include and those we pass unmentioned is often a very narrow one which might easily be shifted either way.

This book is a treatise on a branch of Ichthyology, and Ichthyology is the science of fishes. The word "fish" is a hard one to define because it is used in science with several different grades of meaning. Ordinarily it is the name of a cold-blooded vertebrate which is adapted for life in the water, and has its limbs, if present, developed as fins, never as fingers or toes. This is the broadest correct definition. It excludes the whales, porpoises and seals, which are warm-blooded mammals, looking like fishes only because they lead a fish-like life. It excludes the frogs and sal-amanders of all grades because even those which have gills and live in the water have fingers and toes instead of fins. But for scientific purposes we usually adopt a narrower definition. We exclude the tunicates, which have no skull and lose the backbone in the course of development. We pass by the lancelets, fish-like certainly, but having neither brain nor skull. The higher group of lampreys is also excluded from the circle of fishes, for the lamprey has no jaws, no limbs, and no trace of the bones to which limbs should be hung. This would leave us, then, the following defin-ition of a fish: A "fish" is a cold-blooded vertebrate adapted for life in the water; breathing by means of gills which are attached to bony or cartilaginous gill-arches; having the skull well-developed and with a lower jaw; with the limbs present and developed as fins, or rarely wanting through atrophy; having the exoskeleton developed as scales or bony plates or horny appendages; and with the median line of the body with one or more fins composed of cartilaginous rays connected by membranes.

But a still narrower definition is sometimes necessary, and we may separate from the true fishes the various lower types developed before the formation of the paired fins and jaws of the fishes of to-day.

The sharks are not true fishes, for they have no membrane-bones or gill-covers, and the upper jaw is simply the front of the palate, no upper jaw-bones being developed.

The same is true of the skates, the chimæra and the lung-fishes. The lung-fish, like the bichir of the Nile, another fish-like creature, not a true fish, has, instead of pectoral fins, long-jointed appendages with a fringe of rays along the side. From the structure, as seen in the bichir (*Polypterus bichir*), it is not a great change to the forked limbs of the frog, and it is from air-breathing amphibious fishes like these that the original salamanders and frogs of the coal measures were descended. All these forms, as well as the mailed and helmeted monsters of the Devonian, are fishes in the broad sense of the term, but not in the narrow one of "true fishes." A true fish is an aquatic vertebrate fitted for life in the water, breathing by means of gills, having brain, skull, and lower jaw, the upper jaw formed originally of at least two pieces (premaxillary and maxillary), one on each side, with developed limbs, the pectoral and ventral fins being composed of fin-rays not attached to an elongate jointed axis.

All of those mentioned in this book are true fishes, and each one can verify this definition, although in a few of them the external parts or fin-rays of pectoral or ventral limb are lost altogether.

The nomenclature and arrangement of species in this work agree essentially with that adopted by the present writers in their "Fishes of North and Middle America," with such changes and modifications as more recent investigations and studies seem to require. Perhaps the most important departure from that work is in the use of fewer trinomial names. This is especially to be noted among the *Salmonidæ*. Usually the Sebago salmon and the ouananiche have been regarded as subspecies of the Atlantic salmon and have been given trinomial names—*Salmo salar sebago* and *Salmo salar ouananiche.* Various subspecies of *Salvelinus fontinalis* and of the cut-throat, steelhead and rainbow trouts have been recognized. These forms have, in most cases, perhaps, been regarded as subspecies chiefly because they differed but slightly from related forms. Whether a given form should be regarded as a "species" or a "subspecies" is very much a question of material, both from a geographic and a numerical point of view, as Mr. Robert Ridgway has well said. With greater material, and from properly selected localities, many forms, which have been considered specifically distinct, are shown to be conspecific; and forms that have been regarded as subspecies are in many instances found to be good species or to have no existence at all.

The existence of a subspecies implies greater or less geographic or environmental isolation and the presence of intergrading forms. However great the differences may be between two forms, if complete intergradation is known to exist, the one is regarded as a subspecies of the other. On the other hand, even though the differences are slight, if intergrading is not known to exist, they are to be regarded as distinct species.

Of the various forms of salmon and trout, which we have formerly regarded as subspecies, but few, if any, are known to intergrade with related forms. Although the ouananiche and the Sebago salmon do not differ greatly from the Atlantic salmon or from each other, intergradations are not known. We therefore prefer to regard them as three distinct species, which they probably are.

The same is true with respect to the various forms of trout in the West; most of those which have been recognized as subspecies are certainly distinct species, while others are of very doubtful validity. Among those whose status is problematical are the Kamloops, Kern River, Shasta and Noshee trouts. They may be species, subspecies or nothing. Investigation of the geographic distribution of the various trout is very much to be desired. While it is not likely the number of species will be reduced, their exact relations need to be made out.

B

HOW TO IDENTIFY A FISH

It is easy to know a fish, or even a true fish; but a more interesting question is: What *kind* of a fish is it? There our difficulty begins. We can readily say that a certain specimen is a fish, or even that it is a bass, a perch, a herring, or a trout; but which particular species of the several kinds of bass, perch, herring, or trout is it? *Just what species of fish is it?* This is what every angler, every commercial fisherman, and everyone interested in nature wishes to know, When we get hold of a fish our first desire is to know its name,—*what species it is.* The vague knowledge that a form is something like a perch, a bass, or an eel will not suffice. The works devoted wholly to systematic ichthyology are in the nature of things entirely technical, and they are not easily followed by the untrained student. Though most of our fishes are not difficult of identification, many of them are. There are now known from America north of the Isthmus of Panama more than 3,300 species of fishes and fish-like vertebrates. Many of these are so closely related and the characters separating them so hard to make out, that the difficulties are real and not easily to be overcome except by one trained in the methods of systematic zoology. But fortunately such is not the case with the vast majority of fishes, particularly the food and game species. Most of these are fairly easy to identify. A little time devoted to an examination of the specimen in hand and a careful reading of the keys will enable one to locate it. It has been the aim of the authors of the present work to make a book which any angler or intelligent fisherman can use easily and with satisfaction.

In the first place, in studying a fish, there are some things regarding its anatomy which one must know. He must know the names of the fins, the parts of the mouth and other parts of the head and body; also something about the different kinds of teeth and the bones upon which they are placed, the different kinds of scales and their arrangement, and how to contrast one character with another.

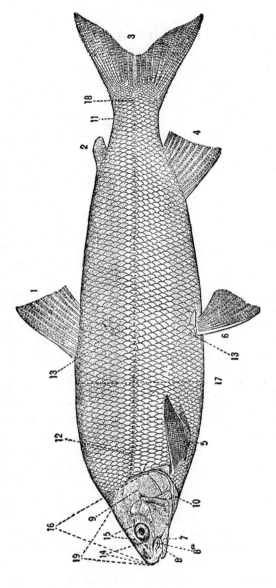

FIGURE OF A WHITEFISH SHOWING THE LOCATION OF PARTS USUALLY REFERRED
TO IN DESCRIPTIONS.

1. Dorsal fin.
2. Adipose fin.
3. Caudal fin.
4. Anal fin.
5. Pectoral fin.
6. Ventral fin.
7. Lower jaw, or mandible.
8. Upper jaw, or maxillary,

8a. Supplemental maxillary.
9. Opercle.
10. Branchiostegals.
11. Caudal peduncle.
12. Lateral line.
13. Series of crosswise scales
    usually counted.

14. Snout.
15. Eye.
16. Head.
17. Depth.
18. Base of Caudal.
19. Distance from snout to nape
    or occiput.

He must in some cases examine the stomach, air-bladder, pyloric cœca, gillrakers and branchiostegals. But though some of these names are long, none of them is difficult to understand and the characters are usually easy to make out.

In the accompanying drawing of a whitefish the important parts of the external anatomy are indicated by name. The whitefish will serve as a type of the great group of soft-rayed fishes to which belong many of the most important families of our game and food fishes.

And the small-mouth black bass, of which a drawing is here given, will answer the same purpose for the spiny-rayed fishes, a still larger and, in many respects, more important group.

With the aid of these two figures one can easily learn about all the external anatomical or other characters used in the present work in the identification of fishes.

These parts are common to most fishes and their names once learned will be found easy to remember. Near the close of the volume will be found a very complete "Glossary," of terms more or less technical, for the use of those who find words with which they are not familiar.

There is also near the close of the book (pp. 541–545), a "Key to the Families of Fishes" which must be used by those who do not at once recognize the family to which the fish under consideration belongs.

All the keys in this work are arranged on the "alternative" basis, which means that either the one or the other of two contrasted statements will be true. The first statement to be considered in using any of the keys is lettered "a", "b", or "c", etc., and the alternative is "aa", "bb", or "cc", etc., the numbering letter being always written double in the alternative. With fish in hand read what is said under "a"; if that be true of your fish, read the first subdivision under "a" which is "b". So long as what is said under the single letter applies to your fish you read on from one subdivision to another until a letter is reached under which there are no subdivisions when you will be brought to a family, generic or specific name. Turn to the page indicated by the figures following this name and you will there find the family, genus or species (as the case may be) to which your fish belongs fully described. Whenever the statement under the single letter is found not to be true of your fish, you then read

xxxi

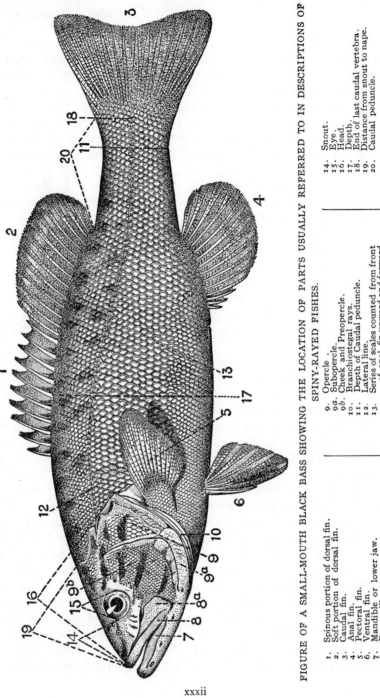

FIGURE OF A SMALL-MOUTH BLACK BASS SHOWING THE LOCATION OF PARTS USUALLY REFERRED TO IN DESCRIPTIONS OF SPINY-RAYED FISHES.

1. Spinous portion of dorsal fin.
2. Soft portion of dorsal fin.
3. Caudal fin.
4. Anal fin.
5. Pectoral fin.
6. Ventral fin.
7. Mandible or lower jaw.
8. Premaxillary.
8a. Maxillary.

9. Opercle.
9a. Subopercle.
9b. Cheek and Preopercle.
10. Branchiostegal rays.
11. Depth of Caudal peduncle.
12. Lateral line.
13. Series of scales counted from front of anal fin upward and forward to lateral line.

14. Snout.
15. Eye.
16. Head.
17. Depth.
18. End of last caudal vertebra.
19. Distance from snout to nape.
20. Caudal peduncle.

the alternative which is under the same letter doubled, and proceed as before. In a few instances there is a second or even
third alternative, the guide letter being written three or four times
to correspond, as, for example, "III" in the Key to Families.

If you do not know to what family the specimen in hand
belongs use the Key to Families at the close of the volume where
all the family names are numbered and paged to correspond with
their position in the text. When the family is found and its
important characters studied, the key following the family diagnosis
will lead one to the right genus. If the specimen agrees with the
generic diagnosis given, you can be sure that no mistake has been
made thus far and the particular species can be determined by the
use of the key following.

These keys and descriptions may at first seem somewhat
difficult but with a little experience they become exceedingly
easy to use and understand.

In descriptions of fishes certain comparative measurements are
made. The length of the head and the depth of the body are
always compared with the standard length of the fish, which is
the distance from the tip of the snout to the base of the caudal
fin. The diameter of the eye, length of snout, maxillary, and
mandible, and (usually) the length of fins, spines or rays, are
compared with that of the head.

In our descriptions of species, we have attempted to bring the
principal comparative measurements first. The expressions "head
4", or "depth 4", mean that the length of the head in the one
case, or the greatest depth of the body in the other, is contained
4 times in the length of the fish measured from the tip of the snout
to the end of the last caudal vertebra, the caudal fin being not
included. "Eye 5" means that the horizontal diameter of the eye
is contained 5 times in the length of the head. "Scales 11–85–25"
means that there are 11 rows of scales between the front of the
dorsal fin and the lateral line, 85 scales in the lateral line itself,
and 25 scales in an oblique series downward and backward from
the lateral line to the origin of the anal fin, or the vent. When
the number of pores in the lateral line is fewer than the number
of scales, we have usually indicated the fact. The fin formulas
are usually shortened as much as possible; thus "D. 10"; "D.
v, 9"; or "D. VIII–13", means that in the first case the fish
has a single dorsal fin of 10 soft or articulated rays; in the second

case a single dorsal fin of 5 spines and 9 soft rays; and the last indicates a fish with two dorsal fins the anterior of which is composed of 8 spines and the other of 13 soft rays. Spines are always indicated by roman letters and rays by figures. The abbreviations for the other fin formulas are similarly explained.

The measurements given in the text are intended to apply to the average of mature fishes. Young fishes are usually more slender, the head and eye larger, and the mouth smaller than in adults.

Those who wish to learn more of what has been written regarding American fishes are referred to the present writers' "Fishes of North and Middle America," a work in 4 volumes of 3,313 pages and about 1,000 illustrations recently published as Bulletin 47 of the United States National Museum; to the "Fisheries and Fishery Industries of the United States" by Dr. George Brown Goode, published in 1884 as a part of the Tenth Census Reports; and to the various Annual Bulletins and Reports of the United States Fish Commission.

C

AMERICAN BAIT MINNOWS

To-morrow we will go a-fishing ; do thou go now and fetch the bait.
—Hymir to Thor.

THE great majority of the "bait minnows" used by anglers in America belong to the *Cyprinidæ,* which is the carp or minnow family proper. Two or three are catfishes, three or four are darters, one or more species of killifish are used to some extent, the skipjack (*Labidesthes sicculus*) is used in some places for certain kinds of fishing, and the young of several species of suckers are seen in the live-box of the dealer in "minnows" or in the bucket of the amateur angler. The mud minnow (*Umbra limi*), which, of course, is no minnow at all, any more than that it is a young dog-fish (*Amia calva*), as many a fisherman will assure you, may also be found among the species offered for sale. And all these have their advantages,—that of *Umbra* being that it will live and remain vigorous under any kind of treatment ; even the game fish will let it severely alone.

Even young bass, perch and blobs may now and then be seen in the live-boxes, and unsophisticated anglers may be inveigled into paying a good round price for them upon the recommendation of the conscienceless dealer who asseverates that they are "just the thing."

With these few exceptions, however, all the small fishes used for bait belong to a single family, the *Cyprinidæ,* an exceedingly large family of fishes, usually small in size, found throughout North America, Europe and Asia. The number of species found in each of these three continents is very great, and the total number of known species in the family is very large. In North America alone the family is represented by about 40 genera and 130 species. There is scarcely a stream or lake which has not from 2 or 3 to 30 or more species of this family. The streams of the Upper Mississippi basin are most abundantly supplied; not only are there numerous species, but individuals abound. In the Wabash basin alone not fewer than 30 different species are found.

Though most of the minnows are species whose individuals attain only a small size, this is not true of all members of the family. While our largest minnows in the Eastern States rarely reach a length of more than a foot or 18 inches, there are species in the West, particularly in the Colorado and Columbia rivers, which attain a length of 4 to 5 feet and a weight of many ponnds. And they are as true minnows as are any of our small species. The term "minnow" does not mean a small fish or a young fish, but it means a member of the *Cyprinidæ* family of fishes, whatever may be its size. The proper name for young fish is fry.

Our genera of *Cyprinidæ* are mostly very closely related and are separated by characters which, although reasonably constant are often of slight structural importance. All the species spawn in the spring and early summer and the spring or breeding dress of the male is often peculiar. The top of the head, and often the fins and other parts of the body are covered with small tubercles, outgrowths from the epidermis. The fins and lower portions of the body are often charged with bright pigment, the prevailing colour of which is red, although

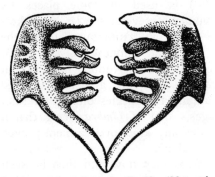

Pharyngeal teeth of the Redfin (*Notropis cornutus*), which has the teeth 2, 4-4, 2, hooked and with narrow grinding surface.

in some genera it is satin-white, yellow, or even black.

Young *Cyprinidæ* are usually more slender than adults of the same species, and the eye is always much larger. The young also frequently show a black lateral stripe and caudal spot which the adult may not possess. The fins and scales are often, especially in individuals living in small brooks or in stagnant water, covered with round black specks, which are immature trematodes and should not be mistaken for true colour markings.

No progress can be made in the identification of minnows without very careful attention to the teeth, as the genera are largely based on dental characters. The minnows have no teeth in the mouth, the jaws, tongue, vomer and palatines being entirely toothless. The only teeth which they possess are on the pharyngeal bones, and are known as pharyngeal teeth.

The pharyngeal bones can be removed by inserting a pin or small hook through the gill-opening, under the shoulder-girdle. The bone may then be carefully cleaned with a tooth-brush, and when dry, examined with a hand-lens and the teeth easily made out. In most cases the teeth will be found to be in two rows, the principal row containing 4 or 5 teeth, and the other row having but 1 or 2, which are usually smaller. There is, of course, a pharyngeal bone on each side, and both must usually be examined. The 2 sides are usually, but not always, symmetrical. Thus, "teeth 2,4-5,1" indicates two rows of teeth on each side, on the one side 4 in the principal row and 2 in the lesser row; on the other side 5 in the main row and 1 in the other. "Teeth 4-4" means a single row of 4 teeth on each pharyngeal bone.

In many of our minnows the teeth, or the principal ones, are "raptatorial,"—that is, hooked inward at the tips. A grinding or masticatory surface is an excavated space or groove, usually at the base of the hook. Sometimes the grinding surface is very narrow and confined to 1 or 2 teeth. Sometimes a bevelled or flattened edge looks so much like a grinding surface as to mislead a superficial observer. In some cases the edge of the tooth is serrate or crenate.

Minnows are found in all sorts of places. Certain species, as the spot-tailed shiner, are confined chiefly to lakes ; others, as the fallfish, are found in the larger streams ; still others, as the creek chub, are found in the smaller streams. In any given stream certain species will be found to frequent the swiftly-flowing waters or the riffles and gravel-bars; others seek the deeper, quiet pools; while yet others will be found among the patches of aquatic vegetation.

Collecting bait minnows: There are, of course, all sorts of ways for collecting or securing bait minnows. The great majority of anglers are doubtless in the habit of depending upon local dealers for bait. Every important fishing resort has one or more persons who are in the business and from whom live minnows may be obtained at prices varying from 25 cents to $2.00 a dozen. And there are dealers who keep nothing but desirable minnows, but the average man who handles live bait is not so particular, and in his live-box may be found all sorts of small fish, and some that are not small, which he recommends in the highest terms to the inexperienced angler.

But many anglers, either by preference or from necessity, collect their own bait minnows, and this custom has much to recommend it ; for one can usually secure better minnows. He can make his own selections as to species and size, his minnows will be fresher and more vigorous than those from the *Saprolegnia*-infested live-box, and, moreover, he who collects his own minnows learns much about their habits and much of nature, which will be no disadvantage to any man.

The best and most satisfactory manner of collecting minnows for bait is by means of the Baird collecting seine. These seines can be had of any desired length from H. & G. W. Lord, Boston, but the angler, will of course, keep within the lawful limit of minnow seines. The peculiarity of the Baird seine is that the middle portion is made with finer mesh than the ends and is made into a bag 2 or 3 feet in length. Seines without the bag, but with the finer mesh in the bunt may be had.

Various other kinds of nets are used, with varying success, but a Baird seine 15 to 25 feet long will prove most satisfactory.

Minnows suitable for live bait can be found in almost any stream or lake that has not been overfished or whose waters are not polluted or made unsuitable for fish by milling, mining, logging or sewage operations. Different species will be found in different streams, some preferring those with colder water, rocky bottom, and swiftly-flowing current, while others have chosen the streams whose waters flow more slowly and are warmer, and whose bottom is of mud or sand or fine gravel. And in the same stream different species will seek out different parts; some prefer the quiet reaches, some the patches of aquatic vegetation, while others delight to dwell in the shallows of the riffles upon the gravel-bars where the water flows swiftly and is well aerated A similar distribution of species will be noticed in the lakes and ponds.

Generally speaking, the species of minnows will be most numerous and individuals most abundant in the warmer streams and lakes.

In the experience of many anglers, creek or river minnows are preferable to those from lakes or ponds, particularly if one is fishing for black bass or wall-eyed pike. The best bait species are those that are found in the swiftly flowing water of the riffles. Not only are the species better, but the fish are more vigorous and active, and more tenacious of life, as well as more silvery or brightly coloured, which are the points chiefly determining the excellence of a bait minnow, as such. To be effective, a bait minnow must be bright or silvery enough to attract the attention of the fish, it must be active to show that it is alive, albeit in distress or under restraint, and its tenacity of life must be great to enable it to withstand the changed and constantly changing environment and the slight physical injury incident to its being impaled upon the hook. The size of the minnows selected will of course be determined by the kind of fishing the angler wishes to do.

In seining for bait minnows a great many small fish will be caught which are not wanted. It would seem that it ought not to be necessary to urge that these should all be returned to the water, but entirely too many bait-gatherers and anglers fail to do so. The seine is hauled out upon the shore, the minnows that are wanted are put into the live-bucket, and the rest of the catch is dumped upon the shore to die. Among the fishes allowed to perish miserably in this way will be found young of many food-and-game species such as both species of black bass, the rock bass, bluegill, and yellow perch, as well as many other species that are either valuable as food or which serve as food for our game fishes. The great scarcity of fish in many streams and small lakes is undoubtedly due in large measure to this wholly inexcusable carelessness and the criminal indifference of those seining for bait.

Various sorts of traps are used for catching minnows. The most common and perhaps the most effective is made of wire and constructed after the manner of the ordinary rat-trap, which permits easy entrance but exit from which is difficult. These traps are, of course, baited, usually with small particles or balls of dough, and are set in places which minnows are known to frequent.

Minnows may be caught also by means of a small dip-net by properly baiting it and allowing it to rest upon the bottom until the minnows are over it in numbers feeding upon the dough with which it has been baited; then by lifting the net quickly the minnows may be secured.

xxxix

In the absence of all better ways good bait minnows, particularly the fallfish, creek chub, river chub, and redfin may be obtained with hook and line, provided the hook used be very small.

The care of live minnows: More bait minnows die from careless handling and disease than are used in actual fishing, but it should be otherwise. With proper attention there should be but little loss with any of the desirable minnows ; most of them are hardy and will do well in confinement.

In the first place, a large minnow bucket is better than a small one, and too many fish should not be put in it at one time; crowding should always be avoided.

The fish must be handled as little as possible and with extreme care; handling or other treatment which results in rubbing off any scales is sure to prove fatal very soon.

The water should be kept cool and well aerated, either by addition of fresh water by pouring, or by pumping air into the water with a bicycle pump. Before putting minnows in the bucket it should be thoroughly cleaned and disinfected, so that no germs may be left from fish which may have died in it.

If you have a live-box in which you keep on hand a larger supply of minnows, it should receive the same attention. It must be set in suitable water, water that is cool and which has a current, if possible, and must be thoroughly cleaned and disinfected as often as possible. Probably the vast majority of fish which die in live-boxes and aquariums do so from the attacks of different species of a fungus belonging to the genus *Saprolegnia*. These are plants closely related in structure to the algæ, and may be regarded as degraded forms which, because of their saprophytic or parasitic habits, have lost their chlorophyl or green colouring matter.

This fungus may develop on any part of the fish, though perhaps most abundantly or more frequently on the tail, fins or head, or where scales have been rubbed off. It may be limited to small definite patches, or may spread all over the fish. In general it forms tufts of white, fluffy threads that radiate out from the body. The mycelium of this fungus develops beneath the scales or skin, and by the time it appears on the surface the fish is past recovery. The only way to do then is to destroy all those evidently affected. The others which may be saved should be removed to another tank or vessel and treated to a saltwater bath.

The salt solution should not be too strong; ordinarily about one part of salt to a thousand of water will prove sufficiently strong. Before the fish are returned to the live-box it should be carefully cleaned and set in a different place.

It is of course much more difficult to keep minnows in the summer than at any other time ; and as it is also easier to get them then there is no necessity for crowding the live-box.

Though there are more than a hundred species of minnows in America and nearly all of them are used to some extent as bait, not more than a dozen or 14 are usually regarded as bait minnows.

While the relative values of the different kinds of bait minnows vary greatly with the locality, nevertheless certain species are recognized by all anglers as particularly suitable for certain game fishes and others for other game fishes.

For muskallunge the best and most popular minnows are the fallfish (*Semotilus corporalis*), large examples of the creek chub (*S. atromaculatus*), and the river chub (*Hybopsis kentuckiensis*). Small suckers are also often used, but perhaps the best of all is the river chub, as it is a hardy vigorous fish which will endure much punishment and is very active and attractive on the hook.

Smaller examples of these same species are excellent for both species of black bass. For bass fishing the following additional species are superior live-bait: Storer's chub (*Hybopsis storerianus*) redfin or common silverside (*Notropis cornutus*), shiner or spottail minnow (*N. hudsonius*), the silverfin (*N. whipplii*), the slender silverside (*N. atherinoides*), and the blunt-nosed minnow (*Pimephales notatus*). In the Potomac and Susquehanna rivers small catfish are extensively used and are very killing. In Maine the grayback or "shore-fish" (*Fundulus diaphanus*) is much used.

But the style of minnow varies much with the locality and the season. In some places and during some seasons crawfish and frogs are the best lures. Frogs are used in New England and in the Great Lakes region. Crawfish are popular in the Great Lakes and throughout the Mississippi Valley. In the small lakes of northern Indiana, justly celebrated for their black bass, the smallmouth prefers a grasshopper in the summer but in the fall the river chub, blunt-nosed minnow and redfin are the best. The large-mouth does not ordinarily take grasshoppers very readily, but the various minnows just named, if of somewhat larger size, are very effective.

Of course many other kinds of small fishes are used as live-bait in different localities and many kinds of live-bait not minnows are used, among which the names of many will occur to the angler who reads these pages,—grasshoppers, frogs, clams, white grubs, angleworms, dobsons, hellgrammite, and even mice.

Perhaps the thorough-going angler will be disposed to scorn all live-bait and use only the artificial fly. And in this he is quite right, for to catch many fish is no longer the desire of the true angler. Only those unworthy the name and whom we no longer respect are disposed to make large catches. Anglers now go a-angling with light tackle and give the fish a chance. They will not catch many fish; the size of the basket is not their aim. They will never take more fish than they can properly use. But they will enjoy fishing only the more on that account. They will get away from offices, counting-rooms, school-books, parlours and five-o'clock teas, out into the open of existence where life is real and where worry and strain and sham are not; where there are green banks and leafy, fragrant woods, singing birds and blue skies. These they will see and feel and enjoy and, returning home, the serious affairs of life will be taken up again with lighter heart and cleaner soul.

"It is not all of fishing to fish."

D

FISHING WITH THE FLY*

LY FISHING is the art of presenting to a fish a bunch of feathers tied to a hook in such a manner that the fish will believe that the aforesaid bunch is something edible and become "permanently attached" to it.

The seductiveness of the presentation of the artificial fly depends greatly on the ability of the fisherman to cause his line to fall gently on the water within reasonable distance of the spot where his prospective victim is lying in wait for something to eat to pass by.

Fly fishing is the highest branch of angling. Its appurtenances are the most artistic of all fishing tackle and its practice utilizes the most graceful of all motions involved in fishing. It is a perpetual joy to its votaries, and, like chess, while the elementary moves are easily learned, there is always room for improvement.

The requisite tackle is simple, beautiful and, comparatively speaking, inexpensive. The man of moderate means is perfectly equipped with a ten-dollar outfit, while the wealthy angler may gratify his artistic taste in the ownership of an equipment costing fifteen times as much and both may meet on the stream on exactly equal terms. The float, sinkers, spoons, bait boxes and swivels of the bait fisherman form no part of the fly-caster's outfit. A light rod with the reel seat below the hand—a simple single-action reel, 25 to 60 yards of waterproof enameled fly line, a couple of 6 foot leaders of single silkworm gut, an assortment of flies and a book to hold them, a creel, and a short-handled landing-net complete his equipment. He has no bait to procure and no worry, trouble or bother in transporting and keeping it alive; the success of his day's outing depends on his skill, the use of the simple equipment given, and his knowledge of the habits of the fish he pursues.

The novice who has never tried to cast a fly will get perhaps as much assistance as he can receive from printed matter out of the following simple instructions:

---

* This chapter has been furnished by Mr. E. T. Keyser.

Take your rod from the case, attach your single-action reel to the butt of the rod on the same side as the guides, in such a position that with the reel on the under side of the butt the handle will be at the right hand. Join the tip and the middle joint together, keeping the guides of both in line, pressing the ferrules gently together, avoiding a twisting motion which is apt to injure the rod; then bring the second joint and butt together in the same manner. Draw 3 or 4 yards of line from the reel and thread it through the guides and tip. Attach the free end of your line to the upper leader loop with a knot as indicated in illustration (1). The advantage of this knot lies in the fact that

1   Knot for attaching leader to line for fly-fishing.

any amount of tension on line or leader will serve only to draw it more tightly, but a slight pull on the loose end (A) will at once release the knot. Make an assortment of three flies, using dark or dull coloured flies for bright days or shallow water and bright gaudy flies for dark days or deep streams. Pass the loop of the fly snell over the leader loops, then bringing the body of the fly through the latter. The leader should be moist and pliant before using; otherwise it will snap when casting and your flies will either decorate some nearby tree-top or sail down the stream entirely unconnected with the rest of your tackle. For casting from a boat or on a comparatively open stream the ordinary over-hand cast which is the simplest may be used. Hold the butt of your rod in your right hand with your reel underneath. Strip sufficient line from your reel to enable your end or dropper fly to come to the butt of your rod. Hold the hook of your dropper fly in the left hand, pulling it backwards on a line with, and sufficient distance below the butt of your rod, to bend the tip in a half circle. Hold your rod almost horizontally, with a slight upward inclination to the tip. Release the dropper fly. The spring of the rod tip will cause the line to spring forward its full length and the flies to light on the water. With the thumb and the fore-finger of the left hand grasp the line above the reel, stripping a couple of feet of it. Raise the rod with a gradual quickening motion until the tip of the rod passes backward over the right shoulder and back of one's head. This will raise the flies from the water and, as they rise, the resistance of the water will take up the slack of the line which has just been stripped from the reel. Rising from the surface of the stream, line, leader and flies will swing over and behind you in a manner similar to a coach driver's whip-lash. Continue the motion of the rod in an elliptical course which will bring the tip forward and to the left until the tip lies again before you—at an angle of about 25 degrees. Then let it cease its motion. By this time if the cast is properly made, the line is out straight ahead of you and the flies have dropped on the surface of the water at a point 2 feet ahead of the spot where they lay before making the cast.

The trick in making this style of cast is to have the line straight out behind you at the same instant that the rod is at its furthest backward position; for if the forward motion is made before the line is straightened out, it will snap like a coachman's whip and good-by leaders and flies. In practising have a companion watch you and shout "forward" at the very instant when the line is at the correct position for the forward cast. A little practice with a watcher to warn will enable you to know intuitively what is the correct time to commence the forward motion of the rod.

Keep the right elbow close to the body. Let all motion be in the forearm and wrist until flies almost touch the water. Use as much as possible the elasticity of the rod to shoot flies and line forward. Keep the rod tip at an angle of 25 degrees until the flies almost touch the water. Then lower it gently just sufficient to allow the flies reaching the surface without splash. If the cast is not long enough, strip a couple more feet of line from the reel and proceed as before until the cast is long enough to suit you or you have as much line out as you can manage.

The position of the rod and the actual path of the flies through the air, from the time of leaving the water until touching it again, will be readily understood by referring to Figure 2. No. 1 is the first position of the rod with the fly resting on the water, No. 2 shows the rod at the end of the backward motion, and No. 3 in its position just before the fly drops to the surface of the water. The path of the flies themselves, from the time they rise from the water until their return to it, is indicated by the dotted lines, the fly moving in the direction of the arrow.

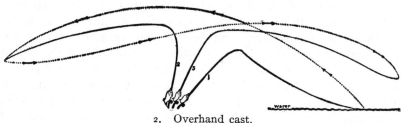

2.   Overhand cast.

It is not always possible to be able to make this kind of cast without danger of entangling the flies in the brushwood back of you and it is often desirable to be able to drop the flies under a projecting bush or tree.   For dropping under an overhanging obstruction flipping the fly as described when first getting it into the water is a good scheme.

The method of making this "flip" cast will be readily understood by referring to diagram No. 3, showing relative position of rod and line and the dotted line indicating the path of the flies through the air.

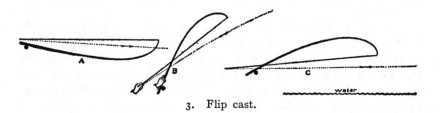

3.   Flip cast.

A very powerful method of getting one's fly out against a head wind is in swiftly raising the rod from nearly a horizontal to a vertical position and then down and away from one with a forceful switching motion.   This throws the line up overhead and then downward and out in front of the caster, the line and the flies cutting through the breeze.   This explanation is scarcely as plain as the diagram No. 4.

The underhand cast, as illustrated in cut No. 5, differs from the overhand in that the path of the fly on leaving the water instead of being upward, is brought back by the motion of the rod from position 1 to 2, about on a level with the reel, and on

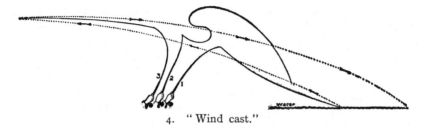

4. " Wind cast."

reaching its furthest backward point by the motion of the rod from positions 2 to 3, the fly sweeps upward, forward, and then downward to the water, as indicated by the dotted line, in a parabolic curve. Roughly speaking, while the path of the fly in the overhand cast may be said to describe almost a figure 8 in the air, in the underhand method it moves in an irregular ellipse.

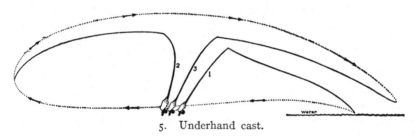

5. Underhand cast.

The switch casting shown in Figure No. 6 will be more easily understood by reference to the diagram than from the lengthy explanation which will be required to describe it. 1, 2, 3 and 4 show the various positions of the rod from the time the fly is on the water until the time it is just about to return to the surface. The heavy lines show approximately the shape which the line assumes at the different positions of the rod, while the dotted line indicates the course of the flies which travel in the direction of the arrow points. The switch cast, when mastered, is a method that enables one to get a tremendous amount of line out; it will also require considerable practice.

xlvii

There are several other very beautiful and useful casts, which nothing but actual practice under an expert will enable one to acquire. By all means fish up stream, if possible. Trout lie with their heads toward the head of the stream, waiting for their food to float toward them. Their vision above and ahead is singularly acute, but extremely poor toward the rear. Cast above them and let the flies float down over them. They are not as likely to see you as if you were in front, and they will not be disturbed by the dirt and debris which you set in motion and which float down stream.

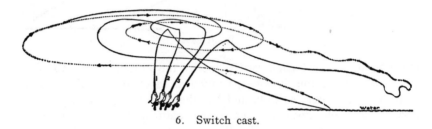

6. Switch cast.

In spring and early summer trout may be found in comparatively shallow water among the ripples. Of course, where the current is very strong in these ripples, or miniature rapids, it may sometimes be desirable to fish for them from up stream, but this practice is to be avoided when possible.

The tackle and methods, as indicated above, are identical for both trout and black bass, with the exceptions, while the trout fly rod may run from 9 to $10\frac{1}{2}$ feet in length and for practical purposes weigh from 6 to $7\frac{1}{2}$ ounces, the bass rod should be about 10 feet in length, and requiring more backbone, should weigh from 8 to 10 ounces. Trout and bass flies are almost identical in their patterns, but while trout flies should be tied on sproat hooks ranging in size for ordinary work from 8 to 10, or for clear much fished streams, on even No. 12, the bass casting flies are tied on Nos. 2, 3, 4 and 5. The most useful may be named as follows: Coachman, professor, soldier, grizzly-king, queen of the water, and ibis, while the green, brown, yellow and red hackles, together with the white hackle for evening use or on very dark days, will be found excellent stand-bys.

While for ordinary streams flies tied on 8 to 10 sproat hooks and the regulation single trout leaders will be found satisfactory, for work on very clear and much fished waters, when the trout have by actual experience or hereditary knowledge become shy, midges or very tiny flies on No. 12 hooks and very finely drawn leaders will more successfully deceive them. On such streams the English method of dry-fly fishing is often the only style of casting that will put trout in the creel.

The usual style of trout-fly fishing consists in wading the stream and making casts in likely places—at the foot of riffles, at the edges of stumps, logs and brush and beneath overhanging bushes and banks. The dry-fly fisher, on the contrary, waits until he perceives a rising fish and then presents his fly in such a manner that it will float over it. In order to have the flies float, they must be dry, and to keep them dry the angler goes along his way casting them backward and forward through the air, never letting them touch the water until actually presenting them to the fish. This continual swinging enables him to have a quantity of line out and under instant control and also dries the flies after each unsuccessful immersion.

Some fishermen drag the flies over the water at the end of each cast, believing that the motion resembles that of an aerial insect endeavoring to escape to land, and flies are often tied with heads toward the hook barb so that, on being drawn over the water, the resistance of their legs and wings will cause them to flutter as if alive.

Other anglers declare that the more attractive method is to allow the flies to float quietly, and to enable them to remain on the surface, the bodies of some flies are wound over strips of cork.

Trout, black bass, grayling and salmon, are the principal American fishes whose capture may be sought with the fly. Both the grayling and salmon may be dismissed with a word. The former, while game, is found in comparatively few waters. The latter requires expensive tackle, boats, guides, and the rights to fish in the waters which it inhabits rent at so high a figure that comparatively few fishermen can afford to indulge in the pastime of bringing them to gaff. Trout and bass, like one's poor relations, are always with us, scarcely any portion of this country is without its trout or bass water, and the poorest man may occupy his vacation in submitting the fly to their critical taste. The little sunfish or pumpkin-seed of our ponds and fresh water streams possesses game qualities not generally recognized. Although usually fished

xlix

for with worms, this beautiful little fellow will take the fly, his preference being one in which orange or yellow predominates, such as the yellow drake, California red hackle, yellow may or ouananiche. On a light fly-rod, swinging his broad side against the strain of the line which he makes cut the water in a hissing circle, Mr. Pumpkin Seed will often give the fisher a pleasant afternoon when trout and bass are not rising.

Many other species of fresh-water fishes will take the fly, some of them readily and with a rush, others somewhat gingerly. Among those we have taken with the fly may be mentioned

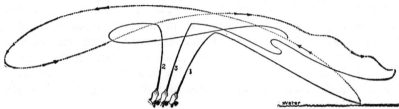

"Clark's spey cast" is a difficult, but beautiful cast to make. Mr. Clark, from whom it takes the name, is credited with throwing fifty yards.

the crappie, calico bass, rock bass, warmouth bass, bluegill, red-eared sunfish, white lake bass, and yellow perch. And the cisco of Lake Tippecanoe and the small Wisconsin lakes takes the fly beautifully for a few days in June, as has been shown by that excellent and versatile angler, William C. Harris.

THE PADDLEFISHES

Family I.   Polyodontidæ

BODY fusiform, scarcely compressed; skin smooth, scaleless; snout lengthened and expanded into a long, thin, flat blade or spatula, the inner part formed by the produced nasal bones, the outer portion with a reticulate bony framework, the whole somewhat flexible; mouth broad and terminal, but overhung by the broad spatulate snout; border of mouth formed by the premaxillaries, the maxillaries being obsolete; jaws and palatines with numerous fine, decidous teeth in the young, scarcely evident in the adult; no tongue; spiracles present; opercle rudimentary, its skin produced behind in a long, pointed flap; no pseudobranchiæ; gills 4½; gillrakers long, in a double series on each arch, the series divided by a broad membrane; gill-membranes connected, but free from the isthmus; a single broad branchiostegal ray; no barbels; nostrils at the base of the blade and double; a well-developed and continuous lateral line, its lower margin with short branches; dorsal fin placed posteriorly, of soft rays only; anal fin similar, somewhat more posterior; tail heterocercal, the lower lobe, however, well-developed, the tail being thus nearly equally forked; sides of the upper caudal lobe armed with small, rhombic plates; pectoral fins moderate, placed low; ventrals many-rayed, abdominal; air-bladder cellular, not bifid; pyloric cœca a short, broad, branching, leaf-like organ; intestine with a spiral valve; skeleton chiefly cartilaginous.

This family contains but two known species—*Psephurus gladius*, a singular inhabitant of the fresh waters of China, and the paddlefish found in the United States.

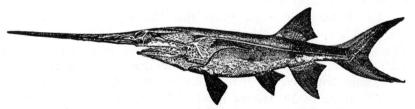

Paddle-fish; Spoon-bill Cat

Polyodon spathula   (Walbaum)

The Paddle-fish is one of the most singular and interesting fishes occurring in American waters.   Its home is in the bayous and lowland streams of the Mississippi Valley from Texas and Louisiana on the south to Minnesota and Wisconsin on the north. It is not uncommon in the Ohio and its larger tributaries, and in the Missouri basin it is found at least as far west as western South Dakota. It is particularly abundant in the streams of Arkansas, the lower Ohio and the Mississippi north to St. Paul. A single example has been recorded from Lake Erie which it doubtless reached through the Wabash and Erie Canal.

The paddle-fish reaches an immense size. Mr. William C. Harris, in his "Fishes of North America," records an individual taken in Lake Tippecanoe, Indiana, which was 6 feet 2 inches in total length, 4 feet in greatest circumference, and which weighed 150 pounds; and we have a photogaph of another caught in Chautauqua Lake, whose length and circumference were exactly the same as in the Tippecanoe specimen, but whose weight was somewhat less, it being only 123½ pounds.

Another example obtained in Lake Manitau, Indiana, weighed 163 pounds, which is the largest on record. Still another, a male, caught by us in White River, South Dakota, was 4 feet 5 inches in total length and weighed 18 pounds. Mr. F. R. Mueller, a wholesale fish dealer of Chicago, who has made a specialty of this species, says he has seen examples as long as 4½ feet and weigh-75 to 80 pounds. He states that the average length is 3 feet and the weight 30 pounds. Mr. Mueller's figures doubtless refer to female fish at spawning time when they are much heavier than the males.

In 1817, the distinguished naturalist, Charles Alexandre Le Sueur, described a specimen, 4 feet 8 inches in total length, which he obtained in the Ohio River, but adds that the species grows to somewhat larger size.

Dr. Kirtland, in 1845, states that Dr. Engelman of St. Louis examined a specimen, 5 feet 10 inches long, weighing 79 pounds. The shovel of this specimen was 16½ inches long and 4 inches wide, 4 inches from the tip He further states that another example taken at the same time weighed "more than 90, or even 100 pounds."

According to Mr. Horace Beach of Prairie du Chien, Wisconsin, the paddle-fish is not uncommon in the river at that place, where it attains a maximum length of somewhat more than 4 feet and a weight of 30 pounds.

The young of the paddle-fish are scarcely, if at all, known. Indeed, we have never seen or heard of an example under 6 or 8

2

inches in length, and individuals so small as that are but rarely seen. Specimens under a foot in length are very greatly desired by naturalists.

The little that is known regarding the spawning time or place of this fish indicates that, in the lower Mississippi Valley, the spawning season is during March and April, while in the Ohio and northward it is during the latter part of May and June. Among a large number of fish examined at Louisville, Kentucky, during the third week in May, only a few were fully ripe. At that time the fish were running up stream, swimming near the surface, and evidently seeking their spawning grounds, which are thought to be in the ponds and bayous along the river. At this time they are caught in seines lightly leaded so as to fish the surface. At other seasons the paddle-fish may be caught on set-lines.

Not until quite recently has this fish been regarded as possessing any food value. True, the negroes of the South have long held it in high esteem along with the channel cat and the goujon, but it is only within the last four or five years that it has had a market value. It now finds a ready sale in the markets and at a fair price. Its flesh is firm, like that of the sturgeon, which it resembles also in flavor. Indeed, in some places the meat of the paddle-fish is smoked and sold as sturgeon.

But the paddle-fish is valued chiefly, not for its flesh, but for the roe, which is made into caviar. The eggs are greenish-black in color, about three times the size of shad eggs, and very numerous. They bring a high price and are said to make a good quality of caviar.

The principal centres at which this industry is now carried on are along the Mississippi River in Mississippi and Tennessee, at Louisville, Kentucky and at Lake Pepin.

Head, with opercular flap, more than half length of body; head, without flap, $\frac{1}{5}$ length of body; spatula $\frac{1}{8}$ to $\frac{1}{4}$ total length, longest in the young. Dorsal fin with 50 to 60 rays; anal 50 to 65; ventral 45. Opercular flap very long and pointed, nearly reaching the ventrals; premaxillary extending to beyond the small eye; gill-rakers very numerous and very slender; paddle broad; caudal fulcra 13 to 20, of moderate size; skin mostly quite smooth, a few small rhombic plates on the tail; ventrals near middle of body, the dorsal fin well behind them; anal larger than dorsal and more posterior, both somewhat falcate; fin-rays slender; a minute barbel at each spiracle; isthmus papillose in the young. Colour nearly uniform pale olivaceous or leaden-gray.

3

THE STURGEONS

Family II. Acipenseridæ

On the white sand of the bottom
Lay the monster, Mishe-Nahma,
Lay the sturgeon, King of Fishes.
—*Hiawatha's Fishing.*

BODY long, subcylindrical, armed with 5 rows of long bucklers, each with a median carina which terminates in a spine, which sometimes becomes obsolete with age; a median dorsal series and a lateral and abdominal series on each side, the latter sometimes deciduous; between the rows the skin is rough with small irregular plates; head covered with bony plates joined by sutures; snout produced, depressed, conical, or spatulate; mouth small, inferior, protractile, with thickened lips; no teeth; 4 barbels in a transverse series on the lower side of the snout in front of the mouth; eyes small; nostrils large, double, in front of eyes; gills 4; an accessory opercular gill; gill-membranes united to the isthmus; no branchiostegals; fin-rays slender, all articulated; ventral fins with fulcra, many-rayed and behind middle of body; tail heterocercal, the lower caudal lobe developed, the upper covered with rhomboid scales.

Large fishes of the seas and fresh waters of northern regions, most of the species being migratory. Two genera and 20 species are known, although more than 100 nominal species have been described.

a. Spiracles present; snout subconic;......... ....*Acipenser,* 5
aa. Spiracles obsolete; snout subspatulate;......*Scaphirhynchus,* 13

GENUS ACIPENSER LINNÆUS

The Sturgeons

A small spiracle over each eye; snout subconic, more or less depressed below the level of the forehead; rows of bony shields distinct throughout, the tail not depressed nor mailed.

Of the true sturgeons there are about 16 species, of which 5 occur in our waters.

a. Plates between ventrals and anal fin small, in 2 rows, of 4 to 8 plates each;........................*transmontanus,* 5

aa. Plates between ventrals and anal fin large, in 1 row, or in 2
    rows anteriorly and 1 posteriorly, of 1 to 4 plates each.
b. Space between dorsal and lateral shields with rather large stel-
    late plates in 5 to 10 series.
c. Shields all roughly striated and ridged; colour decidedly greenish;
                                                    medirostris, 7
cc. Shields not roughly striated nor ridged; colour grayish; *sturio*, 8
bb. Space between dorsal and lateral shields with minute spinules in
    very many series.
d. Last dorsal shield of moderate size, more than $\frac{1}{2}$ the one
    before it; ....*rubicundus*, 10
dd. Last dorsal shield very small, less than $\frac{1}{2}$ length of the one
    before it; ....*brevirostris*, 12

White Sturgeon; Oregon Sturgeon

Acipenser transmontanus (Richardson)

Pacific Coast of America from Monterey, California, north to
Alaska, ascending the Sacramento, Columbia and Fraser rivers in
numbers in the spring.

The white sturgeon, also known under several other names,
among which may be mentioned Columbia River sturgeon, Sacramento sturgeon, and Pacific sturgeon, attains an enormous size
and is one of our largest fishes. The largest examples of which
we have record were 13 feet long and weighed 1,000 pounds.
These were taken in Snake River, Idaho, whence numerous individuals, weighing 100 to 650 pounds each, have been reported.
Formerly very large sturgeon were not uncommon in the Columbia River, at Grays Harbor, and elsewhere on our Pacific
Coast, but the average size of those caught now probably does
not exceed 5 feet in length and 125 pounds in weight. An
example, 11 feet 2 inches long, was 2 feet across the head, and
another, 35 inches long, weighed 7½ pounds.

No careful study of the habits of this sturgeon has been made.
Until recent years it was known to ascend the larger rivers of
our Pacific Coast in great numbers, but, owing largely to destructive methods of fishing in vogue for many years, the species is
now not at all abundant.

It is doubtless true that the white sturgeon, like most other
sturgeons, is anadromous in its habits, living ordinarily either in
salt water or in the river-mouths except at spawning-time, when

it ascends the larger rivers for considerable distances, but it is also true that some individuals remain in fresh water throughout the year. They have been taken in Snake River in Idaho at least from March to October inclusive. It is said that they appear at Upper Salmon Falls just after high water in the spring and remain until winter, if not longer. They are most plentiful in spring when the water is muddy.

Very little has been recorded regarding the food of this sturgeon, though it doubtless consists largely of small animals and plants which are sucked in through the tube-like mouth. Small fish also seem to form no inconsiderable part of their diet. A young sturgeon, 25 inches long, had 11 minnows in its stomach, and in the stomach of larger examples were found several suckers, each about a foot in length. In the lower part of the Columbia River the sturgeon are said to feed largely on sardines, smelts, and other small fish, and lamprey eels are said to make excellent sturgeon bait.

The season for the sturgeon fishery in the Columbia River extends from April to November. The fish are caught on setlines, in pounds, and to some extent in gillnets. The usual price is 4 to 5 cents a pound dressed, while the roe brings 25 to 30 cents a pound. The fish are either frozen and shipped East or the flesh is smoked. The roe is made into caviar, the manufacture of which is explained in connection with the consideration of the common American sturgeon.

Only a few years ago the sturgeon of the West Coast were regarded with great disfavour by the salmon fishermen, who were greatly annoyed by the sturgeon getting in their nets. As they had no commercial value, they were knocked in the head and thrown away. But about 1888 their value began to be appreciated, and since that year every effort has been made to obtain them. The catch, however, has never been large, and the sturgeon fisheries of the West Coast are now quite depleted.

Head 4 in length; depth 7; dorsal rays 44 to 48; anal 28 to 30; dorsal plates 11 to 14; lateral 36 to 50; ventral 9 to 12. Snout sharp in the young, becoming rather blunt and short in the adult in which it is considerably shorter than rest of head; barbels rather nearer tip of snout than mouth; gillrakers abo 26, comparatively long; first caudal fulcrum, above and below enlarged and granular; lower lobe of caudal rather sharp and long, nearly as long as upper.

Colour, dark-grayish, scarcely olive-tinged, and without stripes.

Green Sturgeon

Acipenser medirostris (Ayres)

The geographic range of the green sturgeon is approximately the same as that of the white sturgeon. It probably does not occur much south of San Francisco and is not common north of the Straits of Fuca. It is not so abundant as the white sturgeon and does not attain so large a size.

Its habits do not differ materially from those of the white sturgeon. As a food-fish, however, it is of very inferior rank; indeed, it is commonly believed to be poisonous, but this belief is without any warrant. Its flesh, however, is dark, has a strong, disagreeable taste, and an unpleasant odour, and is regarded as quite inferior to that of the white sturgeon. In the Columbia River it is said to reach a length of 7 feet and a weight of 350 pounds, though the average size is considerably smaller. In the Sacramento they run from 35 to 150 pounds.

This sturgeon is rarely found in fresh water, but is practically limited to salt or brackish waters. It is seen about the river-mouths during August and September.

There appear to be no regular fisheries for it, the flesh bringing only a nominal price, and the roe not being utilized at all.

Head $4\frac{1}{4}$; depth $7\frac{1}{2}$; D. *33* to *35*; A. *22* to *28*; dorsal plates *9* to *11*; lateral *26* to *30*; ventral *7* to *10*. Shields with a strongly hooked spine, the surface very rough; space between lateral and dorsal rows of shields with about 5 series of stellate plates interspersed with smaller ones; last dorsal shield moderate, more than half as large as next to last; snout sharp in the young, becoming blunt with age, usually rather shorter than rest of head; barbels nearly midway between tip of snout and mouth; gillrakers scarcely longer than broad, about 17 in number; upper lobe of tail with some scattered plates; caudal fulcra not enlarged; lower caudal lobe short and blunt, scarcely more than half length of upper; anal fin nearly as long as dorsal and mostly behind it.

Colour, olive-green, with an olive stripe on the median line of belly and one on each side above the ventral plates, these stripes ceasing opposite the vent.

Common Sturgeon

Acipenser sturio (Linnæus)

The early records of this country make frequent mention of this sturgeon. William Penn and the botanist, Peter Kalm, were impressed by its large size and immense numbers, and make frequent reference to it in their notes and letters. As late as 1820 thousands of this huge fish might be seen in the lower Delaware.

Not until about the middle of the century just closed did the sturgeon begin to receive attention as a food-fish. Mr. John N. Cobb states that nearly all the older fishermen of the Delaware River say that in their boyhood days few, except coloured people, ate sturgeon, though occasionally a family would fry a few steaks and serve them with cream. The roe was considered worthless except as bait for eels or perch, or to feed to the hogs. From 3 to 4 cents a pound were the best retail prices that could be obtained for the meat and usually only 25 or 30 cents could be had for a whole fish. About 1870, however, the meat of the sturgeon began to command a fair price, since which time the price has greatly increased and the abundance of the sturgeon has decreased proportionally. In 1890 the average catch of sturgeon in the Delaware River was 60 per net; since that year the decrease has been gradual and rapid, until in 1899 the catch was only 8 fish to the net. The total catch for the Delaware River in 1890 amounted to 5,023,175 pounds, while in 1897 (the last year for which complete statistics are available), the amount was only 2,428,616 pounds. The taking of the roe for caviar began in this country as early as 1853, and the smoking of sturgeon was begun about four years later.

In the sturgeon fishery gillnets are used exclusively, and these are always drifted. The fishermen go out 2 or 3 hours before slack water and put their nets overboard. As the sturgeon is a bottom feeder, the net is weighted so that it sinks, wooden buoys called "dabs" attached to the cork line by means of ropes being used to mark the location of the net. The fishermen drift along behind their net, and when a buoy indicates that a fish has been captured, that section of the net is taken in, the fish hauled into the boat, and the net reset.

The sturgeon is taken aboard by means of long-handled hooks of round iron. Though of great size, they struggle very little when gilled or when being brought into the boat, and are generally rolled in like a log. The net is usually fished but once a day, and is taken up at slack water, the fishermen returning to camp with the ebb tide.

By far the most valuable part of the sturgeon is the roe, from which is prepared the very expensive commercial product called caviar. The manner of preparation is, briefly, as follows: After the eggs have been removed from the fish, they are placed in large masses upon a stand, the top of which is formed of a small-meshed screen. On the under side is placed a zinc-lined trough, about 18 inches deep, 2 feet wide, and 4 feet long. The operator gently rubs the mass of eggs back and forth over the screen, whose mesh is just large enough to let the eggs drop through as they are separated from the enveloping membrane. They thus fall into the trough, from which they are drawn off into tubs through a sliding door in one end of the trough. After all the roe has been separated, the tub is removed, and a certain proportion of the best Luneburg salt is added and mixed with the eggs by careful stirring with the hands. This is the most delicate part of the whole process, and the best results can be obtained by that proficiency which comes from long experience. After adding the salt, the eggs at first become dry, but in 10 or 15 minutes the salt has drawn from the eggs their watery constituents and a copious brine is formed, which is poured off when the tub becomes too full. The salted eggs are then poured into fine-meshed sieves which hold about 10 pounds each, where they are allowed to drain for 8 to 20 hours. The eggs have now become the caviar of commerce, which is put in casks or cans of various sizes. The cask usually holds 135 pounds, the price of which has increased from $9 to $12 in 1885 to $105 in 1899.

Head $3\frac{1}{2}$; depth $5\frac{3}{4}$; snout 2 in head; eye very small, about

14 in head; D. 38; A. 27; dorsal plates 10 to 14; lateral 27 to 29; ventral 8 to 11. Shields not strongly striated; stellate plates small, in about 10 rows, with smaller ones interspersed; last dorsal shield more than half length of one before it; snout rather sharp, about as long as rest of head, becoming shorter and blunter with age; barbels short, not reaching mouth, inserted nearly midway between mouth and tip of snout; gillrakers small, slender, pointed, sparse, not longer than pupil; lower lobe of tail rather sharp; anal more than half as long as the dorsal fin and placed mostly below it; anterior rays of pectoral thickened. Olive gray, paler below.

Maximum length about 10 feet; weight 500 pounds. This is the common sturgeon of our Atlantic Coast and coastal rivers, and ranges from Maine to South Carolina. It is most abundant in the Delaware and occurs in some numbers in all the larger streams of this coast, particularly in the Hudson, Susquehanna, and James. The species is migratory in habit, spending much time in salt water in or near the bays, and running up the rivers to brackish or fresh water at spawning time.

Lake Sturgeon

Acipenser rubicundus. (Le Sueur)

The lake sturgeon is found as an inhabitant of the Great Lakes and the larger rivers connected therewith, Lake of the Woods, and many of the Canadian lakes. It was formerly abundant in the upper Mississippi Valley and is still found in some numbers in the Mississippi and in the lower portions of the Ohio, Missouri, and its other large tributaries. It is now perhaps most abundant in the Lake of the Woods, where the annual catch in 1894 on the United States side amounted to 1,059,267 pounds. Since then the decrease has been very rapid, until in 1899 the catch was only 197,033 pounds. Among the Great Lakes it is most abundant in Lakes Erie and Ontario and least so in Lake Superior, whose deeper, colder water is less favourable for its growth than the more shallow, warmer water of the other lakes named. The lake sturgeon is the largest and one of the most important fishes of the Great Lakes, but it is now much less abundant than formerly. The average length of the examples now taken is less than 5 feet, though examples 6 feet long have been occasionally taken, and rarely individuals 9 feet in length have been reported. The average weight probably does not exceed 40 or 50 pounds, and about 100 pounds is the present maximum weight.

It delights to frequent comparatively shoal water where, according to Milner, it feeds upon the smaller gasteropods, such as thin shelled *Physa*, *Planorbis* and *Valvata*, and the more firm *Limnea* and *Melantho*. Though it is primarily a bottom feeder, it is known that small fishes constitute a not inconsiderable portion of its food. On August 9, 1894, Professor A. J. Woolman examined the stomachs of 55 sturgeon at Garden Island, Lake of the Woods, of which number 28 contained one or more crawfish, 6 had insect larvæ, 6 had mollusks, and 22 were empty. Among the miscellaneous objects found were a fish-egg in one, a fish-vertebra in another, a hazelnut in one, and gravel in eight!

Head $3\frac{1}{2}$; depth $5\frac{3}{4}$; eye 9 to 10 in head; snout about 2; D. 35; A. 26; dorsal shields 11 to 16; lateral shields 30 to 39; ventral shields 8 to 11. Body rather elongate; snout slender and long in the young, becoming quite blunt with age, when it is considerably shorter than rest of head; shields large, rough and with strongly hooked spines in the young, becoming comparatively smooth in old individuals; skin with minute spinules in many series; ventral shields growing smaller with age, and finally deciduous; anal fin $\frac{2}{3}$ length of dorsal, beginning near its middle.

Short-nosed Sturgeon

Acipenser brevirostris (Le Sueur)

The short-nosed sturgeon ranges from Cape Cod southward to Florida, and rarely it has been reported from the coast of Texas. It is more southern in its distribution than the common sturgeon. Though not abundant anywhere, it is taken most frequently from New Jersey southward. Examples are occasionally taken in Indian River and elsewhere on the east coast of Florida, and it is said to be not uncommon in the Suwanee and other rivers on the Gulf coast of that state.

This sturgeon is much smaller than the common sturgeon. The largest examples seen by Le Sueur were only 33 inches long, while the largest obtained by Ryder was but 23 inches. It probably does not attain a greater length than 3 feet, and seems to be not much used for food.

Its habits so far as known do not differ from those of the common species. Its colour alone is usually diagnostic. The young of the common sturgeon is never dark-coloured, while the characteristic dirty olive-green or brownish, with a shade of green in it, is always seen in the common sturgeon at all stages of its growth.

Head about 4; depth $5\frac{1}{2}$; eye 9 to 10 in head; snout about $3\frac{1}{4}$; D. 41; A. 22; dorsal shields 8 to 11; lateral 22 to 33; ventral 6 to 9. Body elongate; snout very short and obtuse, $\frac{1}{3}$ to $\frac{1}{4}$ length of head; barbels short and simple; skin between rows of shields with many rows of prickle-like plates; shields rather large and smoothish; anal fin about half size of dorsal and wholly below it. Colour, dusky or even dark above, paler below. Length 2 to 3 feet.

GENUS SCAPHIRHYNCHUS HECKEL

Snout broad, depressed, and shovel-shaped; caudal peduncle very long, strongly depressed, broader than deep; rows of bony bucklers confluent below the dorsal fin, forming a complete coat of mail on the tail, which is produced in a long filament beyond the caudal fin, this longest in the young; gillrakers somewhat fan-shaped; no pseudobranchiæ.

The single species of this genus is an inhabitant of the United States, but others closely related, forming the genus *Kessleria*, are found in Central Asia.

Shovel-nosed Sturgeon

Scaphirhynchus platorynchus (Rafinesque)

The shovel-nosed sturgeon is known only from the upper and middle Mississippi Valley. It is probably most abundant in the larger streams of the Central States, especially in the Ohio, Illinois and Missouri. During the month of May it is caught in considerable numbers at the Falls of the Ohio. At that time it is running up stream and, as it then swims near the surface, the fishermen capture it by means of seines weighted to fish the top rather than the bottom. It is found associated with the paddlefish and the Ohio shad, which run at the same time. The shovelnose is also taken on set-lines baited with cut-bait or small fish.

According to the books, this species reaches a length of 8 feet, but we have never seen an example even approximating that size. Numerous specimens examined by us in the Wabash and Ohio rivers did not show any exceeding 4 feet in total length. The average length of 62 individuals examined by us at Louisville was 2 feet and the average weight $2\frac{1}{3}$ pounds. The largest example among these was a female, 28 inches long, and weighing $4\frac{1}{4}$ pounds. Examples from the Wabash River, seen at

Terre Haute, were $1\frac{1}{2}$ to 4 feet long and weighed only 3 to 12 pounds!

The female shovel-nose, as is the case with all other sturgeons, is usually considerably larger than the male. The flesh finds a ready sale, it being cut into steaks or smoked. The roe, however, is the most valuable part of the fish, and, though the amount furnished by a single fish is not large, it is highly prized, it being made into caviar. Not until recently has it been utilized for this purpose, but now the more progressive fishermen in the Mississippi Valley are careful to save the roe of both the shovel-nose and the paddle-fish, as well as that of the common lake sturgeon.

Head 4; depth 8; snout $1\frac{1}{2}$; eye very small; D. 32; A. 20; dorsal shields 15 to 20; lateral 41 to 46; ventral 11 to 13. Body elongate, tapering into a slender, depressed tail, which is extended beyond the caudal fin in a slender filament, very long in the young, but usually lost in the adult; bony shields opisthocentrous (i. e., with the spine behind the middle), sharply keeled, the series confluent below the dorsal, obliterating the smaller plates between; 2 occipital plates, each with a short keel; a preocular spine and one at the posterior edge of the "shovel"; a few spines on the snout in the young; barbels nearer mouth than tip of snout; none of the fulcra enlarged; dorsal and anal small; the anal little more than half length of dorsal and entirely behind it; gillrakers small and lamellate, ending in 3 or 4 points. Colour, pale yellowish olive.

LAKE STURGEON, *Acipenser rubicundus*

LAKE STURGEON, *Acipenser rubicundus*

SHORT-NOSED STURGEON *Acipenser brevirostris*

THE CATFISHES

Family III. Siluridæ

BODY more or less elongate, naked or covered with bony plates; head with eight barbels, the base of the longest pair formed by the small or rudimentary maxillary; margin of upper jaw formed by premaxillaries alone; opercle present, subopercle absent; dorsal fin short, above or in front of the ventrals; a small fatty or adipose fin back of the dorsal; front ray of dorsal and ventral spinous; air-bladder large, and connected with the organ of hearing by means of auditory ossicles; lower pharyngeals separate.

The family of catfishes is a large one, the total number of recognized genera being more than one hundred, and the number of species nearly one thousand. The majority of the species are fresh-water fishes, inhabiting the rivers of warmer countries, particularly South America and Africa, being especially characteristic of the Amazon region; only a few species are marine and they are mostly tropical. The total number of species known from North and Middle America is one hundred and eight, of which about one-third are salt-water species belonging to the genera *Felichthys, Galeichthys, Sciadeichthys, Aspistor, Selenaspis, Netuma, Tachysurus* and *Cathorops,* only the first two of which have species on the United States coast. In the fresh waters and on the coasts of southern Mexico, Central America, and southward, are about a score of species of the genera *Rhamdia, Pimelodella* and *Pimelodus,* but none of them is of any importance either for food or as a game-fish.

In the United States and Mexico we have about 34 species, only about a dozen of which are of sufficient importance to merit any consideration in the present work. Most of the others are small species known as stone-cats or mad-toms, belonging to the genera *Noturus and Schilbeodes,* characterized by the possession of a poison gland at the base of the pectoral spine, and by the connection of the adipose fin with the caudal.

Of the 30 species of fresh-water catfishes occurring in the United States, all but 4 are confined to the Atlantic, Mississippi Valley and Gulf States. One species *(Ictalurus meridionalis)* is known only from the Rio Usumacinta, in Guatemala; another

15

(*Ameiurus dugesi*) is known from various parts of the great valley of the Rio Lerma in Mexico, a large stream which flows through Lake Chapala into the Pacific Ocean; another *(Istlarius balsanus),* is a very large catfish in the basin of the Rio Balsas, described from Puente de Ixtla, in Morelos, Mexico ; and another *(Ameiurus pricei),* from San Bernardino Creek in southern Arizona, also tributary to the Pacific.

No species of catfish is native to the fresh waters of the Pacific Coast of the United States, though 2 species, *Ameiurus nebulosus and Ameiurus catus,* have been introduced from the East and have become very abundant in the Sacramento and San Joaquin.

a. Adipose fin with its posterior margin free.
b. Premaxillary band of teeth truncate behind, not produced backward at the outer angles.
c. Supraoccipital bone continued backward from the nape, its notched tip receiving the bone at base of dorsal spine, so that a continuous bony bridge is formed under the skin from snout to base of dorsal; tail forked; ....*Ictalurus,* 16
cc. Supraoccipital not reaching interspinal bones, the bony bridge being more or less incomplete;..............*Ameiurus,* 23
bb. Premaxillary band of teeth with a lateral backward extension on each side; ....*Leptops,* 31
aa. Adipose fin keel-like, adnate to the back and continuous with the caudal fin;.............................*Noturus,* 33

GENUS ICTALURUS RAFINESQUE

The Channel Cats

Body elongate, slender, compressed posteriorly ; head slender and conical; mouth small, terminal, the upper jaw the longer; teeth subulate, in a short band in each jaw; dorsal fin high, with one long spine and usually 6 rays ; adipose fin over posterior portion of anal, which is long, with 25 to 30 rays ; ventral fins, each with one simple and 7 branched rays; pectorals, each with a stout spine, retrorse-serrate within, and about 9 rays; caudal fin long, deeply forked, the lobes pointed, the upper the longer. Colour, pale bluish, lead colour, or silvery.

This genus is confined to the fresh waters of North America and contains four known species, all except one *(I. meridionalis,* which may be an *Ameiurus*, known only from the Rio Usumacinta in southern Mexico) being important food-fishes.

a. Anal fin very long, its base nearly one-third length of body, its rays 31 to 33; ....*furcatus*, 17
aa. Anal fin shorter, its rays 24 to 29.
b. Cranial bones lighter, the supraoccipital long and narrow, its upper surface nearly smooth; ....*punctatus*, 21
bb. Cranial bones heavy, the supraoccipital broadly triangular, its upper surface finely grooved; ....*anguilla*, 22

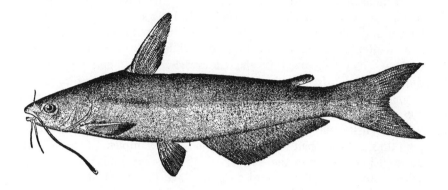

Blue Cat ; Mississippi Cat

Ictalurus furcatus (Le Sueur)

This is the largest and most important of all our catfishes. It is found throughout the Mississippi Valley and the Gulf States in all the larger streams and lakes and bayous. It is particularly abundant along the lower Mississippi, and in the Atchafalaya River in Louisiana, from one to two million pounds being shipped annually from the latter stream. It is not certainly known whether this fish is distinct from the large catfish of the Great Lakes. The blue cat attains an immense size. The largest specimen on record weighed 150 pounds, and was caught in the Mississippi at St. Louis. Examples weighing 80 to 100 pounds have not been infrequent. Very large individuals are not often seen now, however. Of 374 examples weighed and about 2,000 others examined at Morgan City, Louisiana, in 1897, the largest (a ripe female) weighed 35 pounds, but the average weight was

only a few pounds. The species reaches a maximum length of
five feet.

The most important fishery for the blue cat is in the Atchafalaya River, and the industry centres chiefly at Morgan City.
The methods of the fishery are interesting and merit a brief description. Ordinarily the fishing season extends from September
to May, though some fishing may continue throughout the year.
Practically all the fishing is done with "trot lines" and "brush
lines." The length of the former may vary from a few rods to
more than a mile, depending upon the character of the body of
water in which it is set. The snoods are usually 18 inches
long, and placed 3 feet apart. All river fishing during fall
and winter is done at the bottom, while lake fishing is at the
surface. The bait used is classed as "live bait" and "cut bait,"
the former consisting chiefly of fish such as the hickory shad,
mooneye, etc., and crawfish. The "shad" are the best bait, and
100 of them are said to be worth 200 or 300 crawfish. Though
the crawfish will live longer on the hook, the "shad" is more
tempting. "Cut bait" consists of larger examples of these and
other fishes cut into the proper size. Eels are said to make excellent cut bait, but are hard to get. Live bait is most used from
September to November, inclusive, November being the best
month. It is preferred to cut bait at any time, but can be obtained
in quantity only in the fall. Live bait is used, however, whenever
it can be gotten, and occasionally a fisherman is fortunate enough
to secure good supplies during the spring fishing.

These fish are influenced in their movements by the temperature of the water. During the winter they come farther down
the river where the water is warmest, and in the summer they
run farther up stream or into deeper water. During the spring
rise in the Mississippi hundreds of square miles of the adjacent
country become flooded, and then the catfish leave the rivers, lakes
and bayous, and "take to the woods." Here the fishermen
follow them, and "woods" or "swamp" fishing is resorted to.
Short "brush" lines with single hooks are tied to limbs of trees
here and there through the forest, in such a way as to allow
the hook to hang about six inches under water. The trees selected
are usually those along the edges of the "float" roads, and, that
he may readily find his lines again, the fisherman ties a white rag
to each tree to which he has attached a line.

The lines are visited daily, or as often as practicable, and the fish are placed in a live-box, where they are kept until the tug-boats from Morgan City make their regular collecting trips. Then they are transferred to the very large live-boxes or cars carried in tow by the tugs, and are taken to Morgan City, where the fish are dressed, put in barrels with ice, and shipped to the retailers in many States of the Union.

In spite of popular prejudice to the contrary, the flesh of this catfish is of excellent quality, firm and flaky, of very delicious flavour, nutritious in a high degree, and always commanding a fair price. Of all the catfishes it is the one most deserving of cultivation and popular favour, and which could with profit be introduced into other countries. This, however, would probably not meet with the approval of *Punch*, if we may judge by the following protest printed in that periodical, apropos the proposed introduction of the catfish into England.

" Oh, do not bring the Catfish here!
The Catfish is a name I fear.
 Oh, spare each stream and spring,
The Kennet swift, the Wandle clear,
The lake, the loch, the broad, the mere,
 From that detested thing!

" The Catfish is a hideous beast,
A bottom-feeder that doth feast
 Upon unholy bait;
He's no addition to your meal,
He's rather richer than the eel;
 And ranker than the skate.

" His face is broad, and flat, and glum;
He's like some monstrous miller's thumb;
 He's bearded like the pard.
Beholding him the grayling flee,
The trout take refuge in the sea,
 The gudgeons go on guard.

" He grows into a startling size;
The British matron 'twould surprise
 And raise her burning blush

19

> To see white catfish as large as man,
> Through what the bards call 'water wan,'
> Come with an ugly rush!
>
> " They say the Catfish climbs the trees,
> And robs the roosts, and down the breeze
> Prolongs his catterwaul.
> Oh, leave him in his western flood
> Where the Mississippi churns the mud;
> Don't bring him here at all! "

The spawning season of the blue cat in Louisiana is during the months of April and May. Out of 374 fish examined at Morgan City, Louisiana, April 22-24, more than 94 per cent. were spent fish or fish ready to spawn.

In Louisiana this, the most valuable of all our catfishes, is known as the blue cat or poisson bleu. Elsewhere in the Mississippi Valley it is the Mississippi cat, the great forktailed cat or chucklehead cat. Whether the names Florida cat, flannel-mouth cat, etc., apply to this species is not certain, as the blue cat and the large northern catfish *(Ameiurus lacustris)* have not been clearly differentiated.

Head 4 to $4\frac{1}{2}$ in length of body; depth 4 to 5; D.I, 6; A. 32 ; distance from tip of snout to origin of dorsal fin $2\frac{2}{3}$ in body; greatest width of head $1\frac{1}{3}$ in its length; interorbital width 2, equalling width of mouth ; maxillary barbel not reaching beyond head ; humeral process about $\frac{1}{3}$ length of pectoral spine; anal base nearly $\frac{1}{3}$ longer than head, or $\frac{1}{3}$ length of body ; head small; mouth narrow; eye small, wholly anterior, the middle of the head being behind its posterior margin; dorsal a little nearer snout than adipose fin; caudal deeply forked, the upper lobe usually longer and narrower than the lower. Colour, dull olivaceous blue or slaty, pale or whitish below, without spots anywhere; barbels usually the colour of the body, rarely black.

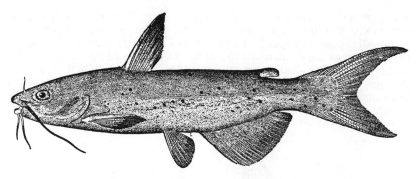

Channel Cat; Spotted Cat

Ictalurus punctatus   (Rafinesque)

Rivers of the Great Lakes region and the Mississippi Valley, and streams tributary to the Gulf of Mexico ; generally abundant in the channels of the larger streams, especially southwestward.

The channel cat has frequently been confused with the preceding species, and its geographic distribution and size have not been definitely made out. It is certain, however, that while the blue cat is a fish of sluggish waters and the lowlands, the channel cat prefers the flowing water of the clearer, purer streams. It does not reach so great a size as the blue cat ; the largest the writers have seen was about 2 feet long. It is doubtful if this species exceeds 25 or 30 pounds in weight.

It is not nearly so abundant as the blue cat in the Atchafalaya River and elsewhere in the South, but in the Wabash, the Tennessee, Cumberland and Gasconade, it is the more common species.

The manner of its capture is the same as for the blue cat.

It is a trimmer, more active fish than any of the related species, and, living as it does in clearer, more swiftly-flowing water, it is more cleanly in its habits, and its flesh is rather firmer, more flaky, and possibly somewhat better in flavour than is that of any other catfish.

The spawning time in the South begins in early April, while in the Wabash it is in June.

Head 4 in length of body; depth 5; body long and slender, the back little elevated; A. 25 to 30; head rather small, narrow, and convex above, so that the eye is little nearer the upper than the lower outline; eye moderate, the posterior edge of the orbit at middle point of head; mouth small and narrow; barbels long, that on maxillary usually reaching beyond gill-opening; spines long; humeral process long and slender, more than half length of pectoral spine, which is strongly serrate behind. Colour, light olivaceous or bluish above, paler on sides, the belly white or silvery ; sides usually, perhaps always, with irregular, small, round blackish spots; fins often with dark edgings.

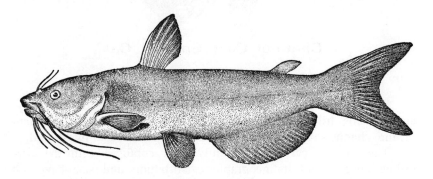

Eel Cat ; Willow Cat

Ictalurus anguilla Evermann & Kendall

This interesting catfish was originally described from the Atchafalaya River, but has since been seen by us in the Ohio at Louisville. It does not appear to be a very common species, not more than thirty examples having as yet been noted. It is, however, well known to the Atchafalaya fishermen, by whom it is prized equally with the blue and channel cats. Its spawning time in Louisiana is in April and May.

Head 4; depth 4.5; eye 7; snout 2.8; maxillary (without barbel) 3; free portion of maxillary barbel longer than head; D. I, 6; A. 24; vertebræ 42; dorsal spine 2 in head; pectoral spine 2; width of mouth 2. Head large, broad and heavy; mouth unusually broad; cheeks and postocular portion of top of head very prominent ; interorbital space flat; body stout, compressed posteriorly, back scarcely elevated; base of dorsal 3.5 in head; longest dorsal ray 1.75 in head; dorsal spine strong, entire on both sides; pectoral spine strong, entire in front, a series of strong retrorse serræ behind ; humeral process 2.2 in pectoral spine ; ventrals barely reaching anal; caudal moderately forked. Colour, uniform pale-yellowish or olivaceous, no spots anywhere. Length 18 inches or less; weight, 3 to 5 pounds.

There is a fourth species of this genus in American waters— *I. meridionalis*, known only from the Rio Usumacinta, in southern Mexico, but nothing is known of its game or food qualities, nor is it certain that the species is not, like *Ameiurus dugesi*, a fork-tailed *Ameiurus*.

GENUS *AMEIURUS RAFINESQUE*

The Bullheads

Body rather stout, the caudal peduncle much compressed ; head large and wide; mouth large, the upper jaw usually the longer; teeth in broad bands on the premaxillaries and dentaries; band on upper jaw convex in front, of uniform width, and without backward prolongation at angle; anal fin of varying length, with 15 to 35 rays; caudal fin truncate in most species, forked in some.

Species several, swarming in every pond and sluggish stream in the Eastern United States and the Mississippi Valley; one or more species introduced on our Pacific Coast, where they are now abundant; one species occurring in China. The species are very variable and not easy to identify. The lack of connection between the supraoccipital and the interspinal buckler is the only characteristic by which this genus can be separated from *Ictalurus*.

Most of the species are small, but they all possess a certain food value and some reach a large size. The species may be distinguished by means of the following key :

a. Caudal fin lunate or forked.
b. Anal rays 25 to 35 .... *lacustris*, 24
bb. Anal rays 19 to 24 ;..... ....*catus*, 25
aa. Caudal fin entire, truncate, or slightly emarginate behind.
c. Anal fin long, of 23 to 27 rays (counting rudiments), its base
        more than ¼ body;........ ....*natalis*, 25

cc. Anal fin moderate, or short, of 15 to 22 rays, its base 4 to 5 in body.

d. Lower jaw projecting ;...........................*vulgaris,* 26

dd. Lower jaw not projecting.

e. Body rather robust, the depth in adult $3\frac{1}{2}$ to $4\frac{1}{2}$ in length ; head not very flat.

f. Pectoral spine long, 2 to $2\frac{1}{2}$ in head; anal rays more than 20; ....*nebulosus,* 26

ff. Pectoral spine short, $2\frac{1}{2}$ to 3 in head; anal short, its rays only 17 to 19, counting rudiments ;..................*melas,* 30

ee. Body slender and low, varying with age, the depth $5\frac{1}{2}$ to 8 in length; head in adult broad and very flat;....*platycephalus,* 31

Great Lakes Catfish

Ameiurus lacustris (Walbaum)

Arctic America and southward, in the Great Lakes and elsewhere. The Southern habitat (Florida, Louisiana) currently assigned to this species has resulted from a confusion of this species with the blue cat *(Ictalurus furcatus),* and it is not certain just what its range really is. It is probably chiefly or even entirely confined to the Great Lakes and northward, including possibly the upper Mississipi.

Nor is it certain what size this species attains. Very large individuals have been seen by the writers in Green Bay, Wisconsin, weighing 20 to 35 pounds. The large ones noted from the South doubtless belonged to the blue cat.

At present the best that can be said is that this species is apparently best represented in the Great Lakes and that it there attains a weight of 15 to 35 pounds. It is a fish of considerable commercial importance, and is usually taken on set lines. It is especially abundant in the northern part of Lake Michigan. In the lakes of British America it is also abundant and its Indian names mean "ugly-fish," while the trappers have called it the "land cod."

Head 4 in length ; depth 5; D.I, 5; A. 25 to 32; P.I,9. Body rather stout; head broad, $\frac{5}{6}$ its length; interorbital width more than half length of head; width of mouth 2 in head; eye moderate, wholly in front of middle of head; top of head quite flat, so that the eyes are much nearer the upper than the lower surface; barbels long, the maxillary barbel reaching beyond head; humeral process short and blunt, about $\frac{1}{3}$ length of pectoral spine; caudal deeply forked, the upper lobe rather longer and narrower than the lower; origin of dorsal a little nearer snout than adipose fin; anal base as long as head. Colour, olivaceous slaty, growing darker with age; sides pale, no spots; anal dusky on edge; barbels black.

White Cat; Potomac Cat

Ameiurus catus (Linnæus)

Delaware River to Texas, most common in the coastwise streams and swamps, especially in the Potomac and about Chesapeake Bay, and in Florida. It has been introduced into California, where it is becoming abundant.

As a commercial fish it ranks with the Great Lakes catfish, and always finds a ready sale at fair prices. The adult fishes are remarkable for their wide head and large mouth.

Anal rays 19 to 22, base of anal $4\frac{1}{2}$ to 5 in body. Body stout, slender in young, the head very broad in the adult; barbels long, except the nasal; caudal fin deeply forked, the upper lobe the longer; humeral process extremely rugose; dorsal fin inserted about midway between snout and adipose fin. Colour, pale olivaceous or bluish, silvery below, without dark spots, but sometimes mottled or clouded. Length 2 feet or less.

Yellow Cat

Ameiurus natalis (Le Sueur)

Great Lakes southward to Virginia and Texas.

This catfish is one of the most common and best known fishes throughout its range. It is usually abundant and extremely variable, several different varieties having been recognized, all agreeing in the long anal of 24 to 27 rays and the squarely cut caudal fin.

We are not sure that *Ameiurus lividus*, the common yellow cat, is not different from the short and chubby original *A. natalis*. We have seen the latter in the United States National Museum but have never taken it in life.

The yellow cat rarely reaches a weight of more than a pound or two, and is usually not distinguished by fishermen from the common bullhead and the black bullhead. All three species frequent similar waters and all are often found in the same stream or lake.

A. 24 to 27. Body rather short and chubby; head short and broad; mouth wide, the jaws subequal. Colour, yellowish, more or less clouded with darker. Length 12 to 18 inches.

Bullpout; Common Catfish

Ameiurus vulgaris (Thompson)

Vermont to Minnesota and Illinois, chiefly northward; not rare, although by no means the common species as its name would denote.

This species closely resembles the common bullhead, not only in structure and general appearance, but in habits as well. It is frequently taken in Lake Champlain and the smaller lakes and ponds of that region, and is of considerable value as a pan-fish.

Head $3\frac{1}{2}$ to 4; depth $4\frac{1}{2}$ to 5; A. 20. Body moderately long; head longer than broad, rather narrow forward; mouth wide; barbels long; profile rather steep, evenly convex, the dorsal region more or less less elevated; lower jaw more or less distinctly projecting; in other respects scarcely distinct from the common bullhead with which it may intergrade. Colour, dark reddish brown or blackish. Length 18 inches.

Common Bullhead; Horned Pout

Ameiurus nebulosus (Le Sueur)

Head $3\frac{4}{5}$ in length of body; depth 4 to $4\frac{1}{2}$; eye $7\frac{1}{2}$ in head; snout $2\frac{1}{2}$; D.1,7; A. 21 or 22. Body rather more elongate than in the yellow cat or in the black bullhead; head heavy; upper jaw usually distinctly longer than the lower; humeral process more than half length of pectoral spine, which is rather long; dorsal inserted somewhat nearer adipose fin than tip of snout; base of anal fin about $\frac{1}{4}$ length of body. Colour, dark yellowish-brown, more or less clouded with darker; sometimes the colour is quite black. Length a foot to 18 inches.

This species ranges from Maine westward through the Great Lakes to North Dakota, and southward to Florida and Texas. In the East and North it is the common bullhead or horned pout; in Pennsylvania it is the Schuylkill cat; and everywhere, the small catfish. It is usually abundant in every pond or small lake and in many streams. It has been introduced into many rivers of the West,—particularly the Sacramento, San Joaquin, Gila, Humboldt, and certain small lakes of southern Oregon, in all of which it readily established itself and is now exceedingly abundant. The species is quite variable.

While this species does not usually much exceed a foot or 15 inches in length, and one or two pounds in weight, examples are sometimes taken several inches longer, and weighing 4 to 6, or even 7 pounds.

"The horned pout," says Thoreau, "are dull and blundering fellows, fond of the mud and growing best in weedy ponds and rivers without current. They stay near the bottom, moving slowly about with their barbels widely spread, watching for anything eatable. They will take any kind of bait, from an angleworm to a piece of tomato can, without hesitation or coquetry, and they seldom fail to swallow the hook. They are very tenacious of life, opening and shutting their mouths for half an hour after their heads have been taken off. They spawn in spring and the old fishes lead the young in great schools near the shore, caring for them as a hen cares for her chickens. A bloodthirsty and bullying set of rangers with ever a lance at rest and ready to do battle with their nearest neighbour."

The following description of the habits of the common bullhead, written as a burlesque by George W. Peck, gives a vivid and truthful idea of the life history and game qualities of this fish:

"It seems that the action of the Milwaukee common council in withdrawing the use of the water works from the fish commissioners will put a stop to the hatching of whitefish. This is as it should be. The whitefish is an aristocratic fish that will not bite a hook, and the propagation of this species is wholly in the interest of the wealthy owners of fishing tubs, who have nets. By strict attention to business they can catch all of the whitefish out of the lake a little faster than the State machine can put them in. Poor people cannot get a smell of whitefish. The same may be said of brook trout. While they will bite a hook, it requires more machinery to catch them than ordinary people can possess without mortgaging a house. A man has got to have a morocco book of expensive flies, a fifteen-dollar bamboo jointed rod, a three-dollar trout basket, with a hole mortised in the top, a corduroy suit made in the latest style, top boots of the Wellington pattern,

27

with red tassels in the straps, and a flask of Otard brandy in a side pocket. Unless a man is got up in that style a speckled trout will see him in Chicago first, and then it won't bite. The brook trout is even more aristocratic than the whitefish, and should not be propagated at public expense.

"But there are fish that should be propagated in the interest of the people. There is a species of fish that never looks at the clothes of the man who throws in the bait, a fish that takes whatever is thrown to it, and when once hold of the hook never tries to shake a friend, but submits to the inevitable, crosses its legs and says, 'Now I lay me,' and comes out on the bank and seems to enjoy being taken. It is a fish that is a friend of the poor, and one that will sacrifice itself in the interest of humanity. That is the fish that the State should adopt as its trade-mark, and cultivate friendly relations with, and stand by. We allude to the bullhead.

"The bullhead never went back on a friend. To catch the bullhead it is not necessary to tempt his appetite with porterhouse steak, or to display an expensive lot of fishing tackle. A pin hook, a piece of liver, and a cistern pole is all the capital required to catch a bullhead. He lies upon the bottom of a stream or pond in the mud, thinking. There is no fish that does more thinking, or has a better head for grasping great questions, or chunks of liver, than the bullhead. His brain is large, his heart beats for humanity, and if he can't get liver, a piece of tin tomato can will make a meal for him. It is an interesting study to watch a boy catch a bullhead. The boy knows where the bullhead congregates, and when he throws in his hook it is dollars to buttons that 'in the near future' he will get a bite.

"The bullhead is democratic in all its instincts. If the boy's shirt is sleeveless, his hat crownless, and his pantaloons a bottomless pit, the bullhead will bite just as well as though the boy is dressed in purple and fine linen, with knee-breeches and plaid stockings. The bullhead seems to be dozing on the muddy bottom, and a stranger would say that he would not bite. But wait. There is a movement of his continuation, and his cow-catcher moves gently toward the piece of liver. He does not wait to smell of it, and canvass in his mind whether the liver is fresh. It makes no difference to him. He argues that here is a family out of meat. 'My country calls and I must go,' says the bullhead to himself, and he opens his mouth and the liver disappears.

28

"It is not certain that the boy will think of his bait for half an hour, but the bullhead is in no hurry. He is in the mud and proceeds to digest the liver. He realizes that his days will not be long in the land, or water more properly speaking, and he argues that if he swallows the bait and digests it before the boy pulls him out, he will be just so much ahead. Finally, the boy thinks of his bait, pulls it out, and the bullhead is landed on the bank, and the boy cuts him open to get the hook out. Some fish only take the bait gingerly, and are only caught around the selvage of the mouth, and they are comparatively easy to dislodge. Not so with the bullhead. He says if liver is a good thing, you can't have too much of it, and it tastes good all the way down. The boy gets down on his knees to dissect the bullhead, and get his hook, and it may be that the boy swears. It would not bé astonishing, though he must feel, when he gets his hook out of the hidden recesses of the bullhead like the minister who took up a collection and didn't get a cent, though he expressed thanks at getting his hat back. There is one drawback to the bullhead, and that is his horns. We doubt if a boy ever descended into the patent insides of a bullhead to mine for limerick hooks, that did not, before his work was done, run a horn into his vital parts. But the boy seems to expect it, and the bullhead enjoys it. We have seen a bullhead lie on the bank and become dry, and to all appearances dead to all that was going on, and when a boy sat down on him and got a horn in his elbow and yelled murder, the bullhead would grin from ear to ear, and wag his tail as though applauding for an encore.

"The bullhead never complains. We have seen a boy take a dull knife and proceed to follow a fish line down a bullhead from head to the end of his subsequent anatomy, and all the time there would be an expression of sweet peace on the countenance of the bullhead, as though he enjoyed it. If we were preparing a picture representing 'Resignation,' for a chromo to give to subscribers, and wished to represent a scene of suffering in which the sufferer was light-hearted, seeming to recognize that all was for the best, we should take for the subject a bullhead, with a boy searching with a knife for a long-lost fish hook.

"The bullhead is a fish that has no scales, but in lieu thereof has a fine India-rubber skin, that is as far ahead of fiddle-string material for strength and durability as possible. The meat of the bullhead is not as choice as that of the mackerel, but it fills up a stomach just as well, and *The Sun* insists that the fish commissioners shall drop the hatching of aristocratic fish and give the bullheads a chance."

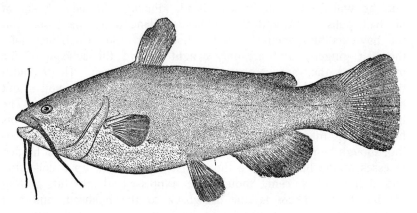

Black Bullhead

Ameiurus melas (Rafinesque)

This is our smallest species of *Ameiurus*, and rarely exceeds 6 to 10 inches in length. It is found in brooks, ponds and lakes, from northern New York westward to Kansas and Nebraska, and south to Texas, and is usually abundant, especially west of the Mississippi. It closely resembles the common bullhead, but can usually be easily distinguished by the smaller anal fin, the light rays and dark membranes of the anal fin, and the smaller size.

Its habits are essentially those of the related species. It thrives in small ponds, especially in those with muck bottom, and on this species in Wyoming County, New York, the senior writer made his first experiments in fish-culture.

Head $3\frac{3}{4}$ in length of body; depth $3\frac{1}{2}$ to $4\frac{1}{2}$; A. 17 to 19. Body very short and deep; head broad behind, rather contracted anteriorly, the front steeply elevated; pectoral spine short, $2\frac{1}{2}$ to 3 in head; base of anal fin short, only about $\frac{1}{5}$ length of body; jaws nearly equal; barbels longer than head; humeral process rather long and rough. Colour, almost black, often varying to yellowish

COMMON BULLHEAD, *Ameiurus nebulosus*

CHANNEL CAT, *Ictalurus punctatus*

YELLOW CAT, *Ameiurus natalis*

COMMON BULLHEAD, *Ameiurus nebulosus*

COMMON REDHORSE SUCKER, *Moxostoma aureolum*

LAKE CARP SUCKER OR QUILLBACK, *Carpiodes thompsoni*

and brown; anal rays white, in marked contrast with the dusky membranes.

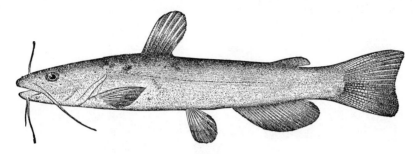

Flatheaded Cat; Brown Cat

Ameiurus platycephalus (Girard)

Head 3½; depth 5½ to 8; A. 16 to 20. Body extremely long, mesially nearly round; head low, flat and broad, especially in old examples, its width 3 to 5 in length of body; upper jaw strongly projecting; dorsal fin high, ⅔ length of head, its spine nearer snout than adipose fin; caudal fin emarginate. Colour, clear olive brown, varying into yellowish or greenish; a dark horizontal bar at base of dorsal. Length 15 to 18 inches.

This is the most slender species of the genus, and is almost entirely herbivorous as to its food, its elongate intestine being usually well-filled with water plants.

It is abundant in the streams of the Carolinas and Georgia from Cape Fear to the Chattahoochee. It is regarded as a good food-fish.

GENUS LEPTOPS RAFINESQUE

Mud Cats

Body elongate, slender, and much depressed anteriorly; head large, very wide, and depressed; skin very thick, entirely concealing the skull; eye small; mouth very large, the lower jaw always projecting beyond the upper; teeth in broad villiform bands on the premaxilliaries and dentaries; adipose fin large, its long base over posterior half of anal; anal fin small; caudal oblong, subtruncate, with numerous accessory rays, recurrent above and behind; pectoral with a broad, compressed spine, serrated on both margins, and with a prolonged fleshy integument, obliquely striated. Only one species known.

Mud Cat; Goujon

Leptops olivaris (Rafinesque)

Body slender, depressed anteriorly; the head very flat, the lower jaw projecting; barbels short; dorsal spine very weak, half the length of the fin; caudal slightly emarginate; anal short, of 12 to 15 rays; humeral process short. Colour, yellowish, more or less mottled with brown and greenish; paler below.

The goujon is a large, coarse fish, said to reach a length of 5 feet, and a weight of 100 pounds. A ripe female examined by us at Morgan City, Louisiana, was 41 inches long and weighed 46 pounds. This fish dressed 27 pounds. Another, 38 inches long, weighed 37 pounds, and still another 37 inches long weighed 36½ pounds.

This species is found in all suitable waters throughout the Mississippi Valley and in the Gulf States from Alabama west and south to Chihuahua. It is a fish of the lowlands, and is most abundant in the lower courses of the large streams and in the bayous and overflow ponds of the lower Mississippi Valley. It is perhaps most plentiful in the lowlands of Arkansas, West Tennessee and Louisiana. In the Atchafalaya River it is, next to the blue cat, the most important food fish. It is caught in the same ways during the same seasons, and is dressed and marketed in the same manner. Its flesh is of fine texture and of exellent flavour, and there is no really good reason for the prejudice against it which obtains in many localities. The fact that it is a large, rather repulsive looking fish, not any too cleanly in its habits doubtless has somewhat to do with this prejudice.

In different parts of its range, the goujon is known by many vernacular names. In Louisiana it is called the goujon or yellow cat, and the latter name is in common use throughout most of its habitat. In the South it is known as the "pieded cat," Opelousas cat, and mud cat, the last of these being also generally used in the North, where it is also called granny cat. The names Bashaw and Russian cat are sometimes heard, but their origin has not been explained.

The goujon is more voracious than the blue cat, and large individuals are apt to feed upon small ones of the latter species when confined in the same live-box. To prevent this, it is said that the fishermen sometimes sew up with wire the mouths of the very large goujon. We have seen, on the Rock Castle River, in Kentucky, the blue cat used as live bait on hooks set for the goujon.

Occasionally large catfishes, of this species and the blue cat, crawl into the hollow cypress logs which are usually left in the water until ready to be sawed. The catfish may be unable to pass on through the log, and, being unable to turn around or back out, remains in the log until it is placed on the carriage, and the presence of the fish is then discovered by the saw crashing into it.

The spawning season of the goujon in Louisiana seems to be during April and the early part of May. As we proceed northward it is correspondingly later, being as late as June in the northern part of its range.

> "Don't talk to me o' bacon fat,
> Or taters, coon or 'possum;
> Fo' when I'se hooked a yaller cat,
> I'se got a meal to boss 'em."
> —*The Darkey and the Catfish.*

GENUS NOTURUS RAFINESQUE

Stone Cats

Teeth as in *Leptops*, the band in the upper jaw having a backward prolongation on each side from the outer posterior angle;

33

adipose fin adnate to the back; a poison gland at the base of the pectoral spine.

This genus, which contains but a single species, is close to *Schilbeodes* (the mad-toms), the species all having the poison gland and the adnate adipose fin, and all being small fish, lurking among weeds in stony brooks.

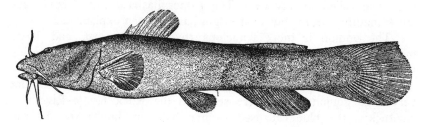

Stone Cat; Little Yellow Cat

Noturus flavus Rafinesque

Head about $4\frac{1}{4}$ in length, its width $5\frac{1}{3}$; depth $5\frac{2}{3}$; distance from snout to origin of dorsal about 3 in length; A. about 16. Body elongate, the head depressed, broad and flat, nearly as broad as long; middle of body subcylindrical; caudal peduncle compressed; a strong keel on back between dorsal fin and adipose fin, the latter deeply notched; dorsal spine very short; pectoral spine retrorsely serrate in front, slightly rough or nearly entire behind, its length $\frac{1}{3}$ distance from snout to origin of dorsal; caudal rounded behind; humeral process very short and sharp.

Colour, nearly uniform yellowish brown, sometimes blackish above; fins edged with yellow. Length, a foot or more. Great Lakes region, and westward and south to Montana, Wyoming and Texas, rather common, especially westward.

This is the only one of the catfishes with adnate adipose fin attaining sufficient size to give it any food value. Ordinarily it is used as food only in those regions where food fishes are not numerous.

Related to the stone cat, are in America, ten or a dozen species of small catfishes belonging to the genus *Schilbeodes*, and known as mad toms. They are all very small, none of them exceeding three or four inches in length, all have the poison gland well developed, and are able to inflict a very painful wound with the pectoral spine.

They live usually in shallow water, in running streams, or lakes, and may often be found hidden under small rocks or other objects affording protection. The species of *Schilbeodes* occur only in the Eastern United States from Vermont to Florida and west to the Dakotas and south to Texas.

Istlarius balsanus is an important food-fish in Morelos and the Mexican States to the Southwest, through which the Rio Balsas flows. In size and appearance it resembles the channel cat. In Jalisco, and in all tributaries of the Rio Lerma and Rio Santiago, *Ameiurus dugesi* is very common, being in size and value as well as in appearance similar to *Ameiurus catus*. The Mexicans call all catfishes Bagre. Those in the streams are Bagre del Rio.

THE SUCKERS

Family IV. Catostomidæ

BODY elongate, usually more or less compressed; head rather conical; opercles normally developed; nostrils double; no barbels; mouth usually greatly protractile and with fleshy lips; jaws toothless; lower pharyngeal bones falciform, armed with a single series of numerous comb-like teeth; branchiostegals 3; gill-membranes more or less united to the isthmus, restricting the gill-openings to the sides; gills 4, a slit behind the fourth; pseudobranchiae present; scales cycloid; lateral line decurved, sometimes absent; head naked; fins not scaly; dorsal fin comparatively long (of 10 to 30 rays); anal fin short; pectorals placed low; ventrals abdominal; no adipose fin; fins without true spines; alimentary canal long; stomach simple and without pyloric cœca; air-bladder large, divided into 2 or 3 parts by transverse constrictions.

The sucker family is a large one, embracing some 15 genera and more than 70 species, 2 of which occur in Eastern Asia, while the others are inhabitants of the fresh waters of North America.

The members of this family are very widely distributed over the United States, there being scarcely a State which has not several species, and at least two extend their range far into Canada and Alaska, while others are found southward into Mexico.

The family includes not only the species commonly known as suckers, but also those known as redhorses, buffaloes, quillbacks, and freshwater mullets. Most of the species do not exceed a weight of 4 or 5 pounds, though some of them reach an immense size.

As food fishes they do not occupy a high rank. Though the flesh is well flavoured, it is exceedingly full of bundles of small fagot-bones, which are very troublesome to one who attempts to eat it. The great abundance and the large size of many of the species, however, render them of considerable commercial importance, thus entitling them to a place in this work.

None of the species has any rank as a game fish. They rarely or never take a hook, except on set-lines. The methods employed in their capture are varied, but haul-seines, gill-nets, pounds and other traps, and set-lines are the kinds of apparatus in most general use.

The habits of all the species are much the same. They are all bottom feeders, feeding chiefly upon vegetation and the less active and soft forms of smaller animal life such as worms, larvæ, and eggs of various kinds.

They are all spring spawners, and nearly all have the habit of running up stream at spawning time. Illinois is called the "Sucker State" because its first settlers came *up the river* in the spring when the suckers were running.

Only the genera and species of some commercial importance are considered at length.

a. Dorsal fin long, with 24 to 30 rays; air-bladder in 2 parts.

b. Fontanelle present; body ovate; scales large.

c. Mouth large, more or less terminal, protractile forward. Large species, dark in color;......................*Ictiobus*, 38

cc. Mouth small, inferior, protractile downward. Smaller species of pale coloration;.........................*Carpiodes*, 41

bb. Fontanelle obliterated by the union of the parietal bones; body elongate;.............................*Cycleptus*, 44

aa. Dorsal fin short, with only 10 to 18 rays.

d. Air bladder in two parts.

e. Lateral line complete; scales small, 55 to 115 in lateral line.

f. Fontanelle nearly or quite obliterated in adult; jaws with hard sheaths; posterior division of air bladder slender; *Pantosteus*, 45

ff. Fontanelle broad and evident at all stages of growth; posterior division of air bladder broad.

g. Nuchal region without a hump, the interneural spines normally developed.

h. Mouth small, inferior, with thick papillose lips;..*Catostomus*, 46

hh. Mouth very large, terminal, oblique; lips thin and nearly smooth.

i. Gillrakers simple, fringe-like;..................*Chasmistes*, 54

ii. Gillrakers broad, shaped like the Greek letter △ (delta), their edges entire and unarmed;....................*Deltistes*, 57

gg. Nuchal region with a high, sharp-edged hump;..*Xyrauchen*, 57

ee. Lateral line interrupted or wanting; scales large, 40 to 50 in a longitudinal series.

j. Lateral line entirely wanting;....................*Erimyzon*, 58

jj. Lateral line more or less developed, especially in adult; *Minytrema*, 59

dd. Air bladder in three parts.
k. Mouth normal, the lower lip entire or merely lobed.
l. Pharyngeal bones moderate, the teeth compressed, gradually larger downward;..........................*Moxostoma,* 60
ll. Pharyngeal bones very strong, with the lower teeth much enlarged, subcylindrical and truncate;.......*Placopharynx,* 64
kk. Mouth singular, the upper lip not protractile, greatly enlarged, the lower lip developed as two separate lobes....
Lagochila, 65

GENUS ICTIOBUS RAFINESQUE

The Buffalo Fishes

Body robust; head very large and strong; fontanelle large; well-open; opercular apparatus well developed, the subopercle broad, the opercle strongly furrowed; mouth large, terminal, protractile; mandible strongly oblique; lips little developed, the upper narrow and smooth, the lower full on the sides, but narrow in front; pharyngeal bones rather weak, the teeth numerous; scales large, thick, and nearly equal over the body; lateral line well developed, slightly decurved anteriorly; dorsal rays numerous, the anterior somewhat elevated; caudal not much forked.

Large, coarse fishes, usually dark in colour, inhabiting chiefly the larger rivers and some of the small lakes of the Mississippi Valley. Only four species known, the three following and a fourth from Guatemala.

a. Mouth large, terminal, protractile forward; lips very thin; lower pharyngeals and teeth weak;........*cyprinella,.* 39
aa. Mouth smaller, more or less inferior, protractile downward, and with thicker lips; lower pharyngeals stronger, the teeth comparatively coarse and large.
b. Back scarcely elevated, the depth 3 to $3\frac{1}{4}$ in length.
c. Mouth rather large and oblique, approaching that of *I. cyprinella,* more oblique than in the next;.................*urus,* 40
cc. Mouth small, inferior;......................*meridionalis,* 41
bb. Back elevated and compressed, the depth $2\frac{1}{2}$ to $2\frac{3}{4}$ in length;
bubalus, 41

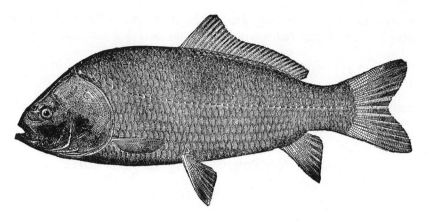

Common Buffalo Fish

Ictiobus cyprinella (Cuvier & Valenciennes)

This species reaches a length of 3 feet, and a weight of 50 pounds or more.

In certain lakes in the Mississippi Valley (notably Lake Washington, Minnesota and the Okeboji lakes in northwestern Iowa) extraordinary runs of very large buffalo fish occur occasionally. These runs take place in the spring at the spawning time of the fish, and usually at the time of a heavy rain when the tributary streams are full and the connecting marshes are flooded. Then these fish come up from the lake, in great numbers, crowding the inlets and spreading over the flooded marshes. They remain only a few days, and soon disappear as suddenly and mysteriously as they came; but their brief stay has been long enough to permit great slaughter by the farmers of the surrounding country, who kill great numbers with pitchforks, clubs and other primitive weapons, and haul them away in wagon loads. After returning to the lakes nothing more is seen of them until the next spring, or possibly not for several years.

In these northern lakes these fish rarely or never take the hook, nor can they be successfully gilled, but in the lower Mississippi Valley they are frequently taken on set-lines baited with balls of dough.

In Louisiana, where they are known as the gourdhead buffalo, they are of considerable commercial interest. The flesh, though nutritious, is coarse and not highly flavoured. This species is also known as the red-mouthed buffalo, and big-mouthed buffalo.

Head 3½; depth 2½ to 3½; D. 27 to 29; A. 9; V. 10; scales 7-37 to 41-6. Body stout, moderately compressed, the outline somewhat elliptical, but the back rather more curved than the belly; opercular apparatus very strong, the opercle itself nearly half length of head. Colour, dull brownish-olive, not silvery; fins dusky.

Black Buffalo; Mongrel Buffalo

Ictiobus urus (Agassiz)

This species is close to the common buffalo, from which it can be distinguished by its smaller, more oblique mouth, and its much darker colour. It occurs throughout the Mississippi Valley in the larger streams, it being most abundant in those of the South, where it is said to spawn in March and April. It reaches a weight of 5 to 35 pounds, and resembles the preceding species in habits and food value. In Louisiana it is sometimes called "chopper."

Head very stout, about 4 in length, strongly convex; depth 3 to 3¼; eye about equal to snout, 5½ in head; D. 30; A. 10; scales 8-41-7. Body much less elevated and less compressed, the head thicker, larger and less pointed, and the eye much smaller than in the small-mouthed buffalo; back not at all carinated; axis of body above ventrals about at the lateral line, and but little farther from the dorsal outline than from the ventral; mouth large, well forward, considerably oblique, approaching that of the common buffalo; mandible longer than the eye; premaxilliaries somewhat below the suborbital; dorsal fin low and less rapidly shortened than in the next species, the longest ray scarcely half as long as base of fin; anal rounded, its rays not rapidly shortened, the middle ones not much shorter than the longest. Colour, very dark, the fins almost black.

Small-mouthed Buffalo; White Buffalo

Ictiobus bubalus (Rafinesque)

This is the most abundant and best known of all the buffalo fishes. It reaches a weight of 35 pounds or more and a length of 3 feet. It is found in all the larger rivers of the Mississippi Basin and in some of the small lakes, where its habits are essentially the same as those of the big-mouthed buffalo, the latter species, however, being less of a bottom feeder than either of the two others here described. In the South all three species spawn in March and April; as we go northward the spawning season is correspondingly later, it being in May and June in Minnesota and Wisconsin.

Head 4; depth $2\frac{1}{2}$; snout $3\frac{1}{8}$; eye 5; D. 28 or 29; A. 10 or 11; V. 10; scales 8 or 9-35 to 39-5 or 6, 12 or 13 before the dorsal. Body short and compressed, the dorsal strongly arched and subcarinate from occiput to origin of dorsal fin; ventral outline only slightly convex; head small; mouth small, subinferior, and protractile downward; lips papillose; opercle strongly striate; caudal peduncle deep and compressed, its least depth $1\frac{3}{4}$ in head; axis of body above the ventrals, below the lateral line, and nearly twice as far from back as from belly; fins moderate, the first 7 or 8 dorsal rays lengthened, as long as head, rays of short portion $3\frac{1}{2}$ in head; longest anal ray $1\frac{1}{6}$; pectoral short, not reaching base of ventral, $1\frac{2}{5}$ in head; ventrals longer, 1.1 in head; caudal deeply lunate, the lobes longer than head. Colour, pale, almost silvery; fins scarcely dusky.

Ictiobus meridionalis is a southern species known only from the Rio Usumacinta, Mexico.

GENUS CARPIODES RAFINESQUE

The Carp Suckers

This genus is very close to *Ictiobus*, the species being smaller, the colour paler, and the dentition weaker, but there are no important technical characters separating the two groups.

Of the five species referred to under this genus, one occurs in the Potomac and Delaware and the streams about Chesapeake Bay, one in the St. Lawrence basin, and the other three in the Mississippi Valley and Texas. Only two of the species are of any commercial value.

a. Body subfusiform, the depth about 3 in length;......*carpio*, 42
aa. Body ovate-oblong, the back elevated, the depth about $2\frac{1}{2}$ in length.

b. Opercles strongly striate.
c. Lips thin, silvery-white in life, the halves of the lower lip meeting in a wide angle, as in *C carpio.*
d. Head large, the snout blunt, the nostril near its tip; eye large, $3\frac{1}{2}$ to 4 in head............................*difformis,* 42
dd. Head small and pointed, the snout projecting; eye small, 5 to $5\frac{1}{2}$ in head............................*thompsoni,* 42
cc. Lips full, thick, reddish in life, the halves of the lower meeting at an acute angle; first ray of dorsal usually very long.
velifer, 43
bb. Opercles nearly smooth; otherwise essentially as in *C. velifer.*
cyprinus, 43

Carp Sucker

Carpiodes carpio (Rafinesque)

The carp sucker is the largest of the genus, reaching a weight of 2 or 3 pounds. It occurs in the Ohio Valley and southward to central Texas, but does not appear to be very abundant anywhere.

It is used for food along with the other members of the family, but is perhaps inferior to most of them. It is caught on setlines and in seines.

Head 4 to 5; depth $2\frac{2}{8}$ to 3; eye $4\frac{1}{2}$ in head; D. 30; A. 7; scales 36. Body more fusiform than in any other species, compressed, but not much arched; head rather short; muzzle short, but projecting beyond the mouth; anterior rays of dorsal short, and notably thickened and long at the base, especially in the adult, the first ray nearer muzzle than base of caudal fin, the longest ray a little more than half base of fin; caudal moderately forked.

C. difformis is an unimportant species occurring in the Ohio Valley and westward in the upper Mississippi Valley. It closely resembles the quillback, but differs in the character of the lower lip.

C. tumidus is perhaps a distinct species found in the lower Rio Grande and southward.

Lake Carp

Carpiodes thompsoni Agassiz

This fish occurs in the Great Lakes and lakes tributary to the St. Lawrence. It reaches a considerable size; an example taken in Lake Champlain about April 23 was 21 inches long and weighed 7 pounds. It was a nearly ripe female and the roe alone weighed 2.5 pounds.

The food value of the flesh of this fish is essentially the same as that of the species of *Ictiobus*.

By the fishermen of Lake Champlain this species is known as "buffalo," "carp sucker," or "drum."

Head 4 to 4.5; depth 2.5; eye small, 5 to 5.5 in head; D. 27; A. 7; V. 10; scales 8-39 to 41-6. Body short and stout, the back much arched; head small, the snout pointed; lips thin and white, meeting at a wide angle; tip of lower jaw much in advance of nostrils; maxillary reaching vertical at front of orbit; scales closely imbricated; dorsal rays considerably elevated, $\frac{2}{3}$ as long as base of fin; origin of dorsal fin about midway of body.

C. velifer, the quillback, spearfish, sailfish, or skimfish, is a small species found pretty well throughout the Mississippi Valley. It is distinguished from other species in the same waters by the produced first dorsal ray and the character of the lower lip whose halves meet at an acute angle.

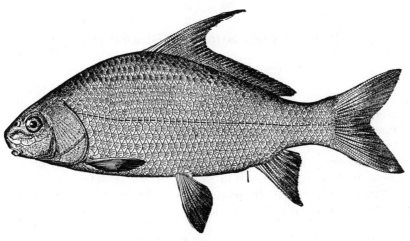

Eastern Carp Sucker

Carpiodes cyprinus (Le Sueur)

In the Potomac and the streams about Chesapeake Bay occurs *C. cyprinus*, the Eastern carp sucker, which resembles *C. velifer* except that its opercles are smooth. Neither of these species is of much or any food-value.

GENUS CYCLEPTUS RAFINESQUE

This genus differs from *Ictiobus* and *Carpiodes*, the only other genera having a long dorsal fin, in having the fontanelle obliterated by the union of the parietal bones, and in the very elongate body. Only one species is known.

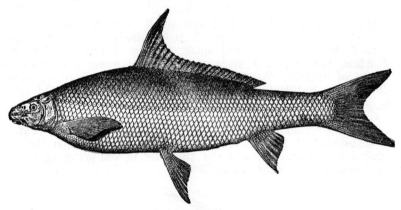

Gourd-seed Sucker; Blackhorse

Cycleptus elongatus (Le Sueur)

This singular and interesting fish is known only from the Mississippi Valley, where it is rather common in the larger streams.

It reaches a length of 2 to 2.5 feet, and is perhaps more highly esteemed as a food-fish than any other member of the family. It is usually caught in seines or on set-lines.

Besides the vernacular names given above, it is also known as "Missouri sucker," "sweet sucker," and "suckerel."

Head 6 to 8.5; depth 4 to 5; eye 6 to 7 in head; D. 30; A 7 or 8; V. 10; scales 9-56-7. Body unusually long and slender, moderately compressed, not much elevated; caudal peduncle long; head very small, short and slender, its upper surface rounded; mouth small, entirely inferior, overlapped by the projecting snout; upper lip thick, pendant, covered with several rows of tubercles; lower lip moderate, formed somewhat as in *Catostomus*, but less full, incised behind; jaws with rudimentary cartilaginous sheath; eye small, behind middle of head, not high up; suborbital bones small and narrow; opercle smooth and narrow; isthmus moderate; gillrakers moderate, soft; pharyngeal bones strong, the teeth rather wide apart, increasing in size downward; scales about equal over the body, with wide, exposed surfaces; lateral line nearly straight, well developed; fins rather large, the dorsal beginning in front of ventrals and ending just before anal, strongly falcate in front, the length of the first and second developed rays more than half base of fin, the following rays rapidly shortened to about the eighth, the remaining rays all short; caudal fin large, widely forked, the lobes equal; anal fin quite small, low and scaly at the base; pectoral long and somewhat falcate; air-bladder in two parts, the anterior short, the other long; sexual peculiarities marked, the males in spring with black pigment and the head covered with small tubercles. Colour very dark, the males in spring almost black.

GENUS PANTOSTEUS COPE

The Mountain Suckers

This genus resembles *Catostomus,* from which it differs chiefly in having the fontanelle nearly obliterated, and in having a more or less developed cartilaginous sheath on each jaw. The species are all western, chiefly in the Rocky Mountain region and westward, mostly in rocky brooks in the arid districts. The 8 known species are each of rather small size, and scarcely valued as food.

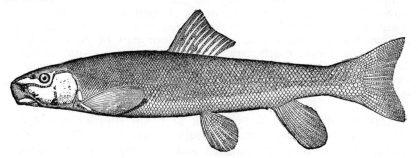

Mountain Sucker

Pantosteus jordani Evermann

Pantosteus arizonæ reaches a length of 9 inches, and is known only from Salt River at Tempe, Arizona. *P. generosus,*

45

known as the mountain sucker, is abundant in the streams in the Salt Lake basin, and southwest in the Sevier basin. It reaches 8 or 10 inches in length. *P. plebeius* reaches a foot in length and is found in the Rio Grande basin and southward into Chihuahua. It is very common. *P. delphinus*, the blue-headed sucker, attains the length of a foot, and is abundant in the upper portion of the basin of the Colorado. *P. guzmaniensis* is known only from Lake Guzman, Chihuahua. *P. jordani* grows to a foot or more in length, and is found pretty generally distributed in clear streams in the upper portions of the Missouri and Columbia basins. It is of more value as a food fish than any other species of the genus. *P. aræopus* from the rivers of Nevada and the Kern River, California, and *P. clarki* from the Gila basin, are rare and little known species.

GENUS CATOSTOMUS LE SUEUR

Fine-scaled Suckers

Body rather elongate, more or less fusiform, subterete; head rather long; eye small and high up; mouth rather large, inferior; upper lip thick, papillose, protractile; lower lip greatly developed, with broad, free margin, usually deeply incised behind, so that it forms two lobes which are often more or less separated; opercle moderate; pharyngeal bones moderate, the teeth rather short, compressed, rapidly diminishing in size upward; scales small and crowded anteriorly; lateral line nearly straight and well developed; origin of dorsal nearly midway of body; anal short and high; ventrals inserted under middle or posterior part of dorsal; caudal forked, the lobes nearly equal; sexual peculiarities not marked, the fins usually higher in the male and the anal somewhat swollen and tuberculate in the spring; breeding males in most species with a rosy or orange lateral band.

Species about 20, all belonging to North America except one *(C. rostratus* Tilesius*)* which is said to occur in Siberia. Our species are not well differentiated and are difficult to distinguish.

In the following key have been included only those which are of commercial value:

a. Head transversely convex above, the orbital rim not elevated; scales in lateral line 60 or more.

b. Scales very small, much reduced and crowded anteriorly, the number in lateral line 80 to 115.

c. Upper lip broad, with 5 or 6 rows of papillæ.

d. Dorsal fin with 11 to 13 rays and very high; *Latipinnis,* 47

dd. Dorsal fin with 10 to 12 rays and only moderately developed; . . . .*griseus,* 48

cc. Upper lip comparatively thin and narrow, with 2 to 4 rows of papillæ.

e. Scales in lateral line 95 to 115; . . . .*catostomus,* 49

bb. Scales small, but larger than in the preceding group, the number in lateral line 56 to 75.

f. Scales in lateral line 70 to 75; lower lip broad.

g. Dorsal fin short, of 11 to 13 rays; head small, conical; *occidentalis,* 50

gg. Dorsal fin long, of about 15 rays; head large; . . .*macrocheilus,* 50

ff. Scales in lateral line larger, 58 to 70 in number; lower lip with about 4 rows of papillæ.

h. Mandible short, $3\frac{1}{2}$ to $3\frac{2}{3}$ in head; upper lip narrow; *commersonii,* 51

hh. Mandible longer, 3 to $3\frac{1}{8}$ head; upper lip broader; . .*ardens,* 52

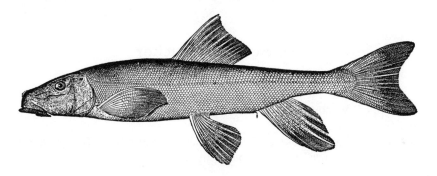

Flannel-mouth Sucker

Catostomus latipinnis Baird & Girard

This sucker is known only from the Colorado River of the West, and its larger tributaries. It is said to be quite abundant and ascends the rivers in spring.

As a food fish it is of some importance, particularly to the Indians.

Head $4\frac{3}{4}$; depth $5\frac{1}{4}$; D. 11 to 13; scales 17-98 to 105-17. Body elongate, the caudal peduncle long and slender; head rather slender, with prominent snout and rather contracted, inferior mouth; outline of mouth triangular, the apex forward; lips very thick, greatly developed, the lower incised to the base, its posterior margin extending backward to opposite the eye; tubercles on lower lip small behind; jaws with a slight cartilaginous sheath; eye small and high up; scales long and low, posteriorly rounded; fins greatly developed, especially in old males, the free border of the dorsal deeply incised; height of vertical fins in the male greater than length of head; origin of dorsal nearer snout than base of caudal; caudal very strong, the rudimentary rays unusually developed. Colour, dark olive, abruptly paler below; sides and fins largely orange in both sexes, the anal and lower lobe of caudal tuberculate in breeding males. Length 2 feet or less.

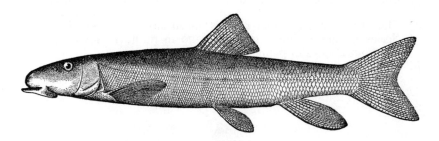

Platte River Sucker

Catostomus griseus (Girard)

Upper Missouri River basin, particularly abundant in the Platte and the Yellowstone.

This species is close to *C. catostomus*, apparently differing chiefly in the larger mouth and the broader upper lip.

Head 4 in body; depth $5\frac{1}{2}$; D. 10 to 12; scales 16-90 to 110-14. Body long and slender, subterete, compressed behind, the form essentially that of *C. catostomus*; head large, the interorbital space broad and flat, $2\frac{1}{2}$ in length of head; eye small, high up and rather posterior; mouth large, about as in *C. latipinnis*, the upper lip very large, pendant, and with 5 to 8 series of tubercles; lower lip incised to base, the lobes long; horny sheath pretty well developed; dorsal fin not long, nor especially elevated, its origin rather nearer base of caudal than tip of snout; caudal long and strongly forked; anal long and high, reaching base of caudal; ventrals not reaching vent. Colour, dusky brown, sometimes with a dusky lateral band, sometimes irregularly mottled or barred; snout dark. Length 1 to 2 feet.

Long-nosed Sucker; Northern Sucker

Catostomus catostomus (Forster)

The long-nosed sucker is one of the largest of the family, reaching a length of 2 to 2½ feet, and a weight of several pounds. It is found from the St. Lawrence River and the Great Lakes westward in the Upper Missouri basin and to the Upper Columbia, thence northward to Alaska; the most widely distributed sucker; but probably not occurring south of 40° north latitude, except in West Virginia where recently obtained by Prof. W. P. Hay.

In the Great Lakes and northward this species is a food fish of considerable value. It is usually taken in hoop or trap nets, or gillnets.

Its spawning time is in the spring, in most localities as early as May.

Head 4¼ to 4⅔; depth 4¼ to 6; eye 6 to 8; D. 10 or 11; A. 7; scales 14 to 17-90 to 117-13. Body elongate, subterete; head very long and slender, depressed and flattened above, broad at base, but tapering into a long snout, which overhangs the large mouth; lips thick, coarsely tuberculate, the upper lip narrow, with 2 or 3, sometimes 4 rows of papillæ; lower lip deeply incised, the lobes shorter than in *C. griseus*, and the mouth narrower; lower jaw with a slight cartilaginous sheath; eye small, behind middle of head; scales very small, much crowded anteriorly.

Males in spring with the head and anal fin profusely tuberculate; and the side with a broad, rosy band.

49

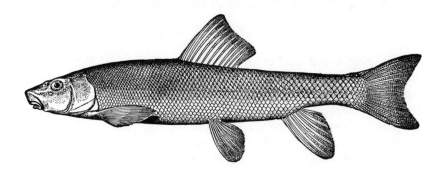

Sacramento Sucker

Catostomus occidentalis Ayres

Streams of California, especially abundant in the Sacramento and San Joaquin rivers. This species was formerly of considerable importance to the Indians, who caught it in great numbers. It reaches a foot in length.

Columbia River Sucker ; Yellow Sucker

Catostomus macrocheilus Girard

Columbia River basin and other rivers and lakes of Oregon and Washington, generally abundant; not known from the Snake River basin above Shoshone Falls. It is abundant in the Redfish Lakes of Idaho and in Flathead Lake of Montana. During the spring and early summer it is found in the streams, but in July or earlier it retires to deeper water, entering lakes whenever opportunity offers. It attains a length of 12 to 17 inches, and is a food-fish of considerable importance, particularly to the Flathead Indians and other Indians in the regions where it is found. Its flesh is sweet, firm and flaky, the fish usually inhabiting cold waters.

At the Redfish Lakes in Idaho this sucker was noticed in August and September toward the close of the day swimming about in great schools at the surface of the water, sometimes with their noses projecting. The schools would gather about the mouth of some inlet and swim slowly about in this way for an hour or more just at sundown. The meaning of this particular habit has not been explained.

Head 4 to $4\frac{2}{5}$; depth 5; eye 5 to 6 in head; snout 2; D. 12 to 14; A. 7; scales 12 to 14-65 to 75-10 or 11, about 40 before the dorsal. Body rather heavy forward, the caudal peduncle slender; snout blunt, overlapping the horizontal mouth which is quite large, with very large lips, the upper full and pendant, with 6 to 8 rows of moderate papillæ; dorsal fin much longer than high; pectoral long and narrow; caudal well forked. Colour, rather dark; a dusky lateral streak; abruptly pale below.

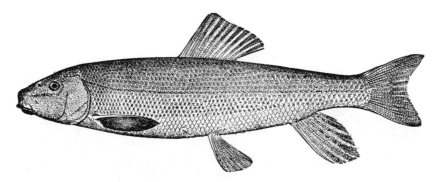

Common Sucker ; White Sucker

Catostomus commersonii (Lacépède)

This is the most abundant sucker in the streams and lakes from Quebec and Massachusetts westward to Montana and Colorado and southward to Missouri and Georgia. Specimens from Montana to Colorado have the lips broader and with more numerous papillæ.

In the smaller streams this species reaches a length of but a few inches, while in the larger streams and lakes it attains a length of 18 inches or more and becomes a food-fish of considerable importance. Though quite bony, its flesh is firm and flaky and very sweet. In some parts of the country this species is caught in large numbers and salted for winter use. It is usually taken by means of seines, traps or gillnets.

In the spring of the year, as the spawning season approaches, they run up the streams in great numbers and spawn upon the riffles. This is, in most parts of its range, in May or June, and the fish is called the "June Sucker."

Head 4 to 4⅔; depth 4 to 5; eye 6 in head; snout 2¼; D. 12; A. 7; scales 10-64 to 70-9. Body rather stout, varying with age. subterete, heavy anteriorly; head moderate, conical, flattish above; snout rather prominent, scarcely overpassing the mouth, which is large, the lips papillose, the upper with 2 or 3 rows of papillæ (4 to 6 in western specimens); scales small, crowded anteriorly, larger on the sides and below. Colour, olivaceous; males in spring somewhat rosy; young brownish, more or less mottled and blotched with dark.

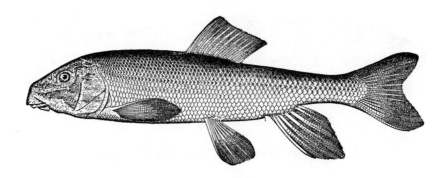

Utah Lake Mullet

Catostomus ardens Jordan & Gilbert

This species is very close to the common sucker, differing chiefly in the larger mouth and lips. Abundant in the Snake River basin above Shoshone Falls and in the lakes and streams of the Great Salt Lake basin. It swarms in myriads in Utah Lake, "the greatest sucker pond in the world." In Heart Lake of Yellowstone Park this fish is infested by a parasitic worm *(Ligula catostomi)* which is often larger than the fish's viscera.

Like all other suckers, this species is a spring spawner, and at that time immense numbers are said to come into the shallow water of Utah Lake, Jacksons Lake and other lakes which it inhabits.

This species reaches a length of 18 inches or more, and holds rank with the others of the genus as a food-fish.

Head $3\frac{2}{8}$; depth $4\frac{1}{2}$; eye small, 7 in head, $3\frac{1}{2}$ in interorbital width; snout $2\frac{1}{4}$ in head; D. 12 or 13; A. 7; scales 12-70 to 72-12. Body rather long, little compressed, the back broad; head broad, conical; mouth entirely inferior, the mandible nearly horizontal; upper lip wide, full, pendant, with 4 to 8 rows of coarse, irregular papillæ; lower lip very broad, coarsely papillose, cut to the base; dorsal fin long and low, its anterior rays $\frac{1}{2}$ longer than the last; pectorals, ventrals and caudal short; anal long. Colour, blackish above, paler below, the fins dark; breeding males with the sides rosy.

Besides the 7 species described above, 12 others of less importance are recognized as occurring in North America.

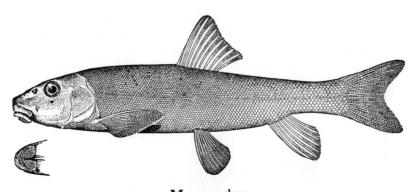

Moogadee

Catostomus pocatello Gilbert & Evermann

One of these, the Moogadee of the Fort Hall Indians of Idaho, is of some food value.

GENUS CHASMISTES JORDAN

Head large, broad and flattish above, the sides vertical; eye small, high up, and rather posterior; mouth very large, terminal, the lower jaw in the closed mouth being very oblique; lower jaw long and strong, more than half length of head, its tip, when the mouth is closed, about on a level with the eye; upper jaw very protractile; upper lip thin and nearly smooth; snout usually elevated above rest of head; the premaxillary spines generally forming a conspicuous nose; lower lip moderate, consisting of a broad flap on each side of the mandible, reduced to a narrow rim in front, the surface of the lip nearly smooth, without papillæ; nostrils large; fontanelle well developed; gillrakers simple, fringe-like; air-bladder in 2 parts. Species of rather large size, inhabiting the Great Salt Lake Basin and the Klamath Lakes of southern Oregon.

Six species are recognized, only 4 of which seem to be of any commercial importance.

a. Scales moderate, 60 to 65 in the lateral line.
b. Scales 9-63-8; dorsal usually 11; nose prominent; *liorus,* 54
aa. Scales small, 75 to 85 in the lateral line.
c. Snout prominent, premaxillary spines strongly protruding, forming a prominently projecting snout;.............*stomias,* 55
cc. Snout not prominent, premaxillary spines not forming a prominent hump.
d. Scales 12-75-11;..................... ....*brevirostris,* 55
dd. Scales 13-80-12;...................................*copei,* 56

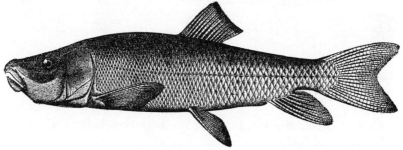

June Sucker of Utah Lake

Chasmistes liorus Jordan

Known only from Utah Lake, where it is exceedingly abundant, contributing, with *Catostomus ardens*, to make that lake the "greatest sucker pond in the world."

Head 3⅖; depth 5; eye 6 to 7; scales 9-63-8; D. 11; A. 7; interorbital space broad, 2¼ in head; width of the open mouth 3½ in head; dorsal elevated in front, its longest ray twice the length of the last and about equal to base of fin; caudal deeply forked, the lower lobe the longer; lower fins small. Colour, dusky above, pale below; back and sides profusely covered with dark punctulations. Length 18 inches or less.

Short-nosed Sucker

Chasmistes brevirostris Cope

This species is known only from the Klamath Lakes of Oregon. It attains a length of 12 to 18 inches and is a food-fish of some value to the Indians, who know it as the " Yen."

Snout 2½ to 2⅖ in head; mandible 1¼ in snout; interorbital width 2⅛ in head; D. 11; A. 9; scales 13-73-12; premaxillary spines not produced to form a hump on the snout; lower lip fold present on the sides of the mandible; each lip with small, inconspicuous, sparse tubercles, in 3 or 4 series on the upper lip; ventrals extending ⅔ distance to vent; scales with strong concentric striæ. Colour, dark above, silvery on lower part of side and on belly; fins all dusky.

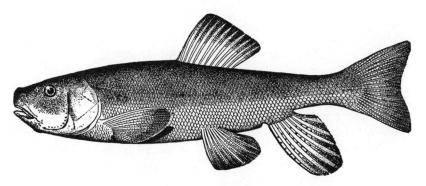

Klamath Lake Sucker

Chasmistes stomias Gilbert

This is another species of *Chasmistes* inhabiting Upper Klamath

Lake, which is a close rival of Utah Lake for the honour of being the "greatest sucker pond in the world."

It is the most abundant species of the genus in the Klamath Lakes. It reaches a length of 15 to 18 inches and is of great value to the Indians, by whom it is known as "Kahptu."

From all other species of the genus, except *C. brevirostris* and *C. copei*, it is distinguished by its small scales (14 or 15-76 to 82-11), and from *C. brevirostris* it differs in the deeper head, larger mandible, more oblique mouth, and by the prominent hump on the snout; mouth inclined at an angle of 40°. Colour, dark above, whitish or silvery below, the two colours separated along a definite line traversing the side midway between lateral line and insertion of ventrals.

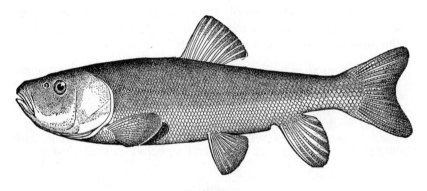

Tswam

Chasmistes copei Evermann & Meek

This is still another species of *Chasmistes*, inhabiting the Klamath Lakes. It closely resembles *C. stomias*, but may be distinguished from that species by its larger head, larger, more oblique mouth, less prominent snout, and very small fins.

This sucker reaches a length of 16 or 18 inches and is used as food by the Klamath Indians. The Indian name is "Tswam."

Head $3\frac{2}{3}$; depth 4; eye $6\frac{1}{5}$; snout $2\frac{1}{2}$; D. 10; A. 7; scales 13-80-12. Head very large, cheek very deep; body stout, back scarcely elevated. Colour, upper parts dark olivaceous; under parts whitish; a dark spot in upper part of axil; dorsal and caudal dark; pectoral dark on inner surface; ventrals and anal plain.

GENUS DELTISTES SEALE

This genus is close to *Chasmistes*, from which it differs chiefly in the structure of the gillrakers, the very long, slender head, the small horizontal mouth, and the thicker lips. The gillrakers are broad and shaped like the Greek letter △ (delta) and their edges are unarmed and entire; lower pharyngeals weak, with numerous small teeth.

The single known species is the Lost River sucker *(D. luxatus)*, which is the most important food-fish of the Klamath Lakes region. It is apparently resident during most of the year in the deeper waters of Upper Klamath and Tule lakes, running up the rivers in March and April in incredible numbers, the height of the run varying from year to year according to the condition of the streams. The Lost River fish are the most highly prized, and are said to be much fatter and of finer flavour than those ascending the tributaries of Upper Klamath Lake.

This species reaches the largest size of any of the Klamath Lake suckers, examples over 3 feet in length and weighing several pounds having been examined. It is of vast importance to the Klamath Indians, who, during the spring run, catch it in immense numbers and cure it for winter use.

An attempt has been made to preserve the meat in cans, but apparently without success. Oil has been extracted from the heads and entrails, said to be worth 60c. to 85c. per gallon.

Head 4; depth $4\frac{4}{5}$; snout $2\frac{2}{5}$ in head; D. 12; A. 7; scales 12-76 to 81-9. Body elongate; head very long and slender, the snout and cheek especially long; mouth inclined upward at an angle of about 35°; fontanelle large; premaxillary spines forming a decided hump on snout near its tip.

GENUS XYRAUCHEN EIGENMANN & KIRSCH

The characters of this genus agree in all respects with those of *Catostomus* except that behind the occiput is a sharp-edged hump produced by the singularly developed interneural bones, giving the adult fish a very grotesque appearance.

Only two species are known, both from the Colorado River. Only one of these is of any food value. The other *(X. uncompahgre* Jordan & Evermann*)* is known only from the type, a specimen 7 inches long, and may be the young of *X. cypho.*

Razor-back Sucker; Hump-back Sucker

Xyrauchen cypho (Lockington)

Known only from the Colorado Basin, where it is quite abundant and of considerable value. It reaches a weight of 8 to 10 pounds.

Head 4; depth 4; D. 13 or 14; A. 7; scales 13 to 15-72 to 77-13. Body stout, compressed, the head low, the profile ascending to the prominent hump; mouth wide, inferior; upper lip with 2 rows of papillæ, the lower deeply divided and with 8 rows; dorsal fin long and low, with concave edge; caudal broad and strong, with numerous rudimentary rays; scales loosely imbricated; anterior part of hump scaleless. Colour, plain olivaceous.

GENUS ERIMYZON JORDAN

The Chub Suckers

This genus may be known by the entire absence of a lateral line and the plain colouration in the adult. The young have a broad black lateral band and are easily mistaken for *Cyprinidæ.*

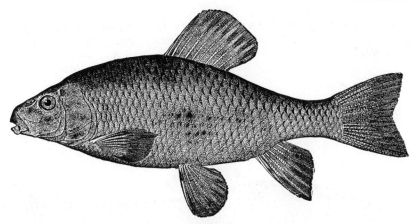

Chub Sucker

Only one species is known, *E. sucetta*, the chub sucker or creekfish, which reaches a length of about 10 inches and is widely distributed from the Great Lakes and New England south to Texas. Those in the northern part of the range have been regarded as a subspecies, *E. sucetta oblongus*.

GENUS MINYTREMA JORDAN

This genus may be known by the incomplete lateral line and the presence of a small blackish spot at base of each scale on side, these forming interrupted longitudinal lines along the rows of scales.

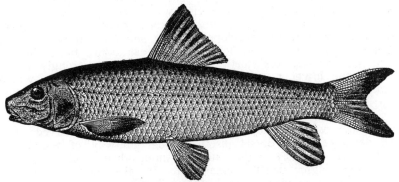

Spotted Sucker

The single species is *M. melanops*, known as the winter sucker or spotted sucker. It reaches a moderate size and is of some value as a food-fish. It occurs in the Great Lakes region and south to North Carolina and Texas, being most common westward.

GENUS MOXOSTOMA RAFINESQUE

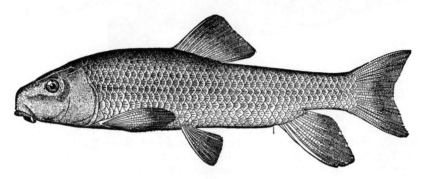

The Redhorses

Body more or less elongate, sometimes nearly terete, usually more or less compressed; head variously long or short; eye usually large; suborbital bones very narrow; fontanelle always open; mouth varying much in size, always inferior in position, the mandible horizontal, or nearly so; lips usually well developed, the form of the lower varying, usually with a slight median fissure, but never deeply cleft; lips with transverse plicæ, rarely broken up into papillæ; jaws without cartilaginous sheath; opercular bones moderately developed, nearly smooth; isthmus broad; gillrakers weak, moderately long; pharyngeal bones rather weak, as in *Catostomus*, the teeth rather coarser and strongly compressed, the lower 5 or 6 more strongly than the others, which rapidly diminish in size upward, each with a prominent internal cusp; scales large, more or less quadrate in form, nearly equal in size over the body, and not especially crowded anywhere; lateral line well developed, straight or anteriorly curved; fins well developed, the dorsal inserted about midway of the body, its first ray usually rather nearer snout than caudal; anal fin short and high, usually emarginate in the male; caudal fin deeply forked; air-bladder with three chambers.

Sexual characters little marked, the males during the spawning season with the lower fins reddened and the anal rays somewhat swollen and tuberculate.

This is a large genus, comprising not fewer than 20 species, all of which occur in the eastern United States in the Atlantic and Gulf drainages. There is no representative of the genus on the Pacific Coast. They inhabit both streams and lakes, but prefer the streams. Their spawning time is in the spring, when they run up the rivers and into the smaller streams, sometimes in very great numbers.

The species are difficult to distinguish and have been unduly multiplied by authors. They are less tenacious of life than the species of *Catostomus*, but equal them in food value.

Of the 20 species only about 5 attain a sufficient size to make them of much value for food. The remaining 15 species, which are mostly of small size, are the following:

Sucking mullet *(M. collapsum)*, lowland streams of North Carolina; thick-cheeked sucker *(M. bucco)*, Missouri River at St. Joseph; Pedee sucker *(M. pidiense)*, Great Pedee River basin; blue mullet *(M. coregonus)*, Catawba and Yadkin rivers; white mullet *(M. album)*, Catawba and other rivers of North Carolina, green mullet *(M. thalassinum)*, Yadkin River; Texas red-horse *(M. congestum)*, rivers of Texas; Mexican mullet *(M. austrinum)* Rio Lerma, Mexico; Yadkin mullet *(M. robustum)* Yadkin River, a doubtful species, perhaps identical with *M. macrolepidotum*, which occurs from Delaware to the Carolinas; picconou *(M. lesueuri)*, Albany River, Canada, and elsewhere in the far north, the most northern species, but not well known; Neuse River mullet *(M. conus)*, Neuse and Yadkin rivers, perhaps not distinct from *M. breviceps*; Tangiopahoa mullet *(M. pœcilurum)*, southern Mississippi to eastern Texas, jump-rocks *(M. rupiscartes)*, rivers from North Carolina to Georgia; and jumping mullet *(M. cervinum)*, rivers of the South Atlantic States from the James to the Neuse, abundant about rapids and rocky pools.

a. Lips full, the folds broken up into evident papillæ;.......
papillosum, 62
aa. Lips plicate, the folds not forming distinct papillæ.
b. Dorsal fin large, of 15 to 18 rays; lower lip V-shaped, somewhat papillose;......................*anisurum*, 62
bb. Dorsal fin smaller, of 10 to 14 rays.
c. Caudal fin with the upper lobe not conspicuously longer than the lower.
d. Dorsal fin with its free margin nearly straight; lower fins always red in life;......................*aureolum*, 63

dd. Dorsal fin with its free margin always more or less incised or concave; lower fins always pale in life.
e. Head moderate, 4⅗ in body; back not elevated;..........
macrolepidotum, 61
ee. Head very short and blunt, 5 in body; back elevated;...
crassilabre, 63
cc. Caudal fin with the upper lobe more or less produced 61
and falcate...............................*breviceps,* 64

White Mullet

Moxostoma papillosum (Cope)

Coastwise streams from the Dismal Swamp to the Ocmulgee River in Georgia; said to be common.

Head 4 to 4½; depth 4 to 4½; D, 12 to 14; scales 6-42-5. Body comparatively stout, the dorsal region somewhat elevated and rounded; eyes rather large, high up and well back, the preorbital space longer than in most species; top of head flat; lips moderate, deeply incised, the folds more broken up than in other species; caudal lobes equal. Colour, silvery; back with smoky shading; lower fins more or less reddish. Length 1 to 2 feet.

White-nosed Sucker

Moxostoma anisurum (Rafinesque)

This species reaches a length of 1½ feet or more, and is not uncommon in the Great Lakes region and southward in the Ohio basin.

Head 3¾ to 4 in length; depth 3 to 4; eye 4 to 5 in head; depth of cheek 2 in head; D. 15 to 18. Body stout, deep and compressed, the back elevated; head short, heavy, flattish and broad above; eye rather large, midway in head; muzzle rather prominent, bluntish, overhanging the large mouth; upper lip thin; fins very large, the dorsal long and high, its height 1⅙ in length of head, its free border straight, the first ray about as long as the fin; pectorals nearly reaching ventrals; upper lobe of caudal narrow, longer than lower. Colour, very pale and silvery; smoky above; lower fins white or pale red.

Common Redhorse

Moxostoma aureolum (Le Sueur)

The common redhorse is found from Lakes Ontario and Michigan to Nebraska and south to Arkansas and Georgia. West of the Alleghanies it is everywhere an abundant and-well-known fish. It reaches a length of 2 feet or more and is the most important food-fish of the genus. In the upper Mississippi Valley states it has always been held in considerable esteem by the farmers, who were in the habit of snaring, seining, or catching them in traps in great numbers in the spring of the year and salting them for winter use.

Like most other well-known species of wide distribution, this sucker has received many common names, among which are the following: mullet, white sucker, large-scaled sucker, and redfin sucker.

Head rather elongate, bluntish, broad and flattened above; body stoutish, varying to moderately elongate; lips rather full, the bluntish muzzle projecting beyond the large mouth; greatest depth of cheek more than half distance from snout to preopercle; dorsal fin medium in size, its free edge nearly straight, its longest ray shorter than the head. Colour, olivaceous; sides silvery, paler beneath; lower fins red or orange.

Sucking Mullet

Moxostoma crassilabre (Cope)

Streams of eastern North Carolina, where it is very abundant. It reaches a length of nearly 2 feet, and, in the spring, is taken in large numbers in the shad seines.

Among the vernacular names applied to it are redhorse, horse-fish, redfin, and mullet.

Head $4\frac{3}{4}$ to 5 in length; depth $3\frac{1}{2}$; eye $3\frac{2}{3}$ to 4; D. 12 or 13; scales 6-42 to 44-5. Body robust, the back elevated and compressed; head short, broad, flattish above; mouth moderate, the lips full, the lower truncate behind; snout short, little projecting; dorsal fin elevated in front, its edge much incised, its first ray longer than the base of the fin and about as long as the head; caudal lobes equal. Colour, silvery, with smoky shading above, some of the scales blackish at their bases; caudal and anal with some red; top of head, humeral bar and a broad shade across dorsal fin, dusky.

Short-headed Redhorse

Moxostoma breviceps (Cope)

Great Lakes and Ohio Valley, abundant in Lake Erie. This species reaches a length of a foot or more.

Head 5 to $5\frac{1}{4}$; depth $3\frac{1}{2}$; eye small, 5 in head; D. 12 or 13-scales 6-45-5. Body deep, compressed; head small; snout short and sharply conic, overhanging the very small mouth; form suggesting that of the white-fish; caudal fin with the upper lobe falcate and much longer than the lower, at least in the adult; dorsal fin short, high, and falcate, the anterior rays $1\frac{1}{3}$ to $1\frac{1}{2}$ times base of fin, the free border much concave; anal long, falcate, reaching beyond base of caudal. Colour, silvery, the lower fins bright red.

GENUS PLACOPHARYNX COPE

Suckers much like *Moxostoma* in all respects, except that the pharyngeal bones are much more developed and the teeth reduced in number, those on the lower half of the bone very large, 6 to 10 in number, nearly cylindric in form, being but little compressed and with a broad, rounded, or flattened grinding surface; mouth larger and more oblique than usual in *Moxostoma*, and the lips thicker. Only one species known.

Big-jawed Sucker

Placopharynx duquesnii (Le Sueur)

This interesting sucker reaches a length of 2 to $2\frac{1}{2}$ feet and is not uncommon from Michigan to Tennessee, Arkansas and

Georgia in the larger streams; it is probably most abundant in the French Broad River and in the Ozark region.

Nothing peculiar in its habits is known, and it ranks with the species of redhorse as a food-fish.

Head 4 in length; depth $3\frac{4}{5}$; D. 12 or 13; A. 9. Body oblong, moderately compressed, heavy at the shoulders; head large, broad, and flattish above, its upper surface somewhat uneven, eye small, behind the middle of the head; mouth large, the lower jaw oblique when the mouth is closed, the mouth, therefore, protractile forward as well as downward; lips very thick, coarsely plicate, the lower lip full and heavy, truncate behind; free edge of dorsal concave, the longest ray longer than base of fin, $1\frac{1}{5}$ in head; upper lobe of caudal narrower than the lower and somewhat longer. Colour, dark olive green, the sides brassy, not silvery; lower fins and caudal orange red.

GENUS LAGOCHILA JORDAN & BRAYTON

This is the most peculiar genus of suckers and may be known readily by the nonprotractile upper lip and the split lower lip. The

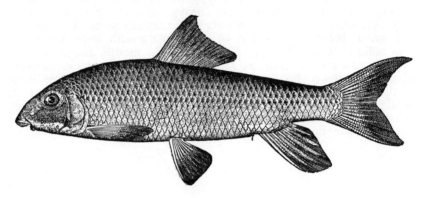

Hare-lip Sucker

single species is the hare-lip sucker, cutlips, split-mouth sucker, rabbit-mouth sucker, pea-lip sucker, or May sucker, *L. lacera*.

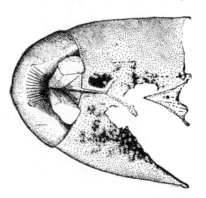

Hare-lip sucker, showing lower lip.

It is found in clear streams in the Mississippi Valley, as the Tippecanoe, Wabash, Clinch, Cumberland, Chickamauga and White River of Arkansas. It is most common in the Ozark region.

THE MINNOWS

Family V. Cyprinidæ

FISHES with the margin of the upper jaw formed by the premaxillaries alone, and the lower pharyngeal bones well developed, falciform, nearly parallel with the gillarches, each with 1 to 3 series of teeth in small number, usually 4 or 5 in the main row, and fewer in the other rows if present; head naked, body scaly, except in a few genera; barbels usually not present, but 2 or 4 small ones present in some genera; belly usually rounded, rarely compressed, never serrated; gill-openings moderate, the membranes broadly joined to the isthmus; gills 4, a slit behind the last; no adipose fin; dorsal fin short in all our species; ventrals abdominal; air-bladder usually large and commonly divided into 2 parts; stomach without appendages, appearing as a simple enlargement of the intestine.

The *Cyprinidæ* constitute a very large family of fishes of moderate or small size, inhabiting the fresh waters of the Old World and North America. The family contains about 200 genera and more than 1,000 species, of which about 225 are found in our waters. This number greatly exceeds that of any other family of fresh-water fishes. Not only are the species very numerous, but the individuals are usually exceedingly abundant.

Most of our species are very small fishes, usually not exceeding a few inches in total length, and, on account of their great uniformity in size, form, and colouration, they constitute one of the most difficult groups in all zoology in which to distinguish genera and species.

Our Eastern species rarely exceed a foot in length, but in the West are several very large species, some reaching a length of several feet, and all of these are of some food value. Several of the smaller species are good "boy's fishes," and one or more species can usually be found on any boy's string. They are all sweet, delicious pan-fishes, albeit exasperatingly bony, and various species of minnows constitute the very best live bait the angler can get.

The spring or breeding dress of the male is often very peculiar; the top of the head and often the fins and portions of the body are covered with small tubercles, outgrowths from the epidermis; the fins and lower parts of the body are often charged with bright pigment, the prevailing colour of which is red, although in some genera it is satin-white, yellowish, or even black.

Although nearly all the *Cyprinidæ* are very small fishes, there are a few species the individuals of which reach a large size.

As so few of the many genera of American *Cyprinidæ* have any commercial species, generic descriptions have been omitted in the hope that the specific descriptions may suffice.

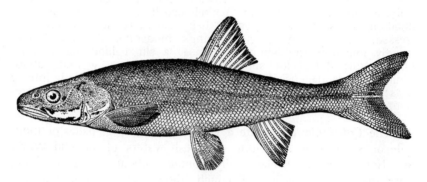

Squawfish

Ptychocheilus oregonensis Richardson

The squawfish is one of the largest of the minnows. It reaches a length of 2 to 4 feet, a size which shows strikingly that "minnows" are not necessarily little fish.

Its geographic range is from British Columbia southward in Pacific Coast drainage to central California. In the Columbia River basin it ascends as far as Shoshone Falls in Snake River, and at least to Flathead Lake in Clarks Fork. It is abundant in the Fraser, and also in the Sacramento, San Joaquin, Salinas, and other lowland streams of California. It is very abundant in the Redfish Lakes, and other lakes of Idaho. During the fall and the latter part of summer large schools of this species could be seen, particularly in the evening, swimming about the mouths of the inlets, usually at a depth of 5 to 40 feet, but toward evening they would come to the surface and feed greedily upon various insects that had fallen upon the surface of the water. Their manner of taking these insects is very much like that of the trout. Frequently they would jump entirely out of the water in their eagerness to secure the falling insect. They will rise to the artificial fly quite freely. By using Royal Coachman and fishing as if for trout excellent sport may be had. They rise to the fly promptly, strike quickly, and fight vigorously for a few moments, after which they allow themselves to be pulled in without much struggle. They will rise to the fly best in the evening, but will at any time take the hook baited with salmon spawn.

During the spring and early summer the Squawfish run out into the streams, where they seem to prefer to spawn, but in the fall and winter the streams connected with lakes are apt to be deserted by this fish. In the winter it is sought as an article of food, and fishing through the ice for squawfish is one of the popular winter amusements at the Idaho lakes. In these lakes it rarely attains a greater weight than about 4 pounds, and the usual weight is not over a pound.

This fish is highly esteemed by the Indians, hence its most popular name. Other names by which it is known are Sacramento pike, chub, big-mouth, box-head, yellow-belly, and chappaul.

Head $3\frac{1}{2}$ to 4; depth $4\frac{2}{3}$ to $5\frac{1}{2}$; eye $7\frac{1}{2}$ in head, $2\frac{1}{2}$ in snout; snout 3; D, 9; A. 8; scales 15 to 17-70 to 80-8, 42 to 60 before the dorsal; teeth 2, 4-5, 2, strong and well hooked, but without grinding surface. Body rather robust, with stout caudal peduncle; head long and pointed; mouth large, the maxillary reaching front of pupil; eye small, much larger in the young; lateral line strongly decurved, much nearer belly than back. Colour, muddy, greenish above, sides somewhat silvery, but chiefly dirty yellowish; belly yellowish or pale; in spring the fins are reddish or orange and the scales more or less dusted with dark specks; young with a black caudal spot.

White Salmon of the Colorado River

Ptychocheilus lucius Girard

This species differs chiefly from the squawfish, which it closely resembles, in the much smaller scales, there being 83 to

90 in the lateral line. There are no other important differences.

Colorado basin; very abundant in the river channels as far up as the mountains of Colorado.

This is the largest of the American *Cyprinidæ*. It reaches a length of 5 feet or more, and a weight of 80 pounds, though examples of this extreme size are infrequent. At Green River, Wyoming, individuals of 8 and 10 pounds are not at all rare. It is known variously as the whitefish, white salmon, or salmon, and in the Colorado basin, where species of food-fishes are not numerous, it is a fish of considerable importance.

Nothing distinctive is known of its habits or methods of capture.

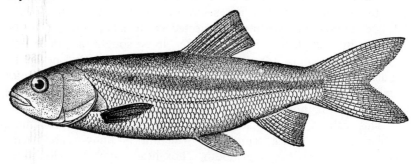

Utah Lake Chub

Leuciscus lineatus (Girard)

Head $3\frac{1}{2}$; depth $3\frac{1}{2}$; eye 7; D. 9; A. 8; scales 10-55 to 65-5; teeth 2, 5-4, 2, short and stout, one of them with grinding surface. Body robust, elevated anteriorly, the sides compressed, although the back is very broad; head broad, the interorbital space flattish; adult with the profile concave, straight or convex in the young; snout broad, elevated at the tip; premaxillary on level of pupil; mouth very oblique, the mandible projecting; maxillary reaching front of eye; scales large, subequal, broadly exposed, firm; lateral line decurved; dorsal nearly median, inserted directly over ventrals; caudal evenly forked, the peduncle long and deep; pectoral short, reaching $\frac{2}{3}$ distance to ventrals; ventrals about reaching vent. Colour, dark, the scales much dotted, the edges quite dark, often forming lines along the rows of scales. Length 12 to 15 inches.

One of the largest and most widely distributed species of the genus, abundant everywhere in the Great Basin of Utah, and in the Snake River basin above Shoshone Falls. In Utah Lake it is exceedingly abundant, as it is also in Jacksons Lake, Yellowstone Lake and other similar waters, where, owing to its large size, it is of some importance as a food-fish. It is said to be very destructive to the eggs of trout, a belief which may be justified by the facts, but we are not aware that the matter has ever been fully investigated.

Besides this species of *Leuciscus* there are in America about 24 other species, all of which are small and of little importance except as boy's fishes. With a few exceptions they are species of the Western States, and are perhaps most valuable to the Indians or in those regions where better fish are rare.

Then in Lake Tahoe, the Klamath Lakes, and various other lakes of Nevada, California and Oregon are found three species of the genus *Rutilus*, closely related to *Leuciscus*, none of them of much food value.

Hornyhead

Hybopsis kentuckiensis (Rafinesque)

The hornyhead is found from Pennsylvania to Wyoming and south to Alabama, on both sides of the Alleghanies; everywhere common in the larger streams, seldom ascending small brooks; one of our most widely distributed and best known minnows.

In different parts of its range it is known as the hornyhead, river chub, Indian chub, or jerker.

Wherever it is found at all, every boy who goes a-fishing is familiar with it. As a game-fish it is the most active and vigorous of its tribe. Any sort of hook baited with an angleworm or white grub is a lure the hornyhead can seldom resist, and he bites with a vim and energy worthy of a better fish. The fight he makes, though it would not wholly satisfy the veteran black bass angler, is quite enough to fill the youthful Walton with unbounded joy and pride. But as his experiences widen his chief interest in the hornyhead lies in the fact that it is one of the best of live baits for nobler fish. For muskallunge, pickerel, walleyed pike, and black bass of either species, as a live bait it is not surpassed; large individuals for muskallunge and increasingly smaller ones for the others, those for the small-mouthed black bass being not over 3 to 5 inches in length.

71

A hardy, active minnow, and of an attractive colour, as a live bait it is unsurpassed.

Head 4; depth $4\frac{1}{4}$; D. 8; A. 7; scales 6-41-4, 18 in front of dorsal; teeth 1,4-4,1, or 1,4-4,0, sometimes 4-4. Body stout, little elevated, and not much compressed; head large, broadly rounded above; snout bluntly conical; mouth rather large, subterminal, little oblique, the lower jaw somewhat the shorter; upper lip below level of eye; maxillary not reaching front of eye; barbel well developed; dorsal fin rather posterior, slightly behind insertion of ventrals: caudal broad, little forked; scales large, not crowded anteriorly; lateral line somewhat decurved. Colour, bluish-olive above; sides with bright green and coppery reflections; a curved dusky bar behind opercle; scales above with dark borders; belly pale but not silvery, rosy in males in spring; fins all pale orange, without black spot; males in spring with a crimson spot on each side of head; adults with top of head swollen, forming a sort of crest covered with tubercles; young with a dark caudal spot. Length 6 to 12 inches.

Cone-head Minnow

Mylopharodon conocephalus (Baird & Girard)

Head $3\frac{1}{2}$; depth $4\frac{2}{3}$; eye 7; snout about 3; D. 8; A. 8; scales 17-74-7. Body elongate, subfusiform, compressed ; head broad and depressed; the snout tapering; mouth horizontal, the jaws about equal, the maxillary extending to the eye; eye small, preorbital elongate; interorbital space as wide as length of maxillary, 3 in head; scales rather small, loosely imbricated ; dorsal fin a little behind ventrals; caudal fin $1\frac{1}{2}$ in head, the lower lobe the longer; caudal peduncle very long, $4\frac{1}{2}$ in length of body. Colour, dark, paler below, no red. This minnow reaches a length of 2 or 3 feet and is of some value as a food-fish. It is found only in the Sacramento-San Joaquin basin.

Columbia Chub

Mylocheilus caurinus (Richardson)

The Columbia chub occurs in the streams and lakes of British Columbia, Washington, Idaho, Montana, and Oregon, chiefly in the Columbia River basin and waters about Puget Sound.

In the Columbia basin it ascends in Clarks fork at least as far as Flathead Lake, and in Snake River to Shoshone Falls.

In the Snake River this minnow is one of the most abundant fishes, and is locally known by the misleading names "fresh-water herring" and "whitefish," and, at one place, they are even called trout. The name "whitefish" for this minnow is rather more than local in its application, as it is used not only on Snake River, but at Flathead Lake and perhaps elsewhere. At the salmon fisheries along the Columbia and Snake rivers it is quite abundant, and, after salmon fishing has begun, schools of 30 to 50 or more can be seen at any time. They are particularly attracted by the offal thrown into the river when the salmon are dressed, and by throwing a few salmon eggs into the water, good-sized schools could be called up at any time.

This fish seldom attains a greater length than a foot, and is, like most members of the family, a bony species; nevertheless, it possesses some importance as a food-fish. At some places in the Columbia basin it is served as "whitefish" at the hotels, and elsewhere it is peddled over the country as "trout" or "fresh-water herring." It takes the hook readily and possesses considerable game qualities. The best bait seems to be salmon spawn, but it will bite at almost anything, a piece of liver, a grasshopper, or a fish's heart or eye. It will fight vigorously for a time, and large individuals will often continue the fight until brought to net.

Head $4\frac{2}{5}$; depth $4\frac{1}{2}$; eye 5; snout $3\frac{1}{2}$; D. 8; A. 8; scales 12-77-7; teeth 1 or 2,5-5,2 or 1. Body moderately slender; head bluntly conic; interorbital space broad, convex; mouth horizontal or nearly so, the maxillary not reaching front of eye; suborbital bone wide; preorbital elongate; teeth hooked in the young, some of them becoming blunt with age. Colour, dark olivaceous above, yellowish silvery on sides, white or pale beneath; a dark or reddish lateral band, below which is a pale stripe, under which is a dark stripe which extends about to vent; fins pale; belly and sides with much red in breeding males.

Fallfish

Semotilus corporalis (Mitchill)

Length a foot to 18 inches. Abundant from the St. Lawrence basin to the James, east of the Alleghanies, in clear, swift streams, rock pools, below dams or falls, and in clear lakes; not found west of the Alleghanies.

The fallfish is much the largest of our eastern *Cyprinidæ*, ranking with the western and some European forms. Though ordinarily not exceeding a foot or 15 inches in length, examples 18 inches or even longer are not rare. An example weighing $3\frac{1}{2}$ pounds has been recorded from Canadian waters, and several examples, each weighing 3 pounds, have been taken in the outlet of Lake Winnepesaukee. The veteran angler, William C. Harris, has taken a 2-pound fish of this species on the artificial fly from Lycoming Creek, Pennsylvania.

Many anglers who are familiar with the fallfish speak enthusiastically of its game qualities. The character of the waters in which it lives and the large size which it attains would readily suggest a minnow of unusual strength and gaminess.

The common names which this fish has received are numerous. The early Dutch settlers of New York called it corporaalen or corporal, and elsewhere it has been variously called chub, roach, silver chub, or wind-fish.

Thoreau says it is a ''soft fish and tastes like brown paper, salted.''

Head 4; depth 4; eye $4\frac{1}{2}$; D. 8; A. 8; scales 8-49-4, 18 to 22 before the dorsal; teeth 2,5-4,2, hooked, without grinding surface. Body oblong, robust, little compressed; head large, convex, the snout bluntly conic; mouth large, terminal, somewhat oblique, the lower jaw included; premaxillary below the level of the eye, the maxillary barely reaching front of orbit; eye moderate, rather high up and anterior; a small barbel on maxillary just above its extremity, not at its tip as in most American minnows, not always evident in the young; scales large, not much crowded anteriorly; dorsal fin somewhat behind middle of body, just behind ventrals, or midway between nostril and base of caudal. Colour, brilliant; steel-blue above, sides and belly silvery; males in spring with the belly and lower fins rosy or crimson; no spots on the fins.

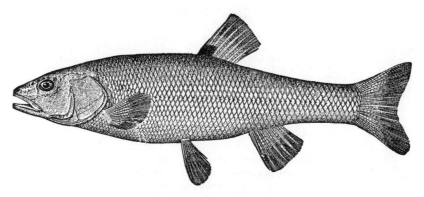

Common Chub

Semotilus atromaculatus (Mitchill)

This fish closely resembles the preceding, from which it may be readily distinguished, however, by the more posterior position of the dorsal fin (midway between middle of eye and base of caudal, and well behind ventrals), the closer crowding of the scales on anterior part of body, and the presence of a large black spot on base of anterior dorsal rays. The scales also are somewhat smaller, the number in the lateral line being usually 50 to 55. Colour, dusky bluish above, side with a vague, dusky band, black in the young, disappearing in the adult; belly whitish, rosy in males in spring; dorsal fin always with a conspicuous black spot on base of anterior rays which is bordered with red in the male; a dark vertebral line; scales everywhere edged with dark punctulations; a dusky bar behind opercle; males with snout coarsely tuberculate in spring; young with a small black caudal spot.

The common chub is found from Maine westward to Wyoming and south to Georgia and Alabama, everywhere abundant, particularly in small creeks, where it is often the largest and most voracious inhabitant.

It reaches a length of a foot or less and is one of the most common species seen on the small boy's string. Its food value is not great, though it serves a useful purpose in many a region where better fish are rare. Moreover, it is an excellent bait minnow for bass, walleyed pike, pickerel, and muskallunge. Among the common names borne by this fish are horned dace, chub, and creek chub.

75

THE TRUE EELS

Family VI.   Anguillidæ

"A youthful eel resided in a tiny tidal pool;
   He was lithe as gutta-percha, and as pliable;
From his actions and contractions he appeared to be a fool,
   But his virtue was completely undeniable."

—Carryl.

THE true eels are characterized by their peculiar fine imbedded scales in association with a conical head and a general resemblance to the conger eels.   The scales are inconspicuous, narrow and placed in series at angles with each other.   The *Anguillidæ* approach more nearly than most of the other eels to the type of the true fishes.   In one respect, that of the minute ova and concealed generation, how-ever, they differ widely from the true fishes.

The single genus of this family is *Anguilla,* with one species in our waters.

Common Eel

Anguilla chrisypa Rafinesque

The brilliant series of investigations by Dr. Johs. Schmidt of Copen-hagen, have resulted in a number of remarkable discoveries in the life history of the common eel.   We cannot do better than quote freely from his valuable report on the "Breeding Places of the Eel."   He says:

It has long been known that the full-grown eels move down in the autumn from their rivers and lakes to the sea; the most important eel fisheries, indeed, are based upon this seaward migration.   The eels do not return again from the sea, but in early spring there appear on the coasts myriads of small young eels, eagerly seeking their way up to fresh-water.   These eel-fry are known in most countries of Europe, and occur in some parts in such quantities as to form the object of a particular industry; for instance, in the River Severn in England, where they are known as "elvers." Until 1896, the elver stage was the earliest stage of development in which the eel was known on the shores of Europe; and it was generally supposed that the elvers arriving in the spring were the offspring of the eels which had migrated during the previous autumn. They are not, however, altogether minute, like the newly hatched larvæ of a cod or herring. . . . We know, then, that the old eels vanish from our ken into the sea, and that the sea sends us in return innumerable hosts of elvers. But whither have they wandered, these old eels, and whence have the elvers come? And what are the still younger stages like, which precede the "elver" stage in the development of the eel? It is such problems as these that constitute the "Eel Question." Two Italian investigators, Grassi and Calandruccio, found that the elver stage is preceded by a larval stage, and that the form described in 1856 by Kaup as *Leptocephalus brevirostris* was not a distinct species but in reality the larva of the common eel. These larvæ are leaf-shaped, transparent as glass, and about $7\frac{1}{2}$ cm. long. By a process of metamorphosis they are transformed into the eel-shaped elver, a reduction in both height and length taking place.

This discovery was of great importance; we have now learned to know a still younger stage than the elver. However, certain points still remained vague. Grassi inferred that the breeding grounds of the eel probably lie in the abyssal depths of the sea; that the ova, suspended in the water, are developed, and here the larvæ live. normally without rising to the upper water layers.

In 1904, Doctor Schmidt began his investigations and was able readily to confirm in every respect Grassi's discovery of the eel larva and its transformation into the elver. He found in surface water west of the Faroes, a Leptocephalus larva $7\frac{1}{2}$ cm. long, the first ever taken outside the Mediterranean. Doctor Schmidt continued his investigations for some 17 years. Without going too much into the details of his studies, it must suffice to state that he found that two species of freshwater eels exist in the Atlantic area—the common European eel (*Anguilla vulgaris*) and the American eel (*Anguilla chrisypa*).

Externally, the two species can hardly be distinguished, but they differ in the number of vertebræ, *A. vulgaris* having on an average about 114.7 while *A. chrisypa* has 107.2. This fact proved of great importance in the investigations at sea, since it was found that the larvæ of both species are mingled together in certain areas in the ocean.

Schmidt found full-grown eel larvæ in quantities in the Atlantic west of Europe from the Faroes to Brittany, west of the 1,000 metre line, but not east of it. In June, the larvæ were full grown, averaging 75 mm. in length. They occurred pelagically in the upper water-layers, and were all metamorphosed. From this he concluded that all the eels of western Europe come from the Atlantic, and that they come from the sea beyond the coastal banks. In 1906, he found that the full-grown larval stages are met with in spring and early summer, that metamorphosis takes place in autumn, and that el-vers appear in winter and spring. He found that the larvæ, during the metamorphosis, become markedly shorter and lighter. He found that the larvæ are always distributed in a particular manner, the younger ones being farthest from the coastal banks; from which it was concluded that the breeding grounds of the eel must be out in the ocean far from the coasts.

The investigations continued in 1913 widely over the Atlantic, with the result that it was shown that the larvæ of the European eel increase in number but decrease in size from east to west, which made it clear that the stock of eels in Europe must originate in an area in the Atlantic far to the west.

In October and November eel larvæ were found about 200 miles south of the Grand Banks to southward of the Bermudas, to about 65° west longitude, and in great numbers. Larvæ of the American eel also were taken sparingly in the same waters.

In 1920 and 1921, Doctor Schmidt resumed his investigations, in March and April and in June and July, chiefly in the western Atlantic. Very tiny larvæ, less than 10 mm. long, were obtained in considerable numbers, and it was evident they could not be very far from the place where the eggs were spawned.

From an examination of the larvæ taken at many different stations Doctor Schmidt was able to conclude that the breeding grounds of the European eel form a continuous area in the western Atlantic between about 22° and 30° N. lat., and about 48° to 65° W. long., the central portion being at about 26° North, or approximately midway between Bermuda and the Leeward Islands. He was also able to conclude that the eels spawn in the spring, that the larvæ require about two years to attain the full larval size, and nearly three years to complete the meta-morphosis. The elvers that appear on the shores of Europe are there-fore about three years old.

The starting-point for the trans-Atlantic migration of the larvæ of the European eel is northeast of Porto Rico and proceeds northeastward,

GOLDEN TENCH, *Tinca tinca*. INTRODUCED

GERMAN CARP, *Cyprinus carpio*. INTRODUCED

COMMON EEL, *Anguilla chrysypa*

COMMON EEL, *Anguilla chrysypa*

the metamorphosis going on *pari passu* until the elver stage is reached at the end of the long journey.

But specimens of the larvæ of both species were frequently taken together, those of the American eel being the larger, from which it is probable that the American eel must spawn earlier or that the larvæ grow more rapidly than the European species. While only American eels were found about Bermuda, the larvæ found about that island were almost all of the European species. These latter do not remain there, they being merely on their way to European waters.

The breeding grounds of both the European and American species lie west of 50° West longitude. While the larvæ of the American species become more abundant from east to west, it is nevertheless true there are areas in which the larvæ of the two species are greatly intermingled. If this be true, a very natural question to ask is: How do the masses of larvæ composed of both species in the western Atlantic sort themselves out so that those individuals which belong to the European species ultimately find their way to Europe while those of the other species reach the shores of America? Doctor Schmidt thinks this question no longer difficult to answer. In the case of the American eel the pelagic larval stage is terminated in about one year; consequently the larvæ have not time to make the journey to Europe, the distance being more than they can cover in that period. It is otherwise with the European eel which takes nearly three times as long for its larval development, as a result of which nearly all of them are far away from the western (American) portion of the Atlantic when the time comes for them, as elvers, to seek the coasts.

We can thus indicate both a geographical and an ethnological cause for the distribution of the two species of freshwater eels. The former lies in the fact that the American species has its center of production somewhat farther west and south than the European species; the latter is the different duration of the pelagic migratory stage. These two facts, in conjunction with the ocean currents as an aid to transport, and later—once the earliest stages of development are past—the active movements of the larvæ themselves, must be regarded as the causes which lead each of the two Atlantic species of eels to find its own side of the ocean, despite the close proximity of their breeding-grounds.

The species of Anguilla are usually termed "freshwater eels," and are reckoned among the freshwater fishes of Europe and America; but, from what we have now learned, it is seen that this is not literally correct. Both from their history and their actual manner of life, these

79

"freshwater eels" are true oceanic fishes, and the remarkable thing in their life-history is not so much the fact of their migrating out into the sea to spawn, as in their leaving it in order to pass their period of growth in an environment of freshwater, so unusual in this group of fishes.

In their feeding habits eels are chiefly scavengers, feeding upon all manner of refuse, but preferring dead fish or other animal matter. They are a very undesirable inmate of rivers in which fish are caught in gillnets. It is said that the destruction of shad and herring by eels in the Susquehanna and other Atlantic coastal streams is enormous. It is not infrequent that when a gillnet is lifted the greater part of the catch consists simply of heads and backbones, the remainder having been devoured by myriads of eels in the short time the net was left out. The spawning shad is considered by them a special delicacy, and are often found emptied at the vent and completely gutted of the ovaries. Sometimes a shad, apparently full, is found to contain several eels of considerable size.

The commercial value of the common eel as a food-fish has long been well established. It justly holds a high rank as an article of food among all who are familiar with it, and in the markets it always brings a good price.

The eel is caught in all sorts of ways—in traps, eel-pots, seines, and on set-lines; and "bobbing for eels" is a classic in angling methods.

Body elongate, compressed behind, covered with imbedded scales which are linear in form and placed obliquely, some of them at right angles to the others; lateral line well developed; head long and conical, 2 to $2\frac{1}{2}$ in trunk; eye small, over angle of mouth; teeth small, subequal, in bands on each jaw, and a long patch on the vomer; tongue free at the tip; lower jaw projecting; gill-openings small and slit-like; nostrils superior, well separated, the anterior with a slight tube; distance from front of dorsal to vent $1\frac{1}{6}$ to 2 in head; pectoral fins $2\frac{5}{6}$ to $3\frac{2}{6}$ in head Colour brown or yellow-olivaceous, nearly plain, paler below, the colour, quite variable.

The common eel reaches a considerable size. An example taken in 1899 in Lake Maxinkuckee measured 43 inches in length, and weighed $6\frac{1}{2}$ pounds. Examples 4 to 5 feet long have been reported, though the average length of those caught probably does not exceed $2\frac{1}{2}$ to 3 feet.

THE CONGER EELS

Family VII.   Leptocephalidæ

THIS family includes those eels which are scaleless, and have
the tongue largely free in front, the body moderately elongate,
the end of the tail surrounded by a fin, the posterior nostril
remote from the upper lip and near the eye, and the pectoral
fins well developed.   All the species are plainly coloured, grayish or dusky brown above, silvery below, and the dorsal edged
with black.

The 3 recognized genera contain about 15 species, inhabiting
most warm seas, usually at moderate depths.   Most of the species
undergo a metamorphosis, the young being loosely organized and
transparent, band-shaped and with a very small head.

a. Vomerine teeth in bands, none of them canine-like.
b. Dorsal fin inserted behind the pectoral, but nearer pectoral
        than vent;..*Leptocephalus,* 81
bb. Dorsal fin beginning over the gill-opening; *Congermuræna,* 81
aa. Vomerine teeth uniserial, some of them canine-like;
                                                                      Uroconger, 81

The 2 species of *Leptocephalus* in our waters are *L. conger*
and *L. caudilimbatus.*   The former is the conger eel which is
generally common on both coasts of the Atlantic, from Cape Cod
to Brazil in America.   It occurs also on the coasts of Africa and
Asia, but is not known from the eastern Pacific.   It reaches a
length of 7 or 8 feet and, though not much used in this country,
it is an important food-fish in Europe.   The other species *(L.
caudilimbatus)* is found in the tropical parts of the Atlantic.   It
is not uncommon in the West Indies where it is used as food,
and it ranges north at least to Pensacola and the Bahamas.   It
also occurs about Madeira.

Five species of *Congermuræna* are found in our limits.   They
are all of small size and of little food value.

Only one species of *Uroconger* is known from our waters.   It is
of no value as a food-fish.

THE MORAYS

Family VIII. Murænidæ

THESE may be distinguished from all other eels by the small round gill-openings and by the absence of pectoral fins. The body and fins are covered by a thick leathery skin, the occipital region is elevated through the development of the strong muscles which move the lower jaw, and the jaws are usually narrow and armed with knife-like or else molar teeth.

The morays inhabit tropical and subtropical waters, and are especially abundant in crevices about coral reefs. Many of the species reach a large size, and all are voracious and pugnacious. The colouration is usually strongly marked, the colour cells being highly specialized.

a. Vertical fins well developed, the dorsal beginning before the vent.
b. Posterior nostril an oblong slit, the anterior in a short tube;
Enchelycore, 83
bb. Posterior nostril circular, with or without a tube.
c. Teeth all, or nearly all, acute, none of those in jaws obtuse or molar-like.
d. Anterior nostrils without tube; vomerine teeth in many series; lips with a free fold;....................*Pythonichthys,* 83
dd. Anterior nostrils each with a long tube; vomerine teeth in 1 or 2 series; lips continuous with skin of head.
e. Posterior nostrils without tube, the margin sometimes slightly raised.
f. Dorsal fin inserted behind the head, over or behind the gill-opening;..*Rabula,* 83
ff. Dorsal fin inserted on the head, considerably before the gill-opening;....................................*Gymnothorax,* 83
ee. Posterior nostrils, as well as anterior, each with a conspicuous tube;..*Muræna,* 83
cc. Teeth mostly obtuse, molar-like;............*Echidna,* 83
aa. Vertical fins rudimentary, confined to the end of the tail.
g. Cleft of mouth short, not half length of head; snout moderate, about half the gape; tail about as long as trunk;
Uropterygius, 83
gg. Cleft of mouth long, nearly half head; snout very short, less than one-fourth the gape; tail very short, about half rest of body;..............................*Channomuræna,* 83

82

Of these 8 genera only *Gymnothorax* contains any species of much importance to us.

The species of *Gymnothorax* are numerous in our waters. They are the most active and voracious of eels, many of them very pugnacious, and most of them live in shallow water about rocks and reefs.

The common spotted moray (*G. moringa*) is found in the West Indies, north to Charleston and Pensacola and south to Brazil. It is the most abundant eel in the West Indies, reaches a length of 2 to 3 feet, and is used extensively for food.

The conger eel of California (*G. mordax*) is found from Point Conception to Cerros Island. It is abundant about the Santa Barbara Island and is remarkable for its ferocity. It is a food-fish of some importance.

There are about 15 other species of *Gymnothorax* in our waters, but none of them possesses much food value.

Enchelycore has one species, common in the West Indies, *Pythonichthys, Rabula, Echidna, Uropterygius,* and *Channomuræna,* have each from 1 to 4 species, in our tropical waters. None is of much food-value.

THE TARPONS

Family IX. Elopidæ

BODY elongate, more or less compressed, covered with silvery cycloid scales; head naked; mouth broad, terminal, the lower jaw prominent; premaxillaries not protractile, short, the maxillaries forming the lateral margins of the upper jaw; an elongate bony plate between the branches of the lower jaw; eye large, with an adipose eyelid; bands of villiform teeth in each jaw and on vomer, palatines, pterygoids, tongue, and base of skull; no large teeth; opercular bones thin, with expanded membranous borders; a scaly occipital collar; gill-membranes entirely separate, free from the isthmus; branchiostegals numerous (20 to 35); gillrakers long and slender; belly not keeled nor serrated, rather broad and covered with ordinary scales; lateral line present; dorsal fin inserted over or slightly behind the ventrals; caudal fin forked; no adipose fin; dorsal and anal depressible into a sheath of scales; pectorals and ventrals each with a very long accessory scale; pyloric cœca numerous.

Genera 3, species 4 or 5, forming 2 well-marked subfamilies, both widely distributed in the tropical seas. The species are not much valued as food, the flesh being dry and bony, but they are among the greatest of game fishes.

In our waters we have two genera, each represented by a single species.

a. Pseudobranchiæ none; body oblong, covered with large scales: anal fin larger than the dorsal; last ray of dorsal produced into a long filament;. . . . .*Tarpon,* 85
aa. Pseudobranchiæ large; body elongate, covered with small scales; anal fin smaller than the dorsal ; last ray of dorsal not produced in a filament;. . . . .*Elops,* 87

GENUS TARPON JORDAN & EVERMANN

Body oblong, compressed, covered with very large, thick, silvery, cycloid scales; belly narrow but not carinated, its edge with ordinary scales; lateral line nearly straight, its tubes radiating widely over the surface of the scales; dorsal fin short and high, inserted behind the ventrals, the last ray long and filamentous; anal fin falcate, much longer than the dorsal, its last ray produced; caudal widely forked, and more or less scaly. Only one species known.

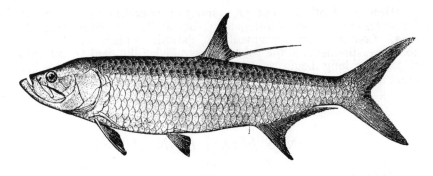

Tarpon

Tarpon atlanticus (Cuvier & Valenciennes)

The tarpon occurs on our Atlantic Coast from Long Island to Brazil, being most common southward, particularly on the coasts of Florida. It is a common fish about Porto Rico, where it evidently breeds.

The tarpon reaches a length of 2 to 6 feet and a weight of 30 to more than 300 pounds. The largest one on record taken with a hook weighed 209 pounds, and the largest taken with a harpoon weighed 383 pounds, if we may believe the record; but examples weighing over 100 pounds are not often seen. Among other names by which the tarpon is known are tarpum, savanilla, savalle sabalo, grand ecaille, and silver king, the last being one of its best and most expressive designations.

The silver king is the greatest of game fishes. There is none more celebrated or deserving of higher praise. Only the few fortunate anglers who, happily situated, are able to spend their winters in Florida or elsewhere on our southern coast, have actually experienced the pleasure of tarpon fishing, but every lover of the rod has heard of the silver king and has hoped that he might some day have an opportunity to test the great fish's strength and skill.

Among the places on our southern coast where excellent tarpon fishing has been obtained are along the west coast of Florida from Punta Gorda southward to Indian River and Lake Worth, about Key West, in Mississippi Sound, and at Galveston and Corpus Christi, Texas. Fort Meyers, on the west coast of Florida has, perhaps, been the most popular resort.

85

Head 4; depth $3\frac{4}{5}$; eye $4\frac{9}{20}$; snout 5; maxillary $1\frac{2}{3}$; D. 12; A 20; scales 5-42-5; branchiostegals 23; dorsal filament longer than the head. Colour, uniform bright silvery, darkish on back. The proportional measurements in the young are somewhat different, in examples of 3 inches long being as follows: Head $3\frac{1}{3}$; depth $4\frac{2}{3}$; eye $3\frac{1}{3}$; snout $4\frac{3}{4}$.

GENUS ELOPS LINNÆUS

Body elongate, covered with small, thin, silvery scales; dorsal slightly behind ventrals, its rays short; lateral line straight, its tubes simple. Large fishes of the open seas, remarkable for the development of scaly sheaths. Only a single species in our waters.

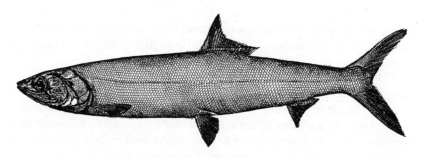

Bony-fish ; Ten-pounder

Elops saurus Linnæus

An abundant and widely distributed fish, found in all tropical seas; common in America north to the Carolinas and the Gulf of California. On our coasts it is probably most numerous in Florida.

It reaches a length of 2 to 3 feet and a weight of several pounds. The young are ribbon-shaped, long, thin, and transparent, passing through a metamorphosis analogous to that seen in the conger eels. They are at first band-shaped, with very small head and loose, transparent tissues. From this condition they become gradually shorter and more compact, shrinking from $3\frac{1}{2}$ inches to 2 inches in length. During these stages the young of this species, the lady-fish, and other fishes which undergo similar changes, are the so-called

" ghost-fishes " which are sometimes thrown up on the beach in large numbers by the waves.

The bony-fish rejoices in a multiplicity of vernacular names, among which are big-eyed herring, piojo, matajuelo real, chiro, Liza, Francesca, ten-pounder, and John Mariggle. Its excellent qualities as a game-fish are only beginning to be appreciated.

Head $4\frac{1}{3}$; depth 5 to 6; eye 4 to 5; snout $4\frac{1}{3}$; maxillary $1\frac{2}{3}$; mandible $1\frac{1}{2}$; interorbital $5\frac{2}{3}$; D. 20; A. 13; V. 15; B. 30; pectoral $1\frac{4}{5}$; ventral 2; caudal $\frac{4}{5}$; scales 13-110 to 120-12; gular plate 3 to 4 times as long as broad. Body very elongate; head small and pointed; mouth very large, the extremely long maxillary reaching far beyond the eye; jaws subequal; caudal lobes long and slender. Colour, bluish above; the sides silvery; white beneath.

THE LADY-FISHES

Family X. Albulidæ

BODY rather long, not much compressed, covered with rather small, brilliantly silvery scales; head naked; snout conic, subquadrangular, shaped like that of a pig and overlapping the small, inferior, horizontal mouth; maxillary rather strong, short, with a distinct supplemental bone; premaxillaries short, not protractile; jaws, vomer, and palatines with bands of villiform teeth; broad patches of coarse, blunt teeth on the tongue; eye large, median in head, a bony ridge above it, and almost covered with an annular adipose eyelid; preopercle with a broad, flat, membranaceous edge; pseudobranchiæ present; gill-membranes entirely separate and free from the isthmus; a fold of skin across gill-membranes anteriorly; no gular plate; lateral line present; belly flattish; covered with ordinary scales; caudal widely forked.

This family contains but a single species.

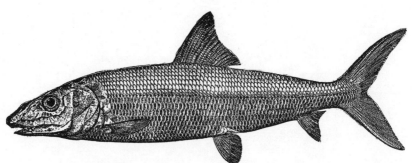

Lady-fish ; Bone-fish ; Banana-fish

Albula vulpes (Linnæus)

This beautiful and active fish is almost universally distributed on sandy coasts in all tropical seas. It ranges northward as far as San Diego and Long Island, and is generally abundant. It is a fish of very attractive appearance, usually litttle valued as food, though in some places, as at Key West, it is held in high esteem. As a game-fish it is highly appreciated by those familiar with it. It resembles, in this respect, the ten-pounder.

The young of this species pass through a metamorphosis, analogous to that seen in the conger eels, the ten-pounder, and the awa. They for a time are elongate, band-shaped, with very small head and loose transparent tissues. From this condition they become gradually shorter and more compact, shrinking from 3 or 3½ inches to 2 inches in length. In the Gulf of California where this species abounds, these band-shaped young are often thrown by the waves on the beach in great masses.

Head 3¾; depth 4; D. 15; A. 8; scales 9-71-7. Upper lobe of caudal the longer; a broad band of peculiar, elongate, membranaceous scales along middle line of back; accessory ventral scale large. Colour, brilliantly silvery on sides, olivaceous above; back and sides with faint streaks along the rows of scales; fins plain; axils dusky. Length 1½ to 3 feet.

THE MOONEYES

Family XI. Hiodontidæ

BODY elongate, compressed, covered with moderate-sized, brilliantly silvery, cycloid scales; head naked, short, the snout blunt; mouth moderate, oblique, terminal, the jaws about equal; premaxillaries not protractile; dentition very complete; premaxillary and dentary bones with small, wide-set, cardiform teeth; maxillaries with weak teeth; a row of strong teeth around the margin of the tongue, the anterior canine and very strong; between these is a band of short, close-set teeth; vomer with a long, double series of close-set, small teeth; similar series on the palatines, sphenoid and pterygoids; eye very large, the adipose eyelid not much developed; preorbital very narrow; nostrils large, those of the same side close together, separated by a flap; gill-membranes not connected, free from the isthmus, a fold of skin covering their base; no gular plate; branchiostegals 8 to 10; gill-rakers few, short and thick; no pseudobranchiæ; lateral line straight; belly not serrated; dorsal fin rather posterior; anal elongate, low; ventrals well developed, caudal strongly forked; no adipose fin; stomach horseshoe-shaped; without blind sac; one pyloric cœcum; air-bladder large; no oviduct, the eggs falling into the cavity of the abdomen before exclusion.

This family contains a single genus, with 3 species, inhabiting the fresh waters of the Great Lakes and the Mississippi Valley. They are all handsome and gamy fishes, of little value as food.

GENUS HIODON LE SUEUR

Characters of the genus included above.

a. Belly in front of ventrals carinated; dorsal with 9 developed rays;..*alosoides*, 91
aa. Belly in front of ventrals not carinated; dorsal with 11 or 12 developed rays.
b. Belly behind ventrals carinated; eye 3 in head;...*tergisus*, 92
bb. Belly nowhere carinated; eye 2½ in head;........*selenops*, 93

Toothed Herring ; La Queche

Hiodon alosoides (Rafinesque)

This fish is found in the upper Mississippi Valley and northward, and is most common northwestward. It prefers the lakes and larger streams. It is a beautiful, attractive fish, reaching a length of 8 to 12 inches.

This and the next species, while of little value as food, are of considerable interest to the anglers of the upper Mississippi Valley states. They are eager biters and take indiscriminately the feathered lures, small spoons, grasshoppers, grubs and other natural bait.

According to Mr. W. C. Harris, they rise freely to the artificial fly in the early spring months, but seem to disregard it as warm weather approaches, at which time they favour the grasshopper above all other lures. In middle Canada they are said to take the fly in the latter part of August, and anglers of that section prize highly the sport of casting for them. In these waters this fish is said to leap, when hooked, repeatedly in the air.

Head $4\frac{1}{2}$; depth $3\frac{1}{2}$; D. 9; A. 32; scales 6-56-7. Body closely compressed, becoming deep in the adult, the ventral edge everywhere carinated; maxillary reaching beyond middle of eye; caudal peduncle rather stouter than in the next species, and the fin not so deeply forked; back less arched and snout blunter than in the other species, the mouth larger and more oblique, the pectorals and the ventrals shorter. Colour, bluish above, sides silvery, with golden lustre.

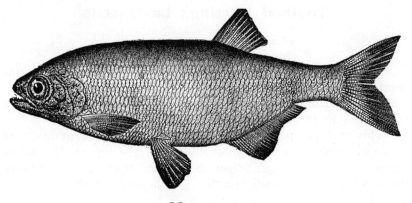

Mooneye

Hiodon tergisus Le Sueur

This fish closely resembles the toothed herring, from which it may best be distinguished by its larger dorsal fin and in having the belly in front of the ventrals not carinated.

The mooneye reaches a length of a foot or more, and is found throughout the Mississippi Valley, the Great Lakes region and northwestward at least to the Assiniboine River. It is usually common in the larger streams and lakes, and is a very handsome fish, not valued as food, the flesh being dry and full of small bones. As a game-fish it does not differ materially from the toothed herring.

Head 4⅛; depth 3; eye 3; D. 12; A. 28; scales 5-55-7. Body oblong, moderately compressed; eye large, the maxillary barely reaching its middle; pectoral fin not reaching ventrals; the latter scarcely reaching vent; belly behind ventrals somewhat carinated, but not in front. Colour, brilliantly silvery, olive-shaded above.

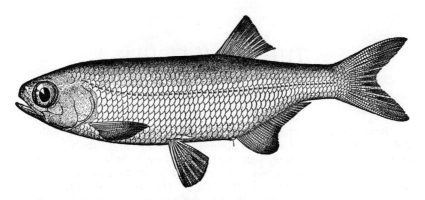

Southern Mooneye

Hiodon selenops Jordan & Bean

In certain southern rivers, the Tennessee, Cumberland and Alabama, is found this species of *Hiodon* which differs from *H. tergisus* chiefly in not having the belly at all carinate. Nothing has been recorded as to its habits.

Head $4\frac{1}{8}$; depth 4; eye $2\frac{1}{2}$; D. 12; A. 27; scales 50. Body more slender than in the other species, little compressed; not much elevated, the belly nowhere carinated; eye very large; pectoral not reaching ventrals; colouration, clear silvery.

THE MILK-FISHES

Family XII. Chanidæ

BODY oblong, compressed, covered with small, firm, adherent scales; lateral line distinct; abdomen broad and flattish; snout depressed; mouth small, anterior, the lower jaw with a small symphyseal tubercle; no teeth; eye with an adipose eyelid; gill-membranes broadly united, free from the isthmus; branchiostegals 4; pseudobranchiæ well developed; an accessory branchial organ in a cavity behind the gill cavity; dorsal fin opposite the ventrals; anal shorter than the dorsal; mucous membrane of the œsophagus raised into a spiral fold; intestine with many convolutions; colour silvery.

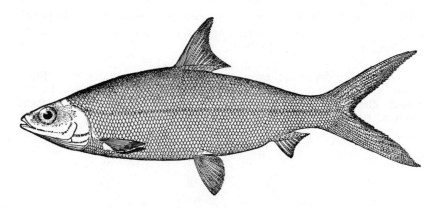

The Awa or Milk-fish

This genus contains 3 species, only one of which is found in our waters. This is *Chanos chanos*, the milk-fish, or awa, a fish of very wide distribution. It is found on most sandy shores of the Pacific and Indian oceans. It is very abundant in the Gulf of California and among the Hawaiian Islands, where it is an important food-fish. In the Hawaiian Islands it is found with the ama-ama, or mullet, in the artificial fish-ponds of the old kings. The awa reaches a length of 2 to 5 feet.

TENPOUNDER, *Elops saurus*

BONEFISH, *Albula vulpes*

SALMON JUMPING A FALLS

THE HERRINGS

Family XIII. Clupeidæ

BODY oblong or elongate, usually much compressed, covered with cycloid or pectinated scales; belly sometimes rounded, sometimes compressed, in which case it is often armed with bony serratures; head naked, usually compressed; mouth rather large, terminal, the jaws about equal; premaxillaries not protractile; teeth mostly small, often feeble or wanting; gillrakers long and slender; gill-membranes not connected, free from the isthmus; branchiostegals usually free, 6 to 15; pseudobranchiæ present; no lateral line; anal fin usually rather long, caudal forked.

This is a large family, embracing about 30 genera and 150 species. Most of the species are saltwater, inhabiting all seas, and usually swimming in immense schools. Many species are anadromous, ascending freshwater streams to spawn, and some species remain in fresh water permanently.

The northern and freshwater species, as in many other families, differ from the tropical forms in having a larger number of vertebræ.

None of the species is considered a game-fish, but many of them are among the most important food-fishes. In American waters the family is represented by 16 genera, and about 38 species, some 10 of which are of commercial importance.

a. Scales with their posterior margins entire and rounded; intestinal canal of moderate length.
b. Vomer with teeth;...............................*Clupea*, 96
bb. Vomer without teeth.
c. Ventral scutes very weak, the belly more or less rounded; ventrals under middle of dorsal;...........*Clupanodon*, 99
cc. Ventral scutes strong, the belly compressed; ventrals below or slightly behind front of dorsal.
d. Premaxillaries meeting at a large angle, so that the tip of the upper jaw does not appear to be notched; cheek longer than deep;................*Pomolobus* 101
dd. Premaxillaries meeting in front at a very acute angle, so that the emarginate front of the upper jaw receives the

slender tip of the lower; fore part of the cheek very deep, deeper than long;......................*Alosa*, 104
aa. Scales with their posterior margins vertical, and pectinate or fluted; intestine elongate;..................*Brevoortia*, 108

GENUS CLUPEA LINNÆUS

The True Herrings

The true herrings have the body elongate, the vertebræ numerous, the ventral serratures weak, and an ovate patch of small but persistent teeth on the vomer. The few species belong to the northern seas, where the number of individuals is very great, exceeding perhaps those of any other genus of fishes. In America there are but 2 species, both of which spawn in the sea.

a. Belly serrate both before and behind ventrals; anal rays 17;............... ....*harengus*, 96
aa. Belly serrate behind ventrals only; anal rays 14;........
pallasii, 99

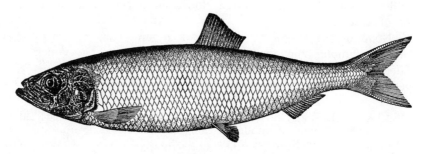

Common Herring

Clupea harengus Linnæus

The herring is beyond question the most important of food fishes in the Atlantic, if not in the world. Distributed as it is throughout the whole of the North Atlantic, it affords occupation for immense fleets of fishing boats, and according to an estimate made by Professor Huxley, the number taken every year out of the North Sea and Atlantic is at least 3,000,000,000, with a weight of at least 1,500,000,000 pounds. This estimate is probably too low. Carl Dambeck estimates the average yield of herring in Norway from 1850 to 1870 at 1,452,000,000 pounds, and the annual yield on the Swedish coast has been put at 300,000,000 pounds. In 1873 the catch on the Scotch coast was 188,000,000 pounds, which employed 45,494 men, using 15,095 boats. In the same period 15,331 boats were used in the English fisheries. If to these we add the yield on the coasts of Ireland, Germany, Belgium, France and America, the total is enormous. But 3,000,000,000 herring is probably no greater than the number contained in a single shoal, if it covers half a dozen square miles, and shoals of much greater size are on record. And, according to Professor Huxley, there must be scattered through the North Sea and the North Atlantic, at one and the same time, scores of shoals, any one of which would go a long way toward supplying the whole of man's consumption of herring.

The herring is found in the temperate and colder parts of the North Atlantic. On our coast it has been found as far south as Cape Hatteras, though it is not abundant south of New England. It rarely enters brackish water, but spawns in the sea. Unlike many other fishes, the herring, as well as other species of *Clupeidæ*, are regarded as particularly delicious at spawning time, and most of the herring fisheries are carried on when the fish are in full roe. The herring fishery in America is entirely a shore fishery. With the exception of a few occasionally taken for bait by the line fishermen on the banks, our herring are all caught in the immediate vicinity of the shore. Although the herring fishery in America has never assumed the importance which it has long held in Europe, the herring is probably no less abundant here than on the other side of the Atlantic. The principal herring fisheries on our coast are north of Cape Cod, and Newfoundland is the most northern point where important fisheries are located. From the Bay of Fundy to Cape Cod the fishing-ground is practically continuous.

The herring fisheries are carried on chiefly by means of brush weirs, gillnets, and torching. The latter method is the most primitive, and is said to be effectual only after the weather has become cool. Formerly a birch-bark torch, now one of oil, was fixed to the bow of the boat, which is rapidly rowed through the water by several fishermen, while another with a large dip-net is stationed in the bow. The fish rise toward the light in numbers so long as the boat is kept moving rapidly, and large quantities are dipped into the boat. At other times the torch is used to lure the fish into the weirs, the light being then extinguished, and the operation repeated as often as necessary. Gillnets, however, are now the appliances chiefly in use in the herring fishery. They are set at some distance below the surface, and anchored at one or both ends. The quantities caught are very great, frequently sufficient to sink the buoys.

The food of the herring consists of small animal organisms, chiefly of two small crustaceans, viz.: copepods, or "red seed," and schizopod crustaceans, or the "shrimp" of the fishermen. Among the enemies of the herring which may be mentioned are the cod, haddock, pollock, hake, dogfish, albacore, squid, porpoises, seals and finback whales, each of which is very destructive.

As a food-fish the herring is of very great importance. It is utilized in many different ways. The great quantities brought to Gloucester, New York and elsewhere in winter from Newfoundland are sold fresh. Those caught on the New England coast are smoked, salted or pickled, packed as sardines or used as bait chiefly in the cod fisheries. On the Maine coast the most important use is as sardines.

Head $4\frac{1}{2}$; depth $4\frac{1}{2}$; eye 4; D. 18; A. 17; scales 57; ventral scutes 28+13; vertebræ 56. Body elongate, compressed; scales loose; cheek longer than high; maxillary reaching middle of eye; upper jaw not emarginate, the lower jaw much projecting; vomer with a small ovate patch of small permanent teeth; palatine teeth small or absent; tongue with small teeth; gillrakers very long, fine and slender, about 40 on lower arm of first arch; eye longer than snout; abdomen serrated in front as well as behind, the serratures weak. Colour, bluish, silvery below, with bright reflections; peritoneum dusky.

California Herring

Clupea pallasii Cuvier & Valenciennes

The California herring, known in some earlier publications as *Clupea mirabilis* Girard, is found in the North Pacific from San Diego to Kamchatka and is everywhere known as "herring." It is scarcely different in size, appearance, or qualities from the Atlantic species. It is found the entire length of our Pacific Coast, being exceedingly abundant northward. All the bays and outlets of Puget Sound are filled with them in summer. South of Point Conception they are seldom seen except in winter. They are so abundant in San Francisco Bay in spring that practically no market can be found for them. At San Diego they spawn in the bay in January. Farther north the spawning season is later. They are fattest and bring the best price in early winter. They are smoked and dried, or salted, or sent fresh to the markets. Sometimes oil is expressed from them.

The California herring is an excellent food-fish, and large quantities are used annually. It reaches a length of 18 inches.

Head $4\frac{1}{3}$; depth 4; D. 16; A. 14; scales 52. Lower jaw strongly projecting, the upper not emarginate; belly scarcely compressed in front of ventrals, serrate only between ventrals and anal; gill-rakers very long and slender; vomerine teeth weaker than in the Atlantic herring; usually a few teeth on tongue and premaxillaries; insertion of dorsal slightly nearer front of eye than base of caudal. Colour, bluish above, silvery on sides and below; peritoneum dusky.

GENUS CLUPANODON LACÉPÈDE

The True Sardines

This genus is close to *Clupea*, which it resembles in form of body and the weak ventral serratures. It differs, however, in having no teeth on the vomer; teeth in jaws mostly weak; scales thin and deciduous; adipose eyelid present; gillrakers very numerous. There are about 6 species in this genus, all confined chiefly to the 2 temperate zones, and all closely related to the

European sardine, *Clupanodon pilchardus*, with which they all agree in richness of flesh.

The 3 genera, *Clupea*, *Clupanodon* and *Pomolobus*, are all closely related and perhaps should be united.

a. Opercle conspicuously striate; side with a series of round black spots;..*cæruleus*, 100
aa. Opercle scarcely striate; side without black spots;
pseudohispanicus, 100

California Sardine

Clupanodon cæruleus (Girard)

This excellent food-fish reaches a length of a foot, and occurs on our Pacific Coast from Puget Sound southward to Magdalena Bay. It is abundant on the California coast, and spawns in the open sea. It resembles the European sardine, but has no teeth, and the belly is less strongly serrate.

Head 4; depth 5; D. 14; A. 17; scales 53; scutes 18+14; vertebræ about 50. Body slender, subfusiform, the back rather broad; ventral serratures very weak; maxillary reaching nearly to middle of eye; mandible little projecting, the tip included; no teeth in mouth; gillrakers longer than the eye, very slender and numerous, close-set, some 50 or 60 on lower limb of arch; a frill of enlarged scales with dendritic striæ about nape and shoulder; insertion of dorsal considerably nearer snout than base of caudal. Colour, dark bluish above, silvery below; a series of round black spots running backward from level of eye, bounding the dark colour of the back; similar smaller spots above, forming lines along the rows of scales; these spots sometimes obscure or wanting, especially in old examples; tip of lower jaw yellow; lower part of dorsal yellowish; peritoneum black; flesh darker and more oily than that of the herring.

Spanish Sardine

Clupanodon pseudohispanicus (Poey)

This is called sardina de España in Cuba and bang in Jamaica. It is found from Pensacola southward and is abundant about Cuba. It is sometimes carried north in the Gulf Stream to Woods Hole and Cape Cod. It reaches 8 inches in length and in the West Indies is of considerable value as a food-fish.

It very closely resembles the European sardine *(Clupanodon pilchardus)*, but is distinguished by the absence of radiating striæ on the opercles. From the California sardine it is distinguished by the smooth opercles, unspotted sides, and the presence of minute teeth on tongue and lower jaw.

GENUS POMOLOBUS RAFINESQUE

The Alewives

This genus is very close to *Clupea* from which it seems to differ only in having no teeth on the vomer.

As here understood this genus contains 4 known species, each of some value as food.

a. Teeth present in the jaws, those on tip of each jaw mostly
    persistent; ....*chrysochloris,* 101
aa. Teeth in jaws disappearing with age.
b. Peritoneum pale.
c. Head long, about 4 in length; ....*mediocris,* 102
cc. Head shorter and heavier, about 4⅔ in length;
                                   pseudoharengus, 103
bb. Peritoneum black; ....*æstivalis,* 104

Fresh-water Skipjack; Blue Herring

Pomolobus chrysochloris Rafinesque

This species is found in all the larger streams of the Mississippi Valley and has been introduced through canals into Lakes Erie and Michigan. As ordinarily seen it is strictly a fresh-water fish, but along the Gulf coast it enters salt water where examples of large size and excessive fatness are occasionally taken. In Lake Erie it is called "sawbelly," from the ventral scutes. This species reaches a length of 15 inches, rarely takes the hook, and is of very little value as a food-fish.

Head 3¾; depth 3¾; eye 4⅓; D. 16; A. 18; scales 52; ventral scutes 20+13. Body elliptical, much compressed; head rather slender and pointed, its upper profile straight; lower jaw strongly projecting, its tip entering the profile; upper jaw emarginate; premaxillary, and often tip of lower jaw, with persistent teeth of moderate size; maxillary large, reaching posterior part of eye; eye large, well covered by adipose eyelid; caudal peduncle slender, the caudal fin well forked; gillrakers comparatively few, short, stout, and coarse, about 23 below angle of arch; opercle with radiating and branching striæ. Colour, brilliant blue above, sides silvery with golden reflections; no dark spots behind opercle; peritoneum pale.

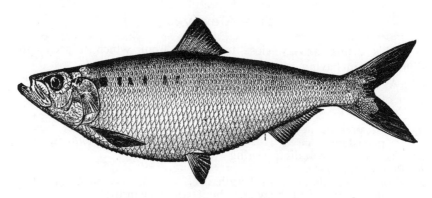

Tailor Herring ; Hickory Shad

Pomolobus mediocris (Mitchill)

This species of herring, which is also known as fall herring and mattowacca, is fairly common from Cape Cod to Florida. The name Mattowacca is said to be derived from the Indian name for Long Island, which was Mattowaka or Mattowax. In the Potomac River it is called "tailor shad" or "fresh-water tailor," in contradistinction to the bluefish which is called "salt-water tailor."

The centre of abundance of the tailor seems to be in the vicinity of Chesapeake Bay where it usually makes its appearance in the rivers in the spring before the shad. Northward it does not usually enter streams, but southward it does so regularly.

It reaches a maximum length of 24 inches, though examples of more than 3 pounds' weight are not often seen.

This species is caught in great quantities in pound-nets and is hawked about the streets of Washington and other cities in the spring, and is often sold as shad to the unsuspecting. Very soon the market for them ceases and they are then used as fertilizer. It is also often sold with the alewife and glut herring, 1 tailor counting as 2 herring.

Head 4; depth $3\frac{3}{8}$; D. 15; A. 21; scales 50; scutes 20+16. Head rather long; lower jaw considerably projecting, the upper emarginate; dorsal fin inserted nearer snout than base of caudal. Colour, bluish silvery; sides with rather faint longitudinal stripes; peritoneum pale.

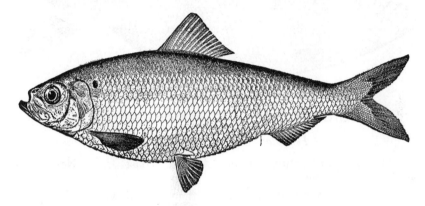

Alewife ; Branch Herring

Pomolobus pseudoharengus (Wilson)

This is known also as wall-eyed herring, big-eyed herring, spring herring, blear-eyed herring, ellwife, Gaspereau, and doubtless by many other names. It is found on our Atlantic coast from the Carolinas northward and is very abundant. It enters fresh-water streams to spawn and the run usually precedes that of the shad by 2 or 3 weeks. It is found also in certain small lakes in New York tributary to the St. Lawrence and in Lake Ontario where it is exceedingly abundant. It seems to be land-locked in these lakes and is greatly dwarfed in size. In Lake Ontario myriads die every year in early summer.

Head $4\frac{2}{3}$; depth $3\frac{1}{3}$; eye $3\frac{1}{2}$; D. 16; A. 19; scales 50; scutes 21+14; gillrakers 30 to 40 below the angle. Body rather deep and compressed; head short, nearly as deep as long; maxillary reaching posterior margin of pupil; lower jaw somewhat projecting, the upper emarginate; eye large; gillrakers long, but shorter and stouter than in the shad; lower lobe of caudal the longer. Colour, bluish above, sides silvery; indistinct dark stripes along the rows of scales; a blackish spot behind opercle; peritoneum pale.

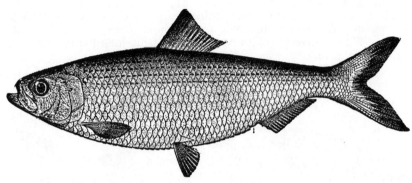

Glut Herring; Summer Herring

Pomolobus æstivalis (Mitchill)

This species occurs on our Atlantic coast from New England to the Carolinas.

It is less abundant northward than the alewife and appears in the streams somewhat later than that species. Southward it is sometimes exceedingly abundant, hence the name "glut herring." Other names by which it is known are blueback, blackbelly, saw-belly, and kyach. As a food-fish it is less valuable than the alewife.

Head 5; depth $3\frac{1}{2}$. Very similar to the preceding, from which it is best distinguished by the black peritoneum; body more elongate, the fins lower, the eye smaller, and the back darker; first ray of dorsal not equal to base of fin.

GENUS ALOSA CUVIER
The Shad

Body deep, compressed, deeper than in related American genera; the head also deep, the free portion of the cheek deeper than long;

jaws toothless; upper jaw with a sharp, deep notch at tip, the premaxillaries meeting at a very acute angle; otherwise as in *Pomolobus*, to
which this genus is closely allied.   There are 2 or 3 American species.

a. Gillrakers very numerous, usually more than 100 on first arch;
sapidissima, 105

aa. Gillrakers less numerous, not more than 70 on first arch;
alabamæ, 108

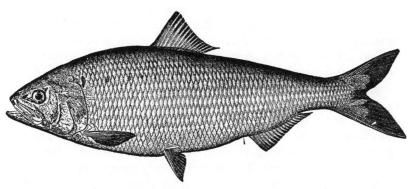

Common Shad ; American Shad

Alosa sapidissima (Wilson)

The shad is found on our Atlantic coast from Florida to Newfoundland, its centre of abundance being from North Carolina to Long
Island.   The principal shad rivers are the Potomac, Susquehanna,
and Delaware.   In the early history of the country the abundance of
the shad excited unbounded astonishment.   Nearly every river on the
Atlantic Coast was invaded in the spring by immense schools, which,
in their upward course, furnished an ample supply of choice food.
But through ever-increasing fishing operations the supply gradually
diminished until 30 years ago when the Federal and various State
governments began hatching the shad artificially.   So successful have
these efforts been that, notwithstanding greatly increased fishing
operations and the curtailment of the spawning-grounds, the supply
in recent years has not only been maintained but largely augmented
in many streams.

One of the satisfactory results of the artificial propagation of useful
food-fishes—satisfactory because they are absolutely proved and cannot be questioned—has been the introduction of the shad into the
waters of our Pacific Coast in which no shad were previously found.

At various times between 1871 and 1880, 619,000 shad fry were planted in the Sacramento River, and in 1885 and 1886 910,000 were placed in the Columbia River. There young shad found the environment congenial, suitable spawning grounds were found, and they have thrived so well that they have spread to San Diego on the South and to Fort Wrangel on the North—a distance of more than 2,000 miles. The shad is now one of the most abundant and most delicious foodfishes in the markets of San Francisco and other west coast cities.

The shad is an anadromous fish which passes most of its life in the sea, performing annual migrations from the ocean to the rivers for the sole purpose of reproduction. Little is known of its life in the ocean, the places to which it resorts are unknown and but little is known regarding its food. In the spring it ascends to suitable spawning grounds, which are always in fresh water, occupying several weeks in depositing and fertilizing its eggs in any given stream. It appears in the St. Johns River, Florida, as early as November, but not in great abundance until February and March. Beginning with the Savannah and Edisto rivers in January, the run in the different streams to the northward is successively later, the height of the run in the Potomac being in April, in the Delaware early in May, and the Miramichi River, in New Brunswick, about the last of May.

The main body ascends when the water temperature is 56° to 66°, the number diminishing when the temperature is over 66°. They come in successive schools, the males preceding the females. Of 61,000 shad received at Washington from March 19 to 24, 1897, 90% were males. Toward the close of the season males were extremely scarce. Formerly the shad ascended many streams much farther than they are now able to go, owing to the erection of many impassable dams, beyond which the fish cannot go.

As the shad enter the rivers only for the purpose of spawning, the fisheries are necessarily prosecuted during the spawning season, and often upon the favourite spawning-grounds. So great is the demand for this delicious food-fish, and so assiduously do the fishermen ply their vocation with many kinds of gear during the period when, under ordinary circumstances, the fish should be protected, that the shad-fisheries would long since have been a thing of the past had it not been for artificial propagation. During the spring of 1900 the U. S. Fish Commission planted in the Atlantic Coast streams a total of 241,056,000 young shad.

The shad is very prolific. Single fish have been known to yield from 60,000 to 156,000 eggs, though the usual number does not exceed 30,000. The eggs are very small, semi-buoyant, and usually require 6 to 10 days for hatching, the time varying with the temperature of the water.

Unlike most other fishes shad roe is considered a great delicacy when fried; and ever since the days of George Washington and John Marshall "planked shad" has been regarded as the acme of success in the preparation of a delicious fish for the table. And a planked shad dinner at Marshall Hall, near Mount Vernon, is quite sure to constitute a feature in the spring programme of many Washington societies.

After entering the rivers, the shad take but little, if any, food previous to spawning, but after casting its eggs it will strike at flies or other small shining objects, and it has been known to take the artifical fly.

Though there is but one species of shad on our Atlantic Coast it has received almost as many vernacular names as there are rivers which it enters, as Potomac shad, Susquehanna shad, Delaware shad, North River shad, and Connecticut shad; and the people on each particular stream regard their shad as the best; and all are right, for the sweetness and delicate flavour of the shad depend much upon its freshness. The shad one gets from a nearby river are apt to reach the table fresher than those shipped from a distance.

The shad is the most valuable river fish of the Atlantic Coast, and, next to the Chinook salmon, the most important species inhabiting the fresh waters of North America. Among all the economic fishes of the United States only the cod and the Chinook salmon exceed it in value. In 1896 the shad catch of the Atlantic seaboard numbered 13,145,395 fish, weighing 50,847,967 pounds, and worth to the fishermen $1,656,580.

Head $4\frac{1}{4}$; depth 3; D. 15; A. 21; scales 60; ventral scutes 21+16. Body comparatively deep; mouth rather large, the jaws about equal, the lower fitting into a notch in the tip of the upper; gillrakers extremely long and numerous, usually about 40+68, the total varying from 93 to 119; fins small, the dorsal much nearer the snout than base of caudal; peritoneum white. Colour, bluish above, sides silvery white; a dark spot behind opercle, and sometimes several along the line dividing the colour of the back from that of the side, these evident when the scales are off; axil dusky. The shad reaches a length of 2 to 2½ feet, though the average weight is less than 4 pounds.

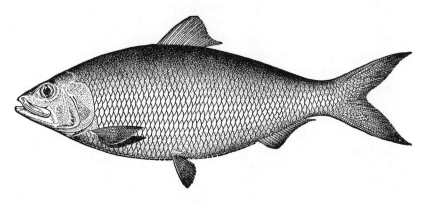

Alabama Shad

Alosa alabamæ Jordan & Evermann

In the Black Warrior River of Alabama, about Pensacola, and doubtless in other rivers flowing into the Gulf of Mexico, is found a species of shad resembling the common shad but differing from it in not having nearly so many gillrakers, in having a sharper, more pointed snout, smaller notch in the upper jaw, more projecting mandible, and more slender maxillary. It also reaches maturity at a considerably smaller size than the common shad, the various examples seen measuring only 15 inches each in total length.

Nothing is known of its habits except that it appears at Tuscaloosa, Alabama, in limited numbers early in April, and that the young have been seen in salt water at Pensacola.

GENUS BREVOORTIA GILL

The Menhadens

Body elliptical, compressed, deepest anteriorly, tapering behind; head very large; cheek deeper than long; mouth large, the lower jaw included; no teeth; gillrakers very long and slender, densely set, appearing to fill the mouth when it is opened; scales deeper than long, closely imbricated, their exposed edges vertical and fluted or pectinated; dorsal fin low, rather posterior; anal fin small; intestine long; peritoneum dusky.

This genus contains only a few species, all inhabiting the Atlantic, and probably spawning in brackish water in the spring. They are coarse, herbivorous fishes, not greatly valued as food, but having several other very important uses.

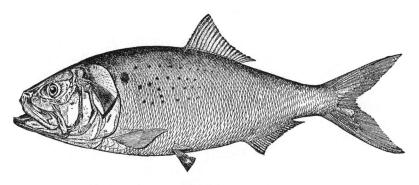

Menhaden; Mossbunker; Pogy

Brevoortia tyrannus (Latrobe)

The menhaden occurs from Nova Scotia to Brazil, and is by far the most abundant fish on the eastern coast of the United States. Several hundred thousand have been taken in a single draft of a purse-seine. A firm at Milford, Connecticut, captured in 1870, 8,800,000; in 1871, 8,000,000; in 1872, 10,000,000, and in 1873, 12,000,000. In 1877, 3 sloops from New London seined 13,000,000. Though this was an unprofitable year the Pemaquid Oil Company took 20,000,000, and the town of Booth Bay alone took 50,000,000.

Though no decrease was visible up to 1880, since that time many fishermen believe a very great decrease has taken place. This, however, has not been proved, and many intelligent observers deny that any appreciable decrease has really occurred.

The food of the menhaden consists almost wholly of plankton—the minute unicellular algæ, and the smaller animals which swarm in untold myriads at the surface of the sea, particularly along the coasts.

The spawning time and method are not well understood. According to Goode, the breeding grounds are probably on the off-shore banks, and the eggs are presumably cast in late winter or early spring. Recently the menhaden has been found breeding in brackish water in Buzzards Bay.

The fecundity of the menhaden is very great, exceeding that of the shad and the herring. More than 140,000 eggs have been taken from one fish.

The enemies of the menhaden are many, and include every predaceous animal swimming in the same waters. Whales and dolphins and sharks follow the schools and destroy multitudes; one hundred have been taken from a shark's stomach. All the large carnivorous fishes feed upon them, the tunny being the most destructive. Dr. Goode, in 1880, estimated the total number of menhaden destroyed annually on our coast by predaceous animals at a million million of millions, compared with which the number destroyed by man is scarcely more than infinitesimal.

As Dr. Goode has so happily said, the menhaden's place in nature is not hard to surmise; swarming our waters in countless myriads, swimming in closely packed unwieldy masses, helpless as flocks of sheep, near to the surface and at the mercy of every enemy, destitute of means of defence and offence, their mission is unmistakably to be eaten.

Besides entering so largely into the food-supply of many important food-fishes, though of little value itself as food for man, the menhaden is nevertheless a fish of very great commercial importance; As a bait fish in the mackerel, cod and halibut fisheries it is unexcelled. In 1877 more than 80,000 barrels, or 26,000,000 fish, valued at $500,000, were used for this purpose. As a source of oil the menhaden is of greater importance than any other marine animal. After the oil is expressed the residue supplies a valuable manure when made into manufactured fertilizers.

Though little valued in the United States as a food-fish, nevertheless many barrels of salted menhaden are shipped to the West Indies, and some are consumed along our own coast. They have been packed in oil, after the manner of sardines, for domestic and foreign consumption. A preparation resembling Liebig's "Extract of Beef" has also been prepared from this fish. And as a food for domestic animals in the form of "fish meal" the menhaden is of value. After all, however, the menhaden must ever be of greatest value as food for other fishes.

The menhaden has received perhaps more common names than any other American fish. Dr. Goode enumerates at least 30 which have been given to it.

Head $3\frac{1}{5}$; depth 3; D. 19; A, 20; scales 60 to 80. Head rather short and heavy; fins comparatively short, the height of the dorsal less than the length of the maxillary; height of anal less than half length of maxillary; pectoral not reaching ventrals; dorsal inserted slightly behind ventrals, or about midway between tip of snout and base of caudal; scales moderate, strongly serrated, irregularly arranged, those before dorsal strongly pectinate; opercle strongly striated; gillrakers much longer than eye. Colour, bluish above, the sides silvery, with a strong brassy lustre; fins usually yellowish; a conspicuous dark scapular blotch, behind which are often smaller spots. Length 12 to 18 inches.

THE ANCHOVIES

Family XIV. Engraulidæ

BODY elongate, more or less compressed, covered with thin, cycloid scales; head compressed; mouth very large, more or less oblique, usually overlapped by the compressed, pointed, pig-like snout; gape very wide, the maxillary long and slender, reaching far beyond the eye, in some species even beyond the head; premaxillaries not protractile, very small and firmly joined to the maxillaries; teeth usually small, sometimes obsolete, usually fine and even, in a single row in each jaw; canines sometimes present; eye large, well forward, no adipose eyelid; opercles thin and membranaceous; gillrakers long and slender; gill-membranes separate or joined, free from the isthmus; pseudobranchiæ present; no lateral line; belly rounded or weakly serrate.

Small, carnivorous shore fishes, usually swimming in large schools on sandy shores; abundant in all warm seas, occasionally entering rivers.

The family contains about 9 genera and 80 species, and is closely related to the *Clupeidæ*.

a. Teeth in jaws all small, if present; no canines.
b. Insertion of dorsal before that of anal.
c. Gill-membranes nearly or quite separate, free from the isthmus.
d. Vertebræ about 41 in number; bones firm; species chiefly tropical;.,................................*Anchovia,* 112
dd. Vertebræ about 45; bones rather feeble; species of temperate regions;................................*Engraulis,* 115
cc. Gill-membranes broadly united, free from the isthmus;
Cetengraulis, 115
bb. Insertion of dorsal behind front of the very long anal; gill-membranes separate;....................*Pterengraulis,* 115
aa. Teeth in jaws unequal, some of them enlarged and canine-like;................................*Lycengraulis,* 115

GENUS ANCHOVIA JORDAN & EVERMANN

The Silvery Anchovies

Body oblong, compressed, covered with rather large, thin, deciduous scales; belly rounded or weakly compressed; snout conical, compressed, projecting beyond the very large mouth; maxillary narrow, little movable, usually formed of 3 pieces, extending backward far beyond the eye, but not beyond gill-opening; anal fin moderate, free from caudal; dorsal inserted about midway of body, behind the ventrals; flesh rather pale and dry and more or less translucent.

This is a large genus, containing 50 or more species, about 20 being found in our waters.

In the following key and descriptions are included only those species which have some food value. None of them possesses any interest to the angler.

a. Anal rays 19 to 24.
b. Silvery lateral band very sharply defined, as broad as eye, not much narrowed anteriorly; A. 20; gillrakers only $\frac{2}{3}$ long as eye; ....*brownii,* 113
bb. Silvery lateral band throughout narrower than the eye; A. 23; gillrakers nearly as long as eye;............*delicatissima,* 113
aa. Anal rays 25 or 26;.............................*mitchilli,* 114

Striped Anchovy

Anchovia brownii (Gmelin)

This little fish reaches a length of 4 to 6 inches and is found from Cape Cod to Brazil. It is very abundant southward in the West Indies and on both coasts of Florida. It is the most abundant American species.

Head $3\frac{3}{4}$; depth $4\frac{3}{4}$; eye $3\frac{1}{2}$; snout 5; D. 15; A. 20; scales 40. Body rather elongate, compressed, not elevated; belly compressed, serrulate; head rather short, the snout projecting much beyond tip of lower jaw; teeth rather strong; maxillary extending beyond base of mandible, but not quite reaching gill-opening; eye large; cheek triangular; gillrakers long; anal fin with a sheath of scales; dorsal inserted nearer caudal than snout. Colour, olivaceous, translucent, sides silvery; the silvery lateral band very distinct and about as wide as eye.

Western Anchovy

Anchovia delicatissima (Girard)

This anchovy reaches a length of 3 inches and occurs on the coast of southern California and southward.

It is locally very abundant and is, as its name indicates, a most delicate little food-fish.

Head $4\frac{1}{4}$; depth $4\frac{3}{4}$; D. 13; A. 23; scales 40. Head short, nearly as deep as long; eye large, much longer than the blunt snout which projects considerably beyond the lower jaw; gillrakers numerous, slender, nearly as long as eye; maxillary reaching past root of mandible; lower lobe of caudal the longer; dorsal inserted midway between base of caudal and front of eye. Colour, very pale olivaceous, translucent, with some dark points, and a silvery lateral band not as wide as eye.

Little Anchovy

Anchovia mitchilli (Cuvier & Valenciennes)

This small fish reaches a length of but 2 to $2\frac{1}{2}$ inches and is the smallest species of anchovy on our coast. It is found from Cape Cod to Texas and is generally abundant on sandy shores and in river-mouths. It is one of the species entering into the composition of "whitebait."

Head $3\frac{4}{5}$; depth 4; eye 3; D. 14; A. 25 or 26; scales 37. Body rather short and deep, strongly compressed, the belly compressed and slightly serrated; head short, compressed and bluntish; snout very short, not longer than pupil; eye very large; maxillary about reaching edge of opercle; teeth in each jaw; cheek broadly triangular, almost equilateral, smaller than eye; opercle short, oblique; gillrakers rather long; dorsal inserted midway between caudal and middle of eye; anal very long; scales thin, caducous. Colour, translucent whitish, the sides silvery with an ill-defined narrow silvery band scarcely wider than pupil; fins rather yellowish ; many dark dots on fins and body.

Sardina Bocona

Anchovia macrolepidota (Kner & Steindachner)

This anchovy occurs from the Gulf of California to Panama and is very abundant about Guaymas where it is often cast up dead on the beach in great numbers. It is one of the largest anchovies, reaching a length of 7 or 8 inches.

Head $3\frac{1}{2}$; depth 3; D. 15; A, 28 to 30; scales 35,-9. Body very short and deep, both dorsal and ventral outlines strongly arched; head $\frac{1}{4}$ longer than deep; snout very short, not longer than pupil and not projecting far beyond lower jaw; maxillary narrow, rounded behind, extending to angle of preopercle; gillrakers fine, long, and very numerous; abdomen slightly compressed; scales adherent; origin of dorsal slightly behind middle of body; ventrals very small; pectorals rather long. Colour, silvery, side with an indistinct bluish band.

GENUS ENGRAULIS CUVIER

This genus contains those spindle-shaped anchovies of the north and south Temperate zones which have the body little compressed, the sides rounded, the vertebræ in increased number (44 to 47), the flesh rather dark, and tender and somewhat oily but not translucent, the bones soft, the appearance and the flesh resembling that of the sardines.

Only one species within our limits.

California Anchovy

Engraulis mordax Girard

This species reaches a length of 7 inches and occurs on our Pacific Coast from south Alaska to Lower California. It is extremely abundant, swimming in large schools. It is one of the largest of the anchovies and the most valuable food-species. The flesh is rich and oily, comparatively dark, and easily torn, as in the sardines.

Head $3\frac{1}{2}$; depth $5\frac{1}{2}$; D. 14; A. 22; Br. 14; scales 40; vertebræ 45. Body spindle-shaped, form resembling that of a sardine, little compressed, rounded above, slightly carinated below, but not serrated; head long, anteriorly compressed, the snout pointed and protruding; head nearly twice as long as deep; eye large, very near the tip of the snout; maxillary extending beyond root of mandible; small teeth on jaws; opercle deeper than long, placed obliquely; gillrakers much longer than eye. Colour, bluish above, silvery on side and below, not translucent; no silvery lateral band.

The 2 species of *Cetengraulis* (*C. mysticetus* and *C. edentulus*) and the one each of *Pterengraulis* (*P. atherinoides*) and *Lycengraulis* (*L. grossidens*) are small tropical fishes of little value.

THE WHITEFISH, SALMON AND TROUT

Family XV. Salmonidæ

THE characters of the *Salmonidæ* are well known and need not be repeated here. As now restricted this is no longer one of the large families of fishes, albeit it is one of the most important, and for beauty, activity, gaminess, quality for food, and size of individuals, different members of the family stand easily with the first among fishes. There are about 10 genera and nearly 100 species.

The *Salmonidæ* are confined to the northern hemisphere, and north of the 40th parallel they are nearly everywhere abundant wherever suitable waters are found. Some of the species, especially the larger ones, are marine and anadromous, living and growing in the sea, and entering fresh waters only for spawning purposes; still others live in running brooks, entering lakes or the sea as occasion serves, but not habitually doing so; others again are lake fishes, approaching the shore, or entering brooks in the spawning season, at other times retiring to waters of considerable depths. Some of them are active, voracious, and gamy, while others are comparatively defenceless and will not take the hook.

The large size of the eggs, their lack of adhesiveness, and the ease with which they may be impregnated, render the members of this family especially adapted to fish-cultural operations.

The *Salmonidæ* are of comparatively recent evolution, none of them occurring as fossils unless it be in recent deposits. The instability of the specific forms and the absence of well-defined specific characters may in part be attributed to their recent origin, as Dr. Günther has suggested.

The family contains 2 well-marked subfamilies, the *Coregoninæ* (the whitefishes and lake herrings) and the *Salmoninæ* (the salmons, charrs and trouts).

Coregoninæ:

a. Mouth not deeply cleft, the mandible articulating with the quadrate bone under or before the eye; dentition more or less feeble or incomplete; scales moderate or large. Species imperfectly anadromous, or confined to lakes or rivers.

b. Jaws toothless or nearly so; scales large; maxillary short and broad, with a broad supplemental bone.

c. Premaxillaries broad, with the cutting edge nearly vertical or directed backward, the lower jaw short and more or less included; cleft of mouth short;........... ....*Coregonus,* 117

cc. Premaxillaries with the cutting edge nearly horizontal and directed forward; lower jaw long, projecting beyond the upper; cleft of mouth long;...................*Leucichthys,* 130

bb. Jaws, vomer, palatines, and tongue with bands of teeth; maxillary very long; lower jaw prominent; anal fin elongate; scales moderate;........ ....*Stenodus,* 142

Salmoninæ :

aa. Mouth deeply cleft, the long lower jaw articulating with the quadrate bone behind the eye; dentition strong and complete; conical teeth on jaws, vomer, and palatines; tongue with 2 series of strong teeth; scales small.

d. Anal fin elongate, of 14 to 17 rays;.......*Oncorhynchus,* 143

dd. Anal fin short, of 9 to 12 developed rays.

e. Vomer flat, its toothed surface plane; teeth on shaft of vomer in alternating rows or in one zigzag row, and placed directly on the surface of the bone, not on a free crest. Species black-spotted;........................*Salmo,* 159

ee. Vomer boat-shaped, the shaft strongly depressed and without teeth; spotted with gray or red.

f. Vomer with a raised crest, armed with strong teeth, extending backward from the head of the bone, free from its shaft; hyoid bone with a broad band of strong teeth. Species spotted with gray, without bright colours;
Cristivomer, 203

ff. Vomer without a raised crest, only the head being toothed; hyoid bone with very weak teeth or none. Species red-spotted, the lower fins with bright edgings; *Salvelinus,* 206

GENUS COREGONUS ARTEDI

The Whitefishes

Recent studies of the whitefishes of America have made it necessary to revise this genus and recognize a larger number of species than have usually been recognized. The additional forms are new species recently described chiefly from the Great Lakes. We now admit the following species:

Saskatchewan Whitefish

Coregonus couesi Milner

This is a strongly marked species, allied to the Oregon whitefish. It is known only from Chief Mountain Lake, Montana, and elsewhere in the headwaters of the Saskatchewan.

Oregon Whitefish

Coregonus oregonius Jordan & Snyder

This species, also known as Chisel-mouth Jack, resembles the Saskatchewan whitefish in the long snout, but has a much larger adipose fin. It was originally described from the McKenzie River, Oregon, and is known only from the lower Columbia basin.

This species reaches a length of eighteen inches or more and is said to be a fine game fish. It is extremely swift and gamey, takes the hook readily, and is reputed to be very destructive to the spawn of salmon.

Yellowstone Whitefish

Coregonus cismontanus Jordan

This species occurs only in the headwaters of the Missouri River where it replaces the Williamson whitefish which it closely resembles and which is found only west of the Rockies.

Stanley's Whitefish

Coregonus stanleyi Kendall

This species is provided with pearly buttons on the scales especially during the breeding season, as in Williamson's whitefish. It is found in the lakes of northern Maine.

Bear Lake Whitefish

Coregonus abyssicola Snyder

This species does not differ greatly from the preceding, but perhaps may be distinguished by the entire absence of spots, even in the 8 to 10 inches long; the head appears to be somewhat shorter and the depth less. Known only from Bear Lake.

Coulter's Whitefish

Coregonus coulterii Eigenmann

This species is a small fish first discovered in 1892 in the Kicking-Horse River at Field, British Columbia, one of the headwaters of the Columbia River. Up to the present time no other specimens have been obtained. It reaches a length of 8 or 10 inches or less, and would doubtless be a good food-fish but for its small size. Nothing distinctive is known as to its habits or game qualities.

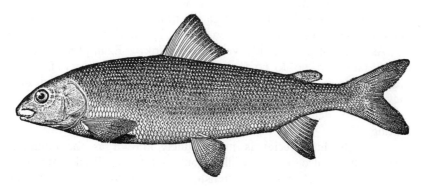

Rocky Mountain Whitefish

Coregonus williamsoni Girard

Two species of whitefish are known from western North America, the species just described and the present one. While Coulter's whitefish is known from but a single locality, the Rocky Mountain whitefish is of very wide distribution, occurring in all suitable waters from the west slope of the Rockies to the Pacific and from Utah to British Columbia. It prefers the cold, clear lakes, such as those of Idaho, Oregon and Washington, but is also found in many streams. Those living in the lakes remain in comparatively deep water except during the spawning season, which occurs in late fall or early winter, when they run out into the tributary streams, in some places in incredible numbers. This is particularly true at Big Payette Lake and in other Idaho lakes.

This species attains a length of a foot or more, and a **weight of** about 4 pounds, though the average is considerably less.

During the spring and early summer they take the fly freely, as well as the baited hook. Though not as game as the trout of the same region, they are sufficiently so to afford much sport, especially when caught from the swiftly flowing streams. The smallness of the mouth of this fish requires the use of hooks of very small size. When bait is used, very small grasshoppers, salmon eggs and small bits of fresh meat of almost any kind have proved effective.

Among the places where excellent sport with this fish may be had, may be mentioned the headwaters of Salmon River and Big Payette Lake in Idaho, streams near Dillon, Montana, lakes Pend d'Oreille and Cœur d'Alene, and Provo River, Utah.

As a pan-fish it holds very high rank. Examples 7 to 10 inches taken in 20 to 60 feet of water are usually very fat, and most delicious, and cannot be surpassed in sweetness and delicacy of flavour. Among the fishes of the Northwest there is none more richly deserving of preservation than this mountain herring.

Though this species is most widely known as the mountain herring, it is also called Williamson's whitefish, Rocky Mountain herring, Rocky Mountain whitefish, and in some places grayling.

Head $4\frac{1}{2}$ to 5; depth 4 to 5; eye $4\frac{1}{2}$; snout $3\frac{1}{2}$ to 4; D. 10 to 12; A. 10 to 12; scales 9 or 10-78 to 88-7 or 8; gillrakers 11 to 15+7 to 10; pectoral $1\frac{1}{5}$; ventral $1\frac{2}{5}$; maxillary 4; mandible 3; longest dorsal ray $1\frac{1}{3}$. Body oblong, but little compressed; head short, conic, the profile abruptly decurved; snout compressed and somewhat pointed at tip, which is entirely below level of eye; preorbital broad, $\frac{2}{3}$ width of eye; maxillary short and very broad, reaching orbit, thus appearing longer than in other species owing to the shortness of the snout; supplemental bone narrow; snout in the males produced and pig-like in the breeding season; adipose fin very large, extending behind the anal; gillrakers short and thick, shorter than the pupil; scales of back and side in breeding season covered with prominent tubercles. Colour, bluish above, silvery on sides, whiter below; breeding males with the under parts white; all the fins tipped with black; caudal and adipose fins steel-blue. The parrmarks persist on the young for a year or more.

The whitefish found in the headwaters of the Missouri River has been described as a subspecies *(cismontanus)* of the preceding, from which it was supposed to differ in its somewhat more slender body, shorter pectoral and ventral, lower dorsal, and smaller scales. The two are probably not distinct.

The waters of the Missouri Basin from which whitefish have been reported are the Yellowstone, Madison, Redrock, Beaverhead, Gibbon and Gallatin rivers, Horsethief Springs, and Big Goose Creek, a tributary of Tongue River, Wyoming.

Broad Whitefish; Muksun

Coregonus kennicotti Milner

This species, known also as Kennicott's whitefish, and the Delta whitefish, was described from Fort Good Hope, British America, in 1883. Since then it has been observed in the Meade, Kuahroo, Kuwuk and Yukon rivers of Alaska, and in Great Bear Lake. These localities indicate its known geographic range.

The broad whitefish is one of the largest species of the genus. It reaches a weight of 30 pounds, and as a food-fish is held in high esteem. It is said by Dr. Dall to be abundant in the Yukon in both winter and summer, and that it spawns in September when it enters the small tributary streams.

Nothing is known as to its game qualities or other habits.

Head $5\frac{2}{3}$; depth $4\frac{2}{3}$; eye $5\frac{1}{2}$; D. 11; A. 14; scales 10-87 to 90-10. Head small and very blunt; mouth inferior, the high blunt snout but little projecting; premaxillaries wide and vertically placed; maxillary reaching slightly beyond vertical at front of eye; preorbital narrow, its greatest width only $\frac{1}{5}$ its length, or $\frac{1}{3}$ diameter of eye; gillrakers 6 or 7+14, short and slender; tongue with a round patch of weak, bristle-like teeth, resembling those of the inconnu; adipose fin large, a wide strip at base covered with small scales. Colour, probably very dark in life; fins all blackish in spirits, with a bluish tinge.

Richardson's Whitefish

Coregonus richardsonii Günther

Only the type specimen of this species is known. It was described from some unknown locality in British America.

It is very similar to the common whitefish, also to the broad whitefish, with which it may prove identical. Nothing is known regarding its habits or food-value.

Menominee Whitefish

Coregonus quadrilateralis Richardson

This species is known as menominee whitefish (Lakes Superior and Michigan), round whitefish (British America), frostfish (Lake Champlain and Adirondack lakes), shadwaiter (Lake Winnepesaukee), pilotfish (Lake Champlain), chivey (Maine), Chateaugay shad (Chateaugay Lake), and blackback (Lake Michigan).

The round whitefish is found in the lakes of New England, westward through the Adirondacks and the Great Lakes, thence northward into Alaska, from which it may be seen that this species is the most widely distributed of the American whitefishes.

The menominee reaches a length of 12 to 15 inches, and a weight of 2 pounds; the average weight of those taken to market, however, does not exceed one pound.

This species, like all others of its genus, spawns in the fall, but nothing distinctive is known of its habits. It is ordinarily found in rather deep water of the lakes, and does not often enter streams. It is not regarded as a game-fish, but as an article of food it ranks with the other smaller whitefishes. Considerable quantities are taken each year in Lake Champlain and the small Adirondack lakes, while in Lakes Huron, Michigan and Superior still larger quantities are caught, gillnets being the gear usually employed for the purpose.

Head 5; depth $4\frac{3}{4}$; eye $5\frac{1}{2}$; D. 11; A. 10; scales 9-80 to 90-8; maxillary $5\frac{1}{2}$; mandible $3\frac{1}{3}$; gillrakers about 7+10, 4 to 5 in eye. Body elongate, not elevated nor much compressed, the back rather broad, the form more nearly round than in any other species; mouth very small and narrow, inferior, the broad maxillary not reaching to opposite the eye; head long, the snout compressed and bluntly pointed, its tip below level of eye; profile not strongly decurved; preorbital wider than pupil; mandible originating under middle of eye; adipose fin small; gillrakers short and stoutish. Colour, dark bluish above, silvery below.

Common Whitefish

Coregonus albus Le Sueur

This is the common whitefish of Lake Erie and Lake St. Clair, from which it has been introduced into all the other Great Lakes and many other lakes. It is the most important and delicious food-fish of our fresh-water lakes. It is very close to *Coregonus clupeaformis*, the whitefish of the other Great Lakes which is commonly known as the Labrador white-fish, from which it differs chiefly in form and colour. Compared with the latter, the Lake Erie whitefish has a smaller head, higher nape, more angular form, and the colour is almost pure olive-white, without dark shades or stripes along the back. The flesh is softer, containing more fat. All these differences may be correlated with the fact that Lake Erie is shallow and its southern shore fed by warm, shallow, muddy, or milky streams.

As no difference appears in technical characters, we regard *Coregonus albus* as a doubtful species, probably not separable from the Labrador whitefish, its distinctions being perhaps purely orthogenetic. On the other hand, it is claimed that the fry of the two can be readily separated. Mr. Harry Marks, superintendent of the United States fish hatchery at Sault Ste. Marie, says that the eggs of the Labrador whitefish are larger and darker than those of the Lake Erie whitefish. The fry are said to be more lively and marked with two dark lines on each side, while those of *C. albus* are plain silvery.

The Labrador or Lake Superior whitefish takes the hook readily, large numbers being caught by local anglers every day in season in the locks at Sault Ste. Marie. *Coregonus albus* takes the hook but rarely if at all.

The eggs of the Lake Erie whitefish have been planted in all the other lakes, and we have recognized specimens we call *Coregonus albus* from Lake Champlain, Lake Ontario, and Lake Superior among the Apostle Islands. The close resemblance between the whitefish, fat, plump, and pale, from the milky waters of Lake Winnipeg and those of Lake Erie has been noticed by many fish dealers. We doubt if any one could distinguish individual specimens from these two localities, although on the average they are different. Possibly *Coregonus albus* is merely an "ontogenetic species," its peculiarities being due to the conditions of food and water in Lake Erie.

The common whitefish lives habitually in the deeper waters of the lake, coming out into more shallow water at spawning time which is from late October into December.

The gillnet grounds extend mainly from about 5 miles off shore to the middle of the lake, the depth ranging from about 12 to 30 fathoms, and the bottom consisting of clay and mud. There is greater or less movement of the fish within these limits, of which the fishermen have cognizance, and which seems to be influenced by changes in the season and weather. In the early spring the best fishing is said generally to be obtained eastward of Dunkirk, in relatively shallow water, the body of fish working westward and into deeper water as the season advances, and again returning to the deeper water as the winter comes on. It is probable, however, that the early spring distribution in abundance is more widespread than the above would indicate, judging from the extent of territory which the fishermen may then occupy. The extent of the gillnet catch varies greatly with the season, caused partly by the condition of the water and partly by the withdrawal of a portion of the fish, as explained further on. The season opens with a large catch, which continues into May, but then falls away into June, when scarcely any fish can be obtained. This circumstance is attributed by the fishermen chiefly to the formation of a slime on the bottom, which also covers the nets and makes it difficult to handle them. These conditions may persist for a week or two in July, when good fishing revives, especially in the deeper waters, in which the best catches of the year are made, during August and September. The remainder of the season affords much poorer return as a whole than the summer, due, undoubtedly, to the spawning run, which takes a large proportion of the fish away from this region.

The two seasonal movements above referred to are both shoreward and toward the western end of the lake, and it is during their continuance that the poundnet catch is made. The spring movement occurs mainly during the latter half of April and in May, although a few stragglers may be found in June. It is felt along both shores as far as the Bass Islands and Kingsville, Ontario, but on the south side of the lake it is most pronounced west of Ashtabula. It extends but a short distance onto the western platform, where only small and irregular catches are now obtained about the Bass Islands and Kelleys Island, although formerly they were more abundant there.

The fall movement is much heavier and much more widespread than the spring, and is actuated by the breeding instinct, which leads the fish to seek spawning grounds, to a large extent, at a great distance from their normal habitat. It begins on a small scale in September, during which month a few individuals are sometimes captured in the poundnets on the platform. It does not become pronounced, however, until in October and, including the up and down runs, continues through November and more or less into December, although very few fish are taken during the last mentioned month; that is to say, the poundnet catch seems to be obtained chiefly, if not almost entirely, from the up run, making it possible that the bulk of the down run keeps farther offshore.

The fall run strikes in along both shores the same as the spring, but at the western end of the lake the fish now become widely distributed over the platform, and a large number pass through the Detroit River into Lake St. Clair. There is considerable difference in the dates of the appearance of the fish at different places, especially on the platform, but this diversity is of only local significance. It is not improbable that during the western movement a certain proportion of the fish also proceed through the deeper waters until they reach the platform, but nothing positive has been learned regarding this matter, as the schools are never followed by the gillnetters as in the case of the herring.

After the whitefish reach their spawning grounds on the western platform, they give rise to an extensive local gillnet fishery of very limited duration. During their passage up the Detroit River, mainly in the latter part of October and the early part of November, they are caught by means of seines, and in Lake St. Clair a few are taken in the pound nets.

It is interesting to note that during the spawning period a large body of fish still remains in the deeper water, where the gillnetters continue to take them, though in smaller quantities than in the summer and in the early fall.

The entire distribution of the spawning grounds of the whitefish in Lake Erie is not known. During the spawning season a part of the fish remain in their normal deep-water habitat, but it is not probable that they spawn there. The regular fall movement carries a very large body to the western platform, where many well-defined spawning grounds occur. These are chiefly rocky reefs and shoals, characterized in part by the water-worn surfaces of the common limestone of the region, the so-called honeycombed rock. Hard gravelly and sandy bottoms in some places are also said to serve the same purpose, but this fact has not been entirely substantiated. The distribution of the grounds on the platform is from the neighbourhood of Kelleys Island to near the Michigan shore, on both sides of the boundary line. Some of the best known are two shoals north of Kelleys Island; the reefs and rocky shores about and in the neighbourhood of North Bass, Middle Bass, Rattlesnake and Green islands; the reefs about the Hen and Chickens, Niagara Reef, and occasional patches off the mainland shores. The depth ranges mostly from about 4 to 20 feet, but is sometimes greater. It is in these places that the gillnet fishing is carried on during the spawning time, and mainly here and in the Detroit River that the eggs have been obtained for the artificial propagation of the species. The fish taken in the Detroit River are mostly bound for Lake St. Clair, although the river itself is said to contain one or more spawning places.

It seems scarcely credible that the great stock of whitefish which has characterized the deeper waters, where the catch has many times exceeded that of all the remainder of the lake combined, can have been maintained solely through the agency of that body of fish which reaches the western platform and it is possible that extensive spawning areas will sometime be discovered farther east. One small ground is known to be located between Dunkirk and Westfield, N. Y., and two others are reported off Port Dover and Port Burwell, Ontario.

The spawning time varies somewhat in different years, dependent on the conditions of the weather and also with respect to the locality. Our information on this subject is mainly limited to the platform, where the dates have been accurately determined in connection with fishcultural operations, as follows: Ripe eggs have been obtained, but only rarely, as early as the latter part of October, the first being taken generally in the early part of November. Spawning may continue into the first week of December, but the last eggs are seldom secured later than December 1, generally a few days before that date. The bulk of the eggs have usually been obtained between the 10th and 25th of November, but sometimes beginning as early as the 5th or 6th and continuing as late as the 28th, which dates may be considered to mark the limitations of the main part of the spawning season. These figures are based on the averages for several years and for the different grounds where eggs are procured for the hatcheries. In any one place the bulk of the spawning may be, and generally is, completed in a much shorter space of time, from 5 to 10 days. They begin to fish for the hatcheries on the Detroit River in the latter part of October, but the fish are not then ripe and are penned until the eggs mature.

The general run of the whitefish taken in Lake Erie ranges from about $1\frac{1}{2}$ to 5 or 6 pounds, but seldom exceeds 4 or 5 pounds. This applies to all parts of the lake, but the average size may differ more or less in different places or in the catch by different kinds of apparatus.

COMMON WHITEFISH OF LAKE ERIE: *Coregonus albus* Le Sueur.
Painting from life of a specimen 17¼ inches long from Lake Michigan, off Berrien Co., Mich.

LAKE HURON HERRING: *Leucichthys sisco huronius* (Jordan & Evermann).
Painting from life of a specimen 12¾ inches long from Lake Michigan, off Berrien Co., Mich.

The species, however, attains a weight of 12 pounds and more, and some have been reported weighing as high as 20 pounds, but these extreme sizes are now practically extinct. Individuals weighing 8 or 9 pounds are considered very large for Lake Erie at the present time.

It has been impossible to ascertain satisfactorily the average size of the fish in the catch of any one fishery. In several fares landed by the gillnet tugs at Dunkirk in August, 1894, the average by actual weigh was found to be between $2\frac{1}{2}$ and 3 pounds, only a very small number weighing as low as $1\frac{1}{2}$ and $1\frac{3}{4}$ pounds, while the largest weighed about 5 pounds. According to the statements of the fishermen, the average weight on the platform ranges all the way from $2\frac{1}{2}$ to 4 pounds, these figures, which are only estimates, being based in part upon the poundnet and in part upon the gillnet catch.

The dealers would prefer to handle no whitefish weighing less than about $1\frac{1}{2}$ pounds, and some would place the minimum size suitable for market as high as 2 pounds.

From the observations of fish-culturists, the smallest fish from which eggs may be obtained on this lake weigh from $1\frac{1}{2}$ to 2 pounds. In that event the general catch of whitefish on Lake Erie may be expected not to include immature fish, and the minimum size desired for market would about correspond with their earliest mature size, $1\frac{1}{2}$ to 2 pounds. It is questionable, however, especially in the case of a rapidly decreasing product, whether its extensive capture in the first year of maturity should be allowed.

It is claimed by some that very large quantities of immature white-fish are caught in certain places, but the evidence in respect to that matter lacks confirmation. According to the testimony, comparatively few whitefish weighing under $1\frac{1}{2}$ pounds reach the platform, the number being somewhat larger in the spring than in the fall, but at no time great enough to make their capture a question for serious consideration. Nothing is definitely known regarding the general distribution and habits of the young, but they are supposed to remain chiefly in the deep waters of the lake. Many are reported to be taken in the herring gillnets in that region, and also in the poundnets on some parts of both the north and south shore, but the men actually concerned in those fisheries deny that the quantity is ever excessive. The subject is important and should be further investigated.

Whitefish reach maturity in the 3d or 4th year. A full-grown individual deposits from 10,000 to 75,000 eggs, depending on the fish's size. A rule for determining the approximate spawning capacity is to allow about 10,000 eggs for each pound of the fish's weight. The eggs are $\frac{1}{8}$ of an inch in diameter, and 36,000 make a fluid quart.

In nature the eggs of the whitefish are subjected to the attacks of many enemies for nearly 5 months. The mud-puppy, commonly known as "lizard" or "water-dog" by the people along the lakes, is especially destructive. During the month of January, 1897, many of these animals were pumped up with the water supply of the Put-in-Bay station. The stomachs of a considerable number of them contained whitefish and cisco eggs, the contents of 1 stomach being 288 whitefish eggs and 4 cisco eggs.

Another voracious destroyer of whitefish eggs is the common yellow perch (*Perca flavescens*). The deck of a boat has been covered with the eggs of the whitefish and cisco pressed out of the stomachs of perch taken from gillnets the last of November on the reefs, where they had gone to feed on the eggs.

The various smaller *Cyprinidæ* and some other fishes, crawfish, and wild fowl make the eggs of fishes a considerable portion of their diet, those which require the longest period in hatching, of course, suffering most.

It has been asserted that the carp is very destructive to the eggs and fry of whitefish and other valuable food-fishes, but Dr. Leon J. Cole who conducted very comprehensive and thorough investigations of the habits of the carp in Lake Erie some years ago found only three whitefish eggs in the stomachs of numerous carp which he examined. His conclusion was that, while the carp may eat some whitefish eggs, the amount is so insignificant as to be practically negligible.

The artificial propagation of whitefish has long since passed the experimental stage and has attained a high degree of perfection. The work can be carried on with great facility, and its value is especially apparent when it is considered that under natural conditions only a very small percentage of the eggs hatch, while through artificial propagation from 75 to 95 per cent are productive. Practically all the eggs taken for hatching purposes are obtained from fish caught by the commercial fishermen, which would otherwise be lost.

In the fiscal year 1897-98 the United States Fish Commission hatched and planted 88,488,000 whitefish fry, and in 1898-99, 152,755,000 fry were hatched and liberated in suitable waters.

The whitefishes are by far the most important group of fresh-water fishes of North America, and probably of the world. The common whitefish is the best of the tribe, but some of the others nearly equal it in merit, and all are more or less esteemed as food. Among the fishes of the Great Lakes the common whitefish ranks next in value to the lake herring, lake trout, and wall-eyed pike. In 1897 the catch in the United States amounted to about 8,000,000 pounds, having a value of nearly $300,000. If to this is added the yield of lake herring and other species of whitefish, the aggregate is over 57,000,000 pounds, having a value of nearly $800,000. The market value of the whitefishes taken in 1898 in the British Provinces was reported as $877,000, a sum representing about 18,400,000 pounds.

The common whitefish reaches a larger size than any other species of whitefish in the United States. Examples weighing over 20 pounds have been taken, but the average weight is under 4 pounds.

Whitefish fishing is done chiefly with gillnets set at or near the bottom in comparatively deep water, although considerable quantities are also taken in pound-nets, trap-nets, and seines. A very large part of the catch reaches the market in a fresh condition, although formerly considerable quantities were salted. The leading centres of the trade are Chicago, Detroit, Sandusky, Cleveland, Erie, and Buffalo, whence the fish are shipped frozen or in ice to all parts of the country.

Head 5; depth 3; eye 4 to 5; D. 11; A. 11; scales 8-74; vertebræ 59; gillrakers usually 10+17 to 19; maxillary 4. Body oblong, compressed, always more or less elevated, becoming notably so in the adult; head small and short, the snout bluntish and obliquely truncated, the tip on the level of lower edge of pupil; width of preorbital less than half that of pupil; maxillary reaching past front of orbit; gillrakers moderate, about 2 in eye. Colour, olivaceous above, the sides white, but not silvery; lower fins sometimes dusky.

Labrador Whitefish

Coregonus clupeaformis Mitchill

This species is the common whitefish of all the Great Lakes, Lake Erie excepted. It is also found in many of the smaller lakes tributary to these. The Otsego whitefish is apparently identical with this species, as is also the whiting of Lake Winnepesaukee.

This whitefish may be recognized by the compressed, elliptical form, rather pointed snout, absence of a hump at the nape except in large examples, and by the presence of a dusky shade on the back, forming more or less distinct streaks along the rows of scales. It varies greatly in size, being mature at $2\frac{1}{2}$ pounds, but attaining a weight of 8 to 12 pounds in Lake Superior. These very large examples are known as bowbacks or humpbacks.

This species is one of the most valuable of our food-fishes. It is probably the only large whitefish native to the Great Lakes system, Lake Erie excepted.

In Jordan & Evermann's Fishes of North and Middle America, the upper lakes were supposed to be inhabited also by the Erie whitefish, and on this supposition the name *clupeaformis* was retained for the latter, while the present species was called *Coregonus labradoricus*. There is very little difference between these two species, if species they really are. In general, *Coregonus clupeaformis* can be told at once by its more elongate, more compressed and more symmetrical body, deepest at the dorsal fin, and scarcely elevated at the nape, by its dark and streaked back, and by its longer pectorals, which reach more than half way to ventrals. The flesh of the Lake Erie fish is fatter and softer.

The whitefishes from the basin of Lake Winnipeg, or Manitoba whitefish, show the general traits of *Coregonus clupeaformis*. In general, however, these are more robust, with larger head, deeped body, and longer fins. The caudal peduncle is deeper than long (the gillrakers are mutilated in all our specimens.) Those from the dark or "muskeeg" water are unusually dark, with dark streaks above and black fins. Those from the milky waters of Lake Winnipeg (about the mouth of the Red River of the North) are all very pale, as pale as the whitefish of Lake Erie. As the water of Lake Erie is similarly milky, discoloured by muddy, clay-bottomed streams, it is a question whether this feature of colouration is really a specific character. Perhaps *Coregonus albus*, as well as this Manitoba form, may be "ontogenetic species," or forms dependent on the food and the character of the water.

Humpback Whitefish

Coregonus nelsonii Bean

This whitefish occurs in Alaska from Bristol Bay northward, where it is said to be not uncommon. According to Dr. Bean, Nelson's whitefish has long been known from Alaska, but it has been confounded with a Siberian species, *C. syrok*, from which it is really very different. The Russian name is Korabati, while the Tenneh tribes of the Yukon call it Kolokuh. Dr. Dall speaks of it as a common species, and says it is rather bony, inferior in flavour, and that it is generally used for dog-food except in times of scarcity.

Head 5; depth 4; maxillary 4; D. 12; A. 12; scales 10-88-8; gill-rakers 26 in number, their length 2 in eye. Allied to *C. clupeaformis*, but distinguished by its arched and compressed back. Colour, plain whitish.

Bonneville Whitefish

Coregonus spilonotus Snyder

Recently Professor Snyder discovered two species of whitefish in Bear Lake, Idaho and Utah. While each had long been known to local fishermen neither of them had ever been described. The present species occurs at a depth of about 100 feet where it is found except during December when it migrates shoreward and spawns in shallow water. It is said not to enter the rivers.

This fish attains a length of a foot or more, and is pale moss-green above, silvery on sides, and white beneath; round, dusky spots, larger than the pupil, from head to tail, absent in adult. It is related to Williamson's whitefish from which it differs in the smaller and more numerous spots, larger scales and longer head. Known only from Bear Lake.

GENUS LEUCICHTHYS DYBOSKI

The Lake Herrings or Ciscoes

This genus is very close to *Coregonus*, from which it differs in the larger mouth, and more produced jaws, the premaxillaries being placed nearly horizontally, and the lower jaw projecting decidedly beyond them. The gillrakers are very long and slender with about 30 on the lower limb of the first arch; vertebræ 55. These characters are associated with greater voracity, and, in general, greater activity of the species.

The species of *Leucichthys* are numerous in northern parts of Asia, Europe, and America, and all are valued as food, though not held in as high esteem as the species of true whitefishes.

a. Caudal peduncle relatively long and slender, its length along lateral line above last ray of anal more than .75 length of head, its length from last ray of anal to first of caudal more than its depth; scales silvery, more or less loosely inserted; body more or less elongate, the depth 3.25 to 5.5 in length; minute teeth on tongue, none on jaws or palatines.

131

b. Species of shore waters, spawning in late autumn, the flesh firm, the skeleton well developed, the mouth small, the maxillary not reaching past middle of eye.

c. Adipose fin very small, usually shorter than eye; body elongate, the caudal peduncle slender, its least depth about 3 in head; body slender, the depth 4.33 to 4.66 in length; body anteriorly long, the pectoral not reaching nearly halfway to ventrals; back lustrous bluish in life, usually not marked with lengthwise streaks.
harengus; osmeriformis

cc. Adipose fin well developed, longer than eye.

d. Body elongate, the depth 4.33 to 4.5 in length; caudal peduncle slender, its least depth about 3 in head; body anteriorly long, the pectoral not reaching halfway to ventrals in the adult; back dark lustrous blue in life, usually marked with dark lengthwise streaks.

e. Body subcylindrical, little compressed, its depth about 4.5 in length, its greatest depth usually before dorsal........*sisco; huronius*

ee. Body more robust and more compressed, its depth about 4 in length, the greatest depth usually near insertion of dorsal.
ontariensis; lucidus; laurettæ; alascanus; pusillus

dd. Body deep and compressed, the depth 3.33 to about 4 in length; caudal peduncle stout, its least depth nearly half head; pectoral reaching more than halfway to ventrals; adipose fin larger, longer than eye; back olive-gray, without distinct dark streaks.

f. Body moderately robust, depth 3.5 to 4 in length; angle at the nape slight, scales relatively thin and loosely attached..*artedi; bisselli*

ff. Body very robust, depth 3.33 to 3.5 in length, with a strong angle at the nape; scales large, regular, and firmly attached; flesh rich, of excellent flavour.................................. *eriensis*

bb. Deep-water forms found in 50 fathoms and upward, spawning in midsummer, the flesh soft and fat, the skeleton relatively feeble, the mouth relatively large; adipose fin rather large.

g. Mouth moderate, the maxillary not extending to middle of eye; premaxillary nearly horizontal, the upper jaw not truncate; head broad, the width between temples rather more than half length of top of head; caudal peduncle stout.

h. Lower jaw distinctly projecting, its tip somewhat produced upward; head thick; eye large; pectoral extending more than halfway to ventrals; depth about 4 in length; adipose fin small; fins with little dark.

i. Head short and slender, 4.66 in length; mouth relatively small; adipose fin rather small............................*supernas*

ii. Head long and thick, 4 to 4.25 in length; mouth large; adipose fin small.

j. Gillrakers more than 40...........................*prognathus*

jj. Gillrakers fewer than 40...........................*johannæ*

hh. Lower jaw included; head long, about 4.5 in length; body moderate, the depth about 4.2 in length; caudal peduncle thick; fins all broadly edged with black.

k. Gillrakers 16 to 19+31 to 35.........................*nigripinnis*
kk. Fins slightly bluish or dusky at tip; gillrakers 14+25..*cyanopterus*
gg. Mouth larger, the maxillary extending about to middle of eye; snout long, subtruncate at tip, the premaxillaries more or less vertically placed, lower jaw included; body slender, the depth more than 4 times in length; caudal peduncle slender; head slender, its breadth at temples half its length above. Colour pale, often some dark on fins except the ventrals.
l. Pectoral not reaching halfway to base of ventrals; snout about equal to eye, about 4 in head; depth of tail much greater than snout; snout more truncate than in next species; scales about 70; colour very silvery....................................... *hoyi*
ll. Pectoral reaching more than halfway to base of ventrals; depth 4.6 to 4.66 in length; snout less truncate than in *L. hoyi*, 3 to 3.5 in head, longer than eye; depth of tail not equal to snout; scales about 77. Colour brassy-silvery, with dark points on all fins save ventrals...................................*zenithicus*
aa. Caudal peduncle short and thick, its length along lateral line above last ray of anal about half head, its length from last ray of anal to first of caudal less than its depth; skeleton and flesh firm; scales dusky, firmly inserted; body deep, compressed, the depth 2.25 to 3.4 in length; no teeth. Colours dark, back and fins dusky.
m. Depth 3.2 to 3.33 in length; adipose fin very small, shorter than eye; caudal peduncle moderate, its depth 2.5 in head ....*manitoulinus*
mm. Depth 2.5 to 3 in length; adipose fin large, longer than eye; body short and deep; caudal peduncle very short and deep, its depth 2 to 2.25 in head................................*tullibee*

Smelt of the New York Lakes

Leucichthys osmeriformis (H. M. Smith)

This small fish has been recorded only from Seneca and Skaneateles lakes, New York, where it is known as smelt. It doubtless inhabits others of the deep-water lakes of northern New York. Nothing is known of its habits; and its small size, 10 inches or less, renders it of little value as food.

Head 4; depth 5 to 6; eye 4; D. 9; A. 13; scales 9-83-10; maxillary 3; mandible 2; gillrakers 20+35, very long and slender, as long as eye. Body very slender, back not elevated; head rather large, its width equal to half its length; eye large, equal to snout; dorsal fin high, its height equal to $\frac{4}{5}$ depth of body, and $1\frac{1}{2}$ times length of base of fin, its origin nearer base of caudal than snout, its free margin nearly straight and vertical; longest anal ray $\frac{4}{5}$ length of base of fin; ventral long, equal to height of dorsal, its length equal to $\frac{3}{4}$ of distance from ventral origin to vent; ventral origin midway between base of caudal and pupil; adipose fin long and slender, of uniform width which is $\frac{1}{3}$ its length; mouth large, lower jaw projecting; teeth on tongue. Colour, grayish silvery above, sides bright silvery, white below; tips of dorsal and caudal dark.

Saginaw Bay Herring

Leucichthys harengus (Richardson)

The herring of bays and shallow waters of lakes Huron and Michigan (Saginaw Bay, Georgian Bay, Green Bay, etc.), until recently confounded with *Leucichthys artedi*, is a distinct species well separated from all the other species of this group by the very small adipose fin. It is a small species, those found in Saginaw Bay rarely exceeding a foot in length and 6 ounces in weight. Of all the species of lake herring this is probably the most numerous in individuals, occupying, as it does, most of the open waters of lakes Huron and Michigan. It is taken in great abundance in Saginaw Bay, where it is largely salted for commercial purposes.

Lake Herring

Leucichthys artedi (Le Sueur)

This important food-fish, named by Le Sueur in honour of Petrus Artedi, the "Father of Ichthyology," the friend and associate of Linnæus, and perhaps the ablest systematic zoologist of the 18th century, abounds in Lake Erie, especially in its southern parts. It ascends to Lake St. Clair and occurs sparingly in Lake Huron. It has also been taken in Lake Ontario.

This species is characterized by its relatively elliptical form with compressed sides, rather stout caudal peduncle, and large adipose fin. All the other species of this subgenus, except Bissell's and the Jumbo herring, are much more slender in all their parts.

The lake herring has the same general habits as the whitefish, but seems to be more widely disseminated during most parts of the year. During the summer and winter it is mainly restricted in Lake Erie to the deeper waters in the middle of the lake, in its eastern half, and along the northern shore east of Rondeau. From the deep-water region there are two great migrations into the shoaler and more changeable portions of the lake. In the spring, when the shoal waters become warmer, the fish emerge from their winter habitat and move shoreward, and upon the edge of the platform, evidently in search of food. The volume of this migration is less than that of the fall run, and is more fluctuating and irregular. Their presence is generally first noticed in early April, and occasionally large lifts are made in the latter part of that month, though the best fishery is in May. Some are caught in June, but by the first of that month the bulk has left the United States coast for deeper water, although on the Canadian shore east of Pointe Pelee they remain throughout the summer. During the summer months the gillnet tugs from Cleveland and eastern ports find them in deep water well out in the lake, the best season off Erie, the principal fishing centre, being from July to September. The fall migration corresponds in a general way with that of the spring, though the incentive is different. Then large bodies of herring seek spawning beds on the platform, over which they become widely distributed. The distribution of their spawning grounds on the platform is less restricted than those of the whitefish, and the herring are not confined to the reefs and rocky bottoms when discharging their eggs. There are doubtless important spawning grounds east of the platform, though their exact location has not been determined.

The spawning of the lake herring takes place in the fall, chiefly in November.

The average weight probably does not exceed a pound, and the maximum weight 2 pounds. It is usually caught in gillnets and pound-nets.

The Cisco of Lake Tippecanoe

Leucichthys sisco (Jordan)

In certain small deep-water lakes in northern Indiana and Wisconsin is a small lake herring described originally from Lake Tippecanoe, Indiana, from which fact it has received its vernacular name. It has been reported also from Crooked, Shriner and Cedar lakes in northeastern Indiana, and from Geneva, La Belle, and Oconomowoc lakes in Wisconsin.

To the angler the cisco of Lake Tippecanoe is by far the most interesting of all the American whitefishes, although, like the mountain herring, the fact that it will rise to the fly or that it can be taken on the hook at all, is not generally known. But its praises have been sung by William C. Harris, the veteran editor of *The American Angler*, and that is praise from Sir Hubert himself.

In Geneva Lake, Wisconsin, this fish is an abundant species, and is regarded by local anglers and others who have had experience with it as one of the most attractive and interesting fishes to be taken with rod and line; and the fact that it can be taken only for a few days each year adds zest to sport already fascinating. Only during the last days of May or the early ones of June, when the Mayfly is on the wing, is the cisco seen. Then the anglers go in boats out on the lake where the water is 50 to 100 feet deep and where experience has shown the cisco may be found. Until casting begins not a fish can be seen, nor the slightest ripple upon the water; but no sooner have a few impaled ephemeras dropped upon the surface than the ciscoes begin to appear. They can be seen coming up from the depths, "their pearly sides burnished by the gleam and glint of the afternoon sun." In a moment the water all about the many boats is a-ripple with eager fish, every hook has been taken, and the happy anglers are busy removing the catch and dropping it into their boats. The Mayfly is the lure in almost exclusive use, though Mr. Harris succeeded in taking a few fish with an artificial fly. The great tenderness of the mouth of the cisco does not permit the angler to play his fish except at the almost certain risk of losing it. So far as we have been able to learn this species has not attracted the attention of anglers elsewhere.

In the small Indiana lakes in which it is found it comes into the inlets or other shallow water for spawning purposes usually between the middle of November and Christmas. The cisco reaches a length of 14 inches and is regarded as a delicious food-fish.

This fish does not differ greatly from the lake herring. The head seems to be longer, the eye smaller and the mandible and the maxillary a trifle shorter. The fish is rather smaller than the lake herring. The colour is not especially different.

Alaska Herring

Argyrosomus alascanus Scofield

This herring is known only from 3 specimens, 1 from salt water at Point Hope, Alaska, and 2 others from freshwater at Grantley Harbour, near Bering Straits.

The species reaches a foot in length. It seems most closely related to the lake herring, from which it differs chiefly in the fewer gillrakers.

Nothing is known regarding its abundance, distribution, or habits.

Mooneye Cisco

Argyrosomus hoyi Gill

This fish, which is thus far known only from Lake Michigan and, possibly from Lake Superior, does not appear to be an abundant species. Until 1894 only 2 specimens were known, but in that year the investigations of the United States Fish Commission showed it to be one of the principal fishes taken in the deep-water gillnet fishery in the western part of Lake Michigan.

Very little is known as to its habits. It seems to be a deep-water species and it is not known to come into shallow water. Examples taken between November 5th and 20th were all ripe or nearly so, indicating that to be their spawning time, and its spawning beds are probably in deeper water than those of other species. Among other names by which this species is known are mooneye, cisco, kieye, chub, and Hoy's whitefish. It reaches a length of 12 or 13 inches and is one of the smallest and handsomest of our whitefishes.

From *A. prognathus*, which it resembles, Hoy's whitefish may be distinguished by the larger eye, the shorter maxillary and the darker colour.

Head $4\frac{1}{2}$; depth $4\frac{1}{2}$; eye $4\frac{1}{5}$ to $4\frac{2}{3}$; snout $3\frac{2}{3}$ to $3\frac{5}{6}$; maxillary $2\frac{3}{5}$ to 3, reaching vertical of middle of pupil; mandible $2\frac{1}{6}$; D. 10; A. 11 or 12; scales 8 or 9-73 to 80-7; gillrakers 14+25 or 26, slender, about 2 in eye; vertebræ 56; B. 8 or 9. Body rather slender, compressed, the back somewhat elevated; mouth large, subterminal, the lower jaw shorter than the upper even when the mouth is open; tip of muzzle rather bluntly truncate, somewhat as in a true *Coregonus*: head rather long, slender, and pointed; suborbital and preorbital long and narrow; distance from tip of snout to occiput $2\frac{1}{5}$ to $2\frac{2}{5}$ in distance from occiput to origin of dorsal fin; fins low; free margin of dorsal very oblique, the length of anterior ray $1\frac{3}{5}$ in head, that of last ray less than half that of first; longest anal ray 2⅔ in head, and more than twice as long as the last; pseudobranchiæ very large; tongue with traces of teeth. Colour, light iridescent blue on back, with a few fine dark punctulations reaching about 2 scales below lateral line; sides and under parts rich silvery, brighter than in any other of our *Coregoninæ*, much as in *Hiodon* and *Albula;* top of head light olivaceous; cheeks silvery; dorsal, caudal and pectorals with some dark on their margins; anal and ventrals white, with some dark dustings; the male perhaps a little richer, more iridescent blue on back, and with the scales a little thicker and less closely imbricated.

Least Whitefish

Argyrosomus pusillus (Bean)

This is perhaps the smallest of American whitefishes, rarely reaching a foot in length and ½ pound in weight. It has the reputation of being more bony than any other species. Its habitat includes practically all of Alaska except the south-eastern portion. It is little used as food except for dogs. Nothing is known as to its habits.

Great Bear Lake Herring

Argyrosomus lucidus (Richardson)

The herring of Great Bear Lake is little known. The only specimens we have seen are 2 obtained in 1894 by Miss Elizabeth Taylor and donated to Stanford University. These are each 16 inches long and are the only specimens received by any museum since Richardson's time, more than half a century earlier.

Lauretta Whitefish

Argyrosomus laurettæ (Bean)

This species is known only from the Yukon River northward to Point Barrow where it is said to be not uncommon. Nothing is known regarding its habits. It is close to *A. lucidus,* but seems to have a longer dorsal fin.

Bloater Whitefish

Leucichthys prognathus (H. M. Smith)

The bloater is known also as bloat, longjaw, silver whitefish, and, sometimes, cisco or ciscoette.

It is known from all the Great Lakes except Lake Erie from which as yet no specimens have been reported. It is probably most abundant in Lakes Ontario and Michigan, where it has good rank as a food-fish. The flesh is firm and of good flavour. By many people it is scarcely less highly esteemed than the common whitefish.

It is highly prized in Lake Ontario where it often brings the same price as *C. albus*; elsewhere it usually sells for a few cents a pound less.

When properly cared for on being caught, this fish is delicious, says Mr. Charles H. Strowger.

"When salted it keeps well, and does not lose its freshness when cooked. A great deal of prejudice against the longjaw is entertained because of the soft and damaged condition in which the fish is usually sold to consumers.

It is a fish that ought to be iced as soon as it is taken from the water and kept cold until used, as it easily softens, and on cooking becomes too greasy for ordinary human palates to enjoy. When fresh caught it is equal, in my judgment, to any fish for delicacy of flavour. It is a splendid fish for baking when of full size, but small-sized fish are always of less value and should not be caught."

The longjaw reaches a length of 8 to 16 inches and a weight of a pound or less. Very little is definitely known regarding the habits of this species. It seems to be an inhabitant of the deeper parts of the lakes and is not often seen in shallow water. In Lake Ontario it is taken only in depths of 200 to 400 feet.

There is much difference of opinion among fishermen as to the spawning time of this fish. Fish with mature roe have been reported as early as May 17, and we have seen ripe fish in late June and July in Lake Ontario. Ripe fish have been reported in July also from Lake Huron.

The indications are that the bloater has a prolonged spawning period and that it is somewhat earlier than that of the common white-fish. Scarcely anything is known as to the location of the spawning beds, except that they are probably in relatively deeper parts of the lake.

Head $4\frac{1}{8}$; depth $3\frac{1}{2}$ to 4; eye 5; maxillary $2\frac{1}{2}$; mandible $1\frac{3}{4}$ to $1\frac{7}{8}$; D. 9 or 10; A. 10 to 12; scales 9-75-8; vertebræ 55; gill-rakers about 15+28. Body oblong, much compressed, back elevated, the body tapering rather sharply toward the narrow caudal peduncle, the adult having a slight hump as in *C. clupeiformis;* mouth large and strong; snout straight, its tip on a level with lower edge of pupil; maxillary long, reaching opposite pupil, its length $3\frac{1}{2}$ times its greatest width; mandible very long, projecting beyond upper jaw when the mouth is closed, reaching to or beyond posterior edge of the eye; head rather short, deep and pointed; cranial ridges prominent; dorsal rather high, the longest ray $\frac{1}{3}$ longer than base of fin; origin of dorsal nearer tip of snout than base of caudal. Colour, sides uniformly bright silvery, with pronounced bluish reflections in life; back dusky; under parts pure white without silvery; above lateral line the upper and lower edges of the scales finely punctulate with dark, the central part unmarked, producing light longitudinal stripes extending whole length of body; fins flesh-colour or pinkish in life, the dorsal and caudal usually showing dusky edges; postorbital area with bright golden reflection; iris golden, pupil black.

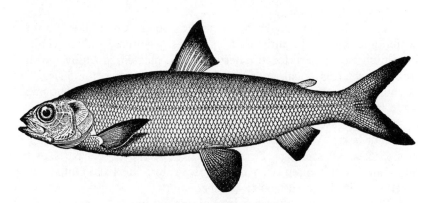

Blackfin Whitefish

Leucichthys nigripinnis (Gill)

The blackfin whitefish is known certainly only from Lake Michigan and Miltona Lake, Minnesota, though it has been reported from other small deepwater lakes of Minnesota and Wisconsin. It has also been reported from Lake Superior, but all the specimens of so-called blackfin or bluefin that we have seen from that lake are the longjaw. The blackfin is probably the most abundant fish of commercial importance in the deeper waters of Lake Michigan. It occurs in schools, like other members of the group, and is associated with the lake trout and other deep-water species.

The spawning season is the same as that of the common whitefish—in November to December. Then the fish come out upon rocky bottom where the eggs are deposited. A favourite resort for blackfin is said to be the Mudhole, a large depression 20 miles east of Sheboygan, in which the depth is about 90 feet. The principal method by which the blackfin is taken is in the gillnets. It is regarded as a good food-fish. It reaches a length of 18 inches, and a weight of one to 2 pounds.

Head 4; depth 4; eye $4\frac{1}{2}$; D. 12; A. 12; scales 9 or 10-73 to 77-7 or 8; vertebræ 57; gillrakers about 18+30, rather long and slender, $1\frac{1}{2}$ in eye or 2 in maxillary. Body stout, fusiform and compressed; head and mouth large; lower jaw slightly projecting; the maxillary $\frac{1}{5}$ greater than eye and reaching vertical of front of pupil; distance from tip of snout to occiput about $3\frac{1}{3}$ in distance from snout to origin of dorsal fin; back not arched, profile from occiput to origin of dorsal fin very gently curved; eye rather large, longer than snout; teeth very feeble but appreciable on the maxillaries and tongue. Colour, dark bluish above, sides silvery, with dark punctulations; fins all blue-black. This species attains a larger size than any of the other ciscoes, and has a larger mouth than any other except the bloater. It may be readily known by its black fins.

Tullibee

Argyrosmus tullibee (Richardson)

This species was first described from Pine Island Lake, Cumberland House, British Columbia. It is now known from Lakes Onondaga (New York), Erie, Superior and Michigan; also from Lake of the Woods, Lake Winnipeg, Albany River, Qu' Appelle River, and other waters northward. It has not been reported from Lake Ontario or Lake Huron.

The tullibee attains a length of 18 or 20 inches, and a weight of $3\frac{1}{2}$ pounds. It ranks high as a food-fish, but its commercial importance is as yet limited.

In the Great Lakes it is not at all common, but in Lake of the Woods it is quite abundant, and considerable quantities are shipped to Sandusky. In the provinces of Assiniboia and Manitoba the fish is taken in large numbers for local consumption, in gillnets and in traps made of brush and stones.

Writing of the tullibee in the lakes of the western territories of Canada, Mr. F. C. Gilchrist, of Fort Qu' Appelle, says:

"In September they will again be found gradually nearing the shoal water, feeding heavily, and plump with fat and the now swelling ovaries. Later on they appear to eat little or nothing, and devote all their time to playing until about the 25th of October, when they have settled down to the business of propagation, which they have finished by November 10. They prefer shallow water close to the shore with clean sand to spawn on, and during the day they may be seen in pairs and small schools, poking along the shores, but at night they come in thousands and keep up a constant loud splashing and fluttering, very strange and weird on a calm night. Two years ago I carefully counted the ova from a ripe fish $2\frac{1}{2}$ pounds in weight, and found there were 23,700, closely resembling whitefish eggs in appearance, but somewhat smaller. After spawning the fish are very thin, lank, dull in colour, and quite unfit for human food."

Mr. James Annin, Jr., in speaking of the tullibee of Lake Onondaga, says they generally commence running up on to the shoals about November 15, and the season extends into December.

They come up to the banks or gravelly shoals and spawn in from 3 to 6 and 7 feet of water. They have never been caught with hook in this lake, and an old fisherman told me that he had tried almost every kind of bait, and had used the very finest gut and the smallest hooks baited with *Gammarus* (freshwater shrimps) and other kinds of natural food—that is he supposed the food was natural to them. At the same time he claims he could see them in large schools lying in the water 8 or 10 feet from the surface.

Head 4 to $4\frac{1}{2}$; depth 3 to $3\frac{3}{5}$; eye 4 to 5; snout about 5; D. 10 to 12; A. 11 or 12; scales 9-68 to 71-8; gillrakers 16 to 18+30 to 34, 1 to $1\frac{1}{2}$ in eye; maxillary $3\frac{1}{2}$; mandible 2 to $2\frac{1}{4}$. Body short and deep, compressed, the dorsal and ventral outlines similarly curved: head small, conic, and compressed; mouth large, lower jaw projecting; middle of upper lip on a level with middle of pupil; maxillary long, moderately broad, reaching anterior edge of pupil, the width about 3 in its length; supplemental maxillary bone well developed, nearly half length of maxillary, its width $2\frac{3}{4}$ in its length; mandible long, reaching posterior edge of pupil; distance from tip of snout to occiput half that from occiput to origin of dorsal fin, which is midway between tip of snout and base of caudal fin; caudal peduncle short, compressed and deep, its least depth about $2\frac{1}{4}$ in head; fins all rather large; height of dorsal $1\frac{1}{5}$ in head, its base $1\frac{2}{5}$ in its longest ray; anal base very oblique, equal to longest ray, which is about equal to base of dorsal fin; pectorals and ventrals long, almost equal to longest dorsal ray; scales firm, considerably enlarged anteriorly; free margins of the scales less convex than in other species, often emarginate, especially on anterior part of body; lateral line straight and in a line with upper rim of orbit; tongue with a patch of fine teeth near the tip ; gillrakers numerous, long and slender. Colour, iridescent bluish above, sides and under parts silvery; older individuals darker above, and with more golden reflections on sides; fins all more or less evidently black-tipped; upper edge of pectoral margined with black. From all other whitefishes the tullibee is easily distinguished by the short, deep body and the closely imbricated scales whose margins are scarcely convex or even emarginate.

Bissell's Whitefish

Leucichthys bisselli (Bollman)

In Rawson and Howard lakes, Michigan, and perhaps in other small lakes of that state, is found a whitefish closely related to the tullibee and possibly intergrading with it; the maxillary seems, however, to be somewhat longer, the scales are smaller, the lower jaw longer, and the supraorbital bone elongate pear-shaped.

Nothing has been recorded as to the habits, size, or abundance of this fish.

The following additional species of lake herrings have been described recently:

Lake Huron Herring

Leucichthys huronius (Jordan & Evermann)

This is the common blueback or Michigan herring of Lakes Huron and Michigan. It occasionally enters Lake Erie where it is recognized as the Lake Huron herring. Its flesh is rather dry and flavourless, something like that of the Menominee whitefish, and it is not to be compared as a food-fish with the Erie herring. It should probably be regarded as a subspecies of *Leucichthys sisco*.

Ontario Herring

Leucichthys ontariensis Jordan & Evermann

This is the ordinary herring of Lake Ontario, and Cayuga Lake, and perhaps of others of the "finger lakes" of New York. It is allied to the Erie herring from which it differs chiefly in the greater length and shorter pectoral.

Jumbo Herring

Leucichthys eriensis (Jordan & Evermann)

This fine fish is found in Lake Erie, especially the north shore where it is extremely abundant. It is not certainly known from any other lake. It has been confounded with the tullibee with which it has nothing in common except the robust form. The name "mongrel whitefish" belongs to this species rather than to the tullibee. The nearest relative of the jumbo herring is *L. artedi*, from which it differs in the much more robust form, deeper nape, smaller head, and firmer scales.

As a food-fish it is far superior to the other lake herrings and is as good as the best whitefish.

Lake Superior Cisco

Leucichthys supernas Jordan & Evermann

This is the Cisco of Lake Superior. It is a silvery fish, found in waters of 50 fathoms or more, and is regarded as an excellent food-fish. It is especially characteristic of the waters west of Keweenaw peninsula where it is found in company with the bluefin and the longjaw.

Lake Michigan Cisco

Leucichthys johannæ (Wagner)

This species, also called the bloater of Lake Michigan, is very common in the northwestern part of Lake Huron in deep waters, and in Lake Michigan throughout its entire length. On these lakes it is not often taken to the markets, and is not highly valued as food. It is a great nuisance to the fishermen, large schools entering the nets, tangling them, although the mesh may be large enough to allow them to escape.

Whether the form in Lake Huron and Lake Michigan is really distinct from the *prognathus* of Lake Ontario is a matter we can not finally determine. Some examples of *johannæ* may be known at once by the few gillrakers, but this character is lost in Lake Huron examples, which, for the present, we are forced to refer to the same species.

Bluefin

Leucichthys cyanopterus Jordan & Evermann

This beautiful species is known only from deep water in Lake Superior. We have examined specimens from off Marquette, Duluth, and Knife River.

Lake Superior Longjaw

Leucichthys ʒenithicus (Jordan & Evermann)

This herring is known only from Lake Superior where it lives in much deeper water than does the ordinary lake herring. The autumn deep-water catch consists chiefly of the bluefin with a considerable percentage of this species. The two species are not always distinguished by the fishermen. From the bluefin it may be distinguished by its larger mouth and the colour. From the mooneye cisco of Lake Michigan it may be known by its less silvery colouration, and the thinner, looser, more dotted scales, longer pectoral, head and jaws, and larger adipose fin.

The flesh of the Lake Superior longjaw is soft but delicate in flavour when fresh, though poor after freezing. It is a good fish for smoking.

Manitoulin Tullibee

Leucichthys manitoulinus Jordan & Evermann

In the northern parts of Lake Huron, particularly about the Manitoulin Islands, the North Channel of Lake Huron, and in Georgian Bay. It may occur in some of the small lakes of northern Minnesota. The species is related to the tullibee of the Lake Winnipeg basin, the body being deep, the head and snout longer, eye larger, and the maxillary longer and larger. As a food-fish it does not rank high, the flesh being rather flavourless.

Inconnu

Stenodus mackenzii (Richardson)

The inconnu is a large, coarse salmonid inhabiting the larger streams of Alaska and northwestern British America. It is known from the Yukon and Mackenzie rivers, and the tributaries of the latter below the cascades; locally abundant and reaching a large size, usually 5 to 15 pounds, but sometimes 30 to 40 pounds. Its large size and comparative abundance render the inconnu of considerable commercial importance, especially in the Yukon since the great development of the gold-fields of that region. Little or nothing is known of the habits of this species.

Head $4\frac{5}{8}$; eye 6; D. 12; A. 14; scales 100; gillrakers 7+17. Eye less than snout, nearly equalling the narrow interorbital; maxillary reaching the vertical of posterior edge of pupil, its length very slightly more than $\frac{1}{3}$ head; supplemental bone long and narrow, nearly as wide as the maxillary, the anterior end notched, the angle above the notch sharply pointed, the lower angle bluntly rounded; the gillraker in the angle very stiff and bony.

GENUS ONCORHYNCHUS SUCKLEY

The Pacific Salmon

Body rather long, subfusiform, and compressed; mouth wide, the maxillary long, lanceolate, usually extending beyond the eye; jaws with moderate teeth, which become in the adult male enormously enlarged in front during the spawning season; vomer long and narrow, flat, with a series of teeth both on the head and the shaft, the latter series comparatively short and weak; palatines with a series of teeth; tongue with a marginal series on each side; teeth on vomer and tongue often lost with age; no teeth on hyoid bone; anal fin comparatively long, of 14 to 20 rays; pyloric cœca very numerous; gillrakers numerous; ova large and comparatively few. Sexual peculiarities very strongly developed, the snout in the adult males greatly distorted during the breeding season, the premaxillaries prolonged, hooking over the lower jaw, which in turn is greatly elongate and somewhat hooked at the tip; the body becomes deep and compressed, a fleshy hump is developed before the dorsal fin, and the scales become embedded in the flesh, and the flesh, which is red and rich in the spring, becomes dry and poor.

There are, in our Pacific Coast waters, five species of salmon, all belonging to the genus Oncorhynchus. They are (1) the king, chinook, quinnat, spring, or tyee salmon; (2) the sockeye, red, or blueback salmon; (3) the coho, silver, or white salmon; (4) the humpback or pink salmon; and (5) the dog, chum, or keta salmon. Each of these five species is more or less abundant, and each of them is the object of important commercial fisheries.

The habits of all the different species of Pacific Coast salmon are essentially the same in many respects. They are all anadromous; that is, they live most of their lives in the sea and enter fresh water only at spawning time to deposit their eggs.

After having spawned *once* they all die, both males and females alike, regardless of whether their spawning beds be hundreds or even thousands of miles from the sea or only a few yards or miles from the sea; none ever lives to return to salt water. The eggs are deposited in shallow nests or on other suitable bottom, usually in water only a few inches, or, at most, a few feet deep, usually in the fall of the year, and usually well toward the headwaters of freshwater streams. The eggs hatch in the winter and following spring, but not until some weeks after the fish that produced them have all died. There is a period of a few weeks each year during which each and every particular salmon family is represented only by a number of eggs. Both parents have died and none of the children has yet been born; there are only eggs to tide the family over. It is evident, therefore, that *no Pacific Coast salmon ever saw either of its parents, or any of its children!*

After the eggs have hatched, the young go down to the sea, some going down as fry, while others remain in fresh water at least one year. In the sea they grow rapidly and, when mature, return to fresh water where they spawn and die, thus completing the life-cycle.

The habits of the salmon in the sea are not easily studied. The chinook and the silver salmon of various sizes may be taken with the seine at almost any season in Puget Sound. They are also taken by trolling and in various waters in Alaska, particularly about Ketchikan. This would indicate that these species do not go far from shore. The chinook salmon takes the hook readily in Monterey Bay, both near the shore and as far as eight to 10 miles off shore. There is reason to believe that these two species do not seek great depths, but remain not far from the rivers in which they were hatched. The blueback and the dog salmon appear to seek deeper water, as the former is seldom taken with the seine in the ocean, and the latter is known to enter the Straits of Fuca at the spawning season, therefore coming in from the open sea.

The runs of the chinook and the sockeye generally begin late in March in the Sacramento and the Fraser rivers, somewhat later northward, and last, with various modifications and interruptions, until the actual spawning season in July to November, the time of the run and the proportionate amount in each of the subordinate runs varying with the different streams.

The salmon that run in the spring are, of course, adults, but their milt and roe are no more developed than in others of the same species that will not enter the rivers until fall. It seems that the contact with cold, fresh water, when in the ocean, in some way causes them to run toward it, even before there is any observable influence to that end exerted by the development of the reproductive organs. High water on any of these rivers in the spring is usually followed by an increased run of salmon. The salmon canners think, and with reason, that salmon which would not have run until later are induced to run by the contact with fresh water. Why contact with fresh water has this effect is not understood. We may call it an instinct of the salmon, which is merely a way of expressing our ignorance. In general, it seems to be true that in those rivers and in those years when the spring run is greatest, the fall run is least to be depended upon. It varies for each of the different rivers and for different parts of the same river.

The manner of spawning is essentially the same for all species. The fish pair off; the male, with tail and side and snout, excavates or forms a broad, shallow "nest" only a few inches deep, in the bed of the stream, often where the current is rather swift but usually where the water is relatively quiet. The depth of the water over the nest may be from a few inches to a few feet. The female swims over the nest, often touching the sides or bottom with her own sides which doubtless aids in the extrusion of the eggs. The male follows closely behind, extruding at the same time the milt which comes in contact with the eggs which are thereby fertilized. The eggs settle down into the interstices among, or become covered by, the gravel. The actual spawning process may extend over a period of several days before all the eggs are deposited. During the spawning operations, through contact with the gravel and as a result of fighting among themselves, the fins and sides of the spawning salmon become more or less worn or abraded, and, sooner or later, a fungus (*Saprolegnia*) appears upon the abraded areas, and the fish becomes a loathsome looking creature. When done spawning the salmon are so weak and worn out that the current carries them downstream tail foremost and they soon die, as already stated, none ever returning to the sea.

The salmon of all kinds are more or less silvery in the spring, spotted or not according to the species. As the spawning season approaches the salmon lose their silvery colour, become more slimy, the scales of the back partly sink into the skin, and the flesh changes from salmon-red to paler, probably from the loss of oil, the degree of paleness varying in different individuals, streams or species. In the Sacramento the flesh is rarely pale, either in spring or fall. In the Columbia, a few with pale flesh are sometimes taken in the spring and more in the fall.

The spring run of chinooks in the Fraser contains very few white-meated fish, but as the season advances the number increases until, in the fall, there is every variation, some having streaks of red meat, others being red anteriorly and pale toward the tail. This seems to be independent of age and sex. The flesh is just as palatable, however, but the canned product does not command as high a price on the market.

As the season advances, the difference between the males and the females becomes more and more marked. In the male the premaxillaries and the lower jaw become more and more prolonged, both jaws becoming, finally, strongly and often extravagantly hooked so that either they shut by the side of each other like shears, or else the mouth cannot be closed. The front teeth become long and canine-like, their growth proceeding very rapidly. The teeth on the vomer and tongue often disappear. The body becomes more compressed and deeper at the shoulders so that a very distinct hump is formed, especially in the humpbacked salmon. The scales disappear, especially on the back, by the growth of spongy skin. The colour changes from silvery to various shades of red and black, or blotchy. These changes are caused by influences connected with the growth of the reproductive organs; they are not caused by fresh water as they take place whether the fish is in fresh water or in the ocean.

Recent studies of the salmon, particularly the sockeye, by Dr. Charles Henry Gilbert of Stanford University, have thrown much light upon their life-histories.

PARENT STREAM THEORY

It has long been maintained by salmon fishermen and others that salmon, when mature, usually, if not invariably, return to the particular stream in which they were hatched. It was generally believed that a great majority of the fish hatched in any particular stream would return to that identical stream when mature and ready to spawn, but that a good many would, or might, go to other streams. Some thought that the salmon return to their own stream because they possess a marvelous geographic or homing instinct, while others maintained that the salmon, after going down to sea as fry or fingerlings, do not wander far from the mouth of the stream in which they were hatched, and that, when they reach maturity they seek fresh water; and the fresh water most easily found is that nearest at hand, which is the water of the stream in which they were hatched; they therefore ascend that particular stream.

While this theory, known as the "Parent Stream Theory," has long been held by many, it was not until recently that its truth was demonstrated. As early as 1906, Chamberlain announced, as one of the conclusions reached from his study of the sockeye at Naha Stream, Yes Bay and elsewhere in Alaska, that "at least the greater part of the supply of any stream must be derived from the fry produced in that stream."

As one of the results of a long series of investigations and observations requiring infinite patience, as well as the greatest care and skill, Dr. Gilbert has demonstrated the validity of the theory not only in its essential features but even in its minutest details. Gilbert says: "The validity of this important theory has been conclusively demonstrated in the case of the larger rivers of the Province. . . . Examination of the scales has removed any possibility of doubt that the progeny of the Fraser River fish return to the Fraser at their maturity, and that this is also true of the fish of each of the large river-basins. It has now been shown . . . that this same principle holds in the case of all the rivers and creeks, however small these may be, and however near together they may enter the sea."

Gilbert's study of the scales has shown that the salmon of each particular stream possess scale characters in common which enable them to be distinguished from the salmon of any other stream, however near the streams may be to each other. He calls attention to the fact that it is only during their life in fresh water that the salmon are subject to obviously diverse conditions. He further says: "It frequently happens that two lakes belonging to different river systems are separated by a few miles only across a low divide. Their physical conditions, it can not be doubted, in so far as these depend on climate, are practically identical. Yet the sockeyes they produce grow each after its own kind while still in freshwater, and exhibit characteristics of growth and habit which distinguish them from their near neighbours across the divide, and ally them closely with all the other like-colonies of their river basins, however distant these may be."

The study of the life-history of a salmon, as recorded in its scales, presents one of the most fascinating of stories. There is none more marvelous in all animate nature. Suppose you should take a trip to British Columbia and Alaska and while there you should visit some of the great salmon canneries. You have heard somewhere that the age of a salmon can be told from its scales. But you are skeptical. To try the thing out, you cut off a piece of skin with a few scales on it from the side of each of three or four salmon at three or four different canneries. You ask the cannery superintendents from what streams those particular fish came. They tell you and you make a note of it. Numbering the samples for identification, you send them to some expert, Dr. Gilbert, let us say, and ask him to examine them and tell you how old each of the fish was and where it came from. When you get Dr. Gilbert's report you will be surprised. He will tell you not only how old each fish was, but he will tell also the particular stream from which it came, if, perchance, it came from a stream whose salmon he has studied. And he will tell you how long it remained in fresh water before it migrated to the ocean—whether it went down to sea while yet in the fry stage the first spring after hatching, or remained in fresh water a year longer and then went down to sea as a yearling or fingerling. If it remained in the lake one summer and one winter, he will tell you whether the summer was a favourable one as to food supply and other conditions which enabled it to grow rapidly. He will tell you how long it lived in the sea—how many summers and how many winters, and this, of course added to the time it spent in fresh water before going to sea, will give its age. And, finally, he will tell you what stream this particular salmon was bound for when it was caught. He will be able to learn all these facts regarding each of the specimens you submit to him from an examination of the scales.

AGE AT WHICH SOCKEYE SALMON MATURE

It has been shown by Gilbert that the Alaska and British Columbia sockeyes, as a rule, mature and return to their home streams to deposit their eggs when four years old. A considerable proportion, however, in certain streams do not return until five years old, and still smaller numbers return at three, six, or even seven years of age. This varies with different streams. For example, it was found that the great majority of the Fraser River sockeyes mature at four years of age, but that, in average years, 10 to 15 per cent. of the run consists of five-year fish. As a result of his study of the sockeyes of Naha Stream, Chamberlain concluded that they are chiefly four-year fish. The Nushagak Bay salmon are either four-year or five-year fish, chiefly the latter.

Attention should here be called to the fact that the salmon return to the stream in which they were liberated when young and in which they were reared through the fry stage or longer. Under natural conditions this, of course, will be the stream in which were laid the eggs which produced them. But when eggs taken in one stream, as, for example, the Yes Bay Stream, are hatched and liberated as fry or fingerlings in another, as the Columbia, for example, they will return not to Yes Bay but to the Columbia.

As the adult salmon return to the stream in which they as fry were liberated and reared, regardless of whether the eggs from which they were hatched came from fish of that stream or not, it is evident that there is no inherited "homing instinct." They return to the stream in which they, as fry, fed, and not to the stream in which their parents fed when fry, unless it be the same stream. The name "Parent Stream Theory" is not well chosen. "Home Stream Theory" has been suggested by Dr. Evermann as a better name.

In view of this important fact, a hatchery which liberates all its output in the stream on which it is located will have no effect upon the run of salmon in any other stream. As Gilbert has said: "In order to maintain the supply of salmon in a given district, it will not be adequate to install a hatchery on any convenient stream into which the entire output of the hatchery will be turned. On the contrary, each stream must be given separate consideration, and must receive its own quota of fry to grow within its boundaries. The original source of the eggs is seemingly a matter of no importance. The destination of the adult salmon is determined by the locality in which the young were reared."

The following key to the species of Pacific Coast salmon will be helpful:

a. Gillrakers 20 to 25, comparatively short and few.
b. Scales very small, more than 200 in a longitudinal series; caudal
    spots large, oblong;.........................*gorbuscha,* 149
bb. scales medium, 138 to 155 in longitudinal series; pyloric cœca
    about 150.
c. Anal rays 13 or 14; black spots small or obsolete; bran-
    chiostegals 13 or 14;.........................*keta,* 150
cc. Anal rays about 16; back and upper fins with round black
    spots; branchiostegals 15 to 19;..........*tschawytscha,* 151
bbb. Scales comparatively large, 125 to 135 in longitudinal series,
    pyloric cœca 50 to 80;.........................*kisutch,* 154
aa. Gillrakers comparatively long and numerous, 30 to 40 in number;
    scales large; lateral line about 130; back in adult usually
    unspotted; clear blue in spring, red in fall; young more or
    less spotted;.........................*nerka,* 155

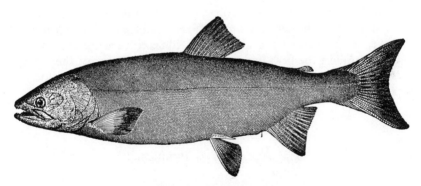

Humpback Salmon
Oncorhynchus gorbuscha (Walbaum)

The humpback salmon reaches a weight of 3 to 6 pounds and is the smallest of the genus. It is found on the Pacific Coast and ascending the rivers of America and Asia from California and Japan northward.

The humpback salmon reaches maturity usually in two years, spawns once, then dies.

In the rivers of Alaska it appears every year in great abundance; in Puget Sound there seems to be a periodicity in its movements, the runs of the alternate, odd years (1887, 1889, etc.) being much larger than in the even years. In the Sacramento River it occurs each year but in very limited numbers and is there known as the lost salmon. Among other names applied to this species are haddo, holia, and dog salmon of Alaska, though it is not the real dog salmon.

Branchiostegals 11 or 12; gillrakers 13+15; A. 15; D. 11; scales 210 to 240, about 170 in the lateral line; pyloric cœca very slender, about 180. Body rather slender, in the female plump and symmetrical, in the fall males very thin and compressed, with the fleshy dorsal hump much developed, the jaws greatly elongated, strongly hooked, and with extravagant canines in front; ventral appendage half as long as the fin. Colour, bluish, sides silvery; back posteriorly, adipose fin, and tail with numerous black spots, those of the caudal fin oblong in form and especially large; fall males red, more or less blotched with brownish. This species may be known at once by the very small scales and the coarse, oblong spots on the tail. In Japan is a very similar species, *Oncorhynchus masau* Brevoort, with equally small scales, but the tail unspotted.

In the early years of the salmon industry, the humpback was not much utilized by the canners, but with the decrease in abundance of the sockeye, the silver and the king, it has come to be more and more in demand. While the flesh has not the rich salmon colour of the sockeye it is nevertheless very palatable and doubtless of equal food value. It is put on the market as "pink salmon."

Dog Salmon

Oncorhynchus keta (Walbaum)

The dog salmon reaches a weight of 8 to 16 pounds. It is found usually in great abundance from the Sacramento northward to Kamchatka and Bering Straits, ascending all suitable streams in the fall, and spawning at no great distance from the sea in the smaller streams, which they enter in marvellous numbers, crowding upon each other in the most appalling manner.

As a food-fish this species is the least valuable of any. The inferiority, however, is more marked when the fish is canned than when otherwise utilized. The flesh is soft, spongy, and pale in colour, and therefore not so attractive in appearance as that of other species. When utilized fresh, the fish takes higher rank. Great quantities are now being frozen and shipped abroad where it is meeting with much favour. Considerable quantities are being dry-salted for the Japanese market, where it is called saké.

Head 4; depth 4; D. 9; A. 13 or 14; scales about 28-150-30; branchiostegals 13 or 14; gillrakers 9+15; pyloric cœca 140 to 185. General form that of the chinook, but the head rather longer, more depressed and pike-like; preopercle more broadly convex behind, and the maxillary extending considerably beyond the eye; gillrakers few, coarse and stout; accessory pectoral scale short, less than half length of fin. Colour, dusky above; sides paler, little lustrous; back and sides with no definite spots, but with fine punctulations which are often entirely obsolete; head dusky, scarcely any metallic lustre on head or tail; caudal dusky, plain, or very finely spotted, its edge usually distinctly blackish; fins all mostly blackish, especially in males; breeding males generally blackish above, the sides brick-red, often barred or mottled.

Chinook Salmon

Oncorhynchus tschawytscha (Walbaum)

Other names by which this fish is known are quinnat salmon, king salmon, Columbia River salmon, Sacramento salmon, tyee, tchaviche, and tschawytscha.

It is found on both coasts of the Pacific, from Monterey Bay, California, and China, north to Bering Straits, ascending all large streams, especially the Sacramento, Columbia and Yukon, in all of which it is very abundant. It ascends the large rivers in spring and summer, moving up without feeding, until the spawning season, by which time many of those which started first may have travelled a thousand miles or more. The run begins in the Columbia River as early as February or March. At first they travel leisurely, moving up only a few miles each day. As they go farther and farther up-stream they swim rather more rapidly. Those that enter the river first are the ones which will go farthest toward the head waters, many of them going to spawning beds in Salmon River in the Sawtooth Mountains of Idaho, more than 1,000 miles from the sea. Those which enter the river later travel more rapidly, but do not go so far toward the headwaters, while those last to pass by Astoria have so long delayed the movement that they are nearly ready to spawn and, consequently, must travel rapidly and enter the first small tributary streams which they reach. Those which go to the headwaters of the Snake River in the Sawtooth Mountains spawn in August and early September; those going to the Big Sandy in Oregon, in July and early August; those going up Snake River to upper Salmon Falls, in October; while those entering the small lower tributaries of the Columbia or the small coastal streams spawn even as late as December. Observations which we have made at various places indicate that wherever the spawning beds may be, spawning will not begin until the temperature of the water has fallen to 54° Fahr. If the fish reach the spawning grounds when the temperature is above 54°, they wait until the water cools down to the required degree.

It has been often stated and generally believed that the salmon receive many injuries by striking against rocks and in other ways while *en route* to their spawning grounds and, as a result from these injuries, those which go long distances from the sea die after once spawning. An examination of many salmon at the time of arrival on their spawning beds in central Idaho showed every fish to be entirely without mutilations of any kind, and apparently in excellent condition. Mutilations, however, soon appeared, resulting from abrasions received on the spawning beds while pushing the gravel about or rubbing against it, and from fighting with each other, which is sometimes quite severe.

The spawning act extends over several days, the eggs being deposited upon beds of fine gravel in clear, cold mountain streams. Soon after they have done spawning both males and females die, each individual spawning only once. This is true of all, whether spawning remote from salt water or only a few miles or yards from the sea. The cause of their dying is not conditioned upon distance from the sea, but is general in its application to all species of Pacific Coast salmon.

The chinook salmon is one of the most desirable and commercially valuable fishes in the world. Of the 5 species of salmon on our west coast it is approached in value only by the blue-back. It reaches an enormous size; examples have been taken in Cook Inlet weighing 100 pounds, and individuals of 40 to 60 pounds weight are not infrequent. The average weight of those taken in the Columbia River has been stated to be 22 pounds, and for those of the Sacramento River, 16 pounds.

The chinook salmon does not take the hook when in fresh water, though it is occasionally taken on the trolling spoon, particularly in the lower Columbia, and at Willamette Falls and in the Sacramento River. In Monterey Bay the chinook salmon is an important game-fish at certain seasons. It is taken exclusively by trolling. The best season is from the middle of May to the end of June, though they may be taken as early as February, and rarely, even in January. The anglers usually use a 30-ply line, a 4-inch hook, a 3 to 5 pound sinker, and let out about 150 feet of line. The sinker is attached by 24-ply line 20 feet above the hook. A sailing speed of about 4 miles an hour, with the hook sunk 20 to 50 feet beneath the surface (depending upon how the fish are running), is most effective. The best time of day is from sunrise to noon. Trolling spoons are rarely used, a hook baited with common sardine being much better. The fish caught range in weight from 8 to 60 pounds, the average being 25 pounds. The fish bite freely, but 25 fish by one line is regarded as a big day's catch. They are very game, and jump out of the water frequently.

This splendid salmon is unknown in Japan, its range extending little south of Kamchatka on the Asiatic side.

Head 4; depth 4; D. 11; A. 16; Br. 15 or 16 to 18 or 19, the number on the two sides always unlike; gillrakers usually 9+14; pyloric cœca 140 to 185; scales 27-146-29, the number in longitudinal series varying from 135 to 155; vertebræ 66. Head conic, rather pointed in the females and spring males; maxillary rather slender, the small eye behind its middle; teeth small, longer on sides of lower jaw; vomerine teeth very few and weak, disappearing in the males; body comparatively robust, its depth greatest near its middle; ventrals inserted behind middle of dorsal; ventral appendage half as long as fin; caudal strongly forked, on a slender peduncle. Colour, dusky above, often tinged with olivaceous or bluish on sides; silvery below; head dark slaty, usually darker than the body, and with few spots; back, dorsal fin and tail usually profusely covered with round black spots, sometimes these are few, but never wholly absent; sides of head and caudal fin with a peculiar metallic tin-coloured lustre; flesh rich salmon-colour in spring, becoming paler as the spawning season approaches. In the late summer and autumn the jaws of the male become elongate and distorted, the anterior teeth become greatly enlarged, and the colour more or less tinged or blotched with dull red.

Silver Salmon

Oncorhynchus kisutch (Walbaum)

The silver salmon is blessed with a large number of vernacular names, among which may be mentioned hoopid salmon, coho, kisutch, skowitz, quisutsch, and bielaya ryba. Next to the chinook and the blueback it is the most important of the genus. It reaches a length of 33 inches, and a weight of 3 to 15 pounds, and is abundant from San Francisco northward along both the American and Asiatic coasts, entering the shorter coastal streams late in the fall. It occurs in Asiatic waters as far south as Japan. In our waters it is especially abundant in Puget Sound, the fjords of Alaska, and in the shorter rivers of Washington and Oregon.

As a food-fish, although scarcely equal to the chinook and sockeye, it is of great importance. Large quantities are canned in Oregon, Washington, and Alaska and put on the market as "coho" or "medium red." Great quantities are utilized fresh.

Its spawning season is later than that of the chinook. They first appear in the southern end of Puget Sound about the first of September, and the run usually lasts until the first or middle of November. An examination of more than 2,000 examples at Celilo on the Columbia River in September and October indicated that their spawning time would not be later than October. This species is common in Japan.

Head 4; depth 4; D. 10; A. 13 or 14; Br. 13 or 14; pyloric cœca very large and few, 45 to 80; scales 25-127-29; gillrakers 10+13, rather long and slender, nearly as long as eye. Body slender and compressed; head short, shorter than in chinook of same size, very conical, the snout bluntly pointed; interorbital space broad and strongly convex; opercle and preopercle strongly convex behind, the preopercle very broad, with the lower limb little developed; eye much smaller than in chinook of same size; maxillary slender and narrow, but extending somewhat beyond the eye; teeth very few and small, only 2 or 3 on the vomer, those on tongue very feeble; fins small. Colour, bluish green on back, the sides silvery, with dark punctulations; no spots except a few rather obscure ones on top of head, back, dorsal fin, adipose fin, and the rudimentary upper rays of the caudal; pectorals dusky, and with dusky edge; sides of head without dark colouration as seen in the chinook; males mostly red in fall, and with the usual changes of form.

The silver salmon is easily distinguished from the chinook, which it most resembles, by its fewer scales, fewer pyloric cœca, and fewer branchiostegals.

Blueback Salmon; Sockeye Salmon

Oncorhynchus nerka (Walbaum)

The blueback salmon is found from the coast of southern Oregon, north to northern Alaska and Kamchatka, and Japan. It has been occasionally reported from the Sacramento and Klamath rivers, but is not at all common south of the Columbia. The principal rivers in the United States which it frequents are the Columbia, Quinialt and Skagit, in each of which very great runs occur. It enters the Fraser in enormous numbers, and is the most abundant and valuable salmon in Alaska.

The runs in the different rivers begin at different times, depending partly upon the distance of the spawning beds from the sea, and the temperature of the water.

The run in the Columbia begins in March or April, and the fish ascend to the headwaters of the Salmon River in Idaho, which they reach in July and August, a journey of some 1,000 miles from the sea. In the Skagit the run begins somewhat later, the fish reaching their spawning grounds in and above Baker Lake in August and September.

The run in the Fraser River is synchronous with that in the Skagit, or possibly a little later. In Alaska most of the streams which it enters are relatively short, and the runs do not begin until a short time before the spawning period. So far as known the blueback enters only such rivers as have lakes in their headwaters, and the spawning beds are always either in the inlets to the lakes or in the lakes themselves; so far as known there is no exception.

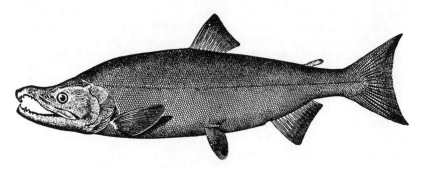

Adult Male Blueback Salmon

In the Columbia River this salmon is called the blueback; in the Fraser it is the sockeye, sawkeye, or sau-qui; in Alaska it is the red salmon or redfish, while among the Russians it is the krasnaya ryba.

In certain small lakes in Idaho, Oregon, Washington, British Columbia and Alaska, is found a dwarf form of the blueback or sockeye, known as little redfish, Kennerley's salmon, walla, or yank. It appears not to differ structurally from the large form. It is mature, however, both males and females, at 12 inches or less, and about one-half pound in weight, and like the regular blueback or sockeye, spawns once then dies. It was formerly believed these small fish were young bluebacks, but their migration up stream from the sea has never been observed. They are now believed to be localized, dwarfed forms which have established themselves in these various lakes where they are physiologically land-locked. Among lakes in which they are known to occur are Alturas, Pettit, Redfish, and Big Payette in Idaho; Wallowa in Oregon; Washington, Sammamish, Ozette, and possibly American and Chelan in Washington; Chiloweyuck, Nicola, François, Fraser, Okanagan, and Kootenai in British Columbia; and Patching Lake, Alaska.

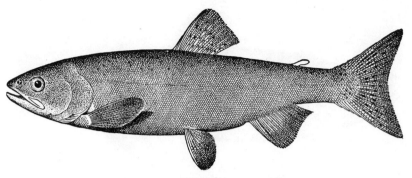

Adult Female Little Redfish

These small redfish are known from the Redfish Lakes of Idaho, Big Payette Lake in Idaho, Wallowa Lake in Oregon, Washington, Sammamish, and Ozette lakes in Washington, and many small lakes in British Columbia and Alaska.

The sockeye or blueback salmon is the most important salmon on our west coast; only the chinook approaches it in value. In Alaska it is by far the most valuable species; how long it can maintain this supremacy is uncertain; so recklessly is the fishery being prosecuted that it is not difficult to see its early fatal depletion.

In Fraser River and Puget Sound the sockeye fishery has already been more than decimated, after having been maintained for many years as one of the greatest fisheries in the world.

This species reaches a length of 15 to 30 inches and a weight of 3 to 11 pounds. For further information regarding the sockeye salmon see pages 143–149.

We have carefully observed the spawning habits of both forms of the redfish and the chinook salmon in the headwaters of Salmon River, Idaho, during two entire seasons, from the time the fish arrived in July until the end of September, by which time all these fish had disappeared. A number of important questions were settled by these investigations. In the first place, it was found that all of these fish arrived upon the spawning-beds in perfect physical condition so far as external appearance indicated, no sores, bruises or other mutilations showing on any of more than 4,000 fish examined. During the spawning, how-

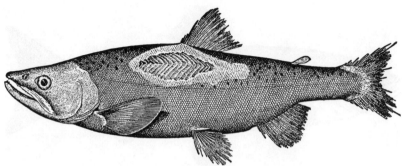

Adult Male Little Redfish, showing condition at end of spawning season

ever, the majority became more or less injured by rubbing against the gravel of the spawning-beds, or by fighting with one another. Soon after done spawning every one of these fish died, not only both forms of redfish, but the chinook salmon as well. There was no tendency to run down stream, but they all died on or near their spawning-beds. The dying is not due to the injuries the fish receive while on the spawning-grounds; many were seen dying or dead which showed no external or other injuries whatever.

The dying of the West Coast salmon is in no manner determined by distance from the sea. Observations made by us and others elsewhere show that the individuals of all the species of *Oncorhynchus* die after once spawning, whether the spawning-beds be remote from the sea or only a short distance from salt water. The cause of the dying is deep-seated in its nature and general in its application. The cause is the same as that which compasses the death of the *ephemera* or may-fly after an existence of but a few hours, or of the corn-plant or melon-vine and all annual plants at the end of one season.

This species, known locally as benimasu or red salmon, is landlocked in a few lakes (Akan, etc.) in Nemuro, in northern Japan, but it is rare on the Asiatic side south of Kamchatka.

Head 4; depth 4; D. 11; A. 14 to 16; scales 20-133-20; Br. 13 to 15; gillrakers 32 to 40, usually 14 or 15+22 or 23, as long as eye; pyloric cœca 75 to 95; vertebræ 64; snout $2\frac{1}{4}$ in head in fall males, $3\frac{1}{2}$ in females; mandible $1\frac{1}{3}$ in head in fall males, $1\frac{3}{4}$ in females. Body long, elliptical, rather slender; head short, snout long, pointed, sharply conic, the lower jaw included; maxil-

ATLANTIC SALMON, *Salmo Salar*

LANDLOCKED SEBAGO SALMON, *Salmo sebago*

lary rather thin and small, reaching beyond eye; teeth all quite small, most of them freely movable; vomer with about 6 weak teeth which grow larger in spawning males; preopercle very wide and convex; opercle very short, not strongly convex; preopercle more free behind than in the chinook salmon; ventral scale about $\frac{1}{2}$ length of fin; caudal fin narrow, widely forked; anal fin long and low; dorsal low; flesh deep red; males becoming extravagantly hook-jawed in the fall, the snout being then much prolonged and much raised above the level of rest of head, the lower jaw produced to meet it. Colour, clear bright blue above; side silvery, this overlapping the blue of the back; lower fins pale, the upper dusky; no spots anywhere on adults in spring; the young with obscure black spots above. Colour of breeding male, dark blood red on back and sides, with dark edges to some of the scales; middle of side darker red, but unevenly so, usually darkest at middle of body; under parts dirty white, with numerous fine dark dustings; entire head light olive, tip of nose and sides of jaws dark; under part of lower jaw white; dorsal fin pale red, anal darker red; adipose fin red; ventrals and pectorals smoky, somewhat red at base. Colour of breeding female, essentially the same, but rather darker on the sides.

The small form of redfish is a rich metallic blue on the back, becoming silvery on the lower sides and under parts; back with a few small black spots. During the breeding season it becomes a dirty red, brightest on the middle of the sides; under parts dirty white; top and sides of head dark greenish olive; snout black; lower jaw white, black at tip; dorsal pale red; anal dirty red; other fins dark smoky. The female is darker than the male and not greatly different in colour from the black-speckled trout.

GENUS SALMO (ARTEDI) LINNÆUS

The Salmon and Trout

Body elongate, somewhat compressed; mouth large; jaws, palatines, and tongue toothed, as in related genera; vomer flat, its shaft not depressed, a few teeth on the chevron behind which is a somewhat irregular single or double series of teeth, which in the migratory species are usually deciduous with age; scales large or small, 100 to 200 in a longitudinal series; dorsal and anal fins short, usually with 10 to 12 rays each; caudal fin truncate, emarginate or forked, its peduncle comparatively stout; sexual peculiarities variously developed, the males in typical species with the jaws prolonged and the front teeth enlarged, the lower jaw being hooked upward and the upper jaw emarginate or perforate; these peculiarities most marked in the larger and migratory species.

The species of this genus are of moderate or large size, black-spotted, and abounding in the colder creeks, rivers and lakes of North America, Europe, and Asia; no purely freshwater species occurring in America east of the Great Plains; 3 Atlantic Coast species, one marine and anadromous.

The non-migratory species (sub-genus *Trutta*) occur in both continents, are extremely closely related and difficult to distinguish, if, indeed, all be not necessarily regarded as forms of a single exceedingly unstable, and variable species. The excessive variations in colour and form have given rise to a host of nominal species.

European writers have described numerous hybrids among the various species of *Salmo*, real or nominal, found in their waters. We have thus far failed to find the slightest evidence of any hybridism among American *Salmonidæ* in a state of nature. Puzzling aberrant or intermediate individuals certainly occur, but such are not necessarily "hybrids."

The following interesting and pertinent observations on the species of trout are taken, with some modification, from Dr. Günther:

There is no other group of fishes which offers so many difficulties to the ichthyologist, with regard to the distinction of the species, as well as to certain points in their life history, as this genus. The almost infinite variations of these fishes are dependent on age, sex and sexual development, food, and the properties of the water. The colouration is, first of all, subject to great variation, and consequently this character but rarely assists in distinguishing a species, there being not one which would show in all stages the same kind of colouration. The young in all the species of the genus are barred, and this is so constantly the case that it may be used as a family character. When the young have passed this "parr" stage the colour becomes much diversified. The males, especially during and immediately after the spawning sea-son, are more intensely coloured and variegated than the females, immature individuals retaining a brighter silvery colour and being more like the female. Food appears to have less influence on the colour of the outer parts than on that of the flesh; thus the more variegated examples are frequently out of condition, whilst well-fed individuals, with pinkish flesh, are of more uniform though bright colours.

The water has a marked influence on the colours. Trout with intense ocellated spots are generally found in clear, rapid rivers and in alpine pools; in the large lakes, with pebbly bottom, the fish are bright silvery, and the ocellated spots are mixed with or replaced by x-shaped black spots; in dark holes, or lakes with peaty bottom, they often assume an almost uniform blackish colouration.

Brackish or salt water has the effect of giving them a bright silvery coat, with or without few spots, none of them ocellated.

With regard to size, the various species do not present an equal amount of variation. Size appears to depend upon the abundance of food and the extent of the water. Thus the migratory species do not appear to vary considerably in size, because they find the same conditions in all the localities inhabited by them. A widely-spread species, however, like our black-spotted trout, when it inhabits a small mountain pool, with scanty food, never attains a weight of more than a few ounces, while in a large lake or river, where it finds an abundance of food, it reaches a weight of 10 to 15 pounds. Such large trout of the rivers and lakes are frequently described as salmon trout, bull trout, silver trout, steelheads, etc.

The proportions of the various parts of the body to one another vary exceedingly, in the same species, with age, sex, and condition. The fins vary to a certain degree. The variation in the number of rays in any one genus (except *Oncorhynchus*) is inconsiderable and of no value for specific determination. Although some species appear to be characterized by comparatively low dorsal and anal fins, yet the proportion of the height of these fins to their length is a rather uncertain character. In most of the species the fin-rays are longer during the stages of growth or development. The caudal fin especially undergoes changes with age. The young of all species have this fin more or less deeply incised, so that the young of a species which has this fin emarginate throughout life is distinguished by a deeper incision of the fin from the young of a species which has it truncate in a young state. The individuals of the same species do not all attain maturity at the same age or size. Finally, to complete our enumeration of these variable characters, we must mention that, in old males, during and after the spawning season, the skin on the back becomes thickened and spongy, so that the scales are quite invisible or hidden in the skin.

After this cursory review of variable characters, we pass on to those which we have found to be constant in numbers of individuals, and in which it is difficult to perceive signs of modification due to external circumstances.

Such characters, according to the views of the zoologists of the present day, are sufficient for the definition of species; at all events, in every description they ought to be noticed. The confused and unsatisfactory state of our knowledge of the *Salmonidæ* is chiefly caused by authors having paid attention to the more conspicuous but unreliable characters and who have but rarely noted any of those enumerated here :

1. The form of the preopercle in the adult fish.
2. The width and strength of the maxillary in the adult; in the young and in females the maxillary is proportionately shorter than in the adult male.
3. The size of the teeth, those of the premaxillaries excepted.
4. The arrangement and permanence of the vomerine teeth.
5. The development or absence of teeth on the hyoid bone. In old examples these are often lost, and their absence in a species usually provided with them is not uncommon.
6. The form of the caudal fin in specimens of a given size, age or sexual development.
7. The size of the scales as indicated by counting the number of transverse rows above the lateral line. The scales in the lateral line are always more or less enlarged or irregular, and the number of scales should be counted higher up; this is one of the most constant and valuable specific characters.
8. A great development of the pectoral fins, when constant in a number of specimens from the same locality.
9. The number of vertebræ.
10. The number of pyloric cœca.
11. The number of gillrakers.

a. Vomerine teeth little developed, those on the shaft of the bone few and deciduous; sexual differences strong; breeding males with the lower jaw hooked upward, the upper jaw emarginate or perforate to receive its tip, size large;..........*salar*, 163
aa. Vomerine teeth well developed, those on the shaft of the bone numerous and peristent; sexual difference less marked, but similar in general character to those in *Salmo salar*.
b. Scales always small, 150 to 200 cross-series; a large deep red or scarlet dash on each side concealed below the inner edge of the dentary bone, this rarely obsolete; mouth large, the maxillary

$1\frac{3}{5}$ to $2\frac{1}{4}$ in head; hyoid teeth usually present but very small. Size various;......................................*clarkii*, 176

bb. Scales moderate, 130 to 180 cross-series; no red on throat; a reddish lateral band usually present; mouth moderate, maxillary 2 in head; hyoid teeth wanting. Size very large;..*gairdneri*, 190

bbb. Scales typically large, in 120 to 130 cross-series; usually no red on throat; a red or yellowish lateral band; mouth small, maxillary 2 to $2\frac{1}{2}$ in head; no hyoid teeth. Size moderate;

irideus, 198

Common Atlantic Salmon

Salmo salar Linnæus

The Atlantic salmon is perhaps the best and most widely known of all game fishes, and it was doubtless this fish which was sought by the earliest anglers. "In Aquitania the river salmon surpasseth all the fishes of the sea," wrote Pliny eighteen hundred years ago. This was the salmon's christening, and though more than 100 species of *Salmonidæ* have been described, the salmon has always stood pre-eminent as a game-fish, like a Scottish chieftain, needing no other name than that of his clan. The luxurious Romans prized highly the salmon streams in their Gallic and British provinces, if we may trust Pliny and Ausonius, and that this fish was well known to the early English is evinced by the many Saxon names, such as "parr," "pearl," "smolt," "grilse," "kipper," and "baggit," given it in different stages of its growth. The Normans brought over the name of Latin origin, which they applied to the perfect adult fish, ready for the banquets of the conqueror. When Cabot discovered Newfoundland in 1497, he found salmon in its waters, but the red men had long before this learned the art of killing them with torches and wooden spears.

Salmon inhabit both coasts of the North Atlantic and all its suitable affluents. How far beyond the Arctic circle they range no one knows, though their occurrence in Greenland, Iceland, northern Scandinavia, and middle Labrador is well established. They occur in Norway, Sweden, Denmark, entering the Baltic and the waters of Russia, and, according to some writers, the White Sea. They abound in all the British Islands, where they are protected and fostered with great success. They are, or were, also common in France, Belgium, Holland, and Prussia, ascending the Rhine as far as Basle. The southern limit of their distribution in Europe is Galicia, the northwestern province of Spain, in latitude 43°. "There is a river in Macedon," says Fluellen, in "King Henry the Fifth," "and there is also moreover a river at Monmouth: it is called Wye, at Monmouth; but it is out of my brains what is the name of the other river; but 'tis all one, 'tis so like as my fingers is to my fingers, and there is salmons in both." But Fluellen was wrong, for there are no salmon in any part of the Mediterranean water system.

On the American side of the Atlantic, the presence of salmon in Hudson Bay and on the Arctic coast is not certain. They range far north on the Labrador coast, and in the waters of the Great Lakes system they ascended as far as Niagara Falls. Nova Scotia, New Brunswick, and Maine have many salmon rivers. New Hampshire, Massachusetts and Connecticut, a very few good ones.

The salmon was at one time very abundant in the Connecticut, and it probably occurred in the Housatonic and Hudson. They have also been taken in the Delaware which probably marks the southern limit of their distribution on our Atlantic Coast.

Salmon were marvellously abundant in Colonial days. It is stated that the epicurean apprentices of Connecticut would eat salmon no oftener than twice a week. "Plenty of them in this country," wrote Fuller, "though not in such abundance as in Scotland where servants (they say) indent with their masters not to be fed therewith above twice a week." There can be no doubt that one hundred years ago salmon fishing was an important food resource in southern New England. Many Connecticut people remember hearing their grandfathers say that when they went to the river to buy shad the fishermen used to stipulate that they should also buy a specified number of salmon. But at the beginning of this century they began rapidly to diminish. Mitchill stated, in 1814, that in former days the supply to the New York market usually came from the Connecticut, but of late years from the Kennebec, covered with ice. Rev. David Dudley Field, writing in 1819, states that salmon had scarcely been seen in the Connecticut for 15 or 20 years. The circumstances of their extermination in the Connecticut are well known, and the same story, with names and dates changed, serves equally well for other rivers.

In 1798 a corporation, known as the "Upper Locks and Canal Company," built a dam 16 feet high at Millers River, 100 miles from the mouth of the Connecticut. For 2 or 3 years fish were seen in great abundance below the dam, and for perhaps 10 years they continued to appear, vainly striving to reach their spawning grounds; but soon the work of extermination was complete. When, in 1872, a solitary salmon made its appearance, the Saybrook fishermen did not know what it was.

At least half of the salmon's life is spent in the ocean. "He is ever bred in fresh rivers," said Isaac Walton, "and never grows big but in the sea." "He has, like some persons of honour and riches which have both their winter and summer houses, this fresh water for summer and the salt water for winter to spend his life in." Most of his tribe, however, are peculiarly fresh-water fishes, though several share his sea-dwelling habits, and others, like the brook trout, descend into salt water when not prevented by temperature barriers. All of the family run into very shoal water, and usually to the source of streams, for spawning purposes. "I am inclined to the view," writes Dr. Goode, "that the natural habitat of the salmon is in the fresh waters, the more so since there are so many instances—such as that of the Stormontfield Ponds in England—where it has been confined for years in lakes without apparent detriment." That the chinook salmon has been kept for years in fresh water ponds in France is another strong evidence of the correctness of this view. The Sebago salmon of the New England lakes, and the ouananiche of Canada never visit salt water, finding ample food and exercise in the fresh waters which they inhabit.

Salmon while in salt or brackish water feed on small shrimps, young crabs, and other crustaceans and their eggs. When in the rivers they are supposed to eat but little, though they will make voracious rushes at the angler's fly.

Dr. W. C. Kendall of the U. S. Fish Commission has made a special study of the Atlantic Salmon and the Sebago salmon, and furnishes us the following regarding their habits:

The assumption that salmon do not feed after entering fresh water is founded upon the fact that seldom is anything found in their stomachs when caught in traps or by hooks. In traps and weirs it is the habit of most fishes either to disgorge the food from fright or, if not immediately removed, to digest it. Most fishes, and salmon ought not to be an exception, take the hook presumably because they are hungry, and except in the case of some gluttonous species, not when gorged with food. It seems more reasonable to believe, and all the evidence is in support of it, that the fish do feed in the early runs, and that they enter the rivers for that purpose. It is hardly credible that salmon would leave regions of abundant food, at a time when there are no other physiological demands, fast for at least 6 months, reproduce, survive and return to another period of feasting. It is also hard to conceive that the fish takes the lure to gratify the angler or just for the fun of the thing.

The belief has become almost proverbial, and is perpetuated in fish literature, that the early summer salmon after entering the rivers remain there until the spawning function is performed. It is well known that in some of the smaller streams there are 2 distinct runs, spring and fall; the first, for some unrecognized purpose, the other for reproduction. In Denny's River, Maine, for example, according to a reliable observer of long residence in the region, the early migrations extend from May 15 to July 30 or thereabouts, and the other from October 1 until November. The first run does not remain in the river. What obtains in small streams ought to hold good in large ones.

The closely related landlocked salmon in Sebago Lake pursues the smelts up the tributary streams as they are on their way to the spawning grounds in the spring, and descends with the return of the smelts to the lake. The fish then bite the hook. In the fall there is another ascent of the streams for spawning purposes, and the fish will very seldom if ever take the hook at that time. The first run is evidently for the purpose of feeding upon the smelts, and, as the early spring run of Atlantic salmon is known to accompany the run of smelts and other species, it would seem to be for the same purpose. We believe the spring run of the Atlantic salmon is a quest for food, and that the fish return to salt water to again ascend the streams late in the fall for spawning purposes.

Though salmon enter the rivers in the spring when the temperature of the water is rising, their spawning takes place on a falling temperature, and usually not until the water has

STEELHEAD TROUT, *Salmo gairdneri*

CUT-THROAT TROUT, *Salmo clarkii*

VON BEHR TROUT, *Salmo fario*.   INTRODUCED

RAINBOW TROUT, *Salmo irideus*

cooled down to about 50° Fahr. In America the more southern rivers are the first to be entered, and the most northern ones last, the range being from April and May in the Connecticut, to even as late as October in the Miramichi.

Ordinarily the salmon will go well toward the headwaters of the streams to establish spawning beds. As the spawning season approaches they lose their trim appearance and their bright colours. They grow lank and misshapen, the fins become thick and fleshy, and the skin, which becomes thick and slimy, is blotched and mottled with brown, green or blue, and vermillion or scarlet. These changes are most apparent in the males, whose jaws become curved so that they touch only at the tips, the lower one developing a large powerful hook. When in this condition, and after spawning, while returning to the sea they are called "kelts."

While the eggs are laid late in the fall, they do not hatch until early the next spring. When the fry are 2 or 3 months old they begin to show the vermillion spots and transverse bars called parr-marks, which entitle the fish to be called a "parr," and which it retains while remaining in fresh water, and sometimes until 7 or 8 inches long. It remains a parr until the second or third spring, when it descends to the sea, assuming at the time a uniform bright silvery colour, and the "parr" becomes a "smolt." After remaining a time in salt water, the time varying from a few months to 2 years, it returns to fresh water either as a "grilse" or "salmon." The "grilse" is the adolescent salmon, weighing 2 to 6 pounds, and is even more graceful than the adult fish. "There is nothing in the water that surpasses a grilse in its symmetrical beauty, its brilliancy, its agility, and its pluck," wrote Thaddeus Norris. "I have had one of 4 pounds to leap from the water 10 times, and higher and farther than a salmon. Woe to the angler who attempts, without giving line, to hold one even of 3 pounds; he does it at the risk of his casting line, or his agile opponent tears a piece from its jaw or snout in its desperate efforts to escape."

Quoting again from Dr. Goode, who can wonder at the angler's enthusiasm over "a salmon fresh run in love and glory from the sea?" Hear Christopher North's praise of a perfect fish: "She has literally no head; but her snout is in her shoulders. That is the beauty of a fish; high and round shoulders, short

waisted, no loins, but all body, and not long of terminating—
the shorter still the better—in a tail sharp and pointed as Diana's
when she is crescent in the sky."

The salmon reaches an immense size. The largest of which
we have seen a record was one of 83 pounds, brought to London in 1821. Perley mentions one of 60 pounds taken long ago
in the Restigouche. In the Penobscot examples of 40 pounds
have been taken, though that weight is very unusual. The
maximum weight of those taken in Maine rivers now does not
exceed 25 pounds, and the average is about 10 pounds.

The catch of salmon by anglers in the Penobscot Pool at
Bangor in 1893 was 87 fish, with a total weight of 1,477$\frac{1}{2}$ pounds.
The largest weighed 30 pounds, and the average was nearly 17
pounds. The catch in 1900 was 67 fish, with a total weight of
970 pounds. The largest weighed 23$\frac{1}{2}$ pounds, and the average
was nearly 14$\frac{1}{2}$ pounds.

Head 4; depth 4; Br. 11; D. 11; A. 9; scales 23-120-21; vertebræ 60; pyloric cœca about 65; gillrakers 8+12=20. Body
moderately elongate, symmetrical, not much compressed; head
rather low; mouth moderate, the maxillary reaching just past the
eye; in young the maxillary is proportionately shorter; preopercle
with a distinct lower limb, the angle rounded; scales comparatively large, rather larger posteriorly, silvery and well imbricated
in the young, becoming embedded in the adult males. Colour, in
adult, brownish above, the sides more or less silvery, with numerous black spots on head, body and fins, and red spots or
patches on sides in males; the "parr" with about 11 dusky or
bluish crossbars, besides red patches and black spots; the colour,
as well as the form of the head and body varying much with
age, food and condition; the black spots in the adult often
X-shaped or XX-shaped.

In the lakes of Maine, New Hampshire and New Brunswick
and in Lake St. John, the Saguenay and neigbouring waters in
Quebec, the salmon is represented by 2 land-locked forms, one
in each region, which are here recognized as species.

Sebago Salmon

Salmo sebago (Girard)

The sebago salmon receives this name from Sebago Lake, the
locality from which it was first described. It originally occurred in

LAND-LOCKED SALMON: *Salmo sebago* (Girard).

Painting from life of a female fish 19 inches long, obtained in Rangeley Stream, Oquossoc, Maine.

4 river basins in Maine and perhaps in a few lakes in the British Provinces.

In Maine the original habitats were Presumpscot River or Sebago Lake basin, Union River or Reeds Pond (now known as Green Lake) basin, Sebec Lake basin and St. Croix River basin which includes the Schoodic Lakes from which the fish derives also the name of "Schoodic salmon"; but it is more commonly called landlocked salmon.

By fish-cultural operations it has become pretty widely distributed, especially in New England and in New York.

As a rule it differs from the sea salmon in the smaller size, rather plumper form, much harder skull-bones, larger scales and different colouration.

The Sebago Lake salmon originally attained the largest size, the Green Lake next, followed by the Sebec Lake, those of Grand Lake of the Western Schoodic Chain being the smallest.

This condition obtains in part to the present day. At least the Sebago Salmon are the largest and the Grand Lake salmon the smallest of the 4 original regions. Though the stocks of Sebec, Sebago and Green lakes have been perhaps, adulterated by introduction of salmon from other waters, that of Grand Lake has been maintained in its primal integrity.

The salmon of Grand Lake seldom exceed a weight of 5 pounds or average more than 2 pounds.

In the fall of 1901, among many salmon taken in the weir at Sebago Lake, for fish-cultural purposes, were one of 23, many of 15 pounds and over, and the average was about 10 pounds.

The habits of the fish are apparently almost in every particular analogous to those of the sea salmon, modified more or less by physical conditions. In Sebago Lake, in the fall, structural and chromatic changes occur, and it ascends tributary streams to spawn. After this function is performed it returns to the lake, which is its ocean, and resorts to deep water.

In the spring, as soon as the ice breaks up, when smelts, upon which it extensively feeds, are running up the streams to spawn, the salmon follow them to the shore and up the larger streams and descend with them. During summer they remain in deep water, though they occasionally appear at the surface coincidently with the surface schooling of smelts.

As a game-fish it ranks high but is reputed to be inferior to the ouananiche of the Grand Décharge.

In lakes it undoubtedly possesses these qualities to a less degree than the ouananiche of the turbulent waters of the Grand Décharge. But this is not due to inherent inactivity but to external conditions.

Rushing waters, single hook and light tackle are $\frac{4}{5}$ of the game qualities of any fish.

The customary angling appliances on Sebago Lake are a stiff rod, a derrick-like reel, a phantom minnow, archer spinner or murderous gang, all of which, combined with the quiet lake or still waters of Songo River, disincline the fish to prolonged antagonism. But let the angler use a light rod, single baited hook or artificial fly in the quick waters of the Presumpscot River or Grand Lake stream, and he will find at least an epitome of the Grand Décharge.

Ouananiche

Salmo ouananiche McCarthy

The ouananiche is another land-locked relative of the Atlantic salmon. While best known as an inhabitant of the Lake St. John region, Mr. Chambers presents evidence showing it to have a much wider distribution than has been generally assigned to it. He reports it from Arnold Bog, and in the lakes of the Goynish, which enters the St. Lawrence north of the island of Anticosti. It is also said to occur in many streams and lakes in the interior of Labrador.

Though in most, perhaps all of these waters the ouananiche would, if it so desired, have free access to the sea, it apparently does not avail itself of that possibility, and is therefore land-locked so far as all questions of geographic distribution are concerned.

The name "ouananiche" is of Montagnais Indian derivation, and is popularly supposed to mean "little salmon." But Mr. Chambers shows that it is probably derived from *ouen-a*, a Montagnais interrogative "Look there! What is that?" The name is frequently written "Winninish," "Winnonish," "Wananishe," and a score of other ways, all variants of the same word.

As a game-fish, those who have had experience with the ouananiche think it has no equal. They may be taken at any time between the going out of the ice and the middle of September, though the best fishing is said to be late in May. During the early part of the season it may be taken with bait of worms, pork, pieces of chub, or even ouananiche itself along the shore of Lake St. John. It is occasionally taken then with the artificial fly, but fly-fishing for the ouananiche is usually not a successful method of capturing it.

According to Mr. Chambers, who has written a delightful volume on the ouananiche, no better direction can be given for angling for the fish in the lake itself than some of the quaint instructions for catching salmon, of Thomas Barker, in *Barker's Delight, or the Art of Angling:*

"The angler that goeth to catch him with a line and hook must angle for him as nigh the middle of the water as he can with one of these baits: He must take 2 bob-worms, baited as handsomely as he can, that the 4 ends may hang meet of a length, and so angle as nigh the bottom as he can, feeling your plummet run on the ground some 12 inches from the hook: if you angle for him with a flie (which he will rise at like a trout) the flie must be made of a large hook, which hook must carry six wings, or four at least; there is judgment in making these flyes. The salmon will come at a gudgeon in the manner of a trouling, and cometh at it bravely, which is fine angling for him and good. You must be sure that you have your line of twenty-six yards of length, that you may have your convenient time to turne him, or else you are in danger to lose him: but if you turne him you are very like to have the fish with small tackles; the danger is all in the running out both of salmon and trout, you must forecast to turn the fish as you do a wild horse, either upon the right or left hand, and wind up your line as you finde occasion in the guiding the fish to the shore."

At the Grand Décharge the ouananiche will take the fly at any time, but not so freely after the middle of July. In the northern tributaries of Lake St. John they may be taken at the surface during July and August.

The Rev. Henry Van Dyke writes thus entertainingly of the ouananiche:

"But the prince of the pool was the fighting ouananiche, the little salmon of St. John. Here let me chant thy praise, thou noblest and most high-minded fish, the cleanest feeder, the merriest liver, the loftiest leaper and the bravest warrior of all creatures that swim! Thy cousin, the trout, in his purple and gold with crimson spots, wears a more splendid armour than thy russet and silver mottled with black, but thine is the kinglier nature. His courage and skill, compared with thine,

'Are as moonlight unto sunlight,
And as water unto wine.'

"The old salmon of the sea who begat thee long ago in these inland waters became a backslider, descending again to the ocean, and grew gross and heavy with coarse feeding. But thou, unsalted salmon of the foaming floods, not land-locked as men call thee, but choosing of thine own free will to dwell on a loftier level in the pure, swift current of a living stream, hath grown in grace and risen to a better life.

"Thou art not to be measured by quantity but by quality, and thy five pounds of pure vigour will outweigh a score of pounds of flesh less vitalized by spirit. Thou feedest on the flies of the air, and thy food is transformed into an aerial passion for flight, as thou springest across the pool, vaulting toward the sky. Thine eyes have grown large and keen by peering through the foam, and the feathered hook that can deceive thee must be deftly tied and delicately cast. Thy tail and fins, by ceaseless conflict with the rapids, have broadened and strengthened, so that they can flash thy slender body like a living arrow up the fall. As Launce-lot among the knights, so art thou among the fish, the plain-armoured hero, the sun-burnt champion of all the water-folk."

According to Eugene McCarthy, who has written much and entertainingly concerning the ouananiche, this fish when hooked will jump out of the water 5 or 6 times on an average, and sometimes will jump 10 or 12 times.

"And such jumps! Two or 3 feet out of the water, often toward the fisherman, then a rush deep down—a pause—a succession of jerks that would seem to tear the hook loose—a wild rush of varying distance, and a run back, almost to the angler's feet. A fish weighing $3\frac{1}{2}$ or 4 pounds will make a fight lasting 10 or 15 minutes, often longer, and that means hard work for every moment for the fisherman."

The average size of the ouananiche is $2\frac{1}{2}$ to $3\frac{1}{2}$ pounds, though examples weighing 8 pounds are often taken.

The ouananiche does not differ greatly from the Atlantic salmon, and is apparently even more closely related to the Sebago salmon. Some ichthyologists and many anglers have maintained that all 3 are identical, and that the Sebago salmon and the ouananiche are not worthy even of a subspecific rank. But specific or subspecific rank is not determined by the *amount* or *greatness* of differences, but rather by their *constancy*. However small the differences may be, if they are real and constant, and do not intergrade, they indicate specific distinctness; however great they may be, if not constant, or if they show intergradation, they can be of no more than subspecific value. Subspecific characters are usually associated with more or less definite geographic or environmental isolation, and the characters of the subspecies and those of the parent species* will intergrade where the two habitats join or overlap.

It seems certain that both the Sebago salmon and the ouananiche are geographically isolated forms, each possessing characters by which it is readily distinguished from the other, and from the Atlantic salmon as well. Whether the differential characters intergrade or not has not been fully determined. If they do not, then each should rank as a full species, and bear a binomial instead of a trinomial name. Comparing the ouananiche with the grilse of the Atlantic salmon, Mr. Walter M. Bracket, as quoted by Mr. Chambers, says the eye of the former "is much larger, the profile rounder, the dark spots larger and much more numerous. In fact, the grilse is much more of an aristocrat than his freshwater cousin, being finer in his proportions and much purer in colour—due, no doubt, to his different habitat and food." But Mr. Bracket's use of the term ouananiche includes the Sebago salmon also.

Mr. Chambers says of the ouananiche, "Its fins are larger and stronger [than those of *Salmo salar*]. . . . Its tail is unusually broad. . . . The eye of the ouananiche is much larger than that of the ordinary salmon, the St. Andrew's cross-marks upon the sides are closer together, and there are larger and more distinct

---

* Used for convenience for the earlier described form, which may, in reality, be the derived form.

black spots upon the gill-covers, in shape both round and irregular."

Mr. J. G. A. Creighton says "the teeth in the ouananiche are larger than in *Salmo salar*, . . . the fins are proportionately much larger, especially the tail. . . . The eye is remarkably large, about three-quarters of an inch in diameter in the adult, with a pupil $\frac{1}{4}$-inch in diameter. These measurements are much greater than in the sea-salmon of 15 to 20 pounds' weight."

The evidence seems to indicate that the ouananiche is specifically distinct from the Atlantic salmon and from the Sebago salmon, and for the present we prefer to so regard it.

The Trout of Western America

In the western part of America are found more than a score of trout of the genus *Salmo* all closely related and difficult to distinguish. There are representatives in the headwaters of the Rio Grande, Arkansas, Platte, Missouri, and Colorado; also in the Great Salt Lake basin, throughout the Columbia basin, and in all suitable waters from southern California and Chihuahua to Alaska and Kamchatka.

It has been the custom of some to regard the trout of western America as falling into three more or less distinct groups or series. This is now known to be no longer justified; nevertheless it possesses a certain convenience. They have been termed the cutthroat series, the rainbow series, and the steelhead series.

The steelhead, or *gairdneri* series, is found in the coastwise streams of California and in the streams of Oregon and Washington, below the great Shoshone Falls of Snake River. In the lower course of the Columbia and in neighbouring streams they are entirely distinct from the cutthroat or *clarkii* series, and no one would question the validity of the 2 species. In the lower Snake River and in other waters east of the Cascade range, the two forms or species are indistinguishable, being either undifferentiated or else inextricably mixed.

The original "rainbow trout" was described in 1855 under the name *Salmo iridea* by Dr. Gibbons, from San Leandro Creek near Alameda, California, while the original "steelhead" was described in 1836 under the name *Salmo gairdneri* by Sir John Richardson, from the Columbia River at Fort Vancouver. It is now known that the small trout found in the coastal streams of California are identical with the young of the steelhead of the California coast and probably of the Columbia also.

This being true, the so-called rainbows of our coastal streams are simply the young steelheads that did not run down to sea to grow large, take on silvery colours and return when mature to freshwater streams to spawn, but remained in fresh water where they took on more brilliant colours and reached maturity at a smaller size. Therefore, Richardson's name antedating that given by Gibbons, has priority, and the trout of our California coastal streams must be called *Salmo gairdneri*. Whether you call them steelheads or rainbows does not matter greatly.

But in McCloud River and other tributaries of the upper Sacramento is a rainbow trout which Dr. Jordan named *Salmo shasta*, the real rainbow of the fish-culturists, very distinct from the San Leandro Creek fish, very brilliantly coloured, never descending to the sea, and in every' way well deserving to be known as *the* Rainbow Trout.

It seems not improbable that the American trout originated in Asia, extended its range southward to the upper Columbia, thence to the Yellowstone and the Missouri *via* Two-Ocean Pass; from the Missouri southward to the Platte and the Arkansas, thence from the Platte to the Rio Grande and the Colorado, and then from the Colorado across the Sierras to Kern River, thence northward and coastwise, the sea-running forms passing from stream to stream as far north as the Fraser where the Kamloops trout would mark one extreme of the series, and re-entering as a distinct species waters long occupied by typical *clarkii*.

KEY TO THE SPECIES OF CUT-THROAT TROUT:

a. Black spots almost as numerous on the head as on the posterior part of the body.
b. Scales usually about 160 to 170.
c. Spots rather large, irregular and profusely scattered, usually none on the belly.
d. Red marks under dentary bones always present.
e. Black spots encroaching somewhat on belly;...........*clarkii*, 176
ee. Black spots not encroaching on belly;.................*lewisi*, 179
dd. Red marks under dentary bones obsolete or nearly so; *gibbsii*, 179
cc. Spots rather large, sparsely scattered, some on belly and lower side of head;....................................*henshawi*, 180
bb. Scales very small, about 200 transverse series;.......*tahoensis*, 181

bbb. Scales large, usually about 145.   Body profusely but finely
  spotted, the spots numerous both anteriorly and posteriorly;
  virginalis; jordani; bathœcetor, 182-183
aa. Black spots placed chiefly on posterior half of body.
f. No black spots except on tail;...............*declivifrous,* 184
ff. Black spots on body.
g. Scales not very small, about 160; spots of moderate size
  (Rio Grande Basin);......................*spilurus,* 185
gg. Scales very small, about 180.
h. Spots rather large; lower fins distinctly red, rarely orange.
i. Spots very numerous; a red lateral band (Colorado Basin);
  pleuriticus, 186
ii. Spots less numerous, none anteriorly (Waha Lake);
  bouvieri, 187
iii. Spots few and large, chiefly on the tail (Arkansas and
  Platte rivers);..........................*stomias,* 188
hh. Spots all small; lower fins bright yellow; a yellow lateral
  shade (Twin Lakes, Colorado);............*macdonaldi,* 188

Cut-throat Trout

Salmo clarkii Richardson

The cut-throat trout, probably the parent form from which all
others of the series have been derived, is found in all the coastwise
streams and lakes from northern California to British Columbia
and possibly into southeastern Alaska.   In the Columbia River basin
it is found as far up the Snake River as Shoshone Falls and into the
headwaters of the Pend d' Oreille.   In the waters about Puget Sound
it is very abundant, as it is, in fact, throughout most of its range.

It is known variously as cut-throat trout, black-spotted trout,
Columbia River trout, and by many other local names.

In the earlier books this species was identified with the *Mykiss*
of Kamchatka and was called *Salmo mykiss* or *Salmo purpuratus.*
But recent investigations have shown that it is not identical with the
Kamchatkan species, and that there is a wide region between
Kamchatka and southeast Alaska in which no trout are found.

The cut-throat trout and all of this series spawn in the spring
and early summer.   Those in the streams seek the shallow waters
of the smaller creeks while those of the lakes come to the shallow
waters near shore or upon the bars; in many cases they ascend
tributary streams.

The silver trout of Lake Tahoe and the yellow-finned trout of Twin Lakes probably spawn in deeper water.

The cut-throat trout and its different derived forms vary greatly in the sizes at which they reach maturity, the chief factors being, of course, the size of the body of water they inhabit and the amount of the food supply.

Those species or individuals, dwelling in lakes of considerable size where the water is of such temperature and depth as insure an ample food-supply, will reach a large size, while those in a restricted environment where both the water and food are limited, will be small directly in proportion to these environing restrictions. The trout of the Klamath Lakes, for example, reach a weight of at least 17 pounds, while in Fish Lake in Idaho mature trout do not exceed 8 to $9\frac{1}{4}$ inches in total length or one-fourth pound in weight. In small creeks in the Sawtooth Mountains and elsewhere they reach maturity at a length of 5 or 6 inches, and are often spoken of as brook trout under the impression that they are a species different from the larger ones found in the lakes and larger streams. But as all sorts of gradations between these extreme forms may be found in the intervening and connecting waters the differences have not even subspecific significance.

The various forms of cut-throat trout vary greatly in game qualities; even the same species in different waters, in different parts of its habitat, or at different seasons, will vary greatly in this regard. In general, however, it is perhaps a fair statement to say that the cut-throat trout are regarded by anglers as being inferior in gaminess to the eastern brook trout. But while this is true, it must not by any means be inferred that it is without game qualities, for it is really a fish which possesses those qualities in a very high degree. Its vigour and voraciousness are determined largely, of course, by the character of the stream or lake in which it lives. The individuals which dwell in cold streams about cascades and seething rapids will show marvellous strength and will make a fight which is rarely equalled by its eastern cousin; while in warmer and larger streams and lakes they may be very sluggish and show but little fight. Yet this is by no means always true. In the Klamath Lakes where the trout grow very large and where they are often very loggy, one is occasionally hooked which tries to the utmost the skill of the angler to prevent his tackle from being smashed and at the same time save the fish. An instance is on record of a most enthusiastic and skilful angler who required one hour and three-quarters to bring to net a nine and three-quarter pound fish in Pelican Bay, Upper Klamath Lake.

These trout can be taken in all sorts of ways. Trolling in the lakes with the spoon or phantom minnow is the usual method, but they rise readily to the artificial fly, the grasshopper, or a buncn of salmon eggs. In the larger streams they may be caught in any of these ways, while in the smaller streams casting with the fly or with hook baited with grasshopper or salmon eggs is the most successful way.

To enumerate the streams and lakes in the West where one may find good trout-fishing would be entirely impracticable; they are numerous in all the Western States. One of us has found exceptionally fine trout fishing at the Dempsey Lakes in Montana, in and about the Payette and Redfish lakes in Idaho, in Pacific Creek, and in the Klamath Lakes. Near Redfish Lake, in Idaho, is a small lake known as Fish Lake. Its area is about 25 acres. It is nearly circular in form, very shallow, and 9000 feet above sea-level. In this little lake a particularly beautiful form of cut-throat is exceedingly abundant.

In August they could be taken on the artificial fly as rapidly as one could cast, averaging more than one per minute. They bit vigorously, and were very gamy, often jumping 2 or 3 times out of the water. In this region the best fishing in the small streams is in the spring and up to late July. In the small lakes it continues good through the summer. In the streams somewhat larger, summer fishing is fairly good, but not until October is it at its best. But while some seasons are better than others, the angler will quite certainly always find good cut-throat trout fishing at whatever season he cares to try it. The typical cut-throat trout *(Salmo clarkii)* may be described as follows:.

Head 4; depth 4; D. 10; A. 10; cœca 43; scales small, in 150 to 170 cross series. Body elongate, compressed; head rather short; mouth moderate, the maxillary not reaching far beyond the eye; vomerine teeth as usual set in an irregular zig-zag series; teeth on the hyoid bone normally present, but often obsolete in old examples; dorsal fin rather low; caudal fin slightly forked (more so in the young). Colour, silvery olivaceous, often dark steel colour; back, upper part of side and caudal peduncle profusely covered with rounded black spots of varying sizes and shapes, these spots often on the head, and sometimes extending on the belly; dorsal, adipose, and caudal fins covered with similar spots about as large as the nostril; inner edge of the mandible with a deep-red blotch, which is a diagnostic mark; middle of side usually with a diffuse pale rosy wash, this sometimes quite bright, and extending on to side of head; under parts silvery white. The red blotches or washing on the membrane joining the dentary bones of the lower jaw are usually constant, probably always present in the adult, and constitute a most important character.

This species has been called *Salmo mykiss* in various publications by the writers and others, but the true *Salmo mykiss* is allied to *Salmo salar*, and has never been taken outside of Kamchatka.

Yellowstone Trout

Salmo lewisi (Girard)

The Yellowstone or Lewis trout inhabits the Snake River basin above Shoshone Falls, and the headwaters of the Missouri. It is abundant throughout this whole region in all accessible waters, and is particularly numerous in Yellowstone Lake. As already stated the trout of Yellowstone Lake certainly came into the Missouri basin by way of Two-Ocean Pass from the Upper Snake River basin. One of the present writers has caught them in the very act of going over Two-Ocean Pass from Pacific into Atlantic drainage. The trout on the two sides of the pass cannot be separated, and constitute a single species.

Silver Trout

Salmo gibbsii Suckley

In the tributaries of the Columbia, between Shoshone Falls and the Cascades, in the lakes and larger streams, there is a trout which may be called the silver trout. It is particularly common in the Des Chutes River, and in the Payette Lakes in Idaho. Examples about 15 inches long taken in Big Payette Lake, September 27, had the spots small, half circles, few below middle of side; rosy wash on side and opercles, brightest in the male; scarcely any red on throat; belly silvery, back dark-greenish; scales about 140 to 145. On this date, while sailing across this lake, trout could be seen jumping in various places; usually as many as 15 or 20 could be seen at any moment. They would take the trolling-spoon readily, and proved very gamy fish.

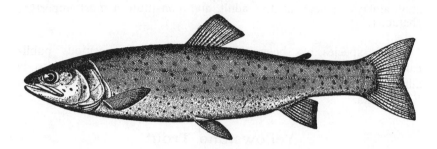

Lake Tahoe Trout; Truckee Trout; "Pogy"; "Snipe"

Salmo henshawi Gill & Jordan

This interesting trout is found in western Nevada and neighbouring parts of California in the region comprised in the basin of the old post-Tertiary Lake Lahontan. It is known from Lakes Tahoe, Pyramid, Webber, Donner and Independence; also from the Truckee, Humboldt and Carson rivers, and from most streams on the east slope of the Sierras. It is also found in the headwaters of the Feather River, where it has probably been introduced.

The Tahoe trout reaches a weight of 3 to 6 pounds, is a food and game fish of considerable importance, and is often seen in the San Francisco markets. It spawns in the spring, entering the shallow water of the streams for that purpose.

Head $3\frac{3}{4}$; depth 4; D. 11; A. 12; scales 27 to 37-160 to 184-27 to 37, usually about 170 in a longitudinal series; caudal fin short, rather strongly forked. Colour, dark green in the pure waters of Lake Tahoe; pale green in the salty waters of Pyramid Lake; side silvery, with a strong shade of coppery red; back about equally spotted before and behind, the spots large and mostly round; spots on side rather distant; belly generally with round spots; head with large black spots above, some even on snout and lower jaw; dorsal and caudal fins spotted; a few large spots on anal; red dashes on lower jaw present; young less spotted.

Silver Trout of Lake Tahoe

Salmo tahoensis Jordan & Evermann

In the deep waters of Lake Tahoe is found a trout of immense size, known to the anglers who are familiar with that lake as the silver trout. So far as known this trout is never seen in the shallow water, but remains at considerable depths, and spawns in the lake itself. It is a large, robust fish, profusely spotted, the spots often oblong, and the general colouration more silvery than in the ordinary Tahoe trout. An example, the type of the species, 2 feet 4 inches long, and weighing $7\frac{1}{2}$ pounds, caught by Mr. A. J. Bayley, presented the following characters.

Head $4\frac{1}{15}$; depth $3\frac{4}{5}$; eye $7\frac{2}{3}$; D. 9; A. 12; Br. 10; scales 33-205-40, 140 pores; P. $1\frac{2}{3}$; maxillary $1\frac{2}{3}$. Body very robust, compressed, unusually deep for a trout, the outline elliptical; head large; eye small, silvery; mouth large, maxillary reaching well beyond the eye; scales small, reduced above and below; caudal fin slightly lunate, almost truncate when spread. Colour, dark green above; belly silvery; side with a broad, coppery shade covering cheek and opercles; sides of lower jaw yellowish; fins olivaceous, a little reddish below; orange dashes between rami of lower jaw moderately conspicuous; back, from tip of snout to tail, closely covered with large, unequal black spots, those on nape and top of head round; posteriorly the spots run together, forming variously shaped markings, usually vertically oblong, which may be regarded as formed of 3 or 4 spots placed in a series, or with 1 or 2 at the side of the other, the longest of these oblong markings being not quite as long as the eye; spots on side of head and body very sparse, those on head round, those behind vertically oblong; belly profusely covered with small black spots which are nearly round; still smaller round spots numerous on lower jaw; spots on caudal peduncle vertically oblong or curved; dorsal and caudal densely covered with oblong spots, smaller than those on body; anal with rather numerous round spots; pectorals and ventrals with a few small spots, the first ray of each with a series of small, faint spots; adipose fin spotted.

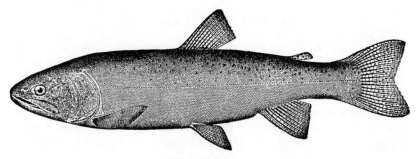

Utah Trout

Salmo utah (Suckley)

In all suitable streams and lakes of the old Lake Bonneville basin, of which the waters of the Great Basin are the present vanishing remnants, is found a trout which is profusely and finely spotted, the spots being numerous anteriorly as well as posteriorly; scales a little larger than usual, in 140 to 150 lengthwise series, and anteriorly less crowded than in the trout of the Rio Grande, or in the green-backed trout. In partly alkaline waters, such as in Utah Lake, this trout reaches a very large size, examples of 8 to 12 pounds being not uncommon. In these waters it is very pale in colour, the dark spots being few and small, and mostly confined to the back.

The Utah trout is found in the streams and lakes of Utah west of the Wasatch Mountains, especially in Bear, Provo, Jordan and Sevier rivers, and in Utah Lake, where it is a very abundant and important food-fish.

Jordan's Trout; Spotted Trout of Lake Southerland

Salmo jordani Meek

In Lake Southerland, west of Puget Sound, is found a black-spotted trout of the cut-throat series which, in colour, seems to resemble the Utah trout. It is, according to Professor D. G. Elliot, a "beautiful and exceedingly gamy trout, taking the fly readily even as late as October, a great leaper when hooked, and fights *à l'outrance*. In appearance it resembles *Salmo gairdneri crescentis* of the neighbouring lake, being fully as brilliantly coloured, but can be at once distinguished by its orange or orange-red fins, red on the jaw, the number and blackness of its spots, and the darker back and top of head. At no stage of its existence that I have seen, from fingerlings to fish weighing over 4 pounds, is there any silvery lustre, but the colours are all bright-hued, some even metallic. It is one of the most attractive of its tribe, and I have had them leap after taking the fly, in such rapid succession and with such dartings about the lake, that it was impossible to imagine where they would next appear. I believe it spawns in the spring, as in the middle of October, the eggs of the females we caught were not enlarged, and showed no indication of the approach of the spawning season."

Head $3\frac{7}{8}$; depth $4\frac{4}{5}$; eye $5\frac{7}{8}$; snout $4\frac{1}{8}$; maxillary $1\frac{3}{4}$; scales 146; D. 10; A. 11; Br. 10 or 11. Body elongate, not much compressed; head short, maxillary not extending far beyond orbit; origin of dorsal fin midway between tip of snout and base of caudal.

Long-headed Trout of Crescent Lake

Salmo bathœcetor Meek

According to Professor Elliot, who collected the type of this species, this is a deepwater fish, keeping always near the bottom, never coming to the surface at any time, and, of course, not taking the fly, or indeed the spoon, or any kind of lure. The only way it can be captured is by the set-lines sunk within a foot of the bottom, and it seems there are only a few places in the lake where it can be caught even by this means. It is a brightly coloured fish, but lacks some of the iridescence of the speckled trout of Crescent Lake, which it otherwise resembles.

Head $3\frac{1}{2}$ to $3\frac{4}{5}$; depth $5\frac{1}{10}$ to $5\frac{3}{4}$; eye $6\frac{3}{4}$ to $7\frac{3}{5}$; snout $3\frac{1}{8}$; maxillary $1\frac{2}{3}$; D. 10; A. 11; scales 150 to 152; gillrakers 7 or 8+11 to 13; Br. 9 to 11. Body slender, head much pointed; maxillary very long and very slender, reaching considerably beyond orbit; teeth on jaws, vomer and palatines large, the dentition strong; mandible very strong; gillrakers short and thick. Colour, much as in the speckled trout of Crescent Lake, but lighter; head, body and tail profusely spotted with black; ventrals and pectorals dark; no red on lower jaw.

This trout differs from *Salmo crescentis* in being more slender, in having the back much less elevated, the head more slender and pointed, the gillrakers shorter, and the maxillary straighter, narrower and longer.

It is probably more closely related to the steelhead trout series than to the cut-throat series, and perhaps should be placed as a subspecies of *Salmo gairdneri.*

Salmon Trout of Lake Southerland

Salmo declivifrons Meek

The general colour of this trout closely resembles that of the blueback trout of Crescent Lake. It is, however, some darker, and has no spots except on the caudal fin. The upper anterior profile is also much more curved.

Head $3\frac{4}{5}$; depth $4\frac{2}{5}$; eye $5\frac{1}{7}$; snout $4\frac{1}{2}$; maxillary $1\frac{2}{3}$; scales 148; D. 10; A. 11; Br. 10; gillrakers 7+10. Body elongate, back elevated, anterior profile much decurved; tip of snout below axis of body; gape nearly horizontal, more so than in other trout; maxillary reaching beyond eye; dentition strong. Colour, dark blue above and on side to lateral line posteriorly, becoming abruptly silvery; belly nearly white; no spots on head or body or elsewhere except few on caudal fin; upper margin of lower jaw black, a dark blue patch on cheek, extending obliquely upward and backward to near upper edge of opercle; pectorals, ventrals and anal yellowish.

Known only from Lake Southerland where it is occasionally taken and where it is called "Salmon trout," according to Professor Elliot, who collected the type. He says, "it is easily recognizable, not only by the sharply curved upper outline of the fore part of the body, but also by its quite different style of colouration, which resembles somewhat that of the blueback of Lake Crescent.

"As there is no water connection between these 2 lakes, and Lake Southerland is 75 feet lower than Crescent Lake, and, moreover, the fish of that lake having no communication with the sea on account of a very high precipitous fall a short distance from its outlet, it cannot be supposed that these two forms are in any way identical. Out of a large number of trout caught by me in Lake Southerland only 2 or 3 of this form were procured, and they were all of small size. This could not be the fault of the lake, which is exceedingly deep and nearly 3 miles in length. It is a gamy fish, takes the fly, leaps out of the water, and is a good fighter for its size." It reaches a length of 10 inches.

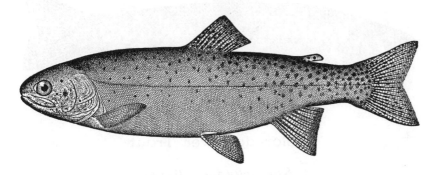

Rio Grande Trout

Salmo virginalis (Girard)

This trout is known only from the upper Rio Grande basin and southward into the mountains of Chihuahua. It is abundant in most mountain streams, but irrigation operations in Colorado and New Mexico have proved very destructive to it on account of the small fish running up the ditches and out upon the fields where they perish. Del Norte and Wagonwheel Gap, Colorado, used to afford excellent trout fishing. The trout were abundant, of good size (2 to $2\frac{1}{2}$ feet), and were very gamy.

Head $3\frac{1}{2}$; depth 4; D. 11; A. 10; scales 37-160-37. Head rather short, its upper surface considerably decurved; interorbital space transversely convex, obtusely carinated, the head more convex than in any other species; mouth large, maxillary reaching past eye; teeth on vomer in 2 distinct series; dorsal fin low in front, high behind, the last ray more than $\frac{2}{3}$ height of first; last ray of anal rather long; caudal with its middle rays about as long as the others. Colour, back and sides profusely covered with round black spots, most developed posteriorly, few on the head, most numerous on the caudal and adipose fins; side with pale blotches. Very much resembling the Colorado River trout except that the scales are considerably larger and less crowded anteriorly.

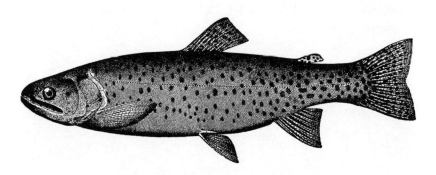

Colorado River Trout

Salmo pleuriticus (Cope)

In all the headwaters of the Colorado is found another representative of the cut-throat trout series. It is abundant throughout western Colorado and in all clear mountain streams in Arizona. It is common in the Eagle and Gunnison where it reaches a good size and is a game-fish of very high rank.

Opercle short, 4⅗ to 5 in head; scales small, 185 to 190 in lateral line. Close to typical *Salmo clarkii*, but the black spots gathered chiefly on posterior part of body, the head being nearly immaculate. The colour is extremely variable, but the lower fins are usually red, sometimes orange; usually a red lateral band. A large, handsome and variable trout, sometimes profusely speckled, sometimes with large spots, and occasionally with strong golden shades.

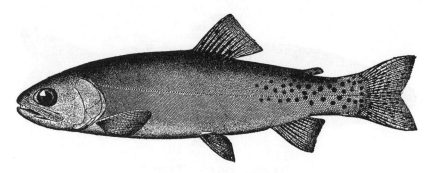

Waha Lake Trout

Salmo bouvieri (Bendire)

This curious and interesting trout is known only from Waha Lake, Idaho, a small mountain lake without any present surface outlet.

These trout reach a weight of 3 pounds though examples of that size are not often seen. The usual size is 6 to 7 inches. They do not take the fly well until the middle of the summer, as the water of Waha Lake is uncommonly cold. Then they rise readily and are as game as most lake trout. The food-quality of this trout is said to be unsurpassed. Professor J. M. Aldrich, of Moscow, Idaho, who has had much experience with the Waha trout, speaks in the highest praise as to its delicacy and delicious flavour.

Head 4; depth $4\frac{2}{3}$; eye 4; D. 10; A. 11; Br. 12; scales 173; maxillary $2\frac{1}{5}$. Similar to typical *Salmo clarkii*, but with dark, spots only on the dorsal, caudal and adipose fins, and on the caudal peduncle behind front of anal, where the spots are very profuse, smaller than the pupil; anterior regions dusky-bluish, not silvery; red blotch on throat very conspicuous; head shorter and deeper than in the typical cut-throat trout, the snout shorter and blunter, not longer than the eye; opercle and preopercle less convex; caudal moderately forked.

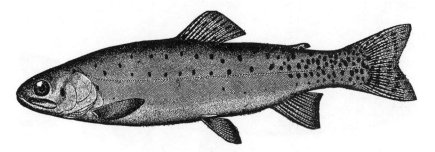

Green-back Trout

Salmo stomias (Cope)

This trout is known only from the headwaters of the Platte and Arkansas rivers and is abundant chiefly in the smaller streams and brooks and in the shallow waters of lakes. It is the common species in Twin Lakes, Colorado and in the waters about Leadville.

It is a small, black-spotted trout, not often exceeding a pound in weight, closely resembling the typical cut-throat trout, but differing chiefly in the much greater size of its black spots which are mainly gathered on the posterior half of the body. Mouth small; scales small, about 180; back deep green, sides sometimes red; flesh deep salmon coloured.

Yellow-fin Trout

Salmo macdonaldi Jordan & Evermann

This interesting and beautiful trout is known only from Twin Lakes, Colorado, where it occurs in company with the green-back trout. The 2 are entirely distinct, the size, colouration and habits being notably different.

The yellow-fin reaches a weight of 8 or 9 pounds while the other rarely exceeds a pound. The former lives on gravel bottom in water of some depth while the latter is a shallow-water trout running into small brooks. The yellow-fin trout is apparently derived from the Colorado River trout which may be descended from the Rio Grande trout which, in turn, is probably derived from the green-back trout of the Arkansas.

As a game-fish the yellow-fin trout has attracted much attention from local anglers by whom it is very highly regarded. It is taken chiefly by trolling, though it rises promptly to the fly and is a splendid fighter.

Head 4; depth $4\frac{1}{2}$ to 5; eye $5\frac{1}{2}$; snout $4\frac{1}{8}$; D. 12; A. 11; Br. 10; scales 40-184-37, about 125 pores. Head long, compressed, the snout moderately pointed; mouth rather large, maxillary $1\frac{3}{4}$ to 2 in head; hyoid teeth present; scales small, irregularly placed. Colour, light olive; a broad shade of lemon-yellow along side; lower fins bright yellow; no red anywhere excépt on throat; posterior part of body, and dorsal and caudal fins profusely covered with small dark spots smaller than the nostril; head and anterior part of body with few spots or none.

KEY TO SPECIES OF STEELHEAD TROUT SERIES:

a. Scales rather small, averaging 150 to 155.
b. Sides bright silvery, usually with a broad flesh-coloured or rosy lateral wash, brightest on opercles. Sea-running forms, reaching a large size;...........................*gairdneri,* 190
bb. No silvery or rosy anywhere. Probably not sea-running;
crescentis, 191
aa. Scales larger, about 130 to 145.
c. Sides very silvery and bright silvery below; a broad band of bright light rose colour; spots few;...........*kamloops,* 192
cc. Sides little silvery; under parts white, not silvery; no rosy lateral band;...................................*beardsleei,* 193

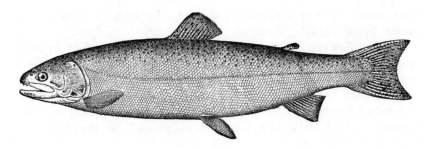

Steelhead Trout

Salmo gairdneri Richardson

This species is variously known as the steelhead, steelhead trout, salmon trout, and hardhead. It is found in all coastwise streams from the Ventura and Santa Clara rivers, Ventura County, California, north to British Columbia, and probably to Sitka. It is especially abundant in the lower Columbia, ascending the Snake River as far as Augur Falls, and the Pend d' Oreille probably to Metaline Falls.

The steelhead is more or less anadromous in its habits, being migratory like the salmon, and ascending rivers fully as far. In California the steelhead is not specifically distinct from the so-called rainbow of the short coastal streams.

The spawning season of the steelhead seems to be a prolonged one and varying greatly with the locality. In the headwaters of Salmon River, Idaho, where there are important spawning beds, spawning takes place in May and early June. In Payette River they spawn a fortnight earlier, and in the shorter tributaries of Snake River from April 15 to May 10. Still lower down the Columbia basin they probably spawn increasingly earlier. Of 4,179 steelheads examined during the last week in September, and the first half of October, at The Dalles, Oregon, 1,531 were males and 2,648 females; 476 males and 900 females were well developed, and probably would have spawned in 4 to 6 weeks. The remaining 2803 apparently would not have spawned until the next spring.

The run of steelheads in the lower Columbia is heaviest from August to November. They reach the Sawtooth Mountains early in May and the headwaters of Payette River early in April; while they reach that portion of Snake River between Weiser and Lower Salmon Falls early in September and remain until spring before they spawn.

In the streams tributary to the northern portion of Puget Sound they arrive in September and October while they do not usually appear in numbers about Seattle until 2 months later.

The steelhead is a large and very important food-fish. The average size of those reaching the Sawtooth Mountains is about 8 pounds, the extremes being 2 and 14 pounds. The maximum weight of the species is probably about 20 pounds, and in streams where it is resident it does not usually exceed 5 or 6 pounds. Unlike the Pacific salmon the steelhead does not die after once spawning, though some individuals probably do. Except during a period following the spawning season, the steelhead ranks as one of the very best of food-fishes. Great quantities are taken every year in the Columbia and either canned or sold fresh. The shipments of steelhead trout to the East have rapidly increased during recent years until they are now very large.

The steelhead ranks very high as a game-fish and trolling for steelheads in the bays, sounds and river-mouths along our Pacific Coast affords excitement and pleasure exceeded among the *Salmonidæ* only by trolling for chinook salmon.

When in fresh water the steelhead does not bite well except where it is resident, but in waters in which it is permanently resident it takes the trolling spoon well and will also rise to the artificial fly; and its large size and gameness make it a fish much sought after by those who have the opportunity.

The steelhead is propagated by the United States Bureau of Fisheries, with marked success. The Bureau has introduced it into Lake Superior and its tributary waters in which it found a congenial home and in which catches of some very large steelheads have been recently made.

Speckled Trout of Crescent Lake

Salmo crescentis Jordan & Beardslee

In Crescent Lake, Clallam County, Washington, is a trout which has been regarded as a subspecies of the steelhead. It reaches a length of 27 inches or more, and a weight of 8 or 10 pounds, and is regarded as an excellent game-fish.

It is very close to the steelhead, from which it differs chiefly in colour, which, in alcohol, is very dark steel-blue above, becoming paler below, and nearly white on belly anteriorly where only the margins of the scales are punctate; no silvery anywhere; lower jaw dusky; a large black blotch on cheek between sub-orbital and premaxillary; sides, top of head, back, and dorsal and caudal fins with few small dark spots; pectorals dusky, slightly spotted at base; anal somewhat dusky, without spots; ventrals dusky with a few spots in the middle; adipose fin with a few spots; lower fins all tipped with paler, probably yellowish red in life; spots all very small and not confined to posterior part of body.

Kamloops Trout ; Stit-tse

Salmo kamloops Jordan

This is an interesting trout found in Kamloops, Okanogan, Kootenai and other lakes tributary to the Fraser and upper Columbia rivers. It is locally abundant, and is a fine large trout, slender in form, graceful in appearance and movement, somewhat different from the common steelhead, but not distinguished by any technical character of importance, and probably intergrading fully with the latter. It is said to be a very fine game-fish, which is taken chiefly by trolling with the spoon.

Head $4\frac{1}{2}$; depth $4\frac{1}{3}$; D. 11; A. 11 or 12; scales 30-135 to 146-26, 65 before the dorsal; gillrakers 6+11 or 12; Br. 11+11. Body elongate, somewhat compressed; maxillary extending beyond eye, its length not quite half head; snout slightly rounded in profile, the profile regularly ascending; teeth moderate, some of those in the outer row in each jaw somewhat enlarged; opercles striate, not much produced backward; dorsal fin rather low, its longest ray slightly greater than base of fin, $1\frac{3}{5}$ in head; anal fin rather larger than usual in trout, its outline slightly concave, its longest ray greater than base of fin, and little more than half head; caudal fin rather broad, distinctly forked, its outer rays about twice length of inner; pectoral rather long, $1\frac{1}{8}$ in head; ventrals moderate, $1\frac{3}{4}$ in head; gillrakers comparatively short and few. Colour, dark olive above, bright silvery below, the silvery colour extending some distance below the lateral line, where it ends abruptly; middle of side with a broad light-rose-colored band, covering about $\frac{1}{8}$ total depth of fish; back above with small black spots about the size of pin heads, irregularly scattered, and somewhat more numerous posteriorly; a few faint spots on top of head; dorsal and caudal fins rather thickly covered with small black spots similar to those on back, but more distinct; a few spots on adipose fin which is edged with blackish; lower fins plain; upper border of pectoral dusky; a vague dusky blotch on upper middle rays of anal.

Blueback Trout of Crescent Lake

Salmo beardsleei Jordan & Seale

One of the most interesting trouts, recently brought to the attention of anglers and ichthyologists by Admiral Beardslee, is the blueback or Beardslee trout of Crescent Lake. This lake is in Clallam County, Washington, in the northern part of the Olympic Mountains, 700 feet above the sea, and the blueback trout is known only from it. This trout lives in deep water. Examples caught by Admiral Beardslee in October were taken at depths varying from 30 to 50 feet. Others caught on April 18 were taken at a depth of 30 to 35 feet, and so far as we have learned it has not been secured in shallow water. The best season for getting this trout seems to be in the spring, probably April to June inclusive, though good catches have been made in October. It is taken only by trolling with the spoon, or, at least, chiefly in that way. They may be taken by trolling with a baited hook, a strip of trout belly being the bait used. Probably various other lures would prove successful. The blueback has the reputation among those who have had the pleasure of catching it of being a very great game-fish. Admiral Beardslee says they fight hard until brought near the surface, when they give up. When landed they are generally puffed up with air, a condition following their quick transferrence from considerable depths to the surface. Examples taken in the spring and put in pools in mountain streams with other trout died very soon, while the others lived.

A 10-pound fish taken by Miss Sara Beazley, of Columbia, Missouri, "made a fierce and prolonged fight, racing along with the boat for a long distance and making several desperate and out-of-the-water leaps and plunges to get away. Miss Beazley followed the plan of rowing along slowly, stopping rowing altogether for a few moments, and then starting off again slowly.

Both large fish were taken just as the boat started up, after one of three brief stops, during which the troll had gone down to a greater depth than when the boat was in motion."

The blueback trout reach a large size. Four examples caught by Admiral Beardslee weighed, 6, 11, 11½, and 11½ pounds respectively. One taken by Miss Beazley measured 29½ inches long and weighed strong 10 pounds. Another caught by Mr. Ben. Lewis, and forwarded by Mr. M. J. Carrigan, of Port Angeles, to Stanford University, was 32 inches long, and weighed 14 pounds.

The flesh is light lemon-colour before cooking, during which process it whitens. It is devoid of the oily salmon flavour, and is very excellent.

KEY TO SPECIES OF RAINBOW TROUT SERIES:

a. Scales well imbricated; upper ray of pectoral usually more or less spotted.

b. Scales comparatively large, 120 to 150 series.

c. Scales decidedly large, in 120 to 130 series; body elongate; no red on throat. Brook forms, mostly of small size; sea-run examples occasionally large; confined to streams of the Coast Ranges.

d. Mouth moderate. Coastwise streams of California; . . . .
irideus gairdneri, 195

dd. Mouth very small. Coastwise streams of Oregon and Washington; . . . .*masoni,* 197

cc. Scales medium, in about 140 series; body rather deep; a small dash of red usually present on the throat. Size medium, 2 to 8 pounds. Streams of the upper Sacramento basin, not running down to sea; . . . .*shasta,* 198

bb. Scales small, in 150 to 185 series. Size large.

e. Back profusely spotted anteriorly as well as posteriorly; some red on lower jaw. Kern River, California; . . . .*gilberti,* 201

ee. Back with the spots chiefly posteriorly; no red on lower jaw. Upper Sacramento basin; . . . .*stonei,* 201 *aa.* Scales very small and not well imbricated; colours brilliant; pectoral, ventral, and anal fins without spots; par marks present.

f. Back and upper two-thirds of side closely covered with small black spots . . . .*whitei*

ff. Back and upper third of side sparsely covered with small black spots . . . .*agua-bonita*

fff. Back and sides unspotted; a few spots on caudal peduncle;

roosevelti

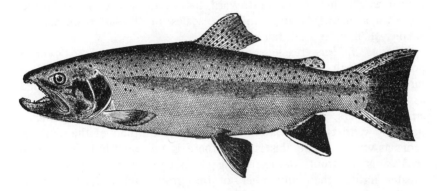

Rainbow Trout

Salmo irideus (*gairdneri*) Gibbons

In mountain streams of the Coast Ranges of the Pacific States and on the west slopes of the Sierra Nevada Mountains are found the various forms of trout which are collectively regarded as constituting the rainbow trout series. Members of this series are distinguished from those of the steelhead series by their larger scales and, generally, by their smaller size and brighter colouration. From the cut-throat series they differ in their larger scales, brighter colouration, and, usually, in the absence of red on the throat. As already stated, however, in some parts of their range these series are inextricably mixed, and present classifications can be regarded only as provisional.

The original rainbow trout, the so-called *S. irideus*, is found only in the small brooks of the Coast Ranges in California, from the Klamath River to the San Luis Ray in San Diego County. It is subject to large local variations, some of these land-locked in peculiar brooks, as in Purissima Creek in San Mateo County, where the individuals are small and brightly coloured, and popularly regarded as a distinct species.

It is thought by some anglers that the young fish hatched in the brooks from eggs of the steelhead remain in mountain streams from 6 to 36 months, going down to the sea with the high waters of spring, after which they return to spawn as typical steelhead trout. Those which are land-locked, or which do not descend, remain rainbows all their lives. As against this view we have the fact that to the northward the rainbow and the steelhead are always distinguishable, and the scales in the latter are always smaller than in typical rainbow trout.

Salmo irideus reaches a weight of a half pound to 5 or 6 pounds, though in most of the streams in which it is found it rarely exceeds 2 or 3 pounds. By many anglers it is regarded as the greatest of all game-fishes. The consensus of opinion among anglers, however, involves and is based upon experience not only with typical *irideus* but with most others of the rainbow series as well. While this is true, there is no doubt but that typical *irideus* is a trout of exceeding gameness and is possibly a greater fighter than any other of the group, when its weight is considered.

But the various forms of rainbow trout, wherever found, may safely be said to have few, if any, equals among the *Salmonidæ*.

In beauty of colour, gracefulness of form and movement, sprightliness when in the water, reckless dash with which it springs from the water to meet the descending fly ere it strikes the surface, and the mad and repeated leaps from the water when hooked, the rainbow trout must ever hold a very high rank. The gamest fish we have ever seen was a 16-inch rainbow taken on a fly in a small spring branch tributary of Williamson River in southern Oregon. It was in a broad and deep pool of exceedingly clear water. As the angler from behind a clump of willows made the cast the trout bounded from the water and met the fly in the air a foot or more above the surface; missing it he dropped upon the water only to turn about and strike viciously a second time at the fly just as it touched the surface; though he again missed the fly the hook caught him in the lower jaw from the outside, and then began a fight which would delight the heart of any angler. His first effort was to reach the bottom of the pool, then, doubling upon the line, he made 3 jumps from the water in quick succession, clearing the surface in each instance from 1 to 4 feet, and every time doing his utmost to free himself from the hook by shaking his head as vigorously as a dog shakes a rat. Then he would rush wildly about in the large pool, now attempting to go down over the riffle below the pool, now trying the opposite direction, and often striving to hide under one or the other of the banks. It was easy to handle the fish when the dash was made up or down stream or for the opposite side, but when he turned about and made a rush for the protection of the overhanging bank upon which the angler stood, it was not easy to keep the line taut. Movements such as these were frequently repeated and 2 more leaps were made. But finally he was worn out after as honest a fight as trout ever made.

The rainbow takes the fly so readily that there is no reason for resorting to grasshoppers, salmon-eggs or other bait. It is a fish whose gameness will satisfy the most exacting of expert anglers and whose readiness to take any proper lure will please the most impatient of inexperienced amateurs.

Western Oregon Brook Trout

Salmo masoni (Suckley)

The common brook trout of the tributaries of the lower Columbia and of coastwise streams of Oregon and Washington is very similar to the typical *irideus* and is readily distinguished from its associates, the steelhead and the cut-throat, by its larger scales. Compared with the cut-throat, it is less slender, the snout is more rounded, there is no red between the branches of the lower jaw, there are no hyoid teeth, the maxillary is broader and shorter, the opercle more evenly convex, there are fewer spots below the lateral line, and the red markings on the sides usually coalesce to form a red lateral band; scales 120 to 130. Apparently merging into the ordinary *irideus* southward, if indeed, the 2 forms are distinguishable.

This trout rarely weighs more than a pound. It is found from Puget Sound to southern Oregon in streams of the Coast Range, and is locally abundant.

It is interesting to note that the type of this gamy little trout was caught by George B. McClellan. In describing it Dr. Suckley says: "I obtained this species at the Cathlapootl River, August

2, 1853, and am indebted for it to the skill of Capt. Geo. B. McClellan, as he took it with the artificial fly at a time when they did not readily bite at any bait."

McCloud River Rainbow Trout

Salmo shasta (Jordan)

The home of this fine trout is in the streams of the Sierra Nevadas from Mount Shasta southward, the limits of its range not well known. It is best known from the McCloud River where it has been handled for many years in the fish-cultural operations of the United States Fish Commission, this being, in fact, the "rainbow trout" of fish-culturists.

Through the operations of the United States Fish Commission this trout has had its range greatly extended. It has been successfully transplanted into many mountain streams in different parts of the United States where it was not previously found, where it grows and multiplies rapidly, as is shown by the many favourable reports. The best results, however, seem to have been obtained from the plants made in Michigan, Missouri, Arkansas, throughout the Alleghany Mountain region, and in Colorado and Nevada. It was introduced into eastern waters in 1880. It is believed this species will serve for stocking streams formerly inhabited by the eastern brook trout in which the latter no longer thrives owing to the clearing of the lands about the sources of the streams, which has brought about changed conditions unfavourable to the eastern brook trout. The rainbow is adapted to warmer and deeper waters, and is therefore suited to many of the now depleted streams which flow from the mountains through cultivated valleys.

Rainbow trout differ widely from brook trout and other pugnacious fishes in that they feed largely upon worms, larvæ, crustaceans, and the like, and do not take so readily to minnows for food. They should be planted in spring or early summer when their natural food is abundant. They will then grow more rapidly and become accustomed to life in the stream, and when worms, larvæ, etc., are no longer to be found, their experience and size will enable them to take anything in the shape of food that may present itself. Fish hatched in December and January can be safely planted in April or May.

The size of the rainbow trout varies greatly, depending upon the volume and temperature of the water, and the amount and character of the food-supply. In the streams of the Sierras, where it is native, it reaches a length of 10 to 30 inches, and a weight of 2 to 8 pounds. The average weight of those caught from streams in the East is probably less than a pound, but examples weighing 6¾ pounds have been taken. In the Ozark region in Missouri they are caught weighing 5 to 10 pounds. In some of the cold mountain streams of Colorado their average weight is but 6 or 8 ounces, while in certain lakes in the same State, where the water is moderately warm, and food is plentiful, they reach a length of 25 to 28 inches, and a weight of 12 or 13 pounds. In the Au Sable River in Michigan they reach a weight of 5 to 7 pounds. The largest example ever produced in the U. S. Fish Commission ponds at Wytheville, Virginia, weighed 6½ pounds.

The average growth of the rainbow trout under favourable artificial circumstances is as follows: One year old, from ¾ to 1 ounce; 2 years old from 8 to 10 ounces; 3 years old from 1 to 2 pounds; 4 years old from 2 to 3 pounds. Like all other fishes, they continue to grow, at least until they are 8 or 10 years old, the rate diminishing with age. Some, of course, grow much faster than others, even under the same circumstances, but the rate of growth, as with all fishes, is largely a question of temperature, food, and extent of water-area. In water at 60°, with plenty of food, fish 1 or 2 years old will double their size several times in a single season; while in water at 40°, with limited food, the growth is very slow indeed.

The rainbow, like the brook trout, will live in water with a comparatively high temperature if it is plentiful and running with a strong current; but in sluggish water, even when the temperature is considerably lower, neither species will do well. The rainbow, however, will live in warmer water than the brook trout, and is often found in streams where the temperature is as high as 75° or even 85°, especially where there is some shade. The water of the streams in which the rainbow is native, varies in temperature from 38° in winter to about 70° in summer. For hatchery purposes spring water, with a temperature from 42° to 58°, is best.

The spawning season of the rainbow trout in California extends from early February to May. A curious change in the season has occurred with those cultivated in the East. In Colorado the season is from May to July, while at Wytheville it extends from early in November to the end of February.

The males are good breeders at 2 years old, but the females rarely produce eggs until the third season.

The number of eggs produced depends upon the age and size of the fish. The maximum from 3-year-old fish, weighing $\frac{1}{2}$ to $1\frac{1}{2}$ pounds, is 500 to 800 eggs; from 6-year-old fish, weighing 2 to 4 pounds, it is 2,500 to 3,000 eggs.

The eggs vary in size from $4\frac{1}{2}$ to 5 eggs to the linear inch, the larger fish usually producing the larger eggs.

All that has been said regarding the game qualities of the typical rainbow trout *(Salmo irideus)* can be said of the rainbow trout of McCloud River. It may lack a little in the wild gameness of typical *irideus*, but that is made good by its larger size.

There is, however, no comparison between the rainbow in its native California mountain streams and those introduced into eastern waters, where the warmer temperature has enervated them, and where they have grown large and fat and sluggish. In the cold waters of Colorado, however, they have lost none of their wild nature and superb game qualities.

Head 4; depth $3\frac{4}{5}$; eye 5; D. 11; A. 11; scales 20 to 24-145-20, about 65 before the dorsal. Body comparatively short and deep, compressed, varying considerably, and much more elongate in males than in females; head short, convex, obtusely ridged above; mouth smaller than in most species of trout, the rather broad maxillary scarcely reaching beyond the eye, except in old males; eye larger than in the steelhead; vomerine teeth in 2 irregular series; dorsal fin moderate; caudal fin distinctly though not strongly forked, more deeply incised than in the typical cut-throat. Colour, bluish above, the sides silvery; everywhere above profusely but irregularly spotted, the spots extending on the sides at least to the lateral line, and covering the vertical fins; top of head well spotted; fins usually not red; almost always a light dash of red on throat; much red or rosy on cheek and opercles; belly partly red in males; side with a broad but more or less interrupted red lateral band, brightest in males.

Kern River Trout

Salmo gilberti (Jordan)

The Kern River trout very closely resembles the McCloud River rainbow, but has the scales smaller, there being as many as 165 transverse series. The body is robust, the mouth moderate.

Colour, back and sides profusely spotted; old examples with more or less orange on lower jaw, this faint or wanting in the young; upper ray of pectoral spotted.

This beautiful trout is known only from Kern River, California, and is abundant in the river channels below the waters inhabited by the golden trout.

The Kern River trout reaches a good size, examples weighing 8 pounds having been recorded. It is a voracious trout, biting freely, and fighting vigorously and with great persistence.

Nissuee Trout; Noshee Trout; Stone's Trout

Salmo stonei (Jordan)

This is a large, voracious trout of the rainbow series found in the upper Sacramento basin, especially in the McCloud River above Baird. It is much larger than typical *irideus*, and reaches a weight of 10 to 12 pounds, but is doubtfully distinct.

Depth 4; A. 11; eye $4\frac{1}{2}$; maxillary about 2; pectoral $1\frac{1}{3}$; scales 140 to 155, about 82 before the dorsal where they are small and embedded; teeth fewer and smaller than in the Shasta trout, those on the vomer in a single zig-zag series. Colour, upper parts plain greenish; spots few and confined chiefly to the posterior part of body; spots small and sparse on dorsal, adipose and caudal fins; a red lateral band usually distinct; cheek and opercles with red; no red on throat.

Golden Trout of Kern River Region

Four species of trout native to the Kern River region of California are now known. The first of these is the Kern River trout (*Salmo gilberti*) which appears to be confined to the main Kern River (see plate facing page 200). The three others are all probably derived from the Kern River species and are popularly known as "golden trout." They are as follows:

Golden Trout of the Little Kern

Salmo whitei Evermann

This beautiful species, named for Stewart Edward White, is the trout found in the western tributaries of the Kern, particularly in the Little Kern and Coyote Creek. It has been introduced into Soda Creek and other waters of the South Fork of the Kaweah, and into other waters west of the Kern. It is abundant in Coyote Creek. It is a small trout characterized by the presence of numerous small dark spots on dorsal and caudal fins, back and upper two-thirds of side, brick red lateral band, lemon-coloured lower side and orange or cadmium belly. It is a small species not often exceeding eight inches in length.

Golden Trout of South Fork of Kern River

Salmo agua-bonita (Jordan)

When this trout was originally described, it was thought that the type specimens came from Volcano Creek, an eastern tributary of Kern River, but it was later learned that they really came from Cottonwood Creek, a tributary of Owens Lake on the east side of the divide, and into which the species had been transplanted from the South Fork of the Kern, the only stream to which it is known to be native. It does not occur in Volcano Creek, but has been transplanted into a number of streams. It resembles *Salmo whitei* from which it may be distinguished by the fewer spots on back and sides, these not extending more than one-third distance down the side, the lower two-thirds of the side being entirely without spots. It is more richly coloured than *Salmo whitei*.

Roosevelt Trout

Salmo roosevelti Evermann

This is the *real* Golden Trout, the most gorgeously coloured trout in all the world, named for Theodore Roosevelt the naturalist. It occurs naturally only in Volcano Creek, an eastern tributary of the Kern, but has been introduced into Rock Creek, Whitney Creek, and other waters on the east side of the Kern.

It is characterized by the extreme smallness of its scales, the gorgeousness of its colouration, and the entire absence of black spots on head and body; the spots being confined to the dorsal and caudal fins, and the caudal peduncle.

This species attains a length of a foot and a weight of a pound in Volcano Creek, while in Rock Creek, into which it has been introduced, it reaches a larger size.

Several new species of trout from the Western states have recently been described as follows:

Crab Creek Trout

Salmo eremogenes Evermann & Nichols

A small trout, reaching a foot in length, of the cut-throat type, known only from Crab Creek near Ritzville, Wash. It apparently is related to the Waha trout.

San Gorgonio Trout

Salmo evermanni Jordan & Grinnell

This is a small species of rainbow trout known only from the upper Santa Ana River, Mount San Gorgonio, southern California. The body is sparsely covered with distinct black spots, the general colour being dull and very dark.

Nelson's Trout

Salmo nelsoni Evermann

Known only from Rio San Ramon in the San Pedro Martir Mountains of Lower California. A small species, the most southern trout known.

Eagle Lake Trout

Salmo aquilarum Snyder

This species, recently described from Eagle Lake, California, is related to the common Lake Tahoe trout, has the body robust, caudal peduncle deep, large and strong fins, large adipose fin, large scales, cheeks red and under parts coppery. Known only from Eagle Lake and its tributary, Pine Creek.

202a

Royal Silver Trout

Salmo regalis Snyder

Deep blue above and silvery on sides, with few or no spots. Known only from Lake Tahoe.

Emerald Trout

Salmo smaragdus Snyder

A slender trout, apparently related to *S. regalis*, entirely without spots, and known only from Pyramid and Winnemucca lakes, Nevada.

GENUS CRISTIVOMER GILL & JORDAN

The Great Lake Trouts

This genus contains only 2 species,—large, coarse charrs, distinguished from *Salvelinus* by the presence of a raised crest behind the head of the vomer and free from its shaft. This crest is armed with teeth, and the hyoid teeth form a strong, cardiform band.

The typical species is a large charr or trout, spotted with gray instead of red, and found in the larger lakes of northern North America.

a. Body elongate, covered with thin skin, there being no special development of the fatty tissue;............*namaycush*, 203
aa. Body deeper, covered with thick skin, there being an excessive development of fatty tissue;................*siscowet*, 205

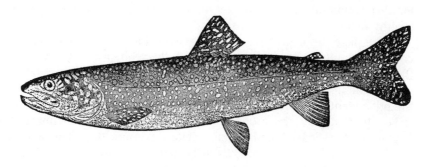

Great Lake Trout; Mackinaw Trout

Cristivomer namaycush (Walbaum)

The namaycush trout is found in most large lakes from New Brunswick and Maine westward throughout the Great Lakes region and to Vancouver Island thence northward to Northern Alaska, Hudson Bay and Labrador. It is known from Henry Lake in Idaho and elsewhere in the headwaters of the Columbia. It is known also from the Fraser River basin, from Vancouver Island, and various places in Alaska.

In addition to the vernacular names already mentioned this fish is known by still others in different parts of its range. In Vermont it is called "longe," in Maine it is the "togue," while among the Canadian Indians it is the "namaycush" or "masamacush."

It is the largest of all the trouts, reaching a length of several feet and a weight of 60 to 125 pounds. The average weight probably does not exceed 15 or 20 pounds.

In the Great Lakes it is exceeded in weight only by the lake sturgeon.

The lake trout is omnivorous in its feeding habits and possesses a ravenous appetite. It greedily devours all kinds of fishes possessing soft fins, and it is said that jack-knives, corncobs and other equally indigestible articles have been found in its stomach.

The eggs and fry of the lake trout suffer from the same enemies as the young of other fishes, but the mature fish are entirely too formidable for other species to prey upon. They are not often troubled with parasites. Occasionally individuals, very thin in flesh and sickly-looking, known as "racers" by fishermen are found swimming near the surface; no sufficient cause has been discovered for this condition, as they are no more afflicted with parasites than healthy fish.

The lake trout fisheries of the Great Lakes are exceeded in commercial importance only by those of the whitefish. At one time the trout was so abundant that it did not command a price at all commensurate with its edible qualities, but as the catches decreased the price went up, until in 1886 it equalled that of its more delicate rival. In that year the artificial propagation of the lake trout was begun by the Federal and certain State governments. The output of the hatcheries increased gradually until, in 1895, that of the Government hatchery at Northville alone amounted to over 11,000,000 eggs; and the species had become so abundant in the lakes in 1896 that the fishing boats ceased operations, the market being glutted, and the price obtainable not justifying the labour involved.

The method of capturing the lake trout is by gillnets, pound-nets, hook and line, and, in winter, by spearing through the ice.

The majority, however, are taken by means of gillnets operated by steam tugs. Some of these tugs carry 5 or 6 miles of nets and catch in one lift from 1,000 pounds to 4 or 5 tons of trout.

GOLDEN TROUT OF VOLCANO CREEK: *Salmo roosevelti* Evermann.

Painting from life of the type, a specimen 12 inches long, taken by Dr. Evermann in Volcano Creek near Mt. Whitney, Cal., July 22nd, 1904.

SODA CREEK GOLDEN TROUT: *Salmo whitei* Evermann.

Painting from life of the type, an example 7¼ inches long, taken in the South Fork of Kaweah River in South Fork Meadows, Cal., July 15, 1904.

McCLOUD RIVER RAINBOW TROUT: *Salmo shasta* Jordan.

This is the species of Rainbow Trout which has been propagated most extensively by the United States Bureau of Fisheries and by the California Fish Commission.

KERN RIVER TROUT: *Salmo gilberti*   (Jordan).

Painting from life of a male fish, 18¼ inches long, weighing 3½ pounds, taken by Dr. Evermann in Kern River, Cal., July 19, 1904.

GOLDEN TROUT OF SOUTH FORK OF KERN RIVER: *Salmo agua-bonita* (Jordan).

Painted from a specimen obtained in South Fork of Kern River, Cal., July 23, 1904. This species was originally described from a specimen which at the time was said to have come from Volcano Creek, but which really came from Cottonwood Lakes into which the species had been introduced from South Fork of Kern River.

GREAT LAKES TROUT: *Cristivomer namaycush* (Walbaum).

Painted from life of a specimen 26 inches long, obtained in Lake Michigan off Berrien Co., Mich

Fishing is done from the time the ice breaks up in the spring until late in the fall.

Lake trout spawn on the reefs and live in deep water at other times. The spawning season begins in Lake Superior late in September, in Lakes Huron and Michigan the height of the season is in early November, and spawning continues into December. The spawning grounds are on the reefs of "honeycomb" rock, 10 to 15 miles off shore, and in water 6 to 120 feet deep. The number of eggs produced is not large; a 24-pound fish produced 14,943 eggs, but the usual number does not exceed 5,000 or 6,000.

As a game-fish the lake trout is held in different degrees of esteem by different anglers. There are those who regard it with slight favour, while with others it is rated as a fish which can give the angler a great deal of sport. It is usually taken by trolling either with the spoon or live minnow, and, as it is a powerful fish, strong tackle is required. Thaddeus Norris, most delightful writer among American anglers, mentions hooking several trout on stout o o Kirby hooks baited with a white rag and a piece of red flannel, and the hooks in every instance but one (a small 8 pound trout) were straightened or broken and the fish lost.

Head $4\frac{1}{4}$; depth 4; eye $4\frac{1}{2}$; Br. 11 or 12; D. 11; A. 11; scales 185 to 205; maxillary 2; interorbital 4. Body long; head very long, its upper surface flattened; mouth very large, the maxillary extending much beyond the eye, the head and jaws proportionately lengthened and pointed; caudal fin well forked; adipose fin small; teeth very strong. General colouration, dark gray, sometimes pale, sometimes almost black, everywhere with rounded pale spots which are often reddish tinged; head usually vermiculate above; dorsal and caudal reticulate with darker.

Siscowet

Cristivomer siscowet (Agassiz)

The siscowet differs from the ordinary Great Lake trout in having a deeper body which is covered with a thicker skin, beneath which is an excessive development of fatty tissue. The scales are somewhat larger and the colour is usually somewhat paler.

This fish is practically confined to Lake Superior where it is abundant in deep water. Occasional examples have been taken in Lakes Huron and Erie.

GENUS SALVELINUS RICHARDSON

The Charrs

Body moderately elongate; teeth of jaws, palatines, and tongue essentially as in *Salmo*, the hyoid patch present or not; vomer boat-shaped, the shaft much depressed, without raised crest, with teeth on the head of the bone but none on the shaft; scales very small, 200 to 250 in a lengthwise series; fins moderate, the caudal forked in the young, truncate in some species in· the adult; sexual peculiarities not strongly marked, the males with the premaxillaries enlarged and a fleshy projection at the tip of the lower jaw.

The scales of the charrs are, in general, smaller than in any other *Salmonidæ*, and they are imbedded in the skin to such a degree as to escape the notice of casual observers and even of many anglers.

> "One trout scale in the scales I lay
> (If trout had scales), and 'twill outweigh
> The wrong side of the balances."—*Lowell*.

Colour, usually dark, with round crimson spots, the lower fins sometimes with marginal bands of black, reddish, and pale.

Species numerous in the clear cold streams and lakes of the northern parts of both continents, sometimes descending to the sea where they lose their variegated colours and become nearly plain and silvery.

The members of this genus are by far the most active and handsome of the trout, living only in the clearest, coldest and most secluded waters. "No higher praise can be given to a *Salmonoid* than to say it is a charr."

As now understood by most ichthyologists this genus is represented in America by 4 species and some 6 or 7 subspecies. Perhaps it is just as well to recognize most, if not all, of these subspecies as full species. This is certainly best in all cases where intergrading has not been proved.

a. Back unspotted, strongly marbled with dark olive or black.
b. Colour, dark olive; side with numerous red spots;

fontinalis, 207

bb. Colour, pale grayish; very few red spots;.....*agassizii,* 210
aa. Back not marbled with darker.
c. Back with red or orange spots like those on sides;
parkei, 210
cc. Back unspotted, the red spots confined to the sides; maxillary usually not reaching beyond the eye.
d. Gillrakers numerous, 6+12 to 16; head rather large, 4 to $4\frac{1}{2}$ in body; body rather stout; belly orange in breeding season.
e. Gillrakers longer and straighter than in the next, $\frac{2}{5}$ length of eye, 7+14 in number;.........................*alipes,* 212
ee. Gillrakers quite short, not $\frac{1}{3}$ length of eye, about 6+12 in number;....................................*aureolus,* 213
dd. Gillrakers fewer, 6+11, small; head small; $4\frac{1}{4}$ to 5 in length; body slender;..............................*oquassa,* 217

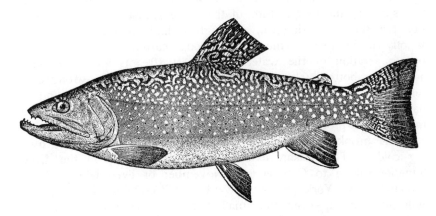

Brook Trout; Speckled Trout

Salvelinus fontinalis (Mitchill)

"And when the timorous Trout I wait
To take, and he devours my Bait,
How small, how poor a thing I find
Will captivate a greedy Mind;
And when none bite, the Wise I praise,
Whom false Allurement ne'er betrays."

The game-fish which has been most written about and which is, perhaps, best and most widely known among the anglers of the world is undoubtedly *Salvelinus fontinalis*. It is one of the most beautiful, active, and widely distributed of American trouts. Its natural range is from Maine to northern Georgia and Alabama in the Appalachian Mountains, and westward through the Great Lakes region to Minnesota; and in Canada from Labrador to the Saskatchewan. It has been extensively introduced into many waters in which it was not native, in the eastern and upper Mississippi Valley States, in the Pacific and Rocky Mountain States, and in many foreign countries as well.

With the possible exceptions of the rainbow and steelhead trouts it is the hardiest member of the salmon family and will make a brave struggle for existence even in an unfavourable environment. Not every stream, however, can be stocked with this species; the temperature of the water must not be too high, nor the flow too sluggish, although a high temperature is not wholly prohibitive, if there is a strong current resulting in the proper aeration of the water. The best streams are those with a gravelly bottom, clear shallow water, steady, fairly strong current with occasional rapids, deeper pools and eddies, abundant natural food, and banks overhung with bushes which afford more or less protection.

The brook trout spawns in the fall when the water is growing colder. The season extends from late August in the Lake Superior region to October and November or even later in New England, New York and southward. At spawning time the fish will push far up even the smallest creeks where the spawning beds are selected upon gravel bottom in shallow water. There the eggs will lie until the next spring—anywhere from 90 to 210 days—when the water begins to grow warmer and the eggs begin to hatch.

The number of eggs produced varies with the age and size of the fish, yearlings usually producing 150 to 250, two-year-olds 350 to 500, and older ones 500 to 2500.

The size of the brook trout varies greatly; in small streams they may be mature at a length of 6 or 8 inches and a weight of but 2 or 3 ounces, while in larger bodies of water and with an abundant food supply they reach 18 inches or even more, and a weight of several pounds. Forty years ago brook trout weighing 4 to 6 and 8 pounds were not uncommon.

But as the trout streams everywhere came to be fished more and more, the trout became smaller and smaller, until now it is a rare trout that escapes the angler's fly until he has reached a greater weight than a pound or two.

The trout are rapidly disappearing from our streams through the agency of the lumberman, manufacturer, and summer boarder. In the words of the late Rev. Myron W. Reed, a noble man, and an excellent angler,—"This is the last generation of trout-fishers. The children will not be able to find any. Already there are well-trodden paths by every stream in Maine, New York, and in Michigan. I know of but one river in North America by the side of which you will find no paper collar or other evidence of civilization. It is the Nameless River. Not that trout will cease to be. They will be hatched by machinery and raised in ponds, and fattened on chopped liver, and grow flabby and lose their spots. The trout of the restaurant will not cease to be; but he is no more like the trout of the wild river than the fat and songless reed-bird is like the bobolink. Gross feeding and easy pond-life enervate and deprave him. The trout that the children will know only by legend is the gold-sprinkled living arrow of the white water; able to zig-zag up the cataract; able to loiter in the rapids; whose dainty meat is the glancing butterfly."

The brook trout is exceedingly variable and many local varieties have been described. The following description will apply well only to typical examples.

Head $4\frac{1}{2}$; depth $4\frac{1}{2}$; D. 10; A. 9; scales 37-230-30; gillrakers about 6+11. Body oblong, moderately compressed, not much elevated; head large, but not very long, the snout bluntish, the interorbital space rather broad; mouth large, the maxillary reaching beyond orbit: eye large, somewhat above axis of body; caudal fin slightly lunate in the adult, forked in the young; adipose fin small; pectoral and ventral fins not especially elongate. Colour, back more or less mottled or barred with dark olive or black, without spots; red spots on side rather smaller than the pupil; dorsal and caudal fins mottled with darker; lower fins dusky, with a pale, usually orange, band anteriorly, followed by a darker one; belly in the male often more or less red; sea-run individuals (the Canadian "salmon trout") are often nearly plain bright silvery.

Dublin Pond Trout

Salvelinus agassizii (Garman)

In certain ponds or lakes in New Hampshire, notably Dublin Pond, Lake Monadnock, Centre Pond, etc., is found a trout whose colouration is pale grayish, and with fewer red spots, thus resembling the lake trout. Otherwise it does not appear to differ from the brook trout, except that the young are said to be rather more slender, the caudal notch slightly deeper, and the sides more silvery. The young are much darker than the adults. This trout reaches a length of 7 or 8 inches.

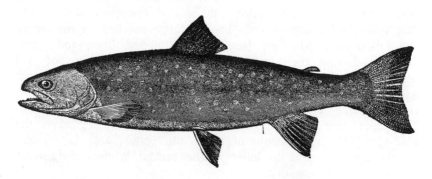

Dolly Varden Trout

Salvelinus parkei (Suckley)

This interesting charr is found in the streams and lakes of Montana, Idaho, Washington, Oregon and California, south to the Sacramento basin, and northward in coastal streams to the Aleutian Islands. It is found only in Pacific drainage. Though resident in fresh water, and scarcely at all migratory, it often descends to the sea, and is frequently taken in salt and brackish waters. In small mountain brooks at Unalaska and elsewhere dwarfed forms occur.

This is the charr which has been known in the books until recently as *Salvelinus malma*, under the belief that it was identical with the *malma* of Walbaum from Kamchatka; but recent investigations have shown the American fish to be distinct from the Kamchatkan species.

In Montana this charr is called salmon trout, in Idaho it is the bull trout, and elsewhere it is charr, western charr, Oregon charr, or Dolly Varden trout, the last being one of the few book names of fishes which have come into general use.

This interesting trout is one of the best known species in the West. It reaches a length of 2 to 3 feet, and a weight of 5 to 12 pounds. An example 26 inches long weighed 5 pounds and 1 ounce. Like its eastern relative it is a voracious fish, feeding freely upon whatever offers, and especially fond of minnows, of which it devours great numbers. At Lake Pend d'Oreille, where the bull trout is an abundant and popular game-fish, we have found 2 species of minnows and one miller's thumb all in the stomach of one fish.

It has been our pleasure to fish for the Dolly Varden trout in many different waters, among which we recall with particular satisfaction the Pend d'Oreille River from the Great Northern Railroad to the international boundary, Lake Pend d'Oreille at Hope and Sand Point, the Redfish Lakes and Upper Salmon River, high among the Sawtooth Mountains of Idaho, and in a little stream near Unalaska, in which dwells a dwarfed Dolly Varden of unusual beauty. During July and August, as well as in early spring, it may be caught in any of these waters. In the smaller lakes it is most abundant about the mouths of the inlets, but the best fishing is usually in the streams, as the fish there will rise to the fly more readily, and are usually more gamy. Anything will serve as a lure—artificial fly, grasshopper or any other insect of fair size, small minnow, a piece of fish or other meat, salmon eggs, trolling spoon or frog, and even the bright coloured leaves of the painted cup or other flower.

The gameness of the Dolly Varden trout varies greatly with the character of the water and the season, just as with any other game-fish. Those taken in lakes are apt to be sluggish, but when taken in cold streams, with a good, strong, steady current, or in the rapids where the water tumbles and boils, then the Dolly Varden displays the superior game qualities which show its kinship with its eastern and better known congener.

Head $3\frac{1}{2}$ to $3\frac{4}{5}$; depth $4\frac{4}{5}$ to 6; eye $6\frac{1}{2}$ to 7; snout 3 to 4; maxillary $1\frac{2}{3}$ to 3; D. 11; A. 9; scales 39-240-36; pyloric cœca large, 45 to 50; gillrakers about 8+12. Body rather slender, the back somewhat elevated, less compressed than in *Salvelinus fontinalis*; head large, snout broad, flattened above; mouth large, the maxillary reaching past the eye; fins short, the caudal slightly forked or almost truncate. General colour, olivaceous, the sides with round red or orange spots nearly as large as the eye, the back with similar but smaller spots, and without reticulations, a feature of colouration which at once distinguishes this from all other American trout; lower fins coloured much as in *S. fontinalis*, dusky, with a pale stripe in front, followed by a darker one. Sea-run examples are silvery, with the spots pale or obsolete.

Long-finned Charr

Salvelinus alipes (Richardson)

In northern Europe, from the Swiss lakes and the lochs of Scotland northward, in all cold waters, is found the Saibling or European charr, *Salvelinus alpinus*. This charr is represented in America by several forms, most of which have usually ranked as subspecies. The first of these is the long-finned charr which inhabits the lakes of Greenland and Boothia Felix about Prince Regent Inlet.

In this charr the body is elongate, the head moderate, the snout long and pointed, with the lower jaw projecting beyond the upper; teeth small; maxillary long and narrow, reaching beyond the eye; preopercle very short, with a very short lower limb; opercle and preopercle very conspicuously and deeply striated; fins much developed, the dorsal much higher than long; pectoral very long, reaching more than halfway to ventrals, which are very long; caudal well forked.

Greenland Charr

Salvelinus stagnalis (Fabricius)

This is another charr occuring in the waters of Greenland, Boothia Felix and neighbouring regions. Body rather elongate; pectoral short, $1\frac{2}{3}$ in head, not reaching half-way to ventrals; dorsal about as high as long, the longest ray $1\frac{3}{4}$ in head; gillrakers $9+15$; slender and nearly straight, the longest $2\frac{1}{8}$ in eye.

Colour, dark green, with lighter irregular green streaks, silvery below; sides everywhere with pale pink spots, the largest smaller than eye; upper fins greenish, the lower fins pink. Sea-run examples nearly plain silvery.

This trout reaches a length of 1 to 2 feet and is a food-fish of considerable importance to the natives of that region.

Arctic Charr

Salvelinus arcturus (Günther)

This charr is known only from Lake Victoria, Floeberg Beach, in lat. 82° 34', and is the most northern Salmonoid known.

It has the body rather slender, head small, snout obtuse, mouth moderate, the maxillary in the male reaching to posterior edge of orbit; teeth small; a band of hyoid teeth; caudal moderately forked; head $4\frac{1}{2}$; depth 5; D. 11; A. 10; Br. 11; pyloric cœca 31 to 44.

Colour, dull greenish, silvery or reddish below; lower fins yellowish; probably no red spots.

Sunapee Trout; American Saibling

Salvelinus aureolus Bean

The golden trout of Sunapee Lake was not known to anglers until about twenty years ago, and it was not described and named until 1888. Through the interesting writings of Dr. John D. Quackenbos and others its name is now a familiar one to anglers everywhere, though but few have a personal acquaintance with the fish in its native waters, for this beautiful trout has a very restricted habitat. So far as known it is native only to Sunapee Lake, New Hampshire, and Flood Pond, near Ellsworth, Maine, but through fish cultural operations it has been introduced into a number of other lakes.

The water of both Sunapee Lake and Flood Pond is exceptionally pure and cold, the bottom temperature varying from 38° to 52°, according to the depth, as giving by Dr. Quackenbos. The maximum depth of each is over 100 feet, the bottom is of white sand and gravel, and there is in each an abundance of crustacea and other fish-food.

These are the environing conditions which have made the Sunapee trout a fish of surprising beauty and gracefulness. According to Dr. Quackenbos who has a more intimate acquaintance with this fish than any other who has written about it, the distinguishing characteristics are as follows: "The presence of a broad row of teeth on the hyoid bone between the lower extremities of the first 2 gill-arches; the absence of mottling on the dark sea-green back, and the excessively developed fins; inconspicuous yellow spots without areola: a square or slightly emarginate tail; a small and delicately shaped head; diminutive, aristocratic mouth, liquid planetary eyes, and a generally graceful build; a phenomenally brilliant nuptial colouration, recalling the foreign appellations of 'blood-red charr,' 'gilt charr,' and 'golden saibling.' As the October pairing time approaches, the Sunapee fish becomes illuminated with the flushes of maturing passion.

"The steel-green mantle of the back and shoulders now seems to dissolve into a veil of amethyst, through which the daffodil spots of mid-summer gleam out in points of flame, while below the lateral line all is dazzling orange. The fins catch the hue of adjacent parts, and pectoral, ventral, anal, and lower lobe of caudal, are marked with a lustrous white band.

"It is a unique experience to watch this American saibling spawning on the Sunapee shallows. Here in all the magnificence of their nuptial decoration flash schools of painted beauties, circling in proud sweeps about the submerged boulders they would select as the scenes of their loves—the poetry of an epithalamium in every motion—in one direction, uncovering to the sunbeams in amorous leaps their golden-tinctured sides, gemmed with the fire of rubies; in another, darting in little companies, the pencilled margins of their fins seeming to trail behind them like white ribbons under the ripples. There are conspicuous differences in intensity of general colouration, and the gaudy dyes of the milter are tempered in the spawner to a dead-lustre cadmium cream or olive chrome, with opal spots. The wedding garment nature has given to this charr is unparagoned. Those who have seen the bridal march of the glistening hordes, in all their glory of colour and majesty of action, pronounce it a spectacle never to be forgotten."

That so conspicuous a game and food-fish could have been aboriginal to Sunapee Lake, and for 100 years have escaped the notice alike of visiting and resident anglers, persistent poachers, and alert scientists is accounted for, as suggested by Dr. Quackenbos, by its habit of remaining almost constantly in deep water, by its spawning on mid-lake reefs late in the fall when angling is out of season and the locality of the beds dangerous of access, and by its comparative scarcity prior to the introduction of black bass in 1868. Quoting still further from Dr. Quackenbos, to whom we are indebted for our account of this fish, "the Sunapee saibling takes live bait readily, preferring a cast smelt in spring, when it pursues the spawning *Osmerus* to the shores. As far as is known, it does not rise to the fly, either at this season, or when on the shoals in autumn. Through the summer months it is angled for with a live minnow or smelt, in 60 to 70 feet of water, over cold bottom, in localities that have been baited. While the smelt are inshore, trolling with a light fly-rod and fine tackle, either with a Skinner fluted spoon, No. 1, or a small smelt on a single hook, will sometimes yield superb sport, as the game qualities of the white trout are estimated to be double those of *fontinalis*.

"The most exhilarating amusement to be had with this charr, after the first hot June days, is in trolling from a sailboat with a greenheart tarpon rod, 300 feet of copper wire of the smallest calibre on a heavy tarpon reel, and attached to this a 6-foot braided leader with a Buell's spinner, or a live minnow on a stiff gang. The weight of the wire sinks the bait to the requisite depth. When the sailboat is running across the wind at the maximum of her speed, the sensation experienced by the strike of a 4 or 5-pound fish bankrupts all description. A strong line under such a tension would part on the instant; but the ductility of the wire averts this accident, and the man at the reel end of the rod experiences a characteristic 'give,' quickly followed by the dead-weight strain of the frenzied Salmonoid. To land a fish thus struck implies much greater patience and skill than a successful battle, under similar circumstances with a 5-ounce 6-strip and delicate tackle. The pleasure is largely concentrated in the strike, and the perception of a big fish 'fast.' The watchfulness and labour involved in the subsequent struggle border closely on the confines of pain. The ductile wire is an essentially different means from a taut silk line. The fish holds the coign of vantage; when he stands back and with bulldog pertinacity wrenches savagely at the pliable metal—when he rises to the surface in a despairing leap for his life—the angler is at his mercy. But, brother of the sleave-silk and tinsel, when at last you gaze upon your captive lying asphyxiated on the surface, a synthesis of qualities that make a perfect fish—when you disengage him from the meshes of the net, and place his icy figure in your outstretched palms, and watch the tropæolin glow of his awakening tones soften into cream tints, and the cream tints pale into the pearl of the moonstone, as the muscles of respiration glow feebler and more irregular in their contraction—you will experience a peculiar thrill that the capture neither of ouananiche, nor *fontinalis*, nor *namaycush* can ever excite. It is this after-glow of pleasure, this delight of contemplation and speculation, of which the scientific angler never wearies, that lends a charm all its own to the pursuit of the Alpine trout.

"Finally there can be no doubt as to the economic value of the American saibling. It is one of the most prolific of our Salmonoids, the female averaging 1200 eggs to the pound, and casting spawn when only 2 ounces in weight. It is also a singularly rapid grower where smelt food abounds. The extreme weight proved to have been attained is about 12 pounds, although accounts exist of much larger specimens weighing from 15 to 20 pounds. As a rule the greater the altitude the smaller the fish, but the more intense the colouration. This charr is exceptionally hardy and easy to propagate. The eggs bear transportation over the roughest roads without injury."

According to Mr. Merrill, of Green Lake, the saibling fry remain perfectly healthy at a temperature which proves very trying to brook trout fry; both the eggs and the fry display wonderful hardiness under the most trying circumstances.

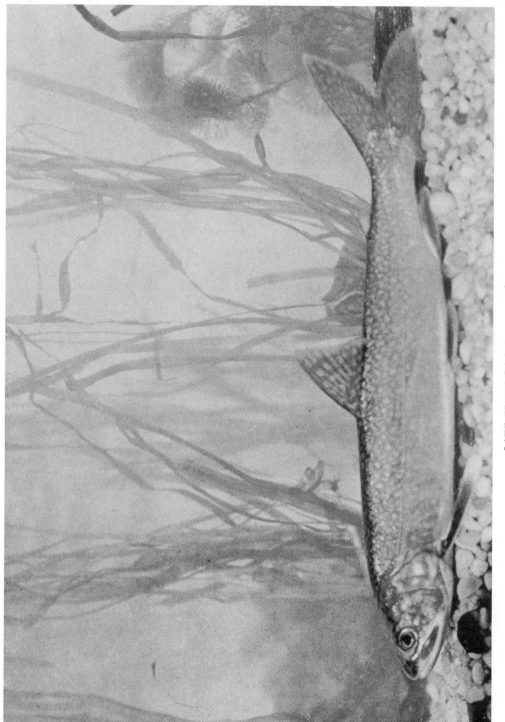

LAKE TROUT, *Cristivomer namaycush*

EASTERN BROOK TROUT, *Salvelinus fontinalis*

The young are persistent hiders; any crevice in the bank or lump of clay affords a hiding place. When fed, they will emerge and rise for their food, but will immediately hide again. In feeding, they remain near the bottom, darting up after their food and going back quickly. They are much cleaner feeders than either trout or salmon, picking up all the food that sinks, allowing none to waste.

Dr. Quackenbos recommends it in the highest terms to fish culturists and regards it as *"facile princeps,* from its rush at the cast smelt to the finish at the breakfast table."

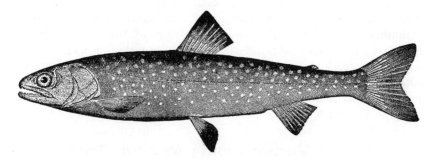

Oquassa Trout; Blueback Trout

Salvelinus oquassa (Girard)

The blueback trout is the smallest and one of the most handsome of the charrs. It rarely exceeds a foot in length and a few ounces in weight, and is known only from the Rangely Lakes in western Maine. Although quite different in appearance, it shows no important structural differences separating it from the European saibling.

Formerly this fish was very abundant, running up the streams in October in immense numbers—running up at night and dropping back before morning, so that none was to be seen in the day time. Then the fish were small, only 6 to 10 inches in length, and 4 to 6 to the pound. Now they are very scarce, and the few that are caught are much larger, sometimes weighing as much as $2\frac{1}{2}$ pounds.

Head 5; depth 5; eye $3\frac{1}{2}$; D. 10; A. 9; scales about 230; gill-rakers about 6+11. Body elongate, considerably compressed, less elevated than in the other species of charrs, the dorsal outline regularly but not strongly curved; head smaller than in any other trout, its upper surface flattish; mouth quite small, the maxillary short and moderately broad, scarcely reaching posterior edge of orbit; jaws about equal; scales small, those along the lateral line somewhat enlarged; pectoral and ventral fins not elongate; caudal fin well forked, in small ones more so than in other species, but more nearly "square" in large individuals; no concentric striæ on opercles. Colour, dark blue, the round red spots much smaller than the pupil, and usually confined to the sides of the body; sides with traces of dark bars; lower fins variegated, as in *S. fontinalis*.

In lakes of Arctic America, about Discovery Bay and Cumberland Gulf, is found another charr, *Salvelinus oquassa naresi* (Günther), usually regarded as a subspecies of the Oquassa trout, from which it does not differ greatly. It reaches a length of a foot or more. Nothing is known of its habits. Colour, greenish above, sides silvery or deep red, with very small red spots, much smaller than the pupil; lower fins deep red, the anterior margins yellowish white; dorsal fin reddish posteriorly.

Lac de Marbre Trout ; Marston Trout

Salvelinus marstoni Garman

This interesting charr was described in 1893 by Professor Samuel Garman, from specimens sent him from Lac de Marbre, Ottawa County, Province of Quebec.

The distribution of this trout has not been determined. If it is identical with the so-called red trout of Canada, as seems probable, it will doubtless be found in most of the suitable waters north of the St. Lawrence and tributary to it. Besides the specimens which Professor Garman had from Lac de Marbre, which is near Ottawa, other examples have been obtained from one of the lakes of the Laurentides Club in the Lake St. John district, others from Lac a Cassette, in Rimouski County, only a few miles from the St. Lawrence, and, more recently, many fine examples were secured by Mr. J. W. Titcomb from Lake Saccacomi and the Red lakes in Maskinonge County, township of St. Alexis des Monts, Quebec.

These red trout were at first thought to be bottom feeders, and that they would not rise to the fly, but they are now known to take the fly readily, and must be classed among the most beautiful and active of American game-fishes.

It is regarded by Professor Garman as allied to the Oquassa trout, from which it differs in the longer maxillary, stronger dentition, deeply notched caudal fin, larger size and different colouration. It seems even more closely related to specimens which have been identified by Dr. Bean with *Salvelinus rossi* of Richardson, which may be identical with the Greenland charr.

Little or nothing has been recorded regarding its game qualities, but its trim appearance and rich colouration, together with the cold water in which it lives, would indicate a fish well worthy the attention of anglers.

Head 5; depth 6; eye about 5; snout $3\frac{3}{4}$; interorbital $3\frac{1}{3}$; D. 13; A. 13; V. 9; P. 14; Br. 11+12; vertebræ 60; gillrakers 8+14. Body subfusiform, compressed, pointed at the snout, slender at the tail; mouth large; maxillary straight, extending almost to posterior edge of eye, bearing strong teeth nearly its whole length; teeth on intermaxillary and mandible stronger; a series of 4 strong hooked teeth on each side of tongue; opercle thin, with few striæ; scales very small, apparently about 230 in the series immediately above lateral line, and more than 250 in a row 5 or 6 scales above this; dorsal and anal slightly emarginate; pectoral and ventral small, base of the latter slightly behind the middle of that of dorsal; caudal peduncle very slender; caudal lobes pointed, the notch very deep. Colour, back dark brown, unspotted, with an iridescent bluish tint; dorsal dark, clouded, without spots or bands; pectoral, ventrals and anal orange in the middle, yellowish or whitish toward bases and at their margins; dark colour of back shading into whitish tinged with pink below lateral line; ventral surface white, no doubt reddish in breeding season; head black on top; cheeks silvery, whitish beneath; caudal fin yellowish toward base, brown distally; faint areas of lighter tint suggest a few spots of red in life along lateral line; flesh pink. It reaches a length of a foot or more.

THE GRAYLINGS

Family XVI. Thymallidæ

THE graylings agree very closely with the *Salmonidæ* in external characters and in habits. They differ notably in the structure of the skull and the presence of epipleural spines on the anterior ribs.

The parietal bones meet at the middle and separate the frontals from the supraoccipital bone. The conventional statement that the graylings are intermediate between the whitefishes and the trout is not born out by the skeleton.

The family contains one genus and about 5 species, all beautiful fishes of the rivers of cold or Arctic regions, active and gamy and delicious as food.

The French call the grayling " un umble chevalier " and say he feeds on gold. "And some think he feeds on water-thyme, for he smells of it when first taken out of the water; and they may think so with as good reason as we do that the smelts smell like violets at their first being caught; which I think is a truth." (Izaak Walton.) And St. Ambrose, the Bishop of Milan, calls the grayling "the flower of fishes."

GENUS THYMALLUS CUVIER

Body oblong, somewhat compressed, not much elevated; head rather short; mouth moderate, terminal, the short maxillary extending past middle of the large eye, but not to its posterior margin; teeth slender and sparse on the maxillaries, premaxillaries and lower jaw; vomer short with a small patch of teeth; teeth on the palatines; tongue toothless or nearly so; scales small and loose; dorsal fin very long and high; caudal well forked; air-bladder very large; pyloric appendages 15 to 18.

Three species, all very closely related, have been recognized in American waters.

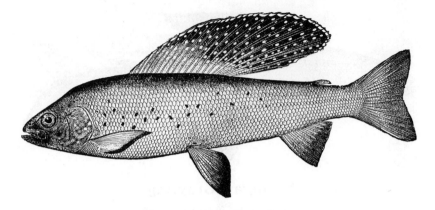

Arctic Grayling; Poisson Bleu

Thymallus signifer (Richardson)

The Arctic or Alaska grayling is known from the Mackenzie, Kowak and other rivers of Alaska, and is said to abound in most clear cold streams even to the Arctic Ocean.

It reaches a length of 18 inches and is an excellent food and game fish.

Head $5\frac{1}{2}$; depth $4\frac{2}{3}$; eye 3; maxillary 6; D. 24; A. 11; scales 8-88 to 90-11; cœca 18. Body elongate, compressed; head rather short, subconic, compressed, its upper outline continuous with anterior curve of back; mouth moderate, the maxillary extending to below middle of eye; jaws about equal; scales moderate, easily detached, lateral line nearly straight; a small bare space behind isthmus. Colour, dark bluish on back, purplish-gray on sides; belly blackish-gray, with irregular whitish blotches; 5 or 6 deep blue spots anteriorly; head brown, a blue mark on each side of lower jaw; dorsal dark gray, blotched with paler, with crossrows of deep-blue spots, edged with lake red; ventrals striated with purplish and whitish.

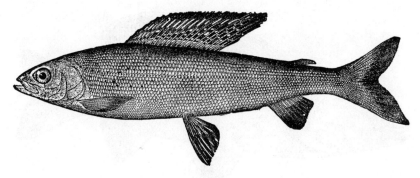

Michigan Grayling

Thymallus tricolor Cope

The Michigan grayling is known from various streams in the southern peninsula of Michigan and from Otter Creek, near Keweenaw, in the northern peninsula. It was formerly very abundant in the Au Sable and Jordan rivers, and other streams of northern Michigan, but through the destructive and wholly inexcusable methods by which the lumbering and logging operations have been carried on in that region these streams have been ruined and the grayling practically exterminated.

The Michigan grayling began to receive the attention of naturalists, fish-culturists, and anglers about 25 years ago, but no great success was ever attained in its artificial propagation. With anglers it has been held in very high esteem.

"There is no species sought for by anglers that surpasses the grayling in beauty. They are more elegantly formed and more graceful than the trout, and their great dorsal fin is a superb mark of loveliness. When the well-lids were lifted, and the sun's rays admitted, lighting up the delicate olive-brown tints of the back and sides, the bluish-white of the abdomen, and the mingling of tints of rose, pale blue, and purplish-pink on the fins, they displayed a combination of colours equaled by no fish outside the tropics." Mr. Fred. Mather describes the colouring of the grayling as follows: "His pectorals are olive-brown, with a bluish tint at the end; the ventrals are striped with alternate streaks of brown and pink; the anal is plain brown; the caudal is very forked and plain, while the crowning glory is the immense dorsal, which is dotted with large, brilliant-red or bluish purple spots,

surrounded with a splendid emerald green, which fades after death—
the changeable shade of green seen in the peacock's tail."

Head about 5; scales 93 to 98; D. 21 or 22, lower and smaller
than in *T. signifer*. Colour, brilliant, purplish-gray; young more
silvery; sides of head with bright bluish and bronze reflections;
anterior part of side with small, irregular, inky-black spots; ventral
fins ornate, dusky, with diagonal rose-coloured lines; dorsal with a
black line along its base, then a rose-coloured one, then a blackish
one, then rose-coloured blackish, and rose coloured, the last stripe
continued as a row of spots; above these is a row of dusky-green
spots, then a row of minute rose-coloured spots, then a
broad dusky area, the middle part of the fin tipped with
rose; anal and adipose fins dusky; central rays of caudal pink, the
outer rays dusky.

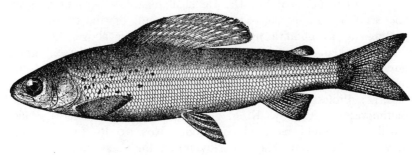

Montana Grayling

Thymallus montanus (Milner)

The Montana grayling is known to occur only in streams
emptying into the Missouri River above the Great Falls, principally in Smith or Deep River and its tributaries, in the Little
Belt Mountains, in Sun River, and in the Jefferson, Gallatin and
Madison rivers and their affluents. Like all other grayling it
prefers cold, clear streams of pure water, with sandy and gravelly
bottoms.

The spawning season of the Montana grayling is in April
and May, depending upon the temperature of the water.

The United States Fish Hatchery at Bozeman, Montana, obtains
eggs of the grayling in Elk Creek, tributary to Red Rock Lake.
At the approach of the spawning season the fish go up the
Jefferson, through Beaverhead and Red Rock rivers, to Red Rock

Lake, 14 miles in length, and through the lake itself to the inlets at its head. After spawning they return through the lake to the rivers below, none stopping in the lake whose waters seem wholly unsuited to them.

At spawning time Elk Creek is fairly alive with grayling on the gravelly shallows, where their large and beautiful dorsal fins are to be seen waving, clear of the water, in the manner of sharks' fins on a flood tide.

The artificial propagation of the Montana grayling was begun at Bozeman in 1898 and, under the able direction of Dr. James A. Henshall, the superintendent, has proved very successful. In 1899, 5,300,000 eggs were taken and 4,567,000 fry were hatched and liberated. The number of eggs varies from 2,000 to 4,000 to the fish.

As to game qualities, Dr. Henshall regards the Montana grayling as fully the equal of the brook trout, or red-throat trout, putting up as good a fight, and often leaping above the surface when hooked. It takes the artificial fly, caddis larvæ, grasshoppers, angleworms and similar bait. The best artificial flies to use are those with bodies of peacock harl, or yellow-bodied flies, as: Professor, Queen of the Water, Oconomowoc, and Lord Baltimore; or Grizzly King, Henshall, Coachman and the like. Small flies should be used, on hooks Nos. 10 to 12. Grayling may be taken from May to November, the best time being in the summer.

The average size of this fish is 10 to 12 inches in length and $\frac{1}{2}$ to 1 pound in weight. The largest Dr. Henshall reports were 20 inches long and weighed 2 pounds.

At present good grayling fishing in Montana can be had in the tributaries of the Smith or Deep River in the Little Belt Mountains, and in the upper parts of the Gallatin, Madison and Jefferson rivers. The best fishing is near the upper canyon of the Madison, and in Odell, Red Rock and other creeks at the head of Red Rock Lake, the sources of the Jefferson.

THE SMELTS

Family XVII. Argentinidæ

THE smelts are small fishes, marine or anadromous, some of them inhabiting deep water; all but one genus confined to the waters of the Northern Hemisphere. There are about a dozen genera with some 15 species, and they may be regarded as reduced *Salmonidæ*, smaller and in every way feebler than the trout, but similar to them in all respects except in the form of the stomach. Most of them are very delicate food-fishes.

a. Ventral fins inserted in front of the middle of the dorsal; mouth large.
b. Scales very small, arranged in the male in villous bands; pectoral broad, of 15 to 20 rays;..............*Mallotus*, 225
bb. Scales large, similar in both sexes; pectoral moderate, of 10 to 12 rays.
c. Teeth feeble, those on tongue very weak; scales small, adherent;............... ....*Thaleichthys*, 226
cc. Teeth strong, those on tongue enlarged, canine-like; scales moderate, loosely attached...................*Osmerus*, 227
aa. Ventral fins inserted under or behind middle of dorsal; mouth rather small.
d. Jaws with minute teeth; similar teeth on tongue and palate; maxillary reaching past front of eye;........*Hypomesus*, 230

GENUS MALLOTUS CUVIER

The Capelins

Body elongate, compressed, covered with minute scales, a band of which, above the lateral line and along each side of the belly, are enlarged, and in mature males they become elongate-lanceolate, densely imbricated, with free, projecting points, forming villous bands. In very old males the scales of the back and belly are similarly modified, and the top of the head and the rays of the paired fins are finely granulated. Mouth rather large, the maxillary thin, extending to below middle of eye; lower jaw projecting; lower fins very large; pectorals large, the base very broad; gillrakers long and slender.

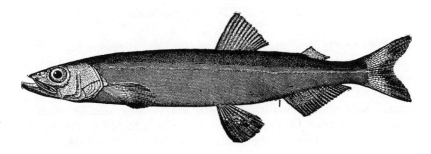

Capelin; Lodde

Mallotus villosus (Müller)

The Capelin is found on both coasts of Arctic America, south to Cape Cod and Alaska. It is also found on the Kamchatkan coast, and is generally abundant northward. It is a most delicious little fish, much valued in the far north.

The eggs of the capelin are deposited in the sand along Arctic shores in incredible numbers. They are washed up on the beaches, and in about 30 days they are hatched. The beach then becomes a quivering mass of little fishes, eggs and sand, from which the little fishes are borne into the sea by the waves.

GENUS THALEICHTHYS GIRARD

This genus is intermediate between *Mallotus* and *Osmerus*, differing from the latter in its rudimentary dentition, and in its small adherent scales. All the teeth are very feeble, slender and deciduous, although occasionally present on all the bones of the mouth; no permanent teeth on the tongue; scales smaller than in *Osmerus*, and more closely adherent, larger than in *Mallotus*, and similar in the 2 sexes. One species.

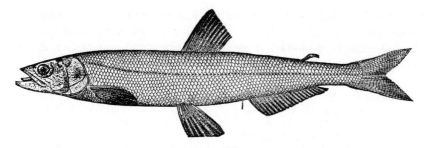

Eulachon ; Candlefish

Thaleichthys pacificus (Richardson)

The Eulachon is found from Oregon northward, ascending the Fraser and other rivers in spring in enormous numbers. An excellent panfish, unsurpassed by any fish whatsoever in delicacy of the flesh, which is far superior to that of any trout; remarkable for extreme oiliness, but the oil has a very delicate, attractive flavour. The oil is sometimes extracted and used as a substitute for cod-liver oil, but it is solid and lard-like at ordinary temperatures. When dried these fish have been used as candles, a wick having been placed in them.

Colour, white, scarcely silvery; upper parts rendered dark iron-gray by the accumulation of dark punctulations. Length, 10 to 12 inches.

GENUS OSMERUS LINNÆUS

The Smelts

Body elongate, compressed; head long, pointed; mouth wide, the slender maxillary extending to past middle of eye; lower jaw projecting; preorbital and suborbital bones narrow; fine teeth on maxillaries and premaxillaries; lower jaw with small teeth, which are larger posteriorly; tongue with a few strong, fang-like teeth, largest at the tip; hyoid bone, vomer, and palatines with wide-set teeth; gillrakers long and slender; scales large and loose; dorsal small, about midway of body, over the ventrals; anal long; vertebræ 40; pyloric cœca few and small.

Small fishes of the coasts of Europe and northern America, sometimes ascending rivers; the flesh of all very delicate and highly valued as food. Five or 6 species and subspecies in our waters.

a. Vomer with a cross-series of small teeth; small, weak species spawning in the sea;......................*thaleichthys,* 228
aa. Vomer with 2 to 4 strong, fang-like teeth; species stronger in habit, ascending streams.
b. Maxillary not reaching posterior margin of eye; depth 6 to 6½ in length; colour plain;....................*mordax,* 229
bb. Maxillary reaching posterior margin of eye; depth 5½; colour brilliant;....................................*dentex,* 230

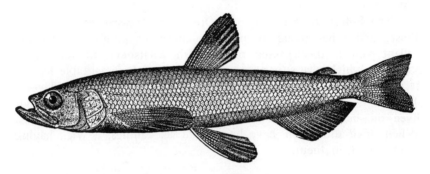

Pacific Smelt

Osmerus thaleichthys Ayres

This interesting little fish is found on our Pacific coast from San Francisco northward to Bristol Bay in Alaska, and is usually common. It is a weak, feeble species, its flesh soft and not keeping well, but of excellent flavour. Colour, olivaceous, the sides silvery and somewhat translucent. Length 8 or 9 inches.

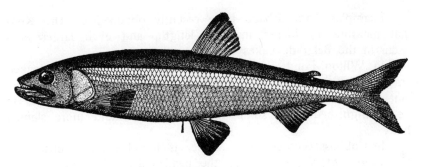

American Smelt

Osmerus mordax (Mitchill)

This is *the* smelt of America. It is found along our Atlantic Coast from Virginia to the Gulf of St. Lawrence, entering streams, and is often land-locked. It is abundant in Lakes Champlain and Memphremagog, and in many other lakes in New England, New Brunswick and Nova Scotia. It enters our rivers and brackish bays during the winter months for the purpose of spawning, when it is caught in immense numbers in nets and by hook and line. In 1622 Capt. John Smith wrote: "Of smelts there is such abundance that the Salvages doe take them up in the rivers with baskets, like sives"; and Josselyn, 55 years later, wrote: "The frostfish [*O. mordax*] is little bigger than a *Gudgeon*, and are taken in fresh brooks; when the waters are frozen they make a hole in the ice, about ½ yard or yard wide, to which the fish repair in great numbers, where, with small nets bound to a hoop about the bigness of a firkin-hoop, with a staff fastened to it, they take them out of the hole." Great quantities are taken along the coast and usually after being frozen, are shipped to the larger cities. Those which have not been frozen are termed "green" smelts, and are much more highly esteemed.

The principal food of the smelt consists of shrimps and other small crustaceans.

Colour, transparent greenish above, sides silvery; body and fins with some dark punctulations. The smelt does not usually exceed 8 or 10 inches in length, but it sometimes exceeds a foot in length and a weight of a pound.

Examples from Sebago Lake recently obtained by Dr. Kendall measure 12 inches in total length, and even larger ones occur in the Belgrade Lakes of Maine.

In Wilton Pond, Kennebec County, Maine, is a land-locked smelt which has been recognized as a subspecies of the common smelt under the name *Osmerus mordax spectrum*. It seems to be distinguished by a somewhat shorter head and more slender body.

In Cobbosseecontee Lake, Maine, is found another subspecies, *O. mordax abbotti*, which has the head still shorter and the body more slender; maxillary reaching posterior margin of pupil.

These subspecies are of doubtful validity.

Rainbow Herring

Osmerus dentex Steindachner

On both coasts of Bering Sea and south to northern China this smelt is found. It is a brilliantly coloured little fish with the flesh of firmer texture than in other species. About Bristol Bay it constitutes an important part of the food of the natives.

Colour, pale olive on back, the scales edged with darker; side above lateral line purple, changing below to blue, and then to violet and gold; under parts silvery, with rosy sheen, the belly satiny-white; fins plain, slightly golden.

GENUS HYPOMESUS GILL

The Surf Smelts

Body rather elongate, moderately compressed, covered with thin scales of moderate size; head rather pointed; mouth moderate, the short maxillary not quite reaching middle of eye, its outline below broadly convex; lower jaw projecting; teeth minute, on jaws, vomer, palatines, and tongue; ventrals inserted directly under middle of dorsal; midway between eye and base of caudal. Small fishes of the North Pacific.

Surf Smelt

Hypomesus pretiosus (Girard)

This smelt attains a length of a foot and is found on the coast of California and Oregon from Monterey northward, usually abundant and spawning in the surf. A firm-fleshed and fat little fish of delicious flavour, scarcely inferior to the eulachon.

Colour, light olivaceous; a silvery band along the lateral line.

Pond Smelt

Hypomesus olidus (Pallas)

This delicious and excellent little food-fish is abundant on both coasts of Bering Sea southward to Japan and the Aleutian Islands. It spawns in fresh-water ponds, and is exceedingly abundant about St. Michaels. From the surf smelt, which it closely resembles, it is distinguished by its higher fins, the longest dorsal ray being only 6 in body; pectoral reaching $\frac{2}{3}$ distance to ventrals, their length 5 in body; ventrals 6 in body. Colour, dusky, little transparent.

THE BLACKFISH

Family XVIII. Dalliidæ

THIS family contains but one genus and a single species, *Dallia pectoralis* Bean, known as the Alaskan blackfish. It is found only in the streams and ponds of northern Alaska and Siberia, abounding in sphagnum ponds and found in countless numbers "wherever there is water enough to wet the skin of a fish." It forms one of the chief articles in the food of the natives

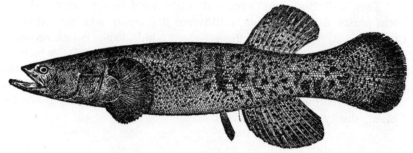

Alaskan Blackfish

who use it also as food for their dogs. It feeds largely upon small plants, worms and crustaceans. Its vitality is extraordinary. It will remain frozen in baskets for weeks and, when thawed out, will be as lively as ever. Turner mentions one swallowed frozen by a dog, thawed out by the heat of the dog's stomach, and vomited up alive. Length about 8 inches.

MONTANA GRAYLING, *Thymallus montanus*

GOLDEN TROUT OF SUNAPEE LAKE. *Salvelinus aureolus*

GREAT BARRACUDA, *Sphyræna barracuda*

THE PIKES

Family XIX. Esocidæ

BODY long, slender, not elevated, more or less compressed posteriorly, broad anteriorly; head long, the snout long and depressed; mouth very large, its cleft forming about half length of head; lower jaw the longer; upper jaw not protractile; premaxillaries, vomer, and palatines with broad bands of strong cardiform teeth which are more or less movable; lower jaw with strong teeth of different sizes; tongue with a band of small teeth; head naked above; cheeks and opercles more or less scaly; gill-openings very wide; gill-membranes separate, free from the isthmus; branchiostigals 12 to 20; scales small; lateral line weak, obsolete in the young, better developed in the adult; pseudo-branchiæ glandular, hidden; air-bladder simple.

Fishes of moderate or large size, inhabiting the fresh waters of Europe, Asia and North America. There is but a single genus with 7 species, one of them cosmopolitan, the others all confined to North America. The species are all noted for their greediness and voracity; "mere machines for the assimilation of other organisms." They are all excellent food-fishes and the larger ones are good game-fishes.

GENUS ESOX LINNÆUS

The characters of the genus included above with those of the family. The 7 species may easily and readily be identified by means of the following key:

a. Cheek entirely scaly; branchiostegals 11 to 16.
b. Opercles entirely scaly; dorsal rays 11 to 14; colour greenish, barred or reticulated with darker.
c. Branchiostegals normally 12 (11 to 13); scales 105 to 108; dorsal rays 11 or 12; anal rays 11 or 12; snout short, middle of eye nearer tip of lower jaw than posterior margin of opercle; species of small size; the fins unspotted.
d. Head short, $3\frac{4}{7}$ in length of body; snout $2\frac{1}{2}$ in head; eye $2\frac{2}{3}$ in snout. Colour, dark greenish, the side with about 20 distinct curved blackish bars; fins pale;....*americanus,* 234

dd. Head longer, $3\frac{1}{4}$ in length of body; snout $2\frac{1}{5}$ in head; eye $2\frac{1}{2}$ in snout. Colour, light greenish, the side with many narrow curved streaks of darker, these usually distinct, irregular, and much reticulated; fins plain; *vermiculatus,* 234

cc. Branchiostegals 14 to 16; scales about 125; dorsal rays 14; anal 13; middle of eye midway between tip of lower jaw and posterior margin of opercle. Colour, greenish, with many narrow dark curved lines and streaks, mostly horizontal and more or less reticulated; fins plain;
reticulatus, 235

bb. Opercles without any scales on the lower half; dorsal rays 16 or 17. Colour, grayish, with many whitish spots, the young with whitish or yellowish crossbars; dorsal, anal, and caudal spotted with black; a white horizontal band bounding naked portion of opercle. Size large;..........*lucius,* 236

aa. Cheeks as well as opercles with the lower half naked; branchiostegals 17 to 19.

d. Sides grayish, with round or squarish blackish spots, not coalescing to form bands;............ ....*masquinongv,* 237

dd. Sides brassy, with narrow dark cross-shades, which break up into vaguely outlined dark spots;.........*ohiensis,* 239

ddd. Sides grayish, unspotted or with very vague dark cross-shades;.............................*immaculatus,* 240

Banded Pickerel

Esox americanus Gmelin

This small pickerel, reaching a length of about a foot, occurs only east of the Alleghany Mountains, from Massachusetts to Florida, the westernmost record being Flomaton, Alabama. It is abundant in all lowland streams and swamps of this region. It takes the baited hook readily but is too small to be of much food or game value.

Easily known by the complete scaling of cheeks and opercles and in having 12 or 13 branchiostegals.

Little Pickerel ; Grass Pike

Esox vermiculatus Le Sueur

The grass pike occurs abundantly throughout the middle and upper Mississippi Valley and in streams tributary to Lakes Erie and

Michigan. It is not known from east of the Alleghanies nor from Texas. Throughout most of its range it is generally common in all ponds, bayous and small sluggish streams, preferring those waters in which there is much aquatic vegetation. It rarely exceeds a foot in length which precludes it being more than a boy's fish.

Br. 11 to 13; scales 105. Colour, green or grayish; side with many curved streaks, sometimes forming bars, but more usually marmorations or reticulations, the colour extremely variable, sometimes quite plain; sides of head usually variegated; a dark bar downward and one forward from the eye; base of caudal sometimes mottled; other fins usually plain.

Common Eastern Pickerel; Green Pike; Jack

Esox reticulatus Le Sueur

This species is found from Maine to Florida, Louisiana, Arkansas and Tennessee, common everywhere east and south of the Alleghanies. In Maine it was probably native only in the southwestern portion of the state, but through the agency of man it is now abundant in practically all the lakes in the southern third of the State, and it is found in some lakes further north. In the other New England States this pickerel is a common and familiar inhabitant of nearly every lake and pond. The same is true of the ponds and lakes of New York, New Jersey and eastern Pennsylvania.

The most southern record is from Crooked Lake, Orange County, Florida. The most western record is from Mammoth Springs, Arkansas, and other tributaries of White River, it being common in the Ozark region. This species attains a length of 2 feet, and a weight of several pounds. In some places it is a game-fish of considerable importance. It is fished for in all sorts of ways. In New England and elsewhere perhaps the most common method is "skittering," using a piece of perch belly, a minnow, a small frog or a frog-leg. In trolling, as in skittering, almost any lure is effective. It will also take the artificial fly, particularly if it be large and bright in colour, and if used somewhat as in skittering. In winter many pickerel are taken through the ice by using live minnow bait.

235

As a food-fish the pickerel occupies a fair rank. Its flesh is firm and flaky and possesses a pleasant flavour, though it is a little dry.

Br. 14 to 16; D. 14; A. 13; scales 125; cheeks and opercles entirely scaly. Colour, green of vary-ing shades; sides with golden lustre, and marked with numerous dark lines and streaks, which are mostly horizontal, and by their junction with one another pro-duce a reticulated appearance; a dark band below eye; fins plain.

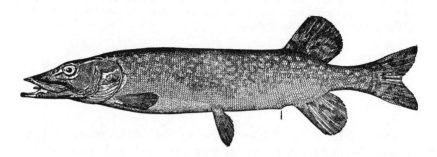

Common Pike; Great Lakes Pike; Pickerel

Esox lucius Linnæus

This is the most widely distributed and most important species of the family. It is found in all suitable fresh waters of northern North America, Europe and Asia. In North America it is found from New York and the Ohio River northward. It is not found on the Pacific coast, except in Alaska. In the small lakes of the upper Mississippi Valley, and in the Great Lakes it is generally common. It is a common fish in Canada, where it is called "eithinyoo-cannooshœoo" by the Creek Indians. It reaches a length of 4 feet and a weight of 40 pounds or more.

Its great size and fairly good game qualities make it a fish which is much prized by many anglers. It is taken in the vari-ous ways by which the eastern pickerel is captured, from which its habits are not materially different. In Europe it is more highly esteemed than with us. Walton devotes an entire chapter to it, concluding with directions how to "roast him when he is caught," and declaring that "when thus prepared he is 'choicely good'—

too good for any but anglers and honest men." In Manitoba it is the jack-fish, according to Mr Ernest Thompson Seton.

One of the best streams for great pike fishing of which we know is the Kankakee. In this sluggish river and its connecting lakes this fish is quite common, and reaches a very large size. The largest example of which we have any record as being taken in the Kankakee weighed 26½ pounds.

Br. 14 to 16; D. 16 or 17; A. 13 or 14; scales 123; cheeks entirely scaly; upper part of opercle scaly, the lower half bare. General colour, bluish or greenish-gray, with many whitish or yellowish spots, which are usually smaller than the eye, and arranged somewhat in rows; dorsal, anal and caudal fins with roundish or oblong black spots; young with the whitish spots coalescing, forming oblique crossbars; a white horizontal band bounding the naked part of the opercle; each scale with a grayish V-shaped mark.

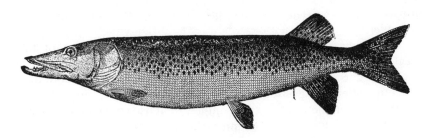

Muskallunge

Esox masquinongy Mitchill

Whence and what are you, monster grim and great?
Sometimes we think you are a "Syndicate,"
For if our quaint cartoonists be but just
You have some features of the modern "Trust."
A wide, ferocious and rapacious jaw,
A vast, insatiate and expansive craw;
And, like the "Trust," your chiefest aim and wish
Was to combine in one all smaller fish,
And all the lesser fry succumbed to fate,
Whom you determined to consolidate.—*Wilcox.*

The muskallunge is native to all the Great Lakes, the upper St. Lawrence River, certain streams and lakes tributary to the Great Lakes, and in a few lakes in the upper Mississippi Valley. It also occurs in Canada north of the Great Lakes. It does not seem to be at all abundant anywhere, as the number taken each year in any one of the lakes is small. It is perhaps most common in Lakes Michigan and Erie, and among the Thousand Islands.

This species is known by many different common names, most of them being variant spellings of the Indian name "nos-conmoge." Among those which deserve mention are: muskallunge, muscalonge, muscallonge, muscallunge, muskellunge, musquellunge, masquinongy, maskinongy and great pike. Muskallunge is the spelling which now seems to be most usually followed.

The muskallunge reaches a length of 8 feet, and is a magnificent fish, by far the largest of its family, reaching a weight of 100 pounds or more. "A long, slim, strong and swift fish, in every way fitted to the life it leads, that of a dauntless marauder."

As a game-fish the muskallunge is regarded as one of the greatest, though the interest in catching a fish of this species is doubtless due more to its immense size than to any extraordinary game qualities. Nevertheless, it is a good fighter, and able to try the skill of the most expert angler. It is an extremely voracious fish, and 80 pounds of muskallunge represents several tons of minnows, whitefish and the like.

The usual method of taking the muskallunge is, of course, by trolling, a stout line, heavy hook and large minnow being used. The best live bait species are the fall-fish, river chub and creek chub; medium-sized suckers are also frequently used.

Br. 17 to 19; D. 17; A. 15; scales 150. General form that of the common pike, the head a little larger; cheek and opercle scaled above, but both naked on their lower half; scaly part of cheek variable, usually about as wide as eye, scales on cheek and opercle in about 8 rows; eye midway between tip of lower jaw and posterior margin of opercle. Colour, dark gray, side with round or squarish blackish spots of varying size on a ground colour of grayish silvery.

Chautauqua Muskallunge

Esox ohiensis Kirtland

The muskallunge of Chautauqua Lake and the Ohio basin differs greatly in appearance from that of the Great Lakes. As the 2 forms are not known to intergrade and as their habitats are entirely distinct, they are best regarded as distinct species. The Chautauqua muskallunge is known chiefly from Chautauqua Lake, though specimens have been reported from a few other places in the Ohio Valley, viz: the Mahoning River, the Ohio at Evansville, and Conneaut Lake. In the early part of the last century when Rafinesque wrote about the fishes of the Ohio River, the muskallunge was apparently more frequently seen in that river than now.

In Chautauqua Lake it is by all odds the most important fish, whether considered from the standpoint of the commercial fisherman or that of the angler. For more than 10 years the State of New York has been propagating this species with notable success, the total number of fry hatched from 1890 to 1898 being 18,325,000. These fry have been planted chiefly in Chautauqua Lake, but large and frequent plants have been made in other waters of New York. Many have been put in Lake Ontario and the St. Lawrence River, and now the angler among the Thousand Islands may expect to find there not only the Great Lakes muskallunge but this species as well.

As a game-fish the Chautauqua muskallunge occupies a high rank, due, doubtless, more to its immense size than to actual fighting power. It is usually taken by trolling either with the spoon or a good-sized minnow. In September the spoon is used; later the minnow becomes more popular.

Writing of this species in 1818 Rafinesque said: "It is one of the best fishes in the Ohio; its flesh is very delicate and divides easily, as in salmon, into large plates as white as snow. It is called salmon pike, white pike, white jack, or white pickerel, and *Picareau blanc* by the Missourians. It reaches a length of 5 feet." Dr. Kirtland says that "epicures consider it one of the best fishes of the West," and another affirms that "as a food-fish there is nothing superior to it. It ranks with the salmon and speckled trout, and surpasses the black and striped bass. The meat is almost as white as snow, fine-grained, nicely laminated, and the flavour is perfect." The quality of the flesh improves upon keeping, and is very much more juicy and of better flavour after a day or 2 on ice.

Colour, nearly uniform dark olive-green on back; upper $\frac{2}{3}$ of side rich brassy green with some metallic green; about 25 faint narrow darker vertical bars extending somewhat below lateral line; lower third of side paler and more brassy, the vertical bars widening into broad darkish blotches, these most greenish on posterior third of body; top of head very dark green; scaled part of head brassy-green, lower part of side of head less brassy and less greenish, it being more silvery, especially on lower part of opercle; rim of lower jaw dusky greenish, rest of lower jaw and throat white; fins dark olive, with numerous darker greenish spots; iris grayish brown. The crossbars are rather broad and do not break up distinctly into diffuse spots, and the fin spots are greenish rather than black. The general colour is a rich greenish brassy with very indistinct darker green crossbars.

Great Northern Pike

Esox immaculatus (Garrard)

This muskallunge is known only from Eagle Lake and other small lakes in northern Wisconsin and Minnesota. From the Great Lakes muskallunge it differs in having the body entirely unspotted, or with vague, dark cross shades. The tail is a little more slender and the fins are a little higher. This form has not been studied critically and its relations to *E. masquinongy* and *E. ohiensis* have not been clearly made out.

THE NEEDLEFISHES

Family XX.   Belonidæ

VORACIOUS, carnivorous, saltwater fishes, bearing a superficial resemblance to the Gar pikes; genera 4 (only 2 in American waters) and species about 50, the majority American.   Their habits are ordinarily much like those of the pikes, but when startled they swim along the surface of the water with extraordinary rapidity, skimming the surface, sometimes leaping from the water with a sculling motion of the tail, sometimes remaining out of the water for long distances, but striking it at short intervals with the caudal fin.   When thus leaping the large species of the tropics are said to be a source of danger to incautious fishermen, sometimes piercing with their long sharp snout the naked bodies of the savages.

Owing to the green colour of their bones, they are not much used as food, though their flesh is excellent.

This family contains 2 genera, *Tylosurus* and *Athlennes*, the former with several species, the latter with but 1.   The only species deserving mention are the common neeedlefish (*T. notatus*),

the billfish (*T. marinus*), and the houndfish or agujon (*T. raphidoma*).   The agujon, of which we present a figure, is an abun·· dant and important food-fish about Porto Rico.   It reaches a length of 3 to 5 feet and is a vigorous, active fish, sometimes dangerous in its leaps from the water, and much dreaded by the fishermen.   The young sometimes stray northward to New Jersey.

THE BALAOS OR HALF-BEAKS

Family XXI.   Hemiramphidæ

HERBIVOROUS fishes of warm seas; mostly shore species, a few pelagic. They feed chiefly on green algæ and, like the related forms, swim at the surface, occasionally leaping in the air. Species of rather small size, rarely exceeding a foot in length. Genera about 7; species about 75. Within our limits there are 4 genera and about 11 species. Most of them are of some food value. This family is doubtfully distinct from *Exocœtidæ* and the 2 should be combined.

The genus *Chriodorus* contains a single species (*C. atherinoides*) which occurs among the Florida Keys. It is abundant at Key West. It reaches a length of 10 inches and is an excellent little panfish.

The genus *Hyporhamphus* contains numerous species in all warm seas. They are all known as half-beaks and swim in large schools usually near shore, where they feed chiefly on green algæ. There are 3 species in our waters, all small and not much used as food, though the flavour is excellent. The com-

mon half-beak (*H. roberti*), of which we give a figure, occurs on both coasts of America, north to Rhode Island and Lower California. It reaches a foot in length.

The balaos (genus *Hemiramphus*) have the body compressed and the sides nearly parallel and vertical. There are 2 species in our waters, both occurring in the West Indies.

The genus *Euleptorhamphus* has the body more slender and more compressed, and the pectoral fins longer. Only 1 species, found in the West Indies, and reaching a length of 2 feet.

THE FLYING-FISHES

Family XXII. Exocœtidæ

FIVE genera and about 65 species of carnivorous or herbivorous fishes, abounding in all warm seas, mostly pelagic, swimming near the surface, and skipping, sailing or flying through the air, sometimes for considerable distances. In our waters there are about 20 species, only the following deserving any special mention in this work.

The most common species off our Atlantic Coast is *Parexocœtus mesogaster*, which also occurs among the Hawaiian Islands. It reaches a length of 7 inches. The sharp-nosed flying-fish *(Fodiator acutus)*, of which we present a figure, is found on both

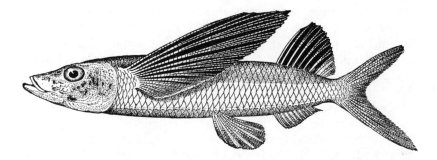

coasts of tropical America. It is common in the Gulf of California, and is a good food-fish.

The common flying-fish *(Exocœtus volitans)* inhabits all warm seas, on our coast north in summer to Newfoundland.

The California flying-fish *(Cypsilurus californicus)*, of which we show a figure on next page, occurs from Point Conception to Cape San Lucas. It is very abundant in summer, and is found in great schools about the Santa Barbara Islands. This is the only flying-fish occurring on our Pacific Coast north of Cape San Lucas. It reaches a length of 18 inches, being the largest flying-fish known, and having the greatest power of flight. Where it goes in winter has not been determined, as it has not been seen out-

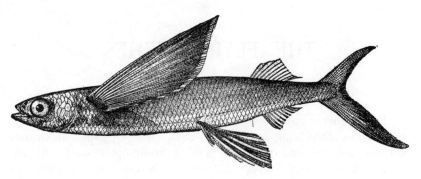

California Flying-fish *(Cypsilurus californicus)*

side of Californian waters. It is an excellent food-fish, and is sometimes taken by thousands off Santa Barbara.

Whether flying-fishes really fly, or merely soar or sail, is a question which has been much discussed. Competent observers have asserted positively that they have a real flight, while others, equally competent, maintain that the movement of the flying-fish in the air is unaccompanied by any vibration of the pectoral fins, and is sustained only so long as is possible from the impetus given upon emerging from the water. Probably the differences in opinion are largely explained by the fact that the different observers have studied different species. Some species, at least the larger ones, have a real flight; the pectoral fins vibrate, and the flight can be prolonged almost indefinitely.

We have often seen the fins vibrating just as do the wings of a bird, and Dr. James E. Benedict and others have caught flying-fish in nets when in the air, and have plainly seen the pectoral fins still vibrating.

Some of the smaller species seem to move quite differently, and it may be that they do not really fly.

The senior author of this work dissents from this common view expressed above, and does not believe that the pectoral fins have any large power of motion of their own, but that they quiver or vibrate only when the muscles of the tail are in action. He has, with Dr. Charles H. Gilbert, had, at Santa Rosa Island, California, the best possible opportunity to observe the motion of *Cypsilurus californicus.*

The flying-fishes live in the open sea. swimming in large schools. They will "fly" a distance of from a few rods to more

244

than an eighth of a mile, rarely rising more than 3 or 4 feet. Their movements in the water are extremely rapid; the sole source of motive power is the action of the strong tail while in the water. No force is acquired while the fish is in the air. On rising from the water the movements of the tail are continued until the whole body is out of the water. While the tail is in motion the pectoral fins seem to be in a state of rapid vibration, but this is apparent only, due to the resistance of the air to the motions of the animal. While the tail is in the water the ventrals are folded. When the action of the tail ceases, the pectorals and ventrals are spread out and held at rest. They are not used as wings, but act rather as parachutes to hold the body in the air. When the fish begins to fall, the tail touches the water, when its motion again begins, and with it the apparent motion of the pectorals. It is thus enabled to resume its flight, which it finishes finally with a splash. While in the air it resembles a large dragon-fly. The motion is very swift, at first in a straight line, but later deflected in a curve. The motion has no relation to the direction of the wind. When a vessel is passing through a school of these fishes, they spring up before it, moving in all directions, as grasshoppers in a meadow before the mower.

During a winter voyage from Norfolk to Porto Rico flying-fish were seen at nearly all times. The species was chiefly *Parexocœtus mesogaster*, and they were particularly abundant between Savannah and the Bahamas, in the Windward and Mona passages, and along the north coasts of Cuba, Santo Domingo, and Porto Rico.

And as one goes from San Francisco to Honolulu in June great schools of the same species greet the vessel as it comes in sight of Diamond Head, and continue to play about it until well within the harbour.

THE SAURIES

Family XXIII.   Scombresocidæ

THIS family contains 2 genera, *Scombresox,* which has the beak longer than rest of head, and *Cololabis,* with the beak about half as long as head.

The single species of *Scombresox, S. saurus,* is known as the saury, skipper, or bluefish.   It is found in temperate parts of the Atlantic, on both coasts, north to Cape Cod and France.   They swim in schools, and are often seen in the open sea.

When pursued by the tunny or mackerels, "multitudes mount to the surface and crowd on each other as they press forward.   When still more closely pursued they spring to the height of several feet, leap over each other in singular confusion, and again sink beneath.   Still further urged, they mount again and rush along the surface, by repeated starts, for more than 100 feet, without once dipping beneath, or scarcely seeming to touch the water.   At last the pursuer springs after them, usually across their course, and again they all disappear together.   Amidst such multitudes—for more than 20,000 have been judged to be out of the water together—some must fall a prey to the enemy; but so many hunting in company, it must be long before the pursuers abandon.   From inspection we could scarcely judge the fish to be capable of such flights, for the fins, though numerous, are small, and the pectoral far from large, though the angle of their articulation is well adapted to raise the fish by the direction of their motions, to the surface."—*Goode.*

The skipper reaches a length of 18 inches, and is a good, wholesome food-fish.

Cololabis brevirostris is found on the California coast from San Francisco southward.   It reaches a length of a foot or more, and is used to some extent as food.

THE SAND ROLLERS

Family XXIV. Percopsidæ

This small family is of special interest because it combines with ordinary *Salmonoid* characters the structure of the head and mouth of the *Percoids*, as may be seen by the accompanying illustration. Only 2 genera known, each with a single species. *Percopsis guttatus*, the common sand roller or trout perch, is found

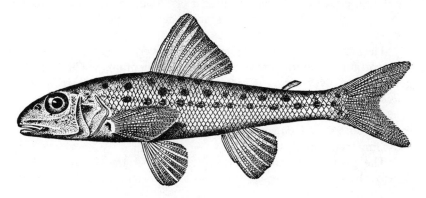

in lakes and suitable streams from Lake Champlain and the Delaware River, west to Kansas and Assiniboia. It prefers cold, clear waters, and is most abundant in the Great Lakes, particularly in Lakes Michigan and Superior. It spawns in the spring, at which time it runs into tributary streams in great numbers. Mr. Andrew Halkett, Naturalist of the Department of Marine and Fisheries, Ottawa, informs us that immense numbers are seen in the Moira River every spring.

Though reaching a length of only 6 or 8 inches, the sand roller takes the hook readily, and is used as a pan-fish. We have seen boys on the Chicago piers catching them in great numbers. *Columbia transmontana* is known only from the Umatilla River at Umatilla, Oregon, and the Walla Walla River at Wallula, Washington, both places in the Columbia River Basin.

THE SILVERSIDES

Family XXV. Atherinidæ

THE silversides are interesting carnivorous fishes, mostly of small size, living in great schools near the shore in temperate and tropical seas; a few species in fresh water; all the species having a silvery band along the side, this sometimes underlaid by black pigment. Genera about 15; species about 70. All of them which are large enough are highly prized as food, hence the common name "fishes of the king," pescados del rey, pesce re, or peixe rey.

The majority of the species, however, are too small and unimportant to merit more than a brief mention. The principal genera are *Atherina, Chirostoma, Menidia, Eslopsarum* and *Labidesthes.*

Atherina contains numerous species 5 or 6 of which are found in our waters. *A. laticeps,* found abundantly at Key West, is the most important species.

The genus *Chirostoma* is represented in the fresh waters of Mexico by several species, the most important of which is the

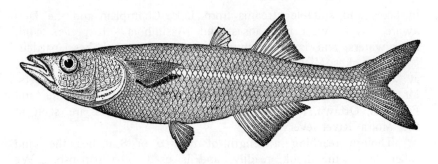

pescado blanco de chalco *(C. humboldtianum),* which is found in the lakes about the City of Mexico and is an important food-fish.

Its flesh is coarser and firmer than in the more transparent members of the family which are called pescado blanco.

The genus *Eslopsarum* is close to *Chirostoma*, differing only in the larger scales. Only 2 species are known, both from fresh waters of Mexico.

The true silversides (*Menidia*) are numerous as to species, there being about a dozen or more in our waters.

They are all of small size, some entering or dwelling in fresh waters, and all of some little value as food.

The more common species enter largely into the aggregation of species known as whitebait.

The genus *Labidesthes* contains one species, *L. sicculus*, a small transparent fish, known as the lake silverside or skipjack, which is abundant in most of the Great Lakes and the small lakes of the upper Mississippi Valley.

In some lakes it is exceedingly abundant, swimming in immense schools at the surface near the shore, or, on occasion, far out in the lake. Late in the fall, even after ice has begun to form around the edges of the lake, these little fishes come in immense schools along the shores where they may be seen swimming slowly about on quiet sunny days. They are easily frightened and the least disturbance causes them to skurry in all directions, many of them skipping over the surface of the water. Large schools may often be seen moving slowly about under the ice in shallow water. Sometimes a strong wind will drive or wash them on shore where large numbers perish. It is a very graceful little fish, reaching 3 to 4 inches in length.

THE MULLETS

Family XXVI.   Mugilidæ

Body oblong, more or less compressed, covered with rather large, cycloid scales; no lateral line, but the furrows often deepened on the middle of each scale so as to form lateral streaks; mouth small, the jaws with small teeth, or none, various in form; premaxillaries protractile; gill-openings wide, the membranes separate, free from the isthmus; branchiostegals 5 or 6; gillrakers long and slender; pseudobranchiæ large; two short dorsal fins, well separated, the anterior of 4 stiff spines, the last one of which is much shorter than the others; second dorsal longer than the first, similar to anal; anal spines 2 or 3, graduated; ventral fins abdominal, not far back; caudal forked; air-bladder large and simple; intestine long; peritoneum usually black.

This important family contains about 10 genera and 100 species, inhabiting the fresh waters and coasts of warm regions, feeding on organic matter contained in mud.   A considerable indigestible portion of mud is swallowed, and in order to prevent larger bodies from passing into the stomach, or such substances passing through the gill-openings, these fishes have the organs of the pharynx modified into a filtering apparatus.   The fish takes in a quantity of mud or sand, and after working it about for some time between the pharyngeal bones, ejects the roughest and indigestible portions.   The upper pharyngeals have a rather irregular form; they are slightly arched, the convexity being directed toward the pharyngeal cavity, tapering anteriorly and broad posteriorly.   They are coated with a thick, soft membrane, which reaches far beyond the margin of the bone, and is studded all over with minute horny cilia.   Each branchial arch is provided with a series of long gillrakers which are laterally bent downward, each series closly fitting to the sides of the adjoining arch; they together thus constitute a sieve admirably adapted to permit a transit for the water, retaining at the same time every solid substance in the cavity of the pharynx.

In our limits 4 genera are represented.

a. Stomach muscular, gizzard-like; teeth slender, usually ciliiform; lower jaw angular in front; species chiefly marine.

b. Orbit with a well developed adipose eyelid, covering part of iris;
Mugil, 251
bb. Orbit without distinct adipose eyelid;.........*Chænomugil,* 256
aa. Stomach not gizzard-like; teeth not ciliiform; lower jaw not angular in front; freshwater species.
c. Teeth in villiform bands;....................*Agonostomus,* 256
cc. Teeth coarse, broad, truncate incisors with their free edges serrate;.................................*Joturus,* 257

GENUS MUGIL LINNÆUS

The Mullets

This genus of well-known fishes is sufficiently characterized above.

a. Soft dorsal and anal almost naked; side with dark longitudinal stripes along the rows of scales; caudal deeply forked; size large.
b. Scales about 33 in longitudinal series;.........*brasiliensis,* 251
bb. Scales about 41 in longitudinal series;..........*cephalus,* 252
aa. Soft dorsal and anal scaled; side without dark stripes along rows of scales; caudal less deeply forked; size smaller.
c. Anal rays III, 9; scales 35 to 45.
d. Scales 42 to 45.
e. Head $4\frac{1}{2}$ in length;..............................*incilis,* 254
ee. Head $3\frac{3}{4}$ in length;...........................*thoburni,* 254
dd. Scales 35 to 38.
f. Pectoral not nearly reaching origin of dorsal;.....*curema,* 254
ff. Pectoral nearly reaching origin of dorsal.
g. Teeth rather wide-set, very small, mostly uniserial, scarcely visible in adult without lens.
h. Scales 38; bare space between dentary bones very large;
hospes, 255
hh. Scales 35 or 36; bare space between dentary bones small;
gaimardianus, 255
gg. Teeth large, in many series above;.............*setosus,* 255
cc. Anal rays III, 8; scales very large, about 33;..*trichodon,* 255

Liza; Lebrancho; Queriman

Mugil brasiliensis Agassiz

This mullet is found from Cuba to Patagonia. It is common in the West Indies and along the coast of Brazil. It is abundant in the Havana market where it is called lebrancho. It is the most abundant mullet seen in the market at San Juan, Porto Rico, and is perhaps the most common species about that island. It reaches a length of 18 inches and is an excellent and important food-fish, the flesh being white and flaky and of delicious flavour.

Head 4; depth $4\frac{4}{7}$; D. IV-I, 8; A. III, 8; scales 35,-12. Body more slender than in any other American species; snout broad and bluntish, the upper profile almost straight and horizontal; interorbital space greatly convex, its width 2 in head; preorbital large, almost covering maxillary; eye hidden anteriorly and posteriorly by a broad adipose membrane; teeth very minute; scales large, especially on top of head, about 21 between origin of dorsal and tip of snout; soft dorsal and anal almost naked; margin of soft dorsal very concave; anal similar to soft dorsal, but slightly less concave; caudal deeply forked. Colour, dusky above, silvery below; a dusky streak along each row of scales, these streaks not so wide as in *M. cephalus*; scales on sides and opercles with dark punctulations; ventrals pale yellowish, the fins otherwise dusky.

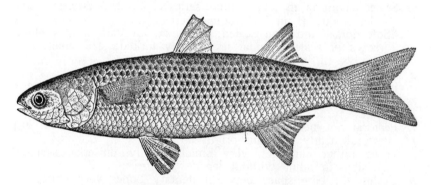

Common Mullet ; Striped Mullet

Mugil cephalus Linnæus

The common mullet is a fish of very wide distribution, occurring on the coasts of southern Europe and northern Africa, on the Atlantic Coast of America from Cape Cod to Brazil, and on our Pacific Coast from Monterey to Chile. It goes in great schools and is everywhere abundant in bays, lagoons, and all sheltered waters. It reaches a length of about 2 feet and is a food-fish of much importance. Although mullets of some species or other are found on every stretch of coast-line in the world in the temperate and tropical zones, it is probable that nowhere else in the world are they so abundant as on our own South Atlantic and Gulf coasts, with their broad margin of partially or entirely land-locked brackish waters, numerous estuaries and broad river-mouths. They abound in the Indian and St. John's rivers of Florida, frequently running up the latter at least to Lake George. Among the Florida Keys and on the west coast of Florida, as well as along the entire Gulf Coast they literally swarm in all suitable places. It is the most generally popular and most abundant food-fish on our southern seaboard. Its abundance puts it within the reach of everybody, blacks as well as whites. "How do you people live?" asked the invalid who had gone to Florida to escape the rigours of the New England winter. "Well, suh, the fac' is, boss," replied his old Negro guide, "in the summuh time we libs on de mullet and in the winter we libs mos'ly on de sick Yankee."

The mullet does not usually take the hook but is caught chiefly in seines, gillnets, or by means of cast-nets, enormous catches being sometimes made. In preparing the mullet for the table it may be either boiled, stewed, baked or fried. Large quantities are salted for local use or shipment north, and many barrels are shipped fresh to northern cities. The mullet roe is also considered a delicacy; and large quantities of mullets are used for bait in the various hand-line fisheries of our southern waters.

The mullet is a bottom-feeder and prefers still, shoal water with grassy and sandy or muddy bottom. It swims along the bottom, head down, now and then taking a mouthful of mud, which is partially culled over in the mouth, the microscopic particles of animal or vegetable matter retained, and the refuse expelled. When one fish finds a spot rich in the desired food, its companions immediately flock around in a manner reminding one of barn-yard fowls feeding from a dish. The mullet eats no fish or anything of any size, but is preyed upon by nearly all other common fishes larger than itself.

Colour, dark bluish above, sides silvery, with a conspicuous dark stripe along each row of scales; under parts pale yellowish; ventral fins yellowish, the other fins more or less dusky.

Trench Mullet

Mugil incilis Hancock

This mullet is known only from brackish waters from the Rio Chagres to Bahia, and is said to be common. We know nothing distinctive regarding its habits.

Galapagos Mullet

Mugil thoburni Jordan & Starks

This small mullet reaches a length of 8 inches or more and is known only from the Pacific Coast of tropical America from Guatemala to the Galapagos Islands. It is close to *M. incilis*, from which it differs chiefly in the larger head.

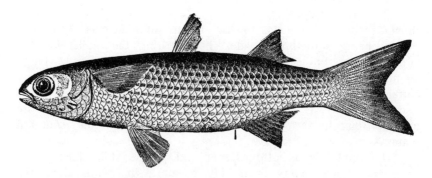

White Mullet; Blue-back Mullet; Liza Blanca

Mugil curema Cuvier & Valenciennes

This mullet occurs from Cape Cod to Brazil on our Atlantic Coast, and on the Pacific side from Chile to Lower California. It is abundant, especially in the tropics, and enters the sea more freely than *M. cephalus*, next to which it is the most important food species of the family in our waters. It is a common fish in the markets of Porto Rico where it is called "Liza" or "Josea." Like the striped mullet, it enters fresh water, specimens having been obtained by us from freshwater streams near Caguas, the interior of Porto Rico.

Colour, dark olive above, with some bluish reflections; silvery below; sides without dark streaks; a small dark blotch at base of pectoral; pectoral and dorsals pale, with numerous small dark punctulations; caudal pale, yellowish at base, the margin blackish; anal and ventrals yellowish; side of head with 2 yellow blotches.

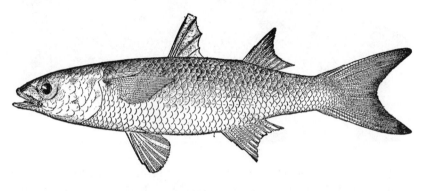

Lisita

Mugil hospes Jordan & Culver

This little mullet is known only from the Pacific Coast of Mexico. It is not uncommon about Mazatlan.

Red-eye Mullet; Liza Ojo de Perdriz

Mugil gaimardianus Desmarest

This species is found from Florida Keys to Cuba, but is not at all common. It reaches a length of about a foot.

Mugil setosus is known only from the Revillagigedo Islands and Mazatlan, it being very abundant about Clarion Island. It closely resembles *M. hospes*, from which it differs widely, however, in its much larger multiserial setæ, and the longer, narrower mouth. It is of no commercial value except locally.

The fan-tailed mullet (*M. trichodon*) is found from Brazil

northward to Key West where it is abundant. It attains a length of 10 inches and is of some little value as food.

The genus *Chænomugil*, distinguished by the absence of an adipose eyelid, has in our waters a single species, *C. proboscideus*,

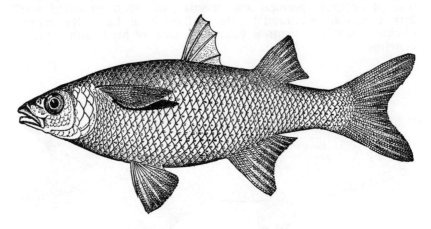

a little mullet, reaching 6 inches in length. It occurs on our Pacific Coast from Mazatlan to Panama. It is not abundant and is not of much food value.

GENUS AGONOSTOMUS BENNETT

The Dajaos

This genus differs from *Mugil* chiefly in not having the stomach gizzard-like. Cleft of mouth extending laterally about to front of eye; teeth small, in villiform bands in each jaw, sometimes also on vomer; edge of lower lip rounded; anal spines usually 2, the first soft ray slender and often taken for a spine. Small, freshwater mullets found in mountain streams in tropical regions. The American species constitute the subgenus *Dajaus*, characterized by the presence of teeth on the palatines.

Four species have been recognized as occurring within our limits, none being of much importance as food.

The dajao (*A. monticola*) is found in freshwater streams of the West Indies and eastern Mexico, and is the most abundant and best

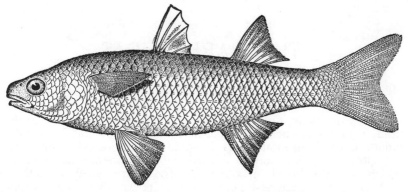

known species of the genus. It is very common in the streams of Porto Rico and is much used as food. It reaches a length of a foot.

Colour, brownish above, scales very dark-edged on upper $\frac{3}{5}$ of side; under parts white; top of head dark; cheeks and opercles white with brassy shades; axil black; a black blotch at base of caudal, disappearing with age; dorsal spines dark; soft dorsal brassy at base, pale at tip; pectoral and ventrals pale; anal yellowish, pale at tip; caudal darker, yellowish at base; peritoneum black.

The genus *Joturus*, characterized by the simple stomach and the coarse truncate incisors, contains only one species. This is the joturo or bobo *(J. pilchardi)*. This species of mullet is an in-

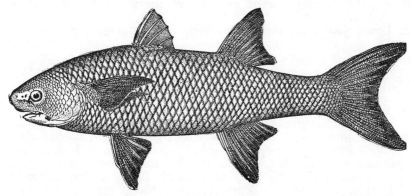

habitant of mountain torrents in the larger islands of the West Indies, also in Costa Rica, and about Vera Cruz and Panama. It attains a length of 2 feet and is one of the largest of the family.

It comes to the Havana market from the Rio Almendares and is a food-fish of some importance.

THE BARRACUDAS

Family XXVII. Sphyrænidæ

Body elongate, subterete, covered with small cycloid scales; head very long, pointed, pike-like, scaly above and on sides; mouth large, horizontal; jaws long, lower projecting; upper jaw not protractile, its border formed by the premaxillaries behind which are the broad maxillaries; large, sharp, unequal teeth on both jaws and palatines, none on vomer; usually a very strong, sharp canine near tip of lower jaw; opercular bones without spines or serrations; gill-openings wide, the membranes not united, free from the isthmus; gillrakers very short or obsolete; pseudo-branchiæ well developed; lateral line well developed and straight.

The family contains a single genus with about 20 species, 6 or 7 of which occur within our limits; only 1 or 2 of them are much valued as food.

a. Scales large, 75 to 85 in lateral line; origin of first dorsal behind root of ventrals, over last third or fourth of pectoral; body compressed;....................*barracuda*, 259
aa. Scales moderate, 110 to 130 in lateral line; body subterete or compressed.
b. Pectoral reaching front of spinous dorsal; maxillary reaching front of orbit.
c. Lower jaw with fleshy tip; teeth very strong; scales 110;
ensis, 259
cc. Lower jaw without fleshy tip; teeth strong; scales 130;
guachancho, 259
bb. Pectoral not reaching front of first dorsal; maxillary not reaching front of orbit.
d. Eye large; teeth small; interorbital area convex; median ridge of frontal groove not well developed;........*picudilla*, 260
dd. Eye small; teeth larger; interorbital area flattish; median ridge of frontal groove prominent;..................*borealis*, 260
aaa. Scales very small, 150 to 170 in lateral line; origin of first dorsal well behind tip of pectoral; body slender, subterete.
e. Body less slender, the depth $7\frac{1}{2}$; scales 160 to 170;.*argentea*, 260
ee. Body very slender, the depth 9 or 10; scales about 150;
sphyræna, 260

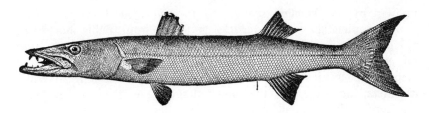

Great Barracuda; Picuda

Sphyræna barracuda (Walbaum)

The great barracuda is found from Brazil northward through the West Indies to Pensacola, Charleston and the Bermudas. It is common in the tropics and is the largest and most voracious of the genus, reaching a length of 6 feet. It is as fierce as a shark and is sometimes very dangerous to bathers. This fish is occasionally taken with hook and line at Key West where it has some value as a food-fish. Its flesh has been reputed poisonous and at times its sale in the Cuban markets has been forbidden. But as a number of the best food-fishes of the West Indies have at one time or another been tabooed by Cuban law, this can not be regarded as conclusive evidence that the flesh of this fish is really unwholesome.

Colour, silvery, darker above; side in young with about 10 dark blotches which break up and disappear with age; some inky spots, usually on posterior part of body, very conspicuous in both old and young; soft dorsal, anal and ventral fins black, except on margins; pectoral plain, except upper margin which is black; fins of young nearly plain.

Another species, *S. ensis*, occurs in the Gulf of California and southward to Panama. It is rather common, reaches a length of 2 feet, and is used as food. It may be readily distinguished from the only other species known from the west coast (the California barracuda) by its larger scales, which are 110 to 130 in lateral line, instead of 166 in the latter.

A third species *(S. guachancho)*, called guachanche or gua-chanche pélon, has about the same distribution as the great barracuda but is occasionally found as far north as Woods Hole. It is a slender species, reaching 2 feet in length, and is not uncommon in the tropics. From *S. barracuda*, it may be known by its smaller scales (120 to 130 instead of 75 to 85).

The picudilla *(S. picudilla)* is found from Bahia northward to the West Indies, chiefly about the coasts of Cuba. It does not seem to be common anywhere. It reaches a length of 18 inches and is closely allied to the northern barracuda, from which it differs, however, in the much larger eye, the smaller teeth, the convex interorbital, and in having the median ridge of the frontal groove well developed.

The northern barracuda *(S. borealis)* is the common species on the Atlantic Coast of the United States from Cape Fear to Cape Cod. It is a small species, rarely used as food, and closely resembles *S. picudilla.*

The California barracuda *(S. argentea)* occurs on our Pacific Coast from San Francisco to Cape San Lucas, very common among the Santa Barbara Islands. About Santa Catalina Island and San Diego it is one of the common and important game-fishes. It reaches a length of 4 or 5 feet. It is a long, slender fish, closely related to the European barracuda, from which it appears to differ chiefly in the somewhat greater depth and smaller scales.

Sphyræna sphyræna is the common species on the coasts of Europe and neighbouring islands. Within our limits it has been reported only from the Bermudas. It is known as spet or sennet.

Trolling for the great barracuda on the Florida coast is a favourite sport. It is done either from a sail-boat or row-boat, and a squit is a choice bait. Or, with boat anchored, they may be taken with tarpon rod and reel, 21 line, and wire snood $1\frac{1}{2}$ feet long. For bait use live mullet, spot, grunt, or other small fish. Do not use a sinker; keep the bait on or near the surface. When the fish bites, let him run a few feet and strike, then play him until he surrenders.

THE THREADFISHES

Family XXVIII. Polynemidæ

Tʜɪs is a small family of tropical fishes bearing superficial resemblances to the *Mugilidæ* on the one hand and the *Sciænidæ* on the other. They may be distinguished by the abdominal ventrals, the presence of 2 dorsal fins, the anterior of spines only, and by having the lower 5 to 8 rays of the ventral fin detached and filamentous. The family contains 4 genera and about 25 species, only 2 of the former and about 5 of the latter being found in our waters.

The 2 genera of this family (*Polynemus* and *Polydactylus*) both have species in our waters, only those of the latter being of any value.

Polydactylus differs from *Polynemus* in the shorter soft dorsal, the serrate preopercle, and the toothed vomer. Numerous species in warm seas, but only 4 within our limits.

a. Pectoral filaments 6, rarely 5; . . . .*approximans,* 261
aa. Pectoral filaments 7; . . . .*virginicus,* 261
aaa. Pectoral filaments 8 or 9.
b. Maxillary less than ½ length of head; pectoral filaments 8;
octonemus, 262
bb Maxillary more than ½ length of head; pectoral filaments usually 9; . . . .*opercularis,* 262

Polydactylus approximans, whose only vernacular name is raton, is found on the Pacific Coast of tropical America from San Diego to Panama. It reaches a foot in length and is a common food-fish at Guaymas, Mazatlan and Panama.

Colour, yellowish white, darker above; pectoral black in adult.

The barbudo or barbu (*P. virginicus*) is an abundant and useful food-fish, found throughout the West Indies and north to the Florida Keys. About Porto Rico it is common and highly esteemed. It reaches a length of a foot.

Colour, whitish-olive above, dirty white below; spinous dorsal dark; soft dorsal and anal pale, with dark punctulations; pectoral with irregular black blotches, the filaments white; ventrals dark, paler on margins.

The threadfish (*P. octonemus*) occurs along our South Atlantic and Gulf coasts from New York to the Rio Grande. It is

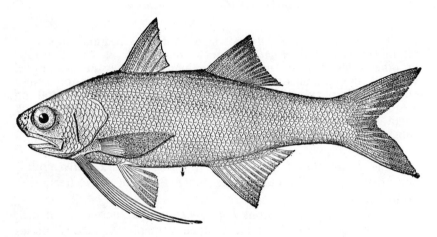

rather rare northward, but is more common on the Texas coast. It frequents sandy shores.

Colour, light olivaceous, tinged with dark punctulations; belly whitish; pectorals pale in the young, black in the adult.

The young of some species of thread-fish, probably *P. octonemus*, are common along the Texas coast where they are often seen in large numbers in shallow water on sandy bottom. These fishes vary greatly with age, the pectoral filaments becoming much shorter with age.

P. opercularis is an unimportant species found on our Pacific Coast from Cape San Lucas to Panama. It is generally common and reaches only a few inches in length.

THE SAND LAUNCES

Family XXIX.   Ammodytidæ

THE sand launces constitute a small family of small, saltwater fishes found chiefly in northern regions.   The single genus, *Ammodytes*, contains 3 or 4 species on our northern coasts.   *A. alascanus* occurs in the North Pacific.   It reaches a length of 6 to 8 inches and is a delicious panfish.

The common sand launce, sand eel, or lant (*A. americanus*)

Common Sand Launce

is abundant on our Atlantic Coast from Cape Hatteras northward. *A. personatus* is another Pacific species, being common from Monterey northward.   It is particularly abundant on sandy shores about Unalaska where we have seined it in very great numbers. All these species are delicious little fishes, the flesh being firm and sweet, similar to that of the smelt.

They swim in immense schools at the surface, and frequently imbed themselves in the sand where they often remain above low-water mark while the tide is out.   Why they do this is not well understood, for they are wanderers, sometimes appearing in immense numbers on the coast and then disappearing as mysteriously as they came.   With their sharp noses and slender bodies they have little difficulty in imbedding themselves several inches deep in the soft sand.   On the sands of Portobello, near Edinburgh, people take advantage of this habit, and when it is discovered that a shoal of sand-eels have hidden in the sand, they sally out, armed with spades, rakes, shovels, and forks and dig them out.   When free of the sand they leap about with great agility, and the fun in catching them probably give rise to the saying, "as jolly as a sand-boy."

THE SQUIRREL-FISHES

Family XXX. Holocentridæ

BODY oblong or ovate, moderately compressed, covered with very strong ctenoid or spinous scales; head with large muciferous cavities; eyes lateral, very large; preorbital very narrow; mouth moderate, oblique; premaxillaries protractile; maxillary very large, with supplemental bone; bands of villiform teeth on jaws, vomer and palatines; opercular and membrane bones of head generally serrated or spinescent along their edges; branchiostegals 8; gill-membranes separate, free from the isthmus; pseudobranchiæ present; no barbels; sides of head scaly; lateral line present; dorsal fin very long, deeply divided, with about 11 strong spines depressible in a scaly groove; anal with 4 spines, the third longest and strongest; ventrals thoracic, with one spine and 7 rays; caudal deeply forked, with sharp rudimentary rays or fulcra at base; vertebræ about 27; pyloric cœca 8 to 25; air-bladder large, sometimes connected with the organ of hearing. General colour red. Genera 4, species about 70, gaily-coloured inhabitants of tropical seas, abounding about coral reefs. Only 4 genera and about 12 species in our waters.

a. Preopercle without conspicuous spine at its angle.
b. Scales very large and rough, about 30;.........*Ostichthys,* 264
bb. Scales moderate, 35 to 45;.... ....*Myripristis,* 265
aa. Preopercle with a conspicuous spine.
c. Suborbital arch simply serrated, scales moderate.
d. Mouth moderate; lower jaw slightly included, its length less than half head;........................*Holocentrus,* 265
dd. Mouth very large; lower jaw projecting, its length more than half head;............................*Flammeo,* 266
cc. Suborbital arch armed with three long spines curved forward............................. ....*Plectrypops,* 267

The genus *Ostichthys* is known by its very large scales. The single species, *O. trachypomus,* is found only in the West Indies, particularly about Cuba, and even there it appears to be rare. Colour, carmine red, darker above; side with about 10 alternate streaks of deep red and rose; fins all red.

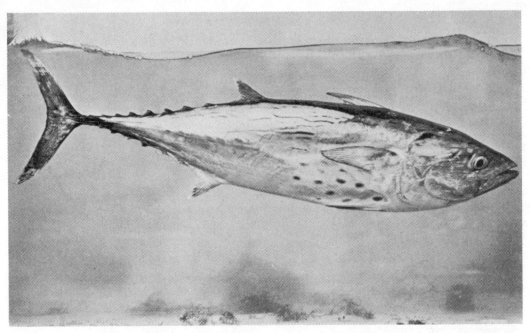

BONITO, *Sarda sarda*.   DEAD

SQUIRREL-FISH. *Holocentrus ascensionis*

KING-FISH OR CERO, *Scomberomorus cavalla.* DEAD

SPANISH MACKEREL, *Scomberomorus maculatus.* DEAD

GENUS MYRIPRISTIS CUVIER

This genus is closely related to *Holocentrus*, from which it differs externally chiefly in the absence of the large spine at the angle of the preopercle. Air-bladder divided into 2 parts by a transverse constriction; pyloric cœca 9.

Species rather numerous in tropical seas; gay-coloured inhabitants of coral reefs and rock pools. Four species in our waters, none of them of much value as food.

The most important of these is the candil, or frère-jacques *(M. jacobus)*, which is a common fish in the West Indies and south to Brazil. It reaches a foot in length, but is of little food-value.

Colour, deep crimson, paler below; a blood-red bar across opercle and base of pectoral, becoming black in spirits; fins red, the vertical ones edged with whitish. A brilliantly coloured fish.

Myripristis occidentalis is a small species, reaching a length of only 6 inches, occurring only on the Pacific Coast of Mexico; said to be common in rock pools about Cape San Lucas.

Colour, reddish, purple above, silvery below, with many dark points, especially along edges of scales; fins pale, except a darker border along spinous dorsal.

GENUS HOLOCENTRUS SCOPOLI

The Squirrel-fishes

Body oblong, moderately compressed, ventral outline nearly straight, the back a little elevated, the caudal peduncle very slender; head compressed, narrowed forward; opercle with a strong spine above, below which the edge is sharply serrate; a strong spine at angle of preopercle; orbital ring, preorbital, preopercle, interopercle, subopercle, occiput, and shoulder-girdle with their edges sharply serrate; mouth small, terminal, the lower jaw slightly included; maxillary broad, striate, with a supplemental bone; eye very large; scales moderate, closely imbricated, the free margins strongly spinous; lateral line continuous; dorsal deeply emarginate, the spines usually 11, depressible in a groove; soft dorsal short and high; anal with 4 spines, the first and second quite small, the third very long and strong, the fourth smaller; caudal widely forked, both lobes with rudimentary rays spine-like; ventrals large, I, 7, the spine very strong.

Species numerous, remarkable for the great development of sharp spines almost everywhere on the surface of the body. About 8 or 9 species in our waters.

Squirrel-fish; Candil

Holocentrus ascensionis (Osbeck)

This fish frequents rocks and reefs throughout the West Indies and is especially abundant in Cuba. It is common about Porto Rico where it attracts at once by reason of its brilliant colouration and the excessive sharpness and completeness of its armature. It is a beautiful fish, reaching a length of 1 to 2 feet, not much valued as food, but often seen in the markets. It occurs as far north as Florida and has been taken at St. Helena.

Head $3\frac{1}{10}$; depth $3\frac{1}{8}$; eye $2\frac{4}{5}$; snout 4; maxillary $2\frac{1}{8}$; mandible 2; interorbital 2 in eye; D. XI, 15; A. IV, 10; scales 4-48-7, 6 before dorsal; cœca 25; vertebræ 11+16. Body considerably compressed, back moderately elevated. Colour, bright rosy-red, paler below; shining longitudinal streaks along rows of scales; fins light red; spinous dorsal largely golden-olive, the edge scarlet; head very red above, a white bar downward and backward from eye; colours all fading in alcohol.

In the Bahamas is found subspecies *rufus*, in which the preopercular spine reaches about to root of pectoral.

GENUS FLAMMEO JORDAN & EVERMANN

This genus is distinguished from *Holocentrus* by the very large mouth and projecting lower jaw which is more than half the head in length. The single known species is the marian,

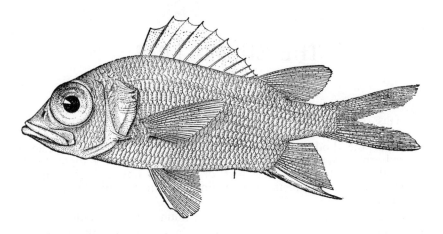

F. marianus, which is found only about Cuba. It is of little importance as a food-fish.

The genus *Plectrypops* differs from *Holocentrus* chiefly in having the preopercle armed with 3 strong teeth which are curved forward. The single species (*P. retrospinis*) is known only from Cuba.

About the coral reefs of the Hawaiian Islands are many different species of squirrel-fishes, all exceedingly brilliant in colouration. In the language of the natives they are called " aleihi." All of the species are more or less red, some being solid red, others red with narrow longitudinal stripes of yellow or white, and others with the fins rich lemon yellow edged more or less with red.

THE SURMULLETS

Family XXXI. Mullidæ

THIS family is briefly characterized by having the ventrals definitely I, 5, thoracic and separate, gill-openings in front of pectorals, the body covered with large, slightly ctenoid scales, the suborbital without a bony stay, 2 dorsal fins remote from each other, both short, the first of 6 to 8 rather high spines, pectoral entire, no finlets, lateral line unarmed, and throat with 2 long barbels.

Genera about 5, species about 40; found in all tropical seas, many of them highly valued as food. In our waters there are 3 genera and about 8 species.

a. Teeth on lower jaw, vomer and palatines;........*Mullus,* 268
aa. Teeth on both jaws; vomer and palatines toothless.
b. Teeth small, subequal, in villiform bands in both jaws;...
Mulloides, 269
bb. Teeth rather strong, unequal, in one or 2 series in each
jaw...*Upeneus,* 270

GENUS MULLUS LINNÆUS

The Surmullets

Villiform teeth on the lower law, and on vomer and palatines, none in the upper jaw, the bone forming a hook over the maxillary well developed; no spines on opercle; interorbital space wide and flat; otherwise as in *Upeneus,* the head rather shorter.

The single species of this genus in our waters is the red mullet, or red goat-fish *(M. auratus)* which is found on our Atlantic coast from Cape Cod to Pensacola. It is occasionally taken in some numbers at Woods Hole, and is sometimes plentiful about Sandy Hook in September and October.

On the Red Snapper Banks off the west coast of Florida it is frequently found in the spewings of snappers and groupers. It reaches a length of 8 inches, and is closely related to the

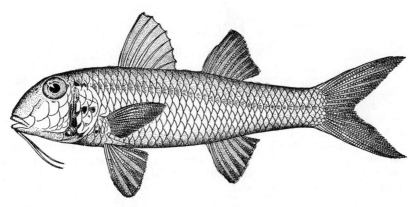

European *M. barbatus,* and even closer to *M. surmuletus,* from which it differs chiefly in having the fins lower, and having a yellow instead of a black dorsal band. It is not abundant enough to be of any value as a food-fish.

Colour, scarlet, becoming crimson where the scales are removed; snout scarlet; side with 2 distinct yellow bands; caudal scarlet; first dorsal with an orange band at base and a yellow band higher up, rest of fin pale; second dorsal mottled scarlet and pale; anal and ventrals plain, pectorals reddish; iris violet, dusky above, sides of head with silvery lustre.

The genus *Mulloides* is distinguished by having its teeth in villiform bands.

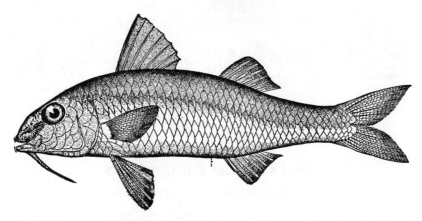

The single species found in our waters is *Mulloides rathbuni,* which occurs in the Gulf of California.

GENUS UPENEUS CUVIER
The Goatfishes

Body oblong, compressed; mouth moderate, nearly horizontal, low, the jaws subequal; eye large, high up, posterior; opercle short and deep, with a posterior spine; each jaw with strong, unequal teeth, in 1 or 2 series; no teeth on vomer or palatines; lips well developed; the bone which forms a hook over the maxillary less developed than in *Mullus;* interorbital space convex and narrow; opercle ending in one spine; barbels nearly as long as head; scales very large, somewhat ctenoid; lateral line continuous; head covered with large scales.

Species numerous in tropical seas. About 7 species within our limits.

a. Teeth in each jaw uniserial (or irregularly biserial above); all the teeth coarse and distinct;..............*maculatus*, 270
aa. Teeth on each jaw biserial, at least in front.
b. Dorsal and caudal with dark crossbands;.............*parvus*, 271
bb. Dorsal and caudal plain yellow;...............*martinicus*, 271

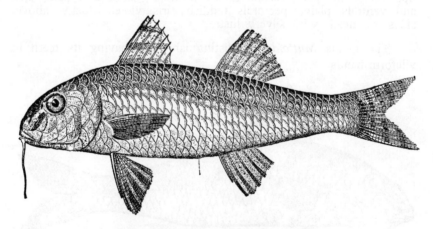

Red Goatfish; Salmonete

Upeneus maculatus (Bloch)

Generally common from Rio Janeiro through the West Indies to Key West. It occurs in abundance about Porto Rico where it is used extensively as a food-fish. It reaches a length of about 10 inches.

Head $3\frac{1}{5}$; depth $3\frac{7}{10}$; eye 4 to 5; snout $1\frac{4}{5}$; maxillary $3\frac{1}{5}$; mandible $2\frac{2}{5}$; interorbital $3\frac{2}{3}$; preorbital $3\frac{1}{3}$; D. VII-I, 8; A. II, 7; pectoral $1\frac{1}{2}$; ventral $1\frac{2}{5}$; caudal $1\frac{1}{8}$; scales 3-30-5. Body little compressed, tapering posteriorly to the long caudal peduncle; snout very long; mouth small, maxillary not nearly reaching eye; throat with 2 long barbels, reaching to margin of preopercle or beyond. Colour, red above, merging into light yellow on the sides, becoming pale-greenish below; oblique bluish streaks on head; several longitudinal rows of light blue round spots, much smaller than pupil, on side, the 2 rows above lateral line plainest; about 4 diffuse blotches of darker red on the side; spinous dorsal light red at base, yellowish outwardly; soft dorsal pale bluish, with some light yellow on membranes and red on middle rays; pectoral chiefly yellow, with red on rays; ventrals pale blue, with streaks of red and yellow on first rays; barbels pink near base, yellow distally.

Upeneus dentatus is a rare species known only from Cape San Lucas, La Paz, Guaymas, and Tres Marias Islands. Colour, dusky above, sides bright rosy, a broad red band extending from eye to caudal. It reaches a foot in length.

Upeneus parvus is another rare species, known only from Cuba. Colour, vermilion above, fading to white below; a yellow band along side, with similar narrower streaks below; ventrals and anal yellow; other fins pale, with dusky cross-bands, 3 on first dorsal, 2 on second, and 5 on each caudal lobe.

Yellow Goatfish; Salmonete Amarilla

Upeneus martinicus Cuvier & Valenciennes

This species occurs from Florida southward among the West Indies, it being known from Key West, Jamaica, Cuba, Martinique, and Porto Rico, about which last island it is less common than the red goatfish. It reaches 12 inches in length and is a good food-fish.

Resembling *U. maculatus* in form, but with slightly larger eye, smaller scales and weaker teeth which are arranged in more than one series. Colour, pale-blue and pink or pale-red, the latter chiefly above, the blue below; a straight yellow band from eye to base of upper caudal rays; a black vertical bar at base of caudal; head with yellow streaks and reddish patches; pectorals red; ventrals, anal, and caudal reddish near base, outer part yellow; dorsals yellow, plainest near tips. These colours fade in spirits.

271

THE MACKERELS

Family XXXII. Scombridæ

Body elongate, fusiform, not much compressed, covered with minute, cycloid scales, those anteriorly forming a corselet; lateral line undulate; head subconic, pointed anteriorly; mouth rather large, premaxillaries not protractile; no supplemental maxillary bone; jaws with sharp teeth; preopercle entire; opercle unarmed; gill-openings very wide, the membranes not united, free from the isthmus; pseudobranchiæ large; branchiostegals 7; dorsal fins 2, the first of rather weak spines, depressible in a groove, the second similar to the anal, the elevated anterior lobe always distinct; anal spines weak; last rays of dorsal and anal detached and separate, forming in each case a series of finlets; caudal peduncle extremely slender, keeled, the caudal lobes abruptly divergent and falcate, the fin adapted for rapid motion; ventral fins I, 5, thoracic and well developed; lower pharyngeals separate; stomach sac-shaped; pyloric cœca numerous; air-bladder small, sometimes absent. Colouration, metallic, often brilliant, the prevailing shade steel-blue.

Genera about 20, species about 60. Fishes of the high seas, many of them cosmopolitan, and all having a wide range; most of them valued as food-fishes, the flesh being firm and oily, but sometimes coarse. Eight genera are represented in our waters by about 15 species.

a. Caudal peduncle without median keel on each side; ......
Scomber, 273
aa. Caudal peduncle with a median keel on each side.
b. Dorsal spines 10 to 16.
c. Body scaleless, except about the lateral line and corselet.
d. Dorsals well separated, the interspace more than half head.
Auxis, 276
dd. Dorsals contiguous, the interspace not one-fifth length of head; ....*Gymnosarda,* 277
cc. Body wholly covered with small scales, those on corselet and lateral line sometimes enlarged.
e. Teeth of jaws slender, subconical, little if at all compressed; gillrakers numerous; corselet distinct; pectorals inserted low.
f. Vomer and palatines with villiform or sand-like teeth; body robust, not compressed.

g. Pectoral short, not reaching much beyond tip of the moderate ventrals; size enormous;.... ....*Thunnus,* 278
gg. Pectoral very long, ribbon-shaped, reaching much beyond front of anal; size moderate;..................*Germo,* 282
ff. Vomer toothless; palatines with a single row of rather strong, conical teeth; body elongate, slightly compressed......
Sarda, 282
ee. Teeth of jaws strong, subtriangular or knife-like, more or less compressed, gillrakers comparatively few; corselet obscure;
Scomberomorus, 283
bb. Dorsal spines about 25;..................*Acanthocybium,* 288

GENUS SCOMBER LINNÆUS

The True Mackerels

Species few, widely distributed, usually swimming in large schools; carnivorous and migratory; everywhere highly valued as food.

a. Air-bladder wanting;........ ....*scombrus,* 273
aa. Air-bladder present;.... ....*japonicus,* 276

Common Mackerel

Scomber scombrus Linnæus

The mackerel inhabits the North Atlantic Ocean. On our coast it ranges from Cape Hatteras to the Straits of Belle Isle; while in European waters it is found from Norway to the Mediterranean and Adriatic.

The mackerel first appear in spring off Cape Hatteras, and later reach the shores of the Middle and New England States and the British possessions, coming in from the sea from a southerly or southeasterly direction. They leave the coast in the same way in fall and winter. It is a wandering fish, and its movements and the causes thereof are not fully understood. It is one of the most abundant fishes on our Atlantic Coast, going in schools often of great extent. It is on record that in 1848 a school was seen one-half mile wide, and at least 20 miles long. Another school, seen in 1877 off Block Island, was estimated to contain 1,000,000 barrels. The schools swim at the surface or near it, and in a rather compact body.

Periods of scarcity alternate with seasons of abundance. The New England catch in 1885 was 330,000 barrels, and the average for the 8 years ending in 1885 was 309,000 barrels. In 1886 it dropped to 80,000 barrels, and in the succeeding 10 years it amounted to only 481,000. The yield in 1898 was 5,769,000 pounds, valued at $307,000, and 15,500 barrels salted, valued at $179,000.

In 1900 the catch landed at Boston and Gloucester amounted to 8,889,294 pounds fresh, valued at $389,952, and 15,965,500 pounds salted, valued at $837,743, or a total of 24,854,794 pounds, valued at $1,227,695. For 1901 the catch landed at these 2 ports amounted to 14,637,615 pounds, valued at $704,375.

The spawning season on our coasts extends from May to July, June probably being the principal month. The spawning grounds are in rather deep water along the coast from Long Island to the Gulf of St. Lawrence. Most of the bays and sounds on the New England Coast contain important spawning-grounds. Prior to spawning, and for several weeks after, the mackerel are lean and poor, and do not make No. 1 fish when salted.

The mackerel feeds upon the small crustaceans and other small animals which swarm in the sea, and is, in turn, fed upon by other fishes, birds, and cetaceans. One of the surface-swimming copepods, known as "red feed" or "cayenne," is a favourite food; when mackerel have been feeding freely on it, they spoil very quickly after being caught, owing to their sides rotting or "burning." Among the fish which the mackerel eat may be named herring, anchovy, sand launce, menhaden, and silversides. Among fishes, sharks are, perhaps, the worst enemies of the mackerel. Other fish-enemies are the bluefish and cod. Porpoises and whales are often seen feeding on the mackerel schools. Large squid do great damage to small mackerel and, among birds, the gannet is especially destructive.

As a food-fish, the mackerel is one of the best and most valuable. On our coast the vessel fishery is carried on chiefly from Gloucester. The vessels go south in the early spring, falling in with the fish when they first appear off our southern coast, and landing their catch fresh at Philadelphia and New York. The fleet next seeks the school off the southern shore of Nova Scotia and follows it to the Gulf of St. Lawrence. Most of the fall fishing is done on the New England shore. Some of the finest fishing vessels in the United States are engaged in this fishery. In recent years the fleet has numbered 150 to 225 vessels, but formerly nearly 1,000 were engaged in this business.

The shore and boat fishing is carried on from New Jersey to Maine, the catch being usually sold fresh.

The local mackerel has so fallen off in recent years that the catch does not supply the home demand, and large quantities are received, both fresh and salt, from Norway, Ireland, and the British provinces.

The United States Fish Commission has undertaken the artificial propagation of the mackerel, but the results have not yet been satisfactory. In 1896, 24,000,000 eggs were collected, but only a small percentage hatched. The mackerel egg is exceedingly small, it being only $\frac{1}{24}$ of an inch in diameter. The eggs average about 40,000 to the fish, but 200,000 have been taken from 1 fish. The largest mackerel would doubtless produce 1,000,000 eggs each. The period of incubation is about 5 days in water at 58°.

Small mackerel are known among fishermen as "spikes," "blinkers," and "tinkers." Spikes are the smallest caught by the commercial fishermen, they being 5 or 6 inches long and 5 to 7 months old, or younger. Tinkers are under 9 inches in length and are supposed to be about 2 years old. Blinkers are intermediate in size and age. Maturity is probably attained in the fourth year.

The common mackerel is so well known as to render a detailed description unnecessary.

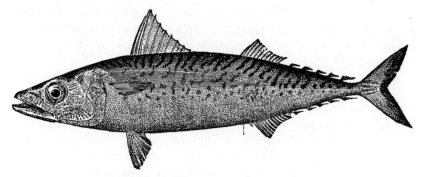

Chub Mackerel; Tinker Mackerel

Scomber japonicus Houttuyn

This mackerel is widely distributed, occurring in both the Atlantic and Pacific, north in the former to England and Maine, and to San Francisco on our west coast. It is very common in the Mediterranean and off southern California.

The history of the chub mackerel on our Atlantic Coast shows great variation in abundance. Up to about 1840 it was apparently an abundant fish, but between 1840 and 1850 it seems to have wholly disappeared from our coast. But in 1879 a considerable school was seen at Provincetown. It again disappeared in 1880, but is not rare at the present time.

This is an excellent food-fish and has been regarded even as superior to the common mackerel.

Colour, blue with about 30 wavy, blackish streaks which reach just below lateral line, some of these forming reticulations enclosing pale spots; more than 20 black specks or mucous pores on base of preopercle, generally arranged in more than 1 row; belly and sides silvery, but always with roundish dusky spots or cloudings in the adult; a black axillary spot.

GENUS AUXIS CUVIER

The Frigate Mackerels

Body oblong, plump, mostly naked posteriorly, anteriorly covered with small cycloid scales, those of the pectoral region enlarged, forming a corselet; snout very short, conical, scarcely compressed; mouth rather small, the jaws equal; teeth very small, mostly in a single series, on jaws only; tail very slender, depressed, with a rather large keel on each side; first dorsal short, some distance from second; second dorsal and anal small, each with 7 or 8 finlets; no air-bladder; gillrakers numerous, very long and slender.

The only species of this genus is the frigate mackerel (*A. thazard*). This fish occurs in all warm seas. On our Atlantic

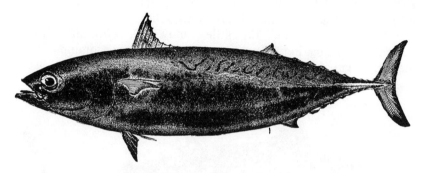

Coast it is seen occasionally as far north as Cape Cod. It appears to be very erratic in its movements, and rarely reaches the United States coasts. It swims in large schools and sometimes appears in immense numbers. In the Adriatic it is called "Timberello."

It resembles in some respects the common mackerel; in other characters it resembles the bonito, the genus *Auxis* being intermediate between *Scomber* and the related genera *Pelamys* and *Orcynus*. It is not much valued as food.

Colour, blue, variegated with darker above, becoming paler with age; belly silvery.

GENUS GYMNOSARDA GILL

The Little Tunnies

This genus differs from that of the great tunnies in the absence of teeth on the vomer, the complete absence of scales outside the corselet, and in the peculiar development, in the form of a network or trellis, of a portion of the abdominal part of the backbone.

Two species of small size in our waters, little valued as food. The first of these, the ocean bonito (*G. pelamis*) occurs in all warm seas, is pelagic, not common anywhere, and on our Atlantic Coast it has been seen as far north as Cape Cod and the Bermudas. It is also frequent in southern California. This species may be distinguished from the next by the distinct curve in the lateral line below second dorsal and in having 4 lengthwise stripes on side below lateral line.

The other species, the little tunny (*G. alleterata*) is also pelagic, occurring in all warm seas. It is not uncommon in the Mediterranean and the West Indies; on our Atlantic Coast it

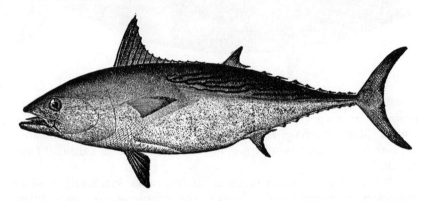

occurs as far north as Cape Cod. It is not known from California. From the ocean bonito it may be readily distinguished by the absence of a curve in the lateral line and in having no stripes.

GENUS THUNNUS SOUTH

The Great Tunnies

Body oblong, robust, with very slender caudal peduncle; head conic; mouth wide, with one series of small, conic teeth in the jaws and bands of minute villiform or sand-like teeth on the vomer and palatines; scales present, those of the pectoral region forming an obscure corselet.

The only known species is the tuna *(Thunnus thynnus).*

This great fish is pelagic in its habits and is found in all warm seas. In the Atlantic it occurs as far north as Newfoundland and the Loffoden Islands, and on the California coast at least to Monterey Bay. It is the "tuna" of the Mediterranean and of California and the "tunny" of the English. On our Atlantic Coast it is the "tunny," "horse mackerel," or "great albacore." They appear on our Atlantic Coast early in summer and remain until October. On some occasions they are very abundant, for so large a fish. During one season one fisherman harpooned 30 of these monsters which weighed in the aggregate at least 30,000 pounds. They are harpooned on the surface of the water, after the manner of taking the sword-fish.

The tuna attains a very great size and is the largest of the mackerel family. A length of 10 or more feet and a weight of 1,500 pounds has been recorded. One taken in 1838, off Cape Ann, was 15 feet long and weighed 1,000 pounds. They do not appear to reach so great a size on the coast of Europe, a 500-pound fish there being considered a monster. Nor do they reach so large a size on the California Coast, the largest example taken with rod and line at Santa Catalina having weighed but 251 pounds. An example measuring 8 feet in length was seen by us at Monterey Bay.

On our Atlantic Coast this fish, there called the horse mackerel, has never attained any reputation as a game-fish, but on the coast of southern California it is one of the monsters much sought by the daring anglers who frequent the famous Santa Catalina resort. Professor Charles F. Holder, who has written so much and so entertainingly concerning the game-fishes of southern California, says "The most sensational fish of these waters is the leaping tuna, which well compares with the tarpon, and personally I prefer it to its Florida and Texas rival, and in my experience, the average large tuna is a match for two tarpons of the same size. The tuna is the tiger of the California seas, a living meteor which strikes like a whirlwind, and when played with a rod that is not a billiard cue or a club in stiffness, will give the average man the contest of his life. My idea of a rod is a 7 or 8½-foot greenheart or split bamboo, with a good cork grip above the reel, the latter of Edward von Hoff make, with a leather pad, break and click. The line should not be larger than a 21-strand, and 600 or 700 feet is enough. The hook either a Van Vleck or a number 9-0 O'Shaughnessy, should have a piano-wire leader 5 or 6 feet in length. The bait, a flying-fish, and you are ready for the game. Your boatman is ready for you at six, the lunch is stowed and you pull out into Avalon Bay over the glass-like sea. The east is a blaze of red, and the placid waters reflect it and the rocks of the precipitous shore. Behind the town that climbs the slopes the mountains reach upward until lost in vagrant fog-masses of burnished silver. The air is soft, like velvet on the cheek, and there is a crispness in the morning strangely at variance with the palms and bananas which top the neighbouring knoll. As your boatman shoves off and clears the beach, he fastens on the big 3-pound flying-fish, the natural food of the tuna, and you gradually pay out until 60, or perhaps 80 feet of line have gone, then fitting the butt of your rod into the leather cap fastened to the seat, rest your thumb upon the leather brake and begin the waiting, which is a part of fishing the world over.

"But it happens, as it often does, that there is no waiting. 'Jim' whispers 'Look out, sir,' and you turn your head to see 3 or 4 flying-fish coming through the air, flushed by the unseen tuna. The blood starts through your veins; your companion, who perchance has never caught a tuna, turns pale and trembles and thinks of the buck fever, recognizing the symptoms; one flying-fish passes over the boat, you duck your head to avoid it, and then soars directly over your bait, and then a mass of white, silvery foam leaps upward. There is a blaze of silver, then loud musical notes, z-e-e-e, z-e-e-e, z-e-e-e, rise on the air as the splendid reel gives tongue, and the fight is on. The tuna turns and rushes seaward, tearing at the line, taking feet, yards, and has 500 feet of line, perhaps, before the boatman has his boat under sternway, and then begins the contest, ranging, according to the individuals, from ten minutes to fourteen hours. At times the game rushes down into the deep channel; again it plays entirely on the surface, varying the performance by repeated rushes at the boat, to turn and dart away again to the melodious clicking of the reel.

"It is big game in every sense of the word, and those who enjoy it are the man and woman who like to face the big game of the forest and mountains. I have seen a fish weighing but

AMBER JACK, *Seriola lalandi*

YELLOW JACK, *Caranx bartholomæi*

RUNNER, *Caranx crysos*

CREVALLE, *Caranx hippos*

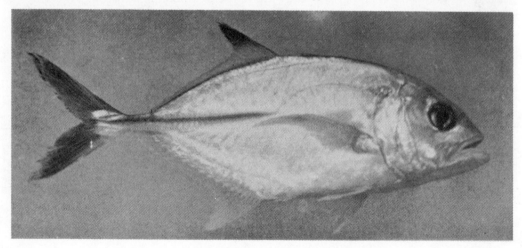

HORSE-EYE JACK *Caranx latus*

125 pounds fight an angler five hours. At that time the fish had towed the boat ten miles off shore, or twenty miles perhaps in all. The angler gave out, the boatman took the rod, and I took the oars and pulled against the fish for two hours, whirling it about in vain efforts to keep the stern to the fish. Then in a heavy and dangerous sea, out of sight of port, a council of war was held. If we continued the contest into the night we should have to make for the mainland, ten miles off, and as a result we surrendered, and the noble fish was ignominiously hauled in by hand, and at the gaffing nearly swamped the boat, being as full of vigour and fight as when it was hooked hours before.

"It was my fortune to hold the record of the largest tuna, 183 pounds, for two years, and as far as I can learn this fish, which fought me four hours and towed me against the oars of my boatman for ten miles, made the hardest fight on record. Its last run was a rush of four miles, and when the magnificent creature was brought to gaff I had reached the limit of endurance; this fish could have towed the heavy boat for hours longer.

"About forty anglers wear the blue button of the Tuna club showing that they have caught tunas weighing over 100 pounds, and from five to ten are added to the list every year, the record being held at present by Colonel C. P. Morehouse of Pasadena, who took a 251-pound tuna in four hours, bringing it to gaff at night in a heavy sea, into which the fish had towed them. If the adventures of the tuna fishermen could be told it would make a volume of thrilling incidents. Some of the large catches are as follows: C. P. Morehouse, 251 pounds; C. F. Holder, 183 pounds; St. J. Earlscliff, 180 pounds; E. L. Doran, 176 pounds; W. C. Arnot, Elmira, N. Y., 140 pounds; J. M. Studebaker, South Bend, Ind., 130 pounds."

The fishermen about the Gulf of Saint Lawrence sometimes take the horse mackerel by means of steel hooks tied to solid lines and baited with herring, especially in the Bay of Chaleur and off Caraquette. The fishing is quite exciting, although tiresome and requiring a good deal of skill, as in the efforts of the fish to escape they pull with such violence as to endanger the lives of the fishermen by dragging them overboard.

GENUS GERMO JORDAN

The Albacores

This genus is close to *Thunnus*, from which it differs chiefly in having the pectoral long and sabre-shaped, the length in the adult about ⅔ that of the body. The only species of this genus is the long-finned albacore *(Germo alalunga)*, a pelagic fish of wide distribution in all tropical seas. It is rarely seen on our

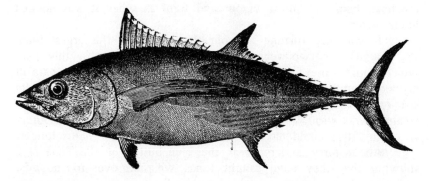

Atlantic Coast but is common in the Mediterranean. On our Pacific Coast it occurs as far north as San Francisco. It is extremely abundant about the Santa Barbara Islands during its spawning season. As a food-fish it is of little value, its flesh being coarse and oily, far inferior to that of the tuna. It is, however, a good game-fish, reaching a length of 3 feet and a weight of 15 or 20 pounds.

GENUS SARDA CUVIER

The Bonitos

This genus is related to *Thunnus* and *Germo*, from which it differs chiefly in having no teeth on the vomer and in the more elongate body. There are 2 species in our waters, fishes of rather large size and metallic colouration.

This genus contains 2 species, *S. sarda* and *S. chilensis.* The first of these is the bonito, a species which lives for the most part in the open sea, wandering hither and thither in large schools, preying upon other pelagic fishes and approaching land only when attracted by abundance of suitable food or for spawning purposes. On our coast it occurs in summer from Cape Cod to Cape Sable, and occasionally off Chesapeake Bay, Cape Hatteras, and in the Gulf of Mexico. It reaches a length of 2 or 3 feet and a weight of 10 to 12 pounds. It is a poor food-fish.

It is distinguished from *S. chilensis* by having 21 spines in the dorsal and the maxillary reaching beyond the orbit.

Colour, dark steel-blue above, with numerous dark narrow stripes obliquely downward and forward from back; under parts silvery.

The California bonito *(S. chilensis)* is found from San Francisco to Patagonia and Japan. It is abundant northward in summer and, as a food-fish ranks with its Atlantic congener, though large numbers are salted and dried. It reaches a length of 2 or 3 feet and a weight of 12 to 16 pounds. During summer and fall it is abundant among the Santa Barbara Islands where, in company with the barracuda, it is taken in large numbers by trolling. It feeds chiefly upon anchovies and squids.

Colour, dark metallic-blue; sides dusky; several blackish stripes running obliquely upward and backward from pectoral region to upper edge of tail, variable in number and direction.

GENUS SCOMBEROMORUS LACÉPEDE

The Spanish Mackerels

Body elongate, wholly covered with rudimentary scales, which do not form a distinct corselet; head pointed, comparatively short and small; mouth wide, the strong teeth in the jaws more or less compressed or knife-shaped; villiform or sand-like teeth on vomer and palatines; maxillary not concealed by preorbital; caudal peduncle with a single keel; spinous dorsal low, of 14 to 18 feeble spines; soft dorsal and anal short, similar, somewhat elevated and falcate, each followed by 7 to 10 finlets; ventrals

283

small; pectoral moderate, near the level of the eye; air-bladder present. Fishes of the high seas, graceful in form and beautiful in colouration; 5 species in our waters.

a. Male with the sides silvery, no spots; female with two rows of brown spots; fins nearly plain;............*concolor*, 284
aa. Each sex with numerous bronze spots on sides; spinous dorsal dark except at base.
b. Soft dorsal inserted in advance of anal;..........*maculatus*, 285
bb. Soft dorsal inserted over anal.
c. Body deep, the depth less than 5 in length.
d. Teeth 26 to 32 on each jaw;......................*sierra,* 286
dd. Teeth about 40 on each jaw....................*regalis*, 286
cc. Body more slender, the depth about 6 in length;........
cavalla, 287

Monterey Spanish Mackerel

Scomberomorus concolor (Lockington)

This species occurs on the coast of California, chiefly in Monterey Bay, where it appears usually in September, disappearing in November. It is never abundant, only a few individuals being seen each season. It attains a length of 30 inches, and a weight of 5 to 8 pounds. It is held in very high esteem as a food-fish, and always brings a high price in market.

Head 5; depth about $4\frac{3}{4}$; eye $5\frac{1}{2}$; D. XVII-16-VIII; A. I, 16-VIII; pectoral 8 in body; teeth about 50 in each jaw. Mouth slightly oblique, the maxillary reaching to posterior edge of pupil; teeth comparatively small, subconic, and little compressed, those on vomer and palatines minute and granular; lateral line slightly wavy, descending obliquely; pectoral inserted rather above axis of body; ventrals small; dorsal spines slender and fragile, the longest 4 in head; dorsal fins separated by an interspace equal to $\frac{1}{8}$ length of base of spinous dorsal; caudal shorter than head, its lower lobe the longer; gillrakers long, 18 below the angle. Colour of male, dark steel-blue, sides silvery, without streaks or spots; female with two alternate series of brown spots, the silvery on sides clouded with dusky; fins nearly plain, dark.

Spanish Mackerel

Scomberomorus maculatus (Mitchill)

The Spanish mackerel is a fish of wide distribution on our Atlantic Coast, ranging north in the fall as far as Cape Ann, and in the south to Brazil. In the West Indies it has been found about Jamaica and Porto Rico, but is probably not known from Cuba. In the Gulf of Mexico and on our South Atlantic Coast it appears irregularly in large schools.

The catch on our Atlantic and Gulf Coasts has been subject to great variations. In the early history of this country the Spanish Mackerel was scarcely known, and not until within the last 30 years has it become of much commercial importance. The catch in 1897 amounted to 1,183,456 pounds, worth $69,778.

It is now one of the most highly prized of all our fishes, and always commands a high price.

Ordinarily it reaches a weight of 6 to 10 pounds, but occasionally very large individuals are taken. The largest we have seen was taken in October, 1901, off Chesapeake Bay, and weighed 25 pounds. It was 41 inches long.

This fish is usually taken in pounds or gillnets, though many are taken by trolling. It is an excellent game-fish. It is a fish of the sunnier climes and comes to us only in the spring, summer and autumn, when it may be seen, sometimes in large schools, swimming at the surface, feeding upon other fishes, often leaping and disporting itself in the sun. The menhaden is probably its principal food, though many other species are eaten.

The Spanish mackerel spawns on the Carolina Coast in April and May and in the lower Chesapeake during the first half of June. Their eggs are very small and very numerous, a 6-pound fish producing about 1,500,000 eggs.

Head $4\frac{1}{2}$; depth $4\frac{1}{2}$; D. XVII-18-IX; A. II-17-IX; maxillary $1\frac{4}{5}$ in head; eye $4\frac{3}{4}$; pectoral $1\frac{3}{4}$; ventral $4\frac{1}{2}$; dorsal and anal lobes subequal, 2 in head. Body elongate, its dorsal and ventral outlines equal; profile straight from snout to dorsal; head small and pointed; mouth large, oblique, the jaws equal; maxillary reaching posterior edge of orbit; teeth large, compressed and sharp, 24 to 26 in each jaw; lateral line undulating, with about 175 pores. Colour, silvery, bluish above; sides with many elliptical spots of dull orange, 2 rows below lateral line and 1 above; spinous dorsal white at base, black above; soft dorsal tinged with yellowish, its margin black; anal white; posterior side of pectoral black, the anterior yellowish with black borders; caudal blackish.

Mexican Sierra

Scomberomorus sierra Jordan & Starks

This species is the Pacific Coast representative of the Spanish mackerel which it very closely resembles and from which it differs only in the more posterior insertion of the soft dorsal and in the colouration. It is known only from Mazatlan, reaches a length of $2\frac{1}{2}$ feet, and is not highly valued as food, but why it is not we are unable to say.

Colour, silvery, dark steel-blue on the back; sides with numerous round spots of the same colour as the back, 3 rows below and 1 above the lateral line; spinous dorsal all black; anal white; posterior surface of pectoral entirely black, anterior yellowish with blackish borders; caudal black. A large example, probably a male, had 5 rows of spots below lateral line, these spots decreasing in size anteriorly toward the belly, but extending nearly to base of ventral fin.

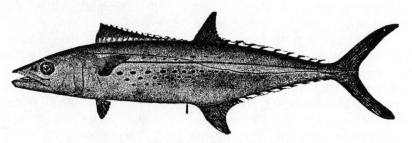

Sierra; Pintado; Kingfish

Scomberomorus regalis (Bloch)

This fine fish is found from Cape Cod to Brazil, but it is not common anywhere except about Florida and Cuba. It grows to 5 or 6 feet in length, 20 pounds or more in weight, and is an excellent game and food-fish. It is found on the south Florida Coast and is caught by trolling. It is not always distinguished by the fishermen from the Spanish mackerel or the cero.

Head $4\frac{1}{4}$; depth $4\frac{1}{2}$; D. XVII-I, 15-VIII; A. II-14-VIII. Body rather elongate, its dorsal and ventral curves about equal; lateral line descending obliquely, undulating along the tail; mouth large, maxillary reaching to below eye; angle of peopercle produced backward; caudal peduncle rather slender, its least depth $5\frac{1}{2}$ in head; caudal fin less widely forked than in the Spanish mackerel; teeth triangular, strongly compressed, about 40 in each jaw; pectoral scaly. Colour, silvery; side with 2 blackish longitudinal bands crossing lateral line below soft dorsal, each posteriorly broken up into longitudinal spots, above and below these are numerous brownish spots in rows, persistent in adult; front of spinous dorsal black.

Kingfish; Cero: Cavalla

Scomberomorus cavalla (Cuvier & Valenciennes)

Of all the host of Florida game-fishes that are used as food this is the greatest. Indeed, there are few game-fishes which excel it in size, strength, swiftness of movement, or fighting powers. The cero is a fish of the tropical seas, often coming in immense numbers to the coasts of Florida and the Carolinas, and ranging north to Cape Cod and south to Brazil and Africa. It is common on our South Atlantic Coast and among the Florida Keys. At Key West it is, next to the grunt, the most important food-fish. It usually appears in November and remains until April, during which time it is caught by trolling. It is said to school at spawning time which is late in winter. As a food-fish it takes a very high rank, the flesh being firm and of excellent flavour.

The cero reaches a length of 5 feet and a weight of 100 pounds. Examples weighing 40 to 50 pounds are not rare. The largest one of which we could find an authentic record at Key West dressed 52 pounds. The average size, however, of those taken about Key West is only about 10 pounds, or perhaps even less. When the Key West fisherman desires large cero he directs his course toward the inshore grounds, lying in about 3 fathoms of water and $1\frac{1}{2}$ to 3 miles from shore, where the water is less clear; and when smaller ones are wanted they are found further off shore along the edge of the Gulf Stream where the water is clearer. The large and smaller one are almost invariably found in separate schools.

The cero is usually caught by trolling and is justly regarded as one of the greatest of all game-fishes. A stout braided line is best, though laid cotton cod-lines are often used. A cod hook with long shank, and a foot or 2 of stout copper or brass wire to withstand the numerous sharp teeth are needed. For bait a strip of white bacon rind, 5 to 8 inches long, cut to resemble a fish, with a slit in the upper end and one in the middle through which it is placed on the hook, the upper end being secured by a fine wire. A block tin squid or a very heavy spinner is, however, a better lure.

In lieu of anything better the hook may be wrapped with white muslin ; tin foil, or anything that the fish can easily see, will answer very well. As a fighter the cero is chiefly famous on account of the marvellous leaps which he makes. Clearing the surface by 10 feet or more is no unusual thing. And Dr. Henshall tells some marvellous stories of its jumping powers, but it is fair to say he does not vouch for them.

Head 5; depth 6; eye large, 2 in snout; D. XV-I, 15-VIII; A. II-15-VIII; pectoral 5; gillrakers very short, less than half diameter of eye, about 8 below angle. Mouth large, maxillary reaching below eye; lateral line decending abruptly below second dorsal; teeth triangular, strongly compressed, about 30 in each jaw. Colour of adult, iron-gray, nearly or quite immaculate; young with the sides with darker yellowish spots; no black blotch on spinous dorsal anteriorly.

GENUS ACANTHOCYBIUM GILL
The Petos

This genus differs from the other Scombroids in the large size of the spinous dorsal, there being about 25 spines instead of 10 to 16 as in the other genera.

The only species is *A. solandri*, known variously as peto, wahoo, and guarapucu, a very large, mackerel-like fish, widely distributed in tropical seas. This great fish reaches our borders only in the West Indies and among the Florida Keys. It reaches a length of 5 or 6 feet and a weight of 50 to 100 pounds, and is known to spawn off Cuba. It is an excellent food-fish and is taken by trolling, but we know nothing regarding its game qualities.

THE ESCOLARS

Family XXXIII. Lepidopidæ

THIS family contains large, mackerel-like fishes with elongate body covered with minute scales.

There are about 9 genera and 17 species, only 3 of which interest us. The first of these is *Ruvettus pretiosus*, a large, deep-water fish, generally valued as food in the tropics. It is abundant about Cuba and the Madeiras, and is often taken in the Mediterranean. It is also occasionally taken off the Grand Banks. Among the common names by which it is known are escolar, rovetto, ruvetto, chicolar, oilfish, scour-fish, and plain-fish. It reaches a weight of 100 pounds.

"The Cubans go 'a-scholaring' ('*á escolarear*') after the fishing for the spearfish has ceased and before that for the red snapper begins."

The flesh is white and flaky, but soft and insipid in the Madeiras, according to Lowe, where its extreme oiliness makes it unwholesome.

Another food species of this family is the rabbit-fish, conejo or Bermuda catfish *(Promethichthys prometheus)*, a large voracious fish of the open sea, found about islands in the tropical Atlantic, chiefly in deep water. In this genus the ventral fin is reduced to a single spine.

THE CUTLASS FISHES

Family XXXIV. Trichiuridæ

BODY extremely elongate, band-shaped, naked, tapering to a point, the ventral fins imperfect or wanting and the spinous and soft parts of the dorsal fin not differentiated. Mouth wide, the jaws armed with strong unequal teeth. Premaxillaries not protractile. Pseudobranchiæ present. Gills 4, a slit behind the fourth; gill-membranes separate, free from the isthmus; lateral line present; dorsal fin very long, low, usually continuous, the rays all similar; caudal fin absent; anal fin very long and low, scarcely rising above the surface of the skin; ventrals thoracic, rudimentary (*Eupleurogrammus*) or wanting; vertebræ in greatly increased number, about 160; air-bladder present; pyloric cœca numerous. Genera 2, species about 6.

The single species in our waters is *Trichiurus lepturus*, known as the cutlass-fish, scabbard-fish, silver-fish, machete, sable,

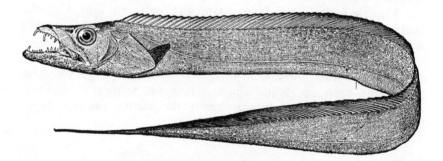

or savola, a long, slender, ribbon-like fish found in the West Indies and north to Virginia. It occurs also on the Pacific Coast about Lower California. It is taken occasionally in the lower Chesapeake and along the South Atlantic Coast. It is not common at Key West and its capture usually excites much interest. In Porto Rico, where it is known by the very appropriate name, machete, it is not rare.

Though not abundant enough to be of commercial importance, it is nevertheless an excellent food-fish.

THE SAILFISHES

Family XXXV.   Istiophoridæ

BODY elongate, much compressed, covered with elongate scutes; bones of upper jaw consolidated into a sword, which is roundish on the edges and spear-like, shorter than in *Xiphias*; jaws with small, persistent granular teeth; ventral fins of 1 or 2 rays each, attached to a pelvic arch; dorsal single or divided into 2 contiguous portions, the first much longer than the second, the fin-rays distinct, the first rays of dorsal distinctly spinous; anal divided, last rays of dorsal and anal suctorial; caudal peduncle with 2 fleshy crests or keels; vertebræ 12+12=24, elongate, hourglass-shaped; neural and hæmal spines flag-like; ribs well developed; air-bladder very large, sacculate, of numerous separate divisions; intestine short, straight; gills reticulated as in *Xiphias*. Two genera, with about 5 species, oceanic, similar in character and habits to the swordfishes, but smaller in size.

The genus *Istiophorus* contains a single species *(I. nigricans)*, known variously as sailfish, spikefish, boohoo, guebucu, voilier, agula volador, etc.

The sailfish occurs in the West Indies and warmer parts of the Atlantic north to Key West and France. It is rather common about the Florida Keys, and examples have been taken at Newport and Savannah. It reaches a length of 6 feet and is an excellent food-fish.

The genus *Tetrapturus*, distinguished from *Istiophorus* by having but one ray in the ventral fin, contains 2 species, the most important of which is *T. imperator*. Among its common names are spearfish, billfish, and aguja blanca.

This great fish reaches a length of 7 feet or more and a weight of 150 pounds. It is found among the West Indies and on our coast occasionally as far north as Cape Cod. It is probably identical with the species found in southern Europe. They swim in deep water, according to Poey, and pass Cuba in pairs in summer.

The spearfish is sometimes taken on the hook. When the fish has swallowed the hook it rises to the surface where it makes prodigious leaps and plunges. At last it is dragged to the boat, secured with a boat-hook, and beaten to death before it is hauled on board. Such fishing is not without danger, for the spearfish sometimes rushes upon the boat, drowning the fisherman, or wounding him with its terrible weapon. The fish becomes furious at the appearance of sharks, which are its natural enemies. They engage in violent combats, and when the spearfish is attached to the fisherman's line, it often receives frightful wounds from these adversaries.

The other species, *T. amplus*, is a rare fish occurring in the West Indies. It reaches a length of 10 feet or more and a weight of 800 pounds. It is the aguja de casta of the Cubans, and would be an important food-fish were it more abundant.

THE SWORDFISHES

Family XXXVI.   Xiphiidæ

THESE are fishes of great size, with long, naked body; upper jaw very much prolonged, forming a "sword," which is flattened horizontally; no teeth in the adult; dorsal fin very long; no ventral fins.

The single species of this family is *Xiphias gladius*, the common swordfish, or espada, a fish of very wide distribution.   It occurs on both coasts of the Atlantic, being most frequent between Cuba and Cape Breton; not rare off Cape Cod and on the Grand Banks; rather common in Southern Europe.   It occurs also in the Pacific, and is occasionally taken about the Santa Barbara Islands.   An enormous fish of the open seas, rivalling the largest sharks in size, and of immense strength of muscle.

The swordfish attracted the attention of the earliest voyagers to America.   As early as 1674, Josselyn, in his "Account of Two Voyages to New England," wrote: "And in the afternoon we saw a great fish called the Vehuella or Sword-fish, having a long, strong and sharp finn, like a sword-blade on the top of his head, with which he pierced our Ship, and broke it off with striving to get loose.   One of our sailors dived and brought it aboard."

The maximum size of the swordfish is 600 to 800 pounds, though examples of more than 400 pounds are not often seen.

The species is rather abundant for so large a fish.   Off the New England Coast 3,000 to 6,000 of these fish are taken every year.   Twenty-five or more are sometimes seen in a single day. One fisherman killed 108 in one year.

The food of the swordfish consists chiefly of the common schooling species of fishes, such as the menhaden, herring, mackerel, bonito and bluefish.   They are said to rise beneath a school of small fish, striking to the right and left with their swords until they have killed a number, which they then proceed to devour.

THE PAPAGALLOS

Family XXXVII. Nematistiidæ

THIS family is related to the *Carangidæ*, from which it is distinguished by the peculiar development of the anal and dorsal spines.

Only a single species, *Nematistius pectoralis*, is known. It

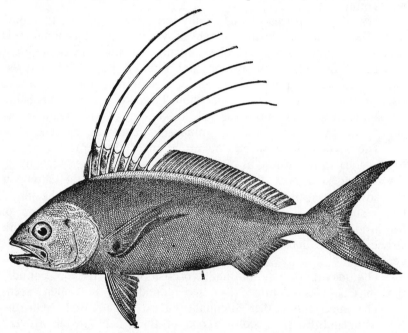

is a large, showily-coloured fish, generally common from the Gulf of California to Panama. It reaches a length of 3 or 4 feet, and is used for food at Guaymas, La Paz, Mazatlan, and perhaps elsewhere. It is known as the pez de gallo, or papagallo, and is one of the most stately fishes in our waters, its long, brightly coloured rays giving it a most striking appearance.

Colour, plumbeous on the back and opercles; sides golden; an indigo-blue crossband on snout, another on forehead, a third from nape to subopercle; a broad indigo band from first dorsal spine to near vent; a curved band from sixth dorsal spine downward and across to base of upper caudal rays; dorsal spines banded with alternate blue-black and white; lower half of pectoral black.

THE PAMPANOS

Family XXXVIII. Carangidæ

BODY more or less compressed, and often elevated, sometimes naked, or more usually covered with small, thin, cycloid scales; head compressed, the occipital keel prominent, usually trenchant; mouth of varying size, the teeth generally small; premaxillaries usually protractile; lateral line complete, anteriorly arched, the posterior part straight, sometimes armed with bony plates; dorsal fins more or less separated, the spinous part rather weak, the spines usually depressible in a groove; anal fin long, similar to the soft dorsal, always preceded by 2 stiff spines, usually separate, but more or less connected with the fin or with each other in the young, these sometimes disappearing with age; often a procumbent spine before the dorsal fin; ventral fins thoracic, well developed, I, 5; caudal peduncle very slender, the lobes widely forked; gill-opening very wide, the membranes usually not connected, free from the isthmus; pseudobranchiæ large, sometimes disappearing with age. Genera about 30, species about 200, abounding in warm seas, often moving north in summer, like the *Scombridæ*. They swim swiftly, often with the dorsal fin above the surface of the water. Most of the species are of wide distribution, and nearly all are valued as food.

The 19 genera represented in our waters by many species are as follows :

a. Premaxillaries not protractile;..................*Oligoplites,* 297
aa. Premaxillaries protractile.
b. Anal fin much shorter than soft dorsal, its base not longer than the abdomen.
c. Dorsal and anal fins without finlets.
d. Membrane of dorsal spines disappearing with age;..*Naucrates,* 298
dd. Membrane of dorsal spines persistent;..............*Seriola,* 299
cc. Dorsal and anal fins each with a detached 2-rayed finlet;
Elagatis, 301
bb. Anal fin about as long as soft dorsal, its base longer than abdomen.
e. Maxillary with a supplemental bone; pectoral long and falcate.
f. Dorsal outline more strongly curved than ventral outline.
g. Dorsal and anal each with a single detached finlet;.*Decapterus,* 302
gg. Dorsal and anal without finlets.
h. Lateral line with well developed scutes for its entire length;
Trachurus, 302
hh. Lateral line with scutes on its straight portion only.

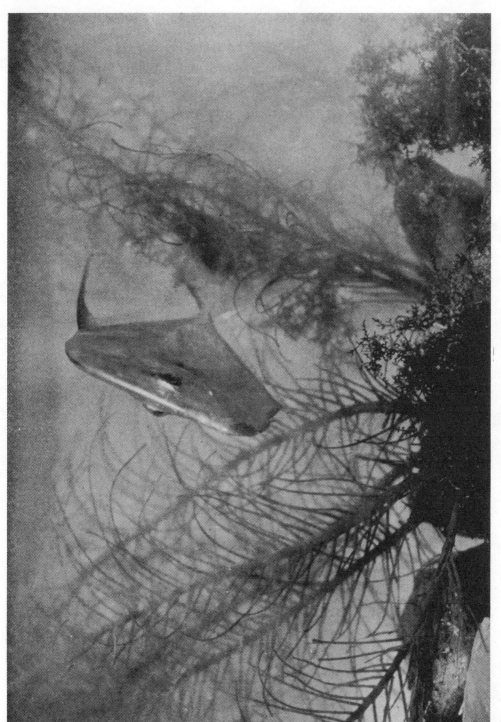

MOONFISH OR LOOK-DOWN, *Selene vomer*

MOONFISH OR LOOK-DOWN, *Selene vomer*

i. Shoulder-girdle with a deep cross-furrow at its junction with the isthmus; body slender;................... *Trachurops,* 303
ii. Shoulder-girdle normal; body deeper.
j. Body oblong or more or less elevated, not as below.
k. Teeth of jaws in few series or one, unequal or at least not forming villiform bands.
l. Maxillary very narrow; head small; teeth on vomer and palatines minute or obsolete;...................... *Hemicaranx,* 303
ll. Maxillary broad; head rather larger; vomer and palatines with teeth;............... .... *Carangus,* 304
kk. Teeth of jaws equally small or wanting, forming villiform bands if present.
m. Teeth very minute, disappearing in the adult; no teeth on vomer or palatines;............................. *Caranx,* 308
mm. Teeth persistent, in bands; vomer and palatines with minute teeth.
n. Soft dorsal with none of its rays produced in filaments;
Carangoides, 308
nn. Soft dorsal with 1 to 6 rays produced in filaments.
o. Body moderately compressed, its edges not trenchant;.. *Citula,* 308
oo. Body deep, greatly compressed, its edges all trenchant.
p. Soft dorsal lobe very high, filamentous;.............. *Alectis,* 308
pp. Soft dorsal lobe low;.... .... *Hynnis,* 309
jj. Body broad-ovate, very strongly compressed;........ *Vomer,* 309
hhh. Lateral line without any scutes;.... .... *Selene,* 311
ff. Dorsal outline less strongly curved than the ventral;
Chloroscombrus, 312
ee. Maxillary without supplemental bone; pectoral short, not falcate.
q. Forehead not much elevated;.................. *Trachinotus,* 313
qq. Forehead more elevated;........................ *Zalocys,* 319

GENUS OLIGOPLITES GILL

The Leather-Jacks

This genus is characterized by the compressed, lanceolate body; slender, unkeeled caudal peduncle; short, compressed, acute head; sharp occipital keel; rather large mouth, with small, sharp teeth in bands on jaws, vomer, and palatines; small, linear, extremely narrow scales which are imbedded in the skin at different angles; unarmed lateral line; and short pectorals.

In our waters there are but 3 species, none of them of much food-value. The common leather-jack or zapatero *(Oligoplites*

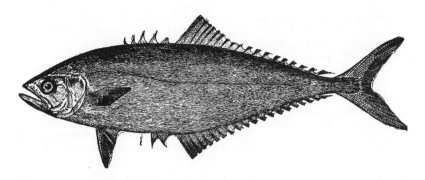

saurus), is found on both coasts of Tropical America, and is common in the West Indies and along the Florida coast, ranging north to New York and Lower California. It reaches a foot in length, and is a very handsome fish, often leaping from the water. It is of very little value as food, the flesh being dry and bony.

The genus *Naucrates* contains the pilot-fish, *N. ductor*, which differs from *Seriola* only in the reduction of the spinous dorsal to a

few (4 or 5) low, disconnected spines. The pilot-fish is a pelagic fish, widely distributed in the open seas. On our Atlantic Coast it is found occasionally from Cape Cod to the West Indies. It reaches 2 feet in length.

GENUS SERIOLA CUVIER

The Amber-fishes

Body oblong, moderately compressed, not elevated; occiput and breast not trenchant; mouth comparatively large, with broad bands of villiform teeth on both jaws, tongue, vomer, and palatines; maxillary with a broad, strong supplemental bone; premaxillaries protractile; scales small; lateral line scarcely arched, forming a keel on caudal peduncle, not armed with bony plates; sides of head with small scales; first dorsal with about 7 low spines, connected by membrane; second dorsal very long, elevated in front; anal similar to soft dorsal but not nearly so long, preceded by 2 very small free spines, which disappear in old fishes; no finlets; ventrals very long; pectorals short and broad.

Species of moderate or large size, often beautifully coloured; most of them valued as food-fishes.

Of the 8 species occurring in our waters 3 or 4 are good food-fishes, and at least one is an excellent game-fish.

a. Head longer than deep, the profile not very steep; a yellow lateral band.
b. Dorsal rays 36 to 38.
c. Mouth rather small, the maxillary barely reaching pupil, $2\frac{2}{3}$ in head; ....*dorsalis*, 300
cc. Mouth large, the maxillary reaching middle of eye, $2\frac{1}{6}$ in head; ....*zonata*, 300
bb. Dorsal rays 30 to 34.
d. Body slender, the depth $3\frac{1}{2}$ to $3\frac{2}{3}$ in length; .....*lalandi*, 301
dd. Body deeper, the depth about 3 in length; ....*dumerili*, 301
aa. Head deeper than long, the anterior profile steep; no yellow lateral band.
e. Dorsal not falcate, its soft rays 32.
f. Body rather elongate, the depth $3\frac{2}{3}$ in length; nuchal band obscure; ....*mazatlana*, 301
ff. Body rather deep, the depth 3 in length; dark nuchal band distinct; ....*fasciata*, 301
ee. Dorsal and anal falcate, their anterior lobes more than half depth of body, the dorsal rays 27 to 30.
g. Nuchal band dark brown or black; ....*rivoliana*, 301
gg. Nuchal band pale yellow; ....*falcata*, 301

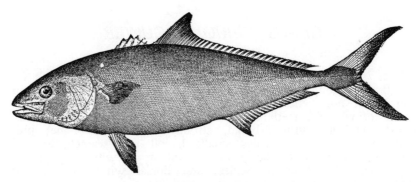

California Yellowtail

Seriola dorsalis (Gill)

The yellowtail is found on our Pacific Coast from Mazatlan and Cape San Lucas north to the Santa Barbara Islands. It usually occurs in abundance about Coronado Island during the spawning season, arriving in July and leaving in the fall. It reaches a length of 3 feet, is an excellent food-fish, and is much sought by anglers. At Coronado Island it is one of the many really great game-fishes.

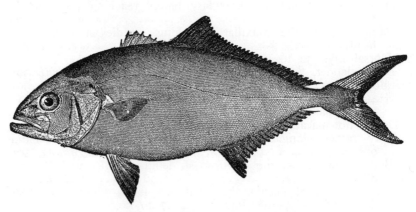

Rudder-fish ; Shark Pilot

Seriola zonata (Mitchill)

This fish is found from Cape Hatteras to Cape Cod. The adult is not common, but the banded young are not rare northward. It attains a length of 2 or 3 feet, but is not highly regarded as a food-fish. It is too rare to be of much interest to the angler.

Colour, bluish above, white below; side with about 6 broad black bars, these forming 3 large blotches on the dorsal and 2 on the anal, these bars growing fainter and disappearing with age; an oblique dark band from the spinous dorsal to the eye, the space above this olivaceous; spinous dorsal black; ventrals mostly black.

Amber-fish ; Coronado

Seriola lalandi Cuvier & Valenciennes

The amber-fish is an immense fish, reaching a length of 5 or 6 feet and a weight of more than 100 pounds, occurring from west Florida to Brazil, and occasionally north to New Jersey. In the Gulf it is rather common and is valued as food.

Colour, dorsal fin dusky, with a light-yellow submarginal band; pectoral fin dusky-yellowish; ventrals yellow and blackish; anal blackish, with pale edge.

Amber-jack

Seriola dumerili (Risso)

This species, also called amber-fish and coronado, is of wide distribution. It occurs both in the Mediterranean and the West Indies. It is rather common about Pensacola and Key West, and is a food-fish of some importance.

Colour, grayish silvery below; a gilt band through eye to caudal, and another through temporal region to front of soft dorsal; fins plain; no dark cross-bands. Very close to *S. lalandi*, but smaller, the body deeper and less compressed; mouth larger than in *S. dorsalis*, but about as in *S. lalandi*.

S. mazatlana, fasciata, rivoliana and *falcata* are unimportant species.

The genus *Elagatis* is close to *Seriola* and contains a single species, *E. bipinnulatus*, a large pelagic fish, reaching a length of $2\frac{1}{2}$ feet. It occurs in most tropical seas and is occasionally seen in the West Indies from which it sometimes strays north to Long Island. It may be known by the 2 small detached finlets and the short anal. It is sometimes called runner.

The genus *Decapterus* contains the mackerel scads of which there are several species, only 5 of which occur within our limits. One of these, *D. punctatus*, known as the scad, round robin or quia-quia, is common on the coasts of Florida and

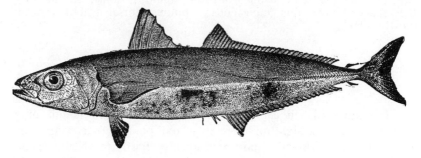

among the West Indies. It reaches a foot in length. Another species is the common mackerel scad, *D. macarellus*, which is found in the warmer parts of the Atlantic. It strays northward on our coast to Cape Cod.

The genus *Trachurus* has only 2 species within our limits, neither of much value as food.

The xurel or saurel, *T. symmetricus*, is common on our Pacific Coast from San Francisco south to the Galapagos. In

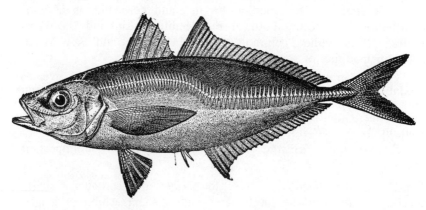

summer it is abundant in the San Francisco markets where it is regarded as a good food-fish. It reaches 2 feet in length.

The other species is *T. trachurus*, which is found in the North Atlantic.   It is rare on our coast.

The genus *Trachurops* differs from *Carangus* chiefly in the more elongate form.   The single species, *T. crumenophthalmus*, is a well-known fish of wide distribution.   In the Atlantic it is

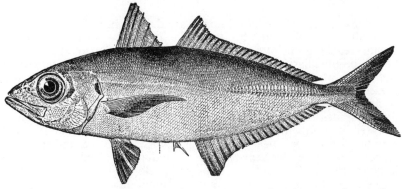

found among the West Indies and occasionally north to Cape Cod.   On the Pacific Coast it occurs from Cape San Lucas southward.   Among the Hawaiian Islands it is an abundant and important food-fish and is known as the akule.   Its common names in American waters are goggler, big-eyed scad, and goggle-eyed jack.

The genus *Hemicaranx* differs from *Carangus* chiefly in the narrow maxillary.   Our waters contain 6 or 7 species, none of great value as food.   The most important is *H. amblyrhynchus*,

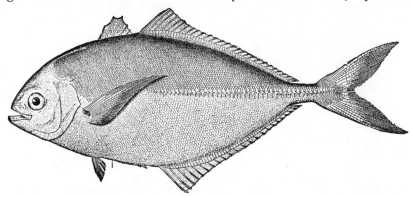

which is found from Cape Hatteras to Brazil.   It is rather common among the West Indies, and is seen now and then on the Florida coast.

GENUS CARANGUS GRIFFITH

The Cavallas

Body ovate or oblong, compressed, the back sometimes considerably elevated; mouth moderate or large, oblique; maxillary broad, reaching below eye, with a well-developed supplemental bone; premaxillaries protractile; teeth in one or few series, unequal, or at least not in villiform bands; villiform teeth usually present on vomer, palatines and tongue, deciduous or wanting in some species; gillrakers long; eye large with an adipose eyelid; dorsal spines rather low, connected; second dorsal long, usually elevated in front, both fins depressible in a groove; anal similar to second dorsal and nearly as long, preceded by 2 rather strong spines, its base longer than the abdomen; caudal fin strongly forked, the peduncle very slender; pectoral falcate; no finlets; scales present, usually very small; lateral line with its posterior portion armed with strong, bony plates, which grow larger on the tail, each plate armed with a spine; a short dorsal branch of lateral line usually present; preopercle entire in adult, serrate in the young; species very numerous in all warm seas, most of them valued as food.

a. Teeth on vomer and palatines persistent.
b. Soft dorsal and anal low, not much elevated in front, little if at all falcate; teeth in jaws in one or few series, with no canines.
c. Lateral line strongly arched, the arched part not half as long as straight portion; . . . .*vinctus,* 305
cc. Lateral line little arched, the arched part not shorter than the straight portion.
d. Body slender, the depth about $3\frac{1}{2}$ in length; colour dark, chiefly bluish; . . . .*ruber,* 305
dd. Body deeper, the depth about $2\frac{4}{5}$ in length; colour pale, mostly golden . . . .*bartholomæi,* 305
bb. Soft dorsal and anal much elevated in front, and more or less falcate; upper teeth in a band, the outer enlarged; lower teeth in one series.
e. Breast naked, except a small rhombic area before ventrals;
hippos, 306
ee. Breast entirely covered with small scales.
f. Body subfusiform, the depth less than $\frac{1}{3}$ the length; teeth of outer series small, not canine-like.
g. Pectoral fin moderate, rarely longer than head; scutes about 50; . . . .*crysos,* 306

gg. Pectoral fin very long, much longer than head; scutes about 40;...*caballus*, 306
ff. Body oblong-ovate, the depth more than $\frac{1}{3}$ the length.
h. General colour silvery; vertical fins not all black.
i. Body moderately elevated, the depth in adult $\frac{1}{2}$ to $\frac{1}{3}$ the length; opercular spot very small or obsolete; no pectoral spot.
j. Body rather slender, the depth about $2\frac{3}{4}$ in the length; dorsal and caudal fins largely black;............*marginatus*, 306
jj. Body deeper, the depth about $2\frac{1}{2}$ in length; caudal fin pale, the dorsal scarcely dusky;.....................*latus*, 306
ii. Body much elevated, the depth in adult $2\frac{1}{4}$ in length; no opercular spot; a dark spot in axil;..........*medusicola*, 307
hh. General colour brassy or blackish; vertical fins black.
k. Anterior profile gibbous, scutes about 28;.........*lugubris*, 307
kk. Anterior profile scarcely gibbous; scutes about 35;........
melampygus, 307
aa. Teeth on vomer and palatines wanting or deciduous;....
guara, 307

Carangus vinctus is known only from the Pacific Coast of Mexico from Lower California to Punta Arenas. It is a well-marked species, abundant about the entrance to the Gulf of California.

Colour, dusky, bluish above, silvery below, with golden and greenish reflections; 8 or 9 vertical dark half-bars from back to below lateral line, the widest about equal to diameter of orbit, and more than twice as wide as the light interspaces; breast blackish; head dusky, end of snout black; a distinct black blotch on upper angle of opercle; fins somewhat dusky, the lower yellow in life; pectoral without spot; axil dusky; anal white at tip.

Carangus ruber is known only from Cuba and St. Croix, in the West Indies; not abundant enough to be of any value as food.

Colour, bluish-olive, silvery below, scarcely yellowish in life; a vaguely defined horizontal stripe of clear blue just below the dorsal; dorsal yellowish-gray, other fins dusky olive; a distinct blackish bar extending along lower lobe of caudal.

Carangus bartholomæi occurs in the West Indies, and occasionally north to Florida and the Carolinas. It is common about Cuba and is of some little value as food.

Colour, bluish silvery, everywhere strongly washed with golden, the young with golden spots; fins all pale yellow; no black on opercle or lower lobe of caudal. It is known as the yellow-jack.

Carangus hippos, the cavalla or jack, is the most abundant and one of the most valuable of the genus. It is found on both coasts of tropical America, north to Cape Cod and the Gulf of California. It occurs also in the East Indies, and is everywhere a food-fish of considerable importance. On our Atlantic Coast it is next in abundance to *C. crysos*.

Colour, olivaceous above, sides and under parts golden; a large faint black spot on lower rays of pectoral; axil with a black blotch; edge of soft dorsal black; upper edge of caudal peduncle dusky.

Carangus crysos, the runner, hard tail, or jurel, reaches a foot or more in length and is found from Brazil north to Cape Cod. It is more abundant northward than any other species of *Carangus*, and is a food-fish of considerable importance, especially in the West Indies.

Colour, greenish-olive, golden-yellow or silvery below; a black blotch on opercle; fins all pale.

Carangus caballus, the cocinero, is the representative of *C. crysos* on the Pacific Coast. It occurs from Panama and Cerros Island northward to San Diego, and is quite abundant from the Gulf of California southward.

Carangus marginatus occurs on the Pacific Coast of Mexico from Mazatlan to Panama, and is not uncommon. From *C. latus*, which it closely resembles, it may be readily known by its less slender form, dark colours, and larger eye.

Carangus latus, the horse-eye jack, inhabits the same waters as the preceding, and is also found on the Atlantic Coast from Brazil to South Carolina and Virginia. It also occurs in the East Indies. It is not of much value as food. The flesh, in some places in the tropics, is reputed poisonous, giving rise to the disease called Ciguatera. It is abundant southward, but further north it is less common than *C. hippos*.

Colour, bluish, sides golden or silvery; a very small, black opercular spot; young sometimes with faint dark crossbands; fins mostly grayish; anterior part of soft dorsal dusky; caudal yellow, no black; no spot on pectoral; no axillary spot.

Carangus medusicola is known only from the vicinity of Mazatlan where it is very common on sandy shores. The young of an inch in length are very abundant in the body-cavity of a large translucent jelly-fish found about the Venados Islands in January. This fish reaches a foot in length and is of some food-value.

Colour, clear blue above, silvery below; no bands or spots anywhere, except a small, black axillary spot, and a blue-green patch on back of caudal peduncle; pectoral bright yellow; anal and caudal yellow, the lobes blackish; ventrals yellow; young with a deep-blue spot above the eye in life.

Carangus lugubris is a rare species found about rocky islands in the tropics in both the Atlantic and Pacific. We have specimens from Clarion Island of the Revillagigedo group, from Cuba, and from off Mobile harbor. It reaches a length of 18 inches or more. It is rather common about Cuba, where it is regarded as poisonous, and its sale in the markets is forbidden. Its specific name, *lugubris*, mournful, is from its dark colour and especially its bad reputation, associated with the much dreaded Ciguatera, a disease resulting from fish-poisoning.

Carangus melampygus is widely distributed about islands in the tropical Pacific and in the East Indies. It is known from the Hawaiian Islands and from the Revillagigedos. It resembles *C. lugubris*, but the anterior profile is scarcely gibbous, and the side has many small dark-brown spots.

Carangus guara is one of the largest species of the genus. It reaches a length of 2 feet or more. It occurs in tropical parts of the Atlantic, in the Mediterranean, along the coasts of Africa, Brazil, and the Madeiras, but it is not certainly known from the West Indies. From other species it may be known by the absence of teeth on the vomer and palatines.

The genus *Caranx* differs from *Carangus* mainly in the dentition, the teeth being very small, granular, and are entirely lost with age; maxillary broad, body compressed, the fins without filaments.

Our single known species is the mojarra dorada, *Caranx speciosus*, which occurs in the Red Sea, the Indian Ocean, and in the tropical Pacific north to Cape San Lucas. It is frequent on sandy shores and is an excellent food-fish. It reaches a length of 2 feet.

Colour, brilliant golden; side with 6 broad, dusky crossbands, a narrow stripe between each pair of broader ones; opercular spot obsolete; a small black spot in axil; caudal lobes dusky on inner edge; no dark caudal spot.

The genus *Carangoides* is close to *Carangus*, but has the persistent teeth all small and in villiform bands on jaws, vomer, palatines, and tongue; lateral line scarcely arched; body oblong, not much elevated; none of the dorsal rays produced. The only known species is *C. orthogrammus*, thus far found only at Clarion Island.

The genus *Citula* differs from *Carangoides* mainly in having one or more of the anterior rays of the soft dorsal produced in filaments. The body has not the distorted form seen in *Alectis* but is more like that of *Carangus*. Species found chiefly in warm seas. The only species in our waters is *C. dorsalis*, the Pacific pompano. This fish occurs on sandy shores from Mazatlan to Panama. It reaches about 2 feet in length, but is not very abundant.

Colour, steel-blue above, silvery below, with golden reflections; fins all pale, tinged with yellowish; axil jet black; ventrals tipped with dusky; opercle dusky along the edge, blackish within; a dark spot on orbit above.

The genus *Alectis* is not essentially different from *Carangus*, the great change in form arising from no important modification of the skeleton. The changes due to age are surprisingly great, the young being almost orbicular, and the dorsal filaments exceedingly long. There are several tropical species. The only one in our waters is *A. ciliaris*, the thread-fish, cobbler-fish or sunfish. This interesting and beautiful little fish occurs on both coasts of tropical America, ranging north to Mazatlan and Cape Cod. It is generally common southward about the Florida Keys and Cuba, and is a food-fish of some importance.

Head $3\frac{1}{3}$; depth $1\frac{1}{4}$ to 2; D. VI-I, 19; A. II-I, 16; scutes 12. Body oval, much compressed, highest at the elevated bases of the dorsal and anal fins; preorbital very deep; mouth nearly horizontal in adult, very oblique in the young; first rays of dorsal and anal filamentous, exceedingly long, in the young much longer than body, becoming shorter with age. Colour, bluish above, golden yellow below; a dark blotch on opercle; a black spot on orbit above; a black blotch on dorsal and one on anal in front.

The genus *Hynnis* is close to *Carangus*, but has the high, compressed, angular body of *Selene*, the dorsal and anal lobes not ending in filaments, and the caudal peduncle armed with a few weak plates as in *Alectis*. There are 2 species in our waters, *H. cubensis*, a rare species known only from Cuba, and *H. hopkinsi* recently described from Mazatlan. It attains a length of 2 feet.

GENUS VOMER CUVIER & VALENCIENNES

The Moon-fishes

This genus is closely allied to *Carangus*, from which it differs only in its distortion of form, and in its weak teeth and very low fins. Body broad-ovate, very strongly compressed, all its outlines sharply trenchant; head very gibbous above the eyes, its anterior profile vertical; lateral line strongly arched, its posterior portion with very weak shields; scales minute; soft dorsal and anal extremely low, not falcate. Young much deeper than the adult, all the fins higher, resembling the next genus. Warm seas; 3 species in our waters. The first of these is *V. dorsalis*, the horsefish, a rare species said to occur on the west coast of Africa, about the Cape Verde Islands, and in the West Indies.

309

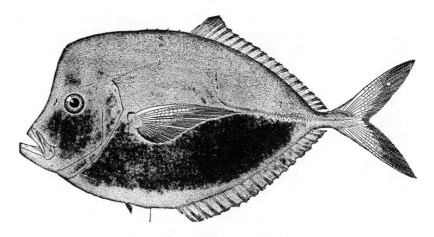

Moonfish; Jorobado

Vomer setipinnis (Mitchill)

This species is found on both coasts of tropical America, from Brazil to Maine, and Peru to Cape San Lucas. It is generally common southward, only the young usually coming northward in the Gulf Stream. It reaches a length of nearly a foot, and is an excellent little food-fish.

Colour, greenish above, golden or silvery below; young with a black blotch at origin of straight part of lateral line.

Corcobado

Vomer gabonensis Guichenot

The corcobado is a fish that was but little known until the recent investigations by the U. S. Fish Commission in Porto Rico, when numerous specimens were obtained. It is now known from Brazil, San Domingo, Jamaica, and Porto Rico; also from the west coast of Africa. It attains a length of 8 or 9 inches, and is a good food-fish. From *V. setipinnis*, which it resembles, it may be distinguished by the much deeper body, larger eye, greater elevation of the occipital region, and the more nearly vertical anterior profile. The young of the two species resemble each other more closely. At a length of 4 inches the difference in relation of depth to length becomes apparent, but under that size the present species is distinguished by its larger eye.

Body ovate, scarcely longer than deep, very greatly compressed; occipital region greatly elevated, making height of body greatest at the eyes; anterior profile nearly vertical from occiput to eye, opposite which it becomes concave; snout protruding. Colour, rich silvery, with an iridescence of steel-blue above and pink below, with a light golden wash below.

GENUS SELENE LACÉPÈDE

The Silvery Moon-fishes

This genus is very close to *Vomer*, from which it differs in the entire absence of scutes on the lateral line. All the species are found in tropical seas, only 2 coming within our limits. The first of these is the Pacific moon-fish *(S. œrstedii)* which is found on the Mexican coast from Mazatlan to Panama. It reaches 15 inches in length, and possesses some food-value. From our Atlantic species it may be distinguished by its smaller fins, the dorsal having 18 and the anal but 15 soft rays.

Lookdown ; Horsehead

Selene vomer (Linnæus)

This is perhaps the most common and best known of the moonfishes. It is found on both coasts of tropical America, from Cape Cod to Brazil, and from Lower California to Peru. Southward it is very common on sandy shores, and is a delicious food-fish, reaching a weight of 2 pounds.

Anterior profile nearly straight from tip of snout to occiput; one or 2 of the dorsal spines very long and filamentous in the young, short in the adult; ventrals and anal variable. Colour, uniform silvery, resembling a sheet of mother-of-pearl in colour and texture.

GENUS CHLOROSCOMBRUS GIRARD

The Casabes

Body oblong-ovate, compressed, not elevated; abdomen prominent anteriorly, its curve being much greater than the curve of the back; occiput and thoracic region trenchant; caudal peduncle very narrow, the fin widely forked; scales small, smooth; lateral line arched in front, armed, or with few small plates; head nearly naked; mouth rather small, oblique, lower jaw scarcely projecting; upper jaw protractile; maxillary broad, emarginate behind, with a large supplemental bone; jaws, vomer and palatines with feeble teeth, mostly in single series; first dorsal of feeble spines, connected by membrane; second dorsal and anal long and low, similar, much longer than the short abdomen; anal spines strong; ventrals small; pectoral falcate; gillrakers long; no finlets. Species, 2 or 3, all American, and of little value as food.

Chloroscombrus orqueta, the xurel de castilla of the Mexicans, has the chord of the curved part of the lateral line considerably longer than the head, and the colour is dusky. This species is found from Lower California to Panama, at which latter place it is rather common. It is of little value for food.

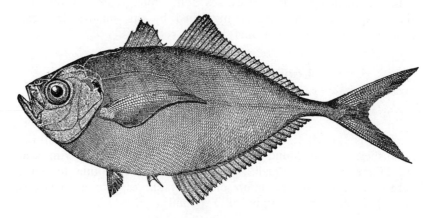

Bumper; Casabe

Chloroscombrus chrysurus (Linnæus)

The bumper is found from Cape Cod to Brazil. It is common on our South Atlantic Coast and about Cuba, and specimens

OLDWIFE, *Trachinotus glaucus*

POMPANO, *Trachinotus carolinus*

were obtained by us in Porto Rico. It is not valued as food, the flesh being thin and dry, and the bones large. Where common it is of some interest as a game-fish, as it takes the hook readily and may be caught either by still-fishing or trolling.

Colour, greenish above, the sides and below golden; caudal peduncle dusky above; dark opercular and axillary spots; inside of mouth black, fins not bordered nor tipped with black.

GENUS TRACHINOTUS LACÉPÈDE

The Pampanos or Pompanos

This is, commercially, the most important genus of the *Carangidæ*, containing, as it does, some of the most delicious of all food-fishes.

Body compressed, moderately elevated, the general outline ovate; caudal peduncle short and rather slender; abdomen not trenchant, shorter than the anal fin; head moderately compressed, very blunt, the snout abruptly truncate; mouth nearly horizontal, maxillary reaching middle of eye; premaxillaries protractile; no distinct supplemental maxillary bone; jaws, vomer, and palatines with bands of villiform teeth, which disappear with age; spinous dorsal represented by 6 rather low spines, connected by membrane in the young but free in adult; second dorsal long, elevated in front, anal opposite and similar to it; 2 stout, nearly free spines in front of anal, and one connected with the fin, these often disappearing with age; scales small and smooth; lateral line unarmed, little arched, no caudal keel.

Species numerous, about a dozen in our waters, most of them of some value as food, and a few among the most highly prized of food-fishes.

a. Dorsal with 19 or 20 soft rays; anal with 17 to 19.
b. Body very much compressed; sides with narrow black crossbars; lobes of vertical fins elongate, reaching past middle of caudal in adult.
c. Snout subtruncate or nearly vertical; profile from supraorbital to front of dorsal fin convex;....................*glaucus*, 314
cc. Snout low, very oblique; profile from supraorbital to front of dorsal scarcely convex........................*rhodopus*, 314

313

bb. Body moderately compressed; sides without narrow black crossbars.

d. Body broad, ovate, the back arched.

e. Lobes of vertical fins much elevated, that of dorsal in adult much longer than head; colour pale.

f. Caudal lobes about $2\frac{2}{3}$ in length of body; . . . .*falcatus,* 315

ff. Caudal lobes longer, about $2\frac{1}{3}$ in body; . . . .*rhomboides,* 315

ee. Lobes of vertical fins low, that of dorsal in adult shorter than head; colour dusky; . . . .*culveri,* 316

dd. Body oblong, the profile not strongly arched.

g. Axil with a jet-black spot; depth about $2\frac{1}{4}$ in length; *kennedyi,* 316

gg. Axil not black; depth about $2\frac{3}{5}$; . . . .*goodei,* 316

aa. Dorsal with 25 to 27 soft rays; anal with 22 to 26.

h. Dorsal with 25 soft rays; anal with 22.

i. Body very deep, half as deep as long; . . . .*argenteus,* 317

ii. Body more slender, the depth $\frac{2}{5}$ the length.

j. Head moderate, about $\frac{1}{4}$ as long as body; dorsal lobe pale; *carolinus,* 317

jj. Head larger, $3\frac{1}{4}$ to $3\frac{1}{2}$ in body; dorsal lobe black; . . . .*paloma,* 319

hh. Dorsal with 27 soft rays; anal with 26; . . . .*cayennensis,* 317

Old Wife; Gaff-topsail Pampano

Trachinotus glaucus (Bloch)

This beautiful fish is found from Virginia to the Caribbean Sea. It is found at Key West and is common about Porto Rico and doubtless about others of the West Indies.

It attains a length of a foot or more, but is not highly valued as food. In Porto Rico, however, it is handled by the fishermen and ranks with the species of *Carangus* in food-value.

Colour, bluish above, golden below; lobes of dorsal and anal black; caudal dark; other fins pale; body with 4 narrow vertical black bars, second and third longest and plainest.

Pampanito

Trachinotus rhodopus Gill

This fish is found from the Gulf of California southward to Panama. It is very common on sandy shores, replacing on the Pacific Coast, *T. glaucus,* which it much resembles.

It reaches a length of 2 feet, but is not much valued as food.

It may be known from *T. glaucus* by the difference in profile, the snout being low and very oblique.

Colour, bluish-green above, silvery below; side with 5 short, narrow, vertical blackish bars, the first 2 nearer together than the others, the last 2 sometimes reduced to spots,—these bands always faint in young in which the vertical fins are also much lower; caudal, dorsal, and anal lobes largely of a bright maroon colour, or orange-brown in life, the anterior edge blackish, shading off into pinkish, this colour present at all ages.

Round Pampano; Indian River Permit

Trachinotus falcatus (Linnæus)

The Round Pampano is found from Cape Cod to Florida, along the coast. It is common southward but occurs northward only in the Gulf Stream.

It reaches a foot or more in length and a weight of 3 pounds, and is a good food-fish. It may be known from the old wife and the pampanito by the absence of dark vertical bars.

Colour, bluish above, silvery below; lobe of dorsal black in young; fins in adult all bluish with lighter tips.

Trachinotus rhomboides, the West Indian round pompano, occurs among the West Indies and southward. It seems to differ from *T. falcatus* in the higher vertical fins.

315

Trachinotus culveri, the Mazatlan pompano, has lower fins than *T. falcatus*, which it closely resembles otherwise.

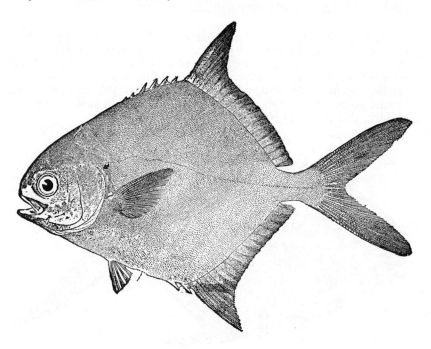

It is known only from the vicinity of Mazatlan. It reaches 8 to 10 inches in length.

Trachinotus kennedyi, the Pacific palmoneta, is another of the rather uncommon species of this genus. It occurs on our Pacific Coast from Magdalena Bay to Panama. It reaches a large size and is of value as a food-fish. It is the Pacific Coast representative of *T. goodei* from which it may be distinguished by the absence of a black axillary spot and the somewhat deeper body.

Permit ; Great Pompano

Trachinotus goodei Jordan & Evermann

The permit is the largest of all pompanos. It reaches a length of 3 feet and a weight of 27 pounds or more. It occurs in the West Indies and north to Florida. It occurs about Key

BLUEFISH. *Pomatomus saltatrix*

CALICO BASS, *Pomoxis sparoides*

ROCK BASS, *Ambloplites rupestris*

West and is occasionally taken in Indian River. It should be remarked, however, that to the Indian River fishermen this species is not distinguished from the common pompano, and that the fish known to them as the "permit" is the round pompano (*T. falcatus*). The permit is an excellent food-fish, not as good as the common pompano, but usually sold as that species and bringing as good a price.

Head 3; depth $2\frac{3}{5}$; D. VI-I, 19; A. II-I, 17; maxillary $2\frac{3}{5}$; ventrals 2. Body oblong, elliptical, moderately compressed; profile nearly straight from procumbent spine to nostril, where it descends nearly vertically, forming an angle, the vertical portion from angle to snout nearly equalling eye; maxillary reaching slightly behind middle of eye; jaws with bands of villiform teeth, disappearing with age; ventrals reaching $\frac{4}{5}$ distance to vent; dorsal and anal fins falcate, the anterior rays less elevated than in the round pompano, but extending beyond middle of fin when depressed; caudal forked, the lobes 3 in body; lateral line nearly straight, slightly curved upward above the pectoral. Colour, bluish-silvery above, silvery below; dorsal, caudal, and anal lobes black; no crossbars.

Trachinotus argenteus, the silvery pompano, is a very rare species, known only from the West Indies south to Brazil. The type specimen was recorded from New York, but probably really came from Brazil. The species is allied to *T. carolinus*, but probably has the body deeper, the depth being half the length in examples 6 inches long, or $2\frac{1}{10}$ in length in the type, a specimen a foot in length.

Common Pompano

Trachinotus carolinus (Linnæus)

The common pompano has its home along our South Atlantic and Gulf Coasts. It is rare in the West Indies and on the coast of Brazil, and does not occur on our Pacific Coast. On the Atlantic Coast it ranges as far north as Cape Cod, but it is not at all common north of New Jersey, and its occurrence that far north is irregular and uncertain. It seems to be most abundant on the South Atlantic and Gulf Coasts, and is particularly common in Indian River and on the west coast of Florida. Of all the fishes of Indian River, the pompano is the most valued and brings the best price to fishermen and dealers. It is present there throughout the year, being most abundant in winter. The best fishing seems to be from late January to April. They are most abundant about the inlets, and play in and out with the tide. They run in bunches or schools, and are easily influenced by changes in temperature. They are a warm-water fish, and a cold snap causes them to leave the river temporarily. The unusual cold of December, 1894, and February, 1895, affected them quite seriously, not only driving them away, but actually killing many. The pompano does not appear to be properly a migratory fish, and when it leaves Indian River it probably does not wander far from the inlets. In summer, however, when the water is warm, many young and some adults are apt to wander north on our coasts at least to Woods Hole. Very little is definitely known regarding the spawning habits of the pompano. On the east coast of Florida they probably spawn in Indian River chiefly in April and May. The food of this fish consists principally of small bivalve mollusks and small crustaceans. They feed extensively about the inlets and in the surf outside. They are often seen rooting or digging for food in the sand or mud, their caudal fins sometimes appearing above the water.

The pompano is less abundant about Key West, but from a little further north on the Gulf Coast to the mouth of the Mississippi it is a common fish, large quantities being brought to the markets of Tampa and Pensacola. On the west side of the Gulf it appears to be uncommon. About Pensacola it seems to be a migratory fish, but southward it is probably not so.

The pompano reaches a length of about 18 inches and a weight of 7 or 8 pounds, though examples of more than 2 or 3 pounds are not now often seen.

As a food-fish there is none better than the pompano, either in the fresh waters or in the seas. This is practically the unanimous verdict of epicures and all others who have had the pleasure of eating the pompano, fresh from the water. The flesh is firm and rich, and possesses a delicacy of flavour peculiarly pleasing to the palate.

The pompano is not a game-fish. " It is mullet-mouthed and never takes a hook except by a mistake," says Genio Scott; but Mr. S. C. Clarke says they have been known to bite at a clam-bait, and Mr. Silas Stearns says they are sometimes taken on the hook about Pensacola.

Head 4; depth $2\frac{1}{3}$ to $2\frac{2}{5}$; eye $4\frac{1}{2}$; snout $4\frac{1}{2}$; D. VI-I, 25; A. II-I, 23; ventrals $2\frac{1}{2}$. Body oblong, compressed, rather robust, the greatest thickness 3 in depth; snout from mouth to horizontal from upper edge of eye nearly vertical, somewhat bluntly rounded; profile from upper edge of snout to procumbent spine evenly convex; mouth nearly horizontal, maxillary reaching middle of eye, its length $2\frac{7}{8}$ in head; no teeth in adult; ventrals reaching $\frac{2}{3}$ distance to vent, about $\frac{1}{2}$ length of pectoral; dorsal and anal fins falcate, anterior rays nearly reaching middle of fins when depressed; dorsal lobe $4\frac{1}{2}$, anal $5\frac{1}{2}$ in body. Colour, bluish above, silvery or slightly golden below; pectoral and anal light orange, shaded with bluish; caudal and upper portion of caudal peduncle with bluish reflections; breast more or less yellowish; top of head bluish.

Trachinotus paloma is an unimportant species, known only from Cape San Lucas, Mazatlan, and San Juan Lagoon. It reaches a length of a foot. As a food-fish it is not distinguished by the Mexican fishermen from other species of the genus. It closely resembles the common pompano, but has the head rather larger, it being $3\frac{1}{3}$ to $3\frac{1}{6}$ in length instead of 4.

Trachinotus cayennensis is another rare species, known only from a single specimen obtained at Cayenne. It is close to *T. falcatus*, but has more numerous fin-rays, D. V-I, 27; A. II-I, 26.

Recently a new genus and species of this family was described from the Revillagigedo Islands by Jordan and McGregor as *Zalocys stilbe*. The genus is close to *Trachinotus*. The single specimen known is 16 inches long.

THE BLUEFISHES

Family XXXIX.   Pomatomidæ

THIS family contains only one genus and one species.

Common Bluefish

Pomatomus saltatrix (Linnæus)

The bluefish is a species of very wide distribution. It occurs in both the Atlantic and Indian oceans, and occasionally enters the Mediterranean Sea. It occurs in the Malay Archipelago, Australia, at the Cape of Good Hope, at Natal, and about Madagascar. It has never been seen on the Atlantic Coast of Europe, nor about Bermuda. On our coast it ranges from central Brazil and the Guianas through the Gulf of Mexico, and north to Nova Scotia, though never seen in the Bay of Fundy. From Cape Florida to Penobscot Bay, bluefish are abundant at all seasons when the temperature of the water is propitious, which probably is above 40°. The menhaden seems to be their principal food and their abundance is largely dependent upon the presence of that species. The bluefish is a pelagic or wandering fish, very capricious in its movements, varying in numbers at particular localities in different years, and sometimes disappearing from certain regions for many years at a time.

The bluefish is a carnivorous animal of the most pronounced type. As Professor Baird has well said, there is no parallel to the bluefish in point of destructiveness to the marine species on our coast. It has been likened to an animated chopping-machine the business of which is to cut to pieces and otherwise destroy as many fish as possible in a given space of time. Going in large schools, in pursuit of fish not much inferior to themselves in size, they move along like a pack of hungry wolves, destroying everything before them. Their trail is marked by fragments of fish and by the stain of blood in the sea, as, when the fish is too large to be swallowed entire, the hinder portion will be bitten off and the anterior part allowed to float or sink. It has been even maintained that such is the gluttony of this fish, that when the stomach becomes full the contents are disgorged and then again filled! It is certain that it kills more fish than it needs or can use. The amount of food they consume or destroy is incredibly great. It has been estimated at twice the weight of the fish in a day, and one observer says that a bluefish will destroy daily a thousand other fish. It has been estimated that there are annually on our coast from New Jersey to Mononomy a thousand million bluefish averaging 5 or 6 pounds each in weight, and that these eat or destroy at the lowest estimate 10 fish each every day, or a total of ten thousand millions of fish destroyed every day. And as the bluefish remain on this coast at least 120 days, the total destruction amounts in round numbers to twelve hundred million millions of fish destroyed in a single season by this species. These would weigh at least three hundred thousand million pounds. And it must be remembered that in this estimate no account has been taken of those destroyed by bluefish under 3 pounds in weight, vastly more numerous and all engaged simultaneously in the same butchery.

The average size of the bluefish caught on the Florida coast is 3 to 5 pounds and the maximum about 15 pounds. The sizes on the North Atlantic Coast run about the same. The largest bluefish of which we have any record weighed 22 pounds, and had a length of 3 feet.

The bluefish is one of the best of food-fishes, ranking in public estimation next to the pompano and Spanish mackerel. It is a standard fish in all the large markets of our eastern states. The flesh is very sweet and savoury but does not keep well. In some places the bluefish is not yet held in high esteem but is rapidly growing in popular favour.

The bluefish is one of the most active and unyielding fishes that swim. "It can jump higher and come down quicker, dive deeper, and stay under longer" than any other salt-water fish of its size, says Nimrod Wildfire. "Look at his clean build, and it is accounted for; his narrow waist and depth of hull, falling off sharply as it approaches the keel, enabling him to keep well to windward, as if he had his centre-board always down. See his immense propeller behind! No fish of his size is more wicked or wild when hooked. I have sometimes struck a 3-pound blue-fish, and thought I had a 6-pound weakfish, until he commenced jumping, and after giving him considerable play, have at last drawn him in by sheer force, with his pluck not the least abated." Thaddeus Norris describes the method of "squidding for bluefish," which he says is the usual way of taking this fish. The *squid* is generally a white bone with a hook at the end, or a piece of pewter. The line is of strong hemp or cotton. With a good breeze when crossing a school of these fish, the sport is highly exciting, and great numbers are sometimes taken. We have taken the bluefish in Indian River by trolling with a large Skinner fluted spoon, and found the sport the most exciting we have ever had with any of the fishes of that river.

THE SERGEANT-FISHES

Family XL.   Rachycentridæ

THE characters of this family are sufficiently shown in the accompanying illustration of the sergeant-fish, *Rachycentron canadus*.

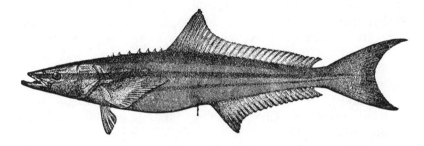

This fish is an inhabitant of warm seas, ranging in summer as far north on our Atlantic Coast as Cape Cod. It is not uncommon from the Chesapeake Bay southward. It is known as sergeant-fish, crab-eater, coal-fish and cobia, and it reaches a length of 4 or 5 feet, and it is edible.

THE DOLPHINS

Family XLI. Coryphænidæ

THIS family contains but one genus with 2 species, found in mid-ocean, where they feed upon other pelagic fishes, such as the flying-fish. They are strong, rapid swimmers, and are widely distributed throughout all tropical and temperate waters. They are often caught by sailors at sea, and are considered excellent food.

It is the custom before eating them to test the flesh by putting a piece of silver into the vessel in which they have been cooked, it being a common belief that if the flesh is poisonous the silver will turn black. Narratives of ocean voyages abound in descriptions of the beautiful colours of the dolphin, and the brilliant changes of hue exhibited by the dying fish. The name dolphin is wrongly applied to these fish, as it belongs properly to a group of small cetaceans.

The single genus, *Coryphæna*, contains 2 species, *C. hippurus*

and *C. equisetis.* The common dolphin, *C. hippurus*, reaches a length of 6 feet. It is a pelagic fish, common on our coast from the Carolinas to Texas, and occasionally north to Cape Cod.

Colour, brilliant in life, the head, body and tail greenish-olive, changing suddenly at death; brownish-olive above, white or golden below, with a series of about 15 bright-blue spots on back along each side of dorsal, the largest on back and head,

WARMOUTH BASS, *Chænobryttus gulosus*

BLUEGILL SUNFISH, *Lepomis pallidus*

RED-EARED SUNFISH, *Eupomotis heros*

forming bands on snout; dorsal purplish blue, with paler oblique lines; other fins tinged with blue; caudal yellow.

The small dolphin, *C. equisetis,* reaches a length of only about $2\frac{1}{2}$ feet. It is found in the open Atlantic. It is rare in the West Indies, and has not been recorded from the coast of the United States.

Colour, sea-green, silvery below, with scattered black spots on the sides and back; a series of distant rounded spots along base of dorsal fin; head with brown stripes.

THE MARIPOSAS

Family XLII. Lampridæ

BODY ovate, compressed, and elevated, covered with minute, cycloid scales; head small, rather pointed; mouth small, terminal; no teeth in adult; premaxillaries protractile; only one dorsal fin, very long, elevated, falcate in front, no spines; anal low, not falcate; both fins depressible in a groove; pectoral fins large, falcate; a pit at base of caudal above and below, as in certain sharks.

Fishes of large size and gorgeous colouration, inhabiting the open sea; highly valued as food, the flesh firm and rich.

The single known species is the opah, mariposa or moon-fish, *Lampris luna*. This interesting fish is found in the open waters of the Atlantic and Pacific. It is frequently taken on the coast of Europe and about Madeira, and is occasionally taken off the coasts of Newfoundland, Maine, and Cuba. It has also been taken at Monterey and other places on the California coast. It reaches a length of 3 to 6 feet and a weight of 50 to 400 pounds. It is called San Pedro-fish, cravo, soho, Jerusalem had-dock, glance-fish, gudlax, and poisson lune, in addition to the names given above. It is one of the choicest food-fishes, the flesh being firm, rich and of delicious flavour.

It is a fish of most gorgeous colouration. "Just imagine the body a beautiful silver," wrote the artist, James Farquhar, half a century ago, "interspersed with spots of a lighter colour, about the size of a sixpence, the eyes very large and brilliant, with a golden ring around them; you will then have some idea of the splendid appearance of the fish when fresh. If Caligula had seen him I might have realized a fortune." The colour in life, as seen by us, is a rich brocade of silver and lilac, rosy underneath; everywhere with round silvery spots; head, opercles and back with ultramarine tints; jaws and fins vermileion; flesh red of varying shades.

THE POMFRETS

Family XLIII. Bramidæ

BODY oblong, more or less elevated, strongly compressed, covered with firm, adherent cycloid, lobate, or emarginate scales, or with a median ridge or spine; mouth very oblique, maxillary broad and scaly; premaxillaries protractile; jaws with bands of slender teeth; dorsal and anal fins similar, long, each with 3 or 4 anterior rays simple, developed as spines; soft dorsal and anal scaly or with a sheath of scales.

Fishes of the open sea, widely distributed and often inhabiting considerable depths, and varying greatly with age.

The single genus in our waters *(Brama)* contains 3 species in our limits, only one of which is of food-value. This is the pomfret, *Brama raii.* This species is of considerable importance as a food-fish. It occurs in the open seas and is widely distributed. It descends to considerable depths. It is rare on our Atlantic Coast but it is not uncommon on the coast of California and north to Puget Sound where it is regarded as an excellent food-fish. It reaches a length of 2 to 4 feet.

Colour, sooty-gray, with some soiled silvery on snout; vertical fins and anal region black, edges of dorsal and anal darker; axil jet black within.

THE FIATOLAS

Family XLIV. Stromateidæ

BODY compressed, more or less elevated, covered with small or minute cycloid scales; anterior profile blunt and rounded; mouth small; premaxillaries not protractile; dentition feeble, no teeth on vomer or palatines; œsophagus armed with numerous horny, barbed, or hooked teeth; opercular bones smooth, not serrate; cheeks scaly; lateral line well developed; dorsal fin single, long, with the spines few or weak, often obsolete; anal fin long, similar to soft dorsal, usually with 3 small spines which are often depressible in a fold of skin; ventrals thoracic, I, 5 in young, but reduced or altogether wanting in adult; caudal well forked.

About 10 genera and 50 species. Fishes usually of small size, found in most warm seas, many of them valued as food. The following are the only genera common in America:

a. Dorsal and anal fins very high in front, the anterior lobe falcate;..*Peprilus,* 328
aa. Dorsal and anal fins only moderately elevated in front, the anterior lobe scarcely falcate.
b. Side of back without conspicuous series of pores abovs lateral line;....................................*Palometa,* 329
bb. Side of back with a conspicuous series of large, wide-set pores above lateral line;..........................*Poronotus,* 330

GENUS PEPRILUS CUVIER

The Butter-fishes

Body ovate or suborbicular, strongly compressed, tapering into a slender caudal peduncle, which has no keel or shield; head short, compressed, the profile obtuse; mouth small, terminal, the jaws subequal; gill-membranes separate, free from the isthmus; usually 1 or more procumbent spines in front of dorsal and anal, each with a free point both anteriorly and posteriorly; pectoral long and narrow; caudal widely forked.

Harvest-fish

Peprilus paru (Linnæus)

This delicious little fish has been found from Cape Cod to Brazil, but it is not abundant anywhere except about the mouth of Chesapeake Bay. At Norfolk, where it is called whiting, it is a fish of considerable commercial importance, and it is one of the most common pan-fishes one sees hawked about the streets of Baltimore, Washington and other middle Atlantic cities. It reaches a length of 6 inches. One interesting fact in the life history of the fish is its habit of swimming beneath the Portuguese man-of-war.

The genus *Palometa* is distinguished from *Peprilus* only by the lower fins. The 3 known species are each of rare occurrence. The first, *P. palometa*, reaches a length of 3 inches and occurs in the Pacific off Columbia. Another species, *P. media*, is known only from Mazatlan. The third species, *P. simillima*, the "California Pompano," occurs on our Pacific Coast from Puget Sound to San Diego. During summer it is abundant, especially about Santa Cruz, and is a

329

highly prized food-fish, the flesh being rich and delicate. It reaches a length of 10 inches. Colour, bluish above, bright silvery below; fins punctulate; anterior lobes of dorsal and anal dusky-edged.

GENUS PORONOTUS GILL

This genus differs from *Palometa* only in the presence of a series of conspicuous, wide-set pores above the lateral line.

There is but a single species in our waters.

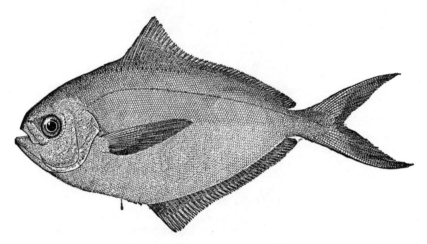

Butterfish; Dollarfish

Poronotus triacanthus (Peck)

This is the butterfish of the coast of Massachusetts and New York, the harvestfish of New Jersey, the dollarfish of Maine, the sheepshead of Cape Cod, the pumpkinseed of Connecticut, and the starfish of Norfork. It occurs from Maine to South Carolina, and is generally common between Cape Cod and Cape Henry. It is a summer visitor, appearing and disappearing with the mackerel. It breeds in early summer and the young are abundant in July, August, and September, swimming about, like the harvestfish, with various jelly-fishes. During the summer certain species of large jelly-fishes, called sun-squalls, are found abundantly on our

Middle Atlantic Coast in waters near shore, and each one is almost invariably accompanied by 10 or 12 or even more young butterfish, seeming to seek shelter under their disks, and perhaps obtaining a supply of food from among the numerous soft bodied invertebrates that are constantly becoming entangled with the floating streamers of their protectors. This position is not always safe for the little fish, as they are sometimes destroyed by the tentacles of their protector which are provided with powerful sting or lasso-cells. Though the fish are, by this commensal arrangement, safe from the attacks of larger fish, they often fall victims to the stinging power of the jelly-fish and are devoured.

THE
BASSES, CRAPPIES AND SUNFISHES.

Family XLV. Centrarchidæ

BODY more or less shortened and compressed, the regions above and below the axis of the body nearly equally developed and corresponding to each other; head compressed; mouth terminal, large or small; teeth in villiform bands, the outer slightly enlarged, no canines; teeth present on the premaxillaries, lower jaw, vomer, usually on the palatines, and sometimes on the tongue, pterygoids and hyoid; premaxillaries protractile; maxillary with a supplemental bone in the large-mouthed species, sometimes minute or obsolete; preopercle entire or somewhat serrate; opercle ending in 2 flat points or prolonged in a black flap at the angle; gills 4, a slit behind the last; pseudobranchiæ small; gill-membranes separate, free from the isthmus; branchiostegals 6, rarely 7; gillrakers variously formed, armed with small teeth; lower pharyngeal bones separate, their teeth conic or sometimes paved; cheek and opercles scaly; body fully scaled, the scales usually not strongly ctenoid, rarely cycloid; lateral line present, usually complete; dorsal fins confluent, the spines 6 to 13, depressible in a shallow groove; anal spines 3 to 9; intestine short; pyloric cœca 5 to 10. Colour, usually brilliant, chiefly greenish; sexes similar; changes with age often great.

This is a family of North American freshwater fishes, with about 12 genera and 30 species, forming one of the most characteristic features of our fish-fauna. Most of the species build nests, which they defend with much courage. They all breed in the spring, and are all valued as food, their importance being in direct proportion to the size which they attain. All are carnivorous, voracious and gamy, some of them being among the greatest of all game-fishes.

a. Dorsal fin scarcely longer than the anal.
b. Dorsal spines 5 to 8; anal spines 6; spinous dorsal shorter
    than soft dorsal; body rather short and greatly compressed;
                                                Pomoxis, 333
bb. Dorsal spines 11 or 12; anal spines 7 or 8; spinous dorsal
    longer than soft dorsal; body short, deep and compressed;
                                                Centrarchus, 337
aa. Dorsal much longer than the anal.

c. Body comparatively short and deep, the depth usually more than ⅔ the length; dorsal fin not deeply emarginate.

d. Tongue and pterygoids with teeth; mouth large, maxillary reaching past middle of eye.

e. Scales cycloid; caudal convex;.............*Acantharchus,* 338

ee. Scales ctenoid; caudal concave.

f. Opercle emarginate behind; anal spines 5 to 8.

g. Lingual teeth in a single patch; gillrakers about 10;.......
Ambloplites, 338

gg. Lingual teeth in 2 patches; gillrakers about 20;...........
Archoplites, 341

ff. Opercle ending in a black convex process or flap; anal spines 3;.................................*Chænobryttus,* 342

dd. Tongue and pterygoids toothless; mouth small, the maxillary barely reaching past middle of eye.

h. Supplemental maxillary bone perfectly distinct;....*Apomotis,* 342

hh. Supplemental maxillary bone rudimentary or wanting.

i. Lower pharyngeals narrow, the teeth usually sharp, not conical;.................................*Lepomis,* 344

ii. Lower pharyngeal bones broad and concave, especially in the adult; teeth more or less blunt or paved;..*Eupomotis,* 350

cc. Body comparatively elongate, the depth in the adult about ⅛ the length; dorsal fin low, deeply emarginate;.........
Micropterus, 355

GENUS POMOXIS RAFINESQUE

Crappie and Calico Bass

Body rather short and greatly compressed; snout projecting; mouth large, oblique; maxillary broad, with a well-developed supplemental bone; gillrakers long and slender; opercle emarginate; preopercle and preorbital finely serrate; scales large, feebly ctenoid; fins large, the anal larger than dorsal; caudal emarginate; branchiostegals 7; lateral line complete.

a. Dorsal spines 6, rarely 5; anal fin plain;......*annularis,* 334

aa. Dorsal spines 7, rarely 8; anal fin strongly reticulated;
sparoides, 335

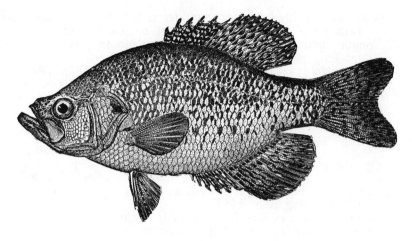

Crappie

Pomoxis annularis Rafinesque

The crappie is found from Vermont and New York westward through the Great Lakes region and Mississippi Valley to the Dakotas and south to Texas. It is therefore a fish of wide distribution and has, in consequence, received many vernacular names. It is called bachelor in the Ohio Valley, campbellite, croppie, and new-light in Illinois, Indiana, and Kentucky; tin-mouth or paper-mouth in northern Indiana and Illinois, and sac-à-lait, and chinquapin perch in the lower Mississippi and Texas. In other places it is known as bridge perch, goggle-eye, speckled perch, shad, and John Demon, the last name being heard in northeastern Indiana. The crappie and the calico bass are confounded by most anglers and fishermen, and many of the vernacular names are, in consequence, interchangeable. Where only one species is found it is quite apt to be known as the crappie. The crappie is found from the St. Lawrence and the Great Lakes south to Texas and west to the Dakotas and Kansas. It is generally abundant in ponds, lagoons, bayous and all sluggish waters, but is much more common in the southern portions of its range. In the lower Mississippi Valley the young of this species literally swarm in the overflow ponds and bayous and vast numbers perish every year when these waters dry up, as many of them do.

The crappie reaches a length of about a foot and, when found in water that is not too warm or too muddy, is regarded as an excellent pan-fish. As it is usually found, however, in muddy water, its flavour is not devoid of the taste of its environment and the species is by many not regarded with very high favour as a food-fish.

As a game-fish it is held in high esteem in the South and at least as far north as Washington. Among Louisiana anglers this fish is said to be a great favourite. It will take a minnow bait as promptly as will a black bass, but is not very pugnacious, and will not make much of a fight; besides, the mouth is very tender and the hook is quite apt to tear out unless the fish is handled with considerable skill. This fact, in the opinion of the expert angler, more highly commends the crappie as it requires greater skill in handling the tackle.

The range of the crappie has been considerably extended through the operations of the United States Fish Commission. Large numbers are reclaimed every year from the overflow ponds along the Mississippi and transplanted into various waters.

Colour, silvery-olive, mottled with dark green, the dark markings chiefly on the upper part of the body and having a tendency to form narrow vertical bars; dorsal and caudal fins marked with green; anal fin pale, nearly plain; fins very high, but lower than in the calico bass.

Calico Bass

Pomoxis sparoides (Lacépède)

The calico bass is found throughout the Great Lakes region and south to New Jersey and Texas. Among the Great Lakes and throughout the upper Mississippi Valley it is an abundant and well-known species. Like its congener, the crappie, it prefers the lakes, ponds, bayous and sluggish lowland streams. The 2 species have essentially the same geographic range, the calico bass, however, being the more common species northward while the crappie is the more abundant in the south.

In the lagoons about Buffalo, N. Y., as well as in the small lakes of Michigan and northern Indiana it is abundant. It is also very abundant in the ponds and bayous in Illinois and large numbers are every year transplanted from the ponds about Meredosia by the United States Fish Commission.

Grass bass, barfish, strawberry bass, bitterhead, banklick bass, and lamplighter are names which have been applied to this fish; in fact, all the names of the crappie have been applied to this species, but the names in most general use are calico bass and strawberry bass.

It reaches a length of a foot or more. In Lake Maxinkuckee we have seen specimens 14 inches long and weighing a pound. The usual size, however, does not exceed 10 or 12 inches and a weight of half a pound. As a food and game-fish the calico bass does not differ appreciably from the crappie. Their habits are essentially the same, both preferring the quiet waters of bayous, ponds and lakes, though this species is more often seen in clearer, colder waters.

At Cedar and Maxinkuckee lakes, in northern Indiana, the calico bass affords much sport to the angler. They bite best in the early spring, in June, and again late in the fall. They may be taken still-fishing with grasshoppers, worms or live minnows, or by trolling with live minnow or spoon. They will at times rise to the artificial fly and we have seen some fine catches made in that way. Trolling is a favourite mode of fishing for this species and the crappie at Lake Maxinkuckee. They take the lure with a rush and vim which promises a more exciting fight than really develops, for they soon give up completely and are lifted into the boat without a struggle. At Cedar Lake they are fished for from flat-bottomed skiffs and from sail-boats, with bait of minnows, worms or pieces of fish. When fishing from a sail-boat the angler uses two lines with spoon-baits or " whirl, " by means of which large catches are made.

Colour, silvery-olive, mottled with clear olive-green, the dark mottlings gathered in small irregular bunches and covering the whole body; vertical fins with dark olive reticulations surrounding pale spots; anal marked like the dorsal; a dusky opercular spot. The calico bass and the crappie resemble each other closely, but are perfectly distinct and well-marked species. The easiest way to distinguish them is by means of the dorsal spines, the crappie having only 5 or 6, while the calico bass always has 7 or 8. The different colouration, particularly of the anal fin, and the difference in the anterior profile are also constant and important differential characters.

GENUS CENTRARCHUS CUVIER & VALEN-CIENNES

This genus contains but one species, *C. macropterus*, the flier or round sun-fish.

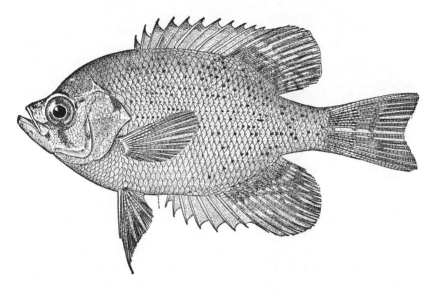

This interesting little sunfish reaches a length of 5 or 6 inches. It inhabits lowland streams, ponds and bayous from Virginia southward near the coast to Florida and Louisiana, and northward sparingly in the Mississippi Valley to Southern Illinois. In the Dismal Swamp region and elsewhere in clear water it is abundant. It is a handsome little fish, and in some places affords considerable sport to local fishermen. It posses considerable gameness and takes the hook baited with angleworm or small cockroach with an avidity which doubtless gave rise to the name "Flier," by which it is most generally known.

Colour, green or greenish, with series of dark brown spots on side below lateral line, forming interrupted, longitudinal lines; a dark spot below eye; soft dorsal and anal reticulated; young with a black ocellus at base of soft dorsal.

GENUS ACANTHARCHUS GILL

This is another genus containing but a single species, the mud sunfish, *A. pomotis.*

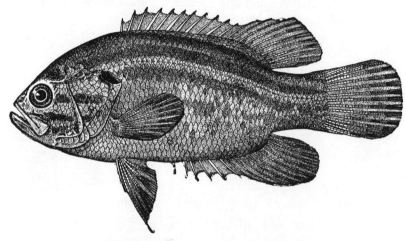

This is another of the small sunfishes found in the lowland streams and sluggish waters of the Middle Atlantic Coast. It occurs from southern New York near the coast to South Carolina; it is locally common, especially in the lower Delaware. It attains a length of about 6 inches and is used to some extent as a panfish. It is inferior in every way to the flier.

Colour, very dark greenish; body usually with 5 rather indistinct blackish longitudinal bands along side; cheek with dark bands which run nearly parallel, the lowest passing across the maxillary around the front part of the lower jaw; a black opercular spot; fins plain dusky.

GENUS AMBLOPLITES RAFINESQUE

The Rock Basses

This genus is characterized by having the body oblong, moderately compressed; mouth large, maxillary broad, the supplemental bone well developed; lower jaw projecting; teeth on vomer, palatines, and tongue; those on tongue in a single patch; pharyngeal teeth sharp; branchiostegals 6; opercle ending in 2 flat points; preopercle serrate at its angle; gillrakers rather long and strong, dentate, fewer than 10 in number, developed only on the lower portion of the arch; scales large, somewhat ctenoid; lateral line complete; dorsal fin much larger than the anal, spines rather low; caudal emarginate.

Rock Bass; Redeye; Goggle-eye

Ambloplites rupestris (Rafinesque)

The common rock bass is one of our most familiar panfishes. It is found from Vermont and New York westward to Manitoba and south to Louisiana and Texas. In the upper Mississippi Valley and in the Great Lakes it is very abundant, and is found in practically every lake, pond and stream. It is found not only in the rivers, but also in the creeks and smaller streams. It prefers clear, cool water, and is therefore least abundant in bayous and shallow, muddy lakes. In the lakes it will be found about patches of potamogeton or other aquatic vegetation. In the streams it most delights to dwell in the quiet water of deep holes where there are large boulders among which some water-plants are growing, or about old stumps or logs where the water is 3 to 6 or 8 feet deep.

The rock bass reaches the length of 12 inches and a weight of 1 to $1\frac{1}{2}$ pounds, though it does not usually attain this size. The average weight probably does not exceed $\frac{1}{2}$ pound. It spawns in the spring, when it constructs a nest on a gravel bed where the water is moderately swift, or on a bar, if in a lake. The parent fish defend the nest with much vigour. This species is pre-eminently a boy's fish, though it is by no means despised by anglers of maturer years, and in the Great Lakes region and upper Mississippi Valley it is one of the better fishes often seen on the small boy's string.

As a game-fish it is rather disappointing. It takes the hook with vim and energy and begins a most vigorous fight which, however, it usually fails to keep up. It can usually be caught at any season and at any time of day; good fishing may be had even at night. Any kind of bait may be used, but

339

small minnows, white grubs, and angleworms are best. It will take the trolling spoon quite readily and the spinner and the bucktail also are successful lures. Minnows may be used either in still-fishing or in trolling. During the summer grasshoppers are a good bait, and pieces of freshwater mussel or yellow perch are excellent. In the fall still-fishing with small minnows usually meets with success. Casting with the artificial fly is not a common method for catching the rock bass, yet we have had many good rises and have taken some fine examples in that way; we have also taken it on the artificial frog. Small crawfish also are a tempting bait.

As already stated, they are pretty gamy when first hooked, and make quite a fight at times, especially at first, and again when brought alongside the boat.

As a pan-fish the rock bass is not equal to the bluegill. Its flesh is softer and less flaky, and is apt to have a muddy taste unless the fish comes from rather cool, clear water. We are inclined to think that those from streams are of better flavour than the ones taken from lakes.

The rock bass has been handled to some extent by the United States Fish Commission, through whose operations it has been introduced into waters which it did not previously inhabit.

Head $2\frac{3}{4}$; depth 2 to $2\frac{1}{2}$; eye $3\frac{1}{2}$ to $4\frac{1}{2}$; snout 4; maxillary $2\frac{1}{3}$; D. XI, 10; A. VI, 10; scales about 6-39-12, 6 to 8 rows on cheek; cœca 7; vertebræ 14+18; gillrakers 7 to 10. Body oblong, moderately compressed, head large; profile in adult somewhat depressed above the eyes; mouth large, the maxillary reaching middle of pupil; gillrakers developed only on lower part of arch; preopercle serrate near its angle. Colour, olive green, conspicuously tinged with brassy, and with much dark mottling; the young irregularly barred and blotched with black, and with very little brassy; the adult with a dark spot on each scale, these forming interrupted black stripes; a black opercular spot; dark mottlings on the soft dorsal, caudal and anal; eye more or less red.

In the Roanoke River of Virginia is found a rock bass closely resembling the common rock bass. It seems to differ only in having the scales on the cheek minute and imbedded and wholly invisible over most of the cheek, and in having the profile over the eyes more concave. No other differences have been noted, and the species are probably not distinct.

The habits of the Roanoke rock bass do not differ from those of the common species.

GENUS ARCHOPLITES GILL

This genus contains a single species, the Sacramento perch, *A. interruptus*, the only species of the family found on our Pacific Coast.

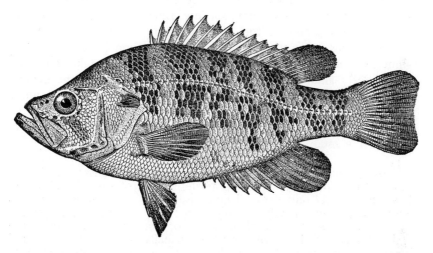

It inhabits the Sacramento and the San Joaquin rivers, and their tributary streams and lakes, and has been abundant throughout its range. It is said, however, probably without reason, that it is being exterminated by the carp and catfish, which infest its spawning grounds. This species reaches a length of 1 to 2 feet, and is regarded as an excellent food-fish. We know nothing as to its game qualities.

Colour, blackish above, side silvery, with about 7 vertical blackish bars, irregular in form and position, and more or less interrupted; body sometimes almost wholly black, sometimes brassy; a black opercular spot; fins nearly plain.

341

GENUS CHÆNOBRYTTUS GILL

This genus has the general form and dentition of *Amblo-plites*, with the convex opercle, 10 dorsal and 3 anal spines of *Lepomis*.

The single species is the warmouth, mud sunfish, or Indian fish, *C. gulosus*. The warmouth is found in the eastern United States from the Great Lakes south to Georgia and Texas and west to Iowa and Kansas, chiefly west of the Alleghanies. It is another of those sunfishes which prefer the bayous, sluggish lowland streams, and shallow, mud-bottomed ponds and lakes. It is abundant in the more shallow lakes in Indiana, Michigan and Wisconsin, and in the ponds and bayous of the South.

It reaches a length of about 10 inches and is not a food or game-fish of much importance. At times it will take the hook pretty freely and will fight fairly well, somewhat after the manner of the rock bass. It will take a live minnow, angleworm, white grub, grasshopper or piece of clam or fish. On account of its usually inhabiting water with muddy bottom its flesh is apt to taste of the mud.

Body shaped much like that of the rock bass; head and mouth large, maxillary reaching posterior line of eye; dorsal spines low, the longest equal to distance from tip of snout to middle of eye; pectoral not nearly reaching anal fin; ventrals barely reaching vent. Colour, dark olive-green, or sometimes rich brick–red and brassy, clouded with darker, usually with red, blue and brassy; a dusky spot on each scale; ventral fins mottled with dusky; a faint spot on last rays of dorsal bordered by paler; 3 oblique dusky or reddish bars radiating from eye; belly yellowish or brassy.

GENUS APOMOTIS RAFINESQUE

This genus is very close to *Lepomis*, from which it differs only in the development of the supplemental maxillary bone which is rudimentary or wanting in *Lepomis;* the mouth is larger in *Apomotis*, the lower pharyngeals narrow, with acute teeth; gillrakers well developed, long and stiff; pectoral bluntish, shorter than head; scales moderate, 33 to 50.

This genus contains 5 known species widely distributed in American waters.

The only one of these species of *Apomotis* which attains sufficient size or that is sufficiently abundant to be of any value as a food or game-fish, is *Apomotis cyanellus*, the blue-spotted sunfish or green sunfish.

This beautiful little sunfish is found wholly west of the Alleghanies and from the Great Lakes to Mexico. It is usually abundant in all suitable waters from central Ohio and Indiana to the Rio Grande.

It is not often found in lakes or large streams but in the smaller creeks, brooks and ponds it is an abundant and well-known little fish. It does not attain a greater length than 6 to 8 inches and a weight of more than 4 or 5 ounces, but it is a sprightly little fish and excellent for the pan. Like the pumpkin-seed it is, where common, a prime favourite with the small boy. It readily takes a hook baited with grub or angleworm and would make a vicious fight for liberty if it were only larger. In the streams of Nebraska, Kansas, South Dakota and south to Texas, where game-fishes are not abundant the green sunfish is a choice pan-fish.

Head 3; depth $2\frac{1}{2}$; D. X, 11; A. III, 9; scales small, 6 or 7–45 to 55–16, 40 to 48 pores, 8 rows on cheek; gillrakers X+10. Body rather elongate, becoming short and deep with age; head large, with projecting snout; mouth rather large, maxillary broad and flat, with a small supplemental bone, reaching nearly to middle of eye; lower jaw projecting; dorsal spines quite low, the highest scarcely longer than snout, 3 to 4 in head in adult, longer in young; opercular spot smaller than eye, broadly margined with bronze, the black confined to the bony part; pectoral short, not reaching anal, $1\frac{1}{2}$ in head; ventrals not reaching vent. Colour, variable, the prevailing shade green, with a strong brassy lustre on sides, becoming nearly yellow below; each scale usually with a sky-blue spot and more or less of gilt edging, giving an appearance of pale lateral streaks; besides these marks, dusky or obscure vertical bars are often present, and the sides are sprinkled with dark dots; vertical fins marked with blue or green, the anal usually edged in front with pale orange; usually a conspicuous black spot on posterior base of dorsal and anal

343

fins, these sometimes obsolete; cheeks with narrow blue stripes; iris red.

The green sunfish can be readily told from all other species by the fact that the black opercular spot covers only the bony or hard portion of the opercle.

Apomotis symmetricus is a pretty and interesting sunfish, not uncommon in the lower Mississippi Valley and Texas, where it is a common pan-fish.

GENUS LEPOMIS RAFINESQUE

Common Sunfishes

Body oblong or ovate, more or less compressed; mouth small, the jaws about equal; maxillary narrow, supplemental bone reduced to a mere rudiment or wholly wanting; teeth on vomer and palatines, none on tongue; lower pharyngeals narrow, the teeth spherical or paved, all or nearly all sharp, few or none of them conical; gillrakers mostly short; preopercle entire; opercle ending behind in a convex black flap, which becomes greatly developed with age in some species; branchiostegals 6; scales moderate; one dorsal fin with 10 spines; anal with 3; caudal fin emarginate. Colour, brilliant, but evanescent.

A genus with about 8 species which are among the most difficult of our fishes to distinguish. The form of the body, development of the ear-flap, and height of the spines vary with age and condition, while the general appearance and the number of scales and fin-rays are essentially the same in all.

a. Pectoral fin short, obtuse, not reaching beyond front of anal, considerably shorter than head.
b. Gillrakers shortish, rather firm; palatine teeth present.
c. Opercular flap in adult very long but narrow; scales 43 to 48; longest dorsal spine about 3 in head; some bluish stripes on head; belly red in adult;.....................*auritus*, 346
cc. Opercular flap short and broad; scales 36 to 40; longest dorsal spine about 2 in head; side with rows of red spots;
miniatus, 346
bb, Gillrakers very soft and weak; palatine teeth obsolete.
d. Dorsal spines rather long, about 2 in head; side with rows of bronze spots;..............................*garmani*, 347
dd. Dorsal spines short, about 3 in head in adult; colour brilliant, variable;...............................*megalotis*, 347
aa. Pectoral fin longer, more or less pointed, not much, if any, shorter than head, reaching to or beyond front of anal.
e. Scales very large, about 35 in lateral line.
f. Opercular spot short, wholly surrounded by a red margin; side with conspicuous red spots;...................*humilis*, 348
ff Opercular spot plain black; body without red spots;
haplognathus, 348
ee. Scales moderate or small, more than 40 in lateral line.
g. Dorsal fin without black spot at base of last rays; opercular flap short; side with chain-like cross-bands;.....*macrochirus*, 348
gg. Dorsal fin with a large black blotch at base of posterior rays; opercular flap large but not long;............*pallidus*, 349

345

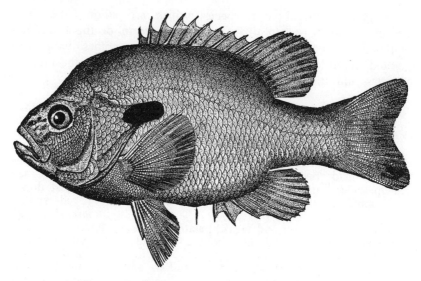

Red-breasted Bream

Lepomis auritus (Linnæus)

The red-breasted bream or yellow-belly is found from Maine to Louisiana and is abundant in all streams east of the Alleghanies. It reaches a length of 6 to 8 inches and is a good little pan-fish. It can be taken readily on the hook baited with angleworm.

Body elongate, not elevated; mouth rather large, oblique, the maxillary reaching past front of eye; gillrakers quite short, X+8 or 9, stiff and rough, set wide apart; opercular flap very long (longer in the adult than in any other sunfish except *L. megalotis*), usually not wider than the eye; lower margin of flap usually pale. Colour, olive; belly largely orange-red; side with reddish spots on a bluish ground; vertical fins chiefly orange or yellowish; head usually with bluish stripes, especially in front of eye, most distinct in adult; fins becoming dusky in spirits; no dusky blotch on last rays of dorsal or anal.

Scarlet Sunfish

Lepomis miniatus Jordan

This handsome little fish is found in the lowland streams along the Gulf Coast from Texas to Florida, passing over even to the

Indian River region. It is probably most abundant about New Orleans. It gets to be about 6 inches in length and is of but little value as a food-fish.

Body oblong and somewhat regularly elliptical; mouth rather large; opercular flap short and broad, entirely black or dark green; gillrakers stout but not very short; pectoral long. Colour, side of male with about 14 rows of red spots, those of lower rows brightest; middle of side with some black spots; some black under pectoral; belly orange with red spots.

In southern Indiana and Illinois is found *L. garmani* which may be not distinct from *miniatus*.

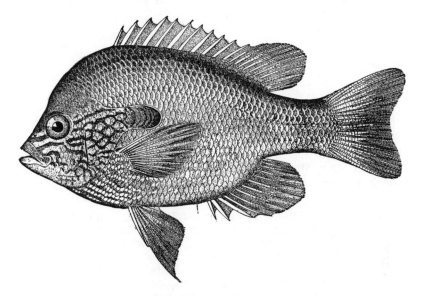

Long-eared Sunfish

Lepomis megalotis (Rafinesque)

One of our most abundant sunfishes from Michigan and Minnesota southward to South Carolina and the Rio Grande. It is found in most streams, especially in clear brooks. It reaches a length of 7 or 8 inches and does not differ essentially from any of the other smaller sunfishes, either as a panfish or in its game qualities.

It is extremely variable in form and colour, but is always one of the most brightly coloured of fresh-water fishes.

347

Body short and deep, compressed, the back very strongly arched in adult, the profile very steep, usually forming an angle above the eyes, but sometimes full and convex; mouth small, oblique, the premaxillary rather below the eye, the maxillary reaching middle of eye; gillrakers very short and soft, weaker than in any other species; dorsal spines very low, the longest little longer than snout, 3 in head; opercular flap in the adult very long and broad, with a pale blue or red margin, which is sometimes very broad, sometimes almost wanting; opercular flap half, or more, longer than the eye in the adult, much shorter in the young. Colour, brilliant blue and orange, the back chiefly blue, the belly entirely orange, the orange on sides in spots, the blue in wavy, vertical streaks; lips blue; cheek orange, with bright blue stripes; blue stripes before the eye, soft parts of vertical fins with the rays blue and the membranes orange; ventrals dusky; iris red.

Red-spotted Sunfish

Lepomis humilis (Girard)

This small, highly-coloured sunfish is found from Ohio and Kentucky west to the Dakotas and south to Texas; locally abundant, especially in sandy streams in the lower Missouri basin. It reaches only about 4 inches in length and, though it will take a hook readily, it is of little importance as a game-fish.

Body oblong, profile not steep; scales large; spines rather high; mucous pores on head very large; opercular flap rather long, broad, and with a very broad red margin which entirely surrounds the black; longest dorsal spine not quite half head; pectoral a little shorter than head; gillrakers rather long and well developed. Colour, bluish, with conspicuous greenish spots and mottlings posteriorly; side with many conspicuous round, salmon-red spots; usually a faint black spot on last rays of dorsal; belly and lower fins red.

Lepomis haplognathus is a rare species known only from Monterey, Nuevo Leon, Mexico. The species is interesting chiefly in that it is the most southern sunfish known.

In the Ohio Valley, and southwestward to Kentucky and Arkansas, is another small sunfish *(Lepomis macrochirus)* reaching a length of 4 or 5 inches. It is related to the bluegill, from which it differs in having no black spot on dorsal or anal

SMALL-MOUTH BLACK BASS, *Micropterus dolomieu*

SMALL-MOUTH BLACK BASS, *Micropterus dolomieu*

SMALL-MOUTH BLACK BASS, *Micropterus dolomieu*
The same individual fish as above, showing the interesting changes in colour markings occurring within a brief time
Photographed at Lake Maxinkuckee, Indiana

fin, in the short opercular flap, and in having chain-like cross-bands on the side. It is a rare species.

Bluegill

Lepomis pallidus (Mitchill)

The bluegill is perhaps the best known and certainly the most important of all our true sunfishes. It is known also as blue bream, blue sunfish, copper-nosed sunfish, dollardee, and doubtless by many other vernacular names. It is found throughout the Great Lakes and in the Mississippi Valley, from western New York and Pennsylvania to Iowa and Missouri, and from Minnesota to Florida and the Rio Grande. It is one of our most variable and widely distributed species, and is found in all lakes, ponds and quiet streams throughout its range. Though found in quiet streams, it is, above all, *the* sunfish of the lakes, whether large or small, but is decidedly more abundant in the smaller ones. In the small glacial lakes of northern Indiana it is found in very great numbers.

The bluegill is the largest of the sunfishes. It reaches a length of 12 to 14 inches, and a weight of nearly a pound. The average weight of those taken at Lake Maxinkuckee is about half a pound, while those at Bass Lake (another famous bluegill lake 10 miles west from Lake Maxinkuckee) do not average more than 3 or 4 ounces. The maximum weight is about $1\frac{1}{2}$ pounds.

As a food-fish the bluegill is of much importance, and of all the species it is the one most often sent to market, where it always brings a good price. As a pan-fish it is excelled, among fresh-water fishes, only by the yellow perch. Its flesh is firm and flaky, and possesses a delicious flavour. And among all the sunfishes it holds the highest rank as a game-fish.

It can be taken at any time in the year, even through the ice in winter. It bites well during the spring and early summer, while from early July until September it is particularly voracious, and fine catches can then be made. It will take any sort of bait, and can be taken with any sort of tackle. Angleworms are probably the best bait, either in still-fishing or trolling, but grasshoppers are also excellent. White grubs, small minnows, small pieces of fish or mussel are good; and they can be taken on the artificial fly, or small trolling spoon.

Most of those who fish for bluegills do so at anchor and with two long cane poles projecting over either side of the stern of the boat. The line always has a float upon it, its distance from the hook regulated by the depth of the water, and the hook is thrown as far from the boat as possible.

The bluegills are usually found in 5 to 15 feet of water on the edges of the bars where there are patches of Potamogeton or other water plants. They usually keep in more or less definite schools, and the patient angler usually lands them all. They do not seize the hook with a rush as does the rock bass, but quietly suck it in, and the fight does not begin until the fish finds that it is hooked, but from then on the fight is of the most vigorous kind, and is kept up to the end with a persistency and viciousness that make the bluegill "the gamest of all fishes for its size."

Colour, rich greenish olive on back, becoming paler on sides; top of head dark greenish; opercles and cheek bluish; opercular flap rich velvety black, a small whitish spot above near its base; side with 3 or 4 broad darker greenish bars; fins all greenish, the pectoral palest, reddish at base; a large black blotch on last rays of dorsal, a similar one on anal; the dark bars become obsolete in the adult; no blue stripes on cheek; no red on fins; old individuals often with the belly coppery red or brassy.

GENUS EUPOMOTIS GILL & JORDAN

This genus is closely related to *Lepomis,* from which it differs only in the blunter and more pavement-like teeth of the lower pharyngeal bones. These bones are usually broader and more concave than in *Lepomis,* the gillrakers are usually shorter and fewer, the supplemental maxillary is reduced or wanting, and the opercular flap is always provided with an orange spot on its lower posterior border. The genus as now understood contains 6 known species.

a. Pectoral fin short, not longer than head, not reaching past origin of anal.
b. Mouth large, maxillary about reaching pupil; supplemental maxillary present; gillrakers hard and of moderate length.

c. Dorsal spines moderate, the longest equalling snout and $\frac{1}{2}$ the orbit; depth $2\frac{1}{3}$; body with 8 or 9 dusky crossbars;
pallidus, 351

cc. Dorsal spines shorter, the longest equalling snout and less than $\frac{1}{3}$ of the orbit;.....................*euryorus,* 351

bb. Mouth smaller, maxillary scarcely reaching orbit; supplemental maxillary absent or reduced to a slight rudiment; gillrakers very short and soft.

d. Pectoral fin slender, nearly as long as head;...*holbrooki,* 352

dd. Pectoral fin obtuse, shorter than head;.........*gibbosus,* 353

aa. Pectoral fin long, slender and pointed, longer than head, reaching middle of anal.

e. Gillrakers long, their ends obtuse; 44 scales in lateral line;
longimanus, 352

ee. Gillrakers short, as in *E. gibbosus,* 39 scales in lateral line;
heros, 354

Eupomotis pallidus, which has received no distinctive common name, occurs in lowland streams from Georgia to Texas. It appears to be rare and only a few specimens are known. It reaches a length of 7 inches.

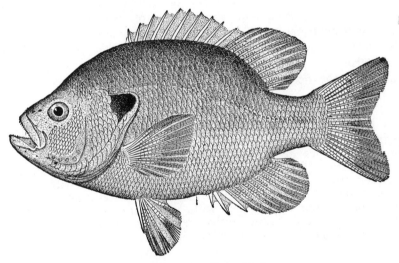

McKay's Sunfish
Eupomotis euryorus (McKay)

This sunfish is known only from southern Michigan, northern Ohio and northern Indiana. It is, preferably, an inhabitant of small lakes, but it has been found also in sluggish streams. In Lost Lake at Maxinkuckee, Indiana, it is abundant in association with the bluegill. It reaches a length of 8 inches, but is of little value as a food or game-fish. It rarely takes the hook and is not sought by even the boy angler. It is, however, a very interesting and handsome fish.

Colour, in spirits, mottled olive, yellowish below; top of head blackish; membranes of vertical fins dusky; ventrals dusky with lighter margins; pectorals pale.

Shell Cracker

Eupomotis holbrooki (Cuvier & Valenciennes)

The habitat of this fish extends from Virginia to Florida in all suitable lowland waters. It is particularly abundant in Florida in which State it seems to be pretty generally distributed. It reaches a length of nearly a foot and is one of the largest and most important sunfishes in the South. Its habits are much the same as those of the bluegill which it also resembles as a food and game-fish. In Florida it is the sunfish which is most frequently taken on the hook, the long cane pole being the rod in most popular use.

Body robust, compressed, elevated, the snout rather produced; maxillary reaching orbit; preopercle slightly toothed; dorsal fin high, the spines about as high as the soft rays, the longest half head; pectoral fin very long, as long as head; gillrakers moderate, obtuse, strongly toothed; opercular flap short, broad, with a broad orange margin below and behind; no palatine teeth; lower pharyngeals broad, the teeth large, with subspherical crowns. Colour, dusky olive, silvery below; throat yellow; fins dark, with yellowish rays; no black spot on dorsal or anal.

Eupomotis longimanus is known only from the St. Johns River, Florida, and is of doubtful validity.

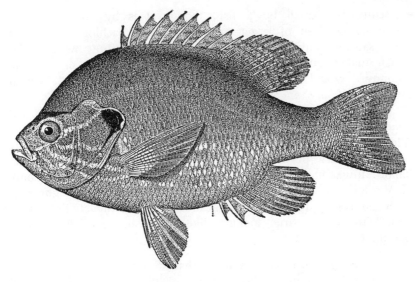

Common Sunfish; Pumpkin-seed

Eupomotis gibbosus (Linnæus)

"Slowly upward, wavering, gleaming
Rose the Ugudwash, the Sunfish;
Seized the line of Hiawatha,
Swung with all his weight upon it.

. . . . .

But when Hiawatha saw him
Slowly rising through the water,
Lifting up his disc refulgent,
Loud he shouted in derision
'Esa! esa! shame upon you,
You are Ugudwash, the Sunfish;
You are not the fish I wanted;
You are not the King of Fishes.'"
—*Longfellow.*

And Hiawatha was quite right. The sunfish is by no means the King of Fishes. But there is no fish which has been oftener sought by the young angler or which has brought more joy to the American boys of every generation. The pumpkin-seed is pre-

353

eminently the small boy's fish, though it is by no means despised by children of larger growth. Never reaching a size that quite satisfies any one except the boy, yet biting with a vim which makes one regret that it is not larger; for a 2 or 3 pound "Sunny," would surely be a fish to try the skill and delight the heart of any angler.

The pumpkin-seed is a familiar inhabitant of clear brooks and ponds from Maine to the Great Lakes and southward east of the Alleghanies to Florida. In the Mississippi Valley it is found only in the northern portion, being fairly abundant in Ohio, Indiana, Illinois, Iowa and northward. It is said to be rather rare south of Virginia. It reaches a length of 8 inches and a weight of 6 or 8 ounces, and is "a very beautiful and compact little fish, perfect in all its parts, looking like a brilliant coin fresh from the mint."

Colour, greenish-olive above, shaded with bluish, the sides spotted and blotched with orange; belly orange-yellow; cheek orange, with wavy blue streaks; lower fins orange, the bluish and orange spotted; opercular flap rather small, the lower posterior part always bright scarlet, a mark which at once distinguishes this species, when adult, from all our other brightly coloured sunfishes.

Eupomotis gibbosus is subject to considerable variations as is to be expected in a species of such wide distribution. Blue stripes and blue markings on the side are very prominent in examples from Hicksville, Ohio, and Marion, Iowa. Examples from Winona Lake, Indiana, have 7 or 8 faint dark bars on side and no blue stripes on cheek.

Red-eared Sunfish

Eupomotis heros (Baird & Girard)

This sunfish is found from northern Indiana to Florida and the Rio Grande. It is an inhabitant of lowland streams and ponds, but does not appear to be common anywhere. It reaches a length of 6 or 7 inches. Nothing is definitely known as to its food and game qualities.

Body robust, moderately elongate, dorsal and ventral outlines equally curved; head rather large, the projecting snout forming

354

a considerable angle above the eyes; mouth rather wide, oblique, maxillary reaching slightly part front of eye; pectoral fin reaching beyond middle of pupil; opercular flap smaller than eye, much as in *E. gibbosus;* gillrakers short and not very stiff; pharyngeal teeth paved, less blunt than in *E. gibbosus.* Colour, dark, greenish above, gradually becoming brassy toward belly which is light brassy; opercular spot greenish black; the flap with a broad, blood-red border in the male, plain in the female; no dark spot on dorsal or anal.

GENUS MICROPTERUS LACÉPÈDE

The Black Basses

Body oblong, compressed, the back not much elevated; head oblong, conic; mouth very large, oblique, the broad maxillary reaching nearly to or even beyond the eye; supplemental bone well developed; lower jaw prominent; teeth on jaws, vomer and palatines in broad villiform bands, the inner depressible; usually no teeth on tongue; preopercle entire, the opercle ending in 2 flat points without cartilaginous flap; branchiostegals normally 6; gillrakers long and slender; scales rather small, weakly ctenoid; lateral line complete; dorsal fin divided by a deep notch, the spines low and not especially strong; anal fin much smaller than the dorsal; pectoral obtusely pointed, the upper rays longest; ventrals below the pectorals and close together; caudal fin emarginate. Size large.

Two species, among the most important of American game-fishes, now largely introduced into European waters.

a. Mouth moderate, the maxillary in adult not extending beyond eye; scales small, about 17 rows on cheek; young more or less barred or spotted; never with a black lateral band;

dolomieu, 355

aa. Mouth very large, the maxillary in adult extending beyond eye; scales rather large, about 10 rows on cheek; young with a blackish lateral band;..............*salmoides,* 357

Small-mouthed Black Bass; Black Bass

Micropterus dolomieu Lacépède

In the felicitous words of Dr. James A. Henshall, the author of the "Book of the Black Bass,"

"The black bass is eminently an American fish; he has the faculty of asserting himself and making himself completely at home wherever placed. He is plucky, game, brave and unyielding to the last when hooked. He has the arrowy rush of the trout, the untiring strength and bold leap of the salmon, while he has a system of fighting tactics peculiarly his own. He will rise to the artificial fly as readily as the salmon or the brook trout, under the same conditions; and will take the live minnow, or other live bait, under any and all circumstances favourable to the taking of any other fish. I consider him, *inch for inch* and *pound for pound*, the gamest fish that swims." And there are few, if any, who will be disposed to take issue in this matter with so experienced and expert an angler as Dr. Henshall.

The black bass is found in most suitable waters from Lake Champlain westward to Manitoba and southward on both sides of the mountains from James River, Virginia, to South Carolina and the Great Lakes to northern Mississippi and Arkansas. Through the operations of the Federal and various State Fish Commissions it has been introduced into many waters to which it was not native. It was planted in the headwaters of the Potomac as early as 1853, and since then it has been successfully introduced into many waters in New England and other states east of the Alleghanies, into many of the Western States, and in England, France, Germany, and other foreign countries.

In nearly all the localities where the black bass has been planted it has done well, and it is now an abundant species not only throughout its natural habitat but in many other places. It is by preference a fish of the clear running streams, and clearer, colder lakes. In the North it is equally abundant in lakes and streams, while in the southern part of its range it will be found only in the cooler streams which possess a good current.

The habits, game qualities and food value of the black bass are so well known, and so much has been written about this splendid fish, that a lengthy presentation of the subject is not given here.

This fish varies greatly in size in different waters. The maximum weight seems to be about 5 pounds. An example caught in Lake Maxinkuckee, 18¾ inches long, and 12 inches in circumference, weighed 4 pounds. The largest ever taken in that lake weighed about 5 pounds.

LARGE-MOUTH BLACK BASS, *Micropterus salmoides*
Photographed at Lake Maxinkuckee, Indiana

YELLOW PERCH, *Perca flavescens*
Photographed at Lake Maxinkuckee

Like all fishes of wide distribution, the black bass presents great variations in colour; but whatever the colour the adult can always be readily distinguished from the large-mouthed black bass by the presence of about 17 rows of scales on the cheek instead of 10 or 11 in the latter species.

Head 2½ to 3½; depth 2¾ to 3½; eye 5 to 6½; D. X, 13 to 15; A. III, 10 to 12; scales 11-72 to 85-25, 67 to 78 pores, about 17 rows on cheek. Body ovate-fusiform, becoming deeper with age; mouth large, but smaller than in the large-mouthed black bass; maxillary ending considerably in front of posterior border of orbit, except in very old examples; scales on cheek minute; those on body small; dorsal fin deeply notched, but less so than in the other species, the ninth spine being about half as long as the fifth, and not much shorter than the tenth; soft dorsal and anal each scaly at the base. General colouration, dull golden green, with bronze lustre, often blotched with darker, especially on head; young with darker spots along the sides, which tend to form short vertical bars, but never a dark lateral band; 3 bronze bands radiating from eye across cheek and opercles; a dusky spot on point of opercle; belly white; caudal fin yellowish at base, then black, with white tips; dorsal with bronze spots, its edge dusky. In some waters the fin-markings are obsolete, but they are usually conspicuous in the young. Southern examples usually have the scales on lower part of sides with faint dark streaks. Adults have all these markings more or less obliterated, the colour ultimately becoming a uniform dead green, without silvery lustre.

Large-mouthed Black Bass; Straw Bass

Micropterus salmoides (Lacépède)

Among the *Centrarchidæ*, the large-mouthed black bass is second only to its cogener, the small-mouthed species, as a game-fish. It is equally well known to anglers, and its range is even greater. From Canada and the Red River of the North it extends southward to Florida, Texas, and even into Mexico. In all suitable waters it is everywhere abundant, but prefers lakes, bayous and other sluggish waters. In the small lakes of the Upper Mississippi Valley it is most abundant in those of moderate or shallow depths. Some small lakes that are rather shallow, whose bottoms are chiefly mud, and whose water is warm, are found to be well suited to the straw bass, and to be entirely without the small-mouthed black bass. But small lakes of considerable depth, cool water and with bottom partly of mud and partly of

357

sand and gravel, such as Lake Maxinkuckee, seem equally well adapted to both species. In the ponds, bayous, lagoons and sluggish streams of the South the straw bass is very abundant. It frequently enters brackish water along the coast, where it seems to be permanently resident.

In the North the maximum weight of the straw bass is about 8 pounds. Examples of that size are rarely seen, however. The average size does not exceed 3 or 4 pounds, though examples weighing 5 or 6 pounds are not at all rare. In the warm waters of the South, particularly in Florida, where the temperatare is equable and food abundant, this fish attains a much greater size. Dr. Henshall gives the maximum weight at 12 to 14 pounds, he himself having seen examples of those weights.

The straw bass, under favourable surroundings, grows very rapidly. The conditions favourable for rapid and large growth are abundant food and waters of warm or moderate temperature and wide extent. The species is very productive. In May, 1892, the Fish Commission placed in one of the rearing ponds at Washington 15 adult large-mouth black bass, 7 or 8 of which were females. These fish spawned in June and at Thanksgiving time, when the young were removed from the pond, there were taken out, by actual count, over 37,000 young, each 3 to 4 inches long and 500 each weighing about one-half pound. These fish had received abundant food, but the 500 larger ones had doubt-less eaten many smaller ones of their own kind.

This fish has received many vernacular names, among which may be mentioned large-mouthed black bass, straw bass, green bass, bayou bass, slough bass, lake bass, moss bass, grass bass, marsh bass, Oswego bass, trout, green trout, welchman, chub, and many others more or less absurd. The most distinctive and expressive name is doubtless "large-mouthed black bass," the only objection to which is its length. For many reasons "straw bass" for this species and "black bass" for the small-mouthed species are excellent names.

The relative merits of the 2 species as game-fishes have been much discussed. This depends upon many factors, as the character of the water with regard to extent, depth, temperature and presence of vegetation, character of bottom, food, season, time of day, personality of the particular fish, and many others. Dr. Henshall regards them as of equal gameness. Our own experience leads us to believe that where the 2 species are found in the same water, the small-mouthed is superior in all those qualities which go together to make a game-fish. The straw-bass is, however, an equally good fighter in some portions of its range and is worthy the highest respect of all who go a-angling.

This bass varies greatly in colour and proportional measurements in different waters. There need be no difficulty, however in identifying any specimen belonging to the species. From the small-mouthed black bass, the only species with which it might be confused, the large-mouthed black bass can always be told by its having only 10 or 11 rows of scales on the cheek.

Head 3 to $3\frac{1}{2}$; depth 3 to $3\frac{1}{4}$; eye 5 to 6; D. X, 12 or 13; A. III, 10 or 11; scales 7–65 to 70–18, about 58 to 67 pores, 10 or 11 rows of scales on cheek. Body ovate-fusiform, becoming deeper with age, moderately compressed; head large; mouth very wide, the maxillary in adult reaching beyond the eye, shorter in the young; scales on body comparatively large; teeth sometimes present on tongue; gillrakers longer than gill-fringes; dorsal fin very deeply notched, its fifth spine $3\frac{1}{4}$ in head. General colour, dark green above, sides and below greenish silvery; young with a blackish stripe along the side from opercle to middle of caudal fin; 3 oblique dark stripes across the cheek and opercles; some dark spots above and below lateral line; caudal fin pale at base, then blackish, and whitish at tip; belly white. As the fish grows older the black lateral band breaks up and grows fainter, and the colour becomes more and more uniform pale dull green, the back being darker.

THE PERCHES

Family XLVI. Percidæ

THE *Percidæ* comprise one of the largest and, from some points of view, one of the most interesting groups of freshwater fishes. Though represented in both Europe and America by numerous species, the great majority are little known to any except to those who really study fishes, while a few of the species are among the best known of the inhabitants of our lakes and streams. These are our yellow perch and wall-eyed pike. The vast majority of the species belong to the subfamily of darters (*Etheostominæ*), all of which are American. They are among the most singular and interesting of our fishes, all being of very small size and most of them of very brilliant colouration. None of the more than 80 species is of any value as food, but some are used as live bait. Descriptions of all the species and much interesting matter concerning their habits may be found in our "Fishes of North and Middle America." In the following keys and descriptions only those few possessing game qualities and food-value are considered.

a. Canine teeth on jaws and palatines; body elongate. *Stizostedion,* 360
aa. Canine teeth none; body oblong....................*Perca,* 364

GENUS STIZOSTEDION RAFINESQUE

The American Pike-perches

Body elongate, fusiform, the back broad; head subconical, long; cheeks, opercles, and top of head more or less scaly; mouth large, the jaws about equal; premaxillaries protractile, but little movable; teeth in villiform bands, the jaws and palatines with long, sharp canines; gill-rakers slender but strong; gill-membranes separate; preopercle serrate, the serræ below turned forward; opercle with one or more spines; dorsal fins well separated, the first with 12 to 15 spines, the second with 17 to 21 rays; last dorsal spine not erectile, but bound down by membrane; anal spines 2, slender, closely bound to the soft rays, which are 11 to 14 in number; ventrals well separated; scales small, strongly ctenoid, the lateral line continuous.

360

This genus contains 2 species, large, carnivorous fishes of the fresh waters of North America, highly valued as food and ranking among our most interesting and important game-fishes.

a. Pyloric cœca 3, of nearly equal length, and each about as long as the stomach....................................*vitreum,* 361
aa. Pyloric cœca 5 to 7, 4 of them much shorter than the stomach, the others smaller and variable ....*canadense, 363*

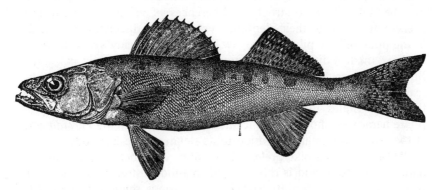

Wall-eyed Pike; Pike-perch

Stizostedion vitreum (Mitchill)

This important fish is a species of wide distribution. It is found from Lake Champlain westward throughout the Great Lakes region and to Assiniboia. It is native also to the small lakes of New York and the Susquehanna and Juniata rivers, east of the Alleghenies. In the Mississippi Valley it occurs in many of the larger streams and small lakes as far south as Georgia and Alabama. Though found in many streams, it is preferably a fish of the lakes, and it reaches its greatest abundance in the Great Lakes, particularly in Lake Erie. In different parts of its range it is known by different names. Among the Great Lakes it is called the wall-eyed pike, yellow pike, doré or dory by the French-Canadians, and pickerel in places where the true pike (*Esox lucius*) is found.

In the Susquehanna and Juniata rivers, and in the small lakes of northern Indiana, it is known as salmon or jack salmon, names absurd and wholly without excuse. Southward in the Mississippi Valley it is the jack. Elsewhere it is called okow, blowfish, or green pike. In the Great Lakes, particularly in Lakes Erie and Ontario, the young of a certain colour are known as blue pike, which commercial fishermen believe to be a wholly distinct species from the yellow pike.   So firmly fixed is this belief that they have little patience with the naturalist who tells them otherwise.   They all admit, however, that they have never found any blue pike with roe, and are unable to point out any differences except that of colour.   And not all of them agree regarding that character.   We have been shown fish which some fishermen said were blue pike which others as stoutly maintained were yellow pike.   It may be stated that no structural differences of value are known, and everything points to their identity.   Formerly no distinction was made in the price of blue pike and yellow pike, but for many years the dealers have made a difference, and now the blue pike is classed as ''soft.'' But this is principally on account of their abundance rather than to any real inferiority of flavour or keeping qualities.   A book-name used by the United States Fish Commission is pike-perch, and a very appropriate name it is, showing at once its relationship with the *Percidæ* and at the same time calling attention to its slender, pike-like body.

The wall-eyed pike prefers clear water, with rock, gravel, sand, or hard clay bottom, and is rarely found in muddy streams or lakes.   It is a voracious fish, feeding largely upon various minnows, but not to any great extent upon the young of the whitefish or other important food-fishes.   It also feeds freely upon crawfishes during the season when in shallow water.

This fish ordinarily inhabits water of moderate depth, deeper than that frequented by the black bass, but more shallow than that sought by the whitefish and cisco.   It varies greatly in size, the maximum length being about 3 feet and the maximum weight about 25 pounds. But examples of this size are very rare.   Specimens weighing even 15 pounds are not common.   It is doubtful if those taken in the Great Lakes average heavier than 10 pounds.   Those taken in Lake Maxinkuckee run from 3 to 7 pounds.   The so-called blue pike average less than 2 pounds.

The spawning-time of the wall-eyed pike is in the early spring, and begins even before the ice goes off.   The spawning-place is in shoal water, usually on the edges of the bars, on hard or gravel bottom.   The eggs are very small, only about $\frac{1}{12}$ inch in diameter, and average about 150,000 to the quart.   The spawning fish at Put-in Bay average about 2 pounds in weight, and produce about 90,000 eggs each.   Larger fish produce proportionally a greater number; and a 20-pound fish would yield about 900,000 eggs.

This is one of the most important fishes propagated by the United States Fish Commission. The principal propagating-station is at Put-in Bay, and the output in 1900 was 89,700,000 eggs, fry, and finger-lings.

Those who are acquainted with the wall-eyed pike as a food-fish hold it in very high esteem. The flesh is firm, flaky, and white, and of delicious flavour.

Colour, dark olive, finely mottled with brassy, the latter colour forming indistinct oblique bars; sides of head more or less vermiculated; lower jaw flesh-coloured; belly and lower fins pinkish; spinous dorsal with a large jet-black blotch on membrane of the last 2 or 3 spines, otherwise nearly plain; second dorsal and caudal mottled — olive and yellowish; base of pectoral dusky, without distinct black blotch.

The colour of this fish is very variable, as is indicated by some of its vernacular names, as yellow pike, gray pike, and blue pike. It can always be told from the sauger by its fewer subequal pyloric cœca.

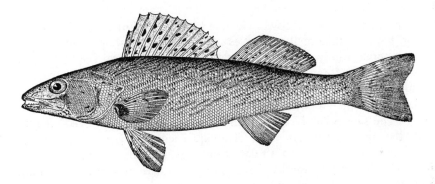

Sauger; Sand-pike

Stizostedion canadense (Smith)

The sauger is found from the St. Lawrence westward through the Great Lakes, and in the Mississippi Valley west to Montana and south to Tennessee and Arkansas. It is especially abundant northward, in the St. Lawrence and the lower Great Lakes, where the typical form is found. In the upper Great Lakes and southwestward is found the sub-species *griseum*, which differs chiefly in the smoother opercles, fewer opercular spines, and the less complete squamation of the head. In the upper Missouri basin is found the subspecies *boreum,* differing only in the more slender head.

The sauger is a much smaller fish than the wall-eyed pike, its length seldom exceeding a foot or 18 inches and its weight a pound or two. It is on this account much less important as a food-fish than the wall-eye. Nor is it much valued as a game-fish, except, perhaps, in the Mississippi Valley, where it is frequently taken by casting and sometimes by trolling.

A few years ago the sauger was, to the few elect who knew where to find it, the choicest game-fish of the lower Wabash River; and we knew a minister who always went "saugering" when he failed in other ways to get the proper inspiration for his next Sunday's sermon. Starting in at the Vandalia bridge, he would direct his oarsman to get out into the current, then row slowly up stream, even to old Fort Harrison and beyond, perhaps to Durkee's Ferry; then, turning, slowly drift with the current home again. Meanwhile, with a small, silvery minnow (a satin-fin, creek chub, or river chub) at the end of 50 feet of line, trolling through the quiet ripples and over the deep pools, he patiently waits for the sauger's strike; and, while waiting, his eyes take in the beauties of the river, the shore, and the sky; ideas come readily, his thoughts fall together in logical sequence, and when Sunday comes, the sermon that he preaches is filled with sunshine, and love, and faith in humanity; and his flock know that their pastor has spent a day upon the river.

The sauger can be easily distinguished from the wall-eyed pike by its having 4 to 7 pyloric cœca of unequal length. Colour, olive-gray, sides brassy or orange, with dark mottlings, most distinct in the young, which are sharply marked; first dorsal with 2 or 3 rows of round black spots, but no black blotch on last spines; second dorsal with 3 irregular rows of dark spots; a large black blotch on base of pectoral; caudal dusky and yellowish.

GENUS *PERCA LINNÆUS*

The River Perch

Body oblong, somewhat compressed, the back elevated; cheeks scaly, opercles mostly naked, the opercle armed with a single spine; preopercle and shoulder-girdle serrated, the former with retrorse, hooked serrations below; premaxillaries protractile; teeth in villiform

WHITE BASS, *Roccus chrysops*

SAUGER, *Stizostedion canadense*
Photographed at Pan-American from specimen from Lake Erie

STRIPED BASS OR ROCKFISH, *Roccus lineatus*

YELLOW BASS, *Morone interrupta*

bands on jaws, vomer, and palatines; no canine teeth; branchiostegals 7; gill-membranes separate; scales small, ctenoid; lateral line complete; dorsal fins entirely separate; caudal emarginate; air-bladder present; pyloric cœca 3.

Three species known, all freshwater fishes of northern regions, only one of them in America.

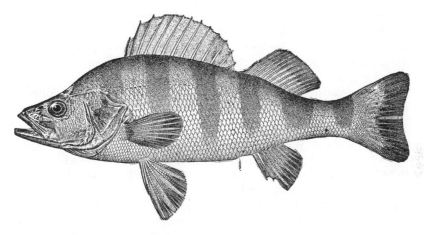

Yellow Perch; Ringed Perch

Perca flavescens (Mitchill)

"I pray you, sir, give me some observations and directions concerning the *Pearch*, for they say he is both a very good and a bold-biting fish, and I would fain learne to fish for him."

—*The Complete Angler.*

The yellow perch is found in the eastern United States, chiefly northward and eastward. It is abundant in the Great Lakes and in the larger coastwise streams and lakes from Nova Scotia to North Carolina; also in most of the small lakes in the upper Mississippi Valley, especially in northern Indiana, Illinois, Michigan, Wisconsin, Minnesota, and Iowa. It is found in some of the streams of this region, but it is by preference a lake fish. It is not known from the Ohio River, nor from the lower Missouri. In most of the New England lakes and those of New York it is an abundant and well-known fish.

Wherever found, this species is the perch *par excellence*. Among other names by which it is known are American perch, raccoon perch, red perch, and striped perch. It is one of the most abundant and best known of freshwater fishes. Its usual length is 10 to 14 inches, and its weight $\frac{1}{2}$ to 2 pounds. Examples of 3 and 4 pounds, however, have been recorded. The largest examples of which we have a definite record are one of $4\frac{1}{4}$ pounds recorded by Dr. Goode, caught in Delaware Bay by Dr. C. C. Abbott, and another reported to us by Mr. F. A. Lucas. It was taken at Moreys Hole, Massachusetts, and weighed 3 pounds 2 ounces. The yellow perch of Europe seems to grow much larger, examples of as great as 8 and 9 pounds having been recorded.

As a pan-fish we do not know of any better among American freshwater fishes. We have experimented with the yellow perch and several other species, including both species of black bass, the blue-gill, wall-eyed pike, and rock-bass, eating each for several days in succession, and found the yellow perch the sweetest and most delicious of them all. One does not tire of it so soon as of the other kinds. Several other persons who tried the same experiment reached the same conclusion. In most parts of its range it is highly esteemed, and in many places it is of very considerable commercial importance. In the Great Lakes, the Potomac River, and the small lakes in the upper Mississippi Valley large quantities are taken, which always find a ready sale.

As a game-fish the yellow perch can be commended chiefly on account of the fact that anybody can catch it. It can be taken with hook and line any month in the year and with any sort of bait, grasshoppers, angleworms, grubs, small minnows, pieces of mussel, or pieces of fish; and it will even rise, and freely, too, on occasion, to the artificial fly; we have taken it "skittering," and also on the trolling-spoon. It is easily taken through the ice in winter, when small minnows are the best bait, as they are perhaps at other times. The yellow perch is not a great fighter,— its small size precludes that possibility,— but it bites well, and a 2-pounder, or one even half that size, is a fish well worth one's while to take. If it be angled for in deep water,— say 25 to 40 feet,— in water that is cold and pure, and with light tackle, it will be found able to make a fight quite enough to please any except the most blasé of anglers.

Besides, the yellow perch is a fish that can be caught by the women and children, who do not, as a rule, seek the more noble game-fishes; and many an inland summer resort is made vastly more attrac-

366

tive because our wives and children who are spending the summer at the little inland lake are always able to bring in good strings of delicious yellow perch. As Thoreau has said in " Walden Pond": " It is a true fish, such as the angler loves to put into his basket or hang on top of his willow twig on shady afternoons, along the banks of the streams." Only the yellow perch is by preferenee a fish of the small lakes rather than of the streams.

This perch is gregarious and may usually be found in schools.

> "Perch, like the Tartar clans, in troops remove,
> And, urged by famine or by pleasure, rove;
> But if one prisoner, as in war, you seize,
> You'll prosper, master of the camp with ease;
> For, like the wicked, unalarmed they view
> Their fellows perish, and their path pursue."

Artificial propagation, in the full sense of the term, has not been attempted with the yellow perch, but mature fish have been placed in aquariums and their naturally fertilized eggs hatched. The eggs are arranged in a very interesting manner, being laid in a single mass, which soon unfolds into a ribbon-like structure. The length of this string is very great, sometimes exceeding 7 feet. One yellow perch in a Fish Commission aquarium at Washington deposited a string of eggs 7 feet 4 inches long, 4 inches wide at one end and 2 at the other. After being fertilized this string weighed 2 pounds 9 ounces, while the weight of the fish before the eggs were discharged was only 1 pound 8 ounces. The eggs are very small, measuring only $\frac{1}{13}$ inch in diameter, and requiring 28,000 to the quart. At Washington the spawning-time extends from the middle of March to the middle of April.

Through the various fish commissions the yellow perch has been introduced quite successfully into a number of small lakes in Washington, Oregon, and California.

Colour on back, olivaceous; sides golden yellow; belly white; side with about 6 or 8 broad dark bars, which extend from back to below axis of body; lower fins largely red or orange, especially in the spring; upper fins olivaceous; a distinct black spot sometimes present on spinous dorsal. The colour varies greatly: the yellow is sometimes very bright, at other times quite pale; and the black bars are much stronger in some waters than in others. There is also frequently a greenish, sometimes coppery, reddish or purplish wash on head and sides; sometimes in mature breeding fish the lower fins are very brilliantly red.

THE ROBALOS

Family XLVII. Centropomidæ

BODY elongate, back considerably elevated, the ventral outline straight, angulated at the anal fin; scales ctenoid, varying in size; lateral line conspicuous, extending on caudal fin; head depressed, pike-like, the lower jaw projecting; villiform teeth, in bands, on jaws, vomer, and palatines; tongue smooth; maxillary broad, truncate behind, with a strong supplemental bone; pseudobranchiæ small; preopercle with a double ridge, the posterior margin strongly serrate, with larger spines at the angle; preorbital and suprascapular serrated; opercle without true spines; dorsal fins well separated, the first with 8 spines, the first and second short, the third and fourth longest; anal with 3 spines, the second strong, the third long and slender; these fins moving in scaly sheaths; caudal forked; air-bladder well developed.

This family contains one genus with about 15 species, all American, and most of them game-fishes and of moderate food-value. The species are all of salt or brackish water, and their habits resemble those of the basses, as their common name, robalo, indicates, robalo being the Spanish name for the European bass. The majority of the species are of little value as food, the flesh being coarse and with little flavour.

Centropomus viridis, the Pacific robalo, occurs from Panama northward to Lower California. It is in most parts of its range a common fish, reaching a length of 2 to 4 feet, and is valued somewhat as a food-fish.

Colour, greenish on back; sides dull silvery; upper fins dusky, lower ones paler; ventrals plain yellowish, scarcely dotted with dusky; no yellow on other fins; lateral line black; some dusky at base of pectoral and behind second anal spine.

C. undecimalis, the common robalo or snook, is the best-known species of the family, as well as the largest and most abundant. It is common on sandy shores throughout the West Indies, and from Florida to Surinam. It occurs at Key West and is common about Porto Rico, entering the lower courses of the rivers, where it is sought by the local anglers. It attains a length of 3 or 4 feet, though examples of that size are not frequent; those usually taken or seen in the markets rarely exceed 2 feet in length. The flesh is white and flaky, and in Porto Rico is highly esteemed as food, but at Key West it is little valued.

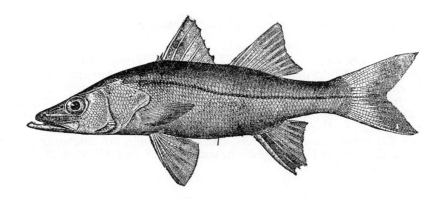

We have never taken the snook with the fly or on the hook, but it is said to take the hook readily and even to rise to the fly. We have been told that the army and navy officers stationed at San Juan, Porto Rico, have good sport trolling for robalos in the mouths of the rivers along the north side of the island.

C. parallelus is known only from Cuba, Santo Domingo, Porto Rico, and Pernambuco. It enters rivers and lakes and may be found long distances from salt water. In Porto Rico it ascends the larger streams well toward the interior of the island. It reaches a foot in length, is a good food-fish, and possesses some game qualities. In Porto Rico it is sought by the local anglers in the lower parts of the Rio de la Plata, the Manati, and the Rio Grande de Arecibo.

THE SEA-BASS

Family XLVIII. Serranidæ

BODY oblong, more or less compressed, covered with adherent scales of moderate or small size, which are usually but not always ctenoid; premaxillaries protractile; teeth all conical or pointed, in bands, present on jaws, vomer, and palatines; pseudobranchiæ large; gill-membranes separate, free from the isthmus; cheeks and opercles always scaly; preopercle usually serrate; opercle usually ending in 1 or 2 flat spines; nostrils double; lateral line single, not extending on the caudal fin; air-bladder present, usually small and adherent to the walls of the abdomen.

This is one of the largest as well as one of the most important families of fishes. It contains about 75 genera and over 400 species, all carnivorous fishes, mostly marine, and found in all warm and temperate seas. Several genera are found in fresh water. In our waters are found 29 genera and about 100 species, nearly all of which are more or less valued as food. Only a few, however, are sufficiently abundant or of sufficient size to justify detailed descriptions in this work.

a. Dorsal fins 2, sometimes slightly joined.
b. Dorsal fins well separated, the spines rather weak; anal III, 12, the spines graduated; lower jaw projecting; base of tongue with teeth ....*Roccus,* 372
bb. Dorsal fins joined, the spines strong; anal III, 9, the spines not graduated; jaws subequal; no teeth on base of tongue.
Morone, 376
aa. Dorsal fin single, sometimes deeply divided.
c. Maxillary with a distinct supplemental bone.
d. Inner teeth of jaws not depressible or hinged.
e. Soft dorsal longer than spinous part; vertebræ $10+14=24$.
f. Dorsal spines 9; caudal lunate ....*Liopropoma.*
ff. Dorsal spines 6; caudal truncate ....*Chorististium.*
ee. Soft dorsal shorter than spinous part; vertebræ 25 to 36.
g. Head not armed with spinigerous ridges; dorsal fin deeply notched.
Stereolepis, 377
gg. Head armed with rough spinigerous crests; dorsal fin low and continuous ....*Polyprion.*
dd. Inner teeth of jaws depressible or hinged.
h. Pectoral unsymmetrical, its upper rays longest..*Gonioplectrus,*
hh. Pectoral symmetrical, rounded, its middle rays longest.

i. Frontal bone of skull with a transverse ridge on posterior part.
Petrometopon, 380

ii. Frontal bone of skull without transverse ridge.

j. Dorsal spines 9 .... *Centropholis.*

jj. Dorsal spines 11, rarely 10 but never 9.

k. Parietal crests not produced forward on the frontals.

l. Scales of lateral line normal, marked by radiating ridges.

m. Cranium narrow above the interorbital space and deeply concave; occipital crest meeting interorbital region .... *Epinephelus, 381*

mm. Cranium very broad and flat above, the interorbital little concave, the occipital crest disappearing before reaching the interorbital region ....*Garrupa, 386*

ll. Scales of lateral line each with 4 to 6 strong, radiating ridges.
Promicrops, 387

kk. Parietal crests produced forward on the frontals.

n. Frontals with a process or knob on each side behind the interorbital area; anal rays III, 8, rarely III, 9.

o. Preopercle with a single antrorse hook or spine near the angle.
Alphestes, 388

oo. Preopercle without antrorse spine ....*Dermatolepis, 389*

nn. Frontals without processes on the upper surface; anal rays III, 11 or 12, very rarely III, 9 or 10...............*Mycteroperca,*

cc. Maxillary without supplemental bone.

p. Gill-rakers comparatively short and wide apart; lateral line not running close to the back (except in *Serranus*).

q. Ventral fins inserted below or more or less behind axil of pectoral.

r. Dorsal fin with 4 or 5 spines produced in long filaments.
Cratinus, 395

rr. Dorsal without long filamentous spines, not more than one of the spines especially produced.

s. Body short and deep, the back elevated, the depth more than $\frac{2}{5}$ the length; preopercle with a few antrorse serræ on its lower limb.
Hypoplectrus, 395

ss. Body comparatively elongate, the depth $\frac{1}{3}$ to $\frac{1}{4}$ the length; no hooked spinules on lower limb of opercle......*Paralabrax, 395*

qq. Ventral fins anterior, inserted more or less in advance of axil of pectoral.

t. Smooth area on top of head very short and small, as seen on removing skin; caudal fin not lunate, but rounded or ending in 3 points....................................*Centropristes, 397*

tt. Smooth area on top of head very large; caudal fin lunate or truncate ....*Diplectrum, 398*

pp. Gill-rakers very long, slender, and close-set; lateral line running close to back ....*Paranthias.*

GENUS ROCCUS MITCHILL

The Striped Bass

Body rather elongate; scales smooth; spines slender; base of tongue with 1 or 2 patches of teeth; anal spines graduated; dorsal fins entirely separate; anal rays III, 11 or 12; lower jaw projecting. Only 2 species, both American and both valued food-fishes.

a. Teeth on base of tongue in a single patch; body rather deep and compressed, the depth more than $\frac{1}{3}$ the length; back arched.
chrysops, 372
aa. Teeth on base of tongue in 2 parallel patches; body rather slender, the depth less than $\frac{1}{3}$ the length; back not arched.
lineatus, 373

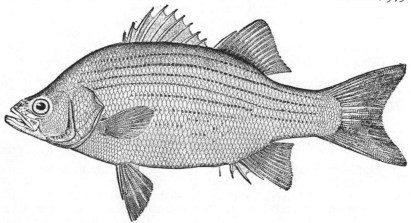

White Bass; White Lake Bass

Roccus chrysops (Rafinesque)

The white bass is found throughout the Great Lakes region from the St. Lawrence to Manitoba, and south in the Mississippi Valley to the Ouachita River in Arkansas. It is generally abundant in the Great Lakes, rare in the Mississippi basin, and not found at all east of the Alleghenies. It does not occur in salt water, but frequents the deep, still waters of the lakes, seldom ascending small streams. It reaches a length of a foot to 18 inches and a weight of 1 to 2 pounds. It is a good food-fish and ranks well as a game-fish. It readily takes the hook when baited with grub, angleworm, or small minnow,

WHITE PERCH, *Morone americana*

CONEY, *Petrometopon cruentatus*

ROCK HIND, *Epinephelus adscensionis*

NIGGER FISH, *Bodianus fulvus*

and will rise to the fly. Thaddeus Norris tells about fly-fishing for the white bass many years ago with a young army officer near Detroit. They met with indifferent success until they tried the mouth of a small creek on the Canadian side, where they caught 25 fish in a short time. They later discovered they had been fishing in preserved waters. The Canadian owner of the land through which the creek flowed was in the habit of seining the fish out of the river and retaining them in the creek (across the mouth of which he had placed netting) until the market price was high enough to please him.

Body rather deep and compressed, the back considerably arched; head subconical, slightly depressed at the nape; mouth moderate, nearly horizontal, the lower jaw little projecting; maxillary reaching middle of pupil, $2\frac{3}{4}$ in head; teeth on base of tongue in a single patch, a patch also on each side of tongue; margin of subopercle with a deep notch; head scaled to between the nostrils; preopercular serræ feeble, strongest at the angle; gill-rakers rather long and slender, as long as the gill-fringes; longest dorsal spine 2 in head; anal spines graduated, the second $\frac{1}{3}$ length of head; middle caudal rays $1\frac{2}{3}$ in outer.

Colour, silvery, tinged with golden below; sides with narrow dusky lines, about 5 above the lateral line, 1 along it, and a variable number below it, these sometimes more or less interrupted or transposed.

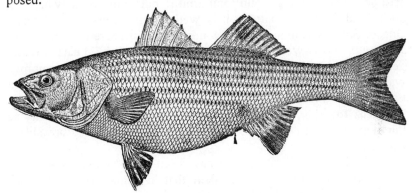

Striped Bass; Rockfish; Rock

Roccus lineatus (Bloch)

" The stately Bass, old Neptune's fleeting Post
That tides it out and in from sea to coast."
— *Wood*, New England's Prospect (1634).

The striped bass occurs on our Atlantic coast north to the St. Lawrence River and south to the Escambia River in western Florida.

It is rather rare in the Gulf of Mexico, and is most common between Cape May and Cape Cod and on the North Carolina coast. It is particularly abundant in the great estuaries and open stretches of large rivers. It is strictly an anadromous fish, living chiefly in salt or brackish water and entering fresh water only at spawning-time. It ascends the Potomac to the Great Falls, and the other rivers of the Middle States until it meets obstructions. In the St. Lawrence it reaches Quebec at least, and there is a record of an example taken in the Niagara River at Lewiston, but this may have been a misidentification of the white bass.

The great abundance of the striped bass excited the wonder of the early colonists.

"The Basse is an excellent fish, both fresh & salte, one hundred whereof salted (at market) have yielded 5 pounds. They are so large, the head of one will give a good eater a dinner, & for daintinesse of diet they excell the Marybones of Beefe. There are such multitudes that I have seene stopped in the river close adjoining to my house with a sande at one tide so many as will loade a ship of 100 tonnes. I my-selfe, at the turning of the tyde have seene such multitudes pass out of a pounde that it seemed to me that one mighte go over their backs drishod." So wrote Captain John Smith; but as his veracity has been questioned in other matters, it is well to give collateral testimony. One of Smith's contemporary divines wrote: "There is a Fish called a Basse, a most sweet & wholesome Fish as ever I did eat; it is alto-gether as good as our fresh Sammon & the season of their comming was begun when we came first to New England in June and so con-tinued about three months space. Of this Fish our Fishers take many hundreds together, which I have seene lying on the shore to my ad-miration; yea, their Netts ordinarily take more than they are able to hall to Land."

Near Norfolk, Virginia, 1500 have been taken at a single set of the seine. At one haul 600 were taken that averaged 80 pounds each. Dr. W. R. Capehart of Edenton, North Carolina, has for many years had the most important striped bass fishery on our coast. During the shad and herring season the striped bass appear in great numbers at the head of Albemarle Sound, where many marvelous catches have been made. At one time about 30,000 pounds were taken at one haul. Many of these weighed 75 to 85 pounds each. At another haul 820 fish weighing 37,000 pounds were taken. Among these were many of 65 pounds, many of 85 pounds, and a few of 90 pounds. In 6 hours' fishing 50,000 pounds were taken May 6, 1876.

On May 6, 1896, 38,000 pounds of rockfish were landed at one haul. Among them were about 600 fish that averaged 60 pounds each, and several that weighed 105 pounds each. The roe of one fish weighed 44 pounds.

Some very large fish have been reported. Dr. Henshall saw one weighed in Baltimore which tipped the beam at more than 100 pounds; one taken at Cuttyhunk weighed 104 pounds; and Dr. Goode records an example caught at Orleans which weighed 112 pounds and which must have been 6 feet long. The average of those seen in the Washington market now does not exceed 5 pounds.

Though the striped bass has undoubtedly decreased greatly in abundance during the century, it is still an abundant fish. The catch on our Atlantic coast for 1897 amounted to nearly one and a half million pounds, valued at $128,000.

The splendid results of the artificial propagation of useful food-fishes are clearly and indisputably shown by the fate of the striped bass on the Pacific coast, where it was planted by the United States and California fish commissions a few years ago. The fish was not native to those waters, and all striped bass now found there are the descendants of those artificially planted. The few fish put in those waters thrived exceedingly, and for several years past the catch has been very large. In 1899 it aggregated 1,234,320 pounds, valued at $61,814.

As a food-fish the striped bass is one of the very best; as a game-fish there is none better. Frank Forester calls it "a gallant fish and a bold biter"; and Genio Scott says it is his favourite of all American game-fishes.

All the published works on fishing in America describe the various methods by which anglers capture this noble fish, and we shall not take space to repeat them here.

Colour, olivaceous, silvery, often brassy-tinged; sides paler, marked with about 7 or 8 continuous or somewhat interrupted blackish stripes, one of them along the lateral line; fins all pale.

The rockfish may be easily distinguished from the white bass, which it most resembles, by its having 2 patches of teeth on its tongue instead of 1, and in not having the back arched.

375

GENUS MORONE MITCHILL

The White Perches

This genus differs from *Roccus* chiefly in having the dorsal fins joined, the spines stronger, the anal rays III, 9 (instead of III, 12), the spines not graduated, the jaws subequal, and no teeth on base of tongue. In all other important respects the 2 genera agree.

The 2 known species are both American and both excellent game- and food-fishes.

a. Body with 7 very distinct longitudinal black lines on side, each interrupted posteriorly ....*interrupta,* 376
aa. Colour, green or olivaceous, and silvery, with faint streaks.
americana, 377

Yellow Bass

Morone interrupta Gill

This handsome fish is found in the lower Mississippi Valley and north to St. Louis and Cincinnati. It occurs also in certain waters in northern Indiana, notably Tippecanoe, Eagle, Pike, Center, and Chapman lakes in Kosciusko County, and in Eel River at Logansport, from which place we have recently examined a specimen. Thirty years ago they were very abundant in the small lakes mentioned, and even now a few are caught every year, usually best after a June freshet.

This species reaches a foot to 18 inches in length and a weight of 5 pounds. Those usually seen do not exceed 1 to 2 pounds, though examples of 3 pounds are not rare. It is a splendid game-fish, even superior to the black bass, in the opinion of some of its admirers; and as a pan-fish it takes very high rank.

Head 3; depth 2⅔; snout 4½; eye 4½; D. X, 12; A. III, 9 or 10; scales 7-50 to 54-11. Body oblong-ovate, the back much arched; head depressed, the snout somewhat pointed, the anterior profile concave; eye large; preorbital finely serrate; mouth small, somewhat oblique, maxillary reaching middle of eye, about 3 in head, somewhat scaly; dorsal and anal spines stout.

Colour in life, brassy yellow, with about 7 very distinct black longitudinal lines, those below lateral line interrupted posteriorly, the posterior parts alternating with the anterior.

NASSAU GROUPER, *Epinephelus striatus*
Photographed at Key West

RED GROUPER. *Epinephelus morio*

RED HIND, *Epinephelus guttatus*

White Perch

Morone americana (Gmelin)

" Nor let the Muse, in her award of fame,
  Illustrious Perch, unnoticed pass thy claim.
  Prince of the prickly cohort, bred in lakes,
  To feast our boards, what sapid boneless flakes
  Thy solid flesh supplies! though overfed,
  No daintier fish in ocean's pastures bred
  Swims thy compeer."
  —*Ausonius.*

This well-known fish is common on the Atlantic coast of America from the Carolinas to the Gulf of St. Lawrence. It thrives in fresh, brackish, and salt water, but is somewhat anadromous, ascending freshwater streams. It is frequently landlocked in coastal ponds, where it becomes purely a freshwater fish. It is found in the lower portions of nearly all the streams from Maine to the Carolinas, and is one of the most popular of game-fishes. It takes the fly readily, though it will not leave the water to do so, and angleworms, grasshoppers, and small minnows are irresistible. As a game-fish it should hold, as it does in some places, a very high rank. It bites vigorously, and as a mad rusher, it is not surpassed. And as a pan-fish many regard it as the best among all our fishes. The only exception we feel disposed to make is the yellow perch.

Colour, olivaceous, varying to dark green; sides silvery or olivaceous, usually with faint paler longitudinal streaks.

GENUS STEREOLEPIS AYRES

The Jewfishes

This genus, characterized by the short, soft dorsal, the absence of spiny ridges on the head, and the continuous but deeply notched dorsal fin, contains one American species, the California jewfish or black sea-bass.

Stereolepis gigas

This huge fish is found on the coast of southern California and north to the Farallones. It is most abundant about Santa Catalina, where it is one of the really great game-fishes taken at that most famous anglers' resort, and Professor Chas. F. Holder has written entertainingly of this wonderful fish. He says the "jewfish is a bottom feeder, and is fished for on the edge of the kelp in 30 or 40 feet of water. The strike comes as a nibble, but when hooked the fish is away with a rush that has been known to demoralize experienced anglers. My largest fish, weighing 276 pounds, was taken in a boat or skiff which weighed 125 pounds, and I was repeatedly almost jerked overboard by the struggles of the bass. When it was gaffed it jerked the gaff from my hands a score of times. It was impossible to take it aboard, so we towed it five miles to port, well illustrating how delightful the most arduous labour becomes when dignified by the term sport. I have seen a 200-pound fish snap the largest shark-line like a thread, and large specimens straighten out an iron shark-hook; yet the skilled wielders of the rod catch these giants of the tribe with a line that is not larger than some eye-glass cords."

Professor Holder's experience with his first California jewfish is worth repeating:

"The anchor was tossed over, the rope ran merrily out, and the hook, baited with a 6-pound whitefish, went hissing down to the big submerged rock.

"'Sometimes he bite, sometimes he don't,' remarked Joe; 'but whether he do or not, we have the fishin' all the same.' And he looked at me inquiringly, to see if I was of that variety of fishermen who are never satisfied unless the fish are always on the line. It so happened that I found pleasure in the mere anticipation; and we sat silent for half an hour, I holding the throbbing line that the ebbing tide played upon as the string of a musical instrument. . . . I glanced at my companion, and was wondering if in his veins ran the blood of the Aztecs or of the Indians whom Cabrillo and others found here centuries ago when Santa Catalina was an empire in itself and owned by them, when suddenly I became aware that the tension of the line I held had increased to a steady pull; then came a jerk that carried my hand into the water.

"'Jewfish, sure!' whispered Joe, awakened from his reverie by my exclamation, 'Slack!'

"I paid out the line, while he seized the anchor-line and made ready to haul up.

"'Give him 10 feet, and then hook!' were my orders.

"I was an old shark fisherman, having caught many of these monsters in the Mexican Gulf, and had taken a Florida jewfish and a tarpon; and I saw that work of a similar kind was before me in this fishing. The line jerked heavily in my hand, then began to run out steadily. When about 6 feet had gone over the gunwale I stopped, gave a glance at the coil to see that all was clear, and when the line came taut jerked the hook into my first jewfish.

"I have every reason to believe that the latter was astonished, as for a single second there was no response; then came a jerk that almost lifted me from the boat, and the line went hissing over the rail like a living thing, playing a merry hornpipe of its own composition. Nothing could stop such a rush, and I simply waited, while Joe pulled up the anchor. When the latter was in, I grasped the line and braced back for the fight. The light boat whirled around like a top, and away we went, like a tug surging through the water, an ominous wave of foam rising high around the bow.

"A 10-foot shark never pulled harder than this gamy fish, and for 5 minutes it was a question who was master. I took it in with the greatest difficulty, gaining 10 feet, only to have the fish rush toward me and then dash away with an impetus that was more than irresistible. Then I would stop him again, slowly making foot by foot, hand over hand, taking a turn on the cleat, slacking and pulling, in attempts to tire the monster — tactics that for a while were of no avail.

"One of the tricks of this fish was to stop and jerk his head from side to side violently, a proceeding that produced an effect equivalent to striking blows at the holder of the line — tremendous jerks that came, one, two, three! then one, two, three! — then the line would slacken as the fish rushed up. And if I took the line in quickly enough to prevent a turn, well and good; if I did not, the fish would turn and dash at the bottom, making everything hum and sing.

"Giving and taking, hauling and easing off, for 20 minutes, I was almost satisfied that I had done my whole duty in the premises, when suddenly the fish rushed up, and recovering, I took in slack, and with a final effort brought the black giant to the surface. For a moment I saw a pair of eyes as large as those of an ox, a rich chestnut black, and then, with a tremendous heave, the fish threw itself over, deluging me with water and half capsizing the boat. It was the last struggle. I kept my hold, and with another haul had the king of Pacific coast fishes at hand's-length, where it rolled and tossed, its huge tail bathing us with spray, protesting against its capture.

"What a wonderful creature it was! The experience of the moment, the sensations, could not have been purchased. It was worth going a long way to accomplish. Imagine, you casters of the black-bass fly, a small-mouthed black bass lengthened out to 6 feet, bulky in proportion, a giant black bass,— one that you would dream about after a good day's fishing,— almost a facsimile of the 5-pounder you have taken pride in, but increased to a size that tips the scales at 347 pounds! Imagine this, and you have the jewfish, black sea-bass, or *Stereolepis gigas*, of the Pacific coast — a noble fish, a gamy fellow, especially adapted to the man who desires animated dumb-bells, or who, sedentary in his habits, requires violent exercise combined with much excitement.

"It has always been doubted that a large jewfish could be taken on a rod; but during the summer of '94 I went to the jewfish grounds one August day with Major Charles Vielé of the United States army, and watched him bring a jewfish of 158 pounds' weight to terms, on a Tufts-Lyon yellowtail rod of 16 ounces and a No. 21 Cuttyhunk line, in just $2\frac{1}{2}$ hours! The struggle was most exciting, and a fine exhibition of skill on the part of the fisherman. We had struck a school of these giants at Silver Cañon, and had we been well equipped could have brought in 6 or 7. As it was we towed in 3 — 1 of 158 pounds, 1 of 227 pounds, and a small one of 100 pounds."

GENUS PETROMETOPON GILL

The Enjambres

This genus is close to *Epinephelus*, from which it differs in the absence of processes and longitudinal ridges on upper surface of the frontals; a curved or angular ridge across the posterior portion of the frontals in front of the supraoccipital, connecting the parietal crests.

There are in our waters 3 species, only 1 being of much value as food. This is the cony or red hind, *Petrometopon cruentatus*.

This beautiful fish ranges from Florida and the West Indies to Brazil. It is common about Cuba and Jamaica, but appears to be rare about Porto Rico. At Key West, where it is called cony, it is rather common about the reefs. It reaches a foot in length and is a good food-fish. It takes the hook readily, and is a very active little fish.

Head $2\frac{1}{2}$; depth $2\frac{4}{5}$; eye $5\frac{1}{2}$; D. IX, 14 or 15; A. III, 8; scales 8-85 to 95-30, about 50 to 55 pores. Body oblong, rather deep and compressed, its width $2\frac{1}{4}$ in its greatest depth; head moderate, a little acute anteriorly, the profile nearly straight from snout to nape, where it is rather convex; mouth rather large, maxillary extending somewhat beyond eye, $1\frac{7}{8}$ in head; lower jaw not strongly projecting; teeth in narrow bands, the depressible teeth of the inner series very long and slender, longer than in any other of our species, those of the lower jaw and front of upper especially enlarged, longer than the small, subequal canines; interorbital space narrow, with a median depression, its width 7 in head; preopercle convex, very weakly serrate; opercle with 3 distinct spines; nostrils small, subequal; scales rather large, mostly strongly ctenoid; dorsal spines slender and pungent, the fourth and fifth highest, $3\frac{2}{5}$ in head; caudal very convex, the middle rays longest; anal rounded.

Colour in life, livid reddish gray, paler below; spots vermilion, usually darker posteriorly, larger anteriorly.

The brown hind may be merely a colour variety of the cony.

GENUS EPINEPHELUS BLOCH

The Groupers

This is one of the most important genera of American fishes.

Body stout, compressed, covered with small, ctenoid scales which are often embedded in the skin; scales of lateral line triangular, cycloid; soft parts of vertical fins generally more or less scaly; cranium narrow above; preopercle moderately serrate behind, its lower limb entire, without distinct antrorse spine; opercle with 2 strong spines; nostrils well separated; mouth large; maxillary large, with a well-developed supplemental bone, its surface usually with small scales; canine teeth few, those in front large; enlarged teeth of inner series in each jaw depressible; gill-rakers short and rather few; caudal fin rounded or lunate; pectorals rounded, shortish; ventrals moderate, inserted below pectorals, close together, each with a strong spine.

Species numerous, most of them of large size, abounding in all tropical seas, and all highly valued as food. The species all possess some game qualities, and, on account of their large size and fighting qualities, afford real sport in their capture. In our waters about a dozen species are known.

a. Nostrils unequal, the posterior much the larger, 3 times diameter of anterior; pyloric cœca numerous.............*mystacinus,* 382

aa. Nostrils subequal, the posterior scarcely the larger; pyloric cœca fewer.

b. Second dorsal spine shorter than third or fourth; caudal more or less rounded.

c. Dorsal spines 10................................*analogus,* 382

cc. Dorsal spines 11.

d. Maxillary naked.

e. Lower jaw strongly projecting.

f. Body and head with red or orange spots........*adscensionis,* 383

ff. Body and head reddish brown, the adult nearly plain..*guaza,* 383

ee. Lower jaw not prominent.....................*labriformis,* 383

dd. Maxillary more or less scaly.

g. Preopercle with a more or less salient angle.

h. Body without orange or dark brown spots; vertical fins without broad black margins.

i. Caudal peduncle without black, saddle-like blotch above.
flavolimbatus, 383

ii. Caudal peduncle with a large, quadrate, saddle-like black blotch above.

j. Eye not surrounded by dark points; no dark cross-bars; lower jaw strongly projecting......................*niveatus,* 384

jj. Eye surrounded by conspicuous dark brown points; body with irregular dark cross-bars; lower jaw little projecting.
striatus, 384

hh. Body covered with small dark orange or brown spots; vertical fins broadly edged with blue-black ....*guttatus,* 384

gg. Preopercle without salient angle............*drummond-hayi,* 385

bb. Second dorsal spine elevated, not shorter than third and fourth; caudal lunate..................................*morio,* 385

Epinephelus mystacinus, the cherna de lo alto, is found among the West Indies and south to Brazil, in rather deep water. It reaches about 2 feet in length, but is not abundant enough to be of much commercial importance. Colour in life, dull olive-brown above, the body grayish brown, crossed by 8 bands of dark olive-brown, the one on caudal peduncle broadest, darkest on back of tail; a dark line along edge of maxillary, and 3 dark bands across cheek; mouth bluish inside. *E. analogus,* the cabrilla pinta, is a west coast species, known from Panama and San Salvador. It is not rare, reaches a foot or more in length, and in life is orange-brown on an olivaceous ground, as in *E. adscensionis,* which this species strongly resembles; no distinct dark edgings to the vertical fins.

Rock-hind; Cabra Mora

Epinephelus adscensionis (Osbeck)

This beautiful and important species is known from southern Florida, Ascension and St. Helena islands, the West Indies, and to Brazil. It has also been recorded from the Cape of Good Hope. It reaches a length of 18 inches, is common in rocky places, and is considered the finest food-fish of the group.

Head $2\frac{2}{8}$; depth 3; eye 6; D. XI, 17; A. III, 7 or 8; scales 12-90 to 110-40, 55 to 60 pores. Body rather robust, little compressed, the greatest thickness 2 in depth; head subconic, acute; mouth rather large, maxillary reaching beyond eye, $2\frac{1}{8}$ in head; lower jaw rather strongly projecting, more prominent than in any other species.

Colour in life, olivaceous gray, with darker clouds; a number of irregular whitish blotches scattered over body; 5 ill-defined, roundish, blackish blotches along side of back, the 4 under dorsal fin extending on fin; head and body everywhere covered with round orange-brown spots of varying size, the centres more orange, the borders brownish, these largest on breast, smallest on lips and under parts, equally distinct everywhere; mouth pale within, the roof with red spots; dorsal light olive, with sparse spots like those on body but smaller; no dark edge to dorsal and anal; numerous white spots on dorsal, most numerous on soft part; caudal pale olive with some paler spots; anal reddish, marked like the dorsal, its spots larger; basal half of pectoral like dorsal, the distal half plain olive; ventrals pale with orange spots.

E. guaza, the merou or méro, is found on the eastern Atlantic from England to the Cape of Good Hope, but has been recorded from our waters only from the coast of Brazil. It is a large fish, reaching a length of 3 feet and a weight of 25 pounds or more.

E. labriformis is a Pacific coast species, known from Cape San Lucas south to the Galapagos Islands. It reaches 2 feet in length and is rather common about rocky places.

The yellow-finned grouper (*E. flavolimbatus*) is known from Cuba and the Snapper Banks off the west coast of Florida. It may be the adult of *E. niveatus*, from which it seems to differ only in colour. In life brownish flesh-colour, unspotted; a clear blue streak from angle of eye to preopercle; no spots or blotches anywhere, and no black on caudal peduncle; whole dorsal with a narrow edge of bright yellow.

The snowy grouper (*E. niveatus*) is known from the West Indies south to Brazil and occasionally north in the Gulf Stream to Woods Hole. Colour, brown with round whitish spots on body, smaller than pupil, regularly arranged in vertical and horizontal series, 4 in former and 5 in latter, these rows sometimes irregular; no distinct spots on breast; a very large black blotch on upper part of caudal peduncle, this sometimes absent.

Nassau Grouper; Hamlet; Cherna Criolla

Epinephelus striatus (Bloch)

This large species is common from Key West to Brazil. It is common about Key West and many large examples are taken. It attains a length of 3 feet and a weight of 50 pounds, though those seen in the Key West market usually do not exceed 10 pounds. It is a good food-fish and is found all the year round about Key West.

Colour in life, rather pale olivaceous gray, paler below, sides with obscure whitish cloudings; side with about 4 irregular broad vertical bars dark brown in colour, each enclosing small whitish spots, these bars darkest on back and extending on dorsal fin; a square jet-black blotch on upper edge of caudal peduncle; a dark band from snout through eye to side below origin of dorsal; another on median line of snout, forking opposite front of eye, the 2 bands extending backward and ceasing on occiput without reaching the other band; cheek light brown with whitish blotches; fins colour of body but lighter; dorsal and caudal with narrow pale yellow border.

The red hind or cabrilla (*E. guttatus*) is found from the Carolinas through the West Indies to Brazil. It is rare on our coast, but is common at Havana.

From related species it may be distinguished by its colour, which in life is light yellowish olive above, whitish below; 3 broad, oblique, obscure olive bands running upward and backward on side; spots on body vivid scarlet, those above darker, edges of scales brown; inside of mouth mostly pale, partly scarlet; belly spotted; dorsal olive-yellow, somewhat clouded, a few red spots on spinous dorsal; soft dorsal broadly edged with black; caudal yellowish, the posterior half black, its edge white; anal like soft dorsal; pectoral light yellow, with rows of small scarlet spots; ventrals red, blackish at tips.

The speckled hind or john-paw (*E. drummond-hayi*) is most abundant on the Snapper Banks in the Gulf of Mexico, but it has been

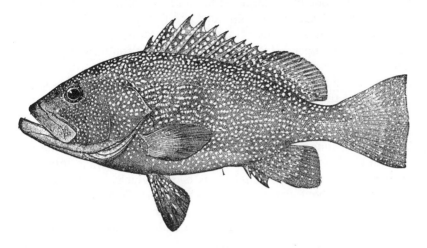

recorded from the Bermudas and Charleston. It attains a weight of 30 pounds, and is an important food-fish in the Pensacola market. It is perhaps the most beautiful in colour of all the groupers.

Colour, dark umber-brown, densely covered with small pearly-white spots, those below smaller and nearly round, all in irregular series; fins not dark-edged, all covered with similar spots, those of the paired fins chiefly on the inner surface; lower side of head flushed with red and unspotted; caudal fin more densely spotted than the body, the terminal spots lavender; pectoral with a subterminal orange band.

Red Grouper; Cherna Americana

Epinephelus morio (Cuvier & Valenciennes)

The red grouper is the most abundant and best-known species of the genus. It is found on our South Atlantic and Gulf coasts from Virginia to Texas and southward to Brazil. It is an easily recognizable species, separated from all others by the elevation of the second dorsal spine. Besides the vernacular names given above, it is known also as cherna, méro, cherna de vivera, nègre, and jaboncillo.

The red grouper is a very handsome fish, bearing some resemblance to the Nassau grouper, but the warm browns on the side of the body and head are richer, while the general appearance is somewhat coarser. It is one of the largest and most important food-fishes of our tropical waters, reaching a length of 2 or 3 feet and a weight of 20 to 40 pounds. It is most abundant on the west coast of Florida, in company with the red snapper. It is also abundant on the south coast of Florida, where it is found throughout the year. The red grouper is more of a bottom fish than the red snapper, and swims more slowly, seldom rising to the surface. It is very voracious, consuming large quantities of crustaceans and small fish. Large crabs and small fishes in perfect condition have been found in their stomachs, and several new species have been obtained in this way. On the Snapper Banks on the west coast of Florida it is caught by the red-snapper fishermen in the same manner in which the red snapper is taken, which is with hook and line, a piece of bone-fish or other fish being used as bait. As a game-fish it does not rank high, its movements being slow, and when hooked it usually has to be hauled in as a dead weight. It will take any kind of bait. When red snappers were more abundant the red grouper did not find a ready sale in Northern markets, though it has always been in good demand at Havana and Key West. The maximum weight of those taken about Key West is about 25 pounds and the average only 8 to 15 pounds.

The red grouper is very tenacious of life, and will live several hours after being taken out of the water, even though exposed to considerable heat. This is one reason why Key West fishermen have preferred red groupers for transportation to Cuba, since they must go a long way to market through warm water, and the groupers bear the crowding and chafing in the live-wells of the smacks better than other species.

GENUS GARRUPA JORDAN

This genus is closely allied to *Epinephelus*, but has the skull very broad and flat; the interorbital little concave, and the median ridge scarcely evident.

The only known species is *Garrupa nigrita*, known as the black jewfish, black grouper, or méro de lo alto, which occurs from Charleston and Pensacola south to Brazil and strays to Sicily.

It is an immense fish, one of the largest known, reaching a

weight of about 500 pounds, and rivaling in size the largest known examples of the spotted jewfish and the California jewfish. No small

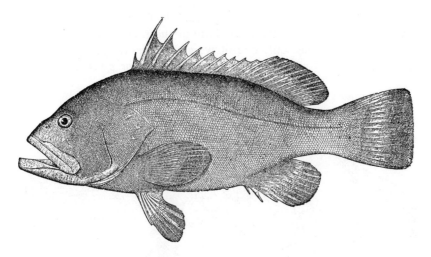

examples have ever been seen, only one weighing less than 100 pounds having been recorded.

Colour, plain chocolate-brown, varying to blackish gray, without markings, or with faint blotches, the lower parts scarcely paler, the distal parts of the vertical fins darker; a dark streak along the edge of the maxillary.

GENUS PROMICROPS GILL

In this genus the cranium is extremely broad and depressed between the eyes, the anterior profile of the head being more or less concave.

Only one species certainly known, the spotted jewfish, *Promicrops itaiara*, a tropical fish of very large size, rivaling the black grouper and the California jewfish in weight. It reaches 2 to 6 feet in length and occurs on both coasts of tropical America north of Florida and the Gulf of California. It is not uncommon in the West Indies, especially about rocks. Colour of adult, nearly uniform dull olive-brown, the spots or bands faint or obsolete.

GENUS ALPHESTES BLOCH & SCHNEIDER

This genus differs from *Epinephelus* chiefly in the presence of a strong antrorse spine on the lower limb of the preopercle. There are but 2 known species, only one of which (*Alphestes afer*) is of much importance. This species, known as the cherna or guaseta, is found

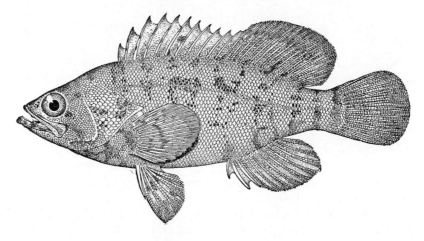

from Cuba to Brazil, and has been recorded also from Africa and the Falkland Islands. It is common about Porto Rico, where it reaches a foot or more in length and is regarded as a good food-fish.

Colour in life, yellowish brown, paler below; upper part of side with about 7 longitudinal stripes of dark brown from head to tail, these becoming rows of round orange spots below; 6 dark inconspicuous vertical bars on body; head with many smaller orange-brown spots; lower part of head and breast with pale bluish spots; fins brownish; ventrals olive edged with darker; other fins obscurely barred; inside of mouth pale.

The other species (*A. multiguttatus*) is very close to *A. afer*, from which it differs in the more slender head, more prominent chin, and the colouration, which is dark olive-brown, the body and head profusely covered with round spots of darker brown about half size of pupil; spots on posterior part of body confluent in horizontal streaks; breast and front of head with few spots; a very faint mustache above maxillary; dorsal and caudal dusky-olive, nearly plain; anal with 2 dusky cross-bands; pectoral yellowish, with 5 dusky cross-bands, its edge pale; ventrals dusky.

This species reaches 8 inches in length and is rather common on our Pacific coast from Mazatlan to Panama.

The genus *Dermatolepis* resembles *Epinephelus*, but it has the body shorter and deeper, the head small and much compressed, the interorbital narrow, the soft dorsal very long, the anal short, and the scales all cycloid, small, and embedded.

Four species are known, 3 of which occur in our waters. None of them is of much value as food. The accompanying illustration of our most interesting species, *D. zanclus*, will serve to indicate the

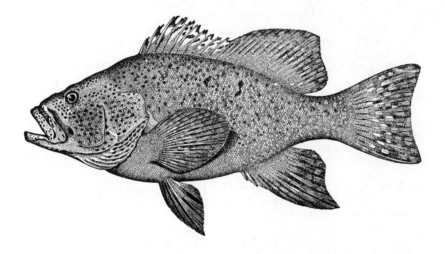

character of this group. This species reaches 2 feet in length, and is known only from Key West.

GENUS MYCTEROPERCA GILL

Cranium broad and transversely concave between the eyes, its lateral crests very strong, nearly parallel with the supraoccipital crest, and extending much farther forward than the latter; lower jaw strongly projecting; anal fin long, usually with 11 or 12 rays; caudal lunate; spines of fins slender, none much elevated; scales small, mostly cycloid, those of the lateral line simple; pyloric cœca few. From *Epinephelus* this genus may be distinguished by its longer anal, larger mouth, and more slender body.

a. Nostrils subequal, well separated

b. Gill-rakers comparatively few and short, 8 to 20 below the angle.

c. Anal fin III, 9 to 11, high and falcate..............*boulengeri,* 391

cc. Anal fin III, 11 or 12, long.

d. Anal fin not angulated, its outline more or less evenly rounded.

e. Angle of preopercle not salient, its teeth scarcely enlarged; gill-rakers $x+8$ to 10.

f. Gill-rakers very few and short, $x+8$ developed; caudal lunate.

g. General colour gray, with red and black markings...*venenosa,* 391

gg. General colour scarlet, with red and black markings....*apua,* 392

ff. Gill-rakers rather slender, about $x+10$; caudal subtruncate.

h. Scales not very small, about 110.

i. Dark blotches on body rather large, often quadrate.....*bonaci,* 392

ii. Dark spots on body very small, close-set........*xanthosticta,* 392

hh. Scales smaller, about 120 to 140...................*jordani,* 392

ee. Angle of preopercle more or less salient, its teeth somewhat enlarged; gill-rakers more numerous, $x+12$ to 14.

j. Scales very small, about 140; caudal distinctly lunate.

microlepis, 392

jj. Scales somewhat larger, about 120; caudal little concave.

interstitialis, 393

jjj. Scales still larger, about 110; caudal deeply lunate. *dimidiata,* 393

dd. Anal fin angulated, its middle rays much exserted, its posterior margin concave ....*xenarcha,* 393

bb. Gill-rakers close-set, very long and slender, 25 to 35 below the angle ....*rubra,* 393

aa. Nostrils very close together, the posterior decidedly larger than the anterior.

k. Gill-rakers very numerous, long and slender, about 24 below the angle ....*pardalis,* 393

kk. Gill-rakers fewer and moderate, 6 to 18 below the angle.

l. Second dorsal spine highest, its length more than $\frac{1}{3}$ that of head.

m. Colour, brown, with grayish reticulations and brown spots.

olfax, 393

mm. Colour, chiefly red..........................*ruberrima,* 393

ll. Second dorsal spine low, shorter than third, the third and fourth highest.

n. Margin of anal fin posteriorly concave, its middle rays much exserted.

o. Gill-rakers rather numerous, 17 to 20 below angle of arch.

p. Outer rays of caudal scarcely produced, not $\frac{2}{3}$ length of head.

rosacea, 393

pp. Outer rays of caudal much produced, more than $\frac{2}{3}$ length of head.

q. Upper canines directed strongly forward, the lower backward; colouration obscure ....*falcata,* 393

qq. Upper canines nearly vertical; colouration brighter ...*phenax,* 394

oo. Gill-rakers few, 8 below angle ....*venadorum,* 394

nn. Margin of anal fin concave posteriorly, the outline of the fin rounded or slightly angular.

r. Gill-rakers rather few, $x+12$; body without dark cross-bars.
s. Scales very small, about 20-140-37; caudal not deeply lunate, eye
    small ....*bowersi,* 394
ss. Scales larger, about 90 to 100 in lateral line; caudal deeply lunate;
    eye larger...................................*calliura,* 394
rr. Gill-rakers very few, short and thick, about $x+6$; body with light
    and dark cross-bars.
t. Ground colour dark olive ....*tigris,* 394
tt. Ground colour bright red. ....*camelopardalis,* 395

The species of this genus are very numerous and most of them very closely related. While all are excellent for food, the scarcity of some and the distance of others from a market leave but few that are of great importance as food-fishes. So many of the species are so closely related that detailed descriptions hardly seem necessary. The key given above will usually be found sufficient for the identification of any of the known species.

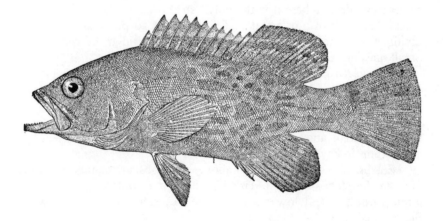

Mycteroperca boulengeri is a small species known only from Mazatlan, where it is rather common in the astillero. It reaches 15 inches in length, is olive-gray in color, covered everywhere with irregular oblong black markings.

M. venenosa, the yellow-finned grouper, rockfish, or bonací de piedra, occurs from the Florida Keys and the Bahamas southward among the West Indies. It is a large, handsome fish, reaching 3 feet in length, and is reputed poisonous. In life it is a clear olive-green, livid blue or pearly below; upper parts everywhere with broad reticulations and curved blotches of bright, clear, light green; entire body and head covered with round orange-brown spots; angle of mouth orange within; iris orange; breast slightly rosy; dorsal olive-brown with whitish blotches.

M. apua, the bonací cardenal, is found from the Florida Keys to Brazil in deeper water than *M. venenosa*, from which it differs only in colour and of which it has usually been regarded as a subspecies. But we have never seen any specimens intermediate between the two, and it seems best to regard them as distinct species.

Colour in life of an example 2 feet long, intense scarlet red above, grayer below; small black spots above, larger red ones below; base of dorsal and caudal deep red, the edge of dorsal, caudal, and anal black; pectoral spotted at base, then blackish, thence broadly yellow. Younger examples scarlet brown above, varying from vermilion to gray.

M. bonaci, the black grouper, bonací arará or aguaji, is found from the Florida Keys through the West Indies to Brazil. It is abundant about Key West, where it is the only fish known as black grouper. It reaches a length of 2 or 3 feet and a weight of 50 pounds. Large individuals are taken with hook and line and are said to be very game. Small ones are seined alongshore.

M. xanthosticta is known only from the Snapper Banks off the west coast of Florida and is rare. It reaches a large size, examples 4 feet in length having been taken.

M. jordani, the cabrilla de astillero or baya, is an important food-fish at Mazatlan and Guaymas. It reaches a length of 2 to 3 feet and is common in bays and protected waters.

Colour, olive-gray, blackish above, with obscure clouds of darker olive in the form of diffuse dark blotches, these oblong quadrate and arranged in 4 series; lower parts pale olive; sides of head with wavy black streaks.

M. microlepis, the gag, occurs from Beaufort, North Carolina, and around the coast of Florida to Pensacola. It is not yet known from the West Indies. At Key West it is a common fish at all times, reaches a weight of 10 pounds, and is highly esteemed.

Colour, variable, those from shallow water being lighter and more variegated; those from deeper water plain brownish gray, paler below, with no distinct spots or rivulations, but with faint traces of darker spotting, which disappear in alcohol; dorsal dark olive, the tip of soft part blue-black, the edge narrowly white; caudal black with bright

YELLOW-FIN GROUPER, *Mycteroperca venenosa*

JEWFISH, *Promicrops itaiara*

BLACK GROUPER, *Mycteroperca bonaci*

blue shadings, its edge white; anal deep indigo blue, olive at base, its edge white; pectoral olive, dusky toward the tip; ventrals blackish, the first ray tipped with white.

M. interstitialis is known only from the coasts of Cuba. It is rather common in the Havana market. It reaches a foot in length and is a good food-fish.

M. dimidiata is a rare species known only from Havana. Specimens only a few inches long have been seen.

M. xenarcha occurs about rocky islands on the Pacific coast from Mazatlan to Peru. It is fairly abundant and reaches 2 feet in length.

M. rubra is of rather wide distribution. It occurs among the West Indies and south to Brazil, in the eastern Atlantic about islands, and in the Mediterranean.

M. pardalis, the cabrilla piritita, is known from the Gulf of California and Mazatlan, where it is rather common about rocky islands; it reaches 2 feet in length.

M. olfax, the yellow grouper, reaches 2 to 3 feet in length, and is rather common about Panama and the Galapagos Islands.

M. ruberrima is a rare species known only from Abingdon Island of the Galapagos group.

M. rosacea is a beautifully coloured but very rare species known only from Angel Island, Gulf of California, and Mazatlan. Colour in life, nearly everywhere brick-red; tips of pectorals dusky.

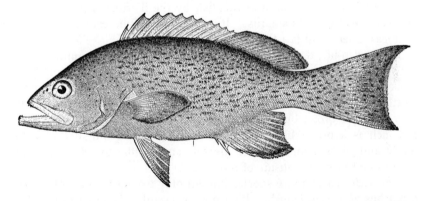

M. falcata, the bacalao or abadejo, is found in the West Indies and north to Bermuda. It grows to 2 or 3 feet in length and is an important food-fish at Havana. Colour in life, brown above, sides grayish brown, faintly covered with darker spots, which disappear in spirits;

eyes and angle of mouth yellowish; ventrals dusky, the outer portion bluish black; pectoral with a whitish edge.

M. phenax, the scamp of Key West and elsewhere in southern Florida, may be told from the preceding by having its upper canines nearly vertical instead of directed forward, and by the different colouration, which is much brighter, being pinkish gray above, paler purplish below; upper parts and opercles thickly covered with small, rounded, irregular spots of dark brown; sides with larger and fainter brown blotches, more or less horizontally oblong and somewhat reticulate; spinous dorsal brownish; soft dorsal darker, faintly spotted, edged with dusky and with a narrow rim of whitish anteriorly; caudal brownish, spotted with darker, its outer rays blackish distally and edged with whitish; pectoral plain, dusky toward the tip, edged with whitish; ventrals pale, tipped with dusky; mouth pale, scarcely greenish. The scamp reaches a length of 2 feet and a weight of 12 pounds or more, though those seen at Key West do not usually exceed 2 or 3 pounds. It is a handsome, trim-looking fish, taking the hook readily and making a good fight.

M. venadorum, the garlopa (garrupa) of the Mazatlan fishermen, is a very large species thus far known only from that place. The type specimen, the skin of which is in the British Museum, weighed 75 pounds, and examples of twice that size have been seen. It is not abundant, but is an important food-fish.

M. bowersi is known only from Culebra Island east of Porto Rico, where it is called rock-hind or rockfish by the Tortola fishermen, and mero cabrilla by the Spaniards. It is a beautiful fish, reaching a length of at least 2 feet, and is a fine food-fish.

Colour in life, dark reddish brown, with many small, round, blood-red spots on body, head, lower jaw, and base of pectoral and anal fins, especially numerous on anal; a few on spinous dorsal; soft dorsal mottled with white and black, with a very narrow white edge inside of which is a broad black band; tip of caudal narrowly white, inside of which is a broad black band, rest of fin mottled and spotted with white and black similar to soft dorsal; anal similar to soft dorsal but with more red spots; inside of mouth pale red.

M. calliura is a rare species known only from the coast of Cuba. It reaches $2\frac{1}{2}$ feet in length. It seems to resemble *M. bowersi*, but differs notably in colour.

M. tigris, the bonaci gato, is found among the West Indies and north to Bermuda. It reaches 2 feet in length and, though not common anywhere, is a good food-fish.

M. camelopardalis is a rare species known only from Havana and resembling *M. tigris*, but the ground colour is bright red.

The genus *Cratinus*, which resembles *Serranus*, has but one species, *C. agassizi*, which occurs about the Galapagos Islands. It reaches 18 inches in length and is peculiar on account of its long, low head.

The genus *Hypoplectrus* has the body more compressed and deeper than in other groups allied to *Serranus*. The skull differs from *Serranus* in the development of the supraoccipital crest, which is much elevated.

Many species have been described, but they nearly all may be simply colour forms of one, *H. unicolor*.

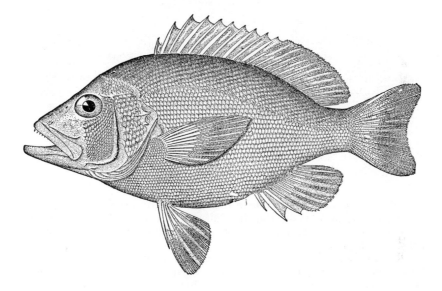

This species, with its various forms, occurs from the Florida Keys southward among the West Indies and to Brazil.

H. lamprurus occurs at Panama and is a rare species. *H. gemma* was described from Garden Key, Florida, and is a doubtful species.

The genus *Paralabrax* has the body robust and covered with ctenoid scales; mouth large, with small lateral canines and no depressible teeth; smooth area on top of head very short and small, not extending much behind the orbits; the long and low supraoccipital crest extending well forward to a line connecting the postfrontal processes; caudal fin always lunate; some of the anterior dorsal spines considerably elevated; dorsal usually X, 14; anal III, 7.

The known species of this genus are confined to the coasts of tropical America, where they are important food-fishes. There are 4 within our limits. *Paralabrax nebulifer*, the johnny-verde, occurs on our Pacific coast from Monterey to Lower California. It is generally common in shallow water, reaches 18 inches in length, and is a food-fish of excellent quality. Its colour is greenish, with irregular pale and dark mottlings and traces of dark oblique cross-bars; suborbital and cheek profusely marked with round orange spots; a dark streak downward and backward from eye; lower side of head salmon colour; lower side of tail with wavy whitish streaks.

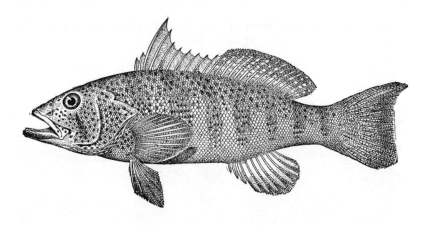

The spotted cabrilla, *P. maculatofasciatus*, occurs from San Pedro, California, to Mazatlan and in the Gulf of California. It is everywhere common on sandy shores, and is an excellent food-fish, reaching a length of 18 inches.

Colour, olive-brown, thickly covered everywhere above with dark hexagonal or roundish spots, so close together that the ground colour appears as reticulations around them; these spots more or less confluent on the back, and more distinct and tinged with orange on sides of head, branchiostegals, and on base of pectorals; about 7 dusky cross-bars on side, in which the spots are deeper in colour and more confluent; a bluish stripe from eye across cheek; lower parts yellow; dorsal and caudal with bronze spots.

P. humeralis is found from Panama southward. It reaches 2 or 3 feet in length, is found in rather deep water, and is a valuable fish.

P. clathratus, the rock-bass of the California coast, occurs from San Francisco southward to Cerros Island. It is the most common species of the genus in those waters, reaches a length of 18 inches and

YELLOW GROUPER, *Mycteroperca oljax*

GAG, *Mycteroperca microlepis*

SCAMP, *Mycteroperca phenax*

SEA BASS, *Centropristes striatus*

a weight of 5 pounds, and is an excellent food-fish. Colour grayish green, with obscure broad, dusky streaks and bars, which form reticulations on the sides, which are often shaded and mottled with bluish and greenish, but usually without distinct spots; a broad, dark, longitudinal shade near axis of body; belly plain silvery gray.

The genus *Centropristes* has the body robust, somewhat compressed, covered with rather large ctenoid scales; mouth large, formed as in *Serranus* and *Paralabrax*, the canines small; preopercle serrate, the lower teeth somewhat antrorse; supraoccipital and parietal with strong crests extending forward to between the postfrontal processes; smooth area on top of head very short and small; dorsal short, X, 11; anal III, 7; caudal usually 3-lobed or double concave; canines very weak.

This genus contains 3 species, one of them a very important food-fish. *C. striatus*, variously known as the black sea-bass, blackfish, hannahill, black-will, and black-harry, is found along our Atlantic coast from Cape Ann to northern Florida. It is common northward and is a well-known food-fish.

The sea-bass is usually a bottom fish, rather sluggish in its movements, and, like the tautog, is often seen lying among loose stones or in cavities in the rocks. They feed upon crabs, shrimps, small fish, and squids. They are voracious feeders, taking the hook freely, and as their mouths are tough, they are not easily lost.

Their spawning-time is probably in the summer, as the fish are full of spawn in the spring, and young fish 1 to 2 inches long are common in the eel-grass along the shores of southern New England in early fall.

The sea-bass grows to a weight of 4 or 5 pounds, though this is unusual; they average less than 2 pounds.

As a food-fish this species holds a high rank. The flesh is flaky and sweet, and keeps well, a feature which makes it a good shipper.

Colour, dusky-brown or black, more or less mottled and with pale longitudinal streaks; dorsal with several series of elongate whitish spots forming oblique light stripes; other fins dusky, mottled; young with a black longitudinal band, which later breaks up, forming dark cross-shades; a large black spot on last dorsal spines.

The tally-wag of the Gulf of Mexico is a distinct species of sea-bass, *C. ocyurus*, occurring in rather deep water, chiefly on the Snapper Banks.

From the common sea-bass this species may be readily distinguished by the much shorter and wider-set gill-rakers, and the colour, which is a pale olive, somewhat darker on the back; side with 3 longitudinal rows of quadrate black blotches, the upper series obscure along base of caudal, the second distinct and placed just below lateral line, the 3 anterior blotches of the series somewhat confluent; the lower series very distinct jet-black and not confluent, placed alongside of belly; caudal fin with middle rays black, the outer pale, all with darker spots.

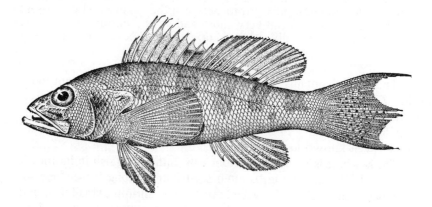

C. philadelphicus, the rock sea-bass, is found on rocky shores of South Carolina, in rather deep water. It is rather common about Charleston, but has not been seen elsewhere. It reaches 8 or 10 inches in length, and may be known by the fleshy filaments on the dorsal spines.

Another species, *C. rufus*, has been described from Martinique, but it is of doubtful validity.

The genus *Diplectrum* is close to *Prionodes*, from which it differs chiefly in the armature of the preopercle, which is provided in the adult with 1 or 2 clusters of strong, straight, divergent spines; smooth area on top of head large; profile of snout rounded; pectoral unsymmetrically rounded, its upper rays longest; ventrals inserted somewhat before axil of pectoral; dorsal spines slender, none of them much elevated; soft dorsal short, the rays X, 12; anal III, 7; caudal lunate.

Several species, all American, and all small, brightly coloured fishes, none of much food-value.

They are all known as squirrel-fishes. *D. formosum*, which is found from Charleston to Montevideo, is one of the best-known spe-

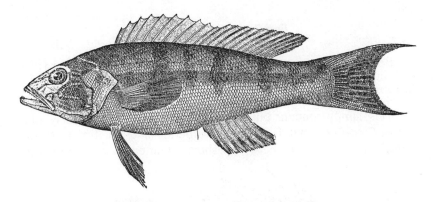

cies. It is quite common on the South Atlantic and Gulf coasts, on both rocky and sandy shores. It is a handsome fish, reaching a length of a foot, and is an excellent food-fish.

399

THE TRIPLETAILS

Family XLIX.   Lobotidæ

BODY oblong, compressed; snout short; eyes well forward; no
teeth on palate; soft parts of dorsal and anal fins equal and opposite,
the former preceded by a much larger spinous portion; vertebræ 12 + 12.

This family contains but 2 or 3 species, large fishes closely allied
to the *Serranidæ*, but lacking the vomerine and palatine teeth, and
with the fore part of the head very short.   Our only important species

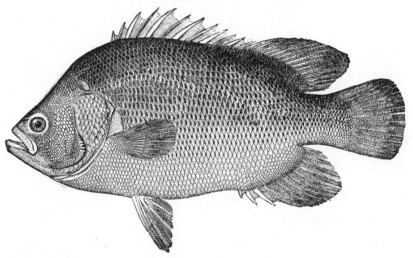

is the flasher or tripletail, which is found from Surinam northward
among the West Indies and occasionally to Cape Cod.   It has been recorded also from the Mediterranean, India, and China.   It is only of
rare occurrence on our coast. In Indian River, Florida, it is taken only
occasionally and is not well known to the fishermen.   It is not uncommon about Porto Rico.   The tripletail is an interesting and attractive fish, reaching a length of 3 feet and a weight of 25 or 30 pounds,
and is a good food-fish.   We know nothing as to its game qualities.

The *Lobotes* on the Pacific coast of Central America (*L. pacificus*)
seems to differ from the tripletail chiefly in the narrower interorbital
and the smaller preopercular serrations.   Little is known of its habits.

THE CATALUFAS

Family L.   Priacanthidæ

BODY oblong or ovate, compressed, covered with small, firm, rough scales, all parts of the body, head, snout, and maxillaries being densely scaled, each scale with a more or less developed plate on its posterior border; mouth large, very oblique, the lower jaw prominent; villiform teeth on jaws, vomer, and palatines, none on tongue; premaxillaries protractile; maxillary broad, without supplemental bone, not slipping under the very narrow preorbital, which is usually serrate; eye very large; posterior nostril long, slit-like, close to the eye; preopercle more or less serrate, one or more spines at its angle; opercle very short, ending in 2 or 3 points; no barbels; gill-membranes separate, free from the isthmus; pseudobranchiæ very large, extending along whole length of opercle; postorbital part of head very short, the opercle small; lateral line continuous, not extending on caudal; dorsal fin continuous, the spines depressible in a groove; anal spines strong, the soft part of fin long, similar to soft dorsal; caudal truncate or lunate; air-bladder large.

Carnivorous fishes of tropical seas, chiefly in deep water; mostly rose-coloured in life.   The family contains 2 genera (*Priacanthus* and *Pseudopriacanthus*) and about 10 species, only 1 or 2 of which are of any food-value.

Priacanthus arenatus, the catalufa or toro, is a beautiful fish found in the West Indies south to Brazil, and occasionally north in the Gulf Stream to Woods Hole.   It has also been reported from Madeira.   On our Southern coast it has been recorded only from Key West.   It is not uncommon about Porto Rico, where it is known as toro or comico. Its usual length is a foot to 15 inches, and it is used as food, its flesh being firm and flaky and of good flavour.   We know nothing of it as a game-fish.   The brilliant red colour and large eye make it a very striking fish.

Head $2\frac{3}{4}$ to $3\frac{1}{4}$; depth $2\frac{4}{5}$; eye $2\frac{2}{3}$; snout 3; maxillary 2; mandible $1\frac{2}{3}$; interorbital $4\frac{2}{3}$; D. X, 14, rarely 13; A. III, 15, rarely 16; pectoral, $1\frac{9}{10}$; ventral $1\frac{1}{10}$; caudal $1\frac{1}{5}$; scales about 94.

Body oblong-ovate; eye very large; mouth extremely oblique; lower jaw strong and prominent; maxillary very broad posteriorly, reaching beyond front of eye; opercle and angle of preopercle each with a flat weak spine; dorsal spines slightly roughened; caudal slightly lunate.

Colour, body and fins nearly everywhere bright red, deepest on ventrals and caudal; base of pectoral yellow; ventral spine pale blue, the rays black-tipped, the membranes mostly dusky; caudal dark-edged; a series of about 12 indistinct dark round blotches just above lateral line; mouth red inside; iris chiefly bright red, a narrow yellow circle about the pupil.

The only other species deserving mention here is the ojudo or big-eye, *P. cruentatus*.

This fish ranges from the West Indies to St. Helena and the Canaries. It is known from Cuba, Jamaica, and Porto Rico, but is not recorded from any point on our Atlantic coast. It reaches a foot in length, and is a good food-fish. It resembles the preceding species, but the body is deeper, the preopercular spine stronger, and the colour different. Colour, silvery, washed with rosy; back with 5 or 6 rosy saddle-like blotches extending on sides to below lateral line; under parts rosy; vertical fins pale at the base, brighter distally; caudal black-edged; pectorals and ventrals rosy, the latter black-tipped.

THE SNAPPERS

Family LI.   Lutianidæ

Body oblong, more or less elevated, covered with moderate-sized, adherent scales, which are more or less strongly ctenoid or almost cycloid; lateral line well developed, concurrent with the back, not extending on the caudal fin; head large, the crests on the skull usually largely developed; mouth moderate or large, usually terminal, low and horizontal; premaxillaries moderately protractile; maxillary long, without supplemental bone; teeth various, unequal and sharp, never incisor-like, some of them sometimes molar; vomer and palatines usually with villiform teeth, but these sometimes molar, sometimes very small, sometimes wanting; pseudobranchiæ large; gill-rakers moderate or long; gill-membranes separate, free from the isthmus; no spines on opercle; side of head usually scaly; dorsal fin usually single, continuous, or deeply notched, sometimes divided into 2 fins, the spines usually strong, depressible in a groove, the spines heteracanthous, i.e., alternating, the one stronger on the right side, the next on the left; anal fin similar to soft dorsal; caudal usually more or less concave; air-bladder present, usually simple; pyloric cœca few; intestine short.

This is one of the largest and most important families among fishes, comprising about 20 genera and some 250 species, inhabiting the shores of the warmer regions.   All are valued as food, and all are active, carnivorous, and voracious.   In our waters are found about 35 species, representing 14 genera, and all of those of sufficient abundance have high value as food-fishes; and several of them are among our most interesting and attractive salt-water game-fishes.

a. Nostrils remote from each other, the anterior tubular and near the end of the snout..........................*Hoplopagrus*, 404
aa. Nostrils close together, placed just before the eye, the anterior not tubular.
b. Interorbital area not flat nor separated from the occipital region.
c. Prefrontals with the articular facets arising from diverging V-shaped ridges.
d. Fronto-occipital crest ceasing anteriorly far from front of frontals.
Lutianus, 405
dd. Fronto-occipital crest continued forward along top of head to nearly opposite nostrils ....*Ocyurus*, 416

cc. Prefrontals with the anterior facets developed from simple tubercles and not V-shaped.

f. Hyoid bone and tongue with teeth; dorsal spines 12 or 13.
Rhomboplites, 417

ff. Hyoid bone and tongue toothless; dorsal spines 10 .. *Apsilus*, 418

bb. Interorbital area flat, separated by a transverse line of demarcation from the occipital region.

g. Head naked above and on snout......................*Etelis*, 419

gg. Head scaly above and on jaws and snout...........*Verilus*, 419

The genus *Hoplopagrus* is close to *Lutianus*, from which it differs chiefly in having the anterior nostril remote from the other.

The single species is the pargo raisero, *H. guntheri.* This

interesting species is found only on the Pacific coast of tropical America, and is known from Guaymas to Panama. It is a common food-fish at Guaymas and Mazatlan. It reaches a foot in length.

Colour, upper parts dark brown, with 6 double bands of brown running obliquely downward and backward, the fourth and fifth pairs appearing as one; breast and belly maroon purple, becoming less distinct on opercles and sides; a large jet-black spot on base of caudal peduncle and extending upon soft dorsal; fins dusky-olive, shaded with pinkish and brown; ventrals black-tipped.

DOG SNAPPER, *Lutianus jocu*

SCHOOLMASTER, *Lutianus apodus*

MUTTON-FISH, *Lutianus analis*

LANE SNAPPER, *Lutianus synagris*

GENUS LUTIANUS BLOCH

The Snappers or Pargos

Body oblong, compressed, the back somewhat elevated; head long, naked above, except for a broad oblique band of scales on nape; nostrils normally close together, neither with a tube; mouth large, the jaws with bands of villiform teeth, besides which is usually an outer series of larger teeth in each jaw; vomer and palatines with villiform teeth; usually one or more patches of teeth on tongue in adult; no molars; preopercle finely serrate, without notch; soft parts of dorsal and anal scaly at base; the dorsal continuous; caudal lunate or forked; parietal crest not confluent with orbital rim.

Species very numerous, Asiatic, American, and African; all very active, predatory fishes, highly valued as food, and many of them possessing good game qualities. In our waters there are about 20 species, most of them food-fishes of importance.

a. Top of head scaled...............................*viridis,* 406
aa. Top of head not scaled.
b. Dorsal spines 10.
c. Vomerine teeth in a diamond-shaped patch..........*jordani,* 407
cc. Vomerine patch of teeth ↑-shaped, or ∧-shaped, not diamond-shaped.
d. Soft dorsal normally with 14 rays, rarely 13.
e. Anal fin rounded, its middle rays less than $\frac{1}{2}$ length of head; no large black lateral spot.
f. Gill-rakers 7 to 9, usually with few rudiments if any.
g. Vomerine teeth forming a ∧- or a ↑-shaped patch, the backward prolongation on median line very short or wanting.
h. Maxillary $2\frac{3}{4}$ in head; preorbital $5\frac{1}{2}$...........*novemfasciatus,* 407
hh. Maxillary $2\frac{2}{7}$ in head; preorbital $4\frac{3}{4}$............*cyanopterus,* 407
gg. Vomerine teeth forming an anchor-shaped patch with a distinct backward prolongation on the median line.
i. Scales above lateral line arranged in series not parallel with lateral line, being oblique and irregular, at least below second dorsal.
j. Body comparatively elongate, the depth $2\frac{3}{4}$ to 3 in length.

griseus, 407

jj. Body deeper, the depth about $2\frac{1}{2}$ in length.
k. Scales moderate, about 9 in an oblique series from first dorsal to lateral line, about 55 in lateral line ....*jocu,* 408
kk. Scales unusually large, only 5 or 6 in an oblique series from first dorsal to lateral line, about 45 in lateral line ......*apodus,* 409

ii. Scales above lateral line in horizontal series which are throughout more or less parallel with it...............*argentiventris,* 409

ff. Gill-rakers more numerous, about 10, with several rudiments before them ....*buccanella,* 409

ee. Anal fin angulated, its middle rays produced, the longest in adult at least ½ as long as head; a black lateral blotch in young.

l. Scales above lateral line arranged in series which are not throughout parallel with it.

m. Teeth on vomer in an anchor-shaped patch, with a median backward prolongation.

n. Iris golden yellow in life; scales 9-52-10...........*vivanus,* 410

nn. Iris rose-red; scales 8-46-14 ....*aya,* 411

mm. Teeth on vomer in a ∧-shaped patch, without a distinct backward prolongation on median line ....*analis,* 413

ll. Scales above lateral line arranged in series which are more or less distinctly parallel throughout with the lateral line.
colorado, 414

dd. Soft dorsal with 12 rays, rarely 13.

o. Mouth moderate, maxillary 2¾ in head; caudal deeply forked.

p. Vomerine teeth in an anchor-shaped patch, with a distinct backward prolongation on median line ....*guttatus,* 414

pp. Vomerine teeth in a ∧- or ↑-shaped patch, the prolongation on median line very short or wanting.

q. Eye small, 5 in head; back less elevated; pectoral short, 1½ in head ....*synagris,* 415

oo. Mouth large, maxillary 2⅗ in head...............*mahogoni,* 415

bb. Dorsal spines 11.................................*aratus,* 416

Lutianus viridis is a rare species known only from the Galapagos,

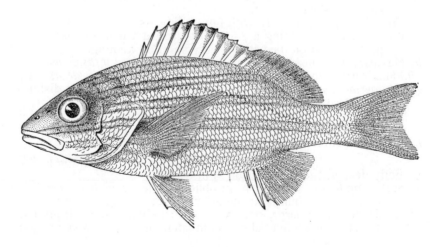

Tres Marias, and Revillagigedo islands. Nothing distinctive is known of its habits. Colour, golden brown, with 5 sky-blue longitudinal stripes, each broadly margined with darker blue; a faint median blue streak from occiput to front of dorsal.

Lutianus jordani is known only from Panama, where it is sometimes taken in considerable numbers. It is a strongly marked species, quite unlike any other, reaching a length of less than 2 feet. It may be readily distinguished from any other species by the diamond-shaped patch of vomerine teeth. Colour, dark purplish olive, scales with silvery spots.

Lutianus novemfasciatus is known from the Pacific coast of tropical America, from Guaymas and Cape San Lucas to Panama; generally common, and a large and valued food-fish, reaching a weight of 20 pounds. It is called pargo prieto.

Colour, back and sides very dark olive-brown, the back with a slaty tinge, the sides often with some faint purplish; belly and lower parts of head white; inside of mouth reddish yellow.

Lutianus cyanopterus is found from Brazil north to Cuba. It is rather common and reaches a length of 2 to 4 feet, being a large, coarse fish, regarded as unwholesome by fishermen.

Colour, dusky-gray, paler below, the belly sometimes reddish; membranes of vertical fins grayish black, especially anal and soft dorsal; ventrals blackish at tip; pectorals plain olivaceous; head dusky above, without markings.

Gray Snapper; Mangrove Snapper

Lutianus griseus (Linnæus)

This is one of the most widely distributed, most abundant, and best known of all the snappers. It is found throughout the West Indies, is abundant on the Florida coast, and strays northward to New Jersey and Woods Hole. It is generally known as the gray snapper, but in Florida and the Bahamas, where the coasts are mangrove-lined, it is called the mangrove snapper; while in the West Indies among the Spanish-speaking people it is the cabellerote or pargo prieto. It inhabits waters of different depths, large examples often being found near the shore, while others equally large are often taken at considerable depths in company with the red snapper. Those from deep water are usually redder than shallow-water examples. In Indian River, Florida, the mangrove snapper is regarded as an excellent food-fish, and is an important commercial fish.

Its average weight there is about 2 pounds, and the maximum about 6 or 7 pounds. At Key West it is the most abundant of all the snappers, and attains a length of 3 feet and a weight of 18 pounds, though the average weight does not exceed 5 pounds. Here it is called gray snapper, and is regarded as a warm-water fish, being found in shallow water in summer, and retiring to deeper water in winter. It is said always to run in schools, and to spawn in July and August, usually on the shoals, the eggs being non-adhesive and separating readily from each other at spawning.

All the snappers are game-fishes of considerable importance, and the gray snapper is one of the very best. Its abundance and wide distribution, the ease with which it may be found at all seasons, together with the readiness and vigour with which it takes the hook and the fairly good fight which it makes, should cause this fish to be much sought after by the anglers who visit our Southern and tropical waters. One of the best places to find it of which we know is in Indian River, from Indian River Inlet southward. Another is in Jack Channel near Key West, where very large ones can be taken by using sardines and pilchards for bait.

Colour, very dark green above, middle part of each scale brassy black, the edge broadly pearly white; below lateral line the duskiness of middle of scale becomes brassy, and lower grayish; blue stripe below eye in very young; top of head blackish olive; dorsal fin bluish black; caudal violaceous or maroon-black, or bluish; anal rosy; pectoral pale flesh-colour. Fishes from deep water are much redder.

Dog Snapper; Jocú

Lutianus jocu (Bloch & Schneider)

This excellent food-fish is known from Bahia north to the Florida Keys, occasionally straying north to Woods Hole. At Key West, where it is not very common, it reaches a weight of 20 pounds, though the average is much smaller. It is found most frequently in fall and winter about Key West. It does not seem to be abundant about Porto Rico, where it is called pargo colorado.

Colour, olivaceous above, rosy or brick-red on side, paler below, much flushed so that the general hue is coppery red; side with very narrow light cross-bars; a line of small round bluish spots below eye and across opercle; dorsal and caudal fins brick-red, the soft dorsal dusky at base; anal and ventrals yellowish.

Schoolmaster; Caji

Lutianus apodus (Walbaum)

The schoolmaster is one of the most richly coloured and beautiful of the snappers, and is withal a very interesting and attractive fish. It is known from Bahia northward through the West Indies to southern Florida. It sometimes strays in the Gulf Stream to Woods Hole. It is found at Key West and in Indian River, but is not common in either place. It is one of the most abundant snappers about Porto Rico, where it is known as pargo amarilla. The species attains a weight of 7 or 8 pounds, though the average is 3 pounds or less. It takes the hook readily and with vigor, and good sport may be had with it "down the bay" near Key West.

Colour of adult, reddish brown on back and top of head, becoming brighter orange-red on side, more orange below; side with about 9 broad greenish white vertical bars from back to lower part of side; top of caudal peduncle with a large blackish blotch; a series of small round dark spots below eye; fins all greenish yellow, the caudal with some orange; young with a sharply defined blue stripe below eye from snout to angle of opercle.

Lutianus argentiventris, the pargo amarilla, is found on our Pacific coast from Mazatlan southward. It resembles the schoolmaster, the dog snapper, and the gray snapper, but is apparently distinct from all of these, the chief difference being that the scales above the lateral line are in series parallel with it.

It reaches a length of 2 feet, is generally common, and is a good food-fish.

Black-fin Snapper

Lutianus buccanella (Cuvier & Valenciennes)

This is a small and strongly marked species, occurring in the West Indies and common in deep water about Havana, in the market of which it is known as sesí or sesí de lo alto.

Colour, crimson in life, silvery below but flushed with crimson; axil and base of pectoral jet-black; eye orange; dorsal crimson, its edge scarlet; caudal orange-yellow, this colour extending upon the caudal peduncle; last rays of soft dorsal and most of anal and ventrals yellow; pectoral, base of anal, and ventral spine pinkish.

Silk Snapper

Lutianus vivanus (Cuvier & Valenciennes)

This handsome snapper is found in the West Indies and is rather common about Havana, where it is known as pargo de lo alto. It reaches a foot or more in length and is of food-value. When fresh it may always be known by the bright yellow colour of the eye, a colour which does not entirely fade in spirits.

Colour in life, bright rose, paler below; some narrow, undulating, light golden streaks following the rows of scales above the lateral line; mouth reddish within; traces of a dark lateral spot in some specimens; dorsal rosy, pale at the base, its edge yellow; caudal rosy, dusky posteriorly, the tip sometimes blood-red; pectoral pale yellow; ventrals and anal pale rosy, the latter yellowish posteriorly.

Red Snapper

Lutianus aya (Bloch)

Of all the snappers, this is by far the most important and best known. It reaches a length of 2 to 3 feet and a weight of 10 to 35 pounds. Its range extends from Long Island to Brazil, but its centre of abundance is in the Gulf of Mexico, in rather deep water on the rocky banks off the west coast of Florida and the coasts of Campeche and Yucatan. On the American coast it is known everywhere as the red snapper. To the Spaniards it is the pargo colorado, while in the Havana market it is the pargo guachinango, or Mexican snapper, because it is brought to that city from the Mexican coast. It is not common in Cuban and Porto Rican waters, and appears to be rare off the coast of Brazil. Off the east coast of Florida and the coast of Georgia it is abundant.

The history of the growth of the red-snapper fishery is an interesting one. In the late forties or early fifties some New London fishermen ventured into the Gulf of Mexico, with their small sloops such as they used in the cod fisheries, none over 15 or 20 tons measurement. They fell in with the red snappers off the west coast of Florida, and made good catches, which they marketed at New Orleans at good prices. Others were induced to leave the whirling tide-rips of the Vineyard Shoals and wet a line on the Snapper Banks. Later, winter voyages were made, in better and more fully equipped smacks, and these for a time held a monopoly of the trade. This trade, however, was local and mostly retail, in New Orleans and Mobile, and not until in the early seventies was an effort made to extend the trade. This was by the Pensacola Ice Company and by Warren & Stearns of Pensacola, while the Hon. Eugene Blackford was active in introducing the red snapper into the New York trade. The business grew rapidly, and in 1898 there were engaged in the red-snapper fishery in the Gulf of Mexico more than 40 vessels.

At first the smacks were provided with wells in which the fish could be kept alive, but now ice is used and the fish are put upon the market in better condition. Pensacola is the centre of the red-snapper trade. From this place the smacks make voyages to the Tortugas and the Campeche banks, some 700 miles distant.

The fish are found by continually throwing the lead when the smack has, by dead reckoning, reached the vicinity of a bank. A man standing on the weather-rail, supporting himself by a hold on the main-shroud, swings the line, to which is attached a baited hook and a 9-pound lead. He releases it as it swings under and forward, and lets it swing to the bottom, and 40 fathoms depth is reached as the hand of the leadsman comes over the lead, although the vessel may be moving forward 3 or 4 knots an hour.

If fish are present and hungry, they snatch at the hook, and one is brought to the surface. As soon as a bite is announced, a dory, with one man provided with fishing-gear, is at once launched, and if the fish bite well the smack is brought back to the spot and either anchored or permitted to drift broadside across the ground. When she drifts away from the fish she is again worked to windward, and the same process repeated until the fish cease biting or the fare is completed. This process of sounding is sometimes followed all day without success; and again, the fish are quickly found. Sometimes six men will catch a thousand fish in a few hours, and at other times two or three hundred fish will be the limit of a day's hard sounding and patient fishing. When the snappers are spawning, they often are so abundant around the smack as to colour the water, but refuse to take the hook, and in such times the only recourse is to search for other schools. The fare is taken to Pensacola as promptly as possible, packed in ice, and shipped to many points in the North and West, from Boston to Denver and from Texas to the Great Lakes. So widely are they shipped that, as one dealer aptly remarks, "No man who is willing to buy a red snapper has lacked the opportunity."

Colour in life, deep rose-red, paler on throat; bluish streaks along rows of scales, above becoming fainter and disappearing with age; fins brick-red; dorsal bordered with orange, with a narrow blackish edge; caudal narrowly edged with blackish; a large blackish blotch above lateral line and below front rays of soft dorsal in the young, usually disappearing with age; axil of pectoral dusky; eye red. The intensity of colour in this species varies much with the locality. Specimens from Porto Rico have the general colour paler and the black lateral blotch more persistent.

Mutton-fish

Lutianus analis (Cuvier & Valenciennes)

This snapper, which is also called pargo or pargo criollo, reaches 2 feet or more in length and a weight of 25 pounds, and is found from Pensacola to Brazil, straying occasionally northward in the Gulf Stream to Woods Hole. It is common at Key West, and in the Havana markets it is the most important food-fish, being always abundant and highly esteemed. About Key West it is found on rock bottom in 3 to 9 fathoms, and is caught with hook and line. They are quite gamy, taking the hook promptly and fighting well. They are found throughout the year, but are scarcest in July and August, which is their spawning-time; the eggs are non-adhesive and the size of a rice-grain.

In Porto Rico this species is highly esteemed. It is called sama or pargo criollo. It is usually taken in the fish-traps set in 5 to 20 fathoms, though considerable numbers of the smaller individuals are caught with the haul-seines in shallow water along the shore.

Colour in life, dark olive-green above, many of the scales with pale blue spots, these forming irregular oblique streaks upward and backward; similar stripes more regular and numerous on caudal

YELLOW-TAIL, *Ocyurus chrysurus*

YELLOW-TAIL, *Ocyurus chrysurus*

MARGATE-FISH, *Hæmulon album*

BASTARD MARGARET, *Hæmulon parra*

peduncle and above anal; in old fishes these blue spots and streaks disappear; belly white, strongly tinged with brick-red; about 6 narrow, dusky vertical bars, a little broader than the interspaces and not well defined, between gill-opening and anal; head bronze-olive, darker above; a broad, undulating, pearly streak from snout below eye to upper edge of gill-opening; a narrow blue streak from eye to nostril; iris fiery red; pectorals, caudal, anal, and ventrals brick-red, the caudal narrowly margined with black and somewhat bronze above; dorsal reddish along the rays and tips of membranes, otherwise yellowish; a distinct lateral blotch just above lateral line and below the first soft ray of dorsal, about as large as pupil, smaller than in other species similarly marked, and seldom disappearing with age; axil and bar across base of pectoral above pale or dusky olive.

Pargo Colorado

Lutianus colorado Jordan & Gilbert

This species reaches the length of $2\frac{1}{2}$ feet, and occurs on our Pacific coast from Guaymas to Panama. It is a common food-fish on that coast, and is highly esteemed.

Colour in life, dark olivaceous above, each scale with the basal half dark olive-brown; head and lower parts of body bright red, especially bright on lower parts of head, the colour extending on the sides for a varying distance; upper jaw and maxillary reddish; upper parts of head dark olivaceous; scales on sides of head without dark spots; a much-interrupted light blue line from middle of preorbital along suborbital, rarely extending behind the orbit; cheek sometimes with bluish spots or lines; inside of mouth red; vertical fins very dark, with more or less reddish; spinous dorsal with a broad median streak of very light slaty blue; pectoral and ventrals reddish, the latter with dusky.

Flamenco

Lutianus guttatus (Steindachner)

This snapper occurs on the Pacific coast from Guaymas to Panama. It is a small species, rarely exceeding a foot in length, and is a common food-fish at Guaymas, Mazatlan, and Panama. It is the Pacific coast representative of the lane snapper, which it somewhat resembles.

Colour in spirits, brown above, the sides bright silvery; a large round black lateral blotch, as large as eye, on lateral line below front of soft dorsal; each scale above lateral line with a faint darker grayish median spot, these forming oblique streaks; side of head often with similar spots; 2 or 3 similar streaks often present below lateral line, these straight and horizontal; each series of scales below lateral line with a narrow yellowish stripe; snout and preorbital with dark vermiculations; fins all pale. In life, light olivaceous above, the markings bronze-olive; side pale crimson, the marks more yellow; belly golden yellow; iris scarlet, eye surrounded by yellow; first dorsal reddish, second with reddish brown markings; caudal deep rich red; lower fins golden; pectoral nearly colourless; side of head pink with golden stripes.

Lane Snapper

Lutianus synagris (Linnæus)

This beautiful species, also known as the red-tailed snapper, is found from Tampa to Colon and Brazil. It is common almost everywhere throughout its range, and in Havana, where it is one of the most popular food-fishes, it is scarcely exceeded in abundance by any other species. Its strongly marked colouration renders it easy of recognition.

Colour in life, rose, tinged with silvery below, slightly olivaceous but not dark above; a large round maroon blotch, larger than eye, just above lateral line and below front of soft dorsal; series of deep golden yellow stripes along side, 3 on head, the upper from snout through eye, and about 10 on body, the lower nearly straight and horizontal, the upper undulating and irregular, extending upward and backward; belly white, its sides largely yellowish; lips red; maxillary partly yellow; tongue yellowish; iris fiery red; caudal deep blood-red; spinous dorsal nearly transparent, with a marginal and basal band of golden; pectoral pinkish; young quite green above.

The lane snapper reaches a maximum weight of about 4 pounds, though the average of those brought to the Key West market is not above ½ pound. The largest seen in Porto Rico was 14 inches long and weighed about 2 pounds. About this island it is known as manchego, mancheva, or raiado, and is highly esteemed as a food-fish.

Mahogany Snapper

Lutianus mahogoni (Cuvier & Valenciennes)

This is a small snapper occurring in the West Indies. It is rather common in the markets of Havana, where it is known as ojanco, in allusion to the large eye. It does not exceed 8 or 10 inches in length.

Colour in life, deep brown, silvery below, everywhere shaded with red, especially on head; eye, which is $3\frac{2}{3}$ in head, scarlet; a large blackish blotch on side, chiefly above lateral line and below first rays of soft dorsal; maxillary yellow on covered parts; narrow bronze streaks following rows of scales, these most distinct above lateral line; dorsal fin pale, edged with blood-red; caudal deep red; anal, ventrals, and pectorals scarlet; the bright colours fade and disappear in spirits, leaving the back dark gray, the lower part silvery, more or less flushed with red.

Pargo de Raizero

Lutianus aratus (Günther)

This species occurs on the Pacific coast of tropical America from Panama to Mazatlan. It is a handsome fish, looking quite unlike the other species of the genus, and is generally common. It reaches a length of 2 feet, and is a good food-fish.

Colour in spirits, dark brown, somewhat paler below; centre of each scale yellowish silvery, these forming conspicuous silvery streaks along the back and sides, most distinct near the middle of the body; fins grayish, rather pale; membrane of soft dorsal dusky; ventrals dusky at tips; young with pale cross-bands formed by enlargement of the silvery spots in certain regions. Colour in life, dark green, the dark stripes on side dark brown, the interspaces yellowish white; belly coppery red; some bluish on cheek; pectoral maroon-red; ventrals salmon-red, the first ray white; anal creamy red.

415

GENUS OCYURUS GILL

The Rabirubias

This genus is allied to *Lutianus,* from which it differs notably in the structure of the skull, especially in the forward extension of the fronto-occipital crest. The single species shows numerous minor peculiarities, as in the form of the body, the large, well-forked tail, the small head, the increased number of gill-rakers, and the presence of pterygoid teeth.

The single species of this genus is the yellowtail or rabirubia, *O. chrysurus.* The yellowtail is found from southern Florida to Brazil, and is generally abundant. It is known from Biscayne Bay, Key West, and nearly all the West Indies. At Key West, where it is known as yellowtail and rabirubia, it is even more abundant than the lane snapper, and is the principal fish served at the hotels and boarding-houses in the fall. It is said to be plentiful throughout the year except during the winter, when cold weather drives them to deep water. During the warmer weather they are found at a depth of 2 fathoms or more, usually in about 5 fathoms, and generally about shoals where there is some mud bottom. The spawning-time is said to be in July, when they are found about the reefs from Miami to the Tortugas.

In Porto Rico it is called colorubia, and is an abundant and important food-fish. It attains a length of 2 feet and a weight of several pounds. At Key West the average weight is not more than a pound.

As a game-fish it is not without merit, it being a ready biter and a vigorous fighter. The commercial fishermen catch it with hook and line, using sardines for bait. At Key West it is hawked about the streets in the early morning, and just at the hour when one most desires to sleep, his slumbers are broken by the monotonous cry, " Yallertail—rabirubia! Yallertail—rabirubia!" first faint and distant, then growing stronger and stronger, passing under your window a distracting yell, and then gradually dying away as the peripatetic vender of the luscious " yallertail " vanishes down the street.

Colour in life, olivaceous above, rather pale and somewhat violet-tinged; a number of large, irregular deep yellow blotches on side of back; a deep yellow stripe from tip of snout straight through eye to caudal peduncle, there broadening and including all of tail above lateral line and behind dorsal fin; above this a pearly purplish area; below it a flesh-coloured or rosy area or band 2 scales broad, then a succession of about 16 narrow streaks alternately flesh-coloured and yellow, growing fainter progressively below; edges of scales yellow, their centres reddish; iris fiery red; lower parts of head flesh-colour, with some yellow spots; maxillary mostly yellow; caudal deep yellow, its edge reddish; dorsal chiefly yellow; anal faintly yellow.

GENUS RHOMBOPLITES GILL

This genus differs from *Lutianus* chiefly in cranial characters and in the extension of the villiform teeth over the pterygoid and hyoid bones. The form of the patch of vomerine teeth is also somewhat peculiar. The genus contains but a single species, *R. aurorubens,* the cagon de lo alto of our Spanish fishermen. It is found from Rio Janeiro northward through the West Indies to the Carolina coast,

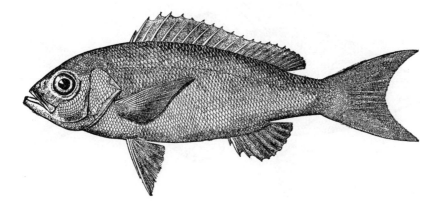

being probably most abundant about Cuba and on the Snapper Banks off the west coast of Florida. It is, however, nowhere very common, but is a good food-fish. Colour in life, vermilion above, paler below, faint brown lines running obliquely downward and forward, following the rows of scales; side with narrow sinuous streaks of golden yellow, some of them longitudinal, others oblique; dorsal rosy, its margin chiefly orange; anal pale at base, rosy at extremity; pectoral yellowish; ventrals rosy; caudal and iris vermilion; inside of mouth dusky.

GENUS APSILUS CUVIER & VALENCIENNES

This very distinct genus has the cranial characters of *Rhomboplites*, with the scaleless fins, peculiar squamation, and dentition of *Aprion*. There are no teeth on the pterygoids, tongue, or hyoid bones. The dorsal fin is short.

In our waters there is but the single species, *A. dentatus*, the arnillo of the Havana fishermen. It is known only from the West Indies, and is not uncommon in the Havana market. It reaches a foot in length, and is a very beautiful little fish, easily distinguished by the generic characters given above. In life this species is dusky-violet above, and on sides paler; inside of mouth and all the fins similar in colour, the anal and ventrals with blackish tips; soft dorsal with some olive shades, the edge grayish.

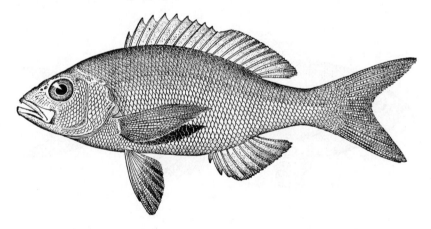

GENUS ETELIS CUVIER & VALENCIENNES

In this genus the dorsal fin is nearly or quite divided into 2 fins by a deep notch, the eye very large, and the preorbital very narrow. It is very closely related to *Aprion*, the skull in the two being almost identical.

There are only two American species, and but one of these of any importance. *E. oculatus*, known in Porto Rico as cachucho, occurs in the West Indies and about Madeira, but is not yet known from Florida or elsewhere on the mainland. It is a species which prefers rather deep water and rocky bottom. It is a beautiful species, reaching a length of 2 to 3 feet, and is an excellent food-fish.

Colour in life, nearly everywhere bright red; pale in spirits, the red nowhere persisting.

GENUS VERILUS POEY

This genus is technically close to *Etelis*, although the single known species is quite different in appearance from *Etelis oculatus*. The cavernous character of the skull is the most striking feature, which, with the nearly divided dorsal, readily distinguishes it.

The only known species is the escolar chino (*V. sordidus*) of the Havana market. It is a rather deep-water species, known only from the coasts of Cuba.

Colour, dusky-gray, slightly paler below; tips of spinous dorsal

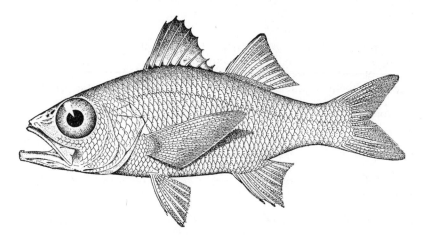

and ventrals jet-black, the fins otherwise coloured as the body; posterior edge of caudal dusky; lining of gill-cavity, peritoneum, and posterior part of mouth jet-black.

THE GRUNTS

Family LII. Hæmulidæ

Body oblong, more or less elevated, covered with moderate-sized scales which are adherent and more or less strongly ctenoid or almost cycloid; lateral line well developed, concurrent with the back, usually not extending on the caudal fin; head large, the crests of the skull usually largely developed; mouth large or small, usually low, horizontal, and terminal; premaxillaries protractile; no supplemental maxillary bone; teeth all pointed, none of them forming marked canines; no teeth on vomer, palatines, or tongue; pseudobranchiæ large; gill-membranes separate, free from the isthmus; opercle without spines; side of head usually scaly; dorsal fin continuous or deeply notched, sometimes divided into 2 fins, the spines usually strong, depressible in a groove, the spines heteracanthous, that is, alternating, the one stronger on the right side, the other on the left; anal similar to soft dorsal, with 3 spines; caudal usually more or less concave behind; air-bladder present.

This family is a very large one, the species being very numerous. They are all carnivorous fishes chiefly of warm seas, and most of them highly valued as food. Thirteen genera and about 55 species are represented in our waters.

a. Chin with a central groove behind the symphysis of the lower jaw.
b. Mouth rather wide, the jaws scarlet posteriorly in life; soft parts of vertical fins densely scaled to their margins.
c. Jaws subequal, the lower included; mouth little oblique; gill-rakers comparatively few and short.
d. Dorsal spines 12, rarely 11......................*Hæmulon,* 421
dd. Dorsal spines 13 ....*Bathystoma,* 428
cc. Lower jaw projecting.......................*Lythrulon,* 429
bb. Mouth more or less narrow, not scarlet within; soft parts of vertical fins naked or with scales only on their bases.
e. Anal fin short, its rays III, 7 to 10; dorsal spines rather robust.
f. Body ovate, the depth greater than head; lips thick.
Anisotremus, 430
ff. Body oblong, the depth usually less than length of head; lips not so thick.
g. Soft parts of dorsal and anal with series of small scales on membranes ....*Brachydenterus,* 432
gg. Soft parts of dorsal and anal without scales, except a low sheath at base ....*Pomadasis,* 432
ee. Anal fin long and low, its rays III, 10 to 13; dorsal fin low, not deeply emarginate ....*Orthopristis,* 433

WHITE OR COMMON GRUNT, *Hæmulon plumieri*

YELLOW GRUNT, *Hæmulon sciurus*

PORKFISH, *Anisotremus virginicus*

GENUS HÆMULON CUVIER

The Roncos or Grunts

Body oblong, usually more or less elevated and compressed; mouth wide, the maxillary long and curved, reaching below eye; lower jaw included; chin with a central groove; teeth of jaws conical, the outer series stronger and curved; lips and inside of mouth posteriorly usually bright red or scarlet in life; preopercle serrate, no recurved hooks below; soft parts of vertical fins completely scaled; dorsal spines 12 or 11; second anal spine enlarged, generally larger and longer than the third; caudal forked.

This genus has many species, all American. All have more or less red or orange inside the mouth, the amount of redness being greatest in those species with the largest mouths. Nearly all the species, when young, have 2 or more more or less sharply defined dark longitudinal stripes along the side, 1 or more along top of head, and a dark spot at base of caudal. In a few species these markings persist through life.

All of the species are valued as food, some of them being among our most important fishes.

a. Scales below lateral line anteriorly not especially enlarged.
b. Scales above lateral line anteriorly not much enlarged.
c. Maxillary $2\frac{1}{3}$ to $2\frac{3}{4}$ in head, not reaching centre of eye in adult.
d. Back and sides without yellow or blue stripes.
e. Seven or 8 rows of scales in vertical series from first dorsal spine to lateral line.
f. Mouth rather small, maxillary scarcely reaching eye.
g. Side with about 6 dark vertical bars ....*sexfasciatum,* 422
gg. Side without dark vertical bars....................*album,* 422
ff. Mouth rather large, maxillary reaching pupil...*macrostomum,* 423
ee. Five or 6 rows of scales in a vertical series from first dorsal spine to lateral line.
h. Series of scales from scapular scale extending backward to front of soft dorsal..................................*bonariense,* 424
hh. Series of scales from scapular scale not extending farther backward than middle of spinous dorsal.
i. Depth of body about $2\frac{2}{3}$ in length; pectoral fin short, less than $\frac{2}{3}$ length of head......................................*parra,* 424
ii. Depth of body $2\frac{1}{2}$ in length; pectoral fin long, more than $\frac{3}{4}$ length of head ....*scudderi,* 425
dd. Back and sides with distinct horizontal yellow stripes.
carbonarium, 425

421

cc. Maxillary nearly or quite ½ length of head, reaching centre of eye in adult.
j. Back and sides with rows of round silvery spots, these forming streaks which follow the rows of scales.....*steindachneri,* 425
jj. Back and sides with continuous yellow stripes which are horizontal and do not everywhere follow the rows of scales.
melanurum, 425
jjj. Back and sides of head and body with continuous blue stripes.
sciurus, 426
bb. Scales above lateral line anteriorly much enlarged...*plumieri,* 426
aa. Scales below lateral line anteriorly much enlarged.
flavolineatum, 427

Hœmulon sexfasciatum, the mojarra almejero, reaches a length of 2 feet or more. It is found on our Pacific coast from Guaymas to Panama. It is not very abundant but is a good food-fish. It is the Pacific coast representative of the margate-fish, from which, however, it differs strikingly in colour.

Colour, pearly gray, with 6 or 7 sharply defined dusky cross-bands from back to lower part of side, fading below; cheek, opercles, and anterior part of side with distinct roundish spots of brownish black, largest and best defined on opercle; fins all nearly plain dusky grayish.

Margate-fish; Margaret Grunt

Hœmulon album Cuvier & Valenciennes

This beautiful and important fish is found from southern Florida to Brazil. At Key West it is a common and valued food-fish. It attains a weight of 8 or 10 pounds, the average being 4 to 6 pounds. It is found chiefly in deep water, most abundantly about the reefs. It is said to spawn early in summer on rock bottom, at which time it is said to school. At night it comes into shallower water to feed upon crabs, crawfish, and worms, which seem to be its principal food. Cold is said to affect this fish very greatly, driving it away to deeper or warmer water.

The name margate-fish appears to have been derived from Margate, a well-known seaport and watering-place in England, from which some of the "conchs" or natives of the Bahamas originally came. In the Bahamas and at Key West the name is now variously corrupted into margat, market, margaret, and margarite.

Colour in life, pearly white, olivaceous above and on sides, some-what bluish below; edges of scales above darker; small whitish spots on centres of scales between nape and pectoral; a brownish streak from snout, following curve of back and ending at last soft ray of dorsal; another from forehead above eye, curving upward across side, then downward, and under last dorsal rays joining a broader, more distinct dark band which runs straight from snout through eye and along middle of side to base of caudal; belly and lower part of side with 4 or 5 rows of small pearly spots; fins all olivaceous, bluish, the soft dorsal and caudal darker olivaceous.

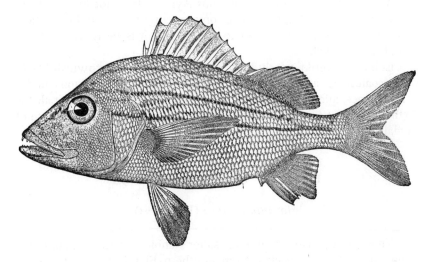

Gray Grunt; Striped Grunt

Hæmulon macrostomum Günther

This grunt is found from Indian River and Clearwater Harbor, Florida, southward to Jamaica and St. Thomas, but does not appear very common anywhere. Not many were seen in Porto Rico, where it is known as corocoro. It reaches a foot or more in length and is a good food-fish.

Colour in life, body dirty silvery with about 9 dark longitudinal streaks, plainest in the young; a median stripe from snout to dorsal fin; first and second lateral stripes from above eye to posterior end of soft dorsal; third from upper rim of orbit to vertical of posterior end of soft dorsal, where it joins the fifth; fourth, which is usually indistinct, from eye across opercle and disappearing on middle of side; the fifth and plainest from eye along middle of side, crossing lateral line, and joining third ends at base of caudal above lateral line; other lines on side more or less broken and indistinct; head dark grayish purple; an inky black spot on inner lower edge of opercle; lower jaw flesh-colour, with numerous fine dark specks; dorsal, caudal, anal, and pectoral yellow, dusky at base; ventrals dark; inside of mouth flesh-colour.

Hæmulon bonariense, the black grunt or ronco prieto, is found in the West Indies and south to Buenos Ayres. It is not known from Florida, and does not appear to be common anywhere. In Porto Rico, where it is known as ronco prieto or arrayado, it is fairly frequent and is highly esteemed.

Colour in spirits, pearly gray, centre of each scale brownish black, these coalescing and forming very sharply defined continuous undulating stripes, about 16 between front of dorsal and front of anal, the sixth extending from the scapular scale to last dorsal spine; base of caudal blackish; other fins dusky.

Bastard Margaret; Ronco

Hæmulon parra (Desmarest)

This grunt, also known as sailor's-choice, ronco blanco, ronco prieto, and arrayado, occurs from southern Florida to Brazil. It has been recorded from many places in southern Florida, the Tortugas, Cuba, Porto Rico, Jamaica, and Brazil. It is an abundant fish about Key West, where it collects in schools in July and August, when it spawns on rock bottom. It reaches 2 pounds in weight and is a good food-fish.

Colour in spirits, dark brown, centre of each scale on upper part of body dark brown surrounded by silvery; free edge of scales paler or purplish brown; lower part of sides and under parts more silvery, but with numerous fine dark specks everywhere; head and fins dark.

BLACK MARGATE-FISH, *Anisotremus surinamensis*

GRAY SNAPPER, *Lutianus griseus*

SCUP, *Stenotomus chrysops*

TOM-TATE, *Bathystoma rimator*

Mojarra Prieta

Hæmulon scudderi Gill

This species occurs on the Pacific coast of America from the Gulf of California to Panama. It is everywhere common, especially about rocks, reaches a length of a foot, and is a good food-fish. It is the Pacific coast representative of *H. parra*, reaches a similar size, is equally abundant, and passes through a similar range of variations and colour changes.

Hæmulon carbonarium, the ronco carbonero, is known from the West Indies, the Bermudas, and Brazil. It seems to be rare about Porto Rico, but is very common at Havana, where it is esteemed as a food-fish. It is a small species, usually not exceeding a foot in length.

Colour in life, light bluish gray, much resembling the common grunt; body with 7 or 8 deep brassy yellow stripes, horizontal above lateral line, those below a little curved, following the rows of scales, 3 above and 3 to 5 below the lateral line, the latter paler; little black under angle of preopercle; caudal blackish yellow at tip; soft dorsal, anal, and ventrals yellowish gray, the distal part blackish; spinous dorsal bluish, deep yellow at base and edge, a yellow stripe along middle; mouth deep red.

Hæmulon steindachneri, the ronco raiado, is a species of rather wide distribution. It occurs on both coasts of tropical America, from the Gulf of California to Panama, and from St. Lucia to Brazil. It is common on the coast of Brazil, and is especially abundant about Mazatlan.

Colour in life, olive or golden brown, golden below, the edges of scales of back with brilliant blue lustre, each scale on back and sides with a median pearly blue spot, these forming very distinct streaks, following the rows of scales; a large, distinct, round blackish blotch on base of caudal fin and caudal peduncle, more distinct than in any other species; a distinct bluish black vertical bar on lower anterior part of opercle, partly concealed by angle of preopercle; fins all bright yellow or golden; ventrals and anal not dark; peritoneum dusky.

Hæmulon melanurum, the jeniguana, is known from the West Indies and south to Brazil. It is rather common at Havana, but was not found by us in Porto Rico. It grows to a foot in length and is a good food-fish.

425

Colour in life, pearly gray; back and side with about 10 horizontal stripes of golden yellow, narrower than the interspaces; a dusky stripe through eye from snout to behind gill-opening; a well-defined black area on back and caudal fin, bounded below by an almost straight line from first dorsal spine to tip of lower caudal lobe; mouth red.

Yellow Grunt; Boar Grunt

Hæmulon sciurus (Shaw)

This common species is found practically everywhere from southern Florida to Brazil. At Key West it is known as boar grunt, and is very plentiful, usually in schools on rocky bottom. It is there caught with hook and line, the hook baited usually with a long worm, which the fishermen obtain from the stem of a tall plant growing on the bars. One fisherman reports catching as many as 500 to 600 in a single day. The best fishing is said to be in August, which is probably the spawning-time. It appears to be abundant about Porto Rico, where it is called cachicata and ronco amarillo. It reaches a foot to 18 inches in length, and a weight of a pound or more. At all places where common it is of much value as a food-fish; and the angler who visits Key West will find it interesting as a game-fish.

Colour in life, yellowish, side with about 10 broad, brassy bands, alternating with somewhat narrower pale blue bands, the fourth of which runs forward across upper edge of orbit, crossing the forehead and joining its fellow on opposite side; cheek and snout with similar blue lines, the one on middle of cheek forking below eye and enclosing an oblong area of the ground colour; spinous dorsal pale yellowish olive, bordered with orange; soft dorsal rusty olivaceous, with orange border; inside of mouth, except tips of jaws, blood-red.

Common Grunt; White Grunt

Hæmulon plumieri (Lacépède)

This is by far the most important of all the grunts. Its range extends from Cape Hatteras and Pensacola to Brazil. It is common everywhere on sandy shores, and it is *par excellence* the grunt of our

South Atlantic States and Florida.   At Key West it is the most abundant of all the food-fishes. and is caught the year round, the best time being in the fall.   Their spawning season is in August and September, at which time they gather into immense schools on shoal, feathery, and rock bottom, where they spawn.   The eggs are said to be "gritty" to the touch and about the size of a No. 10 shot; when ripe they separate and flow freely from the fish.   After spawning, the schools break up and the fish scatter.   They are so abundant, however, that they can usually be found in large numbers on any suitable bottom.   About Key West the white grunt grows to 18 inches in length and 4 pounds in weight, though the average is much less.

About Porto Rico, where it is called cachicata and boca colorado, it is one of the most abundant and useful species, and was seen by us in all the markets of the island.   It is there caught either in fish-traps or haul-seines, while at Key West many are taken with hook and line.   As a pan-fish the common grunt is not excelled.

Colour in life, light bluish; series of scales, each with a small brown or brassy spot, these forming indistinct narrow lines running upward and backward; body of scales above lateral line bluish, the border brownish olive; a brassy band along lateral line; back with some bronze; under parts whitish; about twelve narrow, irregular bright blue lines on head, separated by broad brassy lines, these sometimes extending on body; inner edge of maxillary orange; lower anterior edge of opercle yellow; inside of mouth red or deep yellow; lips dusky; dorsal grayish, with a narrow yellow edge on spinous portion; caudal plain gray; anal gray, tinged with yellow.

French Grunt; Open-mouthed Grunt

Hæmulon flavolineatum (Desmarest)

Found from the Florida Keys south to Brazil, rare in Florida, but generally common throughout the West Indies.   About Porto Rico it is one of the most abundant and valued species.   It is usually found on sandy shores, and is taken in traps, seines, or with the hook.   It reaches a foot in length, and is one of the most strongly marked species of the family.

Colour in life, light bluish gray; a bronze-yellow spot on upper part of each scale, these forming continuous undulating stripes on body and head, wider than the interspaces of ground colour; on the caudal they are nearly straight; on anterior part of body below lateral line, broader and very oblique; a horizontal stripe, crossing the others, along side of back from occiput to last rays of soft dorsal, of the same golden yellow; yellow around eye; yellow shades and streaks on cheek, not strongly marked as in the common grunt and the yellow grunt; top of head with yellow stripes; angle of mouth black, brick-red inside; a large black blotch under angle of preopercle; fins bright golden yellow, the pectoral and spinous dorsal paler. In spirits the ground colour becomes grayish and the stripes brownish or dusky.

GENUS BATHYSTOMA SCUDDER

This genus differs from *Hæmulon* in the presence of 13 dorsal spines; the body is rather elongate, gill-rakers rather numerous, 12 to 18 on lower part of anterior arch, the mouth moderate, the scales small, the frontal foramina long, and the jaws red within.

This genus has 3 species in our waters. The most important of these is the tomtate or red-mouth grunt, *Bathystoma rimator*, which ranges from Cape Hatteras and Pensacola southward through the West Indies to Trinidad. It is abundant about Charleston, S. C., where it is one of the most common food-fishes. Adults are said to be uncommon about Pensacola and Key West, but at the latter place the young swarm everywhere about the wharves and shores. It is as yet not known from Cuba, and does not seem to be at all abundant in Porto Rico. This species is not of large size, seldom exceeding a foot in length. It takes the hook readily, and is an excellent pan-fish. Specimens obtained by us in Porto Rico are 5 to 6 inches in length.

Colour in life, silvery white, slightly bluish above, with iridescent reflections; edges of scales on body light yellow, these forming continuous light yellow stripes, those below lateral line horizontal, those above very oblique; a narrow continuous streak of light yellow above lateral line from head to end of soft dorsal, and another from eye to middle of caudal; head silvery yellowish above; inside of mouth red; no black under preopercle; traces of a black blotch at base of caudal; fins colourless, the lower slightly yellowish.

Another species, *B. aurolineatum*, is found from the Florida Keys to Brazil, its centre of greatest abundance apparently being at Havana, where it is often brought into the market. It has been taken at Garden Key, Florida, but has not been observed at Key West. It reaches a length of only 6 or 8 inches, and is smaller than any other species of this or related genera, except *Brachygenys chrysargyreus*.

Colour in life, dusky-gray, with 7 or 8 yellow longitudinal streaks, the one through eye widest; inside of mouth very red; no dusky spot under the angle of preopercle; fins gray, the dorsal scarcely yellowish.

The third species is the white grunt, *B. striatum*, which is known from the Bermudas, Key West, Cuba, Santo Domingo, and Porto Rico, but is apparently not common anywhere. One specimen was obtained by us at San Juan, Porto Rico. It probably never exceeds a foot in length.

Colour in alcohol, pearly gray, with 5 or 6 continuous brownish streaks (probably golden in life), one on median line from tip of snout to origin of dorsal, one diverging from snout and passing above eye and along side to soft dorsal; another from snout through upper part of eye and terminating near beginning of lateral line; a fourth passing through eye and along middle of side to base of caudal; another crossing opercle and base of pectoral.

GENUS LYTHRULON JORDAN & SWAIN

This genus is closely allied to *Hæmulon*, but differs in the short snout, the high supraoccipital crest, oblique mouth, and increased number of gill-rakers. The form of the body is peculiar, the dorsal and anal long and low and the caudal widely forked. This genus contains but 2 species. The first of these, *Lythrulon flaviguttatum*, is distinguished by having the gill-rakers about $10+22$ and the body oblong, the depth being about $\frac{1}{3}$ the length. This species reaches about a foot in length, and inhabits the Pacific coast of tropical America from the Gulf of California to Panama. It is generally common, and valued as a pan-fish.

Colour in spirits, dark steel-gray, a very distinct small pale spot on each scale of back and side, surrounded by darker; in life these spots are pearly blue; head plain; a small dusky blotch under angle of pre-opercle; fins plain, bright yellow in life. Young with a large black blotch at base of caudal.

The other species, *L. opalescens*, is known only from Mazatlan, where it is rather common in the estuary. It is probably not rare, but has been confounded with the preceding, from which it may be distinguished by the fewer gill-rakers, 8+15, and the deeper body, the

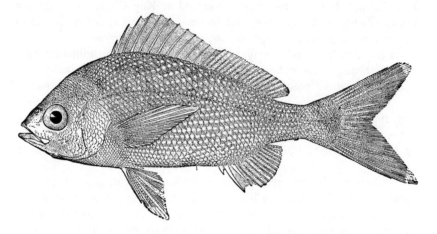

depth being 2⅔ in length.   The species reaches a length of 9 inches or more.

GENUS ANISOTREMUS GILL

Body ovate, short, deep, and compressed; mouth rather small, the lips thick, the maxillary rather short; inside of mouth not red; teeth in jaws only, all pointed, those of the outer series in upper jaw enlarged; chin with a median groove, besides smaller pores; dorsal spines strong; soft rays of dorsal and anal scaly at base; anal spines strong; caudal usually lunate; scales large; lower pharyngeals broad, with coarse, blunt teeth.   This genus, like *Hæmulon*, to which it is closely related, contains numerous species, all of them living on the shores of tropical America.   All of the species undergo considerable change in form with age, and all of them are valued as food-fishes. The young are marked with 2 or 3 blackish lengthwise stripes, which disappear with age, very soon in the brightly coloured species, but persisting longer in those less brightly coloured.

There are in our waters 12 species, several of which are sufficiently abundant to be of commercial value.

Pompon

Anisotremus surinamensis (Bloch)

The pompon is found from southern Florida and Mobile to Brazil. It has been taken by us in Indian River and Porto Rico, and is known also from the Tortugas, Cuba, Jamaica, Martinique, and Surinam. It reaches a length of 2 or 3 feet, and is a good food-fish.

Colour, grayish, darkest on anterior half of body, where each scale is dark brown on its basal half, followed by a white ellipse and a narrow darker border; upper edge of caudal peduncle brown, sides nearly plain whitish; snout and under parts of head lilac-brown; under parts of body rusty brown; fins all brownish, especially soft dorsal and anal.

Pork-fish; Sisi

Anisotremus virginicus (Linnæus)

A very handsome fish ranging from Florida to Brazil; known from Biscayne Bay, Key West, Santo Domingo, Jamaica, Porto Rico, Martinique, and St. Catharine Island. About Key West it is said to school from June to August, which is its spawning season. It is then found about shoals, but soon retires to deeper water. It spawns in the channels among the shoals, where it is caught in great numbers, chiefly in traps and with hook and line. About a month after spawning-time immense numbers of young are said to be found about the shoals.

The species reaches a length of about a foot and a weight of 2 pounds, but those brought to market do not average more than $\frac{1}{3}$ of a pound. In Porto Rico, where it is called sisi, it is not common. It is everywhere regarded as an excellent pan-fish.

Colour in life, side with about 8 broad lemon-yellow longitudinal bars, alternating with similar bars of dirty silvery, the upper 3 or 4 of the yellow lines branching anteriorly, the fifth extending on middle of caudal peduncle; belly silvery white; a broad black bar from origin of spinous dorsal to base of pectoral, continuing on shoulder-girdle to near isthmus; another broad black band from occiput through eye to angle of mouth; cheek metallic or brassy green; top of head brassy;

fins all orange-yellow; spinous dorsal, pectoral, and ventral dusted with brownish; scaly sheath at base of anal rich yellow.

GENUS BRACHYDENTERUS GILL

This genus in most respects resembles *Pomadasis*. Body oblong; scales large, those above in series parallel with the lateral line; mouth small; outer teeth somewhat enlarged; inside of jaws not red; anal spines small or moderate, the second little, if any, longer or stronger than third, and shorter than soft rays; soft dorsal and anal largely covered with small scales; D. XII, 14 to 16. None of the 4 species of this genus is of much importance.

Brachydenterus nitidus is known only from the Gulf of California, Mazatlan, and Panama. It reaches about a foot in length, and is used as food, though it is not abundant. In colour it is silvery, darker above, with dark streaks along the rows of scales, especially distinct below lateral line; a large round dark blotch at beginning of lateral line, about as large as eye.

B. corvinæformis ranges from the West Indies to Brazil, apparently most common about Porto Rico. It reaches a foot in length, and is a good pan-fish.

B. leuciscus is probably the most important species of the genus. It is found on our Pacific coast from Guaymas to Peru. It is very common about Mazatlan and Panama, and is a valued pan-fish.

B. axillaris, the burro blanco, reaches a foot in length, and is known only from Guaymas and Mazatlan, where it is used as food.

GENUS POMADASIS LACÉPÈDE

The Burros

This genus is composed of small shore-fishes, some of its representatives being found in most tropical seas. Several of the species enter fresh waters, and others are found in brackish waters. Numerous species occur on the west coast of Africa and about the Cape Verde Islands, but, so far as known, none enters European waters. The genus is represented in our waters by about 8 species, all of those sufficiently abundant being food-fishes of some little value.

Pomadasis panamensis is a well-marked species occurring on the Pacific coast of tropical America, and rather common at both Panama and Mazatlan. It reaches a foot or more in length, and is a good pan-fish.

Colour, gray silvery; young with 6 very faint cross-bars, one of these below spinous dorsal appearing as a roundish dark spot; lower fins white; a distinct dark blotch on opercle and a fainter one on side below spinous dorsal.

P. bayanus is known only from Panama, the only known specimens having come from the Rio Bayano. Colour, uniform olivaceous above, silvery below; fins plain.

P. productus is a very rare species known only from Cuba. Colour, nearly plain, silvery below.

P. macracanthus occurs on the Pacific coast of tropical America from Mazatlan to Panama. It reaches 15 inches in length, and is used as food. When caught it makes a loud snore-like noise very much like that made by a donkey, hence its common name burro.

P. andrei has been recorded only from the Rio Guayas, near Guayaquil, Ecuador. It is a doubtful species.

P. crocro occurs throughout the West Indies from Cuba to Brazil, and is generally common on sandy shores. Colour, plain olivaceous, silvery below, with about 3 or 4 ill-defined longitudinal dark stripes along side, one from tip of snout to middle of base of caudal.

P. branicki, the burrito, reaching a length of 7 inches, occurs on the Pacific coast of tropical America, from Mazatlan to Peru. It is not uncommon on sandy shores.

The remaining species, *P. ramosus*, is found in the West Indies and south to Brazil. In Porto Rico it is known as ronco blanco, and ascends the streams well toward the interior of the island, specimens having been obtained by us in the Rio Loiza near Caguas more than 25 miles from the coast. This species is said by the native fishermen to utter the grunting noise characteristic of the family. Though of small size, it is nevertheless a good food-fish, and is highly valued.

GENUS ORTHOPRISTIS GIRARD

The Pigfishes

This genus differs from *Pomadasis* in the long anal fin, the smaller scales, and the less development of the dorsal spines. Nearly all the species are American, and some of them are of food-value.

Orthopristis forbesi is known only from Albemarle Island, one of the Galapagos group. Colour in spirits, dark brown above, with bluish reflections, fins dusky except pectorals; caudal edged with light; membrane of opercle dark; preopercle with some dark spots. The known specimens are each about a foot long.

O. reddingi is known only from La Paz, Gulf of California. Colour, pearly gray, darker above; each scale of back and side with a bright bronze spot behind its centre, these forming nearly continuous streaks along the rows of scales, running upward and backward anteriorly and nearly horizontally on side, where they are more or less interrupted or transposed; head plain gray; dorsal with some streaks; ventrals somewhat dusky.

O. chalceus occurs on the coast of tropical America, from the Gulf of California to the Galapagos Islands, and is rather common, especially at Cape San Lucas and Mazatlan. It reaches 18 inches in length, and is a good food-fish. Colour, paler than in related species; pale chalky bluish streaks along the edges of the rows of scales; a pale streak below base of dorsal; fins rather pale, the soft dorsal mottled with darker. The young have broad diffuse dusky cross-bands on the side.

O. poeyi is a rare species known only from Havana. It is close to *O. chrysopterus*, but the body is more slender, and the scales are rather larger.

O. cantharinus is known only from the Galapagos Islands. It reaches a foot in length, and is apparently close to *O. chrysopterus.* Colour, brownish gray above, soiled silvery below; upper parts with 8 diffuse cross-bands, as wide as the interspaces extending to below middle of side; membrane of opercle dark; some dark streaks following rows of scales; dorsal with some dull orange and some pale round spots.

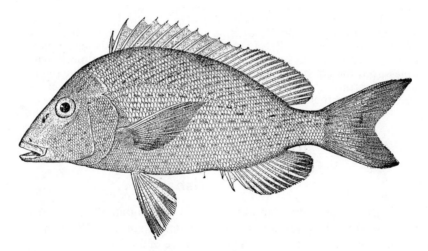

Pigfish; Hogfish

Orthopristis chrysopterus (Linnæus)

This is the most important food-fish of the genus. It reaches a length of 12 to 15 inches, and occurs on the South Atlantic and Gulf coasts of the United States, ranging as far north as Long Island and south to the mouth of the Rio Grande. It is especially abundant on sandy shores, where it is taken in haul-seines. Large numbers are taken along the Carolina coast. It is very highly valued as a pan-fish, and is known in some places as the sailor's-choice.

Colour in life, light blue above, shading gradually into silvery below; preorbital and snout clear sky-blue; a dash of blue on each side of upper lip; each scale on body with a blue centre, the edge with a brown spot, these forming on back and sides very distinct orange-brown stripes along the rows of scales, those above the lateral line extending obliquely upward and backward, those below nearly horizontal; snout with bronze spots; one or two cross-lines connecting front of orbits; 2 or 3 oblique lines on preorbital, besides numerous bronze spots larger than those on body; dorsal translucent with about 3 longitudinal bronze shades, composed of spots, those of soft dorsal most distinctly spot-like; caudal plain, yellowish at base, dusky toward tip; pectorals and ventrals yellowish, the latter darker at tip.

THE PORGIES

Family LIII.   Sparidæ

Body oblong, more or less elevated, covered with rather large adherent scales, which are never truly ctenoid; lateral line well developed, concurrent with the back, not extending on caudal fin; head large; mouth small, terminal, low, and horizontal; premaxillaries little protractile; maxillary short, peculiar in form and in articulation, without supplemental bone; teeth strong, those in front of jaws conical, incisor-like, or molar; lateral teeth of jaws always blunt and molar; no teeth on vomer or palatines; pseudobranchiæ large; gill-membranes separate, free from the isthmus; opercle without spines; sides of head usually scaly; dorsal fin single, sometimes deeply notched, the spines usually strong, depressible in a groove; spines heteracanthous, that is, alternating, the one stronger on the right side, the other on the left, the number 10 to 13; anal fin rather short, similar to the soft dorsal, with 3 spines; ventrals thoracic, with a more or less distinct scale-like appendage at base; caudal fin usually more or less concave behind; air-bladder present.

This is a large family of carnivorous shore-fishes of tropical seas, especially abundant in the Mediterranean, Red Sea, and West Indies. About 12 genera and nearly 100 species are known, and most of them are valued as food.   In our waters are about 24 species representing 7 genera.   Most of them are good food-fishes.

a. Second interhæmal bone enlarged, hollowed anteriorly or pen-shaped, receiving posterior end of air-bladder in its anterior groove.
b. Front teeth narrow, compressed, forming lanceolate incisors.
Stenotomus, 437
bb. Front teeth conical or canine-like ....*Calamus*, 438
aa. Second interhæmal spine normal, not pen-like.
c. First spine-bearing interneural with an antrorse spine in front.
d. Incisors conspicuously notched ....*Lagodon*, 440
dd. Incisors entire or with a shallow notch ....*Archosargus*, 441
cc. First spine-bearing interneural without antrorse spine in front.
Diplodus, 443

GENUS STENOTOMUS GILL

The Scups

This genus is closely related to *Calamus,* having the same quill-like interhæmal bones; the flattened incisors and antrorse dorsal spine mainly distinguishing it. Two species known.

a. Body ovate-elliptical, the depth about the same from the first dorsal spine to the eleventh; pectoral shorter than head, $3\frac{1}{2}$ in body; snout short, $2\frac{1}{4}$ in head......................*chrysops,* 437

aa. Body elongate-ovate, the depth decreasing backward from the first dorsal spine; pectoral about as long as head, $3\frac{1}{5}$ in body; snout long, 2 in head ....*aculeatus,* 438

Common Scup; Scuppaug

Stenotomus chrysops (Linnæus)

This fish is found on our Atlantic coast from the Carolinas to Cape Cod, being especially abundant northward. On the New Eng-

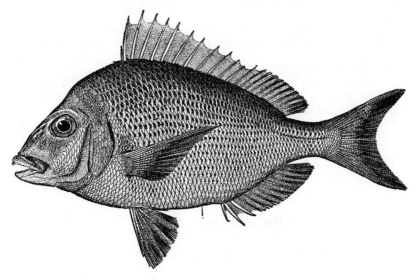

land coast it is usually called scup, while about New York it is the paugy or porgy. Farther south it is the fair-maid, and at Charleston it is the porgy. In New England it is often called scuppaug, a corruption of the Narragansett Indian name mishcuppanog, and an excellent name it is. Though somewhat erratic in its appearance, it is usually quite abundant on our Northern coast. As a food-fish it is one of the commonest and most esteemed. It is a bottom feeder, depending largely upon mollusks of various kinds and worms and small crustaceans.

Colour, brownish, somewhat silvery below, everywhere with bright reflections, but without distinct markings in adult; soft parts of vertical fins mottled with dark in adult; young faintly barred; axil dusky.

The Southern porgy, *Stenotomus aculeatus*, is found from Cape Hatteras southward and on the Gulf coast to Texas. It closely resembles the Northern scup, which it replaces southward.

GENUS CALAMUS SWAINSON

The Porgies

This genus contains some 12 species, all American, all shore-fishes, all closely related, and all excellent food-fishes.

a. Scales comparatively small, 54 to 58 in lateral line.
b. Body very deep, the back elevated, the depth in adult about 2 in length.
c. Preorbital with reticulations of the bluish ground colour around bronze spots ....*calamus*, 438
cc. Preorbital region, snout, cheek, and opercles brassy, crossed by horizontal wavy, non-reticulating lines of violet-blue.
proridens, 439
bb. Body more elongate, the depth $2\frac{1}{6}$ to $2\frac{3}{4}$ in length ..*bajonado*, 439
aa. Scales comparatively large, 45 to 53 in lateral line.
d. Dorsal outline forming a comparatively regular arch ....*penna*, 440
dd. Dorsal outline not forming a regular arch.........*arctifrons*, 440

Saucer-eye Porgy

Calamus calamus (Cuvier & Valenciennes)

West Indies, north to the Florida Keys. It has been recorded from Martinique, Jamaica, Porto Rico, Cuba, and various places in southern Florida.   About Key West and Havana it is generally common, but less abundant than the little-head and jolt-head porgies.   Its Spanish name is pez de pluma or pluma.   At Key West the conchs assure you that its English name is correctly pronounced sasser-eye. It reaches a length of a foot and a weight of a pound or more, though the weight of those seen in market does not usually exceed $\frac{1}{2}$ pound.   It is an excellent food-fish and always commands a good price.   It takes the hook readily, and affords considerable sport as a game-fish.

Colour in life, silvery with bluish reflections; the base and central portion of each scale golden, forming distinct longitudinal stripes, the stripes between these pearly or bluish; rows of scales on cheek and opercles with the pearly stripe median, the golden marginal; a deep violet stripe below orbit, not extending forward on snout nor backward on opercles; preorbital deep dull violet like the snout, the ground colour forming reticulations around conspicuous round brassy spots which cover half the surface; lower jaw dusky-violet; axil golden; fins all pale, vaguely blotched with dull orange; iris golden.

Little-head Porgy

Calamus proridens (Jordan & Gilbert)

West Indies, north to the Florida Keys, and moderately common at Key West.   It is the most brightly coloured species, reaches a foot in length, and may be readily distinguished from the saucer-eye, which it resembles, by the different colouration.   Colour in life, silvery, with bright reflections above, much brighter than any other species; each scale above middle of side with a spot of rich violet-blue on its base, these forming distinct longitudinal streaks; lower parts of body with pale orange spots.

Jolt-head Porgy

Calamus bajonado (Bloch & Schneider)

This, the most abundant species of the genus, is found among the Florida Keys and West Indies.   It is also the largest species, reaching a length of 2 feet and a weight of 8 to 10 pounds.   It frequents smooth rock bottom, upon which it is said to spawn in July and August. About Porto Rico it is one of the most common species, and is found at all times. Because of its large size the bajonado is more important as a food-fish than any of its congeners, though its flesh is rather coarse. It is taken in the hook-and-line fishery and also in various fish-traps.

Colour in life, rather dull brassy, with little blue markings; the middle of each scale shining but scarcely bluish; a blue stripe below eye, narrower and duller than in other species; a second duller streak above this, the 2 meeting on the forehead; preorbital dull coppery, often with irregular and obscure blue lines; axil yellowish.

The white-boned porgy (*Calamus leucosteus*) is a rather deep-water species known only from off the Carolina coast. Colour, smutty silvery; side with vague cross-bars; dorsal and anal with dark blotches; ventrals dusky. In form this species resembles *C. penna*.

The little-mouth porgy or sheepshead porgy (*C. penna*) occurs from southern Florida to Brazil. It is fairly abundant and widely distributed.

The grass or shad porgy (*C. arctifrons*) is a small species, rather common in shallow water among grass-patches at Key West and as far north as Pensacola. Colour, olivaceous, with dark bars or spots, the centres of many scales pearly; 6 yellowish spots along the lateral line; preorbital brownish, usually with dashes of golden yellow; membrane of opercle orange; fins mostly barred or spotted; ventrals pale, faintly barred. Though one of the smallest species of the genus, rarely exceeding a foot in length, it is nevertheless a good and important food-fish wherever found in sufficient numbers. It will take the hook, but it is usually taken in haul-seines.

GENUS LAGODON HOLBROOK

This differs from related genera chiefly in the form of the skull and the notched incisors; otherwise essentially as in *Archosargus*.

The single species is *Lagodon rhomboides*, the sailor's-choice, chopa spina, pigfish, or bream, a small species reaching a length of 6 inches, very abundant on our east coast from Cape Cod to Cuba and Texas. Though small, it is a most excellent pan-fish, and is highly prized wherever found.

Colour in life, olivaceous, the sides bluish silvery; a humeral spot and traces of 6 vertical bars; gilt stripes much less intense than in

SAUCER-EYE PORGY, *Calamus calamus*

LITTLE-HEAD PORGY, *Calamus proridens*

JOLT-HEAD PORGY, *Calamus bajonado*

JOLT-HEAD PORGY, *Calamus bajonado*

Archosargus unimaculatus, much broader than the interspaces; about 7 stripes below the lateral line, those above more or less confluent; dorsal fin pale bluish with a submedian gilt band and a gilt edge; caudal yellow, faintly barred; anal bluish, with a median yellowish band.

GENUS ARCHOSARGUS GILL

The Sheepsheads

This genus, like *Lagodon, Stenotomus,* and *Otrynter,* which show the same character of the procumbent dorsal spine, is confined to American waters. There are 2 colour types in the genus, one group being made up of species with broad black cross-bars, the other of species with longitudinal golden streaks and inconspicuous cross-bars, resembling *Lagodon.*

a. Occipital crest rather thin, its honeycomb structure not exposed. Species with streaks of steel-blue and golden, the dark cross-bars narrow, disappearing with age . . . .*unimaculatus,* 442

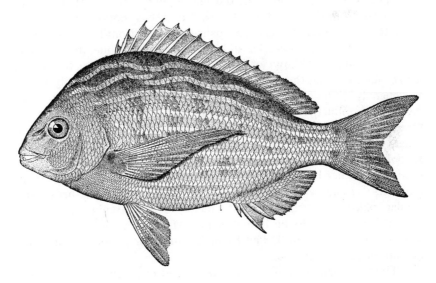

aa. Occipital crest broad, its honeycomb structure plainly exposed at its upper margin. Species without blue or golden markings, but with about 7 broad black cross-bars . .*probatocephalus,* 442

Chopa Amarilla; Salema

Archosargus unimaculatus (Bloch)

This species is found among the Florida Keys and the West Indies, and south to Brazil. It occasionally occurs as far north as Charleston, and it is not uncommon about Key West, Cuba, and Porto Rico. It reaches a foot in length and is a valuable pan-fish.

Colour, olivaceous, silvery below, the upper parts with longitudinal golden stripes, alternating with bluish interspaces; a black humeral spot larger than eye.

Common Sheepshead

Archosargus probatocephalus (Walbaum)

The sheepshead is one of our commonest and best-known fish, its range extending throughout the entire length of our Atlantic and Gulf coast from Cape Cod to Texas, but it has not been recorded from the West Indies. The sheepshead is a bottom-loving species, feeding upon small mollusks and other animals frequenting oyster-beds and muddy shallow waters. From the Chesapeake to Indian River, and again on the Gulf coast from Tampa to Corpus Christi, it is generally abundant in all suitable places. In Indian River it is, next to the mullet, the most abundant food-fish, and is found at all times. Though playing in and out with the tide, and moving somewhat from place to place, it is not properly a migratory fish. It does not school, as the mullets do, but is often found in considerable bunches, brought together by presence of food. Feeding almost wholly upon mollusks, crustaceans, and plants, it frequents oyster-beds and similar places, particularly about inlets. The spawning season in Indian River seems to be in February, extending perhaps into April. The average weight in Indian River is only 3 or 4 pounds, and the maximum 12 to 15 pounds.

Though a salt-water fish, the sheepshead often runs far up fresh-water rivers, particularly the St. Johns in Florida. Throughout its entire range it is regarded as one of the very best food-fishes and is of great commercial importance. There is no more common or

442

better-known fish in the markets of our Atlantic seaboard cities and towns.

As a game-fish the sheepshead is one of the most popular among our salt-water species, and there are many noted places between New York and Biscayne Bay where anglers resort for its capture. As long ago as 1814 Samuel Latham Mitchill, the naturalist-senator of New York, wrote in highest praise of the pleasures of angling for sheepshead: "When a sheepshead is brought on board more joy is manifested than by the possession of any other kind of fish. The sportsmen view the exercises so much above common fishing that the capture of the sheepshead is the most desirable combination of luck and skill; and the feats of hooking and landing him safely in the boat furnish abundant materials for the most pleasing and hyperbolical stories. The sheepshead is a very stout fish, and the hooks and lines are strong in proportion; yet he frequently breaks them and makes his escape."

And good old Thaddeus Norris says: "In fishing with a hand-line, which is the usual mode of taking him, the sheepshead gives one or two slight premonitory jerks, and then a steady pull, when the fisherman gathers in his line as fast as possible, the fish coming along with a heavy drag. When he approaches the boat, there is a desperate contest; there is much probability of his breaking the hook, or his quick downward lunges are apt to snap the line; then the fisher takes in slack or lets the line run through his fingers, as the actions of the fish dictate, and when a proper opportunity offers, throws him into the boat. His pull is at first strong and steady, but as he comes to the surface, his lunges are quick and desperate."

Our personal experience with the sheepshead has been chiefly at Indian River Inlet, one of Senator Quay's favourite fishing-grounds, and about Baldwin Lodge, Mississippi, where the Hon. A. Baldwin and other enthusiastic anglers of New Orleans find royal sport with this and other gamy species.

So well known is the sheepshead that it needs no detailed description.

GENUS DIPLODUS RAFINESQUE

This genus is close to *Archosargus,* from which it differs chiefly in having no procumbent dorsal spine. There are 3 species in our waters, the only one of any importance being the pinfish or spot, *Diplodus holbrooki*. This fish is found on our South Atlantic and

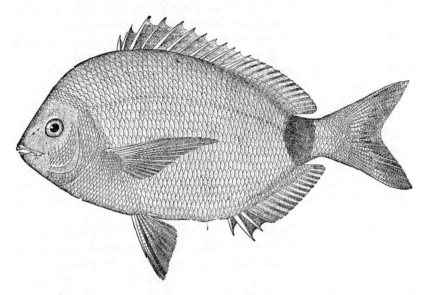

Gulf coasts from Cape Hatteras to Cedar Keys. At Beaufort, North Carolina, it is not uncommon, and the young swarm about the wharves. It is frequent also at Lake Worth, where it is called jimmy. It reaches 8 inches in length and is an excellent pan-fish.

GRASS PORGY, *Calamus arctifrons*

GRASS PORGY, *Calamus arctifrons*
This is the same individual fish as the one above and shows remarkable changes in colour occurring in a few minutes

PINFISH, *Lagodon rhomboides*

PINFISH, *Lagodon rhomboides*

THE MOJARRAS

Family LIV. Gerridæ

BODY oblong or elevated, covered with large, smooth scales; lateral line continuous, concurrent with the back; mouth moderate, extremely protractile, descending when protruded, the spines of the premaxillary extending to above eye, closing a deep groove in top of head; maxillary without supplemental maxillary bone, its surface silvery like the rest of the head; base of mandible scaly; jaws with slender, villiform teeth; no incisors, canines, nor molars; no teeth on vomer or palatines; preopercle entire or serrate; sides of head scaly; dorsal fin single, continuous or deeply notched, the spinous and soft parts about equally developed, a scaly sheath along the base; dorsal spines usually 9 or 10; anal usually with 3 spines, the soft anal similar to the soft dorsal but shorter.

This family contains 6 to 8 genera and about 40 species, all carnivorous fishes of moderate or small size, inhabiting tropical seas.

In our waters 4 of the genera are represented by 17 species, the larger ones being used as food. None of them, however, is of great importance, and they have no value as game-fishes.

a. Second interhæmal spine singularly developed as a hollow cylinder, comparatively short and much expanded, the posterior end of the air-bladder entering its cavity; preopercle and preorbital entire; anal spines 3, the second not much enlarged.

Eucinostomus, 445

aa. Second interhæmal spine normally developed, not hollow, the air-bladder not entering it.

b. Second interhæmal spine very short, bluntish; anal spines 2, both small; preopercle and preorbital entire .... *Ulæma,* 447

bb. Second interhæmal spine long, spear-shaped; anal spines 2 or 3, the second enlarged.

c. Preopercle entire; second anal spine moderate ...... *Xystæma,* 447

cc. Preopercle serrate; second anal spine much enlarged .. *Gerres,* 447

GENUS EUCINOSTOMUS BAIRD & GIRARD

The Mojarritas

This genus, sufficiently defined in the preceding key, is represented in our waters by 5 species, which may be distinguished as follows:

a. Premaxillary groove wholly naked, linear or semioval, sometimes constricted at base, but never scaled.
b. Eye very large, greater than snout, 2⅔ in head; exposed portion of maxillary small, triangular . . . .*dowi,* 446
bb. Eye moderate, about equal to snout, usually more than 3 in head; exposed portion of maxillary triangular in front, oblong behind.
c. Body elongate, the back little elevated, the greatest depth 3¼ to 3½ in length . . . .*pseudogula,* 446
cc. Body deeper and more compressed, the back more elevated, the greatest depth 2⅔ in length.
d. Snout blunt; eye large, scarcely 3 in head; second anal spine large, 2⅔ to 3⅓ in head; premaxillary groove linear . . .*harengulus,* 446
dd. Snout less blunt; eye smaller, more than 3 in head; premaxillary groove linear in young, becoming broader with age; second anal spine shorter, 3¼ to 4½ in head . . . .*californiensis,* 446
aa. Premaxillary groove scaled in front, the scales leaving a naked pit behind . . . .*gula,* 446

Eucinostomus dowi is found on our Pacific coast about Panama and the Galapagos Islands. It reaches 6 inches in length.

E. pseudogula is found among the West Indies, about the Bermudas and south to Brazil. It reaches a length of 7 inches, and is not uncommon.

E. harengulus is one of the most abundant species and is common on our Atlantic coast from north Florida southward to Brazil. It is found about all the West Indies and is abundant about Porto Rico. It reaches 7 or 8 inches in length. It is very close to *E. dowi.*

E. californiensis, the mojarra cantileña, is found on the Pacific coast of Mexico and from Guaymas to Panama, and has been once taken at San Diego. It is exceedingly abundant in shallow bays and estuaries, and enters freshwater streams. It attains a length of 8 inches and is of considerable food-value.

E. gula, known variously as silver jenny, mojarra de ley, mojarra, and petite gueule is excessively common everywhere in shallow water and on sandy shores from the Carolinas to Brazil, and the young stray north to Woods Hole. About Porto Rico it is quite common. It reaches 5 or 6 inches in length and is much used for bait.

All the species of this genus are plain silvery in colour, without any prominent markings.

GENUS ULÆMA JORDAN & EVERMANN

This genus is close to *Eucinostomus*, from which it differs in the form of the second interhæmal. The single species (*Ulæma lefroyi*) is known from the Bermudas, the West Indies, and north on sandy shores to Cedar Keys. It reaches 8 inches in length, and is plain silvery in colour.

GENUS XYSTÆMA JORDAN & EVERMANN

This genus differs from *Gerres* in having the preopercle entire. The single species (*Xystæma cinereum*) is found on both coasts of tropical America, north to Lower California and southern Florida. It is generally common in water of moderate depth, and ascends rivers considerable distances. It reaches a foot or more in length, and is a foodfish of no little importance. In Porto Rico, where it is common, it is called muniama.

GENUS GERRES CUVIER

This genus, distinguished by the long spear-shaped interhæmal, contains 10 American species.

a. Preorbital entire; no distinct dark streaks along rows of scales.
b. Anal spines 2, the rays 9 ....*rhombeus*, 448
bb. Anal spines 3, the rays 8.
c. Premaxillary groove broad, triangular or oval, and free from scales.
d. Body ovate, the outline somewhat regularly elliptical, the depth 2¼
     in length...................................*aureolus*, 448
dd. Body rhomboidal, short and deep, with angular outlines, the
     depth usually more than half the length ....*peruvianus*, 448
cc. Premaxillary groove broad, oval, and covered with scales.
                                        olisthostomus, 448
aa. Preorbital serrate; a distinct dark streak along each row of scales.
e. Scales moderate or large, 34 to 39 in lateral line.
f. Spines moderate, the second dorsal ⅔ to ¾ length of head.
g. Pectoral short, barely reaching vent; second dorsal spine 1⅔ in head;
     caudal shorter than head ....*brevimanus*, 449
gg. Pectoral at least as long as head; caudal longer than head.
h. Pectoral as long as head, not reaching anal, 3 to 3⅓ in body; scales
     38.

i. Third dorsal spine rather longer than second; 10 rows of scales between lateral line and vent; opercle with few if any small scales
   at base..*lineatus,* 449
ii. Third dorsal spine not longer than second; 11 rows of scales between
   lateral line and vent; opercle with numerous small scales at
   base ....*brasilianus,* 449
hh. Pectoral very long, ¼ longer than head, 2½ to 2¾ in body; scales
   35 ....*embryx,* 449
ff. Spines very high, the second dorsal longer than head.*plumieri,* 449
ee. Scales small, 44 in lateral line. ....*mexicanus,* 449

Gerres rhombeus is known from the West Indies and along the
Gulf coast of tropical America.   It has been reported from Martinique,
Jamaica, Santo Domingo, Puerto Cabello, Havana, Aspinwall, Rio
Magdalena, Santa Lucia, Porto Rico, and Bahia.   It reaches a length
of 10 inches, and is generally common.   It is readily known by hav-
ing only 2 anal spines.

G. aureolus is known only from Panama and is very rare.

G. peruvianus is found on the Pacific coast of tropical America
from Mazatlan to Panama and southward.   It attains a small size,
but is abundant.

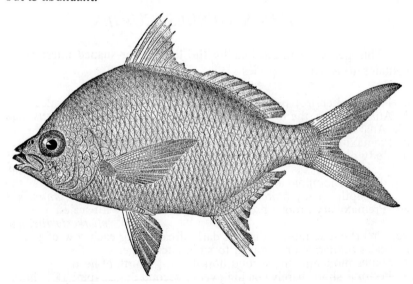

G. olisthostomus, the Irish pompano or mutton-fish, is abundant
through the West Indies, south to Brazil and north to southern Florida.
It reaches a foot in length, and is of some value as a food-fish.

G. brevimanus is a very rare species known only from the Pacific coast of Mexico.

G. lineatus, the mojarra china, occurs on the Pacific coast of Mexico from Mazatlan southward. It reaches a foot in length, and is used extensively as food.

G. brasilianus, the patao, occurs from Cuba to Brazil, reaches a foot in length, and is a food-fish where abundant.

G. embryx is known only from rather deep water off the coast of South Carolina. It reaches a foot in length, but is not common.

G. plumieri is one of the most abundant species, occurring from southern Florida throughout the West Indies and south to Brazil. It attains a length of 10 inches, and is used both as food and bait.

G. mexicanus is known only from the Rio Teapa, Mexico, from which we have recently received specimens, the largest of which is about 10 inches long.

THE RUDDER-FISHES

Family LV. Kyphosidæ

HERBIVOROUS fishes, with incisors only in the front of the jaws; body oblong or elevated, with moderate or small scales; mouth moderate, with incisor-like teeth in front; no molars; premaxillaries moderately protractile; pseudobranchiæ well developed; opercles entire; gill-membranes separate, free from the isthmus; dorsal fin continuous or divided, with 10 to 15 rather strong spines; anal with 3 spines.

A family with a good many species; shore-fishes, feeding largely on green or olive algæ; chiefly found in the Mediterranean and in the Pacific; most of them valued as food. About 6 genera and 10 species within our limits.

a. Soft parts of dorsal and anal fins naked or only partly scaled; teeth in broad bands, all freely movable, none on vomer.
b. Dorsal spines 14 or 15............................*Girella,* 450
bb. Dorsal spines 12 or 13.....................*Doydixodon,* 451
aa. Soft parts of dorsal and anal fins closely scaled; teeth more or less fixed, usually present on vomer.
c. Top of head naked as far back as posterior margin of eyes.
Hermosilla, 451
cc. Top of head as well as its sides and jaws closely scaled.
d. Incisors strong, with horizontal backward projecting roots.
e. Incisor teeth well developed, each with a conspicuous horizontal process or root; caudal fin moderate, about as long as head.
Kyphosus, 452
ee. Incisor teeth small, with inconspicuous roots; caudal much longer than head ....*Sectator,* 453
dd. Incisors very narrow, without evident roots .....*Medialuna,* 453

GENUS GIRELLA GRAY

Body oblong-ovate, compressed, covered with rather large scales; mouth small, with a series of tricuspid, movable incisors, behind which is a broad band of similar smaller ones; no molars; no teeth on vomer or tongue; cheeks with very small scales; opercles and top of head chiefly naked; gill-rakers slender; dorsal fin rather low, XIV, 14, scaled at the base, forming an imperfect sheath; anal fin III, 12, the spines small, graduated; caudal lunate.

This genus contains several species, chiefly on the east coast of Asia. Only one species, *Girella nigricans*, is found on our coast. This species, called the green-fish, occurs on the California coast from Monterey to Cape San Lucas and Guaymas. It reaches a foot in length, is a common and active inhabitant of rock-pools, and is a food-fish of fair quality. In life it is dusky green, paler below; fins dusky greenish; young with a large yellowish blotch on the back on each side of dorsal.

GENUS DOYDIXODON VALENCIENNES

This genus is very close to *Girella*, from which it seems to differ in having the soft dorsal and anal elevated, and only 12 or 13 dorsal spines. The single species in our waters is *D. freminvillei*, a very rare species known only from the Galapagos and the coast of Peru.

GENUS HERMOSILLA JENKINS & EVERMANN

This genus is allied to *Kyphosus*, from which it differs in the weaker gill-rakers, the entire preopercular margin, absence of teeth on

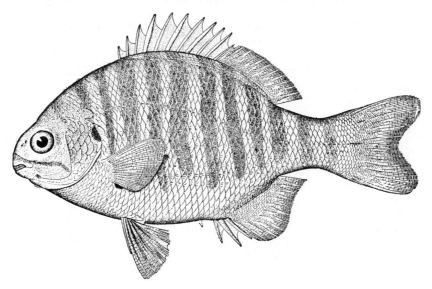

tongue, the larger scales, and the less complete squamation of the head. But one species is known, *H. azurea*, which occurs at Guaymas in the Gulf of California. It reaches a foot in length and is a good food-fish, but not abundant enough to be of much importance. It is one of the most beautiful species of the family.

Colour in life, dark steel-blue, paler below; body with about 12 vertical blackish bars; a dark streak from maxillary to angle of opercle; a black opercular spot; fins mostly dark.

GENUS KYPHOSUS LACÉPÈDE

The Chopas

Body elongate-ovate, regularly elliptical, moderately compressed; head short, the snout blunt; eye large; mouth small, horizontal; maxillary barely reaching eye; each jaw with a single series of rather narrow, obtusely-lanceolate incisors, behind these a narrow band of villiform teeth; fine teeth on vomer, palatines, and tongue; gill-rakers long; preopercle scarcely serrate; scaling very complete, the space between and about the eyes being the only naked part; scales small, thick, ctenoid, 60 to 70 in the lateral line; scales entirely covering soft parts of vertical fins and extending on paired fins; dorsal fin low, with about 11 spines, which are depressible in a groove of scales, the fin continuous, but the last spines low, so that a depression occurs between the 2 parts of the fin whose bases are about equal; anal with 3 spines; caudal moderately forked.

This genus contains about 10 species, chiefly confined to the Pacific, and most of them found in the Indian Ocean; about 5 species within our waters, all food-fishes of excellent flavour.

a. Soft part of anal very long and low, its longest rays $3\frac{1}{2}$ to 4 in head, and 3 in soft part of fin; D. XI, 14 ....*analogus,* 452
aa. Anal fin moderately elevated in front, and rather short, its longest rays $1\frac{1}{4}$ to 2 in base of soft part of fin; D. XI, 11 or 12.
b. Teeth rather narrow and subacute; maxillary short, barely reaching eye, about $3\frac{1}{2}$ in head.
c. Scales moderate, 10-65-20; A. III, 13.................*incisor,* 453
cc. Scales smaller, about 12-67-20; A. III, 11............*elegans,* 453
ccc. Scales rather large, 10-55-16; A. III, 11..........*sectatrix,* 453
bb. Teeth broad and rounded; maxillary rather long, reaching pupil, $3\frac{1}{2}$ in head ....*lutescens,* 453

Kyphosus analogus, the salema, is found on the Pacific coast from the Gulf of California to Mazatlan. It is not rare, reaches a length of

SHEEPSHEAD, *Archosargus probatocephalus*

SHAD PORGY, *Calamus penna*

LITTLE-HEAD PORGY, *Calamus proridens*

BROAD SHAD, *Xystæma cinereum*

18 inches, and is used as food. It is distinguished chiefly by the shape of the anal and the bright gray or steel-blue colouration.

K. incisor, the chopa amarilla, has been recorded from Cuba, Brazil, and the Canaries. It reaches 2½ to 3 feet in length and is a rare species.

K. elegans, the chopa, is found on our Pacific coast from Guaymas to Mazatlan. It is rather common about Mazatlan, especially in the sluggish waters of the astillero. It reaches a foot or more in length.

K. sectatrix is the most important species of the genus. It is of wide distribution, occurring on our South Atlantic and Gulf coasts, among the West Indies, and straying north to Cape Cod and even to the Canaries and Palermo. It is known as the rudder-fish, Bermuda chub, chub, and chopa blanca. It has long been noted for its habit of following vessels, supposedly for the waste food thrown overboard; hence the name rudder-fish. About Key West the chub is locally abundant, preferring the vicinity of shoals and bars. It is said to school in summer. The maximum size is 8 or 9 pounds, the average being only 2 or 3 pounds. As a game-fish this is the most interesting of the family. At Key West it is readily taken with the hook baited with pieces of the spiny crawfish. It bites quickly and makes a splendid fight, its tactics being those of a very large bluegill. Any angler going to Key West or Bermuda should not fail to spend a day in chub-fishing.

The remaining species of this genus, *K. lutescens*, is known only from the Revillagigedo Islands, where it is not rare.

The genus *Sector* Jordan & Fesler is close to *Kyphosus*, from which it differs in its smaller incisor teeth and in the deeply-forked caudal. The single known species, *S. ocyurus*, is very rare, being known only from Panama.

The genus *Medialuna* Jordan & Fesler differs from *Kyphosus* chiefly in the very narrow rootless incisors. The single species, *M. californiensis*, is a handsome fish found on our Pacific coast from Point Conception to Cerros Island.

It is abundant on the rocky coast of southern California, reaches a foot in length, and is an excellent food-fish. Colour, blackish, with steely lustre; paler, often mottled below; side with faint oblique vertical lines of spots; fins blackish.

THE CROAKERS

Family LVI. Sciænidæ

BODY compressed, more or less elongate, covered with rather thin scales which are usually more or less ctenoid; lateral line continuous, extending on caudal fin; head usually large, scaly; bones of head cavernous, the muciferous system highly developed, the surface of the skull very uneven; chin usually with pores, sometimes with barbels; mouth small or large, the teeth in one or more series, the outer sometimes enlarged; canines often present; no incisors or molars; no teeth on vomer, palatines, or tongue; maxillary without supplemental bone; premaxillaries somewhat protractile; nostrils double; pseudobranchiæ usually present and usually large; branchiostegals 7; gill-membranes separate, free from the isthmus; lower pharyngeals separate or united, often enlarged, the teeth conic or molar; preopercle serrate or not; opercle usually ending in 2 flat points; dorsal deeply notched or divided into 2 fins, the soft portion being the longer, the spines depressible into a groove; anal with never more than 2 spines; caudal usually not forked; ear-bones or otoliths very large; air-bladder usually large and complicated (wanting in *Menticirrhus*).

This is a very large and very important family of some 30 genera and 150 species, found on sandy shores in all warm seas; some species ranging northward and a few confined to fresh water. None occurs in deep water and none about rocks. Many of them reach a large size, and nearly all are valued as food. All are carnivorous, and some are of interest as game-fishes. Most of the species make a peculiar noise, variously called croaking, grunting, drumming, or snoring, supposed to be produced by forcing air from the air-bladder into one of the lateral horns. Only the more important genera are included in the following key:

a. Vertebræ 14 or 15 + 10 or 11; abdominal portion of body long.
b. Anal fin long, of 15 to 21 rays ....*Seriphus*, 455
bb. Anal fin moderate or short, of 7 to 13 rays ....*Cynoscion*, 455
aa. Vertebræ 9 to 12 + 13 to 20; abdominal portion of body shorter.
c. Lower pharyngeals separate.
d. Lower jaw without barbels.
e. Teeth well developed, permanent in both jaws.
f. Gill-rakers long and slender ....*Bairdiella*, 460
ff. Gill-rakers short and thick ....*Sciænops*, 461

ee. Teeth very small, subequal, those in lower jaw deciduous or
wanting .... *Leiostomus,* 462
dd. Lower jaw with 1 or more barbels.
g. Lower jaw with slender barbels, usually several in number.
Micropogon, 463
gg. Lower jaw with a single thickish barbel at tip.. *Menticirrhus,* 464
cc. Lower pharyngeals very large and completely united, covered with
coarse, blunt, paved teeth.
h. Lower jaw with numerous barbels; preopercle nearly entire;
marine species .... *Pogonias,* 466
hh. Lower jaw without barbels; preopercle slightly serrate; fresh-
water species .... *Aplodinotus,* 467

The genus *Seriphus,* sufficiently characterized in the foregoing
key, contains but 1 species. This is *S. politus,* the queenfish or white
croaker, which occurs on the Pacific coast from Point Conception to
Cerros Island. It is common on sandy shores, especially about San
Diego. It reaches a foot in length and is an excellent pan-fish.
Colour, bluish above, sides and belly bright silvery, finely punctate;
vertical fins bright yellow in life; base of pectoral blackish.

GENUS CYNOSCION GILL

The Weakfishes

Body elongate, little compressed, the back not elevated; head
conic, rather pointed; mouth very large, terminal, not very oblique,
the lower jaw projecting; maxillary very broad; teeth sharp, not close-
set, in rather narrow bands; tip of lower jaw without canines; upper
jaw with 2 long canines, one of these sometimes obsolete; canines
tapering from base to tip; lateral teeth of lower jaw larger than anterior;
preopercle with its membranous edge serrulate, its bony edge entire;
lower pharyngeals separate, their teeth all pointed; gill-rakers strong,
rather long; pseudobranchiæ well developed; dorsal spines slender,
the fins closely contiguous, the second long and low, more than twice
length of anal.

An important genus of large fishes, chiefly American, closely related to the Old-World genus *Otolithus.* All rank high as food-fishes,
the flesh being rich, but in some species tender and easily torn, hence
the popular name weakfishes.

a. Scales not very small, the lateral line with 55 to 75 pores, the number of scales 55 to 85.

b. Soft portions of dorsal and anal more or less closely scaled.
c. Colour, nearly uniform silvery........................*nothus,* 459
cc. Colour, brownish silvery above, with many dark brown spots arranged in undulating streaks....................*regalis,* 456
bb. Soft portions of dorsal and anal scaleless.
d. Colour, not uniform; grayish or silvery, the back with distinct
   darker spots, lines, or reticulations.
e. Soft dorsal without spots.......................*reticulatus,* 459
ee. Soft dorsal with conspicuous round black spots ....*nebulosus,* 457
dd. Colour, nearly uniform, bluish gray above, silvery below.
f. Caudal fin somewhat lunate in adult, the middle rays shortest, but
   somewhat produced in the young............*parvipinnis,* 460
ff. Caudal fin always double-truncate or double-concave, the middle
   rays somewhat produced ....*macdonaldi,* 460
aa. Scales comparatively small, the lateral line with 70 to 90 pores, the
   number of scales 85 to 150.......................*nobilis,* 458

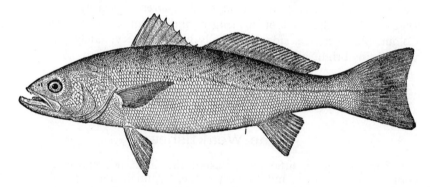

Common Weakfish; Squeteague; Sea-trout

Cynoscion regalis (Bloch & Schneider)

The squeteague is found throughout the entire length of our
Atlantic and Gulf coasts, and ranges as far north as the Bay of Fundy.
It has varied greatly in abundance within the last hundred years, but
is always one of our commonest and best-known fishes. At certain
times and places it is exceedingly abundant. A catch of over 200,000
pounds in one day in 1881 two miles off Rockaway Beach is on record.
It is rare in the Gulf of Mexico, but from Florida to Long Island it is
usually abundant.

Although essentially a coast and still-water fish, the squeteague
sometimes runs up tidal waters and prefers the vicinity of river-

mouths. Though seen in the markets everywhere, this fish is not much valued in the North, but in the South it is highly prized.

As a game-fish the squeteague is the greatest of the family. No salt-water fish of our Atlantic coast affords more sport to the angler than this species. It is only the great freedom with which it takes the bait and the large numbers which may be caught that cause it to fail of the highest appreciation. Its strength and endurance are perhaps not so great as that of the rock, but the strike and first rush are not less vigorous. They take almost any kind of bait, especially clams, soft crabs, or pieces of meat, as well as the trolling-spoon, and bite with a snap. On account of the extreme tenderness of the mouth, they must be handled with extreme care. "His first dash is from the boat and 10 yards of line will be run off in a jiffy. He fights well and at long range if you allow him line, but bear well on him, as the least slacking of the line gives him a chance to disengage the hook, which he sometimes attempts to do by jumping above the water and shaking his head."

Great numbers of weakfish are taken with the hand-line by what is called " drifting "; that is, to sail into a school of them in a mid-tide, and, letting the sheet go, allow the boat to drift while you fish over the sides at half-depth.

The squeteague reaches a maximum weight of 30 pounds, though examples of more than 10 or 12 pounds are very rare, and the average weight is very much less.

This fish is one of the principal species upon which the bluefish feeds, and marvelously great numbers are doubtless destroyed every year by that rapacious fish.

Colour, silvery, darker above, and marked with many small, irregular dark blotches, some of which form undulating lines running downward and forward; back and head with bright reflections; dorsal and caudal fins dusky; ventrals, anal, and lower edge of caudal yellowish, sometimes speckled.

Spotted Weakfish; Spotted Sea-trout

Cynoscion nebulosus (Cuvier & Valenciennes)

This species is associated on the coasts of New Jersey and Virginia with the squeteague, from which it may readily be distinguished by the presence of numerous round black spots on the body posteriorly. It becomes more abundant southward until, off the coast from North Carolina to Georgia, it is one of the most common food-fishes. Owing

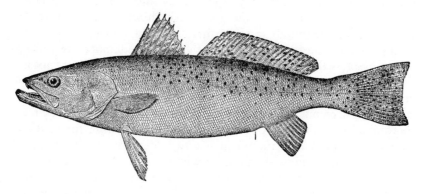

to its shape and spots, it is known on the Southern coast as salmon or spotted sea-trout, names wholly inappropriate. Spotted squeteague is a much better name.

Among the commercial fishes of Indian River this species ranks fourth. Though it is present throughout the year, the largest catches are made during the latter part of winter and early spring. The average weight is 2 to 4 pounds, though the maximum is much greater; we have seen an example at Fort Pierce, Indian River, weighing 13½ pounds.

The spotted squeteague is more migratory in its habits than its relatives. At Beaufort it appears from the South in the spring and passes through the inlets on the flood-tide. Early in May they proceed northward, extending their journeys as far as Long Island. On the North Carolina coast they are perhaps more abundant than any other species, excepting, of course, the mullet.

As a game-fish this species is scarcely inferior to the common squeteague.

California White Sea-bass

Cynoscion nobilis (Ayres)

This important game-fish is perhaps most abundant about Santa Catalina, but ranges north to San Francisco, and occasionally even to

Victoria, Vancouver Island. It reaches a weight of 20 to 80 pounds, and is one of the really great game-fishes. Professor Holder says:

" The season is generally May and June. Of 7 caught in one day by the writer with a 16-strand line each weighed over 50 pounds, and every fish made a play of from 15 to 30 minutes that can only be described by the term magnificent. There is a difference in individuals, but one 51-pound bass, taken after a 25-minute contest, I believe, gave me more pleasure than any catch I ever made.

" The fish played entirely on the surface, and I only saved it by the skill and quick movements of my boatman as the fish repeatedly rushed around the boat. This fish is a beautiful creature in bronze and old-gold tints, and is well called the Santa Catalina salmon, having a close resemblance to that fish and being its equal in every way. The equipment used is, so far as line is concerned, the same as for the tuna, though I prefer a lighter line and a lighter rod. Flying-fish or large smelt is the killing bait, trolled slowly along not 50 feet from the shore. All my catches were made in Avalon Bay not 200 feet from shore, and around the first week in May."

Cynoscion nothus, which is usually called the bastard weakfish, is

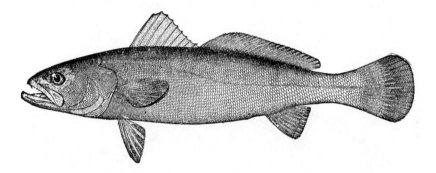

a well-marked species, differing in numerous respects from the others of the genus. It occurs on our South Atlantic and Gulf coasts, and is a good food-fish. Colour, grayish silvery, thickly punctulate above and on sides to level of pectorals, then abruptly silvery, a row of dark points marking the line of division; snout and tip of lower jaw blackish; mouth white within; lower fins white, the upper dusky.

C. reticulatus, the corvina, is found from Mazatlan to Panama. It reaches a length of 3 feet and is a common food-fish on the Pacific coast of Mexico.

C. parvipinnis, the California bluefish, is found on our Pacific coast from the Santa Barbara Islands to Guaymas and Mazatlan. It is common as far north as San Pedro, and is an excellent food-fish, not inferior to the squeteague. Colour, clear steel-blue, without stripes or spots; lower fins yellowish.

C. macdonaldi, the totuava, is the largest species of the genus. It is known only from the Gulf of California, where it is very abundant along the entire eastern shore, congregating in great numbers about the mouth of the Colorado River. It enters the river and is found feeding in shallow water near the shore, where it is easily approached and speared. At the head of the Gulf it is known as the sea-bass, while at Guaymas it is called totuava. It reaches an enormous size, examples weighing 172 pounds having been taken with hand-lines at the head of the Gulf.

GENUS BAIRDIELLA GILL

The Mademoiselles

This genus is characterized by the oblique mouth, little cavernous skull, few rows of small teeth, slender gill-rakers, and the preopercle armed with a plectroid spine.

The numerous species are all American, all small in size and sil-

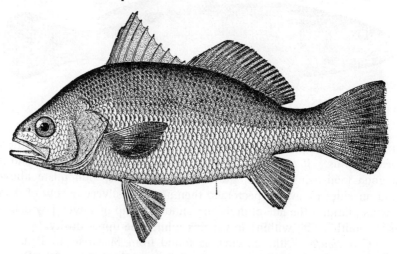

very in colouration. Some of them are remarkable for the great size of the second anal spine, while in others it is quite small.

The only species which is of much food-value is the yellowtail or mademoiselle. It is a well-known fish, very common from New England to Texas on sandy shores. It is most abundant southward. It reaches a foot or less in length and is a most excellent pan-fish.

Colour, greenish above, silvery below; back and sides more or less densely punctate with dark dots, forming narrow, somewhat irregular streaks; fins plain, mostly yellow in life.

GENUS SCIÆNOPS GILL

This genus is very close to *Ophioscion*, from which it differs in the loss of the preopercular spines with age, the serrate edge of the bone becoming entire; caudal truncate or concave; soft dorsal scaleless; slits and pores of upper jaw well developed.

The genus contains but one species, *Sciænops ocellatus*, the reddrum, channel-bass, redfish, bull redfish, or pescado colorado, well

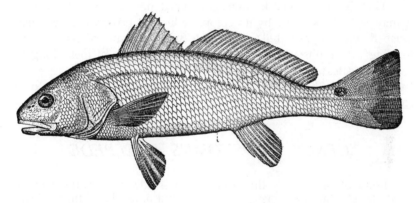

known as an abundant and important food-fish of our South Atlantic and Gulf coasts, from New York to Texas. It is very abundant, especially southward, and is of rare occurrence north of Virginia. It is fifth among the commercial fishes of Indian River, but is rare at Key West. On the Texas coast it is the most abundant food-fish. Its habits have never been fully studied. In Indian River it seems to be resident, being most common in winter and early spring. The larger individuals, such as are usually called channel-bass, appear to leave the river for a brief time during the coldest season, and they also go outside for a time during the warmest period. The spawning season here probably extends from spring to fall and the fish probably spawn inside the river.

The food of the red-drum consists chiefly of small fish such as young mullet, crustaceans, and mollusks.

This fish reaches a length of 4 or 5 feet and a weight of at least 40 pounds, and fish of 12 to 15 pounds are not rare. Fish of greater weight than 15 pounds are, however, coarse and not readily salable. Those of 4 to 6 pounds are best for shipping. As a game-fish the red-drum must take good rank. Mr. S. C. Clarke and others have written its praises, and we ourselves have had exciting experiences with it in Indian River. Still-fishing is the method employed, and any sort of bait will serve, though a piece of a mullet or other fish is best. The bait may lie upon the bottom or dangle a few inches above it. The red-drum may be cautious and slow to take the bait, but when once hooked its strength and size enable it to make a pretty fight.

Though an important commercial fish, its flesh is not of high quality, as it is stringy and lacking in flavour.

This fish is so well known as to need no extended description. It may easily be known by its colour, which is grayish silvery usually washed with coppery red; each scale with a centre of dark points, forming rather obscure irregular, undulating brown stripes along the rows of scales; a jet-black ocellated spot about as large as eye at base of caudal above, this sometimes duplicated, and the body occasionally with ocelli.

GENUS LEIOSTOMUS LACÉPÈDE

Body oblong-ovate, the back compressed; head obtuse; mouth small, horizontal, the upper jaw with a band of feeble teeth, the lower nearly or quite toothless; slits and pores of upper jaw well developed; lower pharyngeals separate, the teeth paved; preopercle with a membranaceous border; D. X — I, 31, the spines slender and rather high, the last connected with the soft rays; A. II, 12, the second spine not large; caudal fin emarginate; gill-membranes slightly connected; gillrakers slender.

This genus differs from *Sciæna* chiefly by the absence of teeth in the lower jaw and by the more paved teeth on the pharyngeals. The single species, *Leiostomus xanthurus*, is a popular and well-known fish on our South Atlantic and Gulf coasts, under the vernacular names spot, goody, lafayette, roach, chub, chopa blanca, and masooka. It is one of the most common pan-fishes on our coast and is excellent in every respect. It occurs as far north as Cape Cod and as far south as Texas, but is very rare in the West Indies.

The spot is a small fish, reaching only 6 to 10 inches in length, and consequently not likely to prove very exciting to the angler, albeit it takes the hook readily and is well worth taking when larger fish refuse to bite.

Colour, bluish above, silvery below; about 15 narrow dark wavy bands extending from the dorsal downward and forward to below lateral line; a round black humeral spot rather smaller than the eye; fins plain olivaceous, the caudal not yellow.

GENUS MICROPOGON CUVIER & VALENCIENNES

The Croakers

Body moderately elongate, compressed, somewhat elevated; pre-opercle strongly serrate; teeth in villiform bands, the outer row in the upper jaw somewhat enlarged; lower jaw with a row of minute bar-bels on each side; gill-rakers short and thickish; spinous dorsal rather short, of 10 or 11 stoutish spines; second anal spine moderate; caudal fin double-truncate; lower pharyngeals narrow, distinct, with sharp conical teeth; air-bladder with long horns.

This is a well-marked genus with about 5 species, all American, distinguished from *Ophioscion* and *Sciænops* by the presence of bar-bels. The species are all closely related, and are similar in form, colour, and size.

The only species of importance is the common croaker, *Micropogon undulatus*. Every one on the Atlantic and Gulf coasts knows the croaker. It is an abundant and important food-fish all the way from Cape Cod to Texas, being most common southward, but not known from the West Indies. At Beaufort, N. C., it is, next to the mullet and the spot, the most common food-fish; and in the markets of Baltimore, Washington, and southward there is no more familiar fish. It appears to be uncommon in Indian River, but is present in limited numbers throughout the year. On the Gulf coast it is exceedingly abundant in all the bays and bayous, where it is found at all times. The croakers live mostly in shallow water on grassy bottom, and feed upon crustaceans and mollusks. They breed in the bays in early winter. They reach a foot in length and are an excellent pan-fish. Commercially they are caught with haul-seines. They take the hook readily and fight fairly well. A slight, pliant rod with a stiffish tip, a reel, a float or not as circumstances require, and hook baited with shrimp or soft crab, will usually prove the proper thing.

Colour, brassy, paler below; middle part of body with short, irregular, dusky vertical bars crossing the lateral line; many dark brown spots on side of back, irregularly placed and not forming continuous streaks along rows of scales; usually some of these coalesce to form 2 dark streaks concurrent with the back.

GENUS MENTICIRRHUS GILL

The Kingfishes

Body rather elongate, little compressed; head long, subconic, the bluntish snout considerably projecting beyond the mouth, which is small and horizontal; both jaws with bands of villiform teeth, the outer of the upper jaw more or less enlarged; chin with a single stoutish barbel; preopercle with its membranaceous edge serrulate; gill-rakers short and tubercular or obsolete; dorsal spines high and slender, 10 or 11 in number; soft dorsal long and low; caudal fin with the lower lobe rounded, the upper sharp; anal with a single weak spine; no air-bladder; lower pharyngeals separate, the teeth varying from sharp to very obtuse.

This genus is one of the most important of the family, containing 9 species, all American. Only a few are of food-value.

a. Gill-rakers obsolete, reduced to tubercular prominences.
b. Mouth rather large, the maxillary reaching middle of eye, $2\frac{3}{4}$ to $3\frac{1}{4}$ in head.
c. Outer teeth of upper jaw decidedly enlarged; spinous dorsal not much elevated, the longest not usually reaching front of soft dorsal, $1\frac{1}{2}$ to $1\frac{2}{3}$ in head.....................*americanus,* 465
cc. Outer teeth of upper jaw less enlarged; spinous dorsal elevated, the longest spine reaching past front of soft dorsal, $1\frac{1}{4}$ in head.
saxatilis, 465

bb. Mouth smaller, the maxillary scarcely reaching eye, $3\frac{1}{3}$ in head.
undulatus, 465
aa. Gill-rakers present, very short and rather slender....*littoralis*, 465

The most important species is the sand whiting or Carolina whiting, *Menticirrhus americanus.* It is found on our South Atlantic and

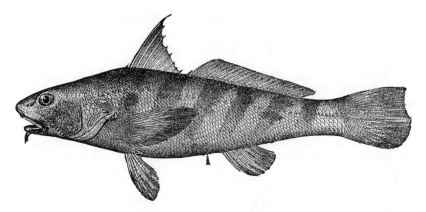

Gulf coasts from the Chesapeake Bay to Texas.   It is very common on sandy shores southward, and is a food-fish of considerable importance.
Colour, grayish silvery, with obscure darker clouds along back and sides, these marks forming dusky bars running obliquely forward and downward to below the lateral line, the bar at the nape saddle-shaped.
The Northern whiting, kingfish, or sea-mink, *M. saxatilis*, is found from Cape Ann to Key West and Pensacola, its centre of greatest abundance being northward.   It is a good food-fish.   Colour, dusky-gray above, sometimes blackish, the back and sides with distinct dark oblique cross-bands running downward and forward, the anterior one at the nape extending downward, meeting the second and thus forming a V-shaped blotch on each side.
The California whiting, *M. undulatus*, occurs from the Santa Barbara Islands southward on sandy shores, and is a food-fish of some value.   *M. elongatus* is found from Mazatlan to Panama and is very common in the surf.   Colour, bluish on back and sides, silvery below, without stripes or bands.
The surf whiting or silver whiting, *M. littoralis*, is found on sandy shores from the Carolinas to Texas and is generally common. Colour, silvery gray above, with bluish and bronze reflections, with-

out spots; a dark bronze shade along sides at level of pectorals, extending to tail and along cheeks; belly below this abruptly white; dorsal fins light brown, the spinous dorsal black at tip, the base narrowly white; caudal pale, its tip usually black.

GENUS POGONIAS LACÉPÈDE

The Sea-drums

Body short and deep, the dorsal outline much elevated, the ventral nearly straight; mouth moderate, the upper jaw the longer; teeth small, in villiform bands, the outer not enlarged; lower pharyngeal bones large, fully united, armed with strong paved teeth; lower jaw with numerous barbels, each about half length of eye; preopercle entire, with a membranaceous edge; dorsal fins slightly connected, the spines high and strong; caudal fin subtruncate; first anal spine

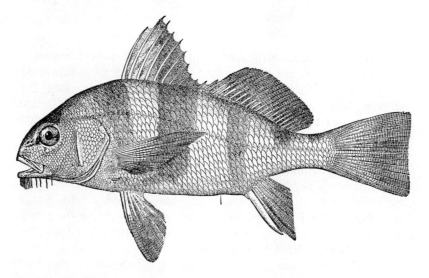

short, the second exceedingly large, nearly as long as the soft rays; pectorals and ventrals long; gill-rakers short and bluntish; pseudobranchiæ large.

This genus contains 2 species, both American, and both large, coarse fishes, among the largest in the family. The more important of the 2 species is the common drum or black drum, *Pogonias cromis*.

The drum is found from New England to the Rio Grande, and is a common and well-known fish on sandy shores everywhere, particularly southward. It is one of the largest food-fishes on our coast. The largest example on record was taken at St. Augustine, Florida, and weighed 146 pounds. Examples weighing 50 to 80 pounds are not rare, though those seen in market weigh only a few pounds. The drum is a sluggish fish, feeding chiefly at the bottom, where their long, sensitive barbels aid them greatly in their search for food, which consists mostly of crustaceans and mollusks, which they easily crush with their strong, paved pharyngeal teeth. They are believed to be very destructive to oyster-beds, particularly southward.

The drum makes a loud drumming noise, especially during the breeding season, a habit shared by many other members of the family. Small fish under about 20 pounds are said not to drum. The males drum loudest, the females in a softer tone, and the drumming is probably for the purpose of attracting the opposite sex.

In the northern portion of its range it is not regarded as a food-fish of any value, but from Chesapeake Bay southward it is held in higher esteem. The flesh is coarse, though tender and of delicate flavour. The roe are considered a great delicacy and are often salted and dried.

The drum is usually taken in seines or traps, but it takes the hook readily when baited with a crab or shrimp, and its large size makes its capture and landing a matter of no little interest to the angler.

The scales of the drum are used to some extent in Florida in the manufacture of the sprays of flowers and other articles of fancy-work which are sold under the name of "fish-scale jewelry." They are large and silvery, and so hard that it is necessary to remove them with an ax or hatchet.

Colour, grayish silvery, with 4 or 5 broad dark vertical bars, these disappearing with age; usually no oblique dark streaks along the rows of scales above; fins blackish.

GENUS APLODINOTUS RAFINESQUE

This genus contains a single species, *Aplodinotus grunniens*, a large freshwater fish occurring in our larger lakes and sluggish streams and bayous from the Great Lakes and west of the Alleghenies southward through the Mississippi Valley to Louisiana, and in lowland streams through Texas to the mouth of the Rio Grande. It has recently been found by us in the Rio Usumacinta, in Tabasco, southern Mexico.

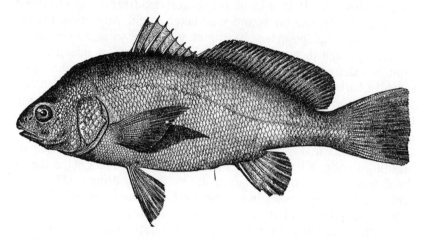

It is most abundant in the Great Lakes and in the lowland streams of Louisiana and Texas. A great number of vernacular names have been bestowed upon this interesting fish. In the Great Lakes it is the sheepshead or freshwater drum; in the lakes of northern Indiana it is called crocus, evidently a corruption of croaker; in the Ohio it is the white perch, gray perch, or simply perch; farther south it is drum or thunder-pumper; and in Louisiana, gaspergou.

It is a bottom fish, feeding chiefly upon crustaceans and mollusks. Northward the freshwater drum is not greatly valued as a food-fish, but in the South it is highly esteemed. Ordinarily we have found the flesh tough and coarse in fibre, and often with a disagreeable shark-like odour.

The gaspergou is one of our largest freshwater fishes, as it reaches a weight of 50 to 60 pounds and a length of 4 feet.

Colour, grayish silvery, dusky above, sometimes very dark; back sometimes with oblique dusky streaks along the rows of scales.

THE SURF-FISHES

Family LVII.   Embiotocidæ

THIS is a large family, all the species of which are viviparous. The young are hatched within the body where they remain closely packed in a sac-like enlargement of the oviduct analogous to the uterus, until born.   These fœtal fishes bear at first little resemblance to the parent, being closely compressed and having the vertical fins exceedingly elevated.   At birth they are $1\frac{1}{2}$ to $2\frac{1}{2}$ inches long, and similar to the adult in appearance, but more compressed and red in colour.

Since the discovery of their viviparity by Dr. Gibbons in 1854, these fishes have been of special interest to zoologists.

They are all fishes of our Pacific Coast, inhabiting bays and the surf on sandy shores, excepting 2 species known from Japan. Several of them are found in brackish water and one inhabits freshwater streams.   The different species reach a length of 6 to 18 inches and are usually very abundant wherever found.   Though extensively used for food, the flesh is rather tasteless and bony. They feed chiefly upon small crustaceans and other invertebrates. None of them ranks high as a game-fish, though most of the species will take the baited hook and are able to make a fairly good fight.   Nearly all the species are handsome fishes, some of them being very richly coloured.

The surf-fish family contains 17 known genera with about 20 species, 2 of which occur only in Japan, all the others being confined to the Pacific Coast of America.

The only species which our space will permit us to mention are the following :

The genus *Hysterocarpus* contains but one species, *H. traski*, a small freshwater fish, locally abundant in the rivers of central

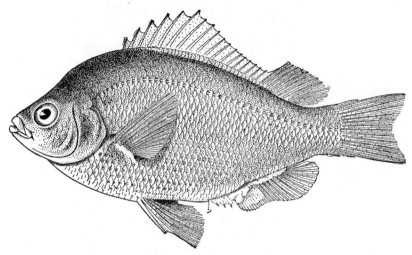

California. It is probably most numerous in the Sacramento.

The genus *Abeona* contains 2 species, *A. minima*, reaching 6 inches in length and found along the entire California coast

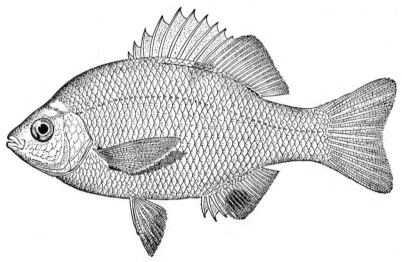

from San Francisco to San Diego. The other species, *A. aurora*, is scarcely larger and is known only from Monterey Bay, where it is abundant.

The genus *Cymatogaster* contains one species, *C. aggregatus*, which is very abundant everywhere from Fort Wrangel to Lower

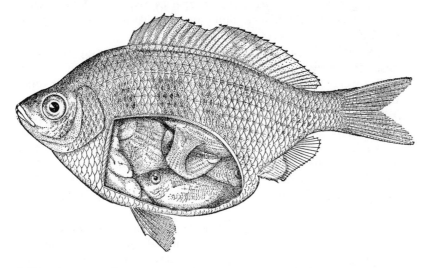

California, especially on sandy or muddy shallows and about wharves. It reaches 6 or 8 inches in length and is one of the most interesting members of the family. It is the common viviparous perch or sparada of the California coast. The above drawing shows a female with a number of young.

The genus *Brachyistius* has only one species, *B. frenatus*, which reaches a length of 8 inches, and is found from Vancouver Island to Lower California. It is rather abundant northward in shallow water.

The genus *Zalembius*, also has a single species, *Z. rosaceus*, which occurs sparingly on the coast of California in deeper water than any of the others, far below the line of the surf. It reaches 8 inches in length and is a beautiful and interesting fish.

Hypocritichthys is another monotypic genus, the single species, *H. analis*, reaching a length of 6 inches, being locally abundant between San Francisco and Point Conception.

The genus *Hyperprosopon* has 2 species. *H. argenteus*, the wall-eyed surf-fish or white perch, is everywhere common on sandy shores from Cape Disappointment to Todos Santos Bay on sandy shores in the surf. It reaches 10 inches in length. *H. agassizii* reaches a somewhat smaller size and is found from San Francisco to Santa Barbara. It is perhaps most common on the coast of San Luis Obispo County.

The genus *Holconotus* has one species, *H. rhodoterus*, which is found in some abundance along the coast from San Francisco to San Diego. It reaches 12 inches in length.

Amphistichus argenteus, the surf-fish, is the only species in its genus. It is very abundant on sandy shores from Cape Flattery to San Diego and reaches a foot in length. The genus *Embiotoca*, upon which the name of the family is based, has one species, the common surf-fish or black perch, *E. jacksoni*, which is rather abundant everywhere from British Columbia to Lower California. Southward it is the most abundant of the larger species. It reaches a foot in length. This interesting species was named for Dr. A. C. Jackson of San Francisco, who, on June 7, 1852, discovered the viviparity of these fishes and first brought the fact to the attention of Professor Agassiz.

The genus *Tæniotoca* contains one species, *T. lateralis*, the blue perch or striped surf-fish, which is found from British Columbia to San Diego. South of Point Conception it is not common, but northward it is very abundant. *Phanerodon* contains 2 species: *P. furcatus*, the white surf-fish which is found from British Columbia to

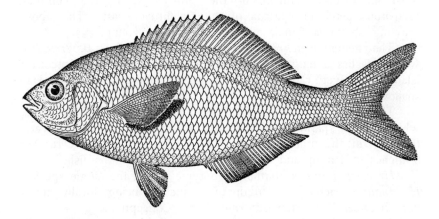

San Diego. It reaches a foot in length and is exceedingly abundant from Cape Mendocino southward. The other species is *P. atripes*, which reaches 10 inches in length and is found from Monterey to San Diego in rather deep water.

The genus *Rachocheilus* contains one species, *R. toxotes*, occurring rather commonly from San Francisco to San Diego. It reaches

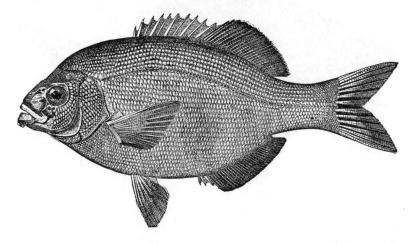

18 inches in length and is one of the largest of the family.

The genus *Hypsurus* has a single species, *H. caryi*, which occurs on the California coast from Cape Mendocino to San Diego. It is a

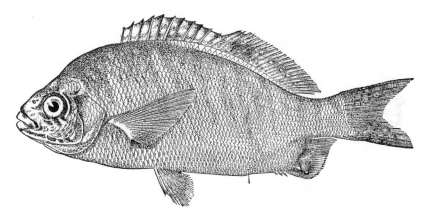

beautiful little fish, 10 inches long, and much used as bait. About San Francisco it is common but south of Point Conception it is rare.

The genus *Damalichthys* contains one species, *D. argyrosomus*, the white perch or porgee of the Pacific Coast. It is everywhere common from British Columbia to Lower California. It is the most

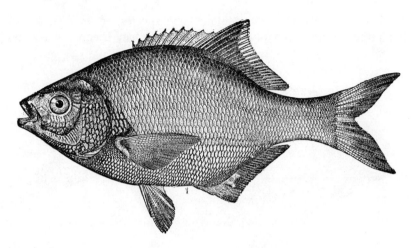

abundant species on the shores of British Columbia where it enters
the inlets in thousands. It reaches a length of 15 inches and is
used to some extent as a food-fish, though its flesh is poor and
has little flavour.

THE CICHLIDS

Family LVIII.   Cichlidæ

The Cichlids are a large family of freshwater fishes of moderate or small size in southern Mexico, Central and South America, resembling in form, size, appearance, habits, and even in many details of structure, the sunfishes or *Centrarchidæ* of the United States, from which they are readily distinguished, however, by having the lower pharyngeals fully united, and only a single nostril on each side. The family contains some 40 genera and 150 species. North of the Isthmus of Panama are found 7 genera, represented by about 60 species. The principal genera are *Cichlasoma*, *Heros* and *Petenia*. The species have not been carefully studied, and little is known of their habits or distribution.

Petenia has with us a single species, *P. splendida*, known only from Lake Peten and the Rio Usumacinta. It is a handsome fish 10 inches long, and much resembling our calico bass in general appearance.

The genus *Cichlasoma* is a large one with 25 or 30 species, north of the Isthmus of Panama, in all the lakes and larger streams of Central America and southern Mexico. The majority of the species are little known and poorly defined.

The genus *Heros* also contains many species, about 25 being within our limits, occupying the same waters as the species of *Cichlasoma*. Only one, *H. cyanoguttatus*, is found as far north as the Rio Grande, this species having been taken at Brownsville, Texas.

All the members of this family are food-fishes of some value, and some of them at least will take the hook.

THE WRASSE-FISHES

Family LIX. Labridæ

BODY oblong or elongate, covered with cycloid scales; lateral line well developed, continuous or interrupted, often angularly bent; mouth moderate, terminal; premaxillaries protractile; maxillary without supplemental bone; anterior teeth in jaws usually very strong and canine-like, often soldered together at base, but not forming a continuous plate; no teeth on vomer or palatines; lower pharyngeals completely united into one bone without median suture, this bone T-shaped or Y-shaped, its teeth conical or tubular; lips thick, longitudinally plicate; nostrils round, with 2 openings on each side; dorsal fin continuous, the spinous portion usually long, the spines usually slender, 3 to 20 in number; anal similar to the soft dorsal, with 2 to 6 spines; branchiostegals 5 or 6; pseudobranchiæ well developed; gills $3\frac{1}{2}$, the slit behind the last arch small or obsolete; gill-membranes somewhat connected, sometimes joined to the narrow isthmus; air-bladder present; no pyloric cœca.

This is one of the very largest families of fishes, the known genera being about 60 and the species about 450. They are chiefly tropical fishes, living among rocks or kelp. Many of them are brilliantly coloured, and some are valued as food. Most of them feed upon mollusks, the dentition being well adapted for crushing shells. Some of the species will take the hook, but none of them ranks high as to game-qualities. In our waters are about 20 genera and 50 species, only a few of which deserve more than mere mention.

The genus *Tautogolabrus* contains 2 species, one in Brazil, the other, the cunner, *T. adspersus*, one of the best known fishes on our North Atlantic Coast from Labrador to Sandy Hook. In southern New England it is called "chogset." Other names

BERMUDA CHUB, *Kyphosus sectatrix*

HOGFISH, *Lachnolaimus maximus*

CROAKER *Micropogon undulatus*

SPOT, *Leiostomus xanthurus*

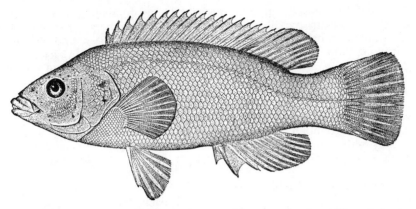

which have been applied to it are blue perch, bergall and berg-gylt. It reaches nearly a foot in length, and its flesh is excellent. These fishes, though useful as scavengers, are a pest to fishermen on account of their habit of nibbling the bait from the hooks.

The genus *Tautoga* contains one species, *Tautoga onitis*, which is an abundant and well-known food-fish from New Brunswick to the Carolinas. East of New York it is usually called the "tautog." On the New York coast it is the "blackfish," and further south the "oyster-fish." Though this well-known fish is quite common in most parts of its range, its centre of abundance seems to be on the southern New England coast. Very large catches have been reported from Narragansett Bay. It is particularly abundant about rocky shores, where it may often be seen quietly resting or even lying on its side in crevices or cavities. It is a sluggish fish at all times, and very apt to hibernate during cold weather.

The tautog reaches a maximum length of 3 feet, though those usually seen are very much smaller.

As a food-fish the tautog is well known and of considerable importance, the catch being made chiefly with handlines. And anglers who visit the seashore find much sport angling for this fish. Standing on a rocky shore, from which one may fish in 5 or 6 fathoms, with hook baited with pieces of crab or lobster, very fine sport can be had.

Head $3\frac{1}{4}$ to $3\frac{1}{2}$; depth $2\frac{2}{3}$ to 3; eye $5\frac{1}{2}$; snout 3; pectoral $1\frac{2}{3}$; ventral 2; D. XVI, 10; A. III, 8; scales 14-60-25. Body somewhat deep and compressed; profile moderately steep, well rounded from snout to dorsal; maxillary reaching vertical from anterior nostril; jaws about equal, with two or three large canines and smaller ones on the side, which gradually diminish in size backward; gillrakers very short and blunt, about 3+6; a patch of small scales behind eye, extending downward to middle of cheek, where there are 5 or 6 series, the head and opercles otherwise naked; pectoral broad and rounded, not quite reaching tips of ventrals; soft dorsal higher than spinous portion; caudal truncate or slightly rounded. Colour, blackish or greenish, the young usually with about 3 pairs of dark bars connected by reticulations; adult often nearly plain blackish; chin white; eye greenish.

The genus *Lachnolaimus* is characterized by the strongly compressed body, the sharp, elevated back, and the long, steep profile; snout sharp; mouth low, horizontal, the jaws narrow; teeth in front prominent, canine-like, in a single series; no posterior canines; cheeks and opercles with imbricate scales; scales of moderate size, thin and adherent; lateral line complete; dorsal with 14 spines, the first 3 strong, falcate, produced in long streamers in the adult, the membranes between these spines very low, the filamentous tips longer than the head; other spines all low, gradually shorter to the eleventh; soft dorsal and anal much produced; caudal lobes falcate; third anal spine strong; pectoral and ventrals short.

This genus contains a single species, *L. maximus*, the hogfish, capitan, or perro perro, a large, showy species usually common throughout the West Indies north to Key West and Bermuda. It is especially abundant about rocky reefs. It was found by us in Porto Rico, where it is called "el capitan." It reaches a weight of 20 pounds, and a length of 2 or 3 feet, though those usually seen in markets are much smaller. It changes greatly in appearance with age. The large adult male is remarkable on account of a heavy black blotch over the forehead and eyes. The name "hogfish" refers to the swine-like appearance of the head, jaws and teeth. Like all other members of this family, it feeds chiefly on small fishes, mollusks and crustaceans.

The hogfish is an important food-fish throughout its range, and is one of the most common and attractive fishes seen in the wells of the fishing-boats of Key West and Nassau. It is a favourite fish in Cuba, though at one time its sale was forbidden by law on account of the supposed poisonous character of its flesh. This opinion obtains to some extent in Porto Rico, but apparently it is only the large individuals that are under the ban.

The genus *Pimelometopon* is close to *Harpe*, from which it differs chiefly in the naked dorsal and smaller scales. It contains 2 species, robust fishes of large size and bright colours. *P. pulcher* is (male) purplish-black on head, dorsal, anal and caudal fins, and posterior part of body forward to vent; lower jaw white; rest of body varying in tint from clear crimson to blackish, with coppery

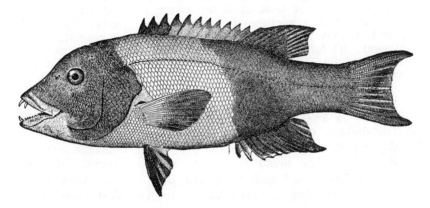

or purplish lustre; female dusky rose-colour, with black areas ill-defined or obsolete. This curious fish, known as the California redfish, or fathead, is very common on the California coast from Point Conception to Lower California. It reaches 12 to 15 pounds in weight, and 3 feet in length, and is taken in large numbers in the kelp off the shore, with hook and line, chiefly by Chinese, who salt and dry them.

THE PARROT-FISHES

Family LX. Scaridæ

BODY oblong, moderately compressed, covered with large cycloid scales; mouth moderate, terminal; teeth in the jaws more or less coalescent at least at base; lower pharyngeals much enlarged, united in a concave or spoon-shaped body, their teeth broadest transversely, and truncate, arranged in mosaic; dorsal continuous, its formula usually IX, 10; anal II, 9; 23 to 25 scales in the lateral line. Sexes similarly coloured, the colouration almost always brilliant.

This is a large family with some 7 genera and more than a hundred species, often of large size, and all are herbivorous and inhabitants of warm seas. The smaller species are found among the algæ in shallow water on sandy shores. Some of the larger ones are found about coral reefs and rocks. The flesh of these fishes is soft and pasty and they are not with us regarded as possessing any food-value. In the West Indies, however, they are utilized to some extent, particularly by the Tortola fishermen who fish about the east end of Porto Rico, where they catch several large species of this family in traps.

Among the natives of the Hawaiian Islands these fishes are highly esteemed. Several species of *Scarus* occur there, known by the natives as lauia, palukaluka, uhuula, etc., and they are eaten raw by the natives who pay very high prices for them.

The species of this family possess no game-qualities and are of so little food-value in the United States that we shall treat them very briefly.

The genus *Sparisoma* is a large one with about 18 species, all but one confined to our waters. They are nearly all of small size, showy colouration and, with few exceptions, of no food-value. The only ones deserving mention here are the following: *Sparisoma abildgaardi*, the red parrot-fish or loro colorado, reaches a foot or more in length. It is found among the West Indies and south to Brazil. It is common about Porto Rico where it is eaten.

S. chrysopterum, the loro verde, cotoro verde, or blue parrot-fish, is known from Brazil and most of the West Indies, It is common about Porto Rico where it reaches a good size and has some value as a food-fish.

S. lorito, the loro, occurs among the West Indies and southward. Obtained by us in Porto Rico, where it is used as food.

S. viride, also known as the loro verde, cotoro, or dark-green parrot-fish, is another West Indian species ranging north to the Bahamas and the Florida Keys. It is common about Porto Rico where it is a food-fish of some value. It reaches 2 feet in length. While all of these species of "loros" or "cotoros" are utilized by the Tortola and St. Thomas fishermen frequenting the grounds about the east end of Porto Rico, they are not so much used in Porto Rico.

The genus *Scarus* is also a large one with many species in all tropical seas. Most of them are large fishes of soft flesh, and of no great value.

Scarus vetula, the old-wife or vieja, reaches a length of 2 feet and is one of the most gorgeous of parrot-fishes. It is generally common throughout the West Indies. In Porto Rico it is used as food. The largest and most important species of the genus is the blue parrot-fish or tumble-rose *(S. cœruleus)*, which reaches a length of 2 or 3 feet and a weight of 12 to 20 pounds. It has the widest distribution of any of our species, being found from Chesapeake Bay southward to Brazil. It is generally common. At the east end of Porto Rico it was not rare, very large examples having been seen by us at Culebra Island. Though evidently not held in high esteem it is doubtless the most important of the parrot-fishes occurring in Porto Rican waters, and its importance is due chiefly to its abundance and large size. Its colour is nearly uniform turquoise-blue throughout.

The genus *Pseudoscarus* contains 5 species all distinguished from species of other genera by their green or blue teeth or jaws. The Guacamaia, *Pseudoscarus guacamaia*, is the only important species. It is found from Florida to Brazil, being common among the Florida Keys, at Havana, about Porto Rico, and nearly everywhere in the West Indies. It reaches 2 or 3 feet in length and ranks with the other large species as an inferior food-fish. *P. perrico* is a large species found on the Pacific Coast of Mexico. It and *Calotomus xenodon* are the only scaroids known from the eastern Pacific. In Hawaii the parrot-fishes, being eaten raw, are very highly esteemed, and even once held as tabu, to be touched only by royalty.

THE SPADE-FISHES

Family LXI.   Ilarchidæ

Body compressed, usually greatly elevated, the anterior profile steep, the caudal peduncle short; scales ctenoid, moderate or small, densely covering soft parts of vertical fins; lateral line present, following curve of back; mouth small, terminal, and horizontal; premaxillaries slightly protractile; maxillary short, without supplemental bone; jaws with bands of slender, pointed, movable, brush-like teeth; nostrils double; preopercle very finely serrate or entire; gill-membranes broadly attached to the isthmus, the openings restricted to the sides; branchiostegals 6 or 7; pyloric cœca few; gillrakers very short; pseudobranchiæ present; dorsal fins 2, somewhat connected, the first of 8 to 11 spines which are depressible in a groove; soft dorsal and anal fins high anteriorly, their bases thickened by a covering of scales; anal spines 3 or 4, short; caudal fin truncate or doubly concave; pectoral short, the rays all branched; air-bladder large, commonly bifurcate in front, and with 2 slender horns behind.

This family contains about 4 genera and 10 or 12 species, all shore-fishes, mostly of large size, inhabiting warm seas, and all valued as food.   Only 2 genera with 3 species in our waters.

The genus *Chætodipterus* has the body much elevated and compressed, the outline nearly orbicular, the anterior profile nearly vertical.   There are 2 species, *C. faber* and *C. zonatus*.   The first of these is the common spade-fish, angel-fish or porgee.

The spade-fish ranges from Cape Cod to Rio Janeiro.   It is occasionally taken near New York, and a few have been caught in traps at Menemsha Bight, near Woods Hole, in August and September.   It is not uncommon about the mouth of Chesapeake Bay and increases in abundance southward to Key West and Pensacola. Among the West Indies it is known from Cuba, Santo Domingo, Jamaica, Martinique and Porto Rico, at which latter place it is called "Paguala" and is common everywhere in suitable places. It has been recorded also from the coasts of Texas and Guatemala.

On the Florida coast the spade-fish is found through summer and fall in bays, about wharves, rock piles and old wrecks wherever crustaceans abound.   In October and November large schools are seen along the sea-beaches, evidently leaving the coast for warmer water, at which time they are caught with haul seines. In that region they probably spawn in early summer and the young are seen until October.

The spade-fish reaches a length of 2 or 3 feet and a weight of 20 pounds, though examples of more than 2 feet are not often seen. Very large examples were at one time regarded as belonging to a different species, *Ephippus gigas*.

Within the last 30 years the spade-fish has come to be one of the most highly prized food-fishes, and it is now held in much esteem by connoisseurs in Washington and New York, and in the markets of most eastern cities when it is most abundant during the summer months.

Large examples of this species are remarkable in having the anterior interhæmal enormously developed into a thick bony mass.

Colour, grayish or bluish; a dusky band across eye to throat; a second, similar but broader band, beginning in front of dorsal and extending across base of pectoral to belly; a third, narrower band extending to middle of side from base of fourth and fifth dorsal spines; a fourth, and broader band, from last dorsal spine to base of anal spines; all these bands growing obscure and finally disappearing with age; ventrals dark.

THE BUTTERFLY-FISHES

Family LXII. Chætodontidæ

BODY strongly compressed, elevated, orbicular, covered with moderate-sized or small scales, which are finely ciliate or nearly smooth; lateral line present, concurrent with the back, not extending on caudal fin; mouth small, terminal, protractile; maxillary very short, irregular in form, divided in two by a longitudinal suture.

Carnivorous fishes of the tropical seas, noted for their singular form, bright colours and great activity. There are 8 or 10 genera and nearly 200 species. They are exceedingly active and their quickness of sense and motion enable them to maintain themselves in the struggle for existence in the close competition that exists among the species about coral reefs notwithstanding their bright colours. In our waters are found about 20 species, only a few of which are large enough to be ranked as food-fishes. On account of their shape, as well as their brilliant colours, most of the species are known as butterfly-fishes, or mariposas where Spanish is spoken.

The genus *Pomacanthus* contains 3 species, each of some importance as a food-fish. *P. arcuatus*, the black angel, is generally common in the West Indies and is occasionally taken as far north as New Jersey, and south to Bahia. It is not rare at Key West and was found by us in Cuba and Porto Rico. It attains a length of nearly 2 feet and a weight of several pounds. Those seen at Key West do not usually exceed 2 or 3 pounds. It is present there throughout the year and is caught chiefly in traps, though it is sometimes speared.

P. paru, the Indian fish, is found among the West Indies and southward, but has not yet been recorded from the United States. *P. ʒonipectus* is the west coast representative of the genus. It is rather common about rocks from Mazatlan to Panama.

The genus *Holacanthus* has numerous species, two of which are of considerable food-importance. The most important species is the rock beauty or palmoneta, *H. tricolor*. It is a most beautiful and interesting fish, rather common throughout the West

PARROT-FISH, *Scarus squalidus*

SPADE-FISH, *Chætodipterus faber*. YOUNG

BLACK ANGEL-FISH, *Pomacanthus arcuatus*. YOUNG

Indies and north to the Bermudas, but it has not been found in the United States. Elegant specimens were obtained by us at Arroyo and Isabel Segunda, Porto Rico, where it is not rare. It reaches a foot or more in length and is used as food.

Colour in life, caudal, pectoral and ventral fins and anterior third of body rich orange-yellow; rest of body black; lips pale blue; soft dorsal and anal fins black, tipped with orange and bordered in front by red; spinous part of dorsal orange in front, then black, the border red.

Holacanthus ciliaris is the blue angel-fish and is found throughout the West Indies and north to Key West where it is called the "yellow angel," which is justified by the broad yellow margins of the scales. It reaches a foot to 18 inches in length and is a very beautiful fish. It is a fair food-fish, usually taken in traps, though it sometimes takes the baited hook.

THE TANGS

Family LXIII.   Teuthididæ

Body oblong, compressed and usually elevated, covered with very small scales; lateral line continuous; tail armed with 1 or more spines or bony plates; eye high up; preorbital very narrow and deep; nostrils double; mouth small and low, each jaw with a single series of narrow incisor-like teeth; vomer and palatines toothless; premaxillaries slightly movable, but not protractile; no gillrakers; pseudobranchiæ large; gill-membranes attached to the isthmus, the openings restricted to the sides; 1 dorsal fin, with strong spines, the spinous part of the fin shorter than the soft part; anal similar to soft dorsal.

Herbivorous fishes of warm seas, usually easily known by the lancet-like spine on side of caudal peduncle.   There are about 5 genera and 80 species, most of the latter belonging to the genus *Teuthis*.   Only a few of the species are of any food-value.   There are in our waters 2 genera with about 6 species, only a few of which are of any value for food.

The American species of *Teuthis* may be distinguished as follows:

a. Outline rhomboid, the depth 1½ in length; colour brown washed with blue;...................... ....*cæruleus*, 486
aa. Outline ovate, the depth about 2 in length; colour brown, never blue.
b. Caudal simply lunate;........ ....*hepatus*, 487
bb. Caudal deeply emarginate.
c. Upper lobe of caudal not filamentous;.... ......*crestonis*, 487
cc. Upper lobe of caudal produced in a long filament;
bahianus, 487

The species of *Teuthis* are known variously as surgeon-fish, doctor-fish, lancet-fish, barbers and tangs; and among Spanish fishermen as Barberos and Médicos—all of the same origin and meaning the same thing; for the barbers were the first "médicos" who combined the practice of phlebotomy with their regular vocation.

T. cæruleus is one of our best known species, as it is quite common from Key West to Bahia.   It is the blue tang and is common about Porto Rico where it is used as food.   It reaches 8 or 10 inches in length and is usually found among algæ in shallow water, though the larger individuals are found at greater depths.

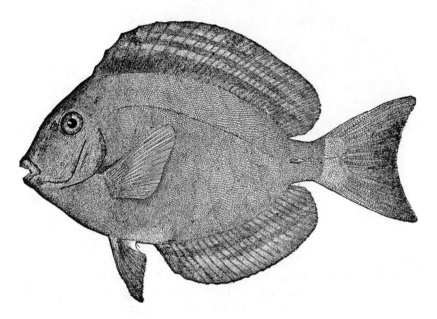

T. *crestonis*, the barbero negro, is known only from Mazatlan where

> "Beyond the headland with its palm tree lone
> Flashes the beacon light of tall Creston;
> The last and haughtiest of the craggy horde,
> Sierra Madre sends forth oceanward."

T. *hepatus* is the common tang and our most abundant species.   It is found from the Carolinas and southern Florida to Brazil.   We found it everywhere about Porto Rico where it is a food-fish of considerable importance.   It reaches a foot in length.

The most important of all our tangs, however, is the ocean tang, T. *bahianus*.   Though not so abundant as the common tang, it is, on account of its larger size, of greater commercial value.   It is found throughout the West Indies and on neighbouring coasts from Florida to Brazil. At the east end of Porto Rico the ocean tang is caught in considerable numbers by the

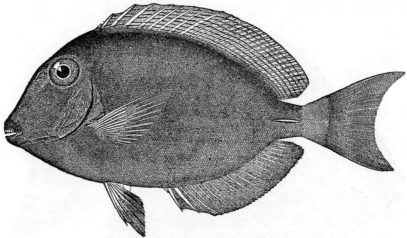

The Ocean Tang, *Teuthis bahianus*

fishermen from Tortola, St. Croix, and St. Thomas. It is usually taken in the native trap-baskets which are baited with large chunks of the white pulp of cactus plants and set in 4 to 10 fathoms of water. Sometimes the fish are "grained" or speared, and occasionally they are caught with hook and line. These fish are corned and taken to Santa Cruz where they bring about $5 a barrel.

BLACK ANGEL-FISH, *Powacanthus arcuatus*

YELLOW OR BLUE ANGEL-FISH, *Holacanthus ciliaris*. ADULT

YELLOW ANGEL-FISH. *Holocanthus ciliaris.* YOUNG.

THE TRUNK-FISHES

Family LXIV. Ostraciidæ

THESE fishes may at once be known by the short, cuboid. triquetous or pentagonal body, covered by a carapace formed of firmly united polygonal bony patches, the jaws, bases of the fins, and the caudal peduncle being the only parts free and covered with smooth skin.

The locomotion of the trunk-fishes is very peculiar. The propelling force is exerted by the dorsal and anal fins, which have a half-rotary, half-sculling motion, resembling that of a screw propeller; the caudal fin acts as a rudder, save when it is needed for unusually rapid swimming, when it is used as in other fishes. The chief function of the broad pectorals seems to be that of forming a current of water through the gills, thus aiding in respiration, which would otherwise be difficult on account of the narrowness and inflexibility of the branchial apertures. When taken from the water one of these fishes will live for 2 or 3 hours, all the time solemnly fanning its gills, and when restored to its native element seems none the worse for its experience, except that, on account of the absorbed air, it cannot at once sink to the bottom (Goode).

The family contains one genus, *Ostracion*, with 4 American species which may be distinguished as follows:

a. Carapace without spines anywhere; . . . .*triqueter*, 490
aa. Carapace with distinct spines, at least on the ventral ridges behind.
b. Frontal spines none.
c. Carapace closed behind the dorsal fin; body everywhere with round dark spots; . . . .*bicaudalis*, 490
cc. Carapace open behind the dorsal fin; body mottled with paler; . . . .*trigonus* 490
bb. Frontal region with 2 strong spines like horns; . .*tricornis*, 490

These fish are all sluggish in their habits, living in shallow water at the bottom about reefs and feeding upon minute animal and plant forms. All 4 of the species occur among the West Indies. They are known variously as trunk-fish, chapin, rock shell-

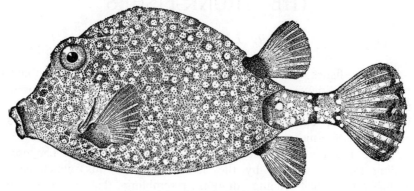

Chapin, *Ostracion triqueter*

fish, plate-fish, cow-fish, and the like. *O. triqueter* is found north to Pensacola, Key West and Bermuda, and is generally abundant. *O. bicaudalis* is a large species, reaching 16 inches in length, and is common among the West Indies, but has not yet been recorded from Florida. *O. trigonus* is the common trunk-fish, very abundant

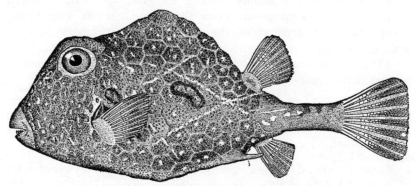

Common Trunk-fish, *Ostracion trigonus*

among the West Indies, and extending its range to Woods Hole and Chesapeake Bay. *O. tricornis* is the common cowfish. Its range extends from Brazil to Charleston, Pensacola, the Chesapeake and, in the Gulf Stream, to Woods Hole. It is even found also on

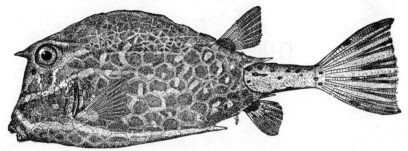

Cow-fish, *Ostracion tricornis*

the African Coast.   Though these fishes are rarely seen in the markets they are all excellent food-fishes, the   flesh   being delicate and

Common Trunk-fish, *Ostracion trigonus*

possessing an unusually pleasant flavour.   A common method of
preparing these fish is first to boil them in salt water,   then clean
out the meat and, after mixing it with cracker crumbs, egg, butter,
and pepper (red preferred), replace it in the shell and bake until
nicely browned.

THE HEAD-FISHES

Family LXV. Molidæ

BODY short and deep, or oblong, compressed, truncate behind, so that there is no caudal peduncle; skin rough, naked, spinous or tessellated; mouth very small, terminal; teeth completely united in each jaw, forming a bony beak without median suture; dorsal and anal fins similar, falcate in front, the posterior parts more or less confluent with the caudal fin; no spinous dorsal; no ventrals, pelvic bones undeveloped; pectoral fins present; belly not inflatable; gill-openings small, in front of the pectorals; an accessory opercular gill; no air-bladder.

Fishes of the open seas, seeming to be composed of a big head to which small fins are attached. There are 3 genera and about 6 species, all pelagic, found in most warm seas, and reaching a very large size. Two genera with 1 species each found in our limits.

a. Body suborbicular, not twice as long as deep; skin thick, rough, gristly, without hexagonal plates; ....*Mola,* 492
aa. Body oblong, about twice as long as deep; skin smooth, tessellated, with smooth hexagonal plates; ....*Ranzania,* 494

The genus *Mola* contains a single species, *Mola mola,* one of the most remarkable among fishes, known as sunfish, headfish, mola, and pez luna, and found in most warm seas. It ranges as far north as England, Cape Cod and San Francisco. It is one of the largest of all fishes reaching a weight of nearly a ton. The largest example on record was taken at Redondo Beach, California, in June, 1893, and was mounted by Mr. T. Shooter of Los Angeles. It was 8 feet 2 inches long and weighed 1800 pounds.

The sunfish are not rare on our Atlantic Coast where they may be seen on almost any calm summer day. They float lazily with one of the bright sides just at the surface, the waves rippling and breaking over them, and the heavy pectoral fin moving slowly to and fro through the air; thus lying they are very conspicuous objects and may be seen long distances. They spend whole days in this position, and may be easily approached and harpooned. From this habit of sunning itself it has received its vernacular name.

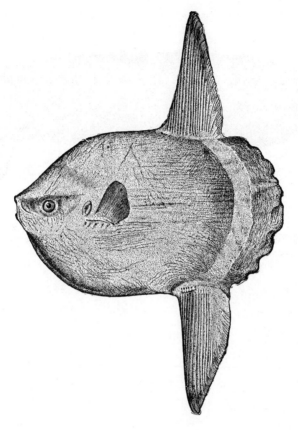

As a food-fish it possesses little value, but oil is sometimes made from their livers.

The genus *Ranzania* contains 2 or more species, one of which, *R. truncata*, is found occasionally off our Atlantic Coast. It reaches

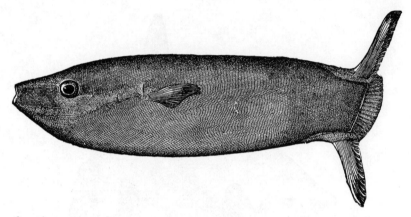

only about 2 feet in length. A similar species, *R. makua*, has recently been described from the Hawaiian Islands by Dr. Jenkins. It occurs also in Japan.

THE ROCKFISHES

Family LXVI. Scorpænidæ

BODY oblong, more or less compressed, the head large, and with one or more pairs of ridges above, which usually terminate in spines; opercle usually with 2 spinous processes, preopercle with 4 or 5; mouth terminal, usually large, with villiform teeth on jaws and vomer; premaxillaries protractile; maxillary broad, without supplemental bone; gill-openings wide, extending forward below; gill-membranes separate, free from the isthmus; scales ctenoid or sometimes cycloid; lateral line continuous, concurrent with the back; a narrow bony stay extending backward from the suborbital toward the preopercle; dorsal fin continuous, sometimes very deeply notched; pseudobranchiæ large; air-bladder usually present.

This is a very large family, with about 30 genera and 250 species, inhabiting all seas, especially abundant in the temperate parts of the Pacific, where they form a large proportion of the fish-fauna. The species are of large or moderate size, and all are non-migratory, living about rocks or among the algæ. Many of the species are of food-value, though some are reputed poisonous. Many of them are viviparous, the young being produced when about ¼ inch long.

The family is most numerously represented on our California coast. In our waters are 8 genera with about 85 species, only a small proportion, however, are of much, if any, food-value. None of them is regarded as a game-fish. We treat the family only briefly.

a. Dorsal spines more than 12.
b. Dorsal spines 15 or 16; vertebræ about 12+19;.... *Sebastes,* 495
bb. Dorsal spines 13 or 14;.....................*Sebastodes,* 496

The only important species of the family on our Atlantic Coast is *Sebastes marinus,* known as the rose-fish, redfish, snapper, red perch, Norway haddock, hemdurgan, bream or John Dory.

It is a fish of wide distribution and is found in northern Europe and from Iceland to middle New Jersey. It is most abundant northward, where it is a shallow water species; southward it is found only in deeper water, and is less common. Its

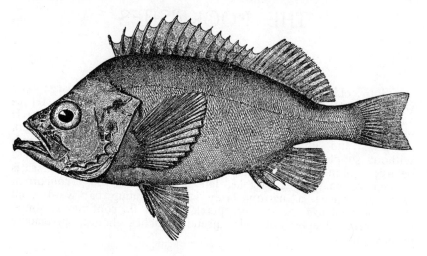

temperature range conforms pretty closely with that of the halibut.

The rosefish reaches 2 feet in length, though the average is much less. Their food consists chiefly of crustaceans, small fish, and mollusks to some extent, and in turn, the young of this species constitute an important part of the food of the cod, and they are at all ages preyed upon by halibut and other large predaceous fishes of cold regions.

The rosefish ranks well as a food-fish, and considerable quantities of them are taken on the New England coast. The most extensive fisheries are on the Greenland coast, where the flesh is highly esteemed, and the spines are used as needles. They may be caught on hand or trawl-lines, with almost any kind of bait. They breed in summer in deep holes in Massachusetts Bay, and elsewhere along the New England coast.

This fish may be known by its nearly uniform orange-red colour, and its spiny head.

The genus *Sebastodes* is the largest in the family, containing as it does not fewer than 56 species, all occurring on our Pacific Coast from Alaska to Lower California. They are all usually known as rockfish, and several are of considerable value as food-fishes. They are all closely related, and only a few of the more important species will be mentioned here. *Sebastodes pau-cispinis*, the bocaccio, large and swift, is abundant in California. *Sebastodes flavidus*, the yellowtail rockfish, reaching a length of 2 feet, is one of the most valuable species. It is abundant from San Francisco to San Diego.

    S. mystinus, the black rockfish, is the most abundant species

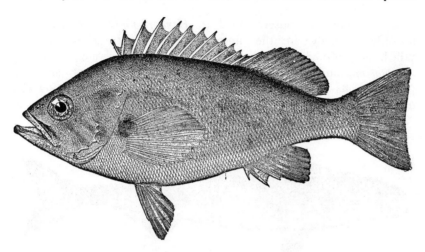

in rather shallow water about San Francisco. Another abundant species is the orange rockfish, *S. pinniger*, found from Puget Sound to San Diego. It reaches 2 feet in length and is a common market-fish; and the rasher, *S. miniatus*, is another important species reaching a length of 2 feet and abundant from San Francisco to San Diego. The red rockfish, *S. ruberrimus*, is the largest species of all, reaching a length of 2½ feet. It is abundant from San Diego to Puget Sound, and is a valued food-fish. Another important species is the yellow-backed rockfish, *S. maliger,* which is found from Monterey to Sitka. It is especially abundant northward, and reaches nearly 2 feet in length. The Spanish flag, *Sebastodes rubrovinctus*, banded red and white, is perhaps the handsomest sea-fish in our waters. Full descriptions of all the species of this genus, 50 in number, may be found in our "Fishes of North and Middle America."

THE SKIL-FISHES

Family LXVII. Anoplopomidæ

THIS family is closely allied to *Hexagrammidæ*, from which it differs chiefly in the normal development of the nostrils which are formed as in fishes generally. There are 2 genera, *Anoplopoma* and *Erilepis*, only the first of which is of any importance. Its single species is *A. fimbria*, a very interesting fish occurring on our Pacific Coast from Monterey Bay to Unalaska.

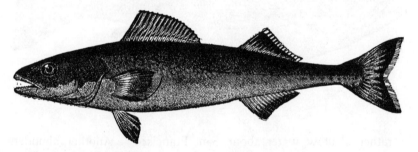

It is the beshow, coal-fish, or skil of that coast, reaches a length of 18 inches, and is used to some extent as food, though the flesh is rather dry and tasteless. About the Straits of Fuca it becomes very fat and is said to be highly appreciated.

THE GREENLINGS

Family LXVIII. Hexagrammidæ

BODY elongate, covered with small ctenoid or cycloid scales;
head conical, scaly, the cranium without spinous ridges above;
preopercle more or less armed, sometimes with entire edges;
third suborbital developed as a bony stay articulating with the
preopercle; mouth large, with acute teeth in jaws, and usually
on vomer and palatines; nostril single on each side, the posterior
opening reduced to a minute pore; pseudobranchiæ well developed;
dorsal fin continuous or divided, the anterior half of many slender
spines; anal fin long, with or without spines; lateral line present,
sometimes several series of pores developed.

Carnivorous fishes, mostly of large size, living in kelp and
about rocks in the North Pacific; some of them highly valued
as food.

Of the 5 genera found in American waters, only 3 contain
food-fishes of any importance.

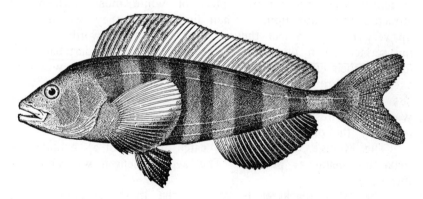

The most interesting species of the family is the Atka mackerel, or Atka-fish, *Pleurogrammus monopterygius.*

This interesting fish is the most important species of the
family. It occurs in the North Pacific, chiefly among the Aleutian Islands. It is not common about Unalaska or the Pribilofs,
but about Atka and Attu it is abundant. It is somewhat erratic

in its movements, and its most eastern record is Belkofski. It is usually found in kelp in 3 to 40 fathoms in spring and early summer, retiring to deeper water later.

Of all the saltwater fishes found about the Aleutian Islands the Atka mackerel is the most interesting to the angler. It takes the hook readily and makes a good fight. The usual method of taking it is by "jigging." On May 28, 1892, we had excellent sport catching these fish near the mouth of the bay at Attu, the most westerly of the Aleutian Islands. We used 3 hooks tied together in a bunch, just above which was tied a piece of white muslin. The line was weighted so that the hooks would descend quickly. When they had reached the bottom, or near it, they would be jerked up and down and the fish, striking at the muslin, would be hooked or would catch the hooks in their mouths. The lines would be let down through the kelp in 15 to 25 feet of water. The fish were in schools and it was easy to get great numbers; in fact, one would be kept very busy hauling in the fish and taking them off the hook. Usually the fish were near the bottom when we began fishing but they soon became excited and would come near the surface where they could be seen swimming about as if greatly disturbed and evidently searching for the piece of white muslin which had attracted their attention. When first hooked they would come up very readily, in fact they seemed to swim upward until near the surface when they would become alarmed and dart back and forth in their efforts to free themselves. Then the sport was very exciting. During 4 hours' fishing 9 persons with 26 lines took 585 fish, or 17 fish to each line per hour. And as our ship was out of fresh meat of every kind, all these fish were soon eaten by the officers and crew.

The average weight of this catch was about $2\frac{1}{3}$ pounds, the maximum being $3\frac{1}{2}$ pounds. The average length was about 18 inches.

The Atka mackerel is one of the most handsome fishes found among the Aleutian Islands. There are 2 patterns of colouration. In one the ground-colour is pale yellowish, the side crossed by 5 nearly jet-black crossbars all continued upon the dorsal fin; anal fin black. In the other the ground-colour is pale chrome-yellow, the vertical base not so dark. Some individuals are dirty gray and the bars are not well defined.

The Atka mackerel, which is of course no mackerel at all, is an excellent food-fish, especially fine when salted. There seems to be no good reason why it may not become the object of an important fishery.

The genus *Hexagrammos*, which contains the true greenlings or rock trouts, differs from *Pleurogrammus* chiefly in having the dorsal fin deeply notched or divided. The species may be known by the presence of 5 lateral lines on each side. All the species attain a considerable size and all are of value as food. They inhabit the North Pacific on both coasts, extending on the American side south to California.

Hexagrammos decagrammus is one of the most valuable species. It is known as the rock trout, boregat, or bodeiron. It reaches

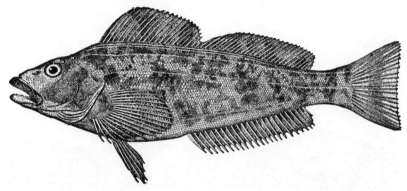

a length of 18 inches and is found from Kadiak Island to Point Conception. It is particularly abundant about San Francisco, and is a common food-fish. The sexes are very unlike in colour.

H. octogrammus, the Alaska green-fish, occurs among the

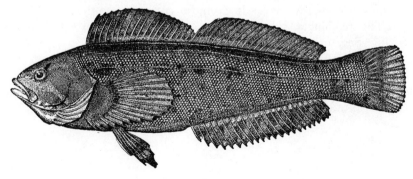

Aleutian Islands and westward to Kamchatka. It is abundant about Unalaska, and is a good food-fish.

H. stelleri, the common greenling, ranges from Kamchatka to San Francisco. It is abundant about Victoria and in Puget

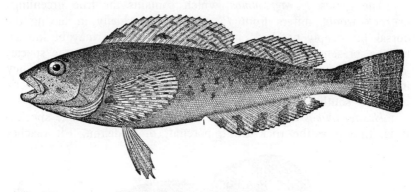

Sound, where it is caught in considerable numbers.

H. superciliosus, the red rock-trout, occurs from Bering

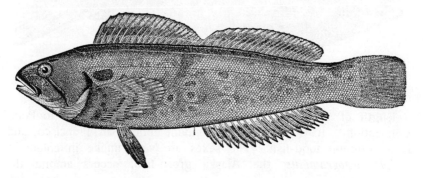

Island to Monterey Bay. It is most common southward.

The remaining species is *H. lagocephalus*, known only from Bering Sea.

The genus *Ophidion*, which may be distinguished from the 2 preceding genera by its single lateral line, contains but one species. This is *O. elongatus*, known as the cultus cod, blue cod, or buffalo cod. The cultus cod is a large, coarse fish, the

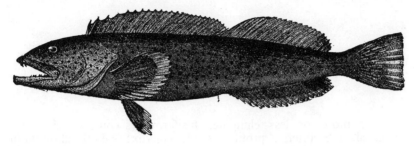

largest of the family, reaching a length of 3 to 4 feet and a weight of 30 or 40 pounds. It is found from Sitka to Santa Barbara and is one of the most common and most important food-fishes of our Pacific Coast. Though the flesh is livid blue or green in colour it is not unwholesome.

THE TILEFISHES

Family LXIX. Latilidæ

BODY more or less elongate, fusiform or compressed; head subconical, the anterior profile usually convex; suborbital without bony stay; cranial bones not cavernous; opercular bones mostly unarmed; mouth rather terminal, little oblique; teeth rather strong, none on vomer or palatines; premaxillaries protractile, each usually with a blunt, posterior canine; maxillary without supplemental bone; pseudobranchiæ well developed; gill-membranes separate, more or less free from the isthmus; scales small, ctenoid; lateral line present, complete, more or less concurrent with the back; dorsal fin long and low, usually continuous, the spinous portion always lower than soft part, but never obsolete; anal very long, its spines few and feeble; caudal fin forked.

Fishes of temperate and tropical waters, some reaching a large size. The 2 genera are *Caulolatilus* and *Lopholatilus*, the former with 22 to 27 rays in the dorsal and anal, the latter with only 13 to 15.

Caulolatilus contains 3 species, the blanquillos, 2 of which occur among the West Indies, the other on the Pacific Coast. None is of sufficient abundance to be of much food-value.

The genus *Lopholatilus* contains but 1 species, *L. chamæleonticeps*, the famous tilefish whose discovery only a few years ago and sudden, almost total disappearance a few months later, has interested commercial fishermen and scientists as well.

The story of the tilefish is a fascinating one. In May, 1879, Capt. Kirby, of the schooner *Wm. V. Hutchings*, while trawling for cod to the southward of Nantucket, took 5,000 pounds of a fish not only new to him, but new to science. The greater part of the fish taken on the first haul of the trawls were thrown away, but as the samples that had been tried proved excellent eating, those subsequently taken were salted down, and when taken to Gloucester a portion was smoked. In July, more tilefish were taken, this time on hand-lines. In 1880 and 1881, while engaged in exploring the sea-bottom off the southern coast of New England, the United States Fish Commission steamer

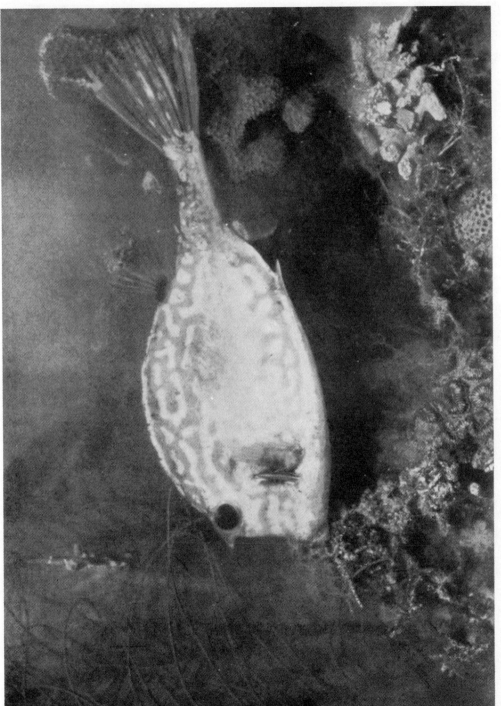

COWFISH, *Ostracion quadricorne*

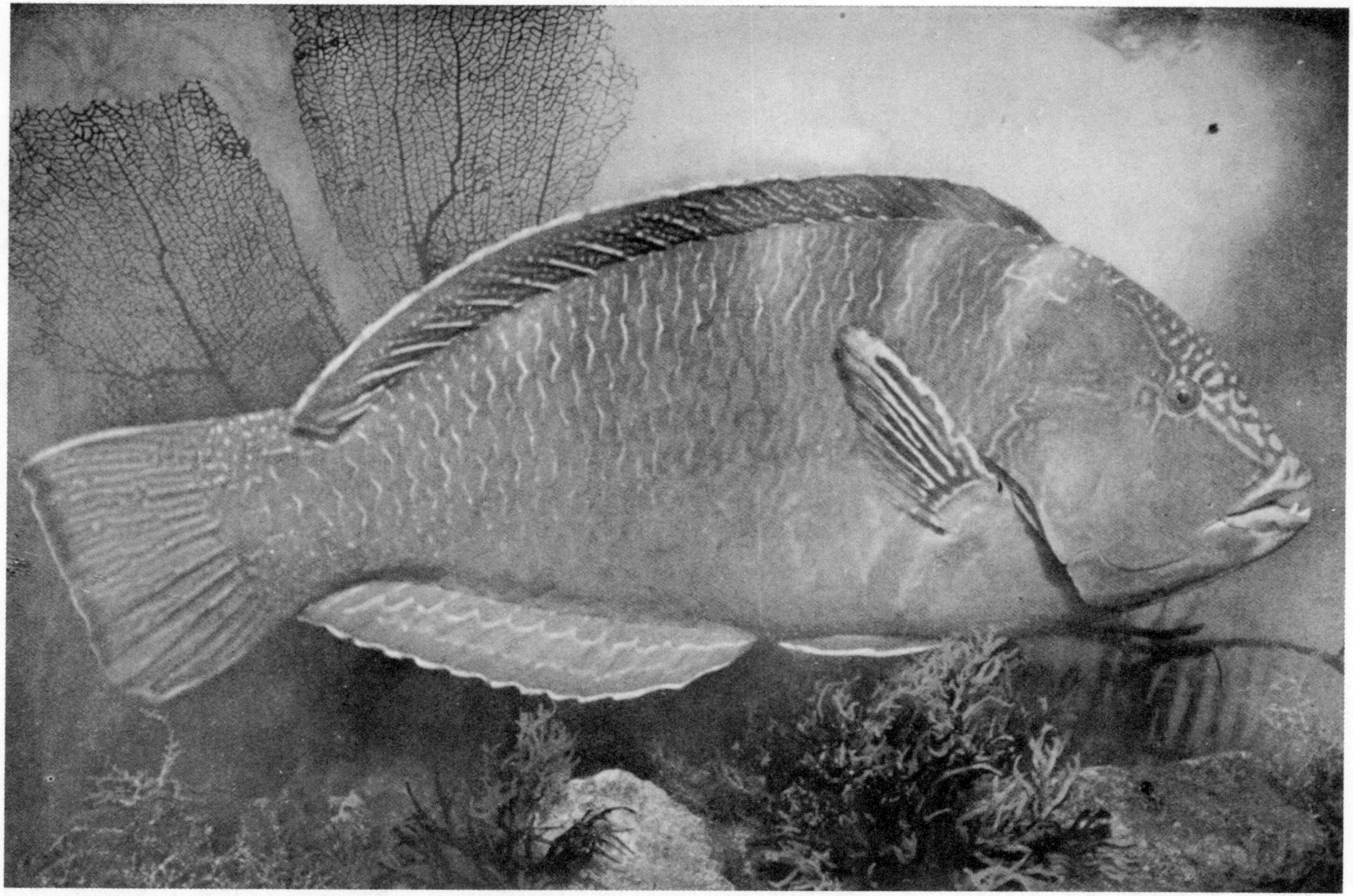

PUDDING-WIFE, *Iridio radiatus*

Fish Hawk took tilefish in several places at depths of 70 to 134 fathoms. The indications of the apparent abundance of a new and edible fish of large size made Professor Baird desirous of obtaining fuller knowledge of its habitat and habits, in the hope that an important new fishery might be developed. Various causes conspired to delay the investigations which he planned until 1882. In March and April of that year vessels arriving at Philadelphia, New York and Boston reported having passed large numbers of dead or dying fish scattered over an area of many square miles, and from descriptions and specimens brought in it was evident that the great majority of these fish were the tilefish. Naturally these fish were not evenly distributed over the area in which they were found, some observers reporting them as scattering, and others as at times so numerous that there would be as many as 50 on the space of a square rod. As one account after another came in, it became evident that a vast destruction of fish had taken place, for vessels reported having sailed 40, 50, and 60 miles through floating fish; and in one case the schooner *Navarino* ploughed for no less than 150 miles through waters dotted as far as the eye could reach with dying fish. Capt. J. W. Collins estimated that an area of 5,000 to 7,500 square miles was so thickly strewn with dead or dying fish that their numbers must have exceeded the enormous number of 1,000,000,000. As there were no signs of any disease, and no parasites found on the fish brought in for examination, their death could not have been due to either of these causes; and many conjectures were made as to the cause of this wholesale destruction of deep-water fishes, such as ordinarily are unaffected by surface conditions. Submarine volcanoes, heat, cold, and poisonous gases were among the agencies suggested. Professor Verrill has noted the occurrence of a strip of water, having a temperature of 48° to 50°, lying on the border of the Gulf Stream slope, between the Arctic current on the one hand and cold depths of the sea on the other.

In 1880 and 1881 Professor Verrill dredged along the Gulf Stream slope, obtaining in this warm belt, as he terms it, many species of invertebrates characteristic of more southern localities. In 1882 the same species were scarce or wholly absent from places where they had previously been abundant; and this, taken in connection with the occurrence of heavy northerly gales and the presence of much inshore ice at the north, leaves little doubt

505

but that some unusual lowering of temperature in the warm belt brought immediate death to many of its inhabitants. This is the more probable since it is a well-known fact that sudden increase of cold will bring many fishes to the surface in a be-numbed or dying condition, and there was no evidence of any shock or earthquake having occurred at that time.

For several years following no tilefish could be found and it was feared the species had become extinct. Although frequent search was made for them it was not until 1892 that they were found again. In that year the *Grampus* took 8 fish and in the following year 53 others were obtained. Thirty more were caught in 1897, and in 1898, when more careful tests were made, the United States Fish Commission caught 342 fish. And every year since 1898 large experimental catches have been made by the Commission and there is now no question but that the tilefish has thoroughly re-established itself, and it is hoped and believed that it may soon become the object of an important fishery. The tilefish grounds are at the edge of the Gulf Stream in about lat. 40° N. and long. 71° W. and in 70 to 80 fathoms.

The tilefish reaches a length of 3 feet and a weight of 30 pounds, and is a superior food-fish in every respect. Everyone who has eaten it praises it very highly. Mr. Willard Nye, an expert in such matters, pronounces it superior to any other fish except the pompano fresh from the water. It is best when boiled or baked.

THE HAKES

Family LXX.   Merluccidæ

Body moderately elongate, covered with small, smooth, deciduous scales; head elongate, depressed and pike-like; mouth terminal, with strong teeth; no barbels; dorsal fins 2, a short anterior and a long posterior one; a long anal fin.   This family contains a single genus with about 4 species, large cod-like fishes of voracious habits, inhabiting moderate depths in northern seas.   *Merluccius merluccius* is the common European hake which strays to Greenland.   *M. bilinearis*, the silver hake, New England hake, or whiting, is common from Newfoundland to Cape Cod, and south to the Bahamas in deep water.   It is of considerable food-value.

The remaining species in our waters is *M. productus*, which

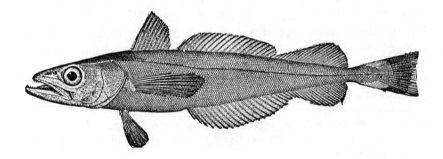

occurs on our Pacific Coast from Santa Catalina to Puget Sound; everywhere abundant and used as food, but it is of coarse and watery texture.

THE CODFISHES

Family LXXI.   Gadidæ

BODY more or less elongate, the caudal region moderate, coniform behind, and with the caudal rays procurrent above and below; vent submedian; scales small, cycloid; mouth large, terminal; chin with a barbel more or less developed; gill-openings very wide; gill-membranes separate or sometimes united, commonly free from the isthmus; no spines in the fins, the rays all reticulated; dorsal fin extending almost the whole length of the back, forming 1, 2 or 3 fins; anal fin long, single or divided; caudal fin distinct, or confluent with the dorsal and anal; ventral fins jugular, each of 1 to 8 branched rays; no pseudobranchiæ; airbladder generally well developed.

This is a large family with about 25 genera and 140 species, many of which are highly valued as food. They inhabit chiefly the northern seas, sometimes venturing into oceanic abysses. One genus (*Lota*) is confined to freshwater lakes and streams. In American waters we have about 36 species representing 19 genera, of which only the following contain food-fishes of any importance to us.

a. Anal divided into 2 separate fins, the dorsal into 3.
b. Lower jaw distinctly projecting; barbel small or obsolete; caudal concave.
c. Subopercle and postclavicle normal, both thin and flat, not enlarged and ivory-like;..................*Pollachius,* 509
cc. Subopercle and postclavicle enlarged, the bone dense and smooth, like ivory;......................*Theragra,* 510
bb. Lower jaw included; barbel well developed; caudal not concave.
d. Lateral line pale; supraoccipital crest moderate.
e. Vent in front of second dorsal; size very small;...*Microgadus,* 511
ee. Vent below second dorsal; typical codfishes of large size;
Gadus, 512
dd. Lateral line black; supraoccipital crest very high;
Melanogrammus, 516
aa. Anal forming a continuous fin or sometimes deeply notched; dorsal not divided into 3 fins.
f. Ventral fins rather broad, each of about 6 rays;........*Lota,* 517
ff. Ventral fins very slender, each with 1 to 3 rays;..*Urophycis,* 518

GENUS POLLACHIUS NILSSON

The Pollacks

Body rather elongate, covered with minute scales; mouth moderate or large, the lower jaw projecting, barbel very small or obsolete; villiform teeth on vomer, none on palatines; teeth in jaws equal, or the outer slightly enlarged; gill-membranes more or less united; subopercle and postclavicle not enlarged and not ivory-like; dorsal fins 3; anal fins 2; caudal lunate; vent under first dorsal.

This genus contains 1 species, *P. virens*, the common pollack,

coal-fish or green cod, which is common northward on both coasts of the Atlantic. It ranges as far south as France and Cape Cod, or even as far as New York on our coast. In the northern parts of its range the pollack is abundant, and at times it is quite common as far south as Cape Cod. It reaches a length of more than 3 feet and a weight of 25 pounds or more. As a food-fish it is not highly esteemed on our coast, partly, no doubt, on account of the fact that it destroys better fish. It is very destructive to the young cod, surrounding the schools and driving the fish to the surface where they fall a prey to the voracious pollacks attacking them from below and hundreds of screeching sea-gulls which with astonishing voracity and precision pounce upon them from above.

The pollack is very productive. According to Mr. E. R. Earll, a fish 3 feet 3½ inches long and weighing 23½ pounds contained 4,029,200 eggs and one of 13 pounds produced 2,569,753 eggs. The eggs, of course are very small. They are buoyant, floating at the surface and hatch in 5 or 6 days. The spawning time of this species on our coast is in the fall.

As a food-fish the pollack is by many highly esteemed. There are those who prefer it to the cod when salted, and others commend it most highly when fresh. The liver yields a valuable oil which is doubtless used extensively in adulterating cod-liver oil.

As a game-fish the pollack has not been fully appreciated. In some localities at least it is a very voracious fish, taking the hook freely and fighting vigorously. In Massachusetts Bay great numbers are caught with a surface bait, but larger fish must be sought at the bottom. North of Cape Cod young pollack afford much sport to fly-fishermen.

The genus *Theragra* is closely allied to *Pollachius*, from which it differs in the thick, smooth and dense subopercle and postclavicle, bones which are squamous in *Pollachius*. There are also differences in the number of the vertebræ.

Of the 2 known species, *T. chalcogrammus*, the Alaska pollack, is the more important.

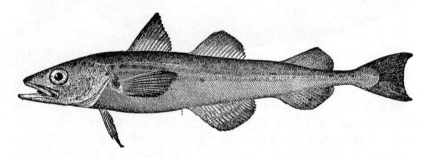

This pollack is found in Bering Sea and neighbouring waters south to Sitka and the Kurils. It is excessively abundant throughout Bering Sea, swimming near the surface and furnishing the greater part of the food of the fur seal. It reaches a length of 3 feet and is doubtless a good food-fish, but no important fishery for it has been established.

South of Sitka this species is replaced by a closely related one, *T. fucenis*, which is abundant in Puget Sound and is found as far south as Monterey Bay.

GENUS MICROGADUS GILL

The Tomcods

These are very small codfishes allied to *Gadus*, but with the vent placed before the second dorsal and with a different structure of the cranium.

There are 2 species.

The first of these is the common tomcod, *M. tomcod*, which is found on our Atlantic Coast from Virginia to Cape Sable. It may be distinguished by the possession of 21 or 22 rays in the dorsal fin.

Though usually known as the tomcod, it is in many places called the frostfish because it is most abundant in early winter

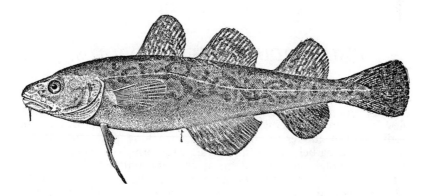

when it approaches the shores and even ascends rivers and creeks for spawning purposes. It has been taken in the Kennebec River 60 miles from its mouth and far above the reach of the tide. When ascending rivers they are taken in large numbers with dip-nets and with hook and line at bridges and wharves.

Though most abundant in winter they may be found along the shore at all seasons.

In form the tomcod is a miniature cod, and there is difficulty in distinguishing the young of the 2 species. The tomcod rarely exceeds a foot in length, feeds upon crustaceans, mollusks and small fishes, and is esteemed in many localities as a delicacy.

The other species is *M. proximus*, the California tomcod,

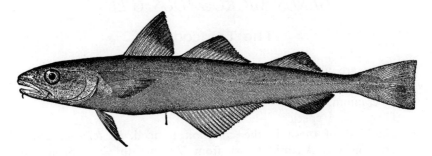

which occurs on our Pacific Coast from Monterey Bay to Unalaska. It is usually abundant and is a useful and valued food-fish. It is easily distinguished from the Atlantic species by the characters given above.

GENUS GADUS (ARTEDI) LINNÆUS.

The True Codfishes

Body moderately elongate, compressed and tapering behind; scales very small; lateral line present, pale; head narrowed anteriorly; mouth moderate, the maxillary reaching past front of eye; chin with a barbel; teeth in jaws, cardiform, subequal; vomer with teeth, none on the palatines; cranium without the expanded crests seen in *Melanogrammus*; no part of the skeleton expanded and ivory-like; dorsal fins 3, well separated; anal fins 2; ventral fins well developed, of about 7 rays each.

Species of northern seas, and all highly valued as food.

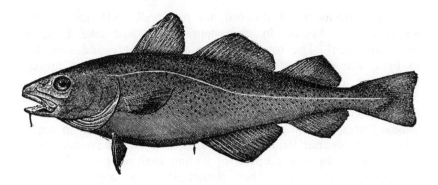

Common Codfish

Gadus callarias Linnæus

This important and well-known fish is found in the North Atlantic and on both coasts, south to France and Virginia. From the earliest settlement of America the cod has been the most valuable of our Atlantic Coast fishes. Indeed, the codfish of the Banks of Newfoundland was one of the principal inducements which led England to establish colonies in America, and in the records of early voyages are many references to the abundance of codfish along our shores. It is even claimed that English vessels visited the fishing grounds near Iceland as early as 1415, and that the Basques knew the Banks of Newfoundland centuries before the discovery of America by Columbus. So important was the cod in the early history of this country that it was placed upon the colonial seal of Massachusetts, and it was also placed upon a Nova Scotian bank-note, with the legend "Success to the Fisheries."

The cod is omnivorous, and feeds upon various kinds of animals, including crustaceans, mollusks and small fishes, and even browses upon Irish moss and other aquatic vegetation. All sorts of things have been found in cods' stomachs, such as scissors, oil-cans, finger-rings, rocks, potato parings, corn cobs, rubber dolls, pieces of clothing, the heel of a boot, as well as many new or rare specimens of mollusks and crustaceans. The belief that the stones are taken in by the cod as ballast, and that the finger-rings, boot-heels, etc., indicate that the cod is a "man-eater," are by no means necessary conclusions.

513

The movements of the cod are not well understood. They go in schools, but not in such dense bodies as mackerel, herring and menhaden. The movements on and off shore and from bank to bank are due chiefly to temperature influences, the presence or absence of food, and the search for proper spawning conditions. In the winter months there is a well-marked movement of large bodies of cod to the shores of New England and the Middle States, and important fisheries are then carried in regions where cod are not found at other seasons. This movement seems to be chiefly for the purpose of finding shallow grounds suitable for spawning purposes. They sometimes make long journeys, as is evidenced by the capture on the New England Coast of cod with hooks in their mouths such as French fishermen use on the Grand Banks. The cod is essentially a deep-water fish, and is usually taken in 20 to 70 fathoms. It has been taken at 300 fathoms depth.

The largest cod recorded from New England weighed $211\frac{1}{2}$ pounds and was over 6 feet long. It was taken on a trawl off the northern coast of Massachusetts in May, 1895. Many examples weighing 100 to 175 pounds have been recorded, but cod weighing even 75 pounds are not at all common. The average weight of the large-size cod caught in the shore-waters of New England is about 35 pounds; on Georges Bank, 25 pounds; on the Grand Bank and other eastern grounds, 20 pounds. The average weight of the small-size cod caught on all these grounds is about 12 pounds.

The principal spawning time of the cod on the New England coast is in the winter, the season beginning as early as November, and continuing until April.

The cod is one of the most prolific fishes. The ovaries of a 21-pound cod have been computed to contain 2,700,000 eggs, and a 75-pound cod, 9,100,000 eggs. The egg is very small, only about $\frac{1}{19}$ to $\frac{1}{17}$ of an inch in diameter, and about 337,000 are required to make one quart. When it is remembered that under natural conditions, in order to maintain the normal number of codfish it is only necessary for two of these eggs to hatch and grow to maturity, it is easily seen that the destruction of eggs is very great. If all the eggs of a 75-pound cod should hatch and grow to maturity, the ocean would soon become packed solid with codfish.

The principal loss is probably due to failure of impregnation, to great numbers being thrown upon the shore by the waves, and to the vast numbers eaten by various animals, including fishes, birds and invertebrates.

Commercially the cod is most important. In the matter of persons engaged, vessels employed, capital invested and value of catch, the taking of codfish in the United States is more extensive than any other fishery for fish proper. At least 600 vessels are engaged taking cod; they carry about 7,000 men, and are valued at $3,000,000. The catch in 1898 amounted to more than 96,000,000 pounds, with a first value of about $2,000,000.

Cod are taken with hand and trawl lines, baited with fish, squid, etc., and fished for from small boats, or the vessel's deck. The principal grounds are the "banks"—Grand, Georges, Western, Quereau, etc.

The cod is propagated artificially on a more extensive scale than any other marine fish. The number of cod fry liberated by the United States Fish Commission up to 1898 was 449,764,000. The output for 1896-97 was 98,000,000, and the unmistakable economic results which have attended these efforts warrant all the time and money devoted to them, and justify the greatest possible expansion of the work.

The common cod is greenish or brownish, subject to great variations, sometimes yellowish or reddish, the back and sides with numerous rounded brownish spots; lateral line pale; fins dark.

Alaska Codfish

Gadus macrocephalus Tilesius

This cod is very abundant in Bering Sea, on both shores, and ranges southward on our coast as far as Oregon on the offshore banks. It is usually found in 15 to 130 fathoms, and is an important food-fish, though not held in as high esteem as the common cod of the Atlantic. Externally, few if any important differences are observable between the two, but the air-bladder or "sound" of the Pacific species is markedly smaller.

Colour, brownish, lighter below; back and sides with numerous brownish spots; first anal and ventral fins dusky, other fins pale.

GENUS MELANOGRAMMUS GILL

The Haddocks

This genus is distinguished from the *Gadus* by its smaller mouth, the produced first dorsal fin, the black lateral line, and especially by the great enlargement of the hypocoracoid, which is dense and ivory-like. The lateral line is always black. The single species is the common haddock, *M. æglefinus*, which is of more restricted distribution than the cod.

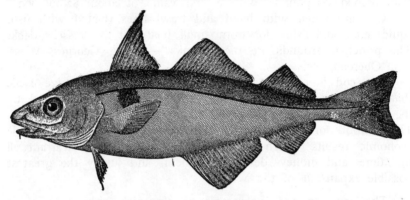

On our coast it probably does not occur north of the Strait of Belle Isle, and the southern limit of its range is off Cape Hatteras in deep water. It is found also from Iceland to France, and is particularly abundant on all the shores of Great Britain and the North Sea. They are abundant on the Massachusetts coast in summer, and it is then that the largest catches are made there as well as on the off-shore banks in the Gulf of St. Lawrence. On our coast there has been great variation in the abundance of the haddock; during some years it abounds, while in others it is very rare, the cause of which is not understood. They are more gregarious than the cod, swimming together in large compact schools from place to place.

The food of the haddock consists largely of invertebrates, although it is really omnivorous, and Professor Verrill has said that a complete list of the animals eaten by the haddock would doubtless include all the species of mollusks belonging to the New England coast fauna. The haddock is rarely seen at the surface, but is a bottom feeder, particularly abundant over clam-banks, hence its German name Schellfisch. It will take the baited hook as it rests on the bottom, while a cod will not notice it until it is raised a little above the bottom. Salted menhaden and stale clams are favourite baits for haddock.

The spawning season on our coast is from April to June, the height being in May. The eggs float at the surface like those of the cod. The size is about $\frac{1}{19}$ of an inch in diameter, and a $9\frac{1}{2}$ pound fish produced 1,839,581 eggs. The usual size of the haddock is about 3 or 4 pounds, and the maximum about 17 pounds.

As a food-fish the haddock has steadily grown in favour until it is now one of the most important. It is especially desirable for boiling or for making chowders. It is well suited for preservation in ice, and enormous quantities are shipped throughout the interior, along with the cod. It is also smoked, salted and dried in large numbers.

Colour, dark gray above, whitish below; lateral line black; a large dark blotch over the pectoral; dorsals and caudal dusky.

GENUS LOTA (CUVIER) OKEN

Body long and low, compressed behind; head small, depressed, rather broad; anterior nostrils each with a small barbel; chin with a long barbel; snout and lower parts of head naked; mouth moderate, the lower jaw included; each jaw with broad bands of equal, villiform teeth; vomer with a broad crescent-shaped band of similar teeth; no teeth on palatines; gill-openings wide, the membranes somewhat connected, free from the isthmus; scales very small, imbedded; vertical fins scaly; dorsal fins 2, the anterior short, the second long and similar to the anal; caudal rounded, its outer rays procurrent.

One of the 2 known species is found in our waters. This is the ling or lake lawyer, *Lota maculosa*. The ling is our only freshwater member of the codfish family. It is found pretty well distributed in the larger lakes of Canada and the northern United States from Maine and New Brunswick to the headwaters of the Missouri, and to Alaska. It is probably most abundant in the

Great Lakes, and has been recorded from the Eagle and St. Francis Lakes, and Lake Temisconti. It has been obtained from various places in the headwaters of the Missouri and Columbia. We have seen specimens from Red Rock Lake in Montana, Lake Chelan in Washington, and from the Fraser and Columbia rivers. It reaches a length of 1 to 3 feet, and though not usually regarded as a food-fish, it is utilized in some places. Properly smoked or salted it is not inferior to other coarse species.

The ling is disposed to stay in the deeper waters of the lakes it inhabits, and is not often seen in the shallows. Among the many common names by which this fish is known may be mentioned ling, lake lawyer, burbot and freshwater cusk.

This species is so unlike any other American freshwater fish that it can readily be identified by the accompanying figure.

GENUS UROPHYCIS GILL

The Codlings, or Hakes

In this genus the body is rather elongate, the head sub-conic, mouth rather large, maxillary reaching to below the eye; lower jaw included; chin with a small barbel; jaws and vomer with broad bands of subequal pointed teeth; palatines toothless; dorsal fins 2, the first sometimes produced at the tip, the second long, similar to the anal; ventrals wide apart, filamentous, each of 3 slender rays, closely jointed, appearing like one bifid filament; gill-membranes somewhat connected, narrowly joined to the isthmus.

This genus contains 6 or 7 species, only 2 of which are of value as food. These are the white hake, *U. tenuis*, and the squirrel hake. These 2 species are found on our Atlantic Coast from

Labrador to Cape Hatteras. They are abundant northward, and are found at a depth as great as 300 fathoms. The two species are very closely related, differing chiefly in the larger scales of the squirrel hake.

They are both ground-fish, remaining close to the bottom, and rarely coming to the surface. According to Captain Atwood they are much more inclined to take the hook by night than by day, and are found on muddy bottom during summer and autumn along the coast of Maine and Massachusetts. They are in best condition during the fall, and if properly prepared are a tolerably good table-fish. They probably spawn in summer, as shown by fish taken then and the size of young seen in the fall.

They are fished for extensively off the New England coast, the amount landed at Gloucester in 1899 aggregating more than 10,000,000 pounds. The white hake constitutes the larger part of the catch. The shore fisheries are by means of hand lines on moonlight nights on muddy bottoms in 10 to 40 or 50 fathoms. The schooner fishery is carried on in much deeper water with trawls and hand-lines. The average size of the hake taken probably does not exceed 5 to 10 pounds, though each species reaches a much larger size. Examples weighing as much as 40 pounds have been reported.

Hake are used extensively for corning, and as boneless cod and shredded cod. They are also smoked in small quantities. They also yield a valuable oil, and the air-bladder or sound is very valuable for the making of isinglass and glue, and even as food.

THE FLOUNDERS

Family LXXII. Pleuronectidæ

Flat fish, with eyes distorted, square, ovoid, rhomboid, long,
Some cased in mail, some slippery-backed, the feeble and
    the strong,
Sedan'd on poles, or dragged on hooks, or poured from tubs
    like water,
Gasp side by side, together piled, in one promiscuous slaughter.
                             —Badham.

BODY strongly compressed, oval or ellipical in outline; head unsymmetrical, the cranium twisted, both eyes being on the same side of the body, which is horizontal in life, the eyed side being uppermost and coloured, the blind side lowermost and usually plain. In the very young the bones of the head are symmetrical, one eye on each side, and the body is vertical in the water, but the cranium very soon becomes twisted so as to bring both eyes on one side. Eyes large and usually well separated; mouth large or small, teeth always present, premaxillaries protractile; pseudobranchiæ present; preopercular margin more or less distinct, not hidden by the skin and scales.

Further description is not necessary, as there is no mistaking a flounder. Everyone who see a flounder recognizes it at once as such, and everyone knows what "flat as a flounder" means. The family is a large one, embracing about 55 genera and nearly 500 species, nearly all of which are carnivorous, inhabiting sandy bottoms in all seas from the Polar regions to the Tropics, and many of them are important food-fishes.

The family divides readily into 3 subfamilies, as indicated in the following key:

a. Ventral fins symmetrical, similar in position and form of base, the one on coloured side not extended along the ridge of the abdomen.
b. Mouth nearly symmetrical, the teeth about equally developed on both sides;..........................*Halibut tribe,* 521
bb. Mouth unsymmetrical, the teeth chiefly on the blind side; eyes and colour on right side;...........*Flounder tribe,* 521

aa. Ventral fins unsymmetrical, dissimilar in position and usually also in form, the one on the eyed side being extended along the ridge of the abdomen; eyes and colour on left side;
Turbot tribe, 532

ANALYSIS OF GENERA OF THE HIPPOGLOSSINÆ, OR HALIBUT TRIBE

a. Vertebræ and fin-rays much increased in number; D. about 100; A. 85; caudal fin lunate.
b. Large teeth in both jaws arrow-shaped, biserial, some of them depressible; upper eye with a vertical range; gillrakers short;
Atheresthes, 522
bb. Large teeth not arrow-shaped, biserial above, uniserial below; gillrakers long and slender.
c. Lateral line without anterior arch; lower pharyngeal teeth uniserial; . . . . *Reinhardtius,* 522
cc. Lateral line with an anterior arch; lower pharyngeal teeth biserial; . . . . *Hippoglossus,* 523
aa. Vertebræ and fin-rays in moderate number; D. fewer than 95; A. fewer than 75.
d. Lateral line without distinct anterior arch. Species of subarctic distribution.
e. Lateral line simple, without accessory dorsal branch.
f. Teeth in upper jaw biserial.
g. Scales comparatively large, thin and deciduous; lateral line 70;
Lyopsetta, 524
gg. Scales small and adherent; lateral line 96; . . . . . *Eopsetta,* 524
ff. Teeth in the upper jaw uniserial; . . . . *Hippoglossoides,* 525
ee. Lateral line with an accessory dorsal branch; . . . . *Psettichthys,* 525
dd. Lateral line with an arch in front. Species chiefly of temperate or subtropical seas; . . . . *Paralichthys,* 526

ANALYSIS OF GENERA OF THE PLEURONECTINÆ, OR FLOUNDER TRIBE

a. Lateral line with a distinct arch in front; . . . . . . *Limanda,* 528
aa. Lateral line without a distinct arch in front.
b. Scales imperfectly imbricated, or else not all ctenoid.
c. Scales rough-ctenoid in the male, more or less cycloid in the female; lower pharyngeals very large, more or less united;
Liopsetta, 531
cc. Scales all in both sexes and on both sides of body represented by coarse, scattered stellate tubercles; . . . . . . *Platichthys,* 531
bb. Scales regularly imbricated, all ctenoid in both sexes:
Pseudopleuronectes, 528

Arrow-toothed Halibut

Atheresthes stomias (Jordan & Gilbert)

The single species of this genus is one of the most remarkable of the flounders. It approaches in form and general characters most nearly to the cod-like fishes, from ancestors of which we suppose the flounders to have descended.

This fish is found from San Francisco to Bering Sea and is most common northward. It is not rare in deep water off San Francisco, where it is caught in considerable numbers in the sweep-nets or paranzelles, used in Drake Bay. About Unalaska and elsewhere northward it occurs in shallower water. It was dredged in abundance by the *Albatross* on both sides of the Alaskan Peninsula and in Bristol Bay in 32 to 406 fathoms; Mr. N. B. Scofield found it in abundance in Chignik Bay, and we have taken it at Unga and Karluk.

This species reaches a length of 2 feet and is a good food-fish.

Greenland Halibut

Reinhardtius hippoglossoides (Walbaum)

The Greenland halibut is found in Arctic parts of the Atlantic and south to Finland and the Grand Banks.

It is known also as the Greenland turbot and little halibut, and is abundant on the Coast of Greenland where it is found in very deep water.

It is said to be found chiefly in the ice-fiords and between the great ice-fields in northern Greenland, and there only in the coldest months in the year. It is fished for by the natives through holes cut in the ice. In South Greenland it is caught on the oceanic banks in 60 to 180 fathoms. In Fortune Bay, Newfoundland, it is abundant in 60 to 300 fathoms, where it is caught chiefly in winter. They are taken also on the outer edge of the oceanic banks in 250 to 300 fathoms, a depth greater than that usually frequented by the true halibut, and where the slope is so nearly vertical that it would seem difficult for them to maintain a hold upon the bottom.

522

This flounder is more symmetrical than any other of the family on our coast, and, moreover, is coloured on both sides, which is unusual in flounders and indicates that this species is in its movements more like ordinary symmetrical fishes and that it can rest with the body in a vertical position.

The flesh of the Greenland halibut is said to be exceedingly palatable, it being firm, white and flaky, and less dry and more delicate than that of the common halibut.

The average weight is 10 to 25 pounds, and the colour is yellowish-brown.

Common Halibut

Hippoglossus hippoglossus (Linnæus)

The halibut is the only member of the genus, and is found in all northern seas. In the North Atlantic it is found as far south as the Cattegat in Europe, and occasionally the English Channel, while on the American side it has been taken as far south as Montauk Point. Its occurrence south of 40° is unusual. Northward its range extends at least as far as Cumberland Gulf, in latitude 64°, and on the coast of Greenland to 71° north. It is abundant also about Iceland and Spitzbergen, in latitude 80°.

The halibut is a fish of the coldest waters. The temperature of the water in which it is taken rarely exceeds 45° Fahr., and it is often as cold as 32°. In the Atlantic it is closely associated with the cod, although usually in somewhat colder water. In the Pacific the halibut ranges from Bering Straits to San Francisco and the Farallones. According to Dr. Bean its centre of abundance is in the Gulf of Alaska, particularly about Kadiak and the Shumagin Islands. A very large and important halibut bank is found in the mouth of the Straits of Fuca, and others have been developed on the Pacific Coast by the *Albatross*. The bulk of the halibut now brought to Puget Sound ports comes from off Cape Flattery, and northward into southeast Alaska. Very important gounds are in Dixon Entrance, about Queen Charlotte Island, and along the coast of British Columbia.

The halibut is one of the very largest of fishes and, of all our species, is equalled in size only by the sword-fish, the tuna, mola, and the tarpon. Captain J. W. Collins says he has never seen examples

523

weighing more than 250 pounds. Captain Atwood mentions one which dressed 237 pounds, and 2 others taken near Race Point which weighed 359 and 401 pounds respectively. Dr. Goode had the record of 10 or 12 captured on the New England coast, each weighing 300 to 400 pounds, and Nilsson records one from the coast of Sweden that weighed 720 pounds. A halibut weighing 350 pounds is about 7 or 8 feet long and nearly 4 feet wide. The male halibut is always much smaller than the female, and rarely exceeds 50 pounds in weight.

Very large fish are not so highly esteemed as those of smaller size. A fat female of about 80 pounds is said by experts to be the most savoury.

The halibut ranks among the most valued food-fishes of the world. In 1898 the halibut landed at Gloucester and Boston amounted to 10,378,181 pounds, valued at $576,382. In 1899 it was somewhat less in quantity (9,025,182 pounds) but valued at $600,000. The halibut fishery on our Pacific coast is also of vast importance. The catch on the coast of Washington, Oregon and California in 1895 aggregated 1,719,315 pounds, valued at $39,818. In 1899 the catch was 6,877,640 pounds, valued at $192,280. And since 1899 the catch has enormously increased, but no exact figures are available.

At the present time the shipment of fresh halibut from the Pacific Coast to the East is an important business. It was only to-day (March 5) that we noticed in the daily papers an account of the running of a fish-train from Vancouver to Boston—the "Halibut Express," "comprising 9 cars of fresh halibut, 1 of Puget Sound salmon, and 1 of Squallish Valley hops," a through fish-train from the Pacific to the Atlantic in 6 days!

The only species of *Lyopsetta* is *L. exilis*. This is a small flounder, rarely exceeding a foot in length and a pound in weight, which is exceedingly abundant in deep water on sandy bottom from San Francisco to Puget Sound. It is taken in the sweep-nets, or paranzelle, in the spring off Point Reyes in enormous numbers, sometimes a ton at a haul. It is less abundant in Puget Sound, though taken in considerable numbers in seines. Its flesh is soft, and the fish does not sell well.

The genus *Eopsetta* contains a single species, *E. jordani*. This flounder, known on the California coast almost exclusively as "sole," is found from Monterey to Puget Sound. It is rare

524

north of Cape Mendocino, but abundant in Monterey Bay, where great numbers are taken by Chinamen on set-lines baited with anchovies. It reaches a length of 18 inches, and a weight of 6 or 8 pounds, the average being about 3 pounds. As a food-fish it is one of the best of the family. Great numbers are dried yearly by the Chinese, who suspend them by strings on a frame placed on the roofs of the houses, as they are too fleshy to dry well on tables. Here they rustle in the wind, and, striking together, produce a sound like the wind among the leaves.

GENUS HIPPOGLOSSOIDES GOTTSCHE

Body oblong, moderately compressed; mouth rather large, with 1 row of sharp teeth in each jaw; no teeth on vomer or palatines; lateral line nearly straight, simple; eyes and colour on right side, except in *H. elassodon.*

This genus contains 3 or 4 species, only 2 of which are of any importance. The sand-dab, or rough-dab, *H. platessoides,* is found in the North Atlantic, and as far south as Woods Hole. It is abundant on the English coast, and is a well-known food-fish in Scandinavia. It is found off the New England coast in rather deep water. It reaches 2 feet in length, and a weight of 3 or 4 pounds. As a food-fish it is highly esteemed, especially in Europe.

H. elassodon occurs from Bering Sea south to Puget Sound. It is common about the wharves at Seattle, Port Townsend and Tacoma, where it takes the hook readily and affords the boys much sport. It reaches a length of 15 or 18 inches, a weight of 2 or 3 pounds, and is a good food-fish.

The single species of *Psettichthys* is *P. melanostictus.* This is one of the most common flounders on the Pacific Coast from Monterey Bay to Sitka, and is everywhere known as " sole." It attains a length of about 20 inches, and a weight of 4 or 5 pounds, the average length being perhaps 15 inches. Although never found in large numbers, it is always present in the markets, and is considered a good food-fish.

GENUS PARALICHTHYS GIRARD

The Bastard Halibuts

Body oblong; mouth large, oblique, each jaw with a single row of usually slender teeth which are more or less enlarged anteriorly; no teeth on vomer or palatines; gillrakers slender; scales small, weakly ctenoid or ciliated; lateral line simple, with a strong curve anteriorly; dorsal fin beginning before the eyes, its anterior rays not produced; both ventrals lateral.

Species numerous, found in all warm seas. Many species inhabiting both coasts of America and the eastern and southern coasts of Asia.

a. Gillrakers in large numbers, about 9+20;....*californicus*, 526
aa. Gillrakers less numerous, about 5 or 6+11 to 21;...*dentatus*, 526
aaa. Gillrakers few, shortish and wide-set, about 2 or 3+8 to 10 in number.
b. Body ovate, more or less compressed and opaque.
c. Dorsal rays numerous, 85 to 93; A. 65 to 73..*lethostigmus*, 527
cc. Dorsal rays in moderate numbers, 70 to 80; A. 54 to 61;
albiguttus, 527
bb. Body oblong, strongly compressed, semitranslucent;
oblongus, 528

The Monterey or bastard halibut, *P. californicus*, reaches a length of 3 feet and a weight of 50 or 60 pounds and is common on the California coast from Tomales Bay to Cerros Island. It is one of the most common food-fishes of that coast where it takes the place occupied by the summer flounder on the Atlantic side. It lives in shallow water, the young abounding near shore. It does not rank high as a food-fish, the flesh of the large ones being tough and coarse, while the young are inferior to most of the so-called Pacific soles.

The summer flounder or plaice, *P. dentatus*, is, next to the halibut, the most important of all the flatfishes on our Atlantic Coast. It is abundant from Cape Cod to the Carolinas. It reaches a length of nearly 3 feet and a weight of about 15 pounds. It has by most writers been confounded with the southern flounder from which it is most easily distinguished by its more numerous

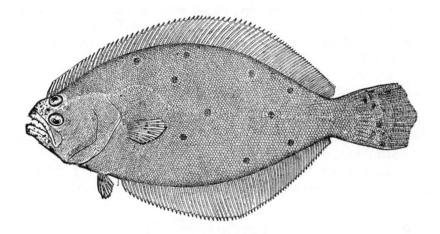

gillrakers and mottled colouration. They are usually found in a depth of 2 to 20 fathoms. In winter they move into deeper water. The largest example of which we have seen a record weighed 26 pounds.

The most extensive fisheries for this fish are on the New England Coast. Great numbers are sometimes caught in seines along shore, though favourite fishing-grounds are on sandy bottom, in 15 to 20 fathoms about Block Island, Marthas Vineyard, and the eastern end of Long Island.

The colour of this flounder in life is a light olive-brown, with numerous small white spots on body and vertical fins; sometimes a series of large white spots along bases of dorsal and anal fins; about 14 ocellated dark spots on side.

The southern flounder, *P. lethostigmus*, is close to the summer flounder with which it has often been confounded. It is the common large species usually abundant from Charleston southward and along the entire Gulf Coast. We have collected it in Indian River and at Tampa, and Mr. Silas Stearns found it abundant in shoal water on the west coast of Florida in summer.

The Gulf flounder, *P. albiguttus*, is rather common on the South Atlantic and Gulf coasts of the United States. It resembles the southern flounder in having few gillrakers, and the summer flounder in the mottled colouration, while from each it is distinguished by its fewer dorsal and anal rays. It attains a length of about 2 feet.

The four-spotted flounder, *P. oblongus*, is rather common on the coast of Cape Cod and neighbouring islands. It is a good food-fish and may be known by the 4 large, horizontal oblong black ocelli, each surrounded by a pinkish border, on side of body.

The genus *Limanda* contains one species, the Alaska dab, *L. aspera*, which is of some food-value.

This is a species of the northern Pacific and Bering Sea and is found on both coasts. On our coast it is generally common as far south as Vancouver Island. In Bristol Bay it is particularly abundant and is regarded as being an excellent food-fish.

There are 3 other species of *Limanda* but none of them of any value commercially except the rusty dab, *L. ferruginea*. This

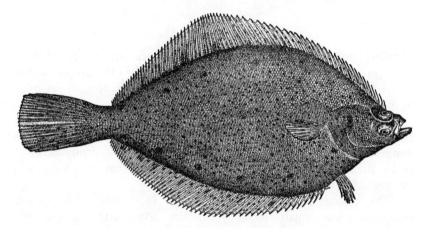

small flounder is found on our Atlantic Coast from New York to Labrador and is not uncommon northward. Though small, it is a good food-fish.

The genus *Pseudopleuronectes* contains one very important species. This is the winter flounder or common flatfish, *P. americanus*.

The winter flounder is one of the most abundant species on our Atlantic Coast, ranging south to the Carolinas and north to Labrador. It is especially abundant in southern New England and New York. It is not a large species, as it rarely exceeds

20 inches in length, and a weight of 5 pounds. Examples more than 12 or 15 inches long are not common.

The winter flounder is very prolific, the number of eggs produced by a large fish being more than a million. The spawning season on our coast is from February to April, and by August the young fish are 1 to 2 inches in length.

The flounder fishery is carried on chiefly during the winter and spring months, large quantities being taken. As a food-fish the winter flounder holds a very high rank; the flesh is white, firm, and of excellent flavour. Next to the halibut it is the most important flatfish of our Atlantic Coast. This species has been more extensively propagated than any other member of the family. The United States Fish Commission obtains the eggs at Woods Hole where its propagation fills in the time between the taking of the cod on the one hand and the lobster on the other. The number of fry hatched in 1900, at Woods Hole, exceeded 87,000,000, which were planted at various points along the New England coast.

The body of this flounder is regularly elliptical, the colour and eyes are on the right side and the upper side of the head is covered with imbricated ctenoid scales similar to those of the body; blind side of head nearly naked. The colour above is dark rusty-brown, either plain or mottled with darker. The young are olive-brown, spotted with reddish; the under parts are white.

529

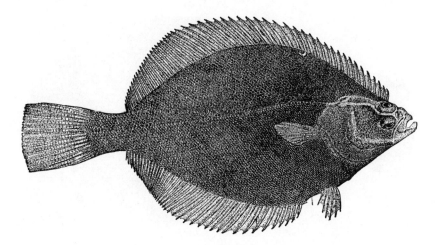

The genus *Liopsetta* is represented by 2 species, the most important of which is known as the Arctic flounder, *L. glacialis*.

This small flounder is found in Bering Sea on both shores, at least as far south on the American side as Bristol Bay. Though small, its great abundance and delicious flavour make it a food-fish of much importance.

The other species, *L. putnami*, is the eel-back flounder. It is found from Cape Cod northward at least to Labrador. It is a

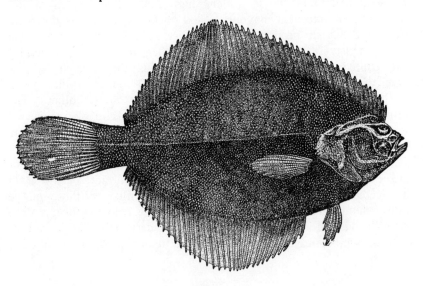

small fish, rarely exceeding a foot in length, but is often seen in the markets. Its flesh is of delicate flavour and the fish finds a ready sale.

The genus *Platichthys* contains a single species, *P. stellatus*, known as the great flounder or starry flounder.

This species occurs on the Pacific Coast of America from middle California to the Arctic Ocean; and south on the Asiatic side to the mouth of the Amur River. Of the small-mouthed flounders it is much the largest species known, as it reaches a weight of 15 to 20 pounds. It is an excellent food-fish, and from its size and abundance it is one of the most important species in the region where found. It constitutes fully one-half the total catch of flounders on our Pacific Coast, and it is equally abundant in Bering Sea. It lives in shallow water and sometimes ascends the larger rivers.

The genus *Glyptocephalus* has 2 species in our waters, only one of which is of importance. This is the pale flounder or craig fluke, *G. cynoglossus*, which occurs in the North Atlantic, south on our coast to Cape Cod. It has been taken in great numbers in rather deep water, on sandy bottom, off the New England coast. Though reaching only a small size, rarely a foot or 18 inches in length, this flounder is an excellent food-fish

531

By many it is said to be not inferior to the European sole. The colour is grayish-brown, the fins dark spotted, the tips of the pectorals dusky.

In the genus *Lophopsetta* (Turbot tribe) we have a single species, *L. maculata*, known popularly as the window pane. It is

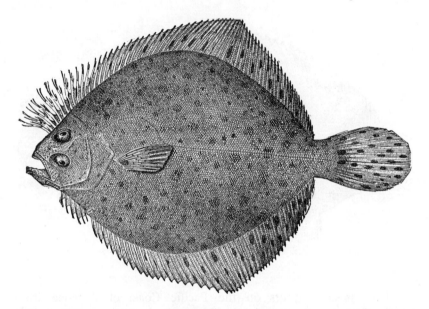

an interesting species, occurring on our Atlantic Coast from Maine to the Carolinas. It attains a weight of 1 to 2 pounds or less and is generally common on sandy bottom. It is a near relative of the valuable European turbot *(Psetta maxima)*.

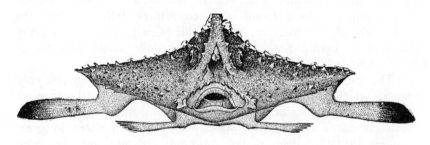

GLOSSARY OF TECHNICAL TERMS*

Abdomen. Belly.

Abdominal. Pertaining to the belly; said of the ventral fins of fishes when inserted considerably behind the pectorals, the pelvic bones to which the ventral fins are attached having no connection with the shoulder girdle.

Abortive. Remaining or becoming imperfect.

Actinosts. A series of bones at the base of the pectoral rays.

Acuminate. Tapering gradually to a point.

Acute. Sharp-pointed.

Adipose fin. A peculiar, fleshy, fin-like projection behind the dorsal fin, on the backs of salmons, catfishes, etc.

Air-bladder. A sac filled with air, lying beneath the backbone of fishes, corresponding to the lungs of higher vertebrates.

Alisphenoid. A small bone on the anterior lateral wall of the brain case.

Amphicœlian. Double-concave; said of vertebræ.

Anadromous. Running up; said of marine fishes which run up rivers to spawn.

Anal. Pertaining to the anus or vent.

Anal fin. The fin on the median line behind the vent, in fishes.

Anchylosed. Grown firmly together.

Angular. A small bone on the posterior end of the mandible.

Antrorse. Turned forward.

Anus. The external opening of the intestine; the vent.

Arterial bulb. The muscular swelling, at the base of the great artery, in fishes.

Articular. The bone of the mandible supporting the dentary.

Articulate. Jointed.

Atlas. The first vertebra.

Atrophy. Nondevelopment.

Attenuate. Long and slender, as if drawn out.

Auditory capsule. The ventrolateral swelling of the skull.

Barbel. An elongated fleshy projection, usually about the head, in fishes.

Basal. Pertaining to the base; at or near the base.

Basibranchials. A lower median series of bones of the branchial arches.

Basioccipital. A median posterior ventral bone of the skull to which the atlas is attached.

Basis cranii. Formed by shelves of bone developed from the inner sides of the prootics which meet and form a roof to the myodome and a floor to the brain cavity.

Bicolour. Two-coloured.

Bicuspid. Having 2 points.

Brachial ossicles. Synonymous with actinosts, q. v.

Branchiæ. Gills; respiratory organs of fishes.

Branchial. Pertaining to the gills.

Branchihyals. Small bones at base of gill arches.

Branchiostegals. The bony rays supporting the branchiostegal membranes, under the head of a fish, below the opercular bones, and behind the lower jaw.

Buccal. Pertaining to the mouth.

Caducous. Falling off early.

Cœcal. Of the form of a blind sac.

Cœcum. An appendage of the form of a blind sac, connected with the alimentary canal at the posterior end of the stomach, or pylorus.

* In the preparation of this Glossary the authors are indebted to Mr. Edwin Chapin Starks for valuable assistance.

Canines. The teeth behind the incisors—the "eye-teeth;" in fishes, any coni-cal teeth in the front part of the jaws, longer than the others.

Cardiform (teeth). Teeth coarse and sharp, like wool cards.

Carinate. Keeled: having a ridge along the middle line.

Carotid. The great artery running to the head.

Catadromous. Running down; said of fresh-water species which run down to the sea to spawn.

Caudal. Pertaining to the tail.

Caudal fin. The fin on the tail of fishes and whales.

Caudal peduncle. The region between the anal and caudal fins in fishes.

Cavernous. Containing cavities, either empty or filled with a mucous secretion.

Centrum. The body of a vertebra.

Cephalic fins. Fins on the head of certain rays; a detached portion of the pectoral.

Ceratobranchials. Bones of the branchial arches just below their angle.

Ceratohyal. One of the hyoid bones.

Chiasma. Crossing of the fibres of the optic nerve.

Chin. The space between the rami of the lower jaw.

Ciliated. Fringed with eyelash-like projections.

Cirri. Fringes.

Claspers. Organs attached to the ventral fins in the male of sharks, skates, etc

Clavicle. The collar bone, or lower anterior part of shoulder girdle, not entering into socket of arm.

Compressed. Flattened laterally.

Condyle. Articulating surface of a bone.

Coracoid. The principal bone of the shoulder girdle in fishes; otherwise a bone or cartilage on the ventral side, helping to form the arm socket. Synony-mous with hypercoracoid, q. v.

Cranial. Pertaining to the cranium or skull.

Ctenoid. Rough-edged; said of scales when the posterior margin is minutely spinous or pectinated.

Cycloid. Smooth-edged; said of scales not ctenoid, but concentrically striate.

Deciduous. Temporary; falling off.

Decurved. Curved downward.

Dentary. The principal or anterior bone of the lower jaw or mandible, usually bearing the teeth.

Dentate. With tooth-like notches.

Denticle. A little tooth.

Depressed. Flattened vertically.

Depth. Vertical diameter (usually of the body of fishes).

Dermal. Pertaining to the skin.

Diaphanous. Translucent.

Distal. Remote from point of attachment.

Dorsal. Pertaining to the back.

Dorsal fin. The fin on the back of fishes.

Emarginate. Slightly forked or notched at the tip.

Endoskeleton. The skeleton proper; the inner bony framework of the body.

Enteron. The alimentary canal.

Epibranchials. The bones directly above the angle of the branchial arches.

Epihyal. One of the hyoid bones.

Epipleurals. Rays of bone attached to the ribs and anterior vertebræ usually touching the skin in the vicinity of the lateral line.

Erectile. Susceptible of being raised or erected.

Ethmoid. A median anterior bone of the skull.

Exoccipitals. Two bones of the skull, one on each side of the foramen magnum

Exoskeleton. Hard parts (scales, scutes) on the surface of the body.

Exserted. Projecting beyond the general level.

Extralimital. Beyond the limits (of this book).

Facial. Pertaining to the face.

Falcate. Scythe-shaped; long, narrow, and curved.

Falciform. Curved like a scythe.

Fauna. The animals inhabiting any region, taken collectively.

Femoral. Pertaining to the femur, or proximal bone of the hinder leg.

Filament. Any slender or thread-like structure.

Filiform. Thread form.

Fontanel. An unossified space on top of head covered with membrane.

Foramen. A hole or opening.

Foramen magnum. The aperture in the posterior part of the skull for the passage of the spinal cord.

Forehead. Frontal curve of head.

Forficate. Deeply forked; scissors-like.

Fossæ (nasal). Grooves in which the nostrils open.

Frontal bone. Anterior bone of top of head, usually paired.

Fulcra. Rudimentary spine-like projections extending on the anterior rays of the fins of ganoid fishes.

Furcate. Forked.

Fusiform. Spindle-shaped; tapering toward both ends, but rather more abruptly forward.

Ganglion. A nerve centre.

Ganoid. Scales or plates of bone covered by enamel.

Gape. Opening of the mouth.

Gill-arches. The bony arches to which the gills are attached.

Gill-openings. Openings leading to or from the branchiæ.

Gillrakers. A series of bony appendages, variously formed, along the inner edge of the anterior gill-arch.

Gills. Organs for breathing the air contained in water.

Glabrous. Smooth.

Glossohyal. The tongue bone.

Graduated (spines). Progressively longer backward, the third being as much longer than the second as the second is longer than the first.

Granulate. Rough with small prominences.

Gular. Pertaining to the *gula*, or upper foreneck.

Hæmal arch. An arch under a hæmal spine for the passage of a blood vessel.

Hæmal canal. The series of hæmal arches as a whole.

Hæmal spine. The lowermost spine of a caudal vertebra, in fishes.

Hæmopophyses. Appendages on the lower side of abdominal vertebræ, in fishes.

Height. Vertical diameter.

Heterocercal. Said of the tail of a fish when unequal; the backbone evidently running into the upper lobe.

Homocercal. Said of the tail of a fish when not evidently unequal; the backbone apparently stopping at the middle of the base of the caudal fin.

Humerus. Bone of the upper arm.

Hyoid. Pertaining to the tongue.

Hyoid apparatus. Formed by a series of bones extending along the inner side of the mandible and supporting the tongue.

Hyomandibular. A bone by which the posterior end of the suspensorium is articulated with the skull; the supporting element of the suspensorium, the mandible, the hyoid apparatus, and the opercular apparatus.

Hypercoracoid. The upper of the 2 bones attached to the clavicle, indirectly bearing the pectoral fin.

Hypleural. The modified last vertebra supporting the caudal fin.

Hypobranchials. Bones of the branchial arches below the ceratobranchials.

Hypocoracoid. The lower of the 2 bones attached to the clavicle behind.

Hypohyals. Small bones, usually 4, by which the respective sides of the hyoid apparatus are joined.

Imbricate. Overlapping, like shingles on a roof.

Imperforate. Not pierced through.

535

Inarticulate. Not jointed.

Incisors. The front or cutting teeth.

Inferior pharyngeals. Synonymous with pharyngeals, q. v.

Infraoral. Below the mouth.

Interhæmal spines. Elements supporting the anal fin.

Interhæmals. Bones to which anal rays are attached, in fishes.

Interhyal. Upper hyoid bone attached to hyomandibular.

Intermusculars. Synonym of epipleurals, q. v.

Interneural spines. Elements supporting the dorsal fins.

Interspinous bones. The interneurals and the interhæmals.

Intermaxillaries. The premaxillaries; the bones forming the middle of the front part of the upper jaw, in fishes.

Interneurals. Bones to which dorsal rays are attached, in fishes.

Interopercle. Membrane bone between the preopercle and the branchiostegals.

Interorbital. Space between the eyes.

Interspinals. Bones to which fin rays are attached (in fishes); inserted between neural spines above and hæmal spines below.

Isocercal (tail). Last vertebræ progressively smaller and ending in median line of caudal fin, as in the codfish.

Jugular. Pertaining to the lower throat; said of the ventral fins, when placed in advance of the attachment of the pectorals.

Keeled. Having a ridge along the middle line.

Lacustrine. Living in lakes.

Lamellæ. Plate-like processes like those inside the bill of a duck.

Larva. An immature form, which must undergo change of appearance before becoming adult.

Lateral. To or toward the side.

Lateral line. A series of muciferous tubes forming a *raised line* along the sides of a fish.

Lateral processes. Synonym of parapophyses, q. v.

Laterally. Sidewise.

Lunate. Form of the new moon; having a broad and rather shallow fork.

Mandible. Under jaw.

Maxilla, or *maxillary.* Upper jaw.

Maxillaries. Outermost or hindermost bones of the upper jaw, in fishes; they are joined to the premaxillaries in front, and usually extend farther back than the latter.

Mesethmoid. Synonym of ethmoid, q. v.

Mesopterygoid. A bone of the suspensorium.

Metapterygoid. A bone of the suspensorium, or chain supporting the lower jaw.

Molars. The grinding teeth; posterior teeth in the jaw.

Muciferous. Producing or containing mucus.

Myocomma. A muscular band.

Myodome. Cavity under the brain for the reception of the rectus muscles of the eye.

Nape. Upper part of neck, next to the occiput.

Nares. Nostrils, anterior and posterior.

Nasal. Pertaining to the nostrils.

Nasal plate. Plate in which the nostrils are inserted.

Neural arch. An opening through the base of the neural spine for the passage of the spinal cord.

Neural canal. The neural arches as a whole.

Neural processes. Two plates rising vertically, one on each side of the centrum of the vertebra, which unite toward their ends and form a spine.

Neural spine. The uppermost spine of a vertebra.

Nictitating membrane. The third or inner eyelid of birds, sharks, etc.

Notochord. A cellular chord which in the embryo precedes the vertebral column.

Nuchal. Pertaining to the nape or *nucha.*

Obsolete. Faintly marked; scarcely evident.

Obtuse. Blunt.

Occipital. Pertaining to the occiput.

Occipital condyle. That part of the occipital bone modified to articulate with the atlas.

Occiput. Back of the head.

Ocellate. With eye-like spots, generally roundish and with a lighter border.

Oid (suffix). Like; as *Percoid*, perch-like.

Opercle, or *operculum.* Gill-cover; the posterior membrane bone of the side of the head, in fishes.

Opercular bones. Membrane bones of the side of the head, in fishes.

Opercular flap. Prolongation of the upper posterior angle of the opercle, in sun-fishes.

Opisthocælian. Concave behind only; said of vertebræ which connect by ball-and-socket joints.

Opisthotic. A bone of the skull to which the lower limb of the post-temporal usually articulates.

Orbicular. Nearly circular.

Orbit. Eye socket.

Osseous. Bony.

Ossicula auditus. Bones of the ear, in fishes.

Osteology. Study of bones.

Oviparous. Producing eggs which are developed after exclusion from the body, as in all birds and most fishes.

Ovoviviparous. Producing eggs which are hatched before exclusion, as in the dogfish and garter snake.

Ovum. Egg.

Palate. The roof of the mouth.

Palatines. Membrane bones of the roof of the mouth, 1 on each side extending outward and backward from the vomer.

Palustrine. Living in swamps.

Papilla. A small fleshy projection.

Papillose. Covered with papillæ.

Parapophyses. The lateral projections on some of the abdominal vertebræ to support ribs.

Parasphenoid. Bone of roof of mouth behind the vomer. Synonym of pre-frontal.

Parietal. Bone of the side of head above.

Parotic process. A posterior lateral process of the skull formed by the pterotic and opisthotic.

Pectinate. Having teeth like a comb.

Pectoral. Pertaining to the breast.

Pectoral fins. The anterior or uppermost of the paired fins, in fishes, corresponding to the anterior limbs of the higher vertebrates.

Pelagic. Living on or in the high seas.

Pelvic girdle. The bones supporting the ventral fins or pelvics.

Pelvis. The bones to which the hinder limbs (ventral fins in fishes) are attached.

Perforate. Pierced through.

Peritoneum. The membrane lining the abdominal cavity.

Pharyngeal bones. Bones behind the gills and at the beginning of the œsophagus of fishes, of various forms, almost always provided with teeth; usually one pair below and two pairs above. They represent a fifth gill-arch.

Pharyngobranchials. Upper elements of the branchial arches, usually bearing teeth.

Pharyngognathous. Having the lower pharyngeal bones united.

Physoclistous. Having the air-bladder closed.

Physostomous. Having the air-bladder connected by a tube with the alimentary canal.

Pigment. Colouring matter.

Pineal body. A small ganglion in the brain; a rudiment of an optic lobe, which in certain lizards (and in extinct forms) is connected with a third or median eye.

Pituitary body. A small ganglion in the brain.

Plicate. Folded; showing transverse folds or wrinkles.

Plumbeous. Lead colored; dull bluish gray.

Polygamous. Mating with more than 1 female.

Postclavicle. A ray composed of 1 or 2 bones attached to the inner upper surface of the clavicle and extending downward.

Postorbital. Behind the eye.

Post-temporal. The bone, in fishes, by which the shoulder girdle is suspended to the cranium.

Præcoracoid. A portion of coracoid more or less separated from the rest.

Præcoracoid arch. An arch in front of the coracoid in most soft-rayed fishes.

Prefrontals. Bones forming lateral projections at the anterior end of the skull.

Premaxillaries. The bones, one on either side, forming the front of the upper jaw in fishes. They are usually larger than the maxillaries and commonly bear most of the upper teeth.

Premolars. The small grinders; the teeth between the canines and the true molars.

Preocular. Before the eye.

Preopercle. The membrane bone lying in front of the opercle and more or less nearly parallel with it.

Preorbital. The large membrane bone before the eye, in fishes.

Procœlian. Concave in front only.

Procurrent (fin). With the lower rays inserted progressively farther forward.

Projectile. Capable of being thrust forward.

Prootic. A bone forming an anterolateral ossification of the brain case.

Protractile. Capable of being drawn forward.

Proximal. Nearest.

Pseudobranchiæ. Small gills developed on the inner side of the opercle, near its junction with the preopercle.

Pterotic. A bone at the posterior lateral process of the skull.

Pterygoids. Bones of roof of mouth in fishes, behind the palatines.

Pubic bones. Same as pelvic bones, q. v.

Pubis. Anterior lower part of pelvis.

Pulmonary. Pertaining to the lungs.

Punctate. Dotted with points.

Pyloric cœca. Glandular appendages in the form of blind sacs opening into the alimentary canal of most fishes at the *pylorus*, or passage from the stomach to the intestine.

Quadrate. A bone of the suspensorium on which the mandible is hinged.

Quincunx. Set of five arranged alternately, thus
```
            *   *
              *
            *   *
```

Radius. Outer bone of forearm.

Ray. One of the cartilaginous rods which support the membrane of the fin of a fish.

Recurved. Curved upward.

Reticulate, Marked with a network of lines.

Retrorse. Turned backward.

Rudimentary. Undeveloped.

Rugose. Rough with wrinkles.

Sacral. Pertaining to the *sacrum*, or vertebræ of the pelvic region.

Scapula. Shoulder blade; in fishes, the bone of the shoulder girdle below the post-temporal

Scapular arch. Shoulder girdle.

Scute. Any external bony or horny plate.

Second dorsal. The posterior or soft part of the dorsal fin, when the two parts are separated.

Septum. A thin partition.

Serrate. Notched, like a saw.

Sessile. Without a stem or peduncle.

Setaceous. Bristly.

Setiform. Bristle-like.

Shaft. Stiff axis of a quill.

Shoulder girdle. The bony girdle posterior to the head, to which the anterior limbs are attached (post-temporal, scapula, and coracoid or clavicle).

Soft dorsal. The posterior part of the dorsal fin in fishes, when composed of soft rays.

Soft rays. Fin rays which are articulate and usually branched.

Spatulate. Shaped like a spatula.

Sphenoid. Basal bone of skull.

Sphenotic. A lateral bone of the skull.

Spine. Any sharp projecting point; in fishes those fin rays which are unbranched, inarticulate, and usually, but not always, more or less stiffened.

Spinous. Stiff or composed of spines.

Spinous dorsal. The anterior part of the dorsal fin when composed of spinous rays.

Spiracles. Openings in the head and neck of some fishes and batrachians.

Stellate. Star-like; with radiating ridges.

Striate. Striped or streaked.

Sub (in composition). Less than; somewhat; not quite; under, etc.

Subcaudal. Under the tail.

Subopercle. The bone immediately below the opercle (the suture connecting the two often hidden by scales).

Suborbital. Below the eye.

Suborbital stay. A bone extending from one of the suborbital bones in certain fishes, across the cheek, or toward the preopercle.

Subulate. Awl-shaped.

Superciliary. Pertaining to the region of the eyebrow.

Superior pharyngeals. Synonym of pharyngobranchials, q. v.

Supplemental maxillary. A small bone lying along upper edge of the maxillary in some fishes.

Supraclavicle. A bone interposed between the clavicle and the post-temporal.

Supraoccipital. The bone at posterior part of skull in fishes, usually with a raised crest above.

Supraoral. Above the mouth.

Supraorbital. Above the eye.

Suprascapular. The post-temporal or bone by which the shoulder girdle in fishes is joined to the skull.

Suspensorium. The chain of bones from the hyomandibular to the palatine.

Suspensory bones. Bones by which the lower jaw, in fishes, is fastened to the skull.

Suture. The line of union of 2 bones, as in the skull.

Symphysis. Point of junction of the 2 parts of lower jaw; tip of chin.

Symplectic. The bone in fishes that keys together the hyomandibular and quadrate posteriorly.

Synonym. A different word having the same or a similar meaning.

Synonymy. A collection of different names for the same group, species, or thing; "A burden and a disgrace to science." (*Coues.*)

Tail. In fishes (usually), the part of the body posterior to the anal fin. (Often used more or less vaguely.)

Temporal. Pertaining to the region of the temples.

Terete. Cylindrical and tapering.

Terminal. At the end.

Tessellated. Marked with little checks or squares, like mosaic work.

Thoracic. Pertaining to the chest; ventral fins are thoracic when attached immediately below the pectorals, as in the perch, the pelvic bones being fastened to the shoulder girdle.

Transverse. Crosswise.

Trenchant. Compressed to a sharp edge.

Truncate. Abrupt, as if cut squarely off.

Tubercle. A small excrescence, like a pimple.

Type (of a genus). The species upon which was based the genus to which it belongs.

Type (of a species). The particular specimen upon which the original specific description was based.

Type locality. The particular place or locality at which the type specimen was collected.

Typical. Of a structure the most usual in a given group.

Ultimate. Last or farthest.

Unicolour. Of a single colour.

Vent. The external opening of the alimentary canal.

Ventral. Pertaining to the abdomen.

Ventral fins. The paired fins behind or below the pectoral fins in fishes, corresponding to the posterior limbs in the higher vertebrates.

Ventral plates. In serpents or fishes, the row of plates along the belly between throat and vent.

Ventricle. One of the thick-walled chambers of the heart.

Versatile. Capable of being turned either way.

Vertebra. One of the bones of the spinal column.

Vertical. Up and down.

Vertical fins. The fins on the median line of the body; the dorsal, anal, and caudal fins.

Villiform. Said of the teeth of fishes when slender and crowded into velvety bands.

Viscous. Slimy

Viviparous. Bringing forth living young.

Vomer. In fishes, the front part of the roof of the mouth; a bone seen immediately behind the premaxillaries.

Zygapophyses. Points of bone affording to the vertebræ more or less definite articulation with each other.

ARTIFICIAL KEY TO THE FAMILIES OF AMERICAN FOOD AND GAME FISHES

The following key is intended simply to facilitate the identification of the species of American fishes which are used as food or which are sought by the angler. No attempt is made to indicate the natural characters or relations of the families, and only those species of any group which are included in the present work are taken into consideration.

I.—VENTRAL FINS PRESENT, ABDOMINAL

  A. Back with an adipose fin behind the single rayed dorsal fin.
  B. Head with 4 to 8 long barbels about the mouth and nostrils; body scaleless; a single spine in each pectoral and in the dorsal fin.
                                          III, Siluridæ, 15
  BB. Head without barbels as described above.
  C. Dorsal, anal, and ventrals each with a small, but distinct spine; scales ctenoid...........................XXIV, Percopsidæ, 247
  CC. Dorsal, anal, and ventrals without spines.
  D. Dorsal fin long and high, of about 24 rays......XVI, Thymallidæ, 220
  DD. Dorsal fin moderate, of fewer than 20 rays.
  E. Stomach with many pyloric cœca..............XV, Salmonidæ, 116
  EE. Stomach with few pyloric cœca; size small......XVII, Argentinidæ, 225
  AA. Back without adipose fin.
  B. Back with a single dorsal fin made up of rays and not preceded by a series of free spines or followed by finlets.
  C. Tail evidently strongly heterocercal.
  D. Body naked; snout with a spatulate blade; mouth wide, without barbels.
             ....   I, Polyodontidæ, 1
  DD. Body with 5 series of body shields; mouth inferior toothless, preceded by 4 barbels.........................II, Acipenseridæ, 4
  CC. Tail not evidently heterocercal.
  E. Pectoral fins inserted high, near axis of body; lower pharyngeals united; lateral line along sides of belly.
  F. Jaws each with long sharp teeth mixed with smaller ones.
                              XX, Belonidæ, 241
  FF. Jaws with small equal teeth, conic or tricuspid.
  G. Lower jaw more or less produced; teeth tricuspid.
                            XXI, Hemiramphidæ, 242
  GG. Lower jaw a little produced; teeth conic; pectorals elongate, forming an organ of flight......................XXII, Exocœtidæ, 243
  EE. Pectoral fins inserted below axis of body; lower pharyngeals separate.
  H. Gill-membranes broadly joined to the isthmus; head naked; no teeth in jaws.
  I. Lower pharyngeal teeth very numerous, in 1 row like the teeth of a comb. (Suckers.)............................IV, Catostomidæ, 36
  II. Lower pharyngeal teeth few, fewer than 8, in 1 to 3 rows. (Carp; Chubs; Minnows.)........................V, Cyprinidæ, 67
  HH. Gill-membranes free from the isthmus.
  K. Head scaly, more or less.
  L. Teeth cardiform; jaws depressed, prolonged....XIX, Esocidæ, 233
  LL. Teeth villiform; jaws short; no lateral line.....XVIII, Dalliidæ, 232
  KK. Head naked ....IX, Elopidæ, 84
  M. Gular plate present.............................IX, Elopidæ. 84
  MM. Gular plate none

   N. Lateral line well developed.
   O. Teeth present, no accessory branchial organ.
   P. Mouth small, horizontal; posterior part of tongue and roof of mouth
         covered with coarse-paved teeth..........X, ALBULIDÆ, 88
 PP. Mouth large, the teeth all pointed, some of them canine, none paved or
         molar ....XI, HIODONTIDÆ, 90
 OO. Teeth none; an accessory branchial organ behind gill cavity.
                                  XII, CHANIDÆ, 94
 NN. Lateral line wanting; no gular plate.
   Q. Mouth moderate, terminal, the maxillary of about 3 pieces; stomach not
         gizzard-like ....XIII, CLUPEIDÆ, 95
 QQ. Mouth subinferior, very large, below a tapering, pig-like snout; maxillary
         very long ....XIV, ENGRAULIDÆ, 112
 BB. Dorsal fins 2, the anterior of spines only, the posterior chiefly of soft rays.
   R. Pectoral fin with 5 to 8 lowermost rays detached and filamentous.
                         XXVIII, POLYNEMIDÆ, 261
 RR. Pectoral fin entire.
   S. Teeth strong, unequal; lateral line present....XXVII, SPHYRÆNIDÆ, 258
 SS. Teeth small or wanting; lateral line obsolete.
   T. Dorsal spines 4, stout; anal spines 3...........XXVI, MUGILIDÆ, 250
 TT. Dorsal spines 4 to 8, slender; anal spine single..XXV, ATHERINIDÆ, 248
BBB. Dorsal fin soft-rayed, followed by a series of detached finlets.
                        XXIII, SCOMBRESOCIDÆ, 246

II.—VENTRAL FINS PRESENT, THORACIC OR SUB-JUGULAR, THE NUMBER OF RAYS DEFINITELY I, 5

   A. Body more or less scaly or armed with bony plates.
   B. Suborbital with a bony stay which extends across the cheek to or towards
         the preopercle; cheek sometimes entirely mailed.
   C. Slit behind fourth gill small or wanting.......LXVI, SCORPÆNIDÆ, 495
 CC. Slit behind fourth gill large; body scaled.
   D. Nostril single on each side, a small pore above it; dorsal fin continuous.
                        LXVIII, HEXAGRAMMIDÆ, 499
 DD. Nostrils 2 on each side; dorsal fins 2......LXVII, ANOPLOPOMIDÆ, 498
 BB. Suborbital stay wanting; cheeks not mailed.
   E. Dorsal spines all or nearly all disconnected from each other.
   F. Body elongate, spindle-shaped..........XL, RACHYCENTRIDÆ, 323
 FF. Body oblong or ovate, compressed.........XXXVIII, CARANGIDÆ, 296
 EE. Dorsal spines (if present) all, or most of them, connected by membrane.
   G. Pectoral fin with 4 to 9 lowermost rays detached and filiform.
                        XXVIII, POLYNEMIDÆ, 261
 GG. Pectoral fin entire.
   H. Dorsal and anal each with 1 or more detached finlets.
   I. Anal preceded by 2 free spines.............XXXVIII, CARANGIDÆ, 296
  II. Anal not preceded by 2 free spines..........XXXII, SCOMBRIDÆ, 272
 HH. Dorsal and anal without finlets.
   J. Lateral line armed posteriorly with a series of keeled plates; 2 free anal
         spines; gill-membranes free from isthmus.
                        XXXVIII, CARANGIDÆ, 296
 JJ. Lateral line armed posteriorly with a sharp, movable, lancet-like spine, or
         with a few bony tubercles; scales small, rough; gill membranes ad-
         herent to isthmus....................LXIII, TEUTHIDIDÆ, 486
JJJ. Lateral line unarmed.
   K. Throat with 2 long barbels (placed just behind chin); dorsal fins 2.
                        XXXI, MULLIDÆ, 268
 KK. Throat without long barbels.
   L. Anal fin preceded by 2 free spines (these obsolete in the very old, joined
         by membrane in the very young).
   M. Preopercle entire; teeth moderate if present.XXXVIII, CARANGIDÆ, 296

MM. Preopercle serrate; teeth unequal, some of them very strong.
XXXIX, Pomatomidæ, 320
LL. Anal fin not preceded by free spines.
N. Nostril single on each side; lateral line interrupted; lower pharyngeals united.
O. Anal spines 3 to 11. Fresh-water fishes......LVIII, Cichlidæ, 475
NN. Nostril double on each side
. Lateral line extending to tip of middle rays of caudal.
. Anal spines 3, the second strong.
P. Dorsal fins 2, separate; body elongate....XLVII, Centropomidæ, 368
RR. Dorsal fin continuous ....LII, Hæmulidæ, 420
QQ. Anal spines 1 or 2, the second large or small....LVI, Sciænidæ, 454
PP. Lateral line not extending beyond base of caudal fin.
S. Gills 3½, the slit behind the last very small or wanting.
T. Teeth in each side of each jaw united, forming a sort of beak.
LX, Scaridæ, 480
TT. Teeth distinct or nearly so, the anterior usually more or less canine.
LIX, Labridæ, 476
SS. Gills 4, a long slit behind the fourth.
U. Teeth setiform, like the teeth of a brush; body elevated, longer than deep, the soft fins completely scaled; gill-membranes attached to the isthmus.
V. Dorsal fin continuous................... LXIII, Chætodontidæ, 484
VV. Dorsal fin divided.........................LXII, Ilarchidæ, 482
UU. Teeth not setiform.
W. Premaxillaries excessively protractile, their basal process very long, in a groove at top of cranium...............LIV, Gerridæ, 445
WW. Premaxillaries moderately protractile or not protractile.
X. Lower pharyngeals united; scales large; anal fin with 3 spines and more than 15 soft rays; preopercle entire. (Viviparous fishes of the Californian fauna) ....LVII, Embiotocidæ, 469
XX. Lower pharyngeals separate.
Y. Pseudobranchiæ wanting or covered by skin.
Z. Dorsal fin of soft rays only, beginning as a crest on the head; caudal widely forked. Pelagic fishes........XLI, Coryphænidæ, 324
ZZ. Dorsal fin with spines anteriorly, not beginning on the head. Fresh-water fishes.
a. Anal spines 3 to 10.....................XLV, Centrarchidæ, 332
aa. Anal spines 1 or 2; body oblong or elongate; length less than 8 inches.
XLVI, Percidæ, 360
YY. Pseudobranchiæ developed.
b. Spinous dorsal of 2 or 3 short spines only; anal without spines; scales small, smooth.......................XLVIII, Serranidæ, 370
b1. Dorsal fin continuous, the spines few and slender..LXIX, Latilidæ, 504
bb1. Dorsal fin not as above
bb. Spinous dorsal, if present, not as above
c. Perch-like fishes, the caudal peduncle not very slender, the scales well developed, ctenoid or cycloid; the dorsal with distinct spines; the anal with at least 1 spine, its soft rays usually few.
d. Maxillary not sheathed by the preorbital, or only partially covered by the edge of the latter; ventral with its accessory scale very small or wanting; pectoral without accessory scale; sheath at base of spinous dorsal little developed; vomer usually with teeth; opercle usually ending in a spine.
e. Anal spines 2 or 1; pseudobranchiæ small; preopercle with a hook-like spine below; vertebræ increased in number (30 to 46). Fresh-water fishes... ....XLVI, Percidæ, 360
ee. Anal spines 3, never 2 nor 1; dorsal fin continuous or divided; vertebræ 24 to 35.

    f. Vomer, and usually palatines also, with teeth.
    g. Anal fin shorter than dorsal; head not everywhere covered with rough scales; postocular part of head not shortened.
                    XLVIII, SERRANIDÆ, 370
  gg. Anal fin scarcely shorter than dorsal and similar to it; head and body everywhere covered with rough scales; body deep, compressed, the posterior part of head shortened.....L. PRIACANTHIDÆ, 401
  ff. Vomer without teeth; dorsal fin continuous; body deep, compressed.
                    XLIX, LOBOTIDÆ, 400
  dd. Maxillary slipping for most of its length under the edge of the preorbital, which forms a more or less distinct sheath; ventrals with an accessory scale; opercle without spines; maxillary without supplemental bone; anal spines 3, rarely 2.
    h. Fishes carnivorous; intestines of moderate length; teeth in jaws not all incisor-like; vertebræ usually 24 or 25.
    i. Vomer with teeth, these sometimes very small; maxillary long.
                    LI, LUTIANIDÆ, 403
    ii. Vomer without teeth; palatines and tongue toothless.
    j. Teeth on sides of jaws not molar; maxillaries formed essentially as in the *Serranidæ;* preopercle mostly serrate......LII, HÆMULIDÆ, 420
    jj. Teeth on sides of jaws molar; maxillaries peculiar in form and in articulation; anterior teeth conical or else more or less incisor-like; preopercle entire ....LIII, SPARIDÆ, 436
  hh. Fishes herbivorous; intestinal canal elongate; anterior teeth in jaws incisor-like; no molars or canines; premaxillaries moderately protractile ....LV, KYPHOSIDÆ, 450
  cc. Mackerel-like fishes, with the caudal peduncle usually very slender, the fin widely forked, the scales various, usually not ctenoid; the dorsal spines various, anal fin long.
    k. Dorsal spines numerous, most of them produced in long filaments; pectorals very long.................XXXVII, NEMATISTIIDÆ, 294
  kk. Dorsal spines mostly low, not more than 2 of them filamentous..
    l. Dorsal fin divided, the spines 6 to 12 in number.
                    XXXIX, POMATOMIDÆ, 320
  ll. Dorsal spines 3 or 4, the fin not divided........XLIII, BRAMIDÆ, 327
AA. Body scaleless, smooth or armed with tubercles, prickles, or scattered bony plates.
  B. Anal preceded by 2 free spines (these lost with age; connected by membranes in the very young)..........XXXVIII, CARANGIDÆ, 296
 BB. Anal without free spines...................XXXII, SCOMBRIDÆ, 272

III.—VENTRAL FINS PRESENT, THORACIC OR JUGULAR, THE NUMBER OF RAYS NOT DEFINITELY I, 5

    A. Eyes unsymmetrical, both on the same side of head.
                    LXXII, PLEURONECTIDÆ, 520
  AA. Eyes symmetrical, one on each side of the head.
    B. Ventral rays with or without spine, the number of soft rays more than 5.
    C. Tail isocercal, the vertebræ progressively smaller to base of caudal; ventrals jugular; no spines in any of the fins.
    D. Jaws and vomer with strong canines; second dorsal and anal deeply notched; no barbel. ....LXX, MERLUCCIIDÆ, 507
  DD. Jaws and vomer without distinct canines; chin usually with a barbel.
                    LXXI, GADIDÆ, 508
  CC. Tail not isocercal, the last vertebræ not reduced in size.
    E. Ventral rays about 15; dorsal fin single, elevated .XLII, LAMPRIDIDÆ, 326
    EE. Ventral rays I, 6 to I, 10; dorsal with spines.
    F. Body covered with firm serrated scales; anal spines 4; dorsal spines not elevated.......................XXX, HOLOCENTRIDÆ, 264

FF. Body uniformly covered with cycloid scales; dorsal spines mostly very high and filamentous.. ....XXXVII, Nematistiidæ, 294
BB. Ventral fins with or without spine, the number of soft rays fewer than 5.
G. Upper jaw not prolonged into a sword.
H. Dorsal fin with some spines or simple rays.... XXXIII, Lepidopidæ, 289
HH. Dorsal fins of soft rays only................LXXIV, Gadidæ, 508
GG. Upper jaw prolonged into a bony sword; dorsal fin long and high; size large.............................XXXV, Istiophoridæ, 291

IV —VENTRAL FINS WHOLLY WANTING

A. Premaxillary and maxillary wanting or grown fast to the palatines; body greatly elongate, eel-shaped; gill-openings restricted to the sides; scales minute or wanting; scapular arch not attached to the skull. Eels.
B. Gill-openings well-developed; tongue present.
C. Skin covered with rudimentary embedded scales, usually linear in form, arranged in small groups, and placed obliquely at right angles to those of the neighbouring groups; pectorals and vertical fins well developed, the latter confluent about the tail; lateral line present; posterior nostril in front of eyes; tongue with its margins free.
VI, Anguillidæ, 76
CC. Scales wholly wanting; eggs (so far as known) of moderate size, much as in ordinary fishes..............VII, Leptocephalidæ, 81
BB. Gill-openings small; no tongue..................VIII, Murænidæ. 82
AA. Premaxillary and maxillary present, often immovably united to rest of cranium.
B. Gill-membranes broadly united to the isthmus, restricting the gill-openings to the sides.
C. Teeth in each jaw confluent into one............LXVI, Molidæ, 492
CC. Teeth separate; body enveloped in a bony box..LXIV, Ostraciidæ, 489
BB. Gill-membranes free from the isthmus.
E. Caudal fin wanting; body naked, greatly elongate.
XXXIV, Trichiuridæ, 290
EE. Caudal fin present.
F. Upper jaw prolonged into a sword; size very large
XXXVI, Xiphiidæ, 293
FF. Upper jaw not prolonged into a sword.
G. Belly with a series of bony scutes along its edge; body much compressed.
XIII, Clupeidæ, 95
GG. Belly not armed with scutes.
H. Body ovate, much compressed. ....XLIV, Stromateidæ, 328
HH. Body oblong or elongate, much longer than deep.
XXIX, Ammodytidæ, 263

INDEX